TO THE STUDENT: A study guide for this textbook is available through your college bookstore under the title *Student Review: Introduction to Management,* Third Edition by Raymond F. Attner and Jim Lee Morgan. This study guide can help you with course material by acting as a tutorial, review, and study aid. If the study guide is not in stock, ask the bookstore manager to order a copy for you.

Introduction to Management

THIRD EDITION

Warren R. Plunkett
Wright College

Raymond F. Attner
Brookhaven College

PWS-KENT
Publishing Company • Boston

To my aunt, Sister Elizabeth Ann, R.G.S.
W.R.P.

To my wife Donnelle—my patience, my inspiration, my commitment
R.F.A.

PWS–KENT
Publishing Company

Editor: Rolf Janke
Production Coordinator: Eve B. Mendelsohn
Interior Designer: Julie Gecha
Cover Designer: Julie Gecha
Manufacturing Coordinator: Margaret Sullivan Higgins
Composition: David Seham Associates
Cover Printer: New England Book Components
Text Printer and Binder: Halliday Lithograph

PWS-KENT Publishing Company is a division of Wadsworth, Inc.

Printed in the United States of America
1 2 3 4 5 6 7 8 9 — 92 91 90 89 88

Library of Congress Cataloging-in-Publication Data

Plunkett, W. Richard (Warren Richard)
   Introduction to management / Warren R. Plunkett,
Raymond F. Attner. — 3rd ed.
     p.   cm.
   Bibliography: p.
   Includes index.
   ISBN 0-534-9176-9
   1. Management. I. Attner, Raymond F. II. Title.
HD31.P55 1988   88-25424
658.4—dc19   CIP

M. BECKETT

Kent Series in Management

Barnett/Wilsted, *Strategic Management: Concepts and Cases*

Barnett/Wilsted, *Strategic Management: Text and Concepts*

Barnett/Wilsted, *Cases for Strategic Management*

Berkman/Neider, *The Human Relations of Organizations*

Crane, *Personnel: The Management of Human Resources,* Fourth Edition

Davis/Cosenza, *Business Research for Decision Making,* Second Edition

Kirkpatrick, *Supervision: A Situational Approach*

Klein/Ritti, *Understanding Organizational Behavior,* Second Edition

Kolde, *Environment of International Business,* Second Edition

Nkomo/Fottler/McAfee, *Applications in Personnel/Human Resource Management:
    Cases, Exercises, and Skill Builders*

Plunkett/Attner, *Introduction to Management,* Third Edition

Punnett, *Experiencing International Management*

Scarpello/Ledvinka, *Personnel/Human Resource Management:
    Environments and Functions*

Starling, *The Changing Environment of Business,* Third Edition

Steers/Ungson/Mowday, *Managing Effective Organizations: An Introduction*

Kent International Dimensions of Business Series

Adler, *International Dimensions of Organizational Behavior*

AlHashim/Arpan, *International Dimensions of Accounting,* Second Edition

Folks/Aggarwal, *International Dimensions of Financial Management*

Garland/Farmer, *International Dimensions of Business Policy and Strategy*

Litka, *International Dimensions of the Legal Environment of Business*

Phatak, *International Dimensions of Management,* Second Edition

Terpstra, *International Dimensions of Marketing,* Second Edition

P
R
E
F
A
C
E

To the Student

This text has been written to introduce you to the concepts, terminology, principles, and theories that are the substance of management—one of the earliest and most fundamental of skills practiced by all peoples throughout human history. Each of us must learn to manage our lives, our careers, and our families. In addition, those of us who are managers by profession must learn to manage the work of others. How well we manage ourselves and the work of others determines, to a great extent, the quality of our lives and that of the lives of others. Managers serve others through the exercise of basic functions and the applications of several skills, all of which are examined in the pages that follow.

As the primary tool in a course on management, this text contains a number of aids to assist you in your studies.

- Seventeen chapters divided into six comprehensive units of related course content.
- Chapter outlines consisting of primary and secondary headings from the contents of each chapter.
- Exhibits and figures designed to highlight and summarize each chapter's essential concepts.
- A list of the "Essential Terms" introduced in each chapter at the beginning and in a glossary defining each term at the end of each chapter and at the back of the text.
- Essential terms appear in boldface type when they are first introduced in each chapter.
- A list of specific "Learning Objectives" to be achieved through the study and discussion of each chapter's contents.
- Chapter summaries including topic sentences that review the essential concepts.
- "Review Questions" at the end of each chapter to help you determine if you have mastered each of a chapter's specific "Learning Objectives."
- A list of "Suggested Readings" at the end of each chapter points to five additional books and five articles in leading journals and business publications that will expand the text's treatment of its concepts, principles, and theories.

• Two cases at the end of each chapter designed to review important points through the application of your understanding to real-life situations and experiences of practicing managers.

The primary goals of this text and your management course are to capture and hold your interest, introduce you to the essential concepts that apply to the practice of management, explain the complexities of management principles and theories through examples and visuals, and allow you to form your own philosophy and unique understanding of management. Upon completion of this course, you should be armed with the essentials necessary to improve your present situation and to enable you to become a better manager of both your own affairs and those of others.

Six Major Units

Part I of this text, "What Does Management Mean?" introduces the subject of management and examines its application to your situation. Chapter 1 answers the questions: What is management? What do managers do? What roles do managers play at work? What skills are needed by managers at different levels? How has management as a field of study evolved?

Chapter 2 talks to you about managing yourself and your career. It asks you to take an inventory of your personal skills, aptitudes, interests, and motivations in order to determine your areas of strength and those in need of improvement. The chapter outlines steps you can take now to plan for the future and the stages you can expect your career to pass through. When you complete it, you will know yourself better and know what you need to do to improve your quality of life.

Chapter 3 looks at the most basic of all human activities—communicating. It examines the process, its components, the barriers that must be anticipated and dealt with, and the roles we all must play as senders or receivers.

Part II, "Planning," also contains three chapters. The first, Chapter 4, examines the need to plan, its importance and impact on the other management functions, and the types of plans managers must formulate. It will help you to put method into your planning efforts and to make your plans more effective. Planning is the first thing we must do regardless of what else we intend to do. Doing it well can prevent many problems, losses, and delays.

Chapter 5 offers you planning tools and techniques. It shows you the various kinds of planning environments you are likely to experience. It examines both quantitative and general planning tools and methods and comments on the usefulness and applications of each.

The last chapter in Part II, Chapter 6, explores how you can improve your decision-making skills. It outlines a rational method for making decisions with a step-by-step approach. It examines various decision-making environments along with the aids and influences on decision-making efforts. After studying this chapter you will be better at making decisions.

Part III, "Organizing," begins with Chapter 7 and a definition of this essential management function. Organizing is examined as a process involving specific steps. Different organizations adopt different approaches to structuring their operations. These, along with the major principles that govern the organizing process, are explored in detail. Chapter 7 looks at the formal organization—the one constructed by managers in order to execute the jobs and tasks that must be done.

Chapter 8 looks at the informal organization—the one constructed by individual employees as a result of their social and work-related interactions with one another. The kinds of informal groups that form are examined along with their natures and activities. The effects that informal organizations have on the formal one in which they exist may be positive, negative, or both. Like formal groups, informal groups have leaders and channels for communicating. Managers are members of both formal and informal groups at work and must be able to work with both.

Part IV, "Staffing and Directing," focuses on how organizations attract and retain good people. Chapter 9 looks at the staffing function and its essential parts: planning for human resources, recruiting, selecting, inducting and orienting, training and developing, and appraising performances. The legal environment for each of these is reviewed along with the principles and practices that affect them.

Chapter 10 is a detailed look at human motivation. It is the first of two chapters focusing on the directing function and takes you through the several important theories about why people do what they do. Managers must not only concern themselves with their own motivations but with the motivations of their subordinates as well. This chapter will add to the insights and understanding that you need to effectively supervise and motivate your subordinates to improve their performances.

The last chapter in Part IV, Chapter 11, looks at leadership—the ability to get others to follow your orders and instructions. The roles leaders must play with their followers are reviewed along with the theories that govern the practice of leadership and the styles that leaders may adopt. This chapter will enable you to spot leadership in others and to know why they are skillful in their execution of the directing function.

Part V, "Controlling and Managing Change," contains three chapters. The first, Chapter 12, looks at controlling as a specific management function. Like the four functions discussed in Parts II, III, and IV, controlling is a process governed by principles and theories. These are examined along with the various types of controls organizations use and the ways in which they can be made effective. As a manager, your efforts at controlling depend upon planning and will help you to prevent and to deal with problems.

Chapter 13 examines the major kinds of controls available to managers: general management controls, financial controls, and production controls. Specific kinds of controls exist to keep track of nearly every activity and operation. Managers must be able to select the one that is right for any given situation. Controls must be used on any important effort that commits resources, whether human or material.

Chapter 14 deals with managing change and conflicts in organizations. As a manager, you will experience many changes in both routines and tasks assigned. This chapter gives you important models that will prove useful in making changes and insuring that changes are evolutionary, not revolutionary. You need to know why people resist change and how organizations and individuals can break down this resistance. Chapter 14 will tell you these and other important concepts.

Part VI, "Contemporary Management: Trends and Issues," is the final section of our text. Chapter 15 looks at management and productivity. It defines the concept of productivity and explores the impact of actions by governments, managements, and labor on it. Each of us has a contribution to make to our organization's ability to produce goods or services. Each of us can be a negative influence on our employer as well. Chapter 15 looks at what has been and is being done by individuals and groups to improve organizational effectiveness and efficiency.

Chapter 16 explores the complex nature of the interactions between managers and their internal and external environments. Managers as individuals and in groups have social and moral responsibilities. What are ethics? What are the legal restraints on managers? How much can society expect from managers and the private sector? These are some of the major issues explored in Chapter 16.

The last chapter, Chapter 17, examines international management. It focuses on the environment of the international manager and the cultural dilemma facing the manager. The chapter provides a thorough analysis of the applications of the five management functions in the international arena.

Two Appendices

Two appendices have been developed to support the six major units. Appendix A, "Managing Your Time," develops the importance of time as a resource, identifies barriers to its effective use, and provides tips on saving time and developing routines. Appendix B, "Managers and Stress," discusses the nature of stress and how it can be managed.

Two Suggestions

Throughout this course and your readings of this text, try to relate what you read and discuss to your past experiences. You have been practicing the art and skills of management all your life. What you are about to learn is merely an extension of your past experiences—a blending of it with the major experiences of others. When you link their experiences with your own, you will be expanding your knowledge and understanding of the world around you without actually having to live through the same experiences. You have a great deal of experience to share with others, just as they have a great deal to share with you. Don't withhold your share of contributions.

While you will be reading each chapter as a separate area of study, try to relate it to what you have read previously. As you read Chapter 3, relate its contents to Chapters 1 and 2. By doing this, you will begin to see that management is a tapestry with many threads that run parallel to and across one another. Planning relates to all the management functions examined after it. Planning, therefore, is part of every other activity just like communicating is. Step back from your study periodically to see the "big picture" that each chapter is a part of.

Good luck to all of you. We wish you the best in life and hope that you get from your work and studies the satisfactions that you seek.

Acknowledgments

We would like to thank the following reviewers who were helpful in preparing the previous editions of this text: A. M. Agnello (Solano Community College), Sr. Marian Batho (Aquinas Junior College), Gus Blomquist (Del Mar College), John Bohan (Clackamas Community College), Arnold J. Bornfield (Worcester State University), Bruce E. Bugbee (Glendale Community College), Charles Chanter (Grand Rapids Junior College), Jim Garaventa (Chemeketa Community College), David A. Gray (University of Texas, Arlington), Theodore L. Hansen, Jr. (Salem State College), Dave Harris (Mission College), Ken Howey (Trident Technical College), Don Hucker (Cypress College), W. J. Jacobs (Lake City Community College), Arthur La Capria, Jr. (El Paso Community College), Norbert Lindskog (The Loop College), Jim Lee Morgan (West Los Angeles College), Joyce P. Moseley (Trident Technical College), George Otto (Truman College), Seiji Sugawara (Mendocino College), Ralph Todd (American River College), W. Emory Trainham (Ashland College), and Sumner M. White (Massachusetts Bay Community College). Finally, we'd like to thank those who provided insightful comments and suggestions that we used to prepare this edition: Douglas Anderson (Ashland College), Anthony J. Alesi (Passaic County Community College), Gary Bacon (North Lake College), Rex L. Bishop (Charles County Community College), Donna Bleck (Middlesex Community College), John Carmichael (Union County College), Linda M. Duckworth (Northeast Mississippi Community College), William H. Graham, Jr. (Catawba Valley Community College), S. Miller Harrison (Durham Technical Community College), Samir T. Ishak (Grand Valley State University), Judith E. Kizzie (Clinton Community College), Gus L. Kotoulas (Morton College), John E. McCarty (New Mexico Junior College), Vladimir G. Marinich (Howard Community College), Leonard Martyns (Chaffey College), Quenton Pulliam (Nashville State Technical Institute), Carol Rowey (Community College of Rhode Island), Sumner M. White (Massachusetts Bay Community College), and Bob Willis (Rogers State College).

Warren Plunkett

Ray Attner

PART IV
Staffing and Directing

PART V
Controlling and Managing Change

PART VI
Contemporary Management: Trends and Issues

What Does Management Mean?

C
H
A
P
T
E
R

1

Management: An Occupation and a Team

OUTLINE

What Is Management?

Levels of Management: The Management Pyramid

Management Functions
- Planning
- Organizing
- Staffing
- Directing
- Controlling
- The Universality of Management Functions

Management Roles

Management Skills

Evaluation of Management Performance

Management Theories
- Foundations of Management Theory
- Classical Management Theory
- Behavioral Management Theory
- Quantitative Management Theory
- Systems Management Theory
- Contingency Management Theory

Management: An Art or a Science? A Profession?

Summary

ESSENTIAL TERMS

conceptual skill   organization
human skill   role
management   system
managers   technical skill

LEARNING OBJECTIVES

After reading and discussing this chapter, you should be able to do the following:

1. Define this chapter's essential terms.
2. Explain why managers are necessary in organizations.
3. List and briefly define the five management functions.
4. Explain the universality of management as it relates to organizations and levels of management.
5. Discuss the roles managers perform.
6. Discuss the skills required of a manager.
7. Discuss the five schools of management thought and relate each to modern-day management.

What Is Management?

Is management necessary? Why? What does a manager actually do? What are some of the characteristics of the field of management? These are questions that the beginning student in management often asks. To answer some of these concerns, just look at yourself. You are a manager of your time, energy, and talents. The decisions you make each day in these three areas will have a far-reaching influence on your career, your life, and the lives of others.

Think of yourself getting up in the morning. You must make decisions at once: You must plan what you want to accomplish during the day, organize the resources to achieve your plan, and periodically check on those activities to see if your plan is being achieved. Realizing it or not, you are performing three of the management functions—planning, organizing, and controlling.

So it is with the persons we call **managers**—those in positions of authority who make decisions to commit their resources and the resources of others toward the achievement of goals.

This chapter, this text, and your course in management are all concerned with making decisions and getting work accomplished. They contain knowledge that you will find of great value in managing your life, family, job, subordinates, and career. This knowledge comes in the form of ideas and principles, as well as the experiences of many who have been managers before you. You will see that there is no "one best way to manage." There are multiple influences in a manager's job and specific skill requirements to accomplish the job. Your challenge as you progress through the text and course is to develop your own philosophy of management from the concepts, principles, and practices cited. Using this approach, you will be prepared to manage yourself and others more efficiently and effectively.

Before defining management and discussing what managers do, we need to examine the environment in which managers conduct their activities and perform the role that separates them from nonmanagers. Managers work in an organization or company. The world is full of organizations: your school, the Dallas Cowboys, the corner drugstore, your neighborhood bank, the Teamsters Union. Organizations can vary in size, structure, resources, personnel, and purposes, but they do have some things in common.

Basically, an **organization** is a group of two or more persons that exists and operates to achieve clearly stated, commonly held objectives. Objectives are goals—targets to shoot for, states of being, or places to be reached through plans and actions. The objectives of an organization have to do with providing goods and services to its members or providing them to others outside the organization. In an organization, it is quite possible that each member might do parts of jobs that each thought important to meet the objectives, while in actuality the members might be working in opposite directions. To prevent this from occurring and to ensure coordination of work to accomplish the objectives, managers are needed. A manager may be the owner/operator/founder of an organization or someone hired to give it direction—to make decisions and commit its resources (personnel, capital, and equipment) to achieve the organization's objectives. The manager is often a connecting link, catalyst, "sparkplug," and driving force for change, coordination, and control in an organization.

Just what do managers do? Are all management jobs the same? If there are differences, what are they? In the following pages, you will examine the answers to these questions and get a better view of the management job.

Management is defined as the process of setting and achieving goals through the execution of five basic management functions that utilize human, financial, and material resources.

There are a number of points to remember in this definition. First, management and managers make conscious decisions to set and achieve goals. Decision making is a critical part of all management activities. Second, management is getting things done through people. Once management acquires the financial and material resources for the organization, it works through the organizational members to reach the stated objectives. Third, to achieve the goals they set, managers must execute the five basic functions: planning, organizing, staffing, directing, and controlling. Each of these we take up later in detail.

Levels of Management: The Management Pyramid

We have been using management in a broad sense to describe all managers. Is management the same throughout the organization? The answer is both yes and no. Managers all perform same management functions but with different emphases because of their positions in the company. In most organizations, the management group consists of several levels of managers, such as those shown in Figure 1.1. The specific titles managers have depend on the organizations they work in and on the actual jobs they perform. In government organizations, such titles as administrator, section chief, and director are quite common. In business, titles such as supervisor, manager, vice-president, and foreman are often used. Titles by themselves have little

FIGURE 1.1
Management's
pyramid structure

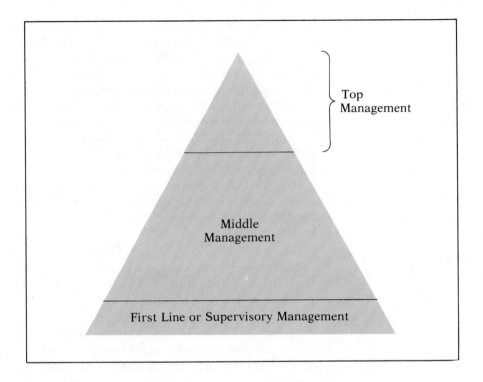

meaning outside the environment in which they are granted. A district
manager of one company could be the equivalent of a regional manager
in a rival firm.

For our purposes, we can divide managers into three basic categories:
top management, *middle management*, and *first-line* or *supervisory management*.
Top management usually consists of the organization's most important
manager—the chief executive officer or president—and his or her immediate
subordinates, usually called vice-presidents. Top management is responsible
for the overall management of the organization. It establishes organizational
or companywide objectives or goals and operating policies, and it directs
the company in relationships with its external environment. Middle managers are all managers below the rank of vice-president but above the supervisory level. These middle managers may be titled regional managers
or group managers in their organizations. Regardless of the title, the main
point is that their subordinates are other managers. They are responsible
for implementing top management objectives and policies. First-line managers or supervisors, those at the operating level, are the lowest level of
management. They are responsible for the management of their specific
work groups and for the accomplishment of the actual work of the organization. Their subordinates are nonmanagement workers—the group
management depends on for the execution of its plans.

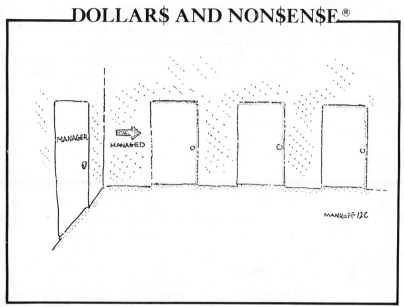

Source: © 1985 United Feature Syndicate, Inc.

Management Functions

We recall from our definition of management that all managers share in the execution of the management functions—planning, organizing, staffing, directing, and controlling. But what do these functions involve? A brief explanation of each of these five functions follows. Separate chapters in this text deal with them in much more detail.

① Planning

Planning is the first function that all managers engage in because it lays the groundwork for all other functions. It identifies the goals and alternatives. It maps out courses of action that will commit individuals, departments, and the entire organization for days, months, and years to come. Planning achieves these ends after setting in motion the following processes: (1) determination of what resources will be needed, (2) identification of the number and types of personnel the organization will need, (3) development of the foundation for the organizational environment in which work is to be accomplished, and (4) determination of standard against which the progress toward the objectives can be measured so that corrections can be made if necessary.

The length of time and the scope of planning will vary according to the level in the company. Top level management planning may cover a period of five or ten years and can be considered long-range planning. The plans at this level may cover expansion of the business and how it will be financed. At lower levels of management, the concern may be a plan for today's activities or planning tomorrow's work schedule.

Each manager's plans are influenced by the plans of other managers. Lower level managers' plans are strongly guided by the directions of the plans of top-level managers. Besides the vertical influence on a manager's plans, there is the horizontal influence of other managers, those on the same level within the same department. Add to these the influence of government rules and regulations, and you can see that planning is more complex than it appears. Planning does not occur in a vacuum. A manager's plans affect, and are affected by, the plans of others on their team and the requirements of government rulings.

Organizing

Organizing as a management function is concerned with (1) assembling the resources necessary to achieve the organization's objectives and (2) establishing the activity–authority relationships of the organization. Planning has established the goals of the company and how they are to be achieved; now, organizing develops the structure to reach these goals.

The activities necessary to achieve the objectives are grouped into working divisions, departments, or other identifiable units primarily by clustering similar and related duties. The result is a network of interdependent units. Each unit (and each person in the unit) should have clearly defined authority, or a clearly defined list of duties, and one person to whom to report. Organizing is not done once and then forgotten. As the objectives of the company change, they will influence the structure of managerial and organizational relationships. One thing is certain in organizing—changes that occur both within and outside the organization will require new approaches, plans, and organizational units.

Staffing

Staffing is concerned with locating prospective employees to fill the jobs created by the organizing process. Staffing initially involves the process of recruiting potential candidates for a job, reviewing the applicants' credentials, and trying to match the job demands with the candidates' abilities. After the employment decision has been made—the position is offered and accepted—staffing involves orienting the new employee to the company environment, training the new person for his or her particular job, and keeping each employee qualified. Staffing also involves the development and implementation of a system for appraising performance and providing feedback for performance improvement. Staffing is also concerned with determining the proper pay and benefits for each job. Many aspects of the staffing function are the responsibility of the personnel department—a staff department most likely to exist in an organization large enough to support such a specialized group.

④ Directing

Directing is aimed at getting the members of the organization to move in the direction that will achieve its objectives. Directing builds a climate, provides leadership, and arranges the opportunity for motivation. Each boss must plan and oversee the work of each of his or her subordinates. The challenge for a manager in directing is to create an environment in which both the employee and the organization will achieve their objectives. To provide this environment, all employees need to be dealt with on an individual basis—one-on-one. Expectations need to be communicated and reinforced. Communication needs to be ongoing and personalized. And each person should be encouraged to participate in the decision-making process.

⑤ Controlling

Controlling deals with establishing standards for performance, measuring performances against established standards, and dealing with deviations from established standards. It attempts to prevent problems, to determine when problems do exist, and to solve the problems that occur as quickly and effectively as possible. Controlling depends on accurate, reliable, and enforceable standards and on monitoring performances by people, machines, and processes. The best controls ensure that work is performed to standards as planned.

The Universality of Management Functions

Regardless of title, position, or management level, all managers do the same job. They execute the five management functions and work through and with others to set and achieve organizational goals. Figure 1.2 shows the concept known as the universality of management. Although all managers perform the same functions, the various management levels require different amounts of time for each function, and the points of emphasis in each function will differ.

Top management.   Top-level management's job is concerned with the "big picture," not the "nitty gritty." The planning function for top-level management consists of developing the major purpose of the organization, the global objectives for organizational accomplishment, and the major policy

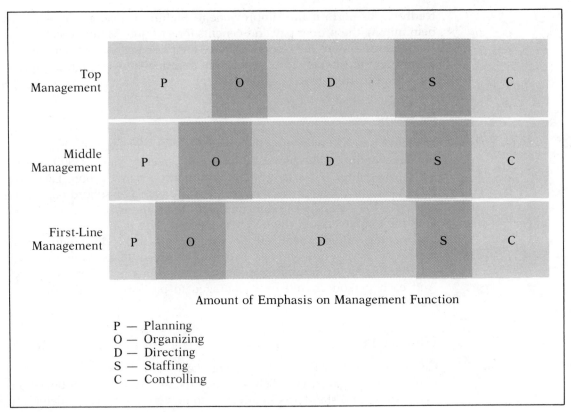

FIGURE 1.2
Universality of management

statements for implementation by middle and first-line managers. Organizing at this level is viewed as developing the overall structure of the organization to support the accomplishment of the plans and then acquiring the resources for the company. The staffing function at the top level of management is concerned with policy development in the areas of equal opportunity in employment and with employee development. Top management is also concerned with acquiring talent to fill upper-management positions. The emphasis in directing is on companywide management philosophy and on cultivating an organizational climate for optimal employee performance. The controlling function at this level emphasizes overall company performance relative to company objectives.

Middle management.   Middle-level management's primary job is to develop implementation strategies for the broad concepts determined by top management. For example, if the top-level managers decide on a 10 percent profit objective, the job of middle managers is to translate that goal into concrete goals of their own so that the desired profit can be attained. Middle managers decide on how to do it, with new products or new customers or new territories. Organizing at the middle level means making specific adjustments in the organization structure and allocating the resources acquired by top management. Staffing focuses on the policy implementation in the areas of equal employment opportunity and employee development programs. Directing is viewed as providing leadership and support for lower level management. Controlling is concerned with monitoring the results of plans for the specific products, regions, and subunits and making the indicated adjustment to achieve organizational objectives.

First-line or supervisory management. Whereas top-level management is concerned with the big picture and middle-level management with its companywide implementation, first-line management is concerned with only its immediate responsibilities. For the first-line manager, planning involves scheduling employees, deciding what work will be done first, and developing procedures to achieve the goals. Organizing may consist of delegating authority or deciding that work done by one group of people should be done by another work group. Staffing at this level consists of requesting a new employee, hiring that employee, and then training the person to perform the job. Directing includes communicating and providing leadership both to the work group and to all employees individually. Controlling at this level focuses on having the manager's work group meet its production, sales, or quality objectives.

Management Roles

Our working definition describes the manager as a person who plans, organizes, staffs, directs, and controls. Implicit in this description is that all managers, regardless of level in the organization or job title—vice-president of marketing, director of accounting services, machine shop foreman, or supervisor of clerical support—perform these functions to some degree. Now we need to know: What does the manager do to carry out these functions? The answer is that she or he must fill various roles.

What are the roles? And what influences which role a manager must assume? A **role** is any one of several behaviors a manager displays as he or she functions in the organization. As a manager attempts to perform the management job, he or she must "wear different hats" in interactions with various members of the organization. These role requirements are influenced by a manager's formal job description and also arise from the values and expectations of the manager's superiors, subordinates, and peers.

Figure 1.3 illustrates how employees rate their managers in performing specific roles. Let's look at some of the roles required of a manager.[1]

- *Figurehead role.* A manager is the head of his or her work unit, be it division, department, or section. Because of this "lead person" position, the manager must routinely perform certain ceremonial duties. For example, the manager may be required to entertain visitors to the organization, attend a subordinate's wedding, or participate in a group luncheon.

- *Leadership role.* The manager is the environment creator. She or he plays this role by working to improve employees' performances, reducing conflict, providing feedback on performance, and encouraging growth.

- *Liaison role.* Managers interact with others besides superiors and subordinates; they work with peer-level managers in other departments, staff specialists, other departments' employees, and outside contacts (suppliers, clients). In this role, the manager is building contacts through which to gather information.

- *Monitor role.* The manager is constantly monitoring the environment to determine what is going on. This information is collected

FIGURE 1.3
Employee rating of management effectiveness in performing management roles

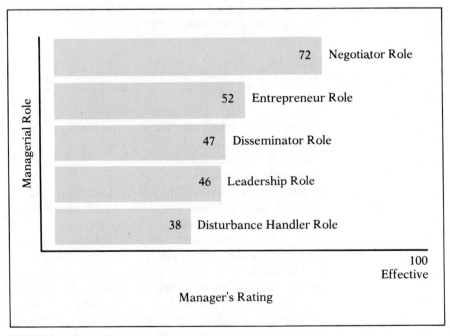

Source: Chicago Tribune, December 14, 1987, sect. 4, p. 1.

both directly, by asking questions, and indirectly, through unsolicited information.

- *Disseminator role.* What does the manager do with the information collected? As disseminator, the manager passes on to subordinates some of the information that would not ordinarily be accessible to them.

- *Spokesperson or representative role.* The manager is the person who speaks for his or her work unit to people outside the work unit. One part of this role is to keep superiors well informed, and a second aspect is to communicate outside the organization.

- *Entrepreneur role.* As the manager is exposed to new ideas or methods that may improve the work unit's operations, she or he assumes the entrepreneur role. In this role, the manager initiates activities that will allow, and encourage, the work unit to use the ideas or methods most advantageously.

- *Disturbance handler role.* What happens when parts of the work environment—schedules, equipment, strikes, reneged contracts—get out of control? The manager must handle these crises as they develop.

- *Resource allocator role.* The manager is responsible for determining who in the work unit gets the resources and how much each person gets. These resources include money, facilities, equipment, and access to the manager's time.

- *Negotiator role.* Managers are required to spend a good part of their time in the negotiator role. Negotiating may be required on contracts with suppliers or simply on trading off resources inside the organization. The manager must play this role because he or she is the only one in the work unit with both the information and authority negotiators need to have.

These multiple roles are what managers actually do as they are completing their managerial functions. In planning and organizing, the manager needs to perform the resource allocator role successfully with money, facilities, and equipment. Staffing requires the manager to focus on the leadership role by providing subordinates with feedback on performance. Directing includes the successful performance of disseminator, entrepreneur, and disturbance handler roles. Controlling is aided through the performance of the monitor role. The ability to perform the multiple role demands makes the difference between a successful manager and an unsuccessful one. Any manager who has a problem wearing any of the many hats of the job is going to have a work unit that is adversely affected to some extent.

Management Skills

As a manager plans, organizes, staffs, directs, and controls in his or her management job, he or she must have mastery of three basic skills. These skills needed by all managers are technical, human, and conceptual.[2]

Technical skill is the knowledge of, and ability to use, the processes, practices, techniques, and tools of the specialty area a manager supervises. For example, if a manager is supervising accountants, the manager would have to have knowledge of accounting. The manager does not need to be a technical expert. Rather, the manager needs enough technical skill to accomplish the job he or she is responsible for.

Human skill is the ability to interact with other persons successfully. A manager must be able to understand, work with, and relate to both individuals and groups in order to build a teamwork environment. The proper execution of one's human skills is often called human relations.

Conceptual skill deals with ideas and abstract relationships. It is the mental ability to view the organization as a whole and to see how the parts of the organization relate to and depend on one another. Conceptual skill is also the ability to imagine the integration and coordination of the parts of an organization—all its processes and systems. A manager needs conceptual skills to see how factors are interrelated, to understand the impact of any action on the other aspects of the organization, and to be able to plan long range.

The importance of having these three skills depends on a manager's level of management in the organization. Technical skill is critical for a manager at the first-line management level and becomes less important as the manager moves up in the organization structure. For example, the supervisor of a word processing department will have to know more technical information about the systems, equipment, and methods of training than the company president, who does not deal in the "how to's" of the department. Figure 1.4 illustrates the relative amounts of each kind of skill needed by the three levels of management.

Human skill is important at every level in the organization. The need to be able to understand and work with people is important at all levels, but the first-line manager's position places a premium on human skill requirements because of the many employee interactions required.

Conceptual skill becomes increasingly important as a manager moves up the levels of management. The first-level manager focuses basically on her or his work group; therefore, the need for conceptual skills is at a minimum. Top-level management is concerned with broad-based, long-range decisions that affect the entire organization; therefore, conceptual skill is most important at that level.

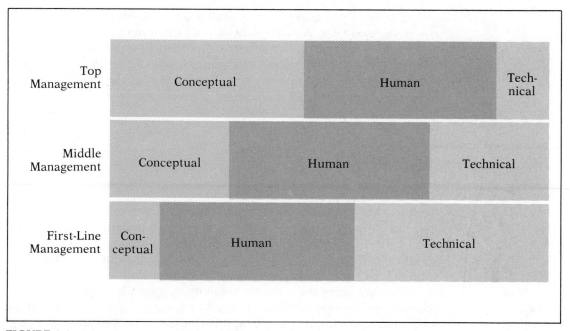

FIGURE 1.4
Proportions of management skills needed at different levels of management
Source: James A. F. Stoner, *Management*, 3rd ed. © 1986, p. 15. Reprinted by permission of Prentice-Hall, Inc., Englewood Cliffs, N.J.

Evaluation of Management Performance

Now that we know what a manager does and the skills needed to perform the job, we want to know: How is the manager judged on his or her own performance? A manager's performance can be measured by two criteria—effectiveness and efficiency.

Effectiveness is defined by Peter Drucker, one of the most respected writers in management, as "doing the right thing."[3] This means a manager has the responsibility for selecting the right goal and the appropriate means for achieving that goal. Thus a manager needs to be able to select the right decision from among all alternatives and then to select the right method from many methods for implementing that decision.

Efficiency is measuring the cost of attaining a given goal. Efficiency is concerned with how resources (money, time, equipment, personnel) are used to get the desired results. If the minimum cost is spent to obtain the desired goal, the manager is being efficient.

The manager's responsibilities require that she or he be both effective and efficient. From an evaluation viewpoint, efficiency is important but effectiveness is vital. A manager who does the wrong things (ineffectiveness) with minimum use of resources (efficiency) is not helping the organization. On the other hand, the manager who makes the right choices but may not have a completely smooth operation as the change is implemented is, despite partial inefficiency, assisting the organization.

Management Theories

After examining management, organizations, a manager's job, roles, and the skills required to do the job, you might be wondering if there is one best approach or theory that can be applied to all management situations. Unfortunately, the answer is no. There is no one best theory just as there is no one best way to manage or study management.

Over the years, the contributions of many people have given us several theories—collections of ideas, concepts, principles, and methods—about what management is and how to approach it as a field of study. One theory emphasizes people. Others emphasize tools such as fundamental truths (principles), mathematics, or systems. Each theory has a different way of looking at organizations, activities, and how people function in organizations, and all the theories have something of value for us.

As a manager, you will be faced with different types of problems—the attitudes of people, work environments, allocation of resources. One theory may be more useful in helping to deal with one problem than another. If we are familiar with all these theories and their present-day applications, it will be easier for us to match the insight achievable through each theory to the appropriate problem. There is no need to reinvent the wheel: Theory is the shortcut to working through problems. Distinct theories or schools of management thought have evolved over the years. We need to examine each, but first let's briefly look at the foundations of management theory.

Foundations of Management Theory

Management did not just start with the Industrial Revolution. People have functioned as groups and have been managed since the beginning of history. Early tribes had leaders and councils of elders, but serious concern for management began only when societies grew larger and more complex. People eventually became specialists and played a role in their government.

Rulers and military men both saw the value of concepts that would allow them to plan, organize, staff, direct, and control for the use of both human and material resources. The Bible, clay tablets from ancient Egypt and Babylonia, and writings from the ancient Greek and Roman worlds all contain records and advice on the art of managing.

Classical Management Theory

The classical school of management had its foundation during the Industrial Revolution, which began in England with the invention of reliable steam-powered machinery and its early applications. This new technology, combined with the concentration of vast amounts of raw material and labor, created a need for management. The writings of the pioneers of the classical school offered others the benefits of their experiences in early factory management. They offered advice on how to improve production operations and their thinking about management as both a science and an art. They have given us the principles and functions of management that are discussed in varying detail throughout this text. Exhibit 1.1 lists the major contributors to the classical school of management theory.

EXHIBIT 1.1
Management's Classical Thinkers

Person	Contributions
(Captain) Henry Metcalf (1847–1917) Classical Scientific	Advocate of administration as a science, based on principles applicable in a variety of environments. Metcalf designed a system for controlling costs and materials that fixed responsibilities and managed the flow of information. Managers, he felt, should record their experiences for the benefit of those who follow, thereby contributing to the study of the science of administration.
Frederick W. Taylor (1856–1915) Classical Scientific	Dedicated to the refinement of scientific principles and their applications to production efforts. Taylor was an early pioneer in time and motion study, whose objective was to remove fatigue and improve efficiency and output. He advocated a system of pay based on output by an individual worker (piece-rate pay). Taylor is often called the Father of Scientific Management.

EXHIBIT 1.1
Continued

Henry L. Gantt (1861–1919) Classical Scientific	Promoted concern for workers and a movement away from authoritarian management. He introduced a task and bonus system of paying wages that paid a fixed wage for below-standard work, a bonus if standards were met, and an additional amount when standards were exceeded. Gantt asserted that methods improvements are best when they are willingly adopted by the people who must apply them. He was the inventor of the Gantt chart for programming production.
Henri Fayol (1841–1925) Classical Administrative	Applied the scientific management concepts to top management and administration. Fayol developed the fourteen basic principles of management that underlie all managerial tasks. (See Exhibit 1.2.) He identified five basic management functions: planning, organizing, commanding (directing), coordinating, and controlling.
Chester I. Barnard (1886–1961) Classical Administrative	Emphasized leadership as the most important task of any manager. He advocated the use of fundamental management principles in any administration position. As an executive in business, government, and not-for-profit institutions, Barnard proved his theories about management and leadership. Barnard felt that after managers set goals and collect resources, they should work at leading so as to gain acceptance for their authority.

One of the pioneers of the classical school was the British mathematician Charles Babbage, who in 1832 published *On the Economy of Machinery and Manufacturers*. In his studies of factory methods, he observed that definite management principles existed, that they had broad applications, and that they could be determined by experience. He thought that the most important principle was "the division of labor amongst the persons who perform the work." Babbage called for the division of work into different processes that could be taught to and mastered quickly by a person.

Babbage and others laid the foundation for the classical management school of thought. The classical school can be looked at as having two branches: classical scientific and classical administrative. Each branch had its points of emphasis, its contributors, and its contributions.

Classical scientific. The scientific management branch arose as a result of a need to increase productivity. With labor in short supply, there was a need to increase the efficiency of workers. The emphasis of scientific management was to try to find the one best way by examining the way work was done, the sequence of the steps, and the skills of the workers.

Frederick Winslow Taylor, American, executive, consultant, production specialist, and efficiency expert (called the Father of Scientific Management), wrote about the applications of scientific methods to factory problems and about the proper uses of human labor and time in executing worker tasks. From his practical experience at Midvale Steel, Simonds Rolling Machine, and Bethlehem Steel, Taylor developed his own work methods and procedures. Introducing time studies to analyze workers' movements on the job, he established how much workers should be able to do with the materials and equipment. From this analysis, he was able to determine the quickest way to do the task. In demonstrating how established scientific principles could be applied, he contributed significantly to what is now known as "scientific management."[4]

Taylor and other scientific management theorists provided a rational approach to examining work-related problems. Both the emphasis on job specialization, as seen on the modern-day assembly lines, and the time and motion studies are the foundations for efficiency in work. Scientific selection and training of workers are the basis for good staffing programs, they felt. The charting systems they advocated for production scheduling have become even more refined with computers.

Classical administrative. We have seen that the classical scientific management branch arose from the perceived need for improving productivity; the classical administrative branch, on the other hand, grew out of the need for guidelines to manage the complex organizations that emerged from the Industrial Revolution. The classical administrative branch emphasized the development of managerial principles rather than work methods.

Henri Fayol, the recognized leader of the classical administrative branch, believed, as did all administrative theorists, that management was not a personal talent but a skill that could be taught. His emphasis was on understanding the principles that underlie good management and on developing a general theory of management practice to serve as a guide to managers. The development of his fourteen principles of management, based on his management experiences, are the foundation for many of today's management practices.[5] (See Exhibit 1.2.) These principles provide

EXHIBIT 1.2
Henri Fayol's General Principles of Management

1. *Division of work:* Specialization allows workers and managers to acquire an ability, sureness, and accuracy that will increase output. More and better work will be produced with the same effort.
2. *Authority:* The right to give orders and the power to exact obedience are the essence of authority. Its roots are in the person and the position. It cannot be conceived of apart from responsibility.
3. *Discipline:* Discipline comprises obedience, application, energy, behavior, and outward marks of respect between employers and employees. It is essential to any business. Without it, no enterprise can prosper. It is what leaders make it.
4. *Unity of command:* For any action whatsoever, an employee should receive orders from one superior only. One person, one boss. In no case is there adaptation of a social organism to a duality of command.
5. *Unity of direction:* One head and one plan should lead a group of activities having the same objective. One head, one plan.
6. *Subordination of individual interest to general interest:* The interest of one person or group in a business should not prevail over that of the organization.
7. *Remuneration of personnel:* The price of services rendered should be fair and satisfactory to both employees and employer. A level of pay depends on an employee's value to the organization and on factors independent of an employee's worth such as cost of living, availability of personnel, and general business conditions.
8. *Centralization:* Everything that serves to reduce the importance of an individual subordinate's role is centralization. Everything that increases the subordinate's importance is decentralization. All situations call for a balance between these two positions.
9. *Scalar chain:* The chain formed by managers from the highest to the lowest is called a scalar chain or chain of command. Managers are the links in the chain. They should communicate to and through the links as they occur in their chains. Links may be skipped or circumvented only when superiors approve and a real need exists to do so.
10. *Order:* This principle is simple advocacy of a place for everyone, and everyone in his or her place; a place for everything, and everything in its place. The objective of order is to avoid loss and waste.
11. *Equity:* Kindliness and justice should be practiced by persons in authority to extract the best that their subordinates have to give.
12. *Stability of tenure of personnel:* Reducing the turnover of personnel will result in more efficiency and fewer expenses.
13. *Initiative:* People should be allowed the freedom to propose and execute ideas at all levels of an enterprise. A manager able to permit the exercise of initiative by subordinates is far superior to one unable to do so.
14. *Esprit de corps:* In unity there is strength. Managers have the duty to promote harmony and to discourage and avoid those things that disturb harmony.

Source: Adapted from *General Principles of Management,* by Henri Fayol. Copyright © 1949 by Pitman Learning, Inc., 6 Davis Drive, Belmont, Calif. 94002. Reprinted with permission.

modern-day managers with general guidelines to organize and administer complex organizations. These basic tenets or principles serve as the theory base for sound administrative structure.

Behavioral Management Theory

The first modern-day author to speak to the subject of concern for people in the work environment was Robert Owen, considered by many the Father of Modern Personnel Management. With the publication of his "An Address to the Superintendents of Manufactories" in 1813, the Scottish manager of textile mills pointed out that the quality and quantity of workers' output were influenced by conditions on and off the job. He demonstrated in his own mills that it made good economic sense to devote as much attention to "vital machines" (people) as to "inanimate machines."[6]

Owen was far ahead of his time. It was not until the contributions of Mary Parker Follett in the 1920s that individual workers were to once again receive the kind of attention and serious study they required. Although not a manager, she wrote so convincingly on the topic of management, with such profound truth and practical guidance, that she quickly was recognized as a major source for modern thinking about problems in personal and group relationships. She believed scientific methods and principles could be applied to human relationships,[7] and she believed people could reach their potentials only through groups.

Elton Mayo was another who emphasized the behavioral aspects of the worker. Through the work conducted at the Hawthorne plant of Western Electric, management was alerted that the social environment of employees had a great influence on productivity. People had needs for recognition and social satisfaction.[8]

The behaviorists took management another step forward. By focusing on employees as individuals, as parts of work groups, as persons with needs to be met by the organization, they forced management to view the work environment from another stance. Modern-day managers view employees as individuals, as resources, as assets to be developed and worked with—not as machines. Exhibit 1.3 lists the major contributors to the behavioral school of management theory.

Quantitative Management Theory

Another management theory school is the quantitative or management science approach. The emphasis of this school is on the application of quantitative or mathematical approaches to management problems. From its roots in World War II scientific research teams, which were assembled to solve highly technological problems, management science has become a part of management activities in most large organizations.

The use of statistical analysis, linear programming for the allocation

EXHIBIT 1.3
Management's Behaviorists

Person	Contributions
Robert Owen (1771–1858)	Asserted that both the quantity and quality of workers' outputs are directly related to conditions on and off the job. It makes sense, Owen said, to concern yourself with your employees' welfare; investments in this effort will return to the business in greater profits.
Mary Parker Follett (1868–1933)	One of the first management thinkers to attempt to apply psychology to business environments. She advocated the application of all teachings of social science to industrial settings. Follett felt that effective leaders motivate others and are able to coordinate plans, actions, and relationships. She promoted the application of scientific methods to human relations problems on the job.
George Elton Mayo (1880–1949)	Conducted studies in industry that identified the social needs in people as strong motivators, along with the need for a sense of participation and membership in a group. His studies pioneered in a search for understanding human motivations to work and while at work.
Douglas M. McGregor (1906–1964)	Industrial psychologist and consultant, McGregor has given us his famous propositions of Theory X and Theory Y, identifying traditional and improved philosophies about employees. (See Chapter 11 for details of these theories.) Theory X assumes the worst about people, whereas Theory Y assumes the best. A manager, using his or her assumptions about people, affects those people and thus their subsequent behavior; what the manager then experiences affects his or her own approach to managing thereafter.

of resources, the development of models before implementing an idea, production scheduling techniques, and financial analysis are all examples of present-day implementation of the quantitative or management science school. An area not addressed effectively by this school is the human relations side of the business.

Systems Management Theory

The systems theory school is built on the premise that the manager of an organization must understand all the various systems that compose the entire operation. A **system** is a group of interrelated parts operating as a whole to achieve stated goals or to function according to a plan or design.

An organization has its subsystems—its various divisions that perform the related tasks necessary for its survival. To understand how any system works, you must know how each of its subdivisions works and what each contributes to the whole. Changes in any one subsystem will usually have consequences for the other subsystems. This systems view of a business organization requires that managers view the entire system with an eye toward understanding how any change they make in their particular subsystems will affect all the other subsystems and the entire system.

In short, no manager, department, or divisional unit in a business is entirely independent of the others within it. This view of the entire operation and its parts is meant to prevent a positive move in one area from negatively affecting another area.

Contingency Management Theory

The contingency theory school is based on the premise that the actions or approaches managers should take depend on the situation and its variables. It looks for the most effective way to deal with any situation or problem. Each situation encountered, although possibly similar to other experiences, has unique characteristics. The contingency theorist uses the classical theories (scientific and administrative), the quantitative (management science) concept, and the systems (interrelatedness) viewpoint to analyze and solve problems. The true contingency approach is an integrative approach. One situation may require a people solution, whereas another may require a logistics solution. The contingency theorists draw on the experiences of the behaviorist in one situation and the knowledge of the quantitative school in another.

The contingency approach to a problem begins with an analysis of a problem, a listing of the circumstances prevailing at the time, the possible courses of action available, and the consequences of each course of action. No two situations are exactly alike and, therefore, no two solutions should be.

Management: An Art or a Science? A Profession?

We have seen what a manager does in the job (the functions), how the job is performed (the roles), the skills required to do the job, and the evolution of management and management theory with current applications. But is management an art or a science? And is it a profession?

Actually, management is neither an art nor a science, but it requires both to be successful. The manager needs to understand people, read situations, reflect on and use applicable experiences—all these are descriptions of management as an art. The application of Fayol's principles, the use of computers for decision making, and statistics analysis —all these are examples of management as a science. Managers work in both areas daily, demonstrating that management is both an art and a science.

Is management a profession? Edgar Schein has defined the characteristics of professionals and has evaluated managers against these characteristics. Professionals, Schein asserts, do the following:

1. They make decisions based on general principles.
2. They attain their status by achieving certain objective standards of performance.
3. They are governed by a strong code of ethics.[9]

Management meets these criteria in some areas and not in others. Management makes use of proven knowledge contributed by practicing managers, social scientists, and other professionals. And the existence of management training at educational institutions and inside organizations indicates that there are generally accepted principles of management to study. (See Exhibit 1.2.) But management does not have a uniformly accepted set of objective performance standards by which to evaluate itself, nor is there a common code of conduct to govern the practices of its members.

For our purposes, it matters little whether or not managers can be certified as professionals at this time. What matters is the general direction management is taking. We need to recognize that, as a field of study, management is growing. More people in the ranks of management today have been exposed to formal training in undergraduate and graduate courses than at any time in the past. Management as a separate field of study is only about sixty years old. The progress made in that short span of time is an indicator of the long-range growth of management.

Summary

- A manager is a paid decision maker—a person hired to commit resources to achieve goals.

- Managers and management utilize human, financial, and material resources through the five major management functions of planning, organizing, staffing, directing, and controlling.

- Most formal organizations contain the three traditional levels of management: top, middle, and operating (first-line, or supervisory).

- Managers at every level perform the same functions. They differ in the time spent on each function and the depth of their involvement with each function.

- To carry out their jobs, managers must be able to perform certain roles. The roles are influenced by a manager's job description and the expectations held by superiors, subordinates, and peers. The ability to perform the multiple role demands is the difference between a successful manager and an unsuccessful one.

- Managers need three basic skills: technical, human, and conceptual. The relative importance of these skills depends on the level of management a manager occupies.

- Managers are evaluated on two criteria: effectiveness (doing the right thing) and efficiency (doing things right).

- Five major management theories have led us to where we are today in the study of management: the classical (scientific and administrative), behavioral, quantitative, systems, and contingency theories.

- Management is neither an art nor a science.

- Management is rapidly evolving into a profession.

Glossary of Essential Terms

conceptual skill   The ability to view the organization as a whole and see how the parts of the organization relate and depend on one another. Deals with ideas and abstractions.

human skill   The ability to interact with other people successfully. To understand, work with, and relate to individuals and to groups of people.

management	The process of setting and achieving goals through the execution of five basic management functions that utilize human, financial, and material resources.
managers	Those in positions of authority who make decisions to commit resources toward the achievement of goals.
organization	A group of two or more people that exists and operates to achieve clearly stated, common objectives.
role	Behaviors a manager is required to enact as he or she functions in the organizational environment. The role is influenced by the job description and the expectations of superiors, subordinates, and peers.
system	A group of interrelated parts, operating as a whole, to achieve stated goals or to function according to a plan or design.
technical skill	The ability to use the processes, practices, techniques, and tools of the specialty area a manager supervises.

Review Questions

1. Can you define this chapter's essential terms? If not, consult the preceding glossary.

2. How do managers assist an organization to achieve its objectives?

3. List and define each of the five major management functions. Why is planning considered the "first" function?

4. How does the term *universality of management* apply to the three levels of management found in most modern-day organizations? How does the execution of the planning function differ in the three levels of management?

5. What is a management role? List and explain four roles managers are required to perform.

6. Identify the three management skills, and explain how the proportions of the skills needed differ at each management level.

7. Identify the major emphasis of each of the five schools of management thought. Explain how each is utilized in modern-day management.

References

1. Henry Mintzberg, "The Manager's Job: Folklore and Fact," *Harvard Business Review* (July–August 1975), pp. 49–61.

2. Robert L. Katz, "Skills of an Effective Administrator," *Harvard Business Review* (September–October 1974), pp. 90–102.

3. Peter Drucker, *Managing for Results* (New York: Harper & Row, 1964), p. 5.

4. *Classics in Management*, rev. ed., ed. Harwood F. Merrill (New York: American Management Association, 1970), p. 56.

5. Ibid., p. 188.

6. Ibid., p. 10.

7. Ibid., p. 280.

8. Elton Mayo, *The Human Problems of an Industrial Civilization* (New York: Macmillan, 1933).

9. Edgar H. Schein, "Organizational Socialization and the Profession of Management," *Industrial Management Review*, 9, no. 2 (Winter 1968), pp. 1–16.

Readings

Albrecht, Karl, with Steven Albrecht. *The Creative Corporation.* Homewood, Ill. Dow Jones Irwin, 1988.

Barcus, Sam W. III and Joseph Wilkinson. *Handbook of Management Consulting Services.* New York: McGraw-Hill, 1987.

Brown, D. S. "Management: How and Where It Originated." *Bureaucrat*, Fall 1987, pp. 28–30.

Brownstone, David and Irene Franck. *The Manager's Advisor*, rev. ed. New York: AMACOM, 1987.

Cowan, Robert A. "When the Thrill Is Gone." *Nation's Business*, March 1988, pp. 31–32.

Grothe, Mardy and Peter Wylie. "Resolved: 'I'll Be a Better Boss.'" *Nation's Business*, January 1988, pp. 43–45.

Hornstein, Harvey A. *Managerial Courage: Revitalizing Your Company Without Sacrificing Your Job.* New York: John Wiley & Sons, 1987.

Kuzela, L. "Management: Making Things Happen." *Industry Week*, August 24, 1987, p. 26.

Pinchot, Gifford III. *Intrapreneuring.* New York: Harper & Row, 1985.

Rhodes, Lucien. "At the Crossroads." *Inc.*, February 1988, pp. 66–76.

C
A
S
E
S

1.1   Kim Tanumi's Ms. Print Shop

Kim Tanumi is about to celebrate her first year as an entrepreneur in the printing business. Her Ms. Print Shop is a franchise that operates throughout two midwestern states. Until recently, she has been operating with herself as the sole voice of authority and has relied on two part-time employees from two local schools as her chief assistants. Though she has trained them to operate the offset press and the other pieces of equipment, Kim has done everything else on her own. All decisions on the price of a job, the scheduling of work, judging quality, and purchasing supplies are made by her.

Lately, however, her business has grown so much that Kim has found this arrangement unsatisfactory. Instead of using her part-timers interchangeably on the equipment, Kim is planning to let Roger concentrate on offset and duplicating and to let Kyle handle the other machines. They would have their jobs expanded to include maintenance, ordering the supplies they needed, and making deliveries of their finished work to neighborhood business customers. When she proposed these changes to her employees, they resisted them. Kyle felt that if their jobs were to grow their pay should, too. Kim responded that their pay was fixed by the going rate for part-timers in the community. Roger wanted to learn more about the ways in which the business's other operations were handled, not just the machines. Kim resisted his demand also. The result was that both employees were very unhappy.

Within two weeks following Kim's rearrangement of the workload, Kyle quit. Roger stayed on, but his attitude changed from cheerful to surly. After interviewing several people, Kim hired a retired man who had worked all of his life in printing and just wanted to keep his skills sharp and his days full. Ben worked out just fine, and after a few weeks, Kim took him on full-time and made him shop manager in charge of all printing operations and Roger. All reporting was then done by Roger through Ben to Kim. Kim reserved the right to go directly to Roger when emergencies arose. This was the source of irritation to both Roger and Ben on more than one occasion during the next few weeks.

pg. 20
using
1, 2

violating
2, 9, 4, 7, 12
13

For Discussion

1. Using Exhibit 1.2, identify the principles of management that Kim is using. Provide examples from the case to support your decisions.

2. Using Exhibit 1.2, identify the principles of management that Kim is violating. Provide examples from the case to support your decisions.

1.2 The President's Remarks

Mario Gonzalez started his company from scratch. He was proud of his accomplishments and let his people know that he was proud of them and their contribution to his company's success. Each quarter of the company's fiscal year ended with an informal luncheon get-together consisting of all the company's managers and Mario. As president, Mario started each meeting with a review of the past quarter's accomplishments for individual persons and the company. Goals that had been reached were stated, and those responsible for achieving them received direct praise and thanks from Mario. Individual managers felt free to voice their opinions and to ask questions. After each luncheon, Mario left his managers with goals for the next quarter and a list of the tasks he viewed as most important. Managers left the meeting knowing who was to do what.

This quarter's meeting ended with the distribution of a one-page handout that contained the following:

1. Find a suitable replacement for the company's vice-president of marketing services within 30 days.

2. Train the existing personnel in accounting to operate the new desktop computers within 45 days.

3. Split the personnel department along functional lines, creating three specialty areas, each headed by its own supervisor. Deadline for change: 45 days.

4. Cut rejects in the production department from 11 to 5 percent within 90 days.

5. Submit proposals for improving morale and motivation on the plant's third shift within 30 days.

For Discussion

1. Which of the items on Mario's list could be classified as planning problems? As organizing problems? As directing problems? As staffing problems? As controlling problems? Explain your answers.

2. Which levels of management will probably be involved in each of the five problems and their solutions? Explain your answers.

Managing Yourself

OUTLINE

Getting to Know Yourself
- Determining Your Skills and Aptitudes
- Determining Your Interests
- Determining Your Motivations

Education and Obsolescence
- Avoiding Obsolescence
- Education and Income

Plans for Improvement
- Constructing Your Plans
- Setting a Timetable
- Implementing Your Plans
- Overcoming the Barriers to Improvement

Planning Your Career
- Thinking About Careers
- Why People Quit Their Jobs
- Making It in Management
- The Sequence of Planning Steps
- Your Present Job

Career Stages
- Stage 1. Trial
- Stage 2. Establishment and Advancement
- Stage 3. Midcareer
- Stage 4. Late Career

Adjusting to Your Employer
- The Socialization Process
- Insiders' Demands
- Outsiders' Demands
- Achieving a Balance

Taking Charge of Your Future

Summary

ESSENTIAL TERMS

aptitude   skill
interest   socialization
obsolescence

LEARNING OBJECTIVES

After reading and discussing this chapter, you should be able to do the following:

1. Define this chapter's essential terms.

2. Describe the importance of, and the means for getting to know your skills, aptitudes, interests, and motivations.

3. Discuss the concept of obsolescence as it relates to your career and what you can do to prevent it.

4. Outline the steps you can take in planning for your future growth and development.

5. Describe the five basic steps you can use to plan your career.

6. Describe the four basic stages you can expect your career to pass through.

7. Describe the socialization process you can expect to experience with each new employer.

Getting to Know Yourself

This chapter is about you and your future. It offers some suggestions and models to help you identify your strengths and weaknesses, to plan for your improvement, to plan your career, and to take charge of your future. The ideas in this chapter can help you continue the growth that you showed you desire by selecting this course in management.

Before you can hope to be successful at managing others, you must be able to effectively manage yourself. To manage yourself—plan, direct, organize, and control your efforts, time, and other resources and choose a staff to help you—you must know yourself well. By using your strengths, working on your weaknesses, and implementing these ideas, you will improve yourself and your ability to manage others. Self-improvement and career planning both begin with identifying your skills.

The first step in getting to know yourself well is to take a personal inventory of your positive and negative characteristics. You need to know what you have working for you and what is working against your progress and ability to perform. By clearly defining your skills, aptitudes, interests, and motivations, you will know who you are and where to begin.

Your skills, aptitudes, interests, and motivations can be defined with the help of friends, your boss, and the organization where you work. People who know you well may have valuable observations of your character and personality to share if you ask them to. Your boss appraises your performance and can help you label your strengths and weaknesses. It is probably reasonable to hope that your boss wants you to overcome your weaknesses and will help you plan for improvement. Your organization's personnel or human resource management department may have a variety of aids available, including career counseling, training programs, and various tests to assess your skills, aptitudes, interests, and motivations.

Determining Your Skills and Aptitudes

A **skill** may be mental or muscular-motor. Mental skills involve the ability to calculate, form clear thoughts, solve problems, organize and plan work, and make decisions. Muscular-motor skills require eye–hand or limb coordination to perform such tasks as typing, writing, operating equipment, and performing physical activities. Skill levels are usually measured through proficiency tests and exercises to see how well the applicant can perform specific tasks and activities. Most of the examinations a person takes in school are proficiency-type tests.

An **aptitude** is a natural tendency, ability, or talent. Aptitudes are areas of your personality that may or may not be developed. They are related to skills because they are the areas skills are developed in. A person with an aptitude for determining spatial relationships has potential to become a skilled mechanic, machinist, artist, or technician. Whether that person does become one of these or not depends in part on that person's interests and the degree to which this aptitude is developed through various experiences, both in and outside a classroom. Exhibit 2.1 shows six basic

EXHIBIT 2.1
Six Basic Aptitudes and the Employment Areas That Relate to Each

Abstract Reasoning	The ability to think logically without using numbers or words. Skilled craftsmen, technicians, engineers, scientists, and computer programmers must have this capacity.
Verbal Reasoning	The ability to think, comprehend, and communicate effectively with words. Authors, teachers, administrators, salespeople, and secretaries require this ability.
Mechanical Reasoning	The ability to recognize the mechanical principles that govern the use of machines and tools. Draftsmen, repairmen, engineers, mechanics, and skilled craftsmen require this ability.
Numeric Ability	The ability to solve mathematical problems and think in numbers. Bank tellers, economists, accountants, designers, and technicians must feel comfortable with numeric reasoning.
Spatial Relationships	The ability to make things three-dimensional and to imagine the shapes and sizes of things. Depth perception and the ability to estimate distances are also part of this aptitude. Drivers, assemblers, draftsmen, scientists, and technicians share this aptitude.
Manual Dexterity	The ability to move the hands skillfully and easily. Nearly every assembly operator, craftsman, and technician needs this aptitude and so do artists and musicians.

Source: U.S. Department of Labor.

aptitudes and the employment areas that relate to each when the aptitudes are developed to marketable skill levels.

Aptitudes and skills are refined by hard work and by educational and practical experiences. Some jobs call for high levels of skills in specific aptitude areas. Others do not. Managers must have highly developed aptitudes in abstract and verbal reasoning and numeric ability. But to begin a career, they may need other aptitudes and skills to qualify for various entry-level positions.

Determining Your Interests

An **interest** is an area of human activity or work that has a special, personal appeal. An area of interest usually captures your attention and curiosity; it draws you in. You get a sense of joy and fulfillment in pursuing it. Your interests are what you would prefer to spend time doing when you are free to choose your activities. Exhibit 2.2 shows a typical item from a preference (interest) test or inventory. Such tests are used to match a person's needs and interests to a specific job environment and the rewards that a job can provide.

Determining Your Motivations

A *motivation* is a psychological need; it may be for security, social activities, esteem, or self-fulfillment. Motivations are your fundamental reasons for engaging in various activities and work. Various tests can help you determine what is really important, not just interesting, in your life and work, but in fact, you already know most of your motives for behaving as you do. Do you seek a job and career that will give you autonomy? Do you want power over others? Do you desire a great deal of human companionship and social relationships? We devote Chapter 10 of this text to the complex subject of motivation and human needs. What is important now is that you recognize, to some extent, what you want from life and your work. Then you can seek jobs and working environments that will lead you to satisfaction of your needs. But you should be aware that what is motivating your behavior now will not always be with you. Motivations change with time, experiences, and your circumstances.

Taking a personal inventory of your needs, abilities, and interests will give you a self-awareness that you probably do not now have. It will arm you to face future decisions about education, jobs, and a career with a larger set of facts to base your decisions on. You won't be rolling dice or jumping at the first opportunity. You will be considering various factors that will enable you to make a more meaningful choice, one that will lead you to a better emotional and financial state.

EXHIBIT 2.2

A Typical Interest or Preference Test Item Designed to Help You Determine Your Motivations

Listed below are several characteristics that could be present on any job. People differ about how much they would like to have each one present in their own jobs. We are interested in learning *how much you personally would like* to have each one present in your job.

Using the scale, please indicate the *degree* to which you would like to have each characteristic present in your job.

Would mildly like having this		Would strongly like having this		Would very strongly like having this	
4	5	6	7	8	9	10

8	1. High respect and fair treatment from my supervisor
8	2. Stimulating and challenging work
8	3. Chances to exercise independent thought and action in my job
10	4. Great job security
8	5. Very friendly co-workers
10	6. Opportunities to learn new things from my work
10	7. High salary and good fringe benefits
10	8. Opportunities to be creative and imaginative in my work
8	9. Quick promotions
10	10. Opportunities for personal growth and development in my job
10	11. A sense of worthwhile accomplishment in my work

Source: J. R. Hackman and G. R. Oldham, *Work Redesign.* © 1980, Addison-Wesley Publishing Co., Reading, Massachusetts. Reprinted with permission.

Once you have a list of your skills, aptitudes, interests, and motivations, you will have a good idea of where you are and where your strengths, both actual and potential, lie. You can begin to construct a plan to improve your skill levels and develop your aptitudes. You will be ready to set specific goals and timetables for reaching them.

Education and Obsolescence

Avoiding Obsolescence

Obsolescence exists when a person or machine is no longer capable of performing to standards or management's expectations. What choices does management have when confronted with an obsolete person or machine? Exhibit 2.3 highlights a company's alternatives. You can see that the best you can hope for from your employer are training and incentives for self-development. In theory, every employee is eligible for training, but in practice, not everyone qualifies for it. Since it is your future we are discussing, you are the one who should be most concerned with it. Don't wait for your employer or others to make the first move. You must take the initiative and maintain it.

A person can become obsolete in attitudes, knowledge, and skills. Obsolescence in any one of these areas may mean trouble for you. An employer needs the services of people who are well schooled and up to date in their chosen fields. Long after your formal schooling ends, you

EXHIBIT 2.3
An Employer's Choices Regarding an Obsolete Person and an Obsolete Machine

Person	Machine
Invest in the person through training and development, and offer incentives for efforts at self-improvement.	Keep the machine, and modify it (when economically feasible to do so) to improve its efficiency and longevity.
Tolerate the person and his or her limitations and inefficiencies.	Keep the machine, and live with its limitations and inefficiencies.
Tolerate the person, but reduce his or her role in the organization by deletion of duties or demotion.	Keep the machine, but reduce its role in production, relegating it to back-up or temporary use.
Discharge the person, and replace him or her with a better-qualified person.	Scrap the machine, and replace it with a more up-to-date model.

Source: W. R. Plunkett, *Supervision: The Direction of People at Work*, 4th ed. Copyright © 1986 by Allyn & Bacon, Needham Hgts., Mass., p. 28. Reprinted by permission.

should be updating your knowledge, attitudes, skills, and abilities with a self-directed program of constant reading and studying about the new developments in your field of specialization.

Personal obsolescence can happen gradually or quite suddenly. Overnight changes can take place that will render a person's performance inadequate. Computers have had this impact on managers as well as workers. When one company buys or merges with another, changes take place rapidly and unpredictably. New skills and knowledge are necessary for the changes in tasks and job descriptions that will take place. Those who possess the potential and have prepared themselves for bigger things will find themselves in great demand and playing more important roles. Others will be looking for new positions with other employers. (See Exhibit 2.4.)

Once begun, your efforts at personal growth should continue throughout your working years. Education by formal and informal means is a lifetime process. The day you stop learning is the day you begin to regress. Continuing your education is the best insurance you can have against the risk of becoming obsolete. Through education, you keep your

EXHIBIT 2.4
If You're Not Getting Ahead on the Job . . .

Sure, the raises come. But there's nothing special for you, nothing to signify a step upward.

And promotions? Well, it's been a long time since the last one.
Meanwhile, the best assignments, the big advancements go to others.

What's gone wrong?

Several things, possibly. And not all of them necessarily are your fault.

Here are ten factors that often explain stalled careers. Look over the list. See which apply to you.

1. Bucking the Boss

Every boss likes candid comment and independent thinking—he says. But how much will he take? There's always an invisible limit. Any chance you've exceeded it?

There are right and wrong ways to dissent and offer differing ideas. You can couch them as contributions toward achieving goals. Or as negative judgments that sound cutting instead of supportive. Which is your way?

Do your proposals create trouble or solve problems? Think about ramifications before you toss out ideas.

Like it or not, the boss is your key to promotion. You don't have to "yes" him, but you ought to make him glad you're around.

continued

EXHIBIT 2.4
Continued

2. Just Cruising

You think you do a good day's work and the company can't complain. Probably you do. And likely it can't. But is that reason to promote you?

Promotions go to those who excel, who show competence or capability beyond the norm. Have you quit putting out signals that distinguish you from the herd?

If you no longer have the zest to give the job more than it asks, perhaps you ought to forget promotion. You may have decided—unconsciously—that you don't want the demands a better job would bring.

3. In the Wrong Company

Sometimes a company just can't—or won't—promote a person in your position. It may be too small. Maybe it's in a shrinking industry or locked into old ways of operating. Perhaps there's nepotism or excessive regard for seniority. Maybe it's an aggressive outfit that raids other companies for good people instead of recognizing its own.

If any of these circumstances hold you back, you're in the wrong company. Start looking for an alert, growing firm that believes in promoting from within.

4. Keeping Yourself Secret

You could shine like the noonday sun in your own branch yet get nowhere because the people who promote don't know you.

Don't trust to natural forces to get the good news around. Watch for chances to get outside your bailiwick. Go to professional gatherings and company meetings. Socialize. Contribute. Watch for activities that bring recognition.

Use tact and discretion, of course. A reputation as a self-promotor won't help. But neither will anonymity.

5. Nursing Disappointment

A cruel truth about how jobs get filled: Only one person gets the job. All others are disappointed.

Know already what it means to lose? Then how did you handle your disappointment? Bitter withdrawal? Animosity? Grudge bearing? Self-pity?

Such responses make temporary defeats permanent. Get off that track. Figure out what went wrong. Ask somebody who was in on the decision. Start thinking about positioning yourself for the next promotion that's coming up.

6. Ducking Tough Duty

How do you define a big job? By the responsibility it entails. You will never look fit for a big job if you duck responsibility that comes your way.

EXHIBIT 2.4
Continued

You know the names for it. Passing the buck. Shifting blame. Letting George do it. Dodging flak. It can also take the form of wanting the last specific detail on a job before you'll do it.

Avoid accepting responsibility where you are and you'll never move up to more of it.

7. Nothing but Replays

Routine is fine if it saves time on small matters to permit more on large ones. But you score no points on replays. And constant replays dull one's ability to innovate, to do things in fresh, better ways.

Look back. Have you come up with anything new lately? Any improvement in procedure or policy? No? Could that explain why no one has come up with the idea of advancing you?

8. Pointing Out Problems

Problems need identifying, but inability to see anything but problems is not a promotable trait.

Some people are naysayers, habitual pessimists, chronic negativists. Launch a new idea and they give 20 reasons why it cannot, ought not, must not be done. And they predict failure if it is.

Have you been showing yourself in this defeatist role? Try looking for how-tos, not why-nots.

9. Overdoing Expertise

Knowing too much about too little can be a trap. Top jobs call for generalists, persons free from specialized perspectives who can handle a broad range of problems.

If you're too specialized, choices narrow to aiming for the best jobs within your specialty, enlarging your qualifications by training or otherwise, or moving to a firm that uses specialists less restrictively.

10. Staying on Too Long

Too long with one firm? It's possible.

One way to keep a career moving is to keep moving yourself. At judicious intervals, not too frequently and not capriciously. Move only to a better situation, better prospects, wider opportunities and preferably all three.

Switching jobs is drastic. But if you're stalled and it's not your fault, a drastic action is needed.

mind alert, and you will be making those necessary refinements so important to flexibility and progress.

Education and Income

Workers with college degrees had an average monthly income of $1,910 in 1984 (the latest year for which figures are available), more than twice as much as was earned each month by those with only a high school diploma.[1] Figure 2.1 shows the wage differences among people, linked to their educational attainment. Although the dollars earned each year may change, the size of the gaps between the groups tends to stay about the same over the years. Education pays.

According to the U.S. Census Bureau, about 21 percent of American adults have earned a degree beyond high school. About 53 percent of all adults have a high school diploma. About 23 percent of college graduates are men with business degrees, and about 15 percent of women college graduates have a business degree. For business managers, the average monthly salary in 1984 was $3,726.

FIGURE 2.1
The relationship between income and education (1984 figures)

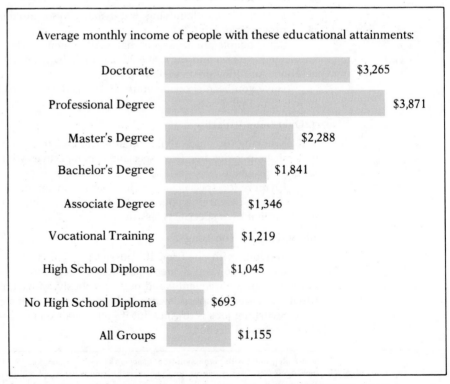

Average monthly income of people with these educational attainments:

Doctorate	$3,265
Professional Degree	$3,871
Master's Degree	$2,288
Bachelor's Degree	$1,841
Associate Degree	$1,346
Vocational Training	$1,219
High School Diploma	$1,045
No High School Diploma	$693
All Groups	$1,155

Source: J. L. Albert, "Census Survey Shows Higher Education Pays," copyright 1987, *USA Today*. Reprinted with permission. Data from U.S. Census Bureau.

Northwestern University's Linquist-Endicott report for 1988 (summarizing the findings of a survey of 226 personnel directors of major U.S. companies) lists the following average starting salaries for the class of 1988:[2]

Bachelor Degrees	Average Annual Salary
Marketing/sales	$22,800
Finance/economics	23,100
Computer sciences	27,400
Business administration	22,900

Plans for Improvement

A personal plan for improvement is essential if you wish to expand your opportunities and avoid becoming out of date. But planning alone will accomplish little. You must have a personal commitment to planning and to accomplishing your plans. You must be willing to commit your resources to the fulfillment of your plans and to revise and update your plans regularly as changes to them or your situation occur.

Constructing Your Plans

Your self-improvement plans should answer the questions who, what, when, where, how, and how much. The question "why" has been answered in the preceding portion of this chapter and by your decision to construct plans for improvement. The "who" includes yourself and everyone else who will play a part in or influence your planning and the execution of your plans. Your family, for example, may have something to say about your plans and some limits to place on them.

The "what" of your plans should contain a specific set of goals, both short- and long-term, that you wish to achieve. These must be specific statements of your intentions, for instance, "to develop my ability to read with the proficiency normal for someone with my level of education." This major goal will lead to the creation of one or more specific minor goals to achieve your major goal, such as "to determine the level of my current ability to read and comprehend what I read" and "to take a specific course in reading (name the course) at a specific place and time (name them)."

One major goal you have now is to complete this course in management with a grade of B or better. To accomplish this, you must accomplish several minor goals, such as "mastering the content of each chapter and unit of study so that I have achieved each chapter's learning objectives and any other tasks set by my instructor."

Setting a Timetable

Unless you answer the question "when" in your plans, you run the risk of losing your initial enthusiasm and commitment through procrastination. In general, the sooner you begin to implement your plans, the better. Set a time for each beginning and each ending. Set a time for checking on your progress toward each of your goals. Use a desk calendar or a master chart, and mark the key dates for beginning, checking on your progress, and completing each task. Refresh your memory periodically by referring to your chart or calendar. Exhibit 2.5 may help you; it is just one example of a chart to keep you on target.

Implementing Your Plans

As soon as your plans are completed (when the basic questions are answered), you are ready to translate them into specific courses of actions that you need to take. Take the actions you have chosen on or before the date you have set for them to begin.

If your progress does not match your plans, don't get discouraged. Planning is always subject to change because it is an effort to predict the future. Revise your goals and plans in line with your experiences, and set new deadlines. Accuracy in predicting your progress is not as important as the progress itself. Find out why your plans have not evolved as you thought they would, and analyze each difficulty you encounter so that you find ways to eliminate or circumvent them in the future.

Overcoming the Barriers to Improvement

Your biggest enemy in planning and executing your plans is yourself. All of us tend to get a little too comfortable with routines. We repeat the patterns in our daily living regularly, preferring the known to the new or unknown. It's always easier to sit than stand. It's more comfortable to sleep late than to get up early. It's usually habit that makes us turn on the television, eat out Wednesdays, and drive to work the same way. Your plans will cause changes to your routines, habits, and patterns: If they don't, your life will not change in any significant ways. Hence it becomes more important than ever before to make the most of the time you have.

You may need the cooperation of others in your life to make your plans work to improve yourself and your situation. Friends, family, and others may have to help in some ways. With the return of adult women to higher education, the routines of many families' daily existences have had to change. Dad has taken up new duties to aid Mom's quest for job skills and a degree. Children have had to pitch in and take on additional responsibilities for their family's welfare. It's not easy making these ad-

EXHIBIT 2.5
Chart for Checking on Progress toward Specific Goals (Keep a Copy at Home and at Work)

Goal		January	February	March	April	May
To improve my business writing skills by mastering grammar, sentence and paragraph structure, and kinds of business letters	Action:	Enroll in English 105, Business Writing		Check on progress		Complete course, May 15
	Start time:	Jan. 19, 5 P.M.				
	Action:					
	Start time:					
	Action:					
	Start time:					
	Action:					
	Start time:					
	Action:					
	Start time:					

justments, but make them you must if your plans are to be completed. It is hard enough to overcome your own resistance to change, let alone other people's efforts to stand in your way.

Employers may affect your plans either positively or negatively. Help with tuition may be possible. Changes in work schedules may be possible, but don't make any plans contingent on such changes until you know that they can occur.

Some bosses can be a big help to your quest for knowledge. Your boss offers a practitioner's point of view in both business and career planning. Sharing your plans with the boss or sharing the knowledge you are gaining through your education may or may not be a good idea. Insecure bosses may view your study of management and your search for higher knowledge as a threat to them or to their operations at work. They may fear your acquisition of higher knowledge because it may mean you want their jobs or you aspire to bigger things. If you are a competent employee filling a job they depend on, they will not be anxious for you to leave through a promotion or otherwise. Be sure you know your boss well and can predict his or her reactions to your intentions before you take that boss into your confidence.

Planning Your Career

Just as you needed to set goals for improving your skills and aptitudes, so too must you set goals for effective career planning. You will need specific short- and long-range (strategic) plans to achieve your goals. Once you know your skills, aptitudes, interests, and motivations, you will have a good idea of what you have going for you and what you want. As part of your planning, you need to seriously think about all the elements of a career, research why people quit jobs they actively sought, and discover what it takes to be successful in a management job. After all, a career is made up of a series of jobs that lead you to ever-increasing competency, responsibilities, and income. It pays in the long run to plan your career.

Thinking About Careers

Sal Divita, a professor of business at George Washington University, recommends that you think about your career in reverse: "Ask yourself what position you want to hold when you retire and then work back from there through jobs it takes to attain that position." Professor Divita further advises that you talk to the person who holds that final job and find out what career path he or she has followed.[3] Avoid looking for a "next job" until you know where you want to be over the long run and what the best path is for getting there.

In their book, *Career-Tracking*, Jimmy Calano and Jeff Salzman offer six tips for keeping your career on the fast track:[4]

1. Look for trouble. Ask yourself in every situation, "What could go wrong?"
2. Take on the undesirable assignment. It'll be yours—your chance to be noticed and to excel.
3. Keep your word.
4. Continuously propose ideas. Look for small, incremental improvements.
5. Find people you can learn from, maybe develop a mentor/protégé relationship.
6. Associate with "positive" people, those excited about life and its possibilities.

Why People Quit Their Jobs

According to the results of a 1987 survey of 1,099 personnel managers, the number one reason given for quitting a job was having a poor opportunity for advancement (66 percent). The Adia Personnel Services survey found four additional reasons: wrong "fit" of person and the job (47 percent), displeasure with the kind of supervision received (46 percent), dissatisfaction with pay (45 percent), and personal problems (25 percent).[5]

Making It in Management

The Interface Group Limited conducted a survey in 1988 to determine what personnel directors from America's largest corporations look for in applicants for management jobs. Of those polled, 60 percent said they looked for experience and knowledge in a field, 22 percent looked for technical skills and an appropriate level of educational achievement, 21 percent looked for the ability to manage, and 12 percent looked for communication skills.[6]

When 100 middle managers were polled by TeleSearch Inc. in 1987, they were asked what they felt had led to their career advancement. Eighty-eight percent named hard work, good job performance, and a bit of luck. Only 9 percent mentioned office politics.[7]

According to a New York University study of 500 executives, there are six keys to being a success as a top executive (vice-president or CEO):[8]

1. An entrepreneurial spirit
2. The ability to manage intracompany rivalry

3. A thorough knowledge of one's company and its markets
4. The ability to identify a successful strategy and then to stick with it
5. Adeptness at identifying and solving problems before they become obstacles
6. Flexibility

The Sequence of Planning Steps

Figure 2.2 contains a sequence of steps for planning a career. It is a model to show moving from where you are now to where you would like to be. Keep in mind that you are qualified or can become qualified to pursue more than one career. There is no such thing as the one right career because your skills, aptitudes, interests, and motivations will work for you in many different areas of employment. Moreover, whatever choices you make are not forever; they can be undone, whenever you elect to make a change, by changing direction.

Step 1: Identify your career objectives.   This step asks you to put specific goals in writing for the short and long term. You must be able to state specifically what it is that you want from your present job and what you hope that job will lead you to in the way of rewards and personal opportunities for growth and development.

Step 2: Analyze jobs and career paths.   This step requires that you research jobs to determine what education, skills, and aptitudes they call for and what their environmental working conditions are. The *Occupational Outlook Quarterly*, published by the U.S. Department of Labor, along with other private and government publications, can help you determine what jobs match your personal qualifications. Few people, if any, match a job perfectly, and few employers look for a perfect fit. What matters most is that the job and the career it allows you to enter are areas that have a strong appeal for you, allowing you to pursue the development of your strongest aptitudes and skills. Exhibit 2.6 matches jobs with the educational requirements and other characteristics that are important to persons considering these jobs as possible employment opportunities.

Libraries, your school's placement office, employment agencies, and job holders are excellent sources of information. If you take a summer job, work part time, or do volunteer service, it can help you gain a close-up view of a job and career area. You will work alongside experienced workers and see what joys and frustrations you and they will undergo. You will be getting paid (probably) to explore areas of interest and can take advantage of the experience that your co-workers possess while acquiring first-hand knowledge of your chosen field.

FIGURE 2.2
Essential steps in planning your career. The last step can lead you to return to a previous step in search of a new job, employer, or career.

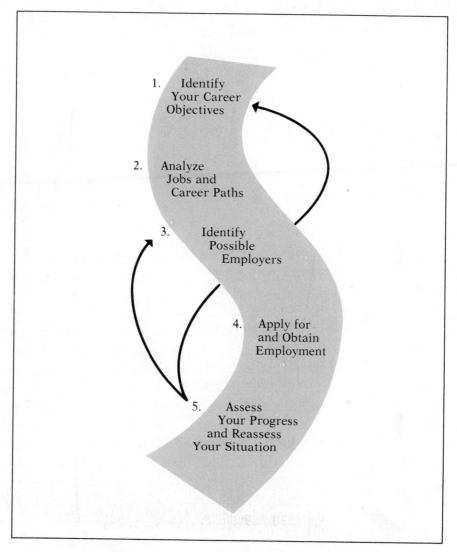

1. Identify Your Career Objectives

2. Analyze Jobs and Career Paths

3. Identify Possible Employers

4. Apply for and Obtain Employment

5. Assess Your Progress and Reassess Your Situation

Career paths are made up of planned job progressions. Entry-level or starter jobs are nonmanagement positions designed to give people experience in doing a job and an understanding of the job's demands and importance. The second job in many career paths is a move to the first level of management, the supervisory level. Some career paths include job rotation through a series of nonmanagement jobs, followed by a rotation through a series of supervisory management positions. Such paths allow people to experience many specialty areas and to develop an overall understanding of the entire organization.

EXHIBIT 2.6
Twenty Basic Jobs: Their Requirements and Characteristics

	1 High school	2 Tech. sch/Apprentice trng.	3 Community college	4 College	5 Problem-solving ability	6 Uses tools, machinery	7 Instructs others
Office Occupations							
Clerical occupations							
Bookkeeping workers	●						
Cashiers							
Collection workers	●						
File clerks							
Hotel front office clerks	●				●		●
Office machine operators	●					●	
Postal clerks						●	
Receptionists	●						●
Computer and related occupations							
Computer operating personnel	●	●			●	●	
Programmers		*	*	*	●		
Systems analysts				●	●		●
Banking occupations							
Bank clerks	●						
Bank officers and managers					●	●	●
Bank tellers							
Insurance occupations							
Actuaries					●	●	
Claim representatives			*	*	●		●
Underwriters					●	●	
Administrative and related occupations							
Accountants					●	●	●
Advertising workers					●	●	
Buyers					●	●	

*Educational requirements vary by industry or employer.

Source: Occupational Outlook Quarterly, U.S. Department of Labor, 1988.

EXHIBIT 2.6
Continued

	8	9	10	11	12	13	14	15	16	17	18	19	20	21	22	23
	Repetitious work	Hazardous	Outdoors	Physical stamina	Generally confined	Precision	Works with detail	Frequent public contact	Part time	Able to see results	Creativity	Influences others	Competition on the job	Works as part of a team	Jobs widely scattered	Initiative
	•				•	•	•		•	•				•	•	
	•				•	•	•	•	•						•	
	•				•		•	•				•		•	•	•
	•						•		•					•	•	
	•				•		•	•						•	•	
	•				•	•	•	•						•	•	
	•			•	•		•								•	
	•				•		•	•	•					•	•	
	•				•	•	•							•	•	
					•	•	•							•	•	
					•	•	•									•
	•				•	•	•							•	•	
					•	•	•	•				•		•	•	•
	•				•	•	•	•	•					•	•	
					•	•	•								•	
				•		•	•	•						•	•	
					•	•	•							•	•	
					•	•	•	•						•	•	
							•	•		•	•	•	•	•	•	•
							•					•	•	•	•	•

Step 3: Identify possible employers. Your possible employers are those that have the kind of jobs and career opportunities you are looking for and are located in an area where you would like to live and work. Consider the climate and cultural, educational, and economic conditions that exist in an area before looking for a job with a specific employer. Once you have a specific area in mind, you are ready to research the employers in the area.

Exhibit 2.7 shows the changes that have taken place in the populations

EXHIBIT 2.7
The Growth of Population and Households in the United States, 1980–1987

State	U.S. Households Number (millions)	Change (1980–1987) (percent)	U.S. Population Number (millions)	Change (1980–1987) (percent)
Alabama	1.48	10.5	4.09	4.9
Alaska	0.17	32.8	0.54	30.7
Arizona	1.24	29.6	3.43	24.6
Arkansas	0.89	9.7	2.40	4.5
California	10.07	16.8	27.53	16.9
Colorado	1.25	18.2	3.31	14.1
Connecticut	1.18	8.7	3.21	3.3
Delaware	0.23	15.0	0.64	8.3
District of Columbia	0.24	-1.9	0.62	-2.6
Florida	4.78	27.8	11.96	23.4
Georgia	2.25	20.6	6.24	13.9
Hawaii	0.34	17.3	1.08	12.2
Idaho	0.35	10.2	1.01	5.8
Illinois	4.27	5.6	11.57	1.4
Indiana	2.04	6.3	5.52	0.7
Iowa	1.07	1.8	2.83	-2.7
Kansas	0.94	8.1	2.47	4.7
Kentucky	1.36	8.2	3.73	1.8
Louisiana	1.56	10.9	4.50	6.1
Maine	0.44	13.1	1.18	5.5
Maryland	1.65	13.4	4.53	7.5
Massachusetts	2.19	7.8	5.84	2.1
Michigan	3.35	5.0	9.19	-0.7
Minnesota	1.58	9.7	4.24	4.2

EXHIBIT 2.7
Continued

State	U.S. Households		U.S. Population	
	Number (millions)	Change (1980–1987) (percent)	Number (millions)	Change (1980–1987) (percent)
Mississippi	0.90	9.9	2.64	4.1
Missouri	1.94	8.2	5.10	3.8
Montana	0.30	6.8	0.81	2.9
Nebraska	0.60	6.4	1.60	1.6
Nevada	0.39	30.6	0.99	25.8
New Hampshire	0.39	21.0	1.05	14.8
New Jersey	2.80	10.2	7.69	4.2
New Mexico	0.53	20.8	1.51	15.1
New York	6.72	6.0	17.76	1.5
North Carolina	2.39	17.0	6.42	9.0
North Dakota	0.24	8.3	0.67	2.9
Ohio	4.03	5.2	10.77	−0.1
Oklahoma	1.24	11.2	3.30	8.2
Oregon	1.07	8.3	2.72	3.4
Pennsylvania	4.44	5.4	11.87	0.6
Rhode Island	0.36	9.1	0.98	4.1
South Carolina	1.19	16.5	3.42	9.7
South Dakota	0.26	8.9	0.71	2.7
Tennessee	1.82	12.5	4.85	5.7
Texas	5.96	20.9	16.94	18.0
Utah	0.51	15.4	1.69	15.0
Vermont	0.20	14.6	0.55	7.2
Virginia	2.17	16.5	5.88	10.4
Washington	1.76	14.3	4.51	9.8
West Virginia	0.70	3.0	1.90	−2.7
Wisconsin	1.78	8.0	4.79	2.1
Wyoming	0.17	6.7	0.51	4.4
Total	**90.03**	**12.0**	**243.31**	**7.4**

Source: "South, West Get Lion's Share of USA's Growing Households," copyright 1988, *USA Today.* Reprinted with permission. Data from U.S. Census Bureau.

of the fifty states and their number of households from 1980 to 1987. Use the chart as a guide to help you decide if the state you are thinking of locating in is one with real growth and, therefore, job opportunities.

Exhibit 2.8 is a 1988 ranking by *Inc.* magazine of growing U.S. cities. In constructing its list, *Inc.* used three criteria: new-business birthrate, percentage growth in private employment, and percentage of young companies experiencing high growth. "For each city, a relative score for each factor was calculated based on a four-year period, then the three numbers were added together for an overall score."[9] You can use *Inc.*'s rankings to help you decide if the city you have in mind is one with growth in its recent past and, therefore, one with possible job prospects.

Finding out about an employer can be done in several ways. The community it is located in will usually have a chamber of commerce or business bureau that can help you determine its local reputation. If a corporation, it will have an annual report of its financial condition. It will be listed in various investment or commercial credit publications and will have an employment history in the area. (An employment history is a record of the

EXHIBIT 2.8
Inc. *Magazine's 1988 Ranking of the Top Thirty Metro Areas*

Metro Ranking

1. Austin, TX (1)	16. Pensacola, FL (31)
2. Manchester-Nashua, NH (8)	17. Fort Myers, FL (22)
3. Orlando, FL (2)	18. South Bend, IN (24)
4. Phoenix, AZ (3)	19. Charleston, SC (14)
5. Atlanta, GA (9)	20. Norfolk-Portsmouth, VA (21)
6. Raleigh-Durham, NC (7)	21. San Antonio, TX (6)
7. Huntsville, AL (10)	22. Jacksonville, FL (16)
8. Washington, DC (11)	23. Boston, MA (25)
9. Dallas-Fort Worth, TX (4)	24. Baltimore, MD (43)
10. San Diego, CA (13)	25. Richmond, VA (58)
11. Nashville, TN (15)	26. El Paso, TX (19)
12. Tucson, AZ (5)	27. Las Vegas, NV (47)
13. Portsmouth-Dover, NH (20)	28. Greensboro, NC (60)
14. Albuquerque, NM (12)	29. Sarasota, FL (28)
15. Tampa-St. Petersburg, FL (23)	30. Memphis, TN (26)

*Inc. magazine's 1987 rankings for the thirty cities are shown in parentheses.

Source: Reprinted with permission, *Inc.* magazine, (March, 1988). Copyright © 1988 by *Inc.* Publishing Company, 38 Commercial Wharf, Boston, MA 02110.

company's hirings and layoffs. Is it known as a good place to work? A bad place? Does it have a history of strikes and labor unrest or employee turnover?) Present employees will give you insights into its reputation for treating its people fairly. The local library can help you find these publications and research a company's history and product lines. If the company deals with unions, these can provide useful information about employment conditions, pay, and benefits.

Step 4: Apply for and obtain employment. Once you have narrowed your choices to the most promising employers, apply to them with a resume and letter of application for specific employment areas. Specify in your letter the job or jobs you believe you are most qualified for and most interested in. State your career objectives. Your resume should contain all the skills, educational experiences, and jobs you have held that relate to the job you are applying for.

If you are applying for a management position, you will want to be familiar first with the material in Exhibit 2.9. It is a list of the qualities many firms see as important to a manager. Although you need not be very strong in all these attributes, your employer will want candidates with strength in most of them.

Two elements critical to obtaining employment are the resume and the employment interview. The resume you prepare will serve the purpose of "opening the door" to a job, and the interview is one of the methods an employer uses to determine the aptitudes and motives you currently have.

Your Resume. A 1987 survey for Robert Half International by Burke Marketing Research polled vice-presidents and personnel directors in 100 of America's largest corporations. According to its findings, the greatest problems found in resumes were[10]

Problems in Resumes	Occurrence
Lies and distortions	36%
Too long	21
Errors and misspellings	19
Lack of specifics	12
Irrelevant material	11
Failure to list job accomplishments	10

Dulany Foster, Jr., president of the National Association for Corporate and Professional Recruiters, advises that you list your name, address, phone number, education, and jobs in the reverse order you held them. Briefly describe your duties and achievements.[11]

The Employment Interview. Your employment interview will follow your application and resume. Like most important events, you must prepare for it. Hopefully, you have researched the company you applied to before you

EXHIBIT 2.9
Ten Attributes That Organizations Look for in Applicants for Management Positions

1. Oral communication skill—effective expression in individual or group situations (includes gestures and nonverbal communications)
2. Oral presentation skills—effective expression when presenting ideas or tasks to an individual or to a group when given time for presentation (includes gestures and nonverbal communication)
3. Written communication skill—clear expression of ideas in writing and in good grammatical form
4. Job motivation—the extent to which activities and responsibilities available in the job overlap with activities and responsibilities that result in personal satisfaction
5. Initiative—active attempts to influence events to achieve goals, self-starting rather than passive acceptance, taking action to achieve goals beyond those called for: originating action
6. Leadership—utilizing appropriate interpersonal styles and methods in guiding individuals (subordinates, peers, superiors) or groups toward task accomplishment
7. Planning and organization—establishing a course of action for self and/or others to accomplish a specific goal: planning proper assignments of personnel and appropriate allocation of resources
8. Analysis—relating and comparing data from different sources, identifying issues, securing relevant information, and identifying relationships
9. Judgment—developing alternative courses of action and making decisions that are based on logical assumptions and reflect factual information
10. Management control—establishing procedures to monitor and/or regulate processes, tasks, or the job and responsibilities of subordinates: taking action to monitor the results of delegated assignments or projects

Source: W. C. Byham, "Starting an Assessment Center the Correct Way." Reprinted from the February 1980 issue of *Personnel Administrator*, copyright © 1980 by The American Society for Personnel Administration, Alexandria, VA.

sent in your application. If not, do so before the interview. Be prepared for such questions as

- Why should we hire you?
- Why did you apply to our company?
- What are your strengths and weaknesses?
- What are your short-term and long-term goals?

- What do you want from work?
- Why do you want a new job?
- What do you like least/best about your current job?

Make a record for yourself about who will be interviewing you and when and where the interview is to take place. Become familiar with the route to the interview in advance, and decide how long it will take you to get there. Dress appropriately for the interview, and arrive a little early. Review your resume, and take along any necessary papers such as your driver's license and social security card.

The interview should be a two-way conversation. You want to give and get information. With courtesy and respect, answer and ask questions clearly. Listen carefully, and make any notes you feel necessary. Be honest and positive. Don't be afraid to detail your accomplishments, but avoid exaggerations. If no job is offered and if you are not refused employment, find out when the interviewer will let you know, and offer to follow up with a call or return visit. Consider each interview a learning experience that will make you a better interviewee.

Be certain that the company you apply to has the job and career opportunities you seek. Find out what help will be given to you in career counseling, training, educational opportunities, and development programs. When hired, give your absolute best to your job, and take advantage of the available opportunities for growth and development.

Step 5: Assess your progress and reassess your situation.   After your first formal performance evaluation, determine what has taken place since you began the job. Have your expectations materialized? Were the promises made kept? Have you grown in skill levels and developed aptitudes? What is your current view of your employer? What are the opportunities for advancement, and what is the possibility of a career with your employer?

Your Present Job

Chances are good that your motivations and career objectives may have changed somewhat since the start of your employment. In the light of your experiences, new goals or career opportunities may have become more important to you, and some adjustment may be needed to your original goals or to their priorities. Before you decide whether your choice of employment has been satisfactory, give yourself at least one full year in the job. This will enable you to see your job through a complete twelve-month cycle and to become eligible for most of your fringe benefits. Don't leave your present position before you know where you want to go and have secured that position.

Career Stages

Few people are lucky enough to find that their first job is in an area and with an employer that suits them permanently. Most of us find two or more jobs before we decide with certainty on a definite career and career path. And most of us pass through four distinct career stages before we retire. Exhibit 2.10 summarizes these stages and the needs they help us satisfy.

Stage 1. Trial

For most of us, this stage begins with the decision to get serious about employment and to seek education and experiences that are directly linked to our search for a career. We examine our skill levels, determine our interests and motives, and seek employment that will match them. For some, this happens in the later years of high school or college. For more and more of us, it happens after several years in unfulfilling jobs. For many women, it happens when children reach school age and time becomes available to pursue interests or start a new career.

Stage 2. Establishment and Advancement

As each of us learns new skills and develops aptitudes, our motivations begin to change. What may not have been too important to us suddenly or gradually takes on importance. After we earn a sense of competence in our chosen fields, we develop the confidence to explore new possibilities and employment areas. New conflicts—between the increasing responsibilities for our families and the increasing competition from our rivals at work—arise about how we spend our time. By the time we reach our late thirties or early forties, we begin to experience the third stage in our careers.

Stage 3. Midcareer

By midcareer, we have found our places in an organization and perform those activities necessary for us to stay abreast of our fields. We find ourselves in various management positions with responsibilities for others at work. Our focus and horizons widen to include more of a total concept about our jobs and our places in the organization as a whole. Priorities may be shuffled in our lives so that we settle down to pursue in earnest what we really value in life and work.

EXHIBIT 2.10
The Four Stages Most Careers Pass Through

Stage	Task Needs	Emotional Needs
Trial	1. Varied job activities 2. Self-exploration	1. Make preliminary job choices 2. Settling down
Establishment and Advancement	1. Job challenge 2. Develop competence in a specialty area 3. Develop creativity and innovation 4. Rotate into new area after 3–5 years	1. Deal with rivalry and competition; face failures 2. Deal with work/family conflicts 3. Support 4. Autonomy
Midcareer	1. Technical updating 2. Develop skills in training and coaching others (younger employees) 3. Rotation into new job requiring new skills 4. Develop broader view of work and own role in organization	1. Express feelings about midlife 2. Reorganize thinking about self in relation to work, family, community 3. Reduce self-indulgence and competitiveness
Late Career	1. Plan for retirement 2. Shift from power role to one of consultation and guidance 3. Identify and develop successors 4. Begin activities outside the organization	1. Support and counseling to see one's work as a platform for others 2. Develop sense of identity in extraorganizational activities

Source: D. T. Hall and M. A. Morgan, "Career Development and Planning." *Contemporary Problems in Personnel,* rev. ed., eds. W. C. Hamner and Frank L. Schmidt (Chicago: St. Clair Press, 1977). Reprinted by permission of John Wiley & Sons, Inc., New York.

Stage 4. Late Career

For most of us, late career is marked by a peak in prestige in our chosen careers. Our focus begins to include outside activities, retirement planning, and grooming younger members of the organization. We begin to help others develop their skills and aptitudes for larger roles in the organization and to groom our own successors. For many upper level managers, late career means consulting positions with other organizations, a position on the board of directors, and a chance to seek identity outside the career environment.

Adjusting to Your Employer

All of us enter our career fields with enthusiasm and varying expectations about what rewards and demands on our time and talents lie ahead. Seldom are our expectations in line with the realities we face once installed in our jobs. Our research and employment interviews have allowed us to create images and impressions of what lies ahead, but often these are distorted because of our own optimism or because of the rosy picture painted by employers who wanted us to accept jobs.

Organizations are a collection of people, and they have all the problems that people have. They, like us, are less than perfect. They are bound by traditional methods, policies, legal requirements, company politics, and union rules. Each of us faces a period of adjustment when we enter a new job and a new work environment. Despite organization efforts to prepare and orient us, surprises await us in the form of too little or too much challenge and responsibility. We must accept that our first entry-level jobs in our chosen careers will be different from what we think they will be. We must be ready for surprises.

The Socialization Process

Socialization is the process through which new members of an organization gain exposure to its values and norms, its policies and procedures, and the behaviors expected from new people. New employees discover for themselves who has the power, what restrictions are on them and what freedoms they have, and how to succeed and survive. Through time and controlled experiences, employers and bosses attempt to define the specific behaviors or roles they expect each new person to assume. Major problems of fit may occur between the employee's and the employer's expectations, needs, and demands. A meeting of the minds must take place if a person is to survive and grow in the new environment.

Organizational psychologist Edgar H. Schein has given us a model of the socialization process;[12] through it, we become accepted and conforming members of an organization. The socialization process consists of the three phases shown in Exhibit 2.11. Phase I forms impressions and expectations in the mind of a job seeker. Phase II is the period of adjustment,

DOLLAR$ AND NONENE™

"Welcome to 'You're Fired.' My first guest is an employee whose brand of fun-loving incompetence has been a delight to everyone in the company but me."

Source: Reprinted by permission of United Feature Syndicate, Inc.

which allows the new employee to match individual needs to those of the organization. Phase III achieves a meeting of the minds and mutual acceptance. Not all employees will survive the last two phases: Faced with conflicts and compromises too great to overcome, employees who cannot adjust and conform may be asked to leave or may leave voluntarily.

The psychological contract Schein describes defines what people are expected to give to the organization and what they can expect to receive in return. It is formed in the mind of the employee and is based on experiences, promises, and personal observations of the ways in which the organization conducts its operations. The terms of the contract are the result of interactions between employee and boss, employee and co-workers, and the employee's first-hand experiences with the organization's efforts to enforce the rules and behaviors it considers essential. A sense of fairness or equity must exist between employee and employer: Each must believe the other is doing its part and giving in proportion to what it expects to receive.[13]

Conflicts can result as the psychological contract comes into being. Co-workers can make demands on an employee that run contrary to management's. Management can say one thing but contradict its position through its actions. A boss may be calling for one level of production but tolerating and even rewarding a lower level. Workers tend to set their own restrictions on their behaviors, deciding what is to be given to an employer and what should be given to each other in order to remain in a social group.

EXHIBIT 2.11
E. H. Schein's Model of the Socialization Process

I. Entry

1. Occupational choice
2. Occupational image
3. Anticipatory socialization to occupation
4. Entry into labor market

II. Socialization

1. Accepting the reality of the human organization
2. Dealing with resistance to change
3. Learning how to work: coping with too much or too little organization and too much or too little job definition
4. Dealing with the boss and deciphering the reward system—learning how to get ahead
5. Locating one's place in the organization and developing an identity

III. Mutual Acceptance: The Psychological Contract

Organizational acceptance

1. Positive performance appraisal
2. Pay increase
3. New job
4. Sharing organizational secrets
5. Initiation rites
6. Promotion

Individual acceptance

1. Continued participation in organization
2. Acceptable job performance
3. High job satisfaction

Source: Edgar Schein, *Career Dynamics,* © 1978, Addison-Wesley Publishing Co., Reading, Massachusetts. Reprinted with permission.

Just how each of us adjusts to conflicting demands depends on our personal needs and goals.

Insiders' Demands

Insiders are people within your working environment: your equals in authority, your subordinates, and higher level managers. Your boss makes demands on your time and loyalty and expects you to comply with reasonable orders and instructions. The boss expects you to respect confidential discussions and information and, in turn, expects you to come to her or him with problems and complaints, not to hear about them second-hand. You, in return, have a right to expect proper instruction, fair evaluations of your performances, and a commitment to your success and advancement when you have proved you are capable of handling greater responsibilities.

A nationwide survey conducted by Burke Marketing Research asked 100 vice-presidents and personnel directors of large companies to identify traits and attitudes that cause subordinates difficulties with their bosses. The number one trait listed was dishonesty. Second came attending to personal business on company time. Being too aggressive and showing arrogance came next. Complaining, absenteeism, and lateness followed. Finally, not following company rules, policies, and instructions irritates bosses the most. Employers "expect a certain amount of commitment, dedication and enthusiasm from their employees. An absence of these qualities or a lack of motivation is likely to inspire similar feelings in your employer when raise and promotion time comes around."[14]

Your subordinates demand your loyalties in return for theirs to you. Before you give them the authority to act, you need to know their capabilities to handle that authority. If you make requests or give orders to subordinates, you arm them to act on your behalf. In performing their routines and executing tasks you delegate to them, they are acting as extensions of your position. Besides being accountable for what they do, you need to be loyal to them when they act as you have taught them or asked them to act. You need to stand behind them when they are wrong because you are at least part of the reason for their being wrong.

Your equals are *peers*—people who have the same positions of authority with your employer as you do. Your equals may adopt the attitude that you are all "in this together" and expect you to be a team player. When they are in the wrong, they may expect you to cover for them—to conceal their mistakes or protect them from the effects of those mistakes. Before getting involved with a coverup, consider the costs of such a move.

Since, logically, your friends at work will be selected from among your equals, you do owe your peers some loyalty. You owe them respect as individuals. You will often be in a position to help them with constructive criticisms and to share your bright ideas. Keep in mind that peers have a way of becoming superiors. Having such friends could be quite helpful in the future.

Outsiders' Demands

Just as outsiders influence the ways in which you execute and perceive your management roles (Chapter 1), they also demand some loyalty from you. When asked to work late, you often run into conflicts between your loyalties to your boss (and employer) and your loyalties to loved ones.

The major claims by outsiders are on your time. Friendships and families need your time. To yourself, you owe time to improve your situation and to further your personal growth and career. You also need time for leisure, rest, and relaxation. When conflicting demands are placed on your loyalties, you will probably have to make compromises.

Achieving a Balance

Along with your loyalties to various groups, you have a set of standards and a code of personal conduct to consider. How do you balance conflicting demands on your loyalties? New positions or states of being may be created or may emerge as a consequence of your actions, with some doors closing while new ones open. It is up to you to do a kind of cost–benefit analysis for each of your possible courses of action. You should know, before choosing, just what costs and benefits you would experience as a consequence of each available course.

You cannot please everyone, but you should be able to honor your commitments and obligations to people before agreeing to take them on. Don't think that you are alone in your efforts at reaching solutions to situations of conflicting loyalty. You are not. You know others who can provide needed insights and with whom you should consult. Let the people involved know of your difficulties. Seek their solutions. Facing disappointments and pain are part of life for everyone, but being deliberately hurt is not. With the employer–employee relationship should come some measure of understanding. With true friendship comes the willingness to put one's self out for a friend. And with a love relationship should come willingness to sacrifice for the other's gain.

Taking Charge of Your Future

Your future is in your hands. You must take the responsibility for it. You have affected it already in many ways, and your actions and plans will continue to do so. Your today is largely a result of your yesterdays. Your tomorrows will be what you want them to be if you take the time and make the necessary plans and sacrifices today.

This chapter has talked to you about improvement. It states that you must know yourself well before you can plan successfully for your future. By emphasizing your strengths and working on your weaknesses, you begin the process of self-development. You will avoid personal obsolescence by planning for your future, not by sitting back and accepting other people's plans for it.

Pursue your interests. Find a job that suits your capabilities and will help to expand them. Read, study, and listen to what others have to offer. Learn from your own experiences and those of others. Observe your boss, your classmates, your peers at work, and others who have something to teach you. Learning from your mistakes and the mistakes of others is never-ending. If you stop learning, you stop growing; you lose your self-respect and the respect of others and fall behind quite quickly in whatever you are doing.

You have seen through your own experiences that few things take care of themselves. Cars, appliances, homes, gardens, humans, and personal relationships need constant attention if they are to remain healthy and attractive. Your career and future need just as much thought and care as your mind and body do. You are the one person best equipped to know what care to give and how to give it. It's up to you.

Summary

- Getting to know yourself is the first step toward improving your present situation and choosing a career. You need to know your skills, aptitudes, interests, and motivations.
- All of us must put our strengths to work while trying to overcome our weaknesses.
- Plans are methods to achieve goals. Goals must be specific if they are to be achieved.
- Making plans for improvement is not enough. Your personal commitment and willingness to sacrifice to achieve your goals are also essential.
- Continuing your education, both by formal and informal means, is the best way to avoid personal obsolescence.
- Most of us pass through four stages in our careers: trial, establishment and advancement, midcareer, and late career. Despite their differences, each is a period for improvement and experimentation.
- Through the socialization process, we attempt to adjust to our jobs and environments with a new employer. We form a psychological contract with our co-workers and our employer that spells out what is to be given and received.
- Conflicting demands on our time and loyalties occur for all of us. They can be balanced effectively if we are honest and open with those causing or affected by the conflicts.
- Your future is your own responsibility. You must plan for it and expect that you will periodically modify and update the plans.

Glossary of Essential Terms

aptitude A fundamental capacity or talent—such as reasoning, verbalizing, and calculating—that may be innate or acquired.

interest Areas of activity that capture your imagination and curiosity and have a special appeal.

obsolescence The condition in which a person or machine is no longer capable of performing to management's expectations.

skill Mental or muscular-motor ability to do something well; a specific proficiency.

socialization The process through which new members of an organization gain exposure to its values and norms, its policies and procedures, and the behaviors expected from new people.

Review Questions

1. Can you define this chapter's essential terms? If not, consult the preceding glossary.
2. Why is it important for us to get to know our individual interests, aptitudes, and motivations?
3. What are the consequences of personal obsolescence? How can personal obsolescence be avoided?
4. Your future is in your hands. What are you doing about controlling its outcomes? What can you do, that you are not now doing, to improve your future?
5. Looking at Figure 2.1, determine where you are along its path. What should your next steps be?
6. What career stage are you in now? What should you be doing to prepare for the next stage?
7. Describe how you have experienced the socialization process in school or with an employer. What were the results?

References

1. J. L. Albert, "Census Survey Shows Higher Education Pays," *USA Today,* October 2, 1987, p. 11A.
2. Carol Kleiman, "Sunny Forecast for Class of '88," *Chicago Tribune,* December 18, 1987, sect. 2, p. 1.

3. Mark Memmott, "Forward Thinkers Plan Careers Backward," *USA Today*, October 7, 1987, p. 5B.

4. James M. Odato, "Tips to Keep Career on the Fast Track," *USA Today*, March 9, 1988, p. 4B. See J. Calano and J. Salzman, *Career-Tracking* (New York: Simon & Schuster, 1988).

5. Marcy Eckroth Mullins, "Why Employees Quit," *USA Today*, February 29, 1988, p. 5B.

6. Rod Little, "USA Snapshots: Experience Counts," *USA Today*, February 19, 1988, p. 1B.

7. "At Work: Hard Work Remains Key Rung on Corporate Ladder," *USA Today*, November 4, 1987, p. 4B.

8. Mark Memmott, "At Work: 6 Keys to Exec Success," *USA Today*, March 18, 1987, p. 9B.

9. "Metro Report: Hot Spots: *Inc.*'s Annual Ranking of America's Cities," *Inc.*, March 1988, p. 74.

10. Karen Loeb, "USA Snapshots: The Trouble with Resumes," *USA Today*, October 2, 1987, p. 1B.

11. "At Work: Resume Report: Keep It Simple," *USA Today*, December 2, 1987, p. 4B.

12. Edgar H. Schein, *Career Dynamics: Matching Individual and Organizational Needs* (Reading, Mass.: Addison-Wesley, 1978).

13. Ibid., pp. 94–97.

14. Nadia Cohen, "What Employers Dislike the Most," *Chicago Tribune*, January 20, 1985, sect. 8, p. 1.

Readings

Barlett, B. "The Bypassed Manager." *Management Today*, June 1987, pp. 82–84.

Bartolome, Fernando and Laurent, Andre. "The Manager: Master and Servant of Power." *Harvard Business Review* no. 6, (November–December 1986), pp. 77–81.

Birch, David. *Job Creation in America*. New York: Free Press, 1987.

"The Economy of the 1990s/Special Report." *Fortune*, February 2, 1987, pp. 22–24, 26–32, 35–38, 42–44, 58–63.

Fields, Debbie and Alan Furst. *One Smart Cookie*. New York: Simon & Schuster, 1987.

Harragan, Betty Lehan. *Games Mother Never Taught You: Corporate Gamesmanship for Women*. New York: Warner Books, 1987.

"Hotspots: *Inc.*'s Annual Ranking of America's Cities." *Inc.*, March 1988, pp. 74–76, 80–81.

Johnson, Raymond C. *The Achievers: The Art of Self-Management for Success*. New York: E. P. Dutton, Truman Talley Books, 1987.

Parkhouse, Gerald C. "Inside Outplacement—My Search for a Job." *Harvard Business Review*, no. 1 (January–February 1988), pp. 67–73.

Rogers, Buck with Levey, Irv. *Getting the Best Out of Yourself and Others.* New York: Harper & Row, 1987.

C
A
S
E
S

(2.1) Stalled Progress

Ellen is not happy with her present situation and let her husband know it. She reentered the workforce four years ago after an absence of some fifteen years. Six years ago, Ellen returned to school to brush up on her secretarial skills. She took courses in word processing and office management and paid for her schooling with part-time work as a lab assistant at her college and a partial scholarship. After her youngest child entered high school, Ellen found a full-time job as an executive secretary for a branch manager of a nationwide computer service firm.

Ellen is an excellent secretary and has been told so with both words and deeds. Her boss, Marge Henderson, has given Ellen annual raises of about 10 percent for each of the four years she has served Marge. But Ellen's duties have not changed since she began as a secretary, and she has just discovered that Marge is receiving a promotion to the company's home office. To date, Marge has said nothing about taking Ellen with her.

During the last two years, Ellen has made her desire for something greater known to just about anyone who will listen to her. She has consistently tried to change office procedures where she felt they needed changing but has been unsuccessful in most of her efforts. In Ellen's words, "Marge just wants to play it safe. She won't change her hair style unless she gets an OK from the home office first." Ellen was denied a promotion to the regional office about a year ago and has nursed her disappointment since.

In her discussion about her unhappiness with her husband, Ellen noted that no one knew a secretary's job better than she did. No one in her branch had her level of skills. For these reasons, Ellen believed, none of the other secretaries would socialize with her except on rare occasions. Her job has kept her isolated from other office personnel, limiting her contacts with them to general meetings and routine business contacts.

Ellen's husband noted that she was dwelling on the negative lately and that she was not very pleasant to be with. Ellen responded that she had lost the old zest that she had when she returned to work but that her frustration with her lack of progress was becoming too much to bear. Ellen's husband suggested either she find a job she could love again or he would find more reasons to work late.

For Discussion

1. Using Exhibit 2.4, analyze why you think Ellen has not progressed on the job.
2. What suggestions do you have for Ellen?

2.2 Our Workforce: Where Do You Fit In?

In 1987, about 111 million employed Americans helped to produce that year's gross national product: $3.9 trillion (using 1982 dollars as the measure). In the same year, 47 percent of the employed labor force consisted of white males, and 53 percent consisted of women and minority group males. Managers, professionals, and clerical workers represented 40 percent of employed persons, and 32 percent worked in manufacturing-related jobs. Of the more than 25 million jobs created in our economy since 1970, 88 percent were in services. Between 1987 and 1995, about 90 percent of all new jobs will be in services. From 1970 to 1987, our employed workforce has grown about 40 percent. In March 1988, 114.1 million Americans were employed, and 6.8 million were unemployed, giving us a total workforce of 120.1 million.*

In 1987, there were about 35 million "contingent workers" (temporaries, part-timers, independent consultants) in our labor force. Along with the service sector, this is one of the fastest growing segments in our nation's workforce. Companies use contingent workers to fill in at peak periods, to avoid labor costs, and to avoid unionization of their workforces.** Contingent workers work for different employers throughout the year for as little as part of one day and for as much as six months or more. In 1988, about 800,000 Americans earned their pay each day as temporaries.

Fourteen of the twenty fastest growing occupations between 1988 and 1995 will require some form of vocational or technical training or a two-year community college degree. Among these are computer programmers, medical and dental assistants, computer service technicians, electrical and electronics technicians, food service workers and managers, and managers of hospitality businesses like motels and hotels.* Most of these fields offer a blend of schooling and work experience. And most community colleges have programs that will let you get college credit for your previous and current job experiences.

Finally, consider these facts: By the time you reach your 40s, you can expect to change your career three times and to work at between six and eight different jobs. These figures are national averages.* For most Americans, staying in one career track and working for one employer for their entire lives are things of the past.

For Discussion

1. Have the above facts about people at work affected your thinking about a career? If so, in what ways?

2. What do you think are the advantages to having a job as a temporary? The disadvantages?

3. What are the primary advantages that go with full-time employment? Which are most important to you?

---

*U.S. Department of Labor, Bureau of Labor Statistics.
**Marie Morelli and Mark Memmott, "Fewer of Us Are Full-Time Employees," *USA Today*, October 14, 1987, p. 5B.

Communicating

OUTLINE

ESSENTIAL TERMS

communication

communication barriers

feedback

impersonal communication

interpersonal communication

medium

message

receiver

sender

LEARNING OBJECTIVES

After reading and discussing this chapter, you should be able to do the following:

1. Define this chapter's essential terms.

2. Diagram the communication process, and explain the importance and relationship of each component to the others.

3. Explain the responsibilities of the sender and the receiver in the communication process.

4. List and explain the barriers to communication, and suggest remedies to overcome these barriers.

5. List and briefly explain the Ten Commandments of Good Communication.

What Is Communication?

What is the purpose of communication in business? What are the problems that can occur in communicating? How can you overcome these problems? What does a manager need to know when involved in communication?

Communicating with others is at the heart of every business activity and of the very process of living. It is the thread that ties the actions of the individual or organization to its desired objectives. It is also the way we humans have of sharing our feelings, thoughts, wants, and needs. When plans go wrong, it's a pretty sure bet that communication difficulties are part of the problem. In this chapter, we look at communication as a process that enables us to share our ideas with others. We also examine the barriers that interfere with effective communications, how to overcome these barriers, and what a manager needs to think about when involved in communication.

Communication Defined

What is communication? **Communication** is the transmission of information and understanding from one person or group to another. The goal is to get a set of information and the understanding of that information from one person or group to another person or group. The critical factor in measuring the effectiveness of communication is *common understanding*. If common understanding exists after the communication has happened, it can be said that effective communication has taken place. Understanding exists when both parties involved in the communication have a mutual agreement as to not only the information but also the meaning of the information.

If the goal of communication is that simple—common understanding or mutual agreement—why do people constantly have problems in communicating with one another? One reason is that communication involves two or more people in a very sensitive process. Let us consider what this process looks like and why it is so sensitive.

The Communication Process

The person who wants to send the message or signal to another is the **sender**. The person for whom the message is intended is the **receiver**. The information that the sender is sending (transmitting) to the receiver is the **message**. The way a receiver sends, verbally or in writing, is the **medium** or channel. The receiver uses **feedback** either to prompt clarification or to let the sender know that the message has been received as intended.

Figure 3.1 shows, in graphic form, the communication process. The sender prepares a message containing information for the receiver. A medium or channel is selected, and the sender transmits the message. The receiver gets the message and should, through feedback, either seek clarity on the message or let the sender know that the message was received as intended. This looks like a very simple process, but in actuality it is very sensitive. Why? Let's look at the process again in depth.

Initially, a sender has some ideas or thoughts that he or she would like to communicate (see Figure 3.2). The sender will then take these thoughts and ideas, develop a message, select a medium, and send the message. The sender ought to do all these things with a sensitivity to the receiver: Who is the person (the receiver)? How does the person think? What is the best way to communicate with the person? If the sender has not been sensitive, there is potential for ineffective communication.

Suppose Diana, Princess of Wales, walked up to your taco stand and asked for two tacos. Don't you think that the message is too imprecise and the medium—oral communication, face to face—too unsettling for you to feel confident about filling the order at once?

When the receiver gets the first message, another set of sensitive events takes place. The receiver attempts to translate the message and interpret what it means. Now the receiver must become a sender—looking for clarification of any unclear parts of the message or acknowledging the

FIGURE 3.1
The communication process

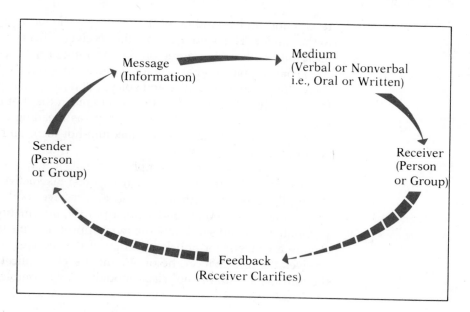

FIGURE 3.2
Communication in
action

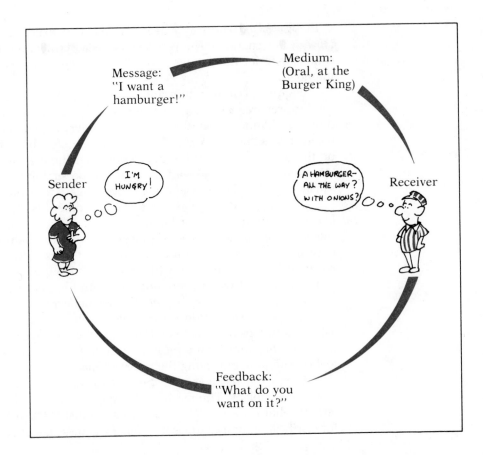

receipt and understanding of the message. The receiver is using feedback to the sender. The sender is now the receiver. This process should repeat itself until both parties agree on the meaning of the message.

For example, after asking for clarification about the tacos, you get this reply: "Oh, make them nice and spicy, but don't put any of those little red things on them." You "translate" this to mean that hot red peppers are to be omitted; you "interpret" the message as meaning that your customer wants what you designate as a medium-hot taco, and you can proceed with preparing two of them.

This process is more complicated than it may appear. If communications are to be effective, both parties must take active and passive roles during the process. Both must send and receive. Both must be sensitive to the other. The initial sender must put the information in the most appropriate form and send it by the most appropriate means. Such decisions require a concern for and knowledge of the receiver. When the receiver receives the information, he or she must seek clarification of any part of the information that is not clear enough to give complete understanding.

The receiver needs to send, as feedback, information to the sender. If no feedback returns to the original sender, the individual or group should ask for feedback to be certain that understanding has taken place. Until the sender has such assurance, the process continues. If it ends without the assurance of understanding, the process could be ineffective.

What does this mean to you as a communicator? What are the specific responsibilities of the sender and receiver in the communication process?

Communication Responsibilities

Responsibilities of the Sender

Responsibility #1. Be sure of the purpose of communicating. Before initiating the process, the sender has two basic questions to answer: Is communication necessary? What are the goals of communicating?

Is communication necessary? The sender must be certain that the idea or information in hand is worth the effort of communicating. Since communication of all kinds can distract and confuse as well as inform, the sender should be certain that what she or he has is valuable enough to share with others. This evaluation seems basic, but it is often overlooked; the result is an overloading of the formal channels of communication with redundant and unnecessary conversations, memos, and reports.

What are the goals of communicating? After the sender determines that what is to be shared is necessary for others to see or hear, he or she must decide what is the purpose or goal of the communication: Is it simply to pass information for present or future reference? Is it to introduce a change of some kind? Is it to provoke action from others? Whatever it is, the sender should be precise in his or her understanding of what is to be accomplished. With such certainty, the sender will be able to choose the proper words, audience, and medium for the message. The sender must keep referring to the goal while preparing to communicate and when communicating. This will help her or him focus on the necessary words or receivers in the process of communicating. The goal or goals will enable the sender to determine if the communication is effective. Exhibit 3.1 provides examples of goals for three different receivers of messages.

Responsibility #2. Know the receiver. Once the sender has determined that the communication is necessary and what specific results are desired, he or she must look at the intended audience to construct the message properly and to determine who the specific receivers should be. This step avoids making receivers of persons who should not be bothered by the message. It also helps tailor the message's form and content to a particular

EXHIBIT 3.1
Some Possible Major Goals of Communications to Three Types of Receivers

When Communicating with Superiors
- To provide responses to their requests
- To keep them informed of your progress
- To solicit their help in solving problems
- To sell them on your ideas and suggestions for improvements
- To seek clarification of their orders and instructions

When Communicating with Peers
- To share ideas for improvements
- To coordinate your activities with theirs
- To provide them with assistance
- To get to know them as individuals

When Communicating with Subordinates
- To issue orders and instructions
- To persuade and sell them on changes
- To appraise their performances
- To compliment, reward, and discipline
- To clarify your intentions, orders, and instructions
- To get to know them as individuals

person or group. The aim throughout all these steps is to eliminate unnecessary words and persons from the communication process.

Responsibility #3. Construct the message with the receiver in mind. Once the target audience has been identified, the sender needs to do some thinking, perhaps research, about that person or group. The sender can put himself or herself in the receiver's position while constructing the message so as to avoid words or references that will trigger emotions or distract the audience from the information and understanding intended. The sender should try to put the message into words that the audience will understand and choose only those words. Let the goal be known to the audience as close as possible to the beginning of the communication.

Before making contact with the receiver, the sender should know something about the receiver's background in regard to the message. What has preceded this message (events, other communications, etc.) that will color the receiver's view of the message? What interests and abilities does the receiver have that might help or hinder reception?

Responsibility #4. Select the proper medium. The sender needs to select the most appropriate medium. The choice of a medium to carry the message depends in part on the content of the message, who the receiver will be, the receiver's location and environment at the time of transmission, and the time chosen to transmit the message. The content of the message may dictate that a personal visit be used rather than a phone call or letter. Or in routine correspondence, a letter or memo is most appropriate. Exhibit 3.2 shows various choices using the written medium.

The receiver may dictate that a specific medium be used. Keep in mind that each of us has four separate and distinct vocabularies: we each have a written, a spoken, a heard, and a visual vocabulary. Because this is so, it would be best to communicate in writing to a receiver who assimilates information most efficiently when it is presented in written form. In addition, if the receiver has indicated a preferred medium, by either instruction or common practice, the sender should comply even if he or she thinks it may be inappropriate for the message. A preference for a written memo rather than a verbal communication is an example. If the receiver requests the communication, the sender should use the medium requested.

The receiver's location and environment can influence the choice of

EXHIBIT 3.2
Communication in the Written Medium

Letter	For correspondence with persons or groups outside the organization. Be sure to use prescribed formats for your official correspondence—form letters, block style, and so on.
Memo	For routine correspondence with superiors, subordinates, and peers. Your memos should contain the date, name(s) of intended receiver and the receiver's title, subject of the correspondence, the message, and the identity (name and title) of the sender. Limit to one page if possible.
Outline	For indicating the structure of a lecture, report, or agenda and to order major and minor points. Outlines are especially useful to develop a table of contents and to summarize.
Report	For reporting the results of an investigation or routine and ongoing activities. Formats vary from fill-in-the-blanks to manuscript with and without statistical data. Be sure to use prescribed formats.

a medium as well. A noisy factory may be a bad place for a face-to-face conversation. A luncheon meeting may be a poor environment for the presentation of a detailed document of research findings.

What are the types of mediums to work with? Do they have advantages and disadvantages? Two types a manager works with are impersonal—where you do not meet the receiver face to face or voice to voice—and interpersonal or face-to-face mediums. Each has its value.

Examples of **impersonal communications** include memos, letters, directives, and other kinds of written messages that are delivered in other than a face-to-face environment between the sender and receiver. The in-basket, mailbox, and bulletin boards at work contain impersonal communications. Impersonal communications usually offer no immediate opportunity for feedback between sender and receiver. The sender is absent at the time the receiver receives the message. This means feedback becomes more difficult and time consuming.

Receivers may not give the kind of attention they should to impersonal communications; the important communications get mixed with the unimportant ones. There is an air of informality and a lack of the sense of urgency when messages are received. Therefore, an impersonal means to communicate should not be used if the message is urgent and in need of the receiver's immediate attention. Impersonal communications should also not be used for any complex or lengthy message that may require clarification. Any message needing immediate feedback should be delivered in person through face-to-face or voice-to-voice means.

What should be communicated impersonally at work? In general, any communication that requires no or minimum feedback—any message that does not need elaboration. A few examples include acknowledgment of receipt of a message, a notice of a paid holiday, memos for files, an announcement that something is or is not going to happen, simple orders, and requests for information or visitations. Impersonal communication is acceptable for communicating about routine and noncontroversial subjects.

Examples of **interpersonal communications** include face-to-face and telephone conversations. This type of communication offers the advantage of immediate feedback. Senders can check on the receiver's comprehension and provide any clarification that may be necessary. When written messages are delivered in person by their authors, they become personal communications.

Interpersonal communications are called for when dealing with urgent matters and matters that require a give and take between senders and receivers. Meetings and conferences are desirable when the issues under discussion affect or require input from more than one person. They allow a means to share ideas, their pros and cons, to solve problems, and to pass on information.

Personal conversations are essential when handing out compliments or criticisms or when giving orders and instructions to subordinates. Thanks for a job well done should be given both in person and in writing. Disciplinary fact finding and grievance processing also require both approaches. Notes are taken in such conversations and become records of the personal exchanges or information and understanding as well as important historical documents. Thus, interpersonal communication provides the best type of communication.

Responsibility #5. The timing of the transmission also affects the sending of a message. Twenty minutes before quitting time is not the right time to communicate lengthy or detailed messages. When meetings run overtime, people are in a hurry or anxious to leave, in order to get on to other things, so messages may be conveyed and received incorrectly. Also, meetings held after lunch or late in the day can be less productive than those held at more opportune times.

Responsibilities of the Receiver

Just as the sender has specific responsibilities in the communication process, the receiver must share in these responsibilities if the two parties are to arrive at a mutual understanding.

Responsibility #1. Listen actively to the sender. The receiver needs to listen attentively to the message the sender has transmitted. This is a two-part obligation: first, to work at paying attention, not letting the mind wander; second, to concentrate on the content of the message, trying to avoid any misinterpretation of the message. The receiver should train himself or herself to pay attention in these ways.

Responsibility #2. Be sensitive to the sender. In what ways should the receiver be sensitive to the sender? By not overreacting to the message and by letting the sender complete the intended message. Another way is to be aware that the sender is trying to communicate this message because it must be important to him or her and in turn important for the receiver to listen. When the receiver considers the sender's feelings, there is a more comfortable climate for communicating.

Responsibility #3. Indicate the appropriate medium. The receiver can aid the communication process by indicating a preference for the medium to be used. This can speed up the communication process, eliminate a lot of trial and error by the sender, and potentially make both parties more comfortable with the communication. A sender's boss may have established several mediums for communication. One example would be the Monday morning meeting for an update or a status report. Another might be the requirement that all reports are to be in writing, in a prescribed format, and delivered in person. Or a union contract can specify that all disciplinary proceedings be put in writing and that specific persons must receive copies.

Responsibility #4.   Initiate feedback. As receiver, we have all been guilty of saying we understood a message when we did not or did not totally understand it. The receiver needs to take the initiative—providing feedback that asks for clarification or acknowledges that the message has been understood and will be acted on if action is called for. How? The receiver can restate the message or ask questions.

About now you may be asking yourself if that is all you need to know: If you are aware of the responsibilities of the sender and receiver, will your communication attempt result in understanding? The answer is that by understanding the process and responsibilities, you will be able to improve communications, but there are still some barriers that may interfere with the process.

Communication Barriers

Communication barriers are any roadblocks that can interfere with effective communication. They interrupt or block communication or prevent mutual understanding. Some barriers arise in interpersonal, face-to-face, communications, while others are unique to organizational structures. A manager functions in an organizational environment, which inevitably requires many face-to-face communication situations as well, so we will examine both types of barriers.

Interpersonal or Face-to-Face Barriers

Leonard R. Sayles and George Strauss have identified common barriers to face-to-face communication.

1. *Hearing what we expect to hear.*   How many times have you been involved in a conversation and tuned out the speaker because you absolutely knew what he was going to say? If you did, you were guilty of letting a barrier arise between you and the sender. This process of expecting something to be said because the situation and people involved seem familiar will seriously inhibit communication.

2. *Ignoring information that conflicts with what we "know."*   We "know" some things to be true. We know we must be at work by 8:00 A.M. We know we need to cooperate with fellow workers. We "know" that everyone who reports to us is satisfied in the work environment even if

that pesky secretary keeps telling us she has heard some people complaining. Blocking out information will definitely limit communication.

3. _Evaluating the source._　The meaning and value of a message is influenced by our evaluation of the source of the message. If the sender has credibility, the message will be received more readily. Communication from a person who has a proven track record is received with more attention than the same message from a rookie. For example, when an experienced old-timer gives instructions to a less experienced newcomer, the message has more value than if it came from a person of experience equal to the newcomer's.

4. _Differing perceptions._　Not all of us come from the same social or cultural backgrounds. We have a different set of experiences, and our values and beliefs are different. Thus, we have different perceptions of the world, and these perceptual differences color our communications. Telling an employee to handle something immediately can mean in the next few seconds, within the day, or when you get to it depending on the employee's perception of the message.

Source: Reprinted with special permission of King Features Syndicate, Inc.

FIGURE 3.3 (Right)
Multiple meanings of words
Source: Reprinted with permission of Macmillan Publishing Co., Inc. from *Communications: The Transfer of Meaning* by Don Fabun. Copyright © 1968, Kaiser Aluminum & Chemical Corporation.

5. *Words have different meanings to different people.*   Consider the words *liberal, conservative, politician, profit,* and *discipline.* Words are only symbols used in communication. For communication to be effective, both the receiver and sender must attribute one symbolic meaning to a word. Figure 3.3 illustrates this point.

Another communication problem associated with the meaning of words is that of jargon or technicalese. A person who works with computers knows what bits and bytes are, a trucker knows what a pup is, and an educator knows what FTE stands for—do you? You are not supposed to, and you don't need to know. Unfortunately, many of us slip into the vocabulary of our jobs when we are communicating with receivers who don't know the jargon. When this is done, it blocks communication.

6. *Conflicting nonverbal communication.*   Along with using words to communicate, all of us talk with our body poses and facial expressions. A person who is frowning while saying, "I really feel great," is actually sending two different messages. And a person who encourages us to elaborate on a story while struggling with a knotted shoelace is also contradicting the spoken message with body language.

7. *Emotional environment.*   Tempers interfere with reason and understanding and cause the roles to change from sender and receiver to opponent and adversary. Attempts at achieving a meeting of the minds can dissolve into name calling and offensive remarks and behavior. Something will be communicated, but the messages the parties take away will probably be damaging to both of them for some time to come. Related to this problem of anger intruding is the danger of being judgmental and evaluating the message. The intent of communicating is to convey information and understanding. The receiver can do that only if she or he listens to the content with an open mind. Being critical of the message will limit this.

8. *Noise.*   Other conversations, the sound of machinery, traffic noises, and irrelevant messages are all part of the working day. Each of these can block messages from being received.*

*Leonard R. Sayles and George Strauss, *Human Behavior in Organizations,* © 1966, pp. 238–246. Adapted by permission of Prentice-Hall, Inc., Englewood Cliffs, N.J.

LEAD

Lead (led), v.² ME. [f. LEAD sb.¹]

1. To cover with or enclose in lead. Also with *over*. 2. To arm, load, or weight with lead 1481. 3. To fix (glass of a window) with leaden cames 1530. †4. To line (pottery) with lead or lead-glaze; to glaze — 1686. 5. *Printing*. To separate lines of type with leads (see LEAD *sb.¹* 8) 1841. 6. *passive* and *intr*. Of a gun barrel: To become foul with a coating of lead 1875.
1. She leaded and paved the Friday Market Cross in Stamford FULLER. Hence LEA · DED *ppl. a.* (of panes of glass) fitted into leaden cames (1855); *Printing*, having the lines separated...

LEAD

Lead (Lid), *sb.²* ME. [f. LEAD *v.¹*]

†1. The action of LEAD *v.¹*; leading — 1510. b. Direction given by going in front; example; esp. in phr. to *follow the l. of* 1863. c. *spec.* in *Hunting*, etc., chiefly in phr. *to give a l.*, i.e. to go first in leaping a fence, etc. 1859. d. A guiding indication 1851. 2. The front or leading place; the place in front *of* (something). Also, the position or function of leading (e.g. a party), leader...

LEAD

Lead (lid), *v.¹* Pa. t. and pa. pple. led. [Com. Teut. wk. vb.: OE. *laedan:* — OTeut. **laidjan*, f. **laida* road, journey (see LOAD, LODE, *sbs.)*, related to OE. *lioan* to go, travel.]

I. To conduct.
1. *trans*. To cause to go along with oneself. †a. To bring or take (a person or animal) to a place. (Phrases like *to l. captive* are now understood in sense 2.) — 1704. b. To carry or convey usu. in a cart,

II. To carry on. †1. To engage or take part in, to perform (dances, songs), to utter sounds. Cf. L. *ducere carmen choros.* — 1493. 2. To go through, pass (life, †a portion of time). Cf. L. *ducere vitam..* Rarely, †To support ...

LEAD

Lead (led), *sb.¹* [OE. *léad* str. neut. = Du· *lood* lead, MHG. *Lót* (mod. G. *lot. loth)* plummet, also solder.]

1. The heaviest of the base metals, of a dull pale bluish-grey colour, easily fusible, soft and malleable. Chemical symbol Pb. Rarely *pl.=* kinds of lead. †b. Sometimes called *black lead* (= L. *plumbum nigrum)* in contradistinction to *white lead (plumbum* album), a name for tin — 1753. 2. See RED LEAD, WHITE...

Organizational Barriers

Besides the interpersonal barriers to communication, other blocks arise because of the nature of organizations.

1. *Management levels*.   The series of management levels in a company can develop natural barriers between the levels. Information can be screened as it moves up and down in the organization either accidentally or intentionally. Figure 3.4 illustrates this point.

2. *Number of people supervised*.   If a manager supervises many people, it may limit the amount of time that he or she can spend with each employee, thus limiting communication. Or sometimes the manager who supervises few employees can inadvertently overcontrol communication.

3. *The rank or position in the organization*.   A natural inhibition of communication can result when a president asks a receptionist to be open and honest about how the company is operating. What happens if the receptionist says the "wrong thing"?

4. *Change in managers*.   Is there a potential barrier when a new manager replaces an incumbent? There may be a change in both style and philosophy of communication. Will the new manager favor oral or written communication? Will the manager prefer one-to-one versus group settings to communicate? Philosophies may differ also. A manager may choose to become actively involved in all communication, which may mean she or he screens information or holds the information tightly.

5. *Manager's interpretations*.   Managers can be influenced by selective interpretation of events depending on their positions in the organization. The perspective of a manager—whether the giver of resources or a contestant for resources—can influence the manager's perception of what is happening and what is communicated, to whom it is communicated, and when it is communicated.

Figure 3.5 shows some of the networks that emerge in organizational communication. It is interesting to observe where the barriers in organizational communication could exist. Note that in the "Y" and the wheel networks, a manager could control information very early. In the chain network, the possibility of screening by levels comes into existence. The circle network provides for more than one source of communication, but still it is limited. Finally, the open network encourages communication among all persons.

The important point in this discussion is not the source of barriers but that they can be controlled by both the sender's and receiver's sensitivity to the communication process.

FIGURE 3.4
Management levels
as barriers

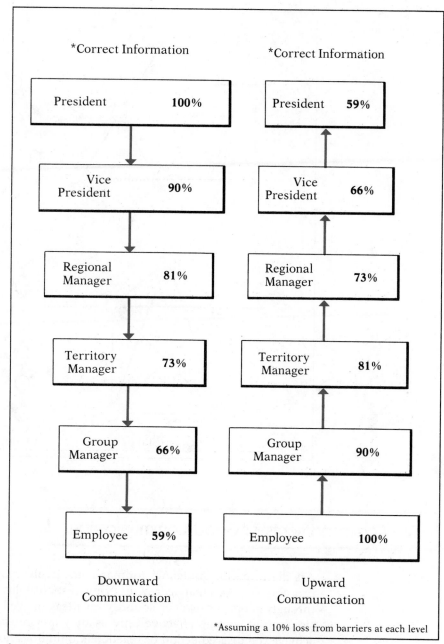

*Assuming a 10% loss from barriers at each level

Source: Adapted from *Human Behavior at Work: Organizational Behavior* by Keith Davis. Copyright © 1982, McGraw-Hill. Used with the permission of McGraw-Hill Book Company.

FIGURE 3.5
Communication
networks

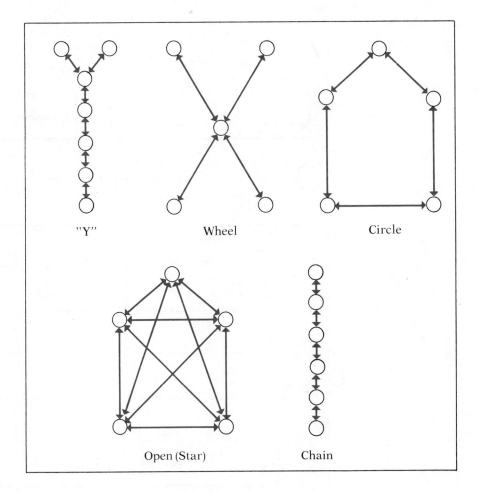

Ten Commandments of Good Communication

Are there specific guidelines for managers involved in the communication process? Yes. As a manager, your prime responsibility is to get things done through people. However sound your ideas or well-reasoned your decisions, they become effective only as they are transmitted to others and achieve the desired action or reaction. Communication, therefore, is your most vital management tool. On the job, you communicate not only with words but also through your apparent attitudes and your actions—because communication encompasses all human behavior that results in an exchange of meaning. How well you manage depends on how well you communicate in this broad sense. These ten commandments are designed to help you improve your skills as a manager by improving your skills of communication with superiors, peers, and subordinates.

1. _Seek to clarify your ideas before communicating_.   The more systematically we analyze the problem or idea to be communicated, the clearer it becomes. This is the first step toward effective communication. Many communications fail because of inadequate planning. Good planning must consider the goals and attitudes of those who will receive the communication and those who will be affected by it.

2. _Examine the true purpose of each communication_.   Before you communicate, ask yourself what you really want to accomplish with your message—obtain information, initiate action, change another person's attitude? Identify your most important goal, and then adapt your language, tone, and total approach to serve that specific objective. Don't try to accomplish too much with each communication. The sharper the focus of your message, the greater its chances of success.

3. _Consider the total physical and human setting whenever you communicate._   Meaning and intent are conveyed by more than words alone. Many other factors influence the overall impact of a communication, and the manager must be sensitive to the total setting in which she or he communicates. Consider, for example, your sense of timing (the circumstances under which you make an announcement or render a decision), the physical setting (whether you communicate in private, or otherwise), the social climate that pervades work relationships within the company or a department and sets the tone of its communications, and custom and past practice (the degree to which your communication conforms to, or departs from, the expectations of your audience). Be constantly aware of the total setting in which you communicate. Like all living things, communication must be capable of adapting to its environment.

4. _Consult with others, where appropriate, in planning communications._   Frequently, it is desirable or necessary to seek the participation of others in planning a communication or developing the facts on which to base it. Such consultation often helps lend additional insight and objectivity to your message. Moreover, those who have helped you plan your communication will give it their active support.

5. _Be mindful, while you communicate, of the overtones as well as the basic content of your message._   Your tone of voice, expression, and apparent receptiveness to the responses of others all have tremendous impact on those you wish to reach. Frequently overlooked, these subtleties of communication often affect a listener's reaction to a message even more than the basic content of the message. Similarly, your choice of lan-

guage—particularly your awareness of the fine shades of meaning and emotion in the words you use—largely predetermines the reactions of your listeners.

6. _Take the opportunity, when it arises, to convey something of help or value to the receiver._   Consideration of the other person's interests and needs—the habit of trying to look at things from his or her viewpoint—will frequently point up opportunities to convey something of immediate benefit or long-range value to the receiver. People on the job are more responsive to the manager whose messages take their own interests into account.

7. _Follow up your communication._   Our best efforts at communication may be wasted, and we may never know whether we have succeeded in expressing our true meaning and intent, if we do not follow up to see how well we have put our message across. This we can do by asking questions, by encouraging the receiver to express his or her reactions, by follow-up contacts, and by subsequent review of performance. Make certain that every important communication has a feedback so that complete understanding and appropriate action result.

8. _Communicate for tomorrow as well as today._   While communications may be aimed primarily at meeting the demands of an immediate situation, they must be planned with the past in mind if they are to maintain consistency in the receiver's view; more important, they must be consistent with long-range interests and goals. For example, it is not easy to communicate frankly on such matters as poor performance or the shortcomings of a loyal subordinate, but postponing disagreeable communications makes them more difficult in the long run and is unfair to your subordinates and your company.

9. _Be sure your actions support your communications._   In the final analysis, the most persuasive kind of communication is not what you say but what you do. When a person's action or attitudes contradict his or her words, we tend to discount what that person has said. For every manager this means good supervisory practice—such as clear assignment of responsibility and authority, fair rewards for fair effort, and sound policy enforcement—serves to communicate more than all the gifts of oratory.

10. _Seek not only to be understood but to understand—be a good listener._   When we start talking, we often cease to listen—in that larger sense of being attuned to the other person's unspoken reactions and attitudes. Even more serious is that we are all guilty, at times, of inattentiveness when others are trying to communicate to us. Listening is one of the most important, most difficult, and most neglected skills in communication. It demands that we concentrate not only on the explicit meanings another person is expressing but also on the implicit mean-

ings, unspoken words, and undertones that may be far more significant. Thus we must learn to listen with the inner ear if we are to know the inner man.*

Summary

- Communicating is part of everything we do in life.
- Communications skills are essential to living and working.
- The communication process attempts to transmit information and understanding from one person or group to another.
- The ingredients to the communication process are the sender, the receiver, the message, the medium, and feedback.
- Understanding exists when the sender and receiver agree on the meaning and intent of the message.
- The sender and receiver have specific responsibilities in the communication process.
- Barriers to effective communications arise from interpersonal and organizational sources.

Glossary of Essential Terms

communication	The transmission of information and understanding from one person or group to another.
communication barriers	Objects or behaviors that can interfere with communication effectiveness.
feedback	A receiver's reaction to a message, through which a receiver becomes a sender.
impersonal communication	Communication in which the participants do not interact directly.
interpersonal communication	Communication delivered in either a face-to-face or voice-to-voice method.

*Adapted, by permission of the publisher, from "Ten Commandments of Good Communication," from *Management Review*, October 1955, © 1955 by American Management Association, New York. All rights reserved.

medium	The method chosen to deliver a message.
message	The information being transmitted in the communication process.
receiver	The person or persons intended as the audience for a message.
sender	The person or persons initiating a message.

Review Questions

1. Can you define this chapter's essential terms? If not, consult the preceding glossary.

2. Construct a diagram of the communication process. Explain the importance of each of its components and the relationship of each component.

3. Identify and explain the five responsibilities of the sender and the four responsibilities of the receiver in the communication process.

4. What are the eight interpersonal barriers to communication? What are the five organizational barriers to communication? Give an example of each.

5. What are the Ten Commandments of Good Communication? Give an example to illustrate each.

Readings

Coplin, Wilbain D. and Michael K. O'Leary. *Power Persuasion.* Reading, Mass.: Addison-Wesley, 1988.

Freston, Patricia and Judy Lease. "Communication Skills Training for Selected Supervisors." *Training and Development Journal,* 41, no. 7, 1987, pp. 67–70.

Glass, Lillein. *Talk to Win: Six Steps to a Successful Vocal Image.* New York: Putnam Publishing, 1987.

Gordon, Bonnie. "Settling Worker Conflicts." *Nation's Business* (March 1988), pp. 70–71.

Hamilton, Cheryl and Cordell Parker. *Communicating for Results.* Belmont, California: Wadsworth, 1987.

Holcombe, Marya and Judith Stein. *Writing for Decision Makers: Memos and Reports with a Competitive Edge,* 2nd ed. New York: Van Nostrand Reinhold, 1987.

Marshall, Verena and Ron Cacioppe. "A Survey of Differences Between Managers and Subordinates." *Leadership and Organizational Development Journal*, 7, no. 4, 1986, pp. 17–25.

Mayfield, Marlys. *Thinking for Yourself: Developing Critical Thinking Skills Through Writing*. Belmont, California: Wadsworth, 1987.

Rosenberg, Arthur M. and Jim Murray. "Can We Talk?" *Modern Office Technology* (February 1988), pp. 40–46(4).

Rossman, M. L. "Bridging the Communications Gap Between Marketing and Operations." *Marketing News*, 21 (July 3, 1987), p. 31.

C A S E S

3.1 Memo Mumbles

Professor Ian Wilson is the chairperson of his college's business department. His faculty members work three basic shifts: morning, afternoon, and evening. Because of this split in work times, Professor Wilson has decided to conduct the regular monthly faculty meeting at two separate times—one in the early afternoon and one in the early evening. Both meetings will have the same agenda. Professor Wilson wrote the following memo to his faculty:

MEMO

TO: All business faculty   Date 4/7
FROM: Professor Wilson
SUBJECT: Regular monthly faculty meeting

1. Our regular meeting this month will be held in two sessions, both with the same agenda—on April 27, Tuesday, and April 29th, Thursday. The meeting on the 29th will be held at noon in room 901. Day faculty will attend. The evening faculty will attend the meeting on the 27th at 5 P.M. in Room 109. Faculty meeting agenda will follow.

2. Faculty with a preference may attend either meeting.

On the morning of the 27th, Wilson placed an agenda on each faculty member's desk. At the 5 P.M. meeting on the 27th, two faculty members arrived 20 minutes late, missing some vital information. After the meeting, Wilson asked them why they were late. Both said that they had waited in room 901 for ten minutes and then returned to the department office and discovered their mistake.

After the meeting on the 29th, Professor Wilson noted that three of his faculty members had not attended either meeting. One, a day faculty member, simply forgot about the meeting. (His agenda was buried under student homework papers.) The other two members told Wilson that they had gone to room 109 at 5 P.M. and waited twenty minutes. When the rest of the faculty failed to appear, they went to the cafeteria to have supper. Both assumed that the meeting had been canceled.

For Discussion

1. Why did these faculty members have the problems they did?
2. As department chairperson, what would you do to make sure all of your faculty attended the meetings?

3.2   Here We Go Again

Ella was thinking about her upcoming dinner party as her boss, Ed Myers, addressed her and her workers about the need for higher quality. "I've heard this all before," thought Ella as she filled in all the *o*'s on her agenda with ink. "What can he possibly say that hasn't been beaten into us ten times. Sure we have rejects, but where does Ed get off telling my people about quality. He hasn't been on the line in twenty years. Just a college boy with a fancy degree in business."

Ed's address was interrupted by Bernice, Ella's most experienced subordinate. "Mr. Myers, I resent your implications that we are not good workers. We work hard and know our jobs. The problems you are talking about are for the maintenance division guys to worry about, not us." Ed was a little shaken by Bernice's comments. "Look, Bernice, when I say 'you people,' I am including everyone involved in making our products. I'll be talking to maintenance next week. But the problem of too many rejects is partly your fault, too. Sure machines are aging, but those maintenance people do a pretty darn good job, and I will not stand for any criticism from you about machine maintenance until you people get your act together."

"Look, Mr. Myers, just tell us what changes you want us to make, and we'll make them. Let's stop criticizing and start changing what's wrong. It's not important to place blame on anyone," said Ella.

Ed Myers was getting angry. After a brief pause, he decided to get specific. "Starting next Monday, we are instituting some changes. Each of you will be expected to inspect your own output at each station. You will not send anything down the line that is not right and ready to take on the next operation. We have hired outside people—experts in quality control—to equip you to take on this vital function."

A flurry of hands went up in the air, and a dozen people began to speak at once. "Won't that slow us down?" and "You've got to change the piece rate system of pay!" were just two of the many objections to Ed's declarations that were raised. Ed interrupted the group with these words, "It's obvious that you have questions. They will be answered in time. But our first priority is to get the quality of the things you make up to standards. You people will conform to the changes management wants or pay the consequences." Ed then left the room.

"What does he mean when he says 'pay the consequences'?" asked Bernice. "I don't know for sure," said Ella, "but what worries me is what the full extent of his management changes might be."

For Discussion

1. What interpersonal or face-to-face barriers are at work in this meeting? Provide examples from the case to support each barrier identified.

2. Did "communication" take place in this meeting? Explain your answer.

3. What do you think about the ways in which Ed Myers handled the questions put to him? Explain your answer.

4. If you were in Ella's place, what would you do now?

Planning

P
A
R
T

II

Planning: The First Function

OUTLINE

ESSENTIAL TERMS

budget   procedure
mission   program
objective   rule
operating plan   strategic plan
planning   strategic planning
policy   tactical plan

LEARNING OBJECTIVES

After reading and discussing this chapter, you should be able to do the following:

1. Define this chapter's essential terms.
2. Explain the importance of planning and its relationship to the other management functions.
3. Differentiate the planning responsibilities of the three levels of management.
4. Explain the difference between strategic and operating planning.
5. List and discuss the seven basic steps in the planning process.
6. Discuss the major barriers to effective planning.
7. Discuss the aids to successful planning.

Why Do You Need a Plan?

Have you ever had too much of a month left over when your money ran out? Have you ever found you were driving with an empty gas tank or on a local road that was undergoing repairs? If you have, you have experienced the results of failing to think about events before experiencing them. While experience is a good teacher, it should have to teach you a lesson only once. After that "negative" experience, you should be able to prevent its repetition. The difference between fools and everyone else is that fools do not learn from their experiences, and thus make the same mistakes more than once.

This chapter is about thinking and looking ahead. It's about trying to predict the future and working with it as it evolves. The previous chapters contain some references to planning, but this chapter is the first of two chapters that are concerned exclusively with planning. In it, we examine what planning is, the importance of planning, the types of plans you will be making, the various processes for planning, barriers to successful planning, and aids to productive planning.

Planning is often called the "first function" of managers because it must be undertaken before other functions. Most managers and organizations cannot afford the luxury of trial and error; it is too costly in terms of the resources expended. Planning helps us avoid errors, waste, and delays, and it aids our efforts at becoming both effective and efficient. Planning involves the execution of several basic steps, which we discuss in detail in the pages that follow. Before planning can be truly useful, the planners must know what they wish to achieve through planning. What exactly is planning? What do we mean by planning?

Planning Defined

Planning is preparing for tomorrow today; it is the activity that allows managers to determine what they want and how to get it: They set goals and decide how to reach them. Some goals, like personal goals, are developed as a result of independent action. Other goals are established through the planning of others. A superior's plans directly affect a subordinate's plans and planning efforts as well as some of the means of approach. Planning, obviously, is not done in a vacuum. Additionally, planning does have limitations placed on it—of funds and of other available resources.

Planning answers six basic questions in regard to any intended activity—what, when, where, who, how, and how much. The "what" is the goal or goals, the things or states of being we do not now have. These may be long-term or short-term goals. The question of "when" is a question of timing; each long-term goal may have a series of short-term goals that must be achieved before the long-term goal can be reached. The "where" issue concerns the place or places where the plans and planning will reach their conclusion. The question of "who" asks which specific people will perform specific tasks essential to the plans. The "how" issue involves methods for reaching short- and long-term goals: What specific steps are to be taken in what sequence; the answer will outline a path to be taken by personnel involved in the planning. The question of "how much" is concerned with the expenditure of resources that are determined to be essential to reach goals. Now that we know what planning involves, let's look at some factors that illustrate the importance of planning.

Importance of Planning

The Primary Management Function

Planning is the primary management function. It sets the stage for resource acquisition and the focus of energy for the entire organization. In planning, managers determine the goals of the organization or work group and develop the overall strategies to achieve them. Planning provides direction and a common sense of purpose for the organization. It helps determine the operations and how those operations will affect the organization before commitments are made.

A simple example can be used to illustrate this point. Can you imagine a business owner approaching a bank loan officer with a request for a start-up business loan without having the mission of the business defined; specific performance objectives for the first year detailed; and an operating plan spelling out financial needs, sales forecasts, inventory requirements, and personnel profiles in hand? If your answer is "absolutely not," you have recognized that planning places everything else in perspective. It is the primary function.

Impact on Other Management Functions

Planning, as we recall, occurs before organizing, staffing, directing, and controlling. Planning generates goals and sets the foundation for organizing of resources and activities to achieve the goals. Additionally, even the structure of the organization is developed to achieve the company's objectives and should change when the objectives change. The plans of the company—whether to maintain the status quo, to expand, or to contract operations—influence human resource planning and the entire staffing process. Planning provides the guidelines for directing the employees and for what is communicated to them. Planning establishes the foundations for the control function because it specifies what is to be accomplished and provides a standard for measuring progress.

Ability to Adjust

Planning allows managers the opportunity to adjust the organization to the environment instead of merely to react to it. The more clearly the company can see into the future, and thus develop both long- and short-range plans, the greater the possibility of the organization continuing in a smooth operating mode. Adjustments to plans, in response to events and circumstances, are less wearing on management and employees than forced reactions and the abruptly conceived need for an entire response system.

Can you imagine the consequences of a football team not having a game plan? Of a country not having a plan of defense? Of a company not having a marketing plan? The existence of plans provides for the chance to adapt rather than to react. Planning increases the possibility of survival in business by minimizing the risks inherent in the future. Chrysler Corporation provides an example of the ability to adjust and readjust through

FIGURE 4.1
Management's
pyramid structure

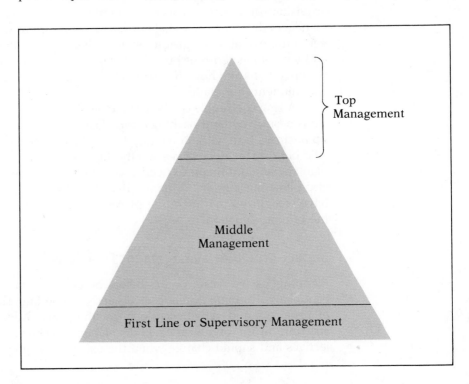

planning. Originally involved in car operations in France, Britain, and Spain, Chrysler was forced to withdraw from these commitments as financial problems mounted in the late 1970s. But plans remained on the drawing board to reenter the market when the long-range forecast for the business improved. Recently, Chrysler implemented new plans and is beginning export operations in West Germany, Belgium, Switzerland, the Netherlands, and Austria.[1]

Unified Framework of Plans

The results of an organization's plans and planning process should provide for a unified framework for the accomplishment of the organization's purpose. If the managerial pyramid (Figure 4.1), with its three levels of management, is used as a model for the planning process, the result should be a hierarchy of plans: The plans for each level from top to bottom should fit into each other (Figure 4.2). In this situation, top-level management has

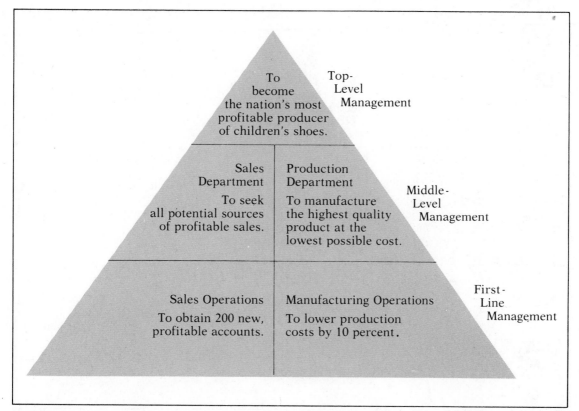

FIGURE 4.2
Hierarchy of plans (objectives) that results in compatible plans

developed its element of a plan (objective) for the total organization. With this as the foundation, the middle-management team can plan for the performance of the functional areas of sales and production. Finally, the first-line management group within the functional areas can develop detailed plans for the individual work units. The outcome—a coordinated hierarchy of plans.

What happens if an individual manager chooses not to plan within this framework? If a middle-level manager develops a set of objectives based on his or her own ambitions, values, or goals that are not in line with top management's objectives, conflicting objectives will result. Figure 4.3 shows a situation in which a sales manager has misinterpreted the intention of top management's goal. Instead of seeking out all potential sources of profitable sales, the sales manager is asking the lower level managers at the operating level to seek out all potential buyers. The salespersons will translate this to mean their goals should be to call on and try to sell to every

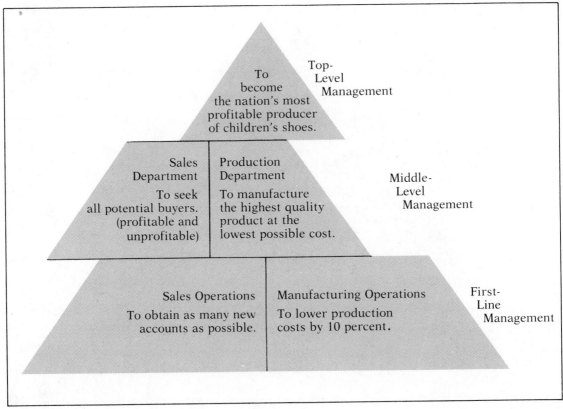

FIGURE 4.3
Conflicting objectives result in incompatible plans

potential buyer, regardless of the potential size of the order or the cost that the company will incur in servicing that order. The result is bound to be that sales to some small, bad-credit, and unprofitable accounts will cause the company losses. Now that we have considered the importance of planning, what are the types of plans, and how are the plans used?

Types and Uses of Plans

Scope of Management Planning

All managers engage in planning their activities and the activities of others. They all plan in basically the same way, but the kinds of plans they develop and the amount of time they spend on planning are different. Top-level managers are concerned with longer time periods and with plans for larger organizational units or divisions. Their planning includes developing the mission for the organization, organizational objectives, and major policy areas. Top-level managers concentrate on the questions of what and how much.

Middle-level managers' planning responsibilities center on translating the broad objectives of top-level management into more specific goals for their work units. These middle-level managers are concerned with the where and when of plans. First-level managers are involved in the scheduling of employees, deciding what work will be done, and developing procedures to reach these goals. These managers concentrate on the who and how of planning. They are concerned with immediate planning times. Figure 4.4 shows the differences between the levels of management with

FIGURE 4.4
Planning and the levels of management: the relationship between planning concerns and the time spent on planning

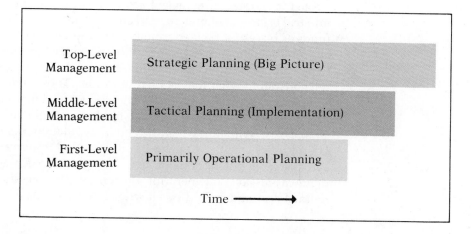

regard to the amount of time each spends planning and the type of planning each does.

Now let's examine the types and uses of plans that managers are involved with.

Strategic Plans

In a business enterprise, a **strategic plan** is one concerned with the entire operation. It requires multilevel involvement. Top management develops the directional objectives for the entire organization; then progressively lower levels of management develop compatible objectives and plans to achieve them. As the planning process moves down the organization, the topics of the objectives and measures of success become more specific.

Strategic planning and the resultant strategic plans look ahead, over the next two, three, five, or even more years; they attempt to prepare the organization for operational success during those years. Just how far into the future an organization's plans will stretch is determined by the degree of certainty managers can have about their plan's key elements.

The strategic plan begins with an organization's mission. The organization's **mission** is a clear statement about why it exists. It holds the key to everything else that will or should happen within the organization. According to Peter Drucker, two questions are essential for every business to answer: What is our business? What should it be?[2] The answer to the first question is determined by the consumer, not the producer. What consumers see, think, believe, and want at any given time must be accepted by management. This question needs to be raised and answered regularly, not just at the beginning of an enterprise.

The second question requires businesses to decide if they are in the right business or if they should change their direction. Some businesses are forced in new directions by accident or by competition. Insurance companies, for example, are doing more than selling insurance. They have created tax-sheltered retirement accounts (IRAs and Keough plans), moved into real estate development, and created mutual funds and money market funds as places for their enormous cash reserves. Productivity, innovation, and profitability considerations all help change a business and open it up to new opportunities and directions. Many companies today bear no direct relationship to what they started out to be. They have merged with other companies, dropped unprofitable lines, and added new ones. B. F. Goodrich Co. provides an example of a drastic change in the mission of an organization. The company, which earned its reputation as a tire maker, sold its Uniroyal tire business to focus its energies and resources on chemicals and aerospace operations.[3] Major and minor moves such as these help to redefine a mission statement for a business. That mission has to be clearly defined and understood by all who sit in positions of authority.

Strategic plans deal with many hard-to-predict future events of great importance to the organization: Will there be a recession? Will inflation continue at its present rates? What will be the situation in our industry with regard to local, state, and federal regulations? These things are difficult enough to predict over a one-year period, let alone a three- or five-year period.

Just as one person's ceiling may be another person's floor, one plan may be the end of one manager's planning efforts but only the beginning of another manager's efforts. Top management's strategic plan for the entire enterprise becomes a building framework and sets the dimensions of lower level planning efforts. In the same way, the marketing department's strategic plan affects the planning by all the managers in that division and, to some extent, the planning by managers in other divisions. Later in this chapter, we take up the process for strategic planning.

Tactical Plans

A **tactical plan** is concerned with what the lower level units within each division must do, how they must do it, and who will have the responsibilities for doing it. Tactics are the means needed to achieve a strategy, to activate it and make it work. Perhaps your strategic plan is to achieve a college degree; your tactical plans to achieve the strategic plan will include successfully completing a series of courses that will earn that degree.

Tactical plans are concerned with shorter time frames and narrower scopes than are strategic plans; they usually span one year or less and represent the short-term efforts required to reach long-term goals, one after another, until the strategic objective is reached.

Although we are discussing strategic and tactical plans separately, they are, in reality, almost inseparable. The "whole" is the strategy, which is made up of a series of tactical plans built on each other to achieve the strategic plan. A coach's strategic plan for victory over an opponent depends on the individual tactical plans—the plays to be used, players to be inserted in various situations, the tactics of the defensive response, and so on.

Operating Plans

An **operating plan** is one that a manager uses to accomplish her or his job responsibilities. It can be a single-use plan or an ongoing plan.

Single-use plans apply to activities that do not recur or repeat. Once the activity is accomplished, the plan is no longer needed. An example of a single-use plan is one to deal with the movement of furniture from one location to another. Once the move is completed, the plans for it are fulfilled. The goal is achieved, and the plans have little or no value in the future.

A **program** is a single-use plan. Like most plans, a program deals with the who, what, where, when, how, and how much of an activity. Your school may have programs for updating its labs, adding new classrooms, making the physical plant more accessible for handicapped students, and so on. In turn, a business may have a program to sponsor a blood donation drive or to automate its office systems. Once a program's goals are achieved, that program ceases to influence organizational behavior.

A **budget** is a single-use plan for predicting sources and amounts of income and how it is to be used. Every organization needs a budget for controlling the use of its financial resources. Budgets may cover any length of time, but they are usually prepared for one-year periods. When its time period ends, the budget loses its value as a planning and control device. It may have historical value, however, because it will usually be used to help in preparing future budgets.

Continuing or *ongoing plans* are usually made once and retain their value over years, undergoing periodic revisions and updates. Ongoing plans are likely to cover the handling of continuing situations, problems, and activities—such as hiring new people, granting credit to customers, and filling out forms. Every plan that repeats, or is continuously in place, in an organization is classified as an ongoing plan.

A **policy** is an example of an ongoing plan. It provides a broad guideline for managers to follow when dealing with important areas of decision making. Policies are usually general statements about the ways in which managers should attempt to handle routine management responsibilities. Exhibit 4.1 shows a personnel policy with regard to hiring potential employees. Note that it does not tell managers what to do, how to do it, or

EXHIBIT 4.1
A Business Policy Statement with Regard to Nondiscrimination

Statement of Policy

THERE SHALL BE NO DISCRIMINATION FOR OR AGAINST ANY APPLICANT OR FOR OR AGAINST ANY CURRENT EMPLOYEE BECAUSE OF HIS OR HER RACE, CREED, COLOR, NATIONAL ORIGIN, SEX, MARITAL STATUS, AGE, OR HANDICAP OR MEMBERSHIP OR LAWFUL PARTICIPATION IN THE ACTIVITIES OF ANY ORGANIZATION OR UNION OR BECAUSE OF HIS OR HER REFUSAL TO JOIN OR PARTICIPATE IN THE ACTIVITIES OF ANY ORGANIZATION OR UNION. MOREOVER, THE COMPANY SHALL ADHERE TO AN AFFIRMATIVE ACTION PROGRAM WITH EACH FUNCTIONAL DIVISION'S CONCERN WITH HIRING PROMOTIONS, TRANSFERS, AND OTHER ONGOING HUMAN RESOURCE ACTIVITIES.

whom to hire. It simply states the view the company wants its managers to adopt when performing their repetitive management functions. Policies guide managers by pointing them in a particular direction.

A **procedure** is the set of step-by-step directions in which activities or tasks are to be carried out. Procedures exist for preparing budgets, getting people paid, handling routine clerical tasks, preparing business correspondence, and so on. Procedures are ongoing plans for the execution of tasks that spell out the "how" for a task or function. Like policies, procedures attempt to promote harmony by means of unified directions and approaches to solving problems or dealing with routine. When followed, procedures guarantee that identical tasks are executed identically, no matter where they are being performed in the organization. Exhibit 4.2 shows a procedure for travel expense reimbursement.

A **rule** is an ongoing, specific plan for controlling human behavior and conduct at work. Rules are "do" and "don't" statements put in place to promote safety of employees and the uniform treatment of and behavior of employees. Unlike policies, rules tell each employee exactly what to do or what kind of behavior is expected in a given situation or environment. For example, a rule that does not permit smoking in an office allows a manager no freedom in decision making. Figure 4.5 illustrates several rules. Both procedures and rules tend to be substitutes for creative thought because they lock people into specific courses of action or modes of acceptable behavior and discourage making adjustments for individual situations. See Exhibit 4.3 for additional insights into the advantages of and requirements for policies, programs, procedures, and rules.

EXHIBIT 4.2
Procedure for Travel Expense Reimbursement

Procedure for Expense Reimbursement
1. Complete operating form XN-12.
2. Attach receipts for the following expenses:
   A. Lodging (all)
   B. Meals (not to exceed $20 per day)
   C. Transportation (where available or itemize, including tolls and parking)
3. Have completed form signed by immediate supervisor.
4. Forward to accounting department within five days of return from trip.

FIGURE 4.5
Rules

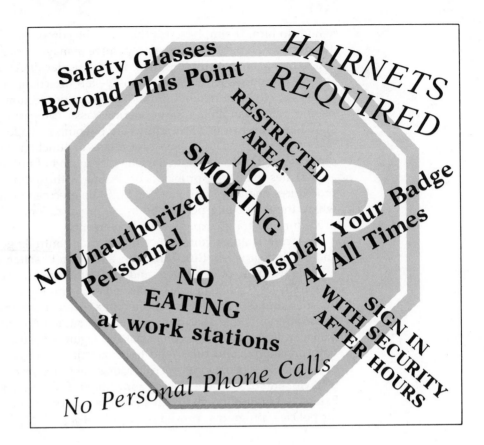

Planning Processes

Just how do managers plan? What steps do they take? What processes are involved? The answers depend on the types of planning processes the managers participate in. All types of planning require a manager to use basically the same planning steps even though the plans being developed may be different: The development of strategic plans uses a process different from the one used for daily operating planning. What then does planning look like? Let's examine the basic planning concept, the operating planning process, and the strategic planning process.

Basic Planning Concept

The basic planning concept answers four questions:

1. What do we want to do?
2. Where are we in relation to that goal?

EXHIBIT 4.3
The Advantages of and the Requirements for Policies, Programs, Procedures, and Rules

	Policies	Programs	Procedures	Rules
Advantages of	Promote uniformity	Provide a plan for an operation from beginning to end	Provide the detail for effective performance	Promote safety
	Save time	Name participants and detail their duties	Promote uniformity	Promote acceptable conduct
	Outline an approach	Coordinate efforts of those seeking the same goal	Save time	Provide security
	Set limitations on management conduct		Provide assistance in training	Provide standards for appraising performance and conduct
	Promote effectiveness for managers and the organization		Provide security in operations	Save time
			Promote effectiveness and efficiency	Aid in disciplinary situations
Requirements for	Should be in writing	Should be in writing in at least an outline format	Should be in writing	Should be in writing
	Need to be communicated and understood	Should answer who, when, where, how, and how much	Should be sufficiently detailed	Must be communicated to and understood by all those affected
	Should provide some flexibility	Should have clear goals, tactics, and timetables	Should be revised periodically	Should be reviewed and revised periodically
	Should be consistent throughout the organization and consistently applied	Needs to be communicated to all those affected by it	Should be communicated and understood by those who need to know them	Should serve needed purposes
	Should support the organization's strategy			
	Based on the mission			

3. Which factors will help or hinder us in reaching the goal?

4. What alternatives are available to us to reach the goal, and which one is the best?

These questions help a manager focus attention on planning and its components. The answers to these four questions are developed through the operating planning process.

Operating Planning Process

Each of us has a planning method that works with some degree of effectiveness. As you examine the following planning process, consider what elements this method has that your method does not have. Then consider adopting anything that will make your approach to planning more effective.

Exhibit 4.4 lists the seven essential steps in what we suggest for a planning process. These steps are basic and are usually taken in the sequence shown.

Step 1: Setting objectives.   When a manager sets **objectives** (goals), he or she is deciding on a target for the energies and efforts of the organization or its subunit. These goals or targets arise from the purposes of the organization (its mission) and therefore differ by type of organization, state of development of the company, overall philosophy of management, and level of the organization at which the objectives are set. Here are some examples of typical objectives with sources.

During the next five years, the company will produce a 10 percent return on investment. (Top level)

To produce the highest quality good at the lowest possible cost. (Middle-level production department)

To reduce turnover by 10 percent. (First level)

To provide the highest quality health care available. (Top level)

To complete the delta project by November 15, 1992. (Middle level)

Regardless of the terminology—objectives, goals, targets—the first step in planning always involves deciding on the expected outcome. In developing the goals, the manager should consider two characteristics: (1) goals should be realistic and specific, and (2) goals should be compatible with other objectives.

The more specific the objectives are, the easier it will be to monitor progress and to note successful completions. Developing goals that cannot be accomplished because of lack of time, talent, or other resources will not be useful to the organization.

EXHIBIT 4.4
Steps in the Operating Planning Process

Step 1: Setting Objectives

Establishing targets for the short- and long-range future.

Step 2: Analyzing and Evaluating the Environment

Analyzing the present position and resources available to achieve objectives.

Step 3: Determining Alternatives

Constructing a list of possible courses of action that will lead you to your goals.

Step 4: Evaluating the Alternatives

Listing and considering the various advantages and disadvantages of each of your possible courses of action.

Step 5: Selecting the Best Solution

Selecting the course of action that has the most advantages and the fewest serious disadvantages.

Step 6: Implementing the Plan

Determining who will be involved, what resources will be assigned, how the plan will be evaluated, and the reporting procedures.

Step 7: Controlling and Evaluating the Results

Making certain that the plan is going according to expectations and making necessary adjustments.

Objectives developed by organizational levels and peer managers should be compatible with one another. Top-level management should set the stage for goal setting by lower level management, thereby ensuring maximum use of resources.

Step 2: Analyzing and evaluating the environment. Once the objectives are established, the manager needs to evaluate the present situation and analyze the organization's environment. Where are we now? What are the limitations in the environment? What resources do we have or are we lacking? Are there any external factors that can influence the objectives and their accomplishment?

In the internal environment of the organization, the manager might want to examine these elements:

1. *Capital.* What is the availability of capital funds in the organization, or what funds could be acquired from the outside?

2. *Company policies, procedures, rules.* Are there policies, procedures, or rules that may restrict the accomplishment of the objectives?

3. *Personnel resources.* What skills and knowledge are available in the organization? Are they adequate, or is it necessary to go outside the company?

4. *Managerial attitudes.* Is the managerial climate supportive or restrictive? If it is restrictive, what can be done to change it?

5. *Facilities.* What facilities are available? Are they adequate?

In the external environment, the manager might want to consider these factors:

1. *Economic conditions.* What data are available to project the general direction of the business cycle? Is the economy heading for a period of recession or expansion? What is the projected rate of inflation?

2. *Technology.* What technology is on the horizon? Will the company's present technology remain competitive for three years? Five years? Eight years?

3. *Labor supply.* If the company depends on skilled labor, is the supply adequate in the immediate service area? If it is not available readily, what can be done to ensure its continued availability based on company objectives?

4. *Sources of supply.* Are the suppliers of raw materials and components readily available? Have there been or are there any potential interruptions in the sources of supply? What alternatives exist?

5. *Government controls.* What is the future direction of government regulations and controls that could affect company operations?

Managers do not plan in a vacuum, even when their planning is concerned with only their individual unit's operations. There are multiple influences and factors to consider in developing plans.

Step 3: Determining the alternatives.   Alternatives are courses of action that are available to a manager to reach a goal. In developing alternatives, a manager should try to create as many roads to the objective as possible. These alternatives are wholly separate ways to reach the objective, not the same plan with variations. For example, suppose your objective is "to have at your disposal the most modern equipment available on the market." What are possible alternatives to achieve this objective? You might (1) purchase the most modern equipment available, (2) rent the current "hot item," or (3) lease-purchase the equipment. Each alternative will achieve the same objective, but which is best for your situation?

Step 4: Evaluating the alternatives.

Each alternative needs to be evaluated to determine which best achieves the objective. To do this, the manager needs to construct a list of advantages (benefits) and disadvantages (costs) for each alternative.

What factors should be considered? For one, you need to know the amount of resources, including time, that each will require. If possible, get a dollar estimate of the cost of each course of action. Then relate this to the dollar value of the goal to be achieved. If $1,000 is spent to gain an $800 goal, the alternative will be ineffective.

In addition to financial factors, consider the effects each alternative is likely to have on organizational members, the organizational unit, and others outside the area of operations. It is possible that certain good and bad side effects will result from the implementation of an alternative.

Are the resources available? Are the resources committed to achieve other goals at the same time they would need to be available to achieve the current goal?

Step 5: Selecting the best solution.

The analysis of each alternative's disadvantages, benefits, costs, and effects should result in determining one course of action that appears better than the others. If no one alternative emerges as clearly the best, consideration should be given to combining parts or the entire content of two or more alternatives. Whatever the course chosen, it should be one that gives you the most advantages and the fewest serious disadvantages.

Step 6: Implementing the plan.

After the optimum alternative has been selected, the manager needs to develop an action plan to implement it. The manager must decide these issues: Who will do what? By what date will the tasks be initiated and completed? What resources, both human and material, will be available for the process? How will the plan be evaluated? What reporting procedures are to be used? What type and degree of authority will be granted to achieve these ends?

Step 7: Controlling and evaluating the results.

Once the plan is implemented, the manager must monitor the progress that is being made, evaluate the reported results, and make any modifications necessary. The environment that a plan is constructed in is constantly changing, so the plans may have to be modified. Or modification may be required because a plan was not quite "perfect" when it was implemented.

This operating planning process is the basic planning tool for managers in the company as they focus their energies on operating problems, present business, present profits, and present resources. What about the future? How does the whole organization interact in the planning process? Through the strategic planning process.

Strategic Planning Process

Earlier in the chapter we discussed strategic plans as plans concerned with the overall undertakings of the entire organization. Strategic planning is initiated and guided by top-level management, but all levels of management must participate for it to work. The purposes of strategic planning are (1) to have the entire organization plan long-range directions and commitments, (2) to provide multilevel involvement in the planning process, and (3) to develop an organization in which the plans of the subunits are harmonious with one another.

As we take up the steps in the strategic planning process, refer to Figure 4.6 to get a picture of how the three levels (top, middle, and first) of management interact to arrive at a workable strategic plan.

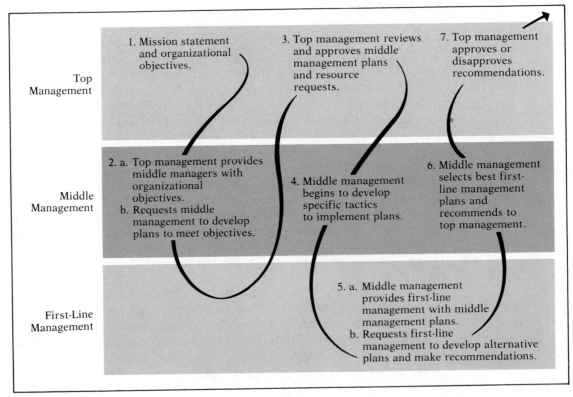

FIGURE 4.6
Strategic planning flow

Step 1: Define the central concept of the business. Top-level management must answer the question "What business are we in?" This is the focal point for the entire organization. "Do we sell hamburgers, or are we in the convenience food business?" is a question that has guided the corporate fortunes of McDonald's, Burger King, Jack-in-the-Box, and Wendy's. Chicken sandwiches, breakfast sausage and eggs, and salad bars are obviously not hamburgers.

When top-level management asks the question, the answer it gets should help identify the product or service and any competitive advantages the company has. The answer can be in terms of quality, location, service, or low cost. All these are elements of the identification.

Step 2: Establish objectives for the organization. Once the concept or mission of the business has been developed, top-level management must develop the objectives for the organization. What exactly will the organization focus on? Profit? Growth and survival? Social responsiveness? Development of individual employees?

Normally, organizations have more than one area of objectives to focus their energies on. The goals should be as specific as possible. The more measurable the goals, the easier it will be for lower level managers to develop their goals.

Step 3: Analyze and evaluate the environment. What is the environment in which the goals have been set? Should the firm plan for expansion of its retail locations downtown if the population is moving to the suburbs? Is it good timing to introduce biodegradable containers if society is concerned about pollution? Is the economy sound, or are people holding on to their money? Answers to these questions will help clarify the climate in which the objectives were set.

A second aspect of this analysis is an assessment of the resources of the organization. What resources are available? Are they adequate? Can we acquire the resources we are lacking?

Step 4: Have the subunits develop their own goals. At this point, top management requests middle-level management to develop their own goals. With top-level management's goals as a guide, middle-level managers develop plans and, in turn, will eventually request the first-line managers to develop their own appropriate goals based on the middle-level managers' plans.

Step 5: Compare lower level goals and close the gap. When middle-level managers have developed their goals and corresponding plans, the top-level managers will review them to determine if they fit and are compatible. Will their accomplishment lead to the achievement of top-level management's goals and the concept of the enterprise? If not, what can be done?

In addition, these lower-level plans are examined to determine if they are consistent with the resources available. If not, top management can decide to seek resources outside the company or possibly to revise the top-level goals. This step is critical to tying the organization together conceptually. (The same process will be used for middle-level and first-level compatibility.)

Step 6: Decide on a plan.   At this point, the management team decides which of the various alternative plans to go with: A firm facing the problem of keeping pace with technology may choose to lease equipment rather than buy—to lessen the chance of it becoming obsolete. A business that is determined to increase its market share by ensuring that the adult population is familiar with its name and product may decide to increase its advertising budget threefold.

Step 7: Implement the strategic plan.   The strategic plan that has been developed on paper is now ready to be put into action. This step requires that all the various subgroups (the middle-level managers and first-level managers) proceed with the detail work—who, when, and where. At this time, the organization should be moving as one big unit, with all parts heading in the same direction.

Step 8: Control and evaluate.   Monitoring and feedback devices are used at all levels of management to watch the progress of the plan and make any changes necessary. The initial plans serve as the standards by which the progress can be measured.

The strategic planning process is critical to the success of an organization. If agreed to and performed correctly, the strategic plan can increase the likelihood that all management will be working with and not against one another. A second benefit is that the entire organization has the opportunity to plan its efforts for a two- to five-year period. This provides a reasonable time in which to measure progress, or in some cases to change the direction, of the company. Strategic planning is a primary concern of top-level management but determines the environment, limits, and direction of planning at all other levels.

Making Plans Effective

Now that we have looked at the planning processes, we want to know if there are some secrets to successful planning. All managers want their plans to be effective, to yield the desired results. What can managers do to increase the potential for success? One step in the right direction is to identify the potential barriers to successful planning and work to overcome them.

Recognize the Planning Barriers

Plans and planning are vulnerable to the negative effects of various barriers. Here are some of the common barriers that inhibit successful planning.

Inability to plan.   Managers are not usually born with the ability to plan, and some managers are not successful planners because they lack the background to plan. Some may not have conceptual ability; this is a more difficult barrier to overcome.

Improper planning process.   Some managers have not been exposed to the idea of planning as a process and do not know how to go about it. This is often the situation with inexperienced managers, but it can be remedied with management training.

Lack of commitment to the planning process.   Another barrier to effective planning is the lack of commitment to planning. Some managers merely react to situations rather than try to anticipate the events through sound planning. The development of plans is hard work, and it is much easier for a manager to claim there is no time for planning than it is to work through the required planning process. Another possible reason for lack of commitment can be fear of failure. One way to overcome this fear is just to try despite the misgivings; experience helps.

Improper information.   Information that is out of date, of poor quality, or of insufficient amount can be a major barrier to planning. Inaccurate information on costs, capital, personnel, time needed, historical performances, or potential developments in the economy can have devastating effects on plans.

Focusing on the present at the expense of the future.   Failure to consider the long term because of emphasis on short-term problems will lead to troubles in coordinating plans and getting ready for the future. Emphasis on the current fiscal year and immediate profit, for example, can turn the manager's attention away from long-range goals and from efforts to guarantee profits in the future. The remedy lies in part with a manager's superior and in part with the top management of the company. A portion of the evaluation of every manager's performance should be devoted to how well each manager plans for the long term. Unless the emphasis comes from the top, strategic planning will take a back seat to tactical planning.

Too much reliance on the planning department.   Much time and money is spent by large businesses on elaborate staffs in planning departments. These departments often are remote from the line managers they exist to serve. Planning can and often does become an end in itself rather than a means to an end—goal achievement. It can be a great temptation to focus on tools and methods of planning as the highest and most reliable parts of planning. What can get lost in the process is the value of the vast experiences acquired by the managers on the line. Planning departments conduct studies, do research, build models, and project probable results, but they do not implement plans. They are aids in planning. Somewhere, somehow, a manager or managers must be able to translate the planning department's output into programs to achieve specific goals at specific times.

Concentrating on only the controllable variables. Managers can find themselves concentrating on the things and events within their powers to control while failing to consider outside factors. The feeling may be that there is little value in attempting to plan by including such variables as the future state of our industry's technology, the future of our economy, future government restrictions, and more because these variables are too difficult to predict accurately. Managers show a decided preference for the known and an aversion to the unknown. But plans are educated guesses about the future. They are only attempts to predict the impact of present decisions on the future and the future's impact on the organization. The longer the range in plans, the greater the need to keep them flexible and to review them at regular intervals so that they can be rewritten in the light of unfolding trends and events.

Besides being aware of the planning barriers, the manager should know about some aids for developing effective plans. These are in addition to those suggested for overcoming the barriers. The traditional aids to planning are getting as much information as possible, using many sources of information, and involving others who can help in the planning process.

Use the Aids to Planning

As much information as possible. The manager increases the probability of having both the proper quantity and quality of information needed by acquiring as much data as possible within the limits of time and money.

Multiple sources of information. A manager is not an expert on every topic. By developing multiple sources of information, the manager can overcome the limitation brought about by focusing on a goal from only one viewpoint. Additional critical information can be received from accounting, legal counsel, personnel, and engineering. All potential sources need to be cultivated.

Involvement of others in the planning process. An effective manager should be eager to involve others in the planning process. Opening the planning process to those who have the ability and interest could result in more and perhaps better plans, in a commitment to the plan through involvement, in development of employees who understand planning as a way of life in a company environment, and in the long-range development of people.

"Well here's the problem, Bob. They installed the pool on the wrong side of the diving board."

Source: Reprinted by permission: Tribune Media Services.

If these aids are implemented, the manager should improve the effectiveness of the plans and planning process.

Summary

- Planning sets goals and selects the means to reach those goals.
- Planning answers the questions of who, what, when, where, how, and how much.
- Plans can be operating (either ongoing or single-use), strategic, and tactical.
- An organization's mission controls its direction and influences its planning at every level.

- Planning involves the execution of seven basic steps: setting objectives, analyzing the environment, determining alternatives, evaluating alternatives, choosing a course or courses of action, implementing the plan, and following up (evaluating).
- The strategic planning process should develop organizational unity by involving all levels of management in a company planning process.
- Barriers to planning can make planning ineffective.
- Aids to planning can help managers plan successfully.

Glossary of Essential Terms

budget	A single-use plan for predicting sources and amounts of income and how it is to be used.
mission	The formal statement about the central purpose behind the organization's existence—its reason to be.
objective	A goal or target that an individual or an organization intends to achieve through planning and plans.
operating plan	A plan that focuses on the implementation or ongoing part of a manager's planning responsibilities.
planning	Setting objectives and determining the means (courses of action) to reach those objectives.
policy	Broad guidelines to aid managers at every level in making decisions about recurring situations or functions.
procedure	Plans that answer how to do something.
program	A single-use plan for solving a problem or accomplishing a group of related activities needed to reach a goal.
rule	Plans that dictate human behavior or conduct at work.
strategic plan	A decision about long-range goals and the course of action to achieve those goals. Strategic plans influence the construction of tactical plans.
strategic planning	Planning that focuses on organizational direction, involving all levels of management.
tactical plan	A decision about short-term goals and the courses of action that will enable an organization to achieve those goals. Tactical plans help achieve strategic goals.

Review Questions

1. Can you define this chapter's essential terms? If not, consult the preceding glossary.

2. What is the importance of planning to the operation of a business? What is the relationship of planning to the functions of organizing, staffing, directing, and controlling?

3. What is the scope of management planning for each of the three levels of management? What specific planning questions are addressed by each level of management?

4. What are the purposes of the operating planning process and the strategic planning process? When would each be used by an organization?

5. List and briefly explain the seven steps in the operating planning process.

6. What are the seven barriers to effective planning? How does each interfere with planning effectiveness?

7. What are the three aids to effectiveness in planning?

References

1. "Chrysler Prepared to Return to Europe," *Chicago Tribune*, January 24, 1988, sect. 7, p. 7.

2. Peter Drucker, *The Practice of Management* (New York: Harper & Row, 1954), pp. 49–61.

3. "Tired of Tires," *USA Today*, December 23, 1987, p. 1B.

Readings

Crosby, Philip B. *Running Things: The Art of Making Things Happen*. New York: New American Library, 1986.

Hamermesh, Richard G. *Making Strategy Work: How Senior Managers Produce Results*. New York: John Wiley & Sons, 1987.

Hax, Arnoldo C., ed. *Planning Strategies That Work*. New York: Oxford University Press, 1987.

Lenz, R. T. "Managing the Evolution of the Strategic Planning Process." *Business Horizon*, 30, no. 1 (January–February 1987), pp. 34–39.

McLimore, J. Fred and Laurie Lauwood. *Strategies . . . Successes . . . Senior Executives Speak Out.* New York: Harper & Row, 1988.

Molz, R. "How Leaders Use Goals." *Illustrated Long Range Planning,* 20 (October 1987), pp. 91–101.

Porter, Michael E. "From Competitive Advantage to Corporate Strategy." *Harvard Business Review* (May–June 1987), pp. 43–59.

Scarborough, Norman and Thomas Zimmerer. "Strategic Planning for the Small Business." *Business: The Magazine of Managerial Thought and Actions,* 37, no. 2 (April–June 1987), pp. 11–19.

Schoonhoven, Claudia Bird. "Combining Strategies Pays Off Fast, Even in Turbulent Markets." *Planning Review,* 15, no. 4 (July–August 1987), pp. 36–41.

Tomasko, Robert M. *Downsizing, Reshaping the Corporation for the Future.* New York: AMACOM, 1987.

C A S E S

4.1 Which Rules Are Rules?

Maura Shaughnessy was counseling her new assistant on the ways in which she wanted her department to operate:

"Listen Steve, when anyone comes in late I want to know about it. It's our policy to record the lateness and keep it on file. That will give us a way of telling how much time is lost and by whom. It will help us build a case for dismissal if it becomes necessary."

"Maura, for heaven's sake, I was late several times before I got promoted. No one ever did anything about it that I am aware of."

"Steve, you know the rule: We dock people's pay after one-half hour of accumulated lateness. Just because your boss was lenient doesn't mean we should ignore company procedures."

"Are there any good reasons for forgiving lateness?"

"Yes. A grievance filed in 1979—the year of the blizzard—established the power to forgive lateness that is widespread and weather-connected."

"What's the rule about leaving early?"

"If your people have a family emergency, like an illness or death in the family, you can authorize an early departure. But see me first before you do."

For Discussion

1. What are this company's policies? Explain your answer.
2. What are this company's procedures? Explain your answer.
3. What are this company's rules? Explain your answer.

4.2 Wilson's Future

"Pop" Wilson (as the vice-presidents at Wilson Products were fond of calling him) was preparing for his monthly meeting with his board of directors. He was facing a deadline of next Tuesday, at which time his annual budget for the coming fiscal year would be presented for approval. Pop was getting ready to turn the day-to-day management over to his son, a vice-president and recent college graduate with a master's degree in economics. He had let "junior" (as the other vice-presidents called him) put the basics of the budget together this year and was reviewing the results when his son, Peter, entered his office.

"Take a chair, son," said Pop cordially. "I have been looking over the figures you gave me yesterday, and I have a few questions."

"I think I know one of them. It has to do with the New Jersey plant, doesn't it?"

"Yes, that's one question. Why are their capital equipment figures missing?"

"Dad, I've talked with them three times this week to jar that information loose. They have had some turnover, and the planning out there is a mess. Jones says to just go with last year's figures if we don't get the information on time for the meeting Tuesday."

"Look, son, I can't do that. Last year they spent half a million on new production equipment. Their spending spree ought to be over by now. We'll cut that figure in half. That's all we can afford for next year, anyway. Now, about the Houston numbers, I . . ." Pop was interrupted by his son.

"Dad, since you bought that company three months ago, I have been trying to interpret their reports. I really think I should get down there again and try to convince them once more to use our accounting system. The categories they use don't fit with those of our other divisions, so we can't integrate the data."

"They don't have to use our system. The numbers are just too high. We have got to get their expenses down and fast. Also, I've cut their request for new people in their design department. They will have to make do with their present staff."

"Dad, if you do that, they will probably delay the production on their new line. The people in Houston told me that new hands were essential if the target date you set is to be reached."

"Son, I can't approve such a large figure. It will cut our profits for next year and force us to dip into past profits. Their high-tech eats up funds faster than any of our other operations."

"That division more than any other is our future. It contributes close to 40 percent of our income now and will be over 50 percent next year if their new line comes out on time. Remember what you said, Dad: 'Our mission is to be the most profitable company in our industry.' "

"That is precisely what I'm thinking about—profits. I've got to show the board members a greater return on our invested dollars than we are showing now. If I go with Houston's request, it will cut into profit sharing bonuses throughout the company."

"If you don't go with Houston's request, the competition will beat us to the market. What will happen to our return on invested capital then?"

For Discussion

1. Which of the barriers to planning is/are illustrated in this case? Provide examples from the case to support your decisions.
2. What do you think of Wilson's mission statement? How would you change the mission statement?
3. What might happen if Pop Wilson does not approve the Houston request for additional funding?

CHAPTER 5

Planning Tools
and Techniques

OUTLINE

ESSENTIAL TERMS

assumptions
brainstorming
breakeven analysis
budgeting
committee
crisis team
critical path
Delphi technique
fixed costs

forecast
game theory
linear programming
network
project management
quality circle
queueing (waiting line) models
simulation
variable costs

LEARNING OBJECTIVES

After reading and discussing this chapter, you should be able to do the following:

1. Define this chapter's essential terms.

2. List and describe the interrelationships among the three variables in planning.

3. Discuss the nature of the managerial planning environment.

4. List and describe five quantitative tools or techniques discussed in this chapter.

5. List and describe the seven general planning tools or techniques discussed in this chapter.

Overview of the Chapter

In Chapter 4, we introduced planning as a management activity and outlined basic planning processes. In this chapter, we explore the various kinds of general and specific tools that managers use to make their planning activities more precise and effective. We begin with an examination of the degree of certainty on which plans are constructed. Next, we look at quantitative (data-related) planning tools and techniques, and last, we turn our attention to more general types of planning tools and techniques.

Determining Degrees of Certainty in Planning

Besides depending on managers' conceptual skills, all plans rest to some extent on three basic elements: objectives, assumptions, and forecasts. Objectives (as we saw in Chapter 4) are the stated ends a manager wishes to achieve. They are what one expects to achieve after executing plans and expending the resources called for. **Assumptions** are the premises or conditions that planners accept as true and real because of their past experiences or those of others. Examples of assumptions are such things as the freezing point of water, the distress of a cat when its tail is pulled, and the distance from Chicago to New York. **Forecasts** are the expectations that planners formulate about the likely or probable state of events or conditions at some time in the future. Forecasts are predictions based on assumptions (the known). They are often summaries of experiences used to project the future. For example, if sales have been rising between 10 and 12 percent over the last three months, a trend may be developing that will help planners forecast the next month's sales increase.

To illustrate the interplay between assumptions and forecasts, consider the weather forecaster on your favorite television news show. The forecaster knows the behavior of the laws of nature and the usual or past behaviors of types of weather systems. Given the current data on upper air currents and the experience of states that are experiencing a particular weather system, the forecaster can predict the conditions most likely to exist over the next several hours or days. The accuracy of the forecast depends on the accuracy of the forecaster's assumptions and the specific future behaviors of the various elements operating to make the weather system. Any changes in expected behaviors can mean an outcome different from the one predicted. Things do not always perform as they did in the past because conditions surrounding past performances may not be duplicated. Besides, new variables are often introduced that cause changes in the behaviors of the other variables. Exhibit 5.1 shows a few predictions that did not turn out.

Forecasting

Forecasting concentrates on predicting the probable outcomes of the activities of the organization. Examples of forecasting challenges for a company might include such questions as these: What will the sales revenue be in

EXHIBIT 5.1
A Few Forecasts That Went Wrong

Not all predictions are of the pie-in-the-sky variety. If anything, as this excerpt of some of the worst predictions of all time from *The Book of Predictions* illustrates, forecasters failed to think big enough:

Galileo's Discovery of Jupiter's Moons

"Jupiter's moons are invisible to the naked eye and therefore can have no influence on the Earth, and therefore would be useless, and therefore do not exist."
—*Pronouncement made by a group of Aristotelian professors who were contemporaries of Galileo's, circa 1610.*

Locomotives

"What can be more palpably absurd than the prospect held out of locomotives traveling twice as fast as stagecoaches?"
—*The Quarterly Review, 1825.*

The Automobile

"The ordinary 'horseless carriage' is at present a luxury for the wealthy; and although its price will probably fall in the future, it will never, of course, come into as common use as the bicycle."
—*The Literary Digest, Oct. 14, 1889.*

The Submarine

"I must confess that my imagination, in spite even of spurring, refuses to see any sort of submarine doing anything but suffocating its crew and floundering at sea."
—*H.G. Wells, British novelist, in "Anticipations," 1901.*

continued

EXHIBIT 5.1
Continued

Radio

"(Lee) De Forest has said in many newspapers and over his signature that it would be possible to transmit the human voice across the Atlantic before many years. Based on these absurd and deliberately misleading statements, the misguided public . . . has been persuaded to purchase stock in his company."
—*A U.S. district attorney prosecuting inventor Lee De Forest for selling stock fraudulently through the United States mails for his Radio Telephone Co., 1913.*

Television

"While theoretically and technically television may be feasible, commercially and financially I consider it an impossibility, a development of which we need waste little time dreaming."
—*Lee De Forest, "Father of the Radio," 1926.*

Repeal of Prohibition?

"I will never see the day when the 18th Amendment is out of the Constitution of the U.S."
—*William Borah, U.S. senator, 1929. (The 18th Amendment was repealed in 1933. Borah was alive to see the day. He did not die until 1940.)*

Hitler

"In this column for years, I have constantly labored these points: Hitler's horoscope is not a war horoscope . . . If and when war comes, not he but others will strike the first blow."
—*R.H. Naylor, British astrologer for the London Sunday Express, 1939.*

The Atomic Bomb

"That is the biggest fool thing we have ever done . . . The bomb will never go off, and I speak as an expert in explosives."
—*Adm. William Leahy, U.S. Navy Officer speaking to President Truman, 1945.*

Landing on the Moon

"Landing and moving around the moon offers so many serious problems for human beings that it may take science another 200 years to lick them."
—*Science Digest, August, 1948.*

The Viet Nam War

"Whatever happens in Viet Nam, I can conceive of nothing except military victory."
—*Lyndon B. Johnson, in a speech at West Point, 1967.*

Source: 11 items from "The 41 Worst Predictions of All Times" in *The Book of Predictions* by David Wallechinsky, Amy Wallace, and Irving Wallace. (Appeared under the title "Forecasters Who Blew It Big" in *Chicago Tribune*.) Copyright © 1981 by David Wallechinsky, Amy Wallace, and Irving Wallace. By permission of William Morrow & Company.

three months? In six months? In a year? Will product X sell more units than last year?

In developing forecasts, managers may rely on internal information or outside resources. In the first instance, when top-level management is developing its budgets, it will base the plans on the forecasts of expected sales and on the revenues generated through these sales. These plans are based on the forecasts of the marketing managers who make the sales projection.

Internal forecasting can also be done through various groups of inside experts who pool their knowledge by forming panels or committees. The typical large business corporation has an executive planning committee composed of various high-level managers who engage routinely in forecasting and planning on the basis of others' forecasts. Often such a committee strives for a consensus—a majority viewpoint or position. Like an appellate court, the committee may issue a majority and a minority report or position for use by the organization's chief executive officer. Both reports always state the assumptions to support their forecast or prediction.

In general, top management committees help establish official information channels for the chief executive officer. Information is gathered, passed, and interpreted by members of the committees. Corporate policies, decisions, and actions are explained, and questions from on high or below are answered. Decisions made with the help of or through committees can be more easily implemented than decisions made individually by a chief executive officer. Committee members tend to weld together, becoming members of a real corporate team with commitment to the results generated by the committee. The differing backgrounds and experiences of the committee members bring a wide range of expertise to bear on planning and other concerns for such committees and provide a direct pipeline to and from the chief executive.[1] We discuss committees in more detail later in this chapter.

In other instances, management may rely on outside sources. Various government bureaus and agencies regularly provide forecasts about specific and overall economic activities, such as the rates of inflation, unemployment, retail sales, consumer spending, interest rates, and the growth of specific industries or job categories. Exhibit 5.2 is such a forecast, provided by the U.S. Department of Labor, Bureau of Labor Statistics. Additionally, various private organizations, such as universities and business associations, provide specific forecasts for specific areas of the country and sections of the economy that can assist managers in attempting to predict the future.

A Few Examples

Nearly every producer of goods and services needs up-to-date market research to help decide what product will sell to whom, in how many units, with what options, and at what price. Over 400 companies perform market

EXHIBIT 5.2
Employment by Occupational Groups, 1986 and Projected Changes to the Year 2000*

Occupation	1986	Projected 2000 Alternatives			Change 1986–2000 Moderate Alternative		
		Low	Moderate	High	Number Change	Percent Change	Annual Rate of Change
Total Employment	111,623	126,432	133,030	137,533	11,407	19.2	1.3
Executive, Administrative, and Managerial Workers	10,583	12,900	13,616	14,105	3,033	28.7	1.8
Education administrators	288	316	325	336	37	12.9	0.9
Financial managers	638	747	792	824	154	24.1	1.6
General managers and top executives	2,383	2,820	2,965	3,052	582	24.4	1.6
Marketing, advertising, and public relations managers	323	402	427	444	105	32.5	2.0
Accountants and auditors	945	1,251	1,322	1,371	376	39.8	2.4
Personnel, training, and labor relations specialists	230	264	278	288	49	21.2	1.4
Professional Workers	13,538	16,438	17,192	17,793	3,654	27.0	1.7
Electrical and electronics engineers	401	544	592	616	192	47.8	2.8
Computer systems analysts	331	544	582	607	251	75.6	4.1
Lawyers	527	676	718	748	191	36.3	2.2
Teachers, preschool	176	233	240	248	64	36.3	2.2
Teachers, kindergarten and elementary	1,527	1,778	1,826	1,883	299	19.6	1.3
Teachers, secondary school	1,128	1,246	1,280	1,320	152	13.4	0.9
College and university faculty	754	703	722	745	-32	-4.2	-0.3
Dentists	151	184	196	203	45	29.6	1.9
Physicians and surgeons	491	645	679	700	188	38.2	2.3
Registered nurses	1,406	1,951	2,018	2,077	612	43.6	2.6

*Low projections are pessimistic estimates, and high projections are optimistic estimates.

Source: U.S. Department of Labor, Bureau of Labor Statistics, 1987.

research for other companies and generate about 3,000 market research reports each year for clients. Their tools include U.S. census data, selected mailing lists for specified groups, camera surveillance of customers in stores, scanner analysis of what certain groups purchase in supermarkets, and customer or consumer testing of various kinds. In addition, most companies have their own market research people or use those employed by their advertising agencies.[2]

The same research people who sample consumer preferences for soap makers have begun looking at what makes a new car successful. Durable Goods Assessor is a system used by Management Decision Systems, Inc. of Boston to make forecasts of products years before they will be available for sale. This system has a 90 percent reliability record for soap and food products and is now being applied to automobiles, according to Robert Klein, senior vice-president of the firm. So far the research for cars has come within plus or minus 25 percent reliability.[3] The tools used include consumer comparisons of upcoming models with existing ones, product information and films of the product in use, and actual cars for potential customers to drive. Klein's firm claims it can tell a manufacturer how many people will like the car, how great the car is compared to another car, how many cars will likely sell, and the type and income of people who are likely to buy the car. When you consider that bringing a new model to the public costs about $1 billion, such research is extremely essential.[4]

The Japanese conduct their market research differently from U.S. firms. Instead of relying on data gathered by professional research firms from people who might become buyers, the Japanese manufacturers rely most heavily on information gathered from their distributors, dealers, and people who have bought or used their products. They stay closely in touch with their distribution channel members, tracking the sales results monthly, weekly, and sometimes daily. They trust their managers' intuition—their feel for the market. At Honda, managers spend up to 50 percent of their time talking with dealers and distributors. These people know the customers' needs best.[5]

The Public Broadcasting System uses outside experts in creating the format for its program "Wall Street Week." Interviewers ask various financial and security analysts to forecast the performance of securities, securities markets, and other areas of interest to investors and financial managers. This method of forecasting, known as the **Delphi technique** (after the Greek prophet or oracle who lived at Delphi in ancient times), uses the opinions of various outside experts who are regularly polled or interviewed and paid for their forecasts. At year's end, the predictions are reviewed and analyzed for accuracy.

If a company uses outside experts, it may contact them by mail or directly and ask them specific questions. The responses are recorded, and trends or majority viewpoints are determined. An expert whose view differs from the majority view may be asked why—to state the assumptions on which the forecast was made. The organization then has to determine which forecasts it will take as its assumptions when planning.

Which sources to use for forecasting (internal, external, or both) depends on the particular organization, its resources, degree of sophistication in forecasting, and the type of forecast needed. Regardless of the sources used, forecasting with a great deal of certainty is difficult mainly because forecasting is done within the framework of an ever-changing environment.

The Planning Environment

When managers forecast, they are trying to predict the future. The dilemma in this situation is that managers cannot hold the future constant: It is ever-changing. In addition, managers must deal with the dimension of time—the longer the period of time a forecast covers, the more vulnerable it is to the elements of uncertainty.

The pressure of a change in forecasting affects all organizations, large or small. Exxon, the world's largest oil company, has trouble forecasting with even near-term accuracy despite its degree of sophistication in the use of planning resources. (Exxon uses outside experts as well as its own analysts in preparing forecasts for energy availability and usage.) Like other companies, Exxon operates in an environment with so many variables that it is powerless to control or influence. During the 1982 analysts' presentation and conference, Exxon's president said, "If you should gain the impression that we feel somewhat less certain than usual about forecasting near-term economic and energy trends, you're absolutely correct. Forecasting oil demand these days can be a bit like solving Rubik's Cube—except that there are no pamphlets available to let one peek at the right answer."[6] Another Exxon official explained to reporters, "It used to be fairly simple to predict where energy would fit in the overall American economic picture, at least in the near term. But now we've got an administration in Washington that has an economic policy that, quite simply, has never been tested before. All bets are off on what's going to happen this year or next."[7]

Faced with an ever-changing environment and less than perfect information, what can managers do to improve the accuracy of plans? The answer is in the selection and application of appropriate planning tools and techniques.

Quantitative Planning Tools and Techniques

In this section, we examine basic tools or planning techniques used by or available to almost every organization and management level. Some require the use of a computer. All have limits and advantages and depend on an individual manager's abilities to apply them to the proper situation. These tools and techniques are quantitative because they require numerical data.

Networks

The purpose of a network is to show all activities needed to complete a project and to enable the planner to calculate the length of time the project will take from start to finish. Once a project begins, the time each activity takes may vary from the time scheduled for it, and adjustments to the network's times may then be made. Some tasks will be completed early, whereas others may be delayed.

Figure 5.1 shows a simple **network** consisting of activities (arrows) and events (circles) to represent a complete project. Events mark the beginning or the end of one or more activities. Activities consist of the mental and physical tasks that must be accomplished to reach an event. Each activity is assigned a time estimate for its completion. Any unit of time may be used, and more than one time estimate may be shown—the most optimistic, the most pessimistic, or an average of the two. In this illustration, we are using optimistic times expressed as production days.

FIGURE 5.1
A network for a project involving the manufacture of two parts and the assembly of those parts into a finished product. Times expressed in production days

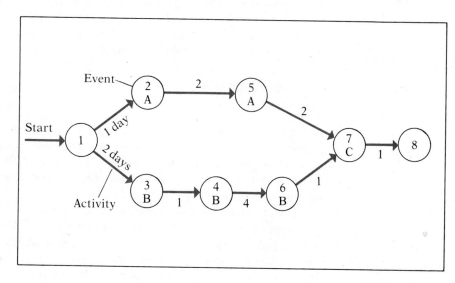

Figure 5.1 represents the manufacture of two parts, A and B, and their assembly into C, a finished component—event 7. Event 1 represents the setup of machinery to manufacture each part. Events 2 and 5 create part A, whereas events 3, 4, and 6 create part B. The total time estimated for the manufacture of part A is the result of the sum of the times needed for events 1, 2, 5, to 7—or five production days total. The total time needed to manufacture part B is the sum of the activity times from event 1 through events 3, 4, and 6 to event 7—or eight days total. Event 7, the production of C, cannot take place until both parts A and B are completed. Therefore, the earliest possible completion time for the project is dictated by the longest time needed for a part's manufacture. Event 7 cannot start until at least eight days after the beginning of the manufacturing operations even though part A will be ready in five days.

As networks are developed, the activities create paths through the diagrams. The **critical path** is the longest path through the diagram from start to finish. It is critical because it represents the earliest possible completion time for the entire project. In Figure 5.1, the critical path runs from event 1 through events 3, 4, 6, 7 and on to 8; it requires a total of nine production days. Once planners know this path, they can try to shorten times for the activities along it to speed up the project's completion. If they were able to shorten the critical path by four days, a new critical path would emerge connecting events 1, 2, 5, 7, and 8. A new completion time of six days would then be possible.

Networks help planners focus on the most time-consuming activities in a project, be it clerical or manufacturing. Networks are dynamic in that times for activities change once the production project begins. Completion dates may be adjusted in the light of changes in times. Networks also show the interrelationship between various parts of a project. They aid in planning both simple and very complex, time-consuming projects. We discuss networks as tools for controlling in Chapter 13.

Operations Research/Management Science Techniques

Other basic tools available to a manager for planning have been developed as part of the output of a field called operations research/management science. Its techniques use both mathematic and scientific techniques to develop models that are able to provide information to forecast changes, determine the outcome of alternative courses of action, and provide an analysis of the alternatives. The techniques include simulations, linear programming, queueing or waiting line models, and game theory. Let's examine each.

A **simulation** is a model of a real or actual activity or process. When we simulate a process, we create a model that will behave like that process.[8] The federal government and many private corporations and universities have computer simulations or models to tell how our economy might change when various changes are introduced into it. Data on a proposed tax cut or increase in the rates of interest charged borrowers can be fed into the computer, and a printout of the areas of the economy that will be affected and how they will change will emerge.

Models may be physical or abstract. The computer model mentioned above is an example of an abstract model. Computer programs, designer drawings, mathematical or chemical equations—all are examples of abstract models. Most of us are more familiar with physical models because they are tangible and three-dimensional. Manufacturers' prototypes (one-of-a-kind, handmade models), architectural models of finished structures, and Detroit's dream cars are just a few examples. Airline pilots and flight attendants are trained in models that simulate not only the appearance but also the behavior of an airplane's instrumentation or passenger compartment under a wide variety of changing conditions.

To use models or simulations, managers must know and understand the process they wish to simulate and the interrelationships of its variables. Simulations through a computer require knowledge of computer simulation techniques. The major advantage of models and simulations is that they avoid the interruptions of normal business operations that real-life experimentation can cause. They avoid the time losses and expenses of employees experimenting with actual company assets. They avoid annoying the customers and taking facilities out of service while training or experimentation is being conducted.

Linear programming attempts to determine the best way to allocate resources when given the possible alternative uses for and limitations on the resources. Programs are called *linear* because of the direct and proportional relationship of the set of variables being programmed. A manager who is contemplating the assignment of overtime to subordinates should know that there will be a direct and proportional relationship between the hours worked and the increase to payroll costs. A direct and proportional relationship will exist as well between the overtime hours and the output of work from the overtime expenditures.

Linear programs attempt to determine the costs in time or money connected with a set of alternatives. A manufacturer may be attempting to determine the best (least costly or fastest) way to ship an order to a customer. Various alternatives (trucks, rail, air freight) are available, and each has an element of time and a specific cost connected or linked to it. Each alternative can be evaluated in terms of its cost in dollars and days. The manager responsible can select a mode of transport on the basis of quantitative measures.[9]

Queueing or waiting line models are used to help managers decide what length of waiting line or queue would be preferable. In a supermarket, or discount store, the length of the checkout line at the cash register and the subsequent time customers must wait in that line are of concern to management. If customers must wait too long, they may choose to do business at another store that provides faster service. The factor that has to be evaluated by management in this situation is the cost of opening other checkout areas to provide faster service. What balance between customer dissatisfaction and operating costs is the best?

Game theory attempts to predict how people or organizations will behave in competitive situations. The purpose of the prediction is to allow strategies to be devised to counter the behavior. Game theory has applications in situations in which organizations compete against one another in price, product development, advertising, and distribution systems. As an example, if a company were able to predict with a degree of accuracy whether and within what time frame a competitor would follow a planned price decrease, the company could decide whether or not to implement the price decrease.

Breakeven Analysis

All businesses need to know at what point their sales revenue or income will allow them to pay all of their bills—their breakeven point—and, therefore, at what point income from sales will exceed expenses, thus yielding a profit. Figure 5.2 shows one way in which any organization can determine its breakeven point. It comprises three main elements marked off by three lines on the chart: the total fixed costs, the variable costs connected to each unit of production, and the revenue or income connected with each unit of sales. Along the left or vertical side of the chart are dollar amounts. Along the bottom or horizontal side of the chart are units of either production or sales.

Fixed costs are those costs unconnected to and separate from the costs of manufacturing a product or selling it. They include such items as insurance premiums, real estate taxes, rent, and administrative wages and salaries.

Variable costs are those costs connected with the manufacture or sale of a product. They include any expense not considered fixed. Fixed costs plus variable costs equal an organization's total costs. In Figure 5.2, the variable cost line begins at the dollar value of fixed costs. Moving from any point on the variable cost line to the dollar amounts shown on the left will give you a reading of total costs, not variable costs. To read variable costs, read total costs and subtract the fixed costs from it.

The data shown on a breakeven chart can also be shown in tabular form. The data shown in the following table are for a small manufacturer of fancy pocket calculators. It has fixed costs of $10,000 per month and variable costs of $20 for each unit it produces. The company can calculate

FIGURE 5.2
A typical breakeven
chart's component
parts

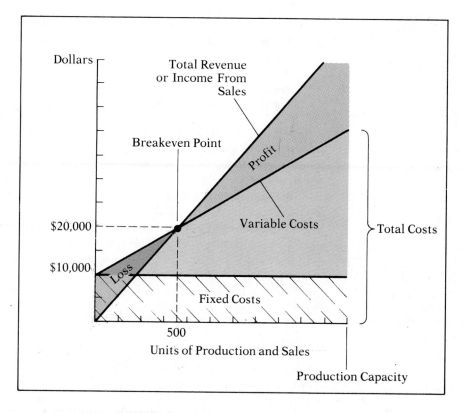

its costs at any given level of production for any month, up to its total
production capacity.

Production Volume	Fixed Costs	+	Variable Costs	=	Total Cost
–0–	$10,000		–0–		$10,000
100	$10,000		$ 2,000		$12,000
500	$10,000		$10,000		$20,000

[Variable Cost: Production Volume (100) × Variable Unit Cost ($20)]

Using these data, the manufacturer can calculate a breakeven point and
profit or loss projection for various sales volumes. Assuming a $40 selling
price, our manufacturer would need a sales volume of 500 units to break
even [Total Revenue: Units Sold (500) × Selling Price ($40)]. Any sales
volume above that figure will give the producer a profit. Here are some
specific figures.

Production Volume	Total Costs	Total Revenue	Profit (Loss)
–0–	$10,000	–0–	($10,000)
100	$12,000	$ 4,000	($ 8,000)
500	$20,000	$20,000	–0–
600	$22,000	$24,000	$ 2,000

If market conditions permitted an increased selling price, the breakeven point would occur on a smaller sales volume. Conversely, if prices are cut to meet competition or to stimulate sales, breakeven would occur at a higher sales volume.

Breakeven analysis enables producers to determine the effect of various changes in costs and sales revenue on their availability of capital and helps them set optimum or maximum selling prices. All costs and selling prices are not entirely under the control of a producer. Actions by competitors, suppliers, carriers, governments, and changes in consumer preferences can affect costs and selling prices as well as sales volumes at any given time. Changes in any of these three variables can be plotted and the net effect determined at a glance.

Budgeting

All of us have to worry about our levels of income and expenses. Each of us has a fixed income but unlimited desires to spend that income. If we are to have enough when we need it, we must make some kind of budget (see Chapter 4) and go through a **budgeting** process. We have to determine the income for a period and the expected expenses for that same period. To allow us to save or invest so that money will be there when we need it at some time in the future, our income must exceed our expenses.

In a business, the primary source of income is the sales of products or services. Once accurate forecasts of sales income are available, money can be allocated to the various parts of the enterprise according to some formula. Who gets what is determined by businesses in various ways. Under grass-roots budgeting, the lowest levels have input and prepare detailed lists of expected areas of expenses that they will or would like to have over the period of time covered by the budget. These estimates are consolidated at one or more levels, and a committee usually reviews and approves or disapproves specific expenditures. A second approach involves top-level management determining what each operating unit has for a total budget. This allocation is then "budgeted" according to the priorities of the department.

Both the top-down and the bottom-up approaches have their relative advantages and appropriate uses. Top-down approaches work well "when business unit managers must be given explicit performance objectives because of economic crises, when unit managers lack the perspective to participate in budget setting, and when the nature of the business requires close coordination between units. In these situations, the knowledge necessary for good budget preparation usually resides at a managerial level one or two steps above that of unit managers."[10]

Bottom-up budgeting places responsibility in the hands of those who have direct knowledge of the environment and the marketplace. The more authority and control over their operations that unit managers have, the more important it is for them to take active parts in creating their budgets. They should know their targets and problems and where resources should be put to use. In addition, managers who have a voice in their budgets are more likely than their counterparts to commit themselves and their units to keeping within it.[11]

Simple top-down and bottom-up approaches are rare. Most companies blend the two as seems appropriate for their particular situations. A blend of the two approaches unites the experience of unit managers with the broad overview and concern of top management for goals, strategies, and available resources. Exhibit 5.3 illustrates the integration of the top-down, bottom-up budget development process. This integration is the quality approach resulting from the utilization of the strategic planning process introduced in Chapter 4. Such an approach allows top management to keep control but incorporates unit managers' contributions before all managers are asked to commit to the final version.[12]

Two options available to an organization in developing budgets are the historical approach and zero-base budgeting. With the historical approach, the amount budgeted the previous year is established as the base figure. This figure is then adjusted upward on the basis of projected percentages. As an example, a firm had $100 budgeted for postage expense last year. As the manager develops the budget, she anticipates a 10 percent increase in mailing. Therefore, she requests this figure. Zero-base budgets force each part of an organization to justify with specifics each of the operations it wishes to fund. Nothing is a given from the previous year, and every request for funds must be backed by a statement of its value to the organization. In Chapter 13, we discuss budgets as controls.

General Planning Tools and Techniques

While quantitative tools and techniques reduce alternatives and outcomes to numeric values, another set of techniques have different advantages: They utilize the stores of experience, expertise, energy, and creativity of people at all levels in an organization to generate ideas and potential

EXHIBIT 5.3
Six Steps to Building a Budget That Blends Top-down and Bottom-up
Approaches Using the Strategic Planning Process

Step 1:

Top management sets forth in broad terms, and sends to the operating unit managers, an overview of the environment, the corporate goals for the year, and the resource constraints.

Step 2:

Each operating unit manager formulates in broad terms the unit's operating plans, performance targets, and resource requirements.

Step 3:

Top management collects, combines, and evaluates information from all the operating units.

Step 4:

Top management assesses and revises targets and resource availabilities, and assigns preliminary estimates to each operating unit.

Step 5:

Operating unit managers plan their activities in detail, determine their resource needs, and prepare their final budgets, which are sent to top management.

Step 6:

Top management combines these unit budgets, tunes them where necessary, approves them, and sends them back to the operating unit managers for implementation.

Source: Reprinted by permission of the Harvard Business Review. Excerpt from "Budget Choice: Planning vs. Control" by Neil C. Churchill (July–August 1984). Copyright © 1984 by the President and Fellows of Harvard College; all rights reserved.

alternatives in the planning process. Whereas quantitative tools use charts, graphs, matrixes, computer programs, and mathematical equations, the tools of general planning use the talents of people in various situations.

Consultants

Earlier in this chapter, we introduced the Delphi technique for forecasting. It uses the funds of knowledge and educated opinions and assumptions of a group of experts outside the business enterprise. These forecasters and all other consultants are outside experts and exist in almost any field. They may be located through management consulting firms, certified public accounting firms, or architectural and computer service companies. Consultants can be called on to examine organization procedures and policies; to analyze, solve, or recommend solutions to problems; and to provide the forecasts that become the manager's assumptions for planning.

The major advantage of using outside experts is that they bring objective viewpoints and analysis to bear on an issue or situation. They are unaffected by the infighting and politics of an organization they are hired to serve. They usually have seen similar problems in other kinds of organizations and are less confined by past practices and the narrow experiences of just one organization's management.

Various government agencies—local, state, and federal—offer advisory services along with an enormous number of useful publications. These publications are available at no or low cost and offer assistance in many areas common to all businesses, such as health and safety, hiring, production and quality control, and management approaches to marketing and finance. The federal government's Small Business Administration specializes in offering management services and advice to our nation's 13.5 million small businesses in the forms of publications, contracted consultants,

"Even a small kingdom, Your Highness, can make effective use of modern management techniques."

Source: Drawing by P. Steiner; © 1982 The New Yorker Magazine, Inc.

and managers (retired or active) from organizations in the private sector who will spend time assisting small business managers. Local and state governments have publications and offices set up to help new businesses locate or deal with the requirements of doing business in particular locales.

Two variations on consultants are the *council* and the *roundtable*. A council will be composed of those people who the manager believes are loyal and committed to the manager's vision of what is to be accomplished. They bring their expertise and advice to the manager they are asked to serve, providing additional insights and observations to each plan or problem under consideration. Councils can be created at almost any level of an organization to serve one or a group of managers. The keys to the success of councils are the willingness of their members to serve and an adequate fund of knowledge that can be brought to bear on the issues to be examined.

The roundtable is a collection of people who consume the output of a manager's unit or enterprise. These may be customers or users within the organization. A retail store manager may ask that customers meet with him or her periodically to offer feedback on how well the store, its merchandise, and its personnel are meeting their needs. The manager of a distribution center may call together the managers of the various stores that his or her facility supplies for the same kind of examination. The mayor of New York has become famous for his often-asked question to New Yorkers he meets: "How am I doing?" Likewise, managers need to know how those they are paid to serve believe they are doing.

Committees

A **committee** is a group of people who volunteer or are appointed to serve as investigators, problem solvers, or decision makers. The leader or chairperson may be elected, appointed, or the person who called for or created the committee. Members bring with them the expertise, experience, and other resources needed for successfully completing their tasks. Committees may be temporary (ad hoc) or permanent (standing). Temporary committees may deal with an issue, and once that issue is resolved, the committee dissolves. Such groups may deal with the move from one facility to another, plan retirement parties, and investigate accidents. Standing committees deal with continuing problem areas such as budgeting, safety, facilities management, and project review and approval.

Brainstorming

Brainstorming is a group effort at generating ideas and alternatives that can help a particular manager make decisions or solve problems.[13] Like the Delphi technique and the use of outside consultants, brainstorming uses the contributions of experts on the particular subject under investigation, but these persons are usually employees of the organization conducting the brainstorming session. Five to ten people are assembled for a roundtable discussion. The leader of the discussion group may or may not be the manager seeking alternatives. The leader must be skilled at running a group brainstorming session, which he or she begins by explaining the purpose of the meeting and the ground rules. Participants are told that no idea offered will be evaluated during the session and that no idea or suggestion is too ridiculous to be aired. Participants must be made comfortable and must feel free to offer an uninterrupted flow of ideas. They are encouraged to build on one another's offerings until all their contributions have been given. Chalkboards, flipcharts, paper, and pens are made available, and all offerings are recorded.

After the session, ideas are sorted, and the best are examined in more detail by the manager who called the session or by the original group or another group of experts. Participants may be asked to research their ideas or to refine or build on them. Credit is given for ideas eventually used.

Besides encouraging the free flow of ideas, brainstorming promotes spirited competition among participants to produce more and better ideas; it spreads enthusiasm, and it provides opportunities to improve on other people's ideas. What may seem absurd to one person can stimulate another to suggest a useful variation.[14] " 'The proof of a good brainstorming session is the number of ideas produced and the way participants feel afterward,' writes Alex Osborn, an advertising executive who codified the technique in the 1940s."[15]

According to Paul Hawken, entrepreneur and author of *Growing a Business*, "good management is the art of making problems so interesting and their solutions so constructive that everyone wants to get to work and deal with them."[16] Hawken says that good problems energize a staff of problem solvers, and when a company has good problems to solve, it attracts bright, unusual people to join in solving them. Some good problems that will fuel a brainstorming group include

- Too much or too little demand for a company's product
- Too many opportunities to expand[17]

Project Management Teams

If you want to add a room to your home, you must accomplish several tasks before your goal can be achieved. Your tasks include hiring an architect to design the structure, getting a building permit, getting bids for the construction, hiring a contractor or individual building specialists, overseeing the project, and paying the people involved. The project must be managed by yourself or another, usually a contractor who will oversee the operations from start to finish.

Project management requires that one person (the project's manager) take charge of the set of activities—planning, controlling, organizing, staffing, and leading them. When Apple Computer Corporation set about the task of designing a new personal computer, it did so with a project team. Its members represented all the essential departments at the company—programmers, engineers, production, and marketing. The project leader was co-founder, and then chief executive officer, Steven Jobs. His team of specialists represented the latest and the best in state-of-the-art computer know-how. The result was the Apple II personal computer, a huge success for the company.

Project managers must worry about three basic things: the time a project will take, the cost of the project, and the quality of performances needed to reach the outcome specified for the project. Bringing a project in on time, on budget, and to set standards are the main tasks facing the project manager. Project teams usually consist of people from several departments or divisions. Thus they cross organizational lines and borrow from several functional areas. Like ad hoc committees, they are set up to do a job, and when they have done it, their members return to their departments or are assigned to a new project team. Project managers often use networks and a matrix form of organization, which we discuss in Chapter 7.

Crisis Teams

A **crisis team** usually consists of key people throughout an organization who can take charge of the organization and make decisions rapidly when an unforeseen, large problem occurs. The chief executive, the top legal officer, a public relations specialist, and heads of departments that are affected by the crisis come together to analyze and decide on strategy and tactics. In 1982, when one or more persons added deadly cyanide to capsules of Extra-Strength Tylenol and placed them on retail store shelves in the Chicago area, the chairman of Johnson & Johnson, makers of Tylenol, quickly created a crisis team of seven members. It met twice each day for the first six weeks of the crisis. The team decided to recall all the capsules, to stop making and advertising Tylenol capsules, to go public on television and in newspapers to regain customer confidence, and to increase the tamper-proof packaging on all of their drug products. By 1984, the company had recaptured nearly all its market share for the pain reliever. The quick corporate response probably saved many lives since at least forty-four tainted capsules were discovered in the recall.[18]

Crisis teams may be standing teams that actually drill or run practice rehearsals by simulating such crises as product tampering, strikes at key facilities, new and costly government regulations, competitors' introductions of product innovations, and large losses through employee theft or embezzlement. Plans are drawn up and procedures written that will help shorten the response time in a real emergency.

Worker Participation Techniques

Many organizations and managers have discovered that those who perform jobs and execute tasks can be extremely useful in uncovering ways in which jobs and tasks can be improved and made more efficient. The past fifteen or so years have seen an explosion in the ways in which employees' first-hand knowledge of business operations can be tapped to provide any number of improvements. Many companies have proved that worker input is valuable and can be obtained when top management is committed to having it and when all levels of the enterprise have been properly trained and prepared to gather workers' inputs.

Experiences in the United States and in other industrial nations, notably Japan, tell us that worker participation programs work best when all employees know what they are expected to do and how they should do it. Unions, too, must back the effort, or it is doomed. When General Motors expanded its worker participation programs in 1977 at its Tarrytown, New York, assembly plant, every manager spent three days learning the program's principles and goals. Some 3,000 hourly workers received twenty-seven hours each of technical and problem-solving training. When General Motors started its Dayton, Ohio, program in 1981, it gave each worker forty hours of training at full pay. Half the training was devoted to the problem-solving and team-building skills needed for GM's participative management programs.[19]

An example of worker participation programs is the **quality circle**, a cooperative effort of workers and supervisor to find ways to improve operations and quality. Quality circles originated in Japan and focus on gaining workers' input and cooperation in programs of cost reduction and methods improvement. Over 750 U.S. corporations use quality circles, and the number is growing rapidly. The fifty-five or so blue- and white-collar circles operating at Northrop Corporation's California Aircraft Division have contributed significantly to reducing by 50 percent the costs of the Boeing 747 parts they make. Hewlett-Packard, an electronics manufacturer, started quality circles in 1979 and now has over 500. Its quality circles, too, have contributed significantly in cost reductions and methods improvements.[20]

The quality circles in most companies have several things in common. They hinge on commitments by all company personnel. They are administered at the supervisory levels of most firms. They involve workers on a voluntary basis, some choosing participation, others choosing to avoid it. Sessions are held regularly, most daily, to focus on only one problem that the supervisor or participants wish to consider. Updates are furnished to all participants regularly so that progress can be seen and contributions noted.

Management by Objectives

Management by objectives (MBO) is a one-on-one approach to improving performances of both individuals and the organization as a whole. It requires face-to-face meetings between managers and subordinates. Subordinates are asked to construct specific goals that will lead to improved performances. Supervisors suggest goals as well. Once specific goals are agreed on, the goals are assigned priorities, and times are set by which they should be achieved. Managers hold follow-up sessions periodically to check on progress and make adjustments as needed. It may be necessary to change priorities as things change or to establish new goals. Additional resources may be needed to accomplish the goals. Individuals are evaluated on the number of goals they achieve, how they achieve them, and how their performances have improved.

MBO is used not only to evaluate individual performances, but also, primarily, as a planning tool. It has applications to any management or worker task, representing a goal-oriented approach to performing any operation. Individuals can use the approach on their own to improve their use of time, their approaches to supervising subordinates, their efforts at organizing, or any other future-oriented area.

Summary

- Plans rest on three basic elements: objectives, assumptions, and forecasts. The more certain and reliable these elements are, the more useful will be the plans that use them.
- All plans begin with specific, stated objectives and use assumptions and forecasts about their outcomes and future conditions.
- Forecasts are based on assumptions and may become assumptions for other planners.
- The dilemma facing managers in planning is that they cannot hold the future constant. The planning environment is ever-changing. The longer the period a forecast is developed for, the more vulnerable it is to uncertainty.
- Quantitative planning tools and techniques depend on mathematical data and often use computers. They are attempts to make plans and planning more precise and less intuitive.

- General planning tools and techniques depend less on numerical data and more on human judgment, experiences, and expertise.
- Both quantitative and general tools and techniques are useful to any organization.

Glossary of Essential Terms

assumptions	The premises or conditions that planners accept as or know to be true and real because of their experiences or those of others.
brainstorming	A group effort at generating ideas and alternatives, using inside experts who focus on one issue or problem.
breakeven analysis	A quantitative planning technique relating costs, revenue, and profit. It determines at what point income and expenses are equal—where an organization breaks even.
budgeting	A planning technique that attempts to formalize in writing the financial resources to be allocated for specific purposes.
committee	A group of people who volunteer or are appointed to serve as investigators, problem solvers, or decision makers.
crisis team	Key people located throughout the organization who come together in an emergency to take charge and make the necessary decisions to deal with its impact on the organization.
critical path	The longest path through a production flowchart or diagram from start to finish.
Delphi technique	A forecasting technique using the opinions of outside experts.
fixed costs	Costs unconnected to and separate from the costs of manufacturing a product or selling it.
forecast	Planners' expectations about the likely or probable state of events or conditions at some time in the future.
game theory	An operations research technique that attempts to predict how people or organizations will behave in competitive situations.
linear programming	A quantitative planning technique that attempts to determine the best way to allocate resources when given the possible alternative uses for and limitations on the resources.
network	A quantitative planning technique using activities and events to chart the flow of a project from start to finish and to calculate the shortest possible completion time for the project.

project management	The overseeing of a project by a project manager who must plan, organize, staff, direct, and control those tasks needed to reach the desired outcome.
quality circle	A general planning technique involving workers and their supervisors in determining ways to improve methods, reduce waste and costs, and improve quality.
queueing (waiting line) models	An operations research technique used to assist managers in deciding what length of waiting line or queue would be preferable.
simulation	A model of a real or an actual activity or process that behaves like the real activity or process.
variable costs	Costs connected to the manufacture or sale of a product.

Review Questions

1. Can you define this chapter's essential terms? If not, consult the preceding glossary.
2. How are a plan's objectives, assumptions, and forecasts related?
3. What factors influence the managerial planning environment? How does each affect the environment?
4. What quantitative tools or techniques are available to help make planning a more precise activity?
5. What are four general, nonquantitative tools or techniques available to help managers plan?

References

1. Richard F. Vancil and Charles H. Green, "How CEOs Use Top Management Committees," *Harvard Business Review*, no. 1 (January–February 1984), pp. 65–66.
2. Robert Garfield, "Researchers Put Us under Microscope," *USA Today*, January 8, 1985, sect. B, pp. 1B–2B.
3. James Mateja, "Predicting the Cars Motorists Are Going to Want," *Chicago Tribune*, December 17, 1984, sect. 3, p. 2.
4. Ibid.
5. Johny K. Johansson and Ikujiro Nonaka, "Market Research the Japanese Way," *Harvard Business Review*, no. 3 (May–June 1987), pp. 16–17.

6. Michael Coakley, "Even Mighty Exxon Mired in Ooze of Oil Uncertainty," *Chicago Tribune*, February 28, 1982, sect. 5, p. 5.

7. Ibid.

8. James P. Fourre, *Quantitative Business Planning Techniques* (New York: American Management Association, 1970), p. 55.

9. For an in-depth look at linear programs and how they work, see Fourre, *Quantitative Business Planning Techniques*, pp. 137–67.

10. Neil C. Churchill, "Budget Choice: Planning vs. Control," *Harvard Business Review*, no. 4. (July–August 1984), pp. 151–52.

11. Ibid., p. 152.

12. Ibid., pp. 152, 154.

13. This concept is generally attributed to Alex F. Osborn, an advertising executive. See his book *Applied Imagination* (New York: Charles Scribner's Sons, 1953).

14. Charles S. Whiting, "Operation Techniques of Creative Thinking," *Advanced Management* (October 1955), pp. 24–30.

15. Joan Detz, "The Adaptive Leader," *Success*, June 1987, p. 46.

16. Paul Hawken, "Problems, Problems," *Inc.*, September 1987, pp. 24–25.

17. Ibid., p. 25.

18. For additional details of the Tylenol crisis, see Leonard Snyder, "An Anniversary Review and Critique: The Tylenol Crisis," *Public Relations Review* (Fall 1983), pp. 24–34 and the Johnson & Johnson Annual Reports for 1983 and 1984.

19. Charles G. Burck, "What Happens When Workers Manage Themselves?" *Fortune*, July 27, 1981.

20. Ibid.

Readings

Einhorn, Hillel J. and Hogarth, Robin M. "Decision Making: Going Forward in Reverse." *Harvard Business Review*, no. 1 (January–February 1987), pp. 66–70.

Halberstam, David. *The Reckoning.* New York: William Morrow, 1986.

Hampton, William J. "What Went Wrong at GM?" *Business Week*, March 16, 1987, pp. 102–108, 110.

Hardaker, Maurice and Ward, Bryan K. "How to Make a Team Work." *Harvard Business Review*, no. 6 (November–December 1987), pp. 112–114, 118–120.

Hawken, Paul. *Growing a Business.* New York: Simon & Schuster, 1987.

Oliver, Thomas. *The Real Coke, The Real Story.* New York: Random House, 1986.

Pickens, T. Boone. *Boone.* Boston: Houghton Mifflin, 1987.

Roman, Mark B. "The Johari Window." *Success* (July–August 1987), pp. 59–61.

Slevin, Dennis P. and Pinto, Jeffrey K. "Balancing Strategy and Tactics in Project Implementation." *Sloan Management Review*, 29, no. 1 (Fall 1987), pp. 33–41.

Thurow, Lester C., ed. *The Management Challenge.* Cambridge, Mass.: MIT Press, 1986.

C A S E S

5.1 Industrial Widgets

Pete Wilson was worried. Since he had put himself in business three years ago by buying the top producer of industrial widgets, profits have shown a slow but steady decline. In looking over the most recent sales figures, Pete realized that a definite trend was forming. He was losing his share of the widget market, and he knew he had to act fast.

Over the past eight months, several events have occurred: His share of the market has dropped from 52 to 43 percent; though the decline in his most important product, widgets, had slowed because of his reduction in their selling prices, sales volume was still on the decline; with the fall in sales and his cut in prices, profits on the widgets had dropped nearly 20 percent. Pete knew if things continued as they were for much longer, he would be at his breakeven point for widgets, and that could force a shutdown and layoffs.

Pete believed his widget was the best on the market, especially since he had cut his selling price to meet the competition. He believed his sales force was a big part of the problem he now faced. Since he had purchased the company, he had made no changes in sales personnel. Their average age was 47 years, and this, he believed, was at the core of falling sales. He felt his sales force was getting lazy and complacent. He was certain after talking with a few of them that they had lost the "old drive." Sure they had experienced a cut in pay because their pay was pegged to selling prices. None of them received a bonus last year because none of them reached their quotas. "Yes," Pete thought, "it's time for some new blood." Pete resolved to begin recruiting younger, more energetic people. That would be phase one of his recovery plan.

For phase two, Pete drafted a proposal to take to his board of directors next month. He would seek its approval to put together a financing plan that would enable his company to make a buyout offer to his biggest rival in widgets, Acme Allied Machinery. Pete reasoned that if he could purchase the product line, research, and know-how of his biggest rival, he would once again dominate the market. Pete had heard through the industrial grapevine that Acme had some new designs on the drawing board. If Pete could acquire them, his future would be secure. He knew he would have to act quickly since his cash and credit positions were shrinking.

With these two strategies, Pete believed he would regain the profit position he had enjoyed three years earlier. His market research, compiled by using government figures on his industry, indicated a growing market for widgets at home and overseas. As soon as he acquired Acme Allied Machinery, he would draft his plans for expansion to overseas markets.

For Discussion

1. What are Pete's major assumptions?
2. What do you think about Pete's two phases to recover his market position?
3. How can Pete improve on his efforts at researching his market?

5.2 Barbara's Brainstorm

Barbara Leyton was excited about the recent seminar the company had sponsored on gaining group participation in improving quality. She was particularly interested in trying the brainstorming session with her people. The director of the seminar had encouraged all the managers in attendance to experiment, and the company's chief executive officer had given the contents of the seminar his full support.

Armed with her notes and her superior's approval, Barbara reserved the conference room, set a date, and sent a memo to her seven subordinate managers and their sixteen subordinates, inviting them to attend "a most exciting exercise in improving our quality of service to our customers." By the time of the meeting, all but two had agreed to participate.

all but 2
too many

Barbara opened the meeting with a brief statement of its purpose. She told the group that they were to feel free to offer any ideas they had on improving services to customers. She promised that all ideas would receive equal treatment and that any ideas adopted would be credited to their proper sources. Barbara stated that the more ideas that were generated the better for all concerned. Barbara began by turning on her tape recorder and offering two quick ideas. Her ideas were quickly endorsed by two others, and another idea was offered by one of Barbara's subordinates. This idea generated a great deal of controversy between two participants. One saw it as an underhanded criticism of his operations. The other saw it as stupid and immature.

Several more ideas were offered with no criticism from the group. Within a few minutes, many ideas about improving nearly every aspect of the company's operations began to flow freely. Critical comments were offered on nearly all recently adopted procedural changes. After about one hour, the ideas stopped, and Barbara terminated the meeting.

During her lunch hour, Barbara replayed the tape of the morning's meeting. As she sat with pen in hand, recording the thoughts that were on the tape, she began to realize several important facts. First, the group had offered only three concrete ideas about customer service improvements. Many of the other ideas had no bearing on the subject of the meeting. Second, Barbara recognized that three voices were dominant throughout the meeting. All were her immediate subordinates. Third, some highly critical remarks were made about the company's top management and the ways in which changes were being made. More than five voices talked about the lack of consultation with people before changes were made or, as one voice put it, "announced on high."

For Discussion

1. Evaluate the effectiveness of the meeting using the text's description of how brainstorming sessions should be conducted.
2. What other techniques could Barbara use to explore ways to improve customer service?

CHAPTER 6

Making Decisions

OUTLINE

ESSENTIAL TERMS

alternative	maximize
decision	payback analysis
decision making	problem
decision tree	programmed decision
limiting factors	satisfice

LEARNING OBJECTIVES

After reading and discussing this chapter, you should be able to do the following:

1. Define the chapter's essential terms.
2. Recognize that decision making is a function of all managers at all levels.
3. Describe the formal decision-making process.
4. Explain the factors in the decision-making environment and the influences on decision making.
5. Discuss the importance of a manager's evaluating the effectiveness of a decision.
6. Discuss four decision-making aids.

What Do You Need to Know About Decisions?

For many years, you have been making decisions. You are reading these words as a direct result of a decision you made to study management. Your entire life is a result of the decisions you have made and of those made by others. A **decision** is the result of making a judgment or reaching a conclusion. Some of your decisions are the result of habitual modes of behavior; some are the result of careful research. Some are made for you, and some are the result of indecision—the failure to decide. The choice to not decide is, in fact, a decision.

In performing their jobs, managers must make decisions. What is decision making? What are the steps in the decision-making process? What aids does a good manager use to make decisions? What influences decision making? Is there a secret to implementing a decision?

This chapter can supply answers to these questions that can make a big impression on your decision making. It is about making decisions in a logical way by following a series of recommended steps. You explore the decision-making process, its setting, and the influences on it. Finally, you examine aids to decision making and the importance of evaluating the effectiveness of decisions.

If you dread decisions, postpone them, or simply feel you could use some extra help on the subject, this chapter is for you. When you have finished reading its ideas, examples, and suggestions, your approach to decision making should be more confident.

What Is Decision Making?

For our purposes, **decision making** is defined as a rational choice among alternatives. There have to be options to choose from; if there are not, there is no choice possible and no decision. Decision making is a process, not a lightning-bolt occurrence. In making the decision, a manager is making a judgment—reaching a conclusion—from a list of known alternatives. Just who makes decisions?

Decision Making Is Universal

Decision making is a part of all managers' jobs. A manager makes decisions constantly while performing the functions of planning, organizing, staffing, directing, and controlling. Decision making is not a separate, isolated function of management but a common core to the other functions.

Managers at all levels of the organization are engaged in decision making. The decisions made by top management, dealing with the mission of the organization and strategies for achieving it, have an impact on the total organization. Middle-level managers, in turn, focus their decision making on implementing the strategies, as well as on budget and resource allocations. Finally, first-level management deals with repetitive day-to-day operations. Decision making is indeed universal.

Managers make big decisions and small ones daily. Whether they realize it or not, they go through a process to make those decisions. Whether planning a budget, organizing a work schedule, interviewing a prospective employee, watching a worker on the assembly line, or making adjustments to a project, the manager is performing a decision-making process.

Importance of Using a Rational Process

Because decision making is such an important part of a manager's job, we need to discover anything that can improve the quality of decision making. One of the most effective measures is to follow a conscious, rational, decision-making process. A manager who makes decisions on a whim will not have the day-to-day decision-making success of the manager who consciously works through the decision-making process.

What is a sound decision-making process, and what is its purpose? Its purpose is to resolve a **problem**, which is the difference between what is and what should be. The process itself is more complicated.

The Decision-Making Process

The decision-making process has seven steps. They are logical and simple in themselves, but they are all essential to the process:

1. Define the problem.
2. Identify the limiting or critical factors.
3. Develop potential alternatives.
4. Analyze the alternatives.
5. Select the best alternative or combination of best alternatives.
6. Implement the solution.
7. Establish a control and evaluation system.

Let's look at each step individually.

1. Define the Problem

What is the particular problem you have to resolve? Defining the problem is the critical step. The accurate definition of a problem affects all the steps that follow; if a problem is inaccurately defined, every other step in the decision-making process will be based on that incorrect point. A motorist tells a mechanic that her car is running rough. This is a symptom of a problem or problems. The mechanic starts by diagnosing the possible causes of a "rough running" engine, checking each possible cause based on the mechanic's experience. The mechanic may find one problem—a faulty spark plug. If this is the problem, changing the plug will result in a smooth running engine. If not, then a problem still exists. Only a road test will tell for sure. Other causes may still exist.

Is there a good method for a manager to use to define the problem? Yes. A manager needs to focus on the problem, not the symptoms. This is accomplished by asking the right questions and developing a sound questioning process. According to Peter Drucker, "the most common source of mistakes in management decisions is the emphasis on finding the right answer rather than the right question."[1]

Figure 6.1 illustrates the *funnel approach* to defining the problem. Initially, a problem is noticed; here, production quotas are not being met by employees. Management now begins the funnel approach by looking for the real reason, not just the symptom. Are hours worked decreasing? No, absenteeism is normal. Is material needed for operations backlogged? No, material is flowing at a normal pace. How is the employees' morale? Are there complaints or concerns? Are the employees functioning satisfactorily. Well, as a matter of fact, there are some rumors of discontent. Is it wages? No. Is it working conditions? No. Is it supervision? Some workers are concerned about the supervision they receive. What are their concerns? The supervisor does not answer the employees' questions on how to perform the technical aspects of the job. An examination reveals that the supervisor lacks technical skills.

Finding a solution to the problem will be greatly aided by its proper identification. The consequences of not properly defining the problem are wasted time and energy. There is also the possibility of hearing, "What, that again! We just solved that problem last month. Or at least we thought we did."

2. Identify the Limiting or Critical Factors

Once the problem is defined, the manager needs to develop the limiting or critical factors of the problem. **Limiting factors** are those constraints that rule out certain alternative solutions. One common limitation is

FIGURE 6.1
Funnel approach to
defining a problem

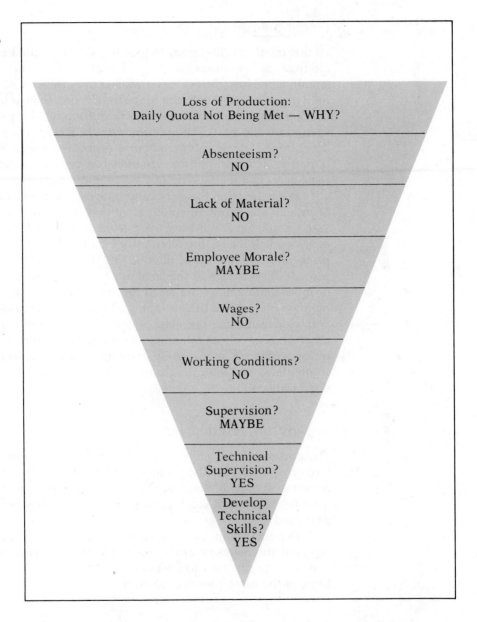

Loss of Production:
Daily Quota Not Being Met — WHY?

Absenteeism?
NO

Lack of Material?
NO

Employee Morale?
MAYBE

Wages?
NO

Working Conditions?
NO

Supervision?
MAYBE

Technical
Supervision?
YES

Develop
Technical
Skills?
YES

time. If a new product has to be on the dealer's shelves in one month, any alternative that takes more than one month will be eliminated. Resources—personnel, money, facilities, and equipment—are the most common limiting or critical factors that narrow down the range of possible alternatives.

3. Develop Potential Alternatives

At this point, it is necessary to look for, develop, and list as many possible **alternatives**—solutions to the problem—as you can. These alternatives should eliminate, correct, or neutralize the problem. Alternative solutions for a manager faced with the problem of trying to maintain scheduled production may be to start an extra work shift, to regularly schedule overtime, to increase the size of the present work force by hiring employees, or to do nothing. Doing nothing about a problem sometimes is the proper alternative, at least until the situation has been thoroughly analyzed. Occasionally, just the passing of time provides a cure.

While building this list of alternatives, it is wise to avoid being critical or judgmental about any alternative that occurs to you or those assisting you. Censorship at this stage can needlessly limit the number of alternatives developed. Initially, the alternatives should be separate solutions to the problem because a set of alternatives that are variations of one another provides less choice in the final analysis. After the initial brainstorming process, variations of the listed ideas will begin to crystalize, and combinations will emerge. In developing alternatives, the goal is to be as creative and wide-ranging as possible. Sources for alternatives include experience, other persons whose opinions and judgments are respected, the practice of successful managers, group opinions through the use of task forces and committees, and the use of outside sources, including managers in other organizations.

4. Analyze the Alternatives

The purpose of this step is to decide the relative merits of each of the alternatives. What are the positives and negatives (the advantages and disadvantages) of each alternative? Do any alternatives conflict with the critical (limiting) factors that you identified earlier? If so, they must be automatically discarded.

Depending on the type of problem and the potential solutions developed, the manager might need to make a more thorough analysis by applying specific decision-making aids. Later in this chapter, we discuss some of the more common decision-making aids.

5. Select the Best Alternative

By this point, the alternatives have been listed along with their corresponding advantages and disadvantages. Which should be selected? Sometimes the optimal solution is a combination of several of the alternatives.

In trying to select an alternative or combination of alternatives, you must, reasonably enough, find a solution that appears to offer the fewest serious disadvantages and the most advantages. Take care not to solve one problem and create another with your choice.

6. Implement the Solution

Managers are paid to make decisions, but they are also paid to get results from these decisions. A decision that just sits there hoping someone will put it into effect may as well never have been made. Everyone involved with it must know what he or she must do, how to do it, why, and when. Additionally, a good alternative half-heartedly applied by uncommitted persons will often create problems, not solve them. Like plans, solutions need effective implementation to yield the desired results. People must be sold on their roles and must know exactly what they must do and why.

Source: ZIGGY © 1987 *Universal Press Syndicate.* Reprinted with permission. All rights reserved.

Finally, programs, procedures, rules, or policies must be thoughtfully put into effect.

7. Establish a Control and Evaluation System

The final step in the decision-making process is to create a control and evaluation system. Ongoing actions need to be monitored. This system should provide feedback on how well the decision was implemented, what the results are—positive or negative—and what adjustments are necessary to get the results that were wanted when the solution was chosen.

For a manager who uses this decision-making process, the probability for success in decisions should be improved. Why? Because it provides a step-by-step roadmap for the manager to move logically through decision making.

Is the decision-making process all a manager needs to master to be successful in decision making? No; the manager must be aware of the environment in which he or she makes decisions. In the following section, we examine the decision-making environment.

The Decision-Making Environment

Decision making, like planning and other management functions, does not take place in a vacuum. There are many factors in the environment that affect the process and the decision maker.

Degree of Certainty

In some situations, the manager has perfect knowledge of what to do about what the consequences of the action will be. In others, the manager has no such knowledge. Decisions are made under the conditions of certainty, risk, and uncertainty. These different decision-making environments require different responses from a manager.

Decision making under conditions of *certainty* means the manager has what is known as perfect knowledge. The manager has had this decision to make before, the alternatives are known, and the consequences of each alternative are fully understood. In this type of decision-making situation, the manager will choose the alternative known to get the best results. Decisions made under conditions of certainty can mean a manager can rely on a policy or standing plan; the decisions will be made routinely.

Decision making under conditions of *risk* provides a more difficult decision-making environment. In this situation, the manager knows what the problem is, knows what the alternatives are, but does not know how each alternative will work out even though he or she knows the odds (probabilities) of possible outcomes. The manager is faced with the dilemma of choosing the best alternative available.

Decision making under conditions of *uncertainty* is the most difficult for a manager. This decision-making situation is like being a pioneer. In this situation, the manager is not able to determine the exact odds (probabilities) of the potential alternatives available. The manager may be dealing with too many variables, or perhaps there are too many unknown facts. Regardless of the reasons, the manager is unable to accurately predict the probable results of choosing any one of the alternatives. What can be done? Reliance on experience, judgment, and other people's experiences can assist the manager in assessing the value of the alternatives.

Decision Strategy: Maximizing or Satisficing?

All managers would ideally like to **maximize** their decisions: They want to make the best possible decision. To accomplish this, managers need to have the ideal resources—information, time, personnel, equipment, and supplies. But managers operate in an environment that normally does not provide ideal resources. They may lack the proper budget or the desired quantity or quality of information.

Managers in the real world do not always have, for example, the time they need to collect all the information they desire about a problem, so they choose to do something more realistic: to **satisfice**—that is, to make the best decision possible with the information available and in the time available. If a manager tries always to maximize decisions, the result may be that a great deal of time is spent gathering information and not making the decision.

Internal Environment

Decisions will never have a chance to affect the organization and solve problems unless they receive acceptance and support. A manager's decision-making environment is greatly structured by superiors, subordinates, and organizational systems.

Superiors. The manager's boss is a major factor in the operating environment. Is the boss one who has confidence in his or her subordinates, wants to be informed on progress, and will support logical decisions after receiving the information? If the answer is yes, then coaching and communicating are the means to help create a good decision-making environment for the subordinate manager to work in.

On the other hand, insecure managers can fear the success of their subordinates, jealously guarding knowledge they possess that might help. In addition, some superiors are so fearful of being accountable for failures that they are reluctant to let their subordinates make any decision of consequence. If this is the environment the manager has to function in, the choices are not easy: Work over the long run to create a climate of mutual trust, continue to live with the frustration and be ineffective as a decision maker, or leave the environment to find a more acceptable situation. Whatever the ultimate choice, a subordinate is being strongly influenced by the leadership environment created by her or his superior.

Subordinates. Subordinates are also a major factor in a manager's decision-making environment. Without the support of subordinates, their appropriate input, and their understanding of the decision, the manager cannot work effectively. What does a manager need to be aware of? The manager must evaluate the level of the subordinates' involvement—which can range from no input to full responsibility for decisions, with the manager just accepting them. The possible degrees of involvement as outlined by Victor Vroom are as follows:

1. The manager solves the problem or makes the decision himself, using information available to him at that time.
2. The manager obtains the necessary information from subordinates, then decides on the solution to the problem. The manager may or may not tell the subordinates what the problem is in getting the information from them. The role played by the subordinates is clearly one of providing the necessary information to the manager, rather than generating or evaluating alternative solutions.
3. The manager shares the problem with relevant subordinates individually, getting their ideas and suggestions without bringing them together as a group. Then the manager makes the decision that may or may not reflect the subordinates' influence.
4. The manager shares the problem with the subordinates as a group, collectively obtaining their ideas and suggestions. Then the manager makes the decision that may or may not reflect the subordinates' influence.
5. The manager shares a problem with the subordinates as a group. Together they generate and evaluate alternatives and attempt to reach agreement (consensus) on a solution. The manager's role is much like that of chairperson. He/she does not try to influence the group to adopt "a" solution, and is willing to accept and implement any solution that has the support of the entire group.*

*Adapted, by permission of the publisher, from "A New Look at Managerial Decision Making," by Victor H. Vroom, *Organizational Dynamics*, Spring 1973, p. 67. © 1973 American Management Association, New York. All rights reserved.

Which one of these options should a manager use? Two factors, suggested by Norman Maier, that will influence the choice are the objective quality of the decision needed and the degree of acceptance of the decision by the subordinates.[2]

A decision is considered to have a high degree of objective quality if it is made in a logical, rational, step-by-step approach. In other words, a decision that can be made by the application of the formal decision-making process, without the inclusion of the opinions of those affected by the decision, meets the objective-quality criteria. An example of a decision necessitating this criteria is one involving a highly technical problem.

A decision is considered to have a high degree of acceptance if it has been made with the input of those affected by it. Decisions requiring the understanding and support of those affected by them meet the requirements for the application of the acceptance criteria. Normally, a decision will have a high degree of acceptance if those people influenced by it have been involved. Examples can include decisions about changing operating procedures, making changes in the work environment, or scheduling vacations. At times, both acceptance and quality criteria can apply to the same decision.

How can a manager know which factors are important in a given decision process? Victor Vroom and Phillip Yetton have provided managers with a series of questions that guide the manager to the appropriate style (see Figure 6.2).

As an example, suppose that a manager, Emil, must develop work schedules; he would approach the process by asking these questions:

A. Is there a quality requirement such as that one solution is likely to be more rational than another? The answer: No; move to D.

D. Is acceptance of the decision by subordinates critical to effective implementation? The answer: Yes, the subordinates are concerned; move to E.

E. If you were to make the decision by yourself, is it reasonably certain that it would be accepted by your subordinates? The answer: No; use option 5.

Emil gets his answers on which option to use in developing the work schedule from the model. In this particular instance, Emil would share the problem with the subordinates as a group. Together they would generate and evaluate alternatives and attempt to reach agreement (consensus) on a solution. Emil should not try to influence the group to adopt "his" solution, and he must be willing to accept and implement any solution that has the support of the entire group. In this situation, as in most situations in a work environment, working with and cultivating the support of em-

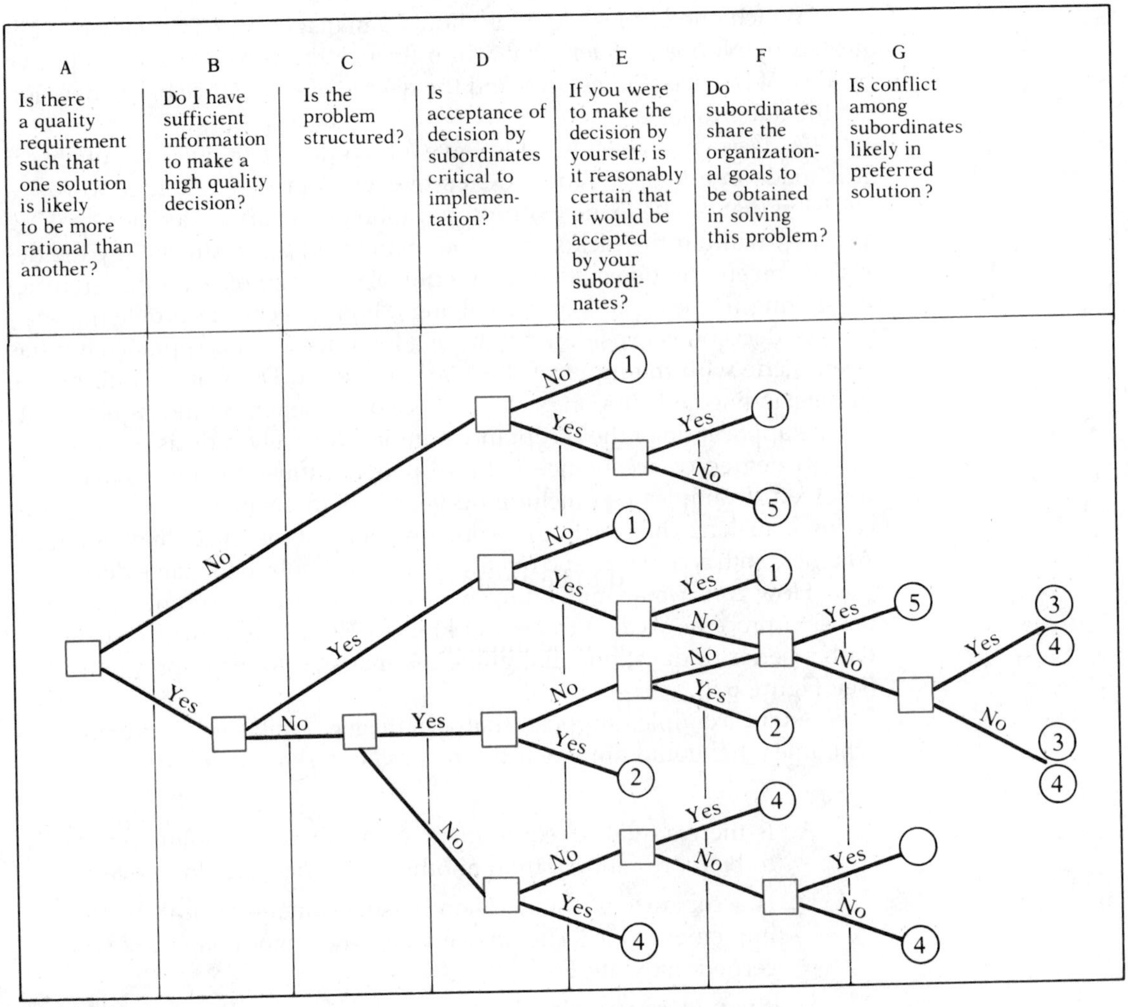

FIGURE 6.2
Victor H. Vroom's guide for choosing an appropriate decision-making style
Source: Adapted, by permission of the publisher, from "A New Look at Managerial Decision Making," by Victor H. Vroom, *Organizational Dynamics,* Spring 1973, p. 70. © 1973 American Management Association, New York. All rights reserved.

ployees for decisions is critical to a manager. High-quality decisions that do not receive support will not be effectively implemented.

Organizational systems. These systems are a final element of the internal environment. Every organization has policies, procedures, programs, and rules that serve as boundaries for a manager's decision making. These factors may be obsolete and may even be the causes of potential or existing problems. If they pose major barriers, it may be a wise strategy to delay a decision and try instead to get the system modified.

External Forces

Besides dealing with the internal factors, a manager must consider external forces, or external environment, in the decision-making process. Customers, competitors, and government agencies are examples of external forces that cannot be controlled and can influence decisions. Just when everything appears to be under control, the economy can take a nose dive and, in turn, weaken sales and revenues. The lesson to be learned here is to keep these factors in sight when making or implementing decisions.

Influences of Manager's Style

In addition to the need to be aware of the environment that decisions are made in, there are other influences on managerial decision making we must acknowledge. Three of these influences are personal attributes (the manager's personal decision-making approach), the ability to set priorities, and the timing of decisions.

Personal Decision-Making Approaches

Not all managers approach decisions the same way. A manager may have a bias for any of the following three approaches. The choice, you will agree, greatly influences the decisions that emerge.

1. *Rational/logical decision model.* This is the approach we recommend in this chapter. It proposes that the manager use a step-by-step process. It focuses on facts and logic while eliminating intuitive judgments. The manager using this method is trying to thoroughly examine a situation or problem in an orderly fashion. Reliance is on the steps and on decision tools such as payback analysis, decision trees, and research.

2. *Nonrational/intuitive decision model.* Some managers prefer to avoid statistical analysis and logical processes in making a decision. These managers are "gut" decision makers who rely on their feelings about the situation. It is hard to eliminate all elements of intuition from decision making, but the manager who relies on intuition for long-range decision making could be courting disaster. The best decisions are often the result of a blend of the decision maker's intuition (based on experience and hindsight) and the rational step-by-step approach.

3. *Predisposed decision model.* This approach is evidenced by a manager who decides on a solution and then gathers the material to support the decision. If a manager has this tendency, there is a strong possibility that he or she may ignore critical information. The results may be that the manager will face the same decision again later.

In a 1987 survey of management executives, 67 percent of the respondents preferred the rational/logical decision model. When making tough decisions, the managers enlist the aid of staff recommendations, statistics, and consultants. The remaining 33 percent of the respondents relied on "gut feelings."[3]

Regardless of the model favored by the manager, a critical element is for the manager to know what his or her tendencies are in decision making and to move toward the rational model. A serious problem can be created when a manager believes he or she is using one approach when in reality he or she is using a different model.

Ability to Set Priorities

There is an old saying: When it rains it pours. The same can be said about decisions. They have a tendency to be called for continuously, possibly in bunches. Thus a factor that can influence a manager's success is the ability to establish priorities for decision making. Each manager may have a different set of criteria. Some managers may give number one priority to the decision having the greatest impact on the organization's goals. Others may assign priorities in terms of what the boss thinks is important. A third approach is to make decisions based on likes and dislikes. The point to remember is that it is necessary to assign priorities to the making of decisions and to know your own reasons for the choices you make.

Timing of Decisions

After a decision is made, it must be translated into action. Good timing plays an important part in successfully implementing a decision, and improper timing can harm the best decision. A manager should be sensitive to the influence of timing to increase the possibility of success. For example, a manager who has made a decision to change the payroll procedures would be unwise to implement that decision in the middle of the payroll run. Regardless of how good the procedures might be, the manager would be wiser to wait until a more opportune time—after the run when everyone affected has time to absorb it and react to it.

Aids to Decision Making

We have been looking at influences on decision making. Now we need to know if there are some aids to decision making available to a manager. Fortunately, there are. Let's examine four of them.

To improve the quality of decisions, a manager has several strategies available. These strategies range from involving other people in decision making to more technological assistance, such as programming routine decisions; another approach is the application of decision tools, like payback analysis and decision trees. Each has a value when applied to the right situation.

Involvement of Others

A manager can choose to involve others in the decision-making process through either individual employee participation or a structured committee. We already touched on this when we considered Vroom's list of degrees of involvement of subordinates. Involvement of individual employees may result in using insights and skills of others who may be better equipped to deal with elements of the decision than the manager is. This process will also help develop the talents of subordinates. A point to consider when involving individual employees is that their inexperience may cause delays. The number of people involved might also slow things down. As a bonus, participation should lead the people involved to feel a commitment to the project.

Involvement in decision making may also be created through the appointment of a committee. As we discussed in Chapter 5, the committee can aid in fact-finding, analysis of problems, and development of alternatives. The committee format has the major advantages of concentrating several minds on a particular problem or set of problems, of involving persons who share or have a stake in a problem's outcome, and of drawing the members into a commitment to the committee's decision.

The Programming of Decisions

Decisions that keep recurring can become **programmed decisions;** that is, the known components can be quantified in routine, decision-making steps or procedures. Typical business decisions that lend themselves to programming are summarizing company records, preparing company reports, handling routine correspondence, and preparing payrolls. Computers can

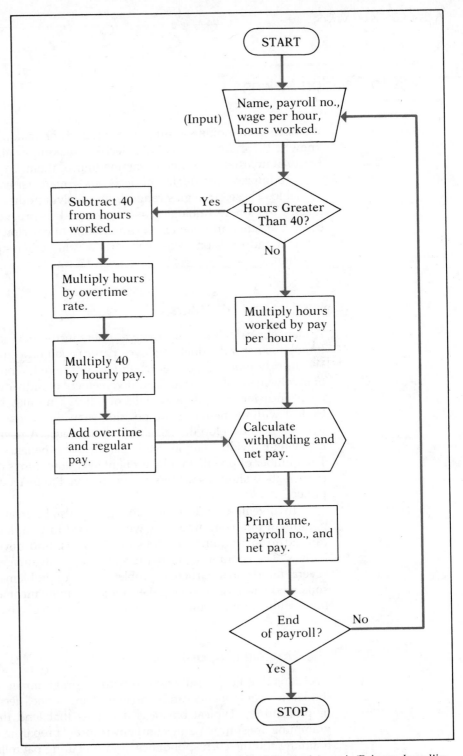

Source: From W. Richard Plunkett, *Introduction to Business: A Functional Approach*. (Dubuque, Iowa: Wm. C. Brown, 1977), p. 149.

be programmed to handle some decisions for you. Figure 6.3 is an example of the model for such a program.

Where computers are not available, other data processing tools can be used. Standard operating procedures (SOPs) can be created to handle the routine, repetitive kinds of decisions that have to be made. The new and unique decisions must be made using managerial intuition, experiences, trial and error, and creative approaches. Most one-of-a-kind problems require a nonprogrammed approach because few, if any, precedents or procedures exist that would apply. It would make little economic sense to program such a decision because of the additional costs in time and other resources.

Using Decision Trees

A **decision tree** is a pictorial representation of a potential decision. It allows the manager to show graphically which actions could be taken and how these actions relate to future events. Figure 6.4 presents an example of the use of a decision tree to show the results of initial and successive decisions.

In this situation, Oscar Vincent is a manager who must decide whether to spend funds to develop a new product or to spend funds on improving an existing product. If the development of the new product is successful, his company will have a competitive edge. But if it fails, the competition may develop the product and damage the company's position in the market because Vincent's company will have neither the next product nor an improved version of the old one.

The process of the decision starts with the initial decision at point A in Figure 6.4. Provided that Vincent decides to authorize the project, point B is the second point for a decision. If no important changes occur in the situation between the initial point A and point B, a decision should be made on the alternative that will be important at that time.

The tree comprises branches from decision points (squares) and chance, or competitive moves (circles). The outcomes are shown to the right of the tree's branches. Decision trees require the manager to draw out only those decisions and events or results that are important. These are ones that have consequences that need to be compared.[4]

An additional refinement for the decision tree approach is to use it for statistical decision theory. This technique requires two elements to be workable: (1) the inclusion of the probability of the occurrence of each alternative and (2) the calculation of the expected value of each alternative (obtained by multiplying the probability of the alternative by the benefit or cost of the alternative).

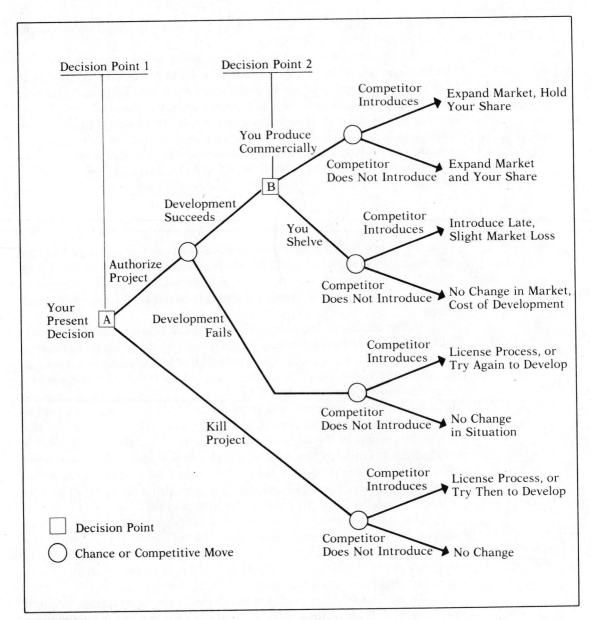

FIGURE 6.4

A decision tree with chains of activities and events

Payback Analysis

If a manager needs to evaluate capital purchasing alternatives, a sound strategy is to apply **payback analysis**, which is an approach the manager uses to rank alternatives according to how long each takes to pay back its initial cost. The strategy is to choose the alternative that has the quickest payback of the initial cost. Exhibit 6.1 illustrates this technique.

In each of the three investments an initial cost is listed along with the revenues derived from the investment for a five-year period. In this case, Machine C appears to be the best investment, at least in terms of the fastest payback: cost divided by annual revenue.

Evaluating the Effectiveness of Decisions

Decisions and decision-making processes are only as good as the results they achieve. The final step in the decision-making process is evaluation and control; this step is intended to provide feedback on the effectiveness of the decision as it is implemented.

Besides this built-in device, are there other devices and indicators of the effectiveness of decisions? Follow-up and feedback techniques—such as accounting information and employee surveys—will provide managers with control mechanisms while giving them a context within which to judge the decisions. The following questions can produce answers that shed light

EXHIBIT 6.1
Payback Analysis

Machine		A	B	C
Initial cost:		$10,000	$9,000	$12,000
Revenues:	Year 1	2,500	2,000	4,000
	Year 2	2,500	2,000	4,000
	Year 3	2,500	2,000	4,000
	Year 4	2,500	2,000	4,000
	Year 5	2,500	2,000	4,000
Payback period:		$\frac{10,000}{2,500} = 4.0$	$\frac{9,000}{2,000} = 4.5$	$\frac{12,000}{4,000} = 3.0$

on the effectiveness of decisions: How many adjustments were necessary? Was any vital information overlooked that would have changed the results? Was the decision accepted by those it affected?

A final comment: Decision making is not just a process of going through the motions of making a decision. Effective decisions are judged on the sincerity of application of the process and the results produced.

Summary

- A decision is the result of making a judgment or reaching a conclusion.
- Decision making is a rational choice among alternatives.
- Decision making is universal to all managers.
- Application of the decision-making process is critical to success in decision making.
- The decision-making process is a seven-step, problem-solving process.
- The manager should be aware of the decision-making environment, which includes the factors of certainty of outcome, resources available, internal environment, and external forces.
- Personal influences on decision making include the manager's decision-making approaches and the ability to set priorities and timing of decisions.
- Aids to decision making include involvement of others and the techniques of programming decisions, decision trees, and payback analysis.

Glossary of Essential Terms

alternative	A potential course of action that is likely to eliminate, correct, or neutralize the cause of a problem.
decision	The result of making a judgment or reaching a conclusion.
decision making	A rational choice among alternatives—making a judgment or reaching a conclusion.
decision tree	A graphic representation of the actions a manager can take and how these actions relate to further events.
limiting factors	Constraints managers work with that rule out potential alternatives.

maximize	Make the best possible decision. Requires ideal resources—information, time, personnel, equipment, and supplies.
payback analysis	Evaluation of investment alternatives by comparing the length of time necessary to pay back their initial costs.
problem	The difference between a desirable situation and what actually happens—the "what is" compared with the "what should be."
programmed decision	Resolution by routine decision-making steps or procedures of a recurring challenge or problem.
satisfice	Make the best possible decision you can with the time and information you have available.

Review Questions

1. Can you define this chapter's essential terms? If not, refer to the preceding glossary.
pg 160 2. What is meant by the statement "Decision making is universal among managers"? Provide an example to support your answer.
pg 161 3. Identify each step in the decision-making process, and describe briefly what should happen in each step.
4. What are the four factors in the decision-making environment that influence the decision-making process and the decision maker?
pg 171 5. What are the three personal decision-making approaches a manager may use? What are the characteristics of each?
pg 177 6. Why is it important for a manager to evaluate the effectiveness of a decision? How does this contribute to the quality of future decisions?
pg 177 7. Under what circumstances would you use payback analysis? What purpose does payback analysis serve?

References

1. Peter F. Drucker, *The Practice of Management* (New York: Harper & Row, 1954), p. 351.
2. Norman R. F. Maier, *Problem Solving Discussions and Conferences: Leadership Methods and Skills* (New York: McGraw-Hill, 1963), pp. 95–110.

3. Mark Memmott, "It Takes Guts for Executives to Make the Tough Decision," *USA Today*, July 21, 1987, p. 7B.

4. *Harvard Business Review*, "Decision Trees for Decision Making," in *Business Classics: Fifteen Key Concepts for Managerial Success* (1975), p. 85.

Readings

Allen, Jane Elizabeth. "How to Solve the Right Problem." *Training*, 24, no. 2 (February 1987), pp. 39ff.

Altier, William J. "Task Forces: An Effective Management Tool." *Management Review*, 76, no. 2 (February 1987), pp. 52–57.

Beeler, J. "The Nuts and Bolts of Decision Making and Problem Solving." *Data Management*, 25 (October 1987), pp. 23–25.

DeBono, Edward. *Six Thinking Hats*. Boston: Little, Brown, 1985.

Drucker, Peter. *The Frontiers of Management: Where Tomorrow's Decisions Are Being Shaped Today*. New York: Harper & Row, 1986.

Lamb, Robert. *Running American Business: Top CEOs Rethink Their Major Decisions*. New York: Basic Books, 1987.

Phillips, Steven and William Bergquist. "Focusing Problem Management." *Training and Development Journal*, 41, no. 3 (March 1987), pp. 87ff.

Quick, Thomas. *Quick Solutions: 500 People Problems Managers Face and How To Solve Them*. New York: John Wiley & Sons, 1987.

Rogers, Henry C. *One-Hat Solution: Rober's Strategy for Creative Middle Management*. New York: St. Martin's Press, 1986.

Schilit, Warren Keith. "An Examination of the Influence of Middle-Level Managers in Formulating and Implementing Strategic Decisions." *Journal of Management Studies*, 24, no. 3 (May 1987), pp. 271–293.

C
A
S
E
S

6.1   First Federal Savings & Loan

The First Federal Savings & Loan is a relatively large organization employing almost a thousand people in several locations throughout the city. In recent years, the company has noticed a significant increase in absenteeism, particularly in the clerical and nonmanagerial ranks. The payroll expense associated with the problem has been growing, and the supervisors and managers have expressed annoyance at constantly having to find someone to fill in for an absent employee. Most attribute the cause of the problem to the generous sick leave policy (twenty paid sick days per year).

For some time, there have been discussions regarding possible ways of reducing the absenteeism. The executive committee of the company has agreed to entertain solutions from all managers and then decide which, if any, should be implemented. It was announced at one of the managers' meetings recently that supervisors and managers should write up their ideas and submit them to the executive committee.

After several weeks, the suggestions were collected and distributed to all managers and supervisors. There was some duplication among the ideas, but the following list is representative of the recommendations:

1. Abolish the present sick leave policy, and have no paid sick leave except for individuals who produce a medical certificate.

2. Reduce the number of paid sick days from twenty to some lower number. (Most recommended ten but a few suggested it be as low as five.)

3. Leave the sick leave policy alone, but point out to employees the problems associated with high absenteeism.

4. Start a demerit system in which sick days taken would be tabulated and translated into demerits. These demerits would then be used in other decisions such as promotions, transfers, and layoffs.

5. Allow employees to trade sick days not taken for vacation days. After a year, unused sick days could be used as vacation days the following year on a ratio of 2:1 (one vacation day for every two sick days).

6. Create a new policy that would state that any absent employee who was discovered not to be sick would be fired.

7. Have a cash bonus system in which employees who had a perfect attendance record for the year would be awarded $100 cash.

8. Publish the names of those with perfect attendance records in the monthly company newsletter.

9. Establish a lottery in which every employee with perfect attendance for the week would be eligible for a draw for $10.

Source: From Jerry L. Gray, *Supervision: An Applied Behavioral Science Approach to Managing People* (Boston: Kent Publishing Company, 1984), pp. 197–198. © 1984 by Wadsworth, Inc. Reprinted by permission of PWS-KENT Publishing Company, a division of Wadsworth, Inc.

For Discussion

1. Has the First Federal management team applied the decision-making process? Explain your answer.

2. What information does First Federal need to solve the problem?

3. How should First Federal acquire the needed information?

6.2 To Ship or Not to Ship

Bill Warren was in a tight spot. If he didn't ship MacNeil's order today, it would not arrive on time to meet the deadline. The order would be lost, and $15,000 would remain unearned. MacNeil was a new customer and had been approved only for a cash sale. The credit department had refused to grant him any credit since he was just coming into the market with no established credit history. The parts that MacNeil had ordered were essential to his completing a large order from his customer. Without Bill's parts in his factory by tomorrow morning, MacNeil would miss his deadline. MacNeil used the post office to send his payment to Bill, but the check did not arrive in today's mail.

MacNeil was frantic as he talked with Bill on the phone. "Bill, I've got to have those parts by tomorrow morning. I sent the check four days ago, and it is certified. Don't worry about it. The bank will not refuse it."

"I wish I could ship, but my boss says that I cannot without your payment first. If this were not your first order with us, we would probably work around this problem. But my boss was firm. No check, no shipment."

"Look, maybe I could wire the money to you, you know, send it by having my bank wire it to yours. If I can arrange that, would that be all right?"

"It would if time were not so important. I've got less than half an hour to go before the last pickup for the airport. If I miss that truck, your parts won't go out until tomorrow morning."

"Bill, isn't there something you can do. I'm desperate! I'll be placing plenty of orders with you guys in the future, but this order is life or death for me. If I don't ship on time, I won't have a future."

For Discussion

1. What is the problem in this case?

2. Using the chapter's seven-step, decision-making process, take over Bill's position, and make your decision.

3. What does this case tell you about the decision-making problems that can and do face managers?

4. How could this situation have been avoided?

Organizing

Organizing: The Formal Organization

OUTLINE

- Span of Control
- Centralization vs. Decentralization

Summary

ESSENTIAL TERMS

accountability	organization chart
authority	organizing
chain of command	power
delegation	responsibility
departmentation	span of control
division of labor	staff authority
functional authority	staff departments
line authority	unity of command
line departments	unity of direction
organization	

LEARNING OBJECTIVES

After reading and discussing this chapter, you should be able to do the following:

1. Define this chapter's essential terms.
2. Explain the relationship between the management functions of planning and organizing.
3. Explain the importance of the organizing process.
4. List and discuss the five steps in the organizing process.
5. Describe and give an example of the five kinds of approaches to organizing.
6. Discuss the concept of authority, its sources and types.
7. Explain the concept of power and its sources.
8. Discuss the following concepts as they apply to organizations:
   - Unity of command
   - Span of control
   - Centralization vs. decentralization
   - Delegation

Who's in Charge?

"You can't tell me what to do; only Larry can, he's my boss!"

"When did the research and development department start reporting to marketing? I thought it was part of the production group."

"All I want is a decision on this engineering drawing. Can't anyone make a decision? Who's in charge here, anyway?"

Were you smiling or frowning as you read those quotations? No matter: If these words sound familiar, you have had practical experience with problems relating to the second managerial function—organizing. A company that has taken the time, energy, and money to develop quality plans needs managers who understand the importance of organizing. Organizing, like planning, must be a process, carefully worked out and applied. This process involves determining what work is needed, assigning those tasks, and arranging them in a decision-making framework (an organizational structure). If this process is not conducted well, the results may be confusion, frustration, loss of efficiency, and limited effectiveness.

In this chapter, we discuss the nature and purpose of organizing, the steps in the organizing process, the important organizing principles, different approaches to organizational structure; and major organizational concepts.

Organizing Defined

Organizing is the management function that establishes relationships between activity and authority. It has four distinct activities:

1. It determines what work activities have to be done to accomplish organizational objectives.
2. It classifies the type of work needed and groups the work into manageable work units.
3. It assigns the work to individuals and delegates the appropriate authority.
4. It designs a hierarchy of decision-making relationships.

The end result of the organizing process is an **organization**—a whole consisting of unified parts (a system) acting in harmony to execute tasks to achieve goals, both effectively and efficiently.

The Relationship Between Planning and Organizing

The managerial functions of planning and organizing are intimately related. Organizing begins with and is governed by plans, and plans state where the organization is going and how it will get there. An organization must be built, or an existing one must be modified, to see to it that the plans are executed and that their goals are reached. The organization must be able to concentrate its resources in a unified way to translate plans from intentions to realities.

The concept that the kind of organization a business should have depends on the kind of results it wants to achieve is not new. It was proposed by Russell Robb in his *Lectures on Organization* published in 1910. An acknowledged leader in the management of public utilities and in the application of management theories, Robb made the following comments about the factors that make an organization:

> . . . we know pretty definitely the factors that make organization. They are structure, lines of authority, responsibility, division of labor, system, discipline; accounting, records, and statistics; and esprit de corps (group spirit), cooperation, team play; but when we attempt to determine the parts played by these factors, we find that their relative importance changes with purposes, conditions, and material. We begin to realize that there is an art of organizing that requires knowledge of aims, processes, men and conditions, as well as of the principles of organization.[1]

An organization structure is a tool of management to achieve plans. As the plans change, the organization structure should be responsive. And even when objectives are similar, what works for one organization will not necessarily work for another.

Zales Jewelers provides an excellent example of the relationship between planning and organizing. In 1980, Zales's organization structure was designed to reflect its organizational goals: product diversification through the development and acquisition of retail consumer product stores. An analysis revealed that Zales was not successful at applying its retail jewelry knowledge to other retail product operations. A decision was made to gradually sell all the nonjewelry businesses—sporting goods, ladies wear, and drug stores. The new company goals—developing, acquiring, and marketing jewelry-related products—were implemented through the development of a modified organizational structure.

What are the results of the organizing process?

Importance of the Organizing Process

Management is very much interested in the successful completion of the organizing process. They are also concerned with the subsequent development, or modification, of an organization structure. Why? For one thing, the organizing process will make it possible to attain the purpose of the organization (as defined previously by the planning function). It also should provide the following real benefits:

1. *A clarified work environment.*   Everyone should know what to do. The tasks and responsibilities of all individuals, departments, and major organization divisions should have been clarified. The type and limits of authority will have been determined.

2. *A coordinated environment.*   Confusion should be minimized and obstacles to performance removed. The interrelationship of the various work units will have been developed. Guidelines for interaction among personnel will have been defined. In addition, the principle of **unity of direction** should be achieved: This principle calls for the establishment of one authority figure for each designated task of the organization; this person has the authority to coordinate all plans concerning that task. The importance of this principle can be illustrated by an example of its absence: It happens all too often that various government agencies develop separate plans on the same topic; no one agency or person is in control of the task or can coordinate plans.

3. *A formal decision-making structure.*   Through the organization chart, the formal superior–subordinate relationships have been developed. This allows the orderly progression up through the hierarchy for decision making and decision-making communications. As a result, the confusion highlighted by one of the chapter's opening questions— "Who's in charge here, anyway?"—should not occur.

By applying the organizing process, management will improve the possibilities of achieving a functioning work environment. What does this organizing process consist of? Let's examine its components.

The Organizing Process

Figure 7.1 provides a series of illustrations that show how the organizing process is applied. As you read and study the following description of the five-step process, refer to this figure to see an example of how the organization structure works.

Step 1. Consider Plans and Goals

As mentioned earlier, plans and their goals affect organizing and its result, the organization. Plans dictate the purposes and activities that organizations have or will have. Some purposes and some activities are likely to remain

EXCELSIOR
WIDGETS CORPORATION

STEP 1
Consider Plans and Goals

To manufacture and market the UNIVERSAL WIDGET at a 10 percent return on investment.

STEP 2
Determine Activities

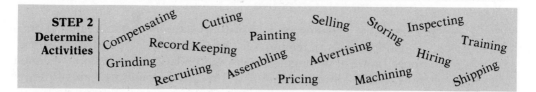

Compensating · Cutting · Selling · Storing · Inspecting · Record Keeping · Painting · Training · Grinding · Advertising · Hiring · Recruiting · Assembling · Shipping · Pricing · Machining

STEP 3
Classify and Group Activities

MARKETING
• selling
• advertising
• storing
• shipping

ACCOUNTING
• record keeping
• pricing

PERSONNEL
• training
• compensating
• hiring
• recruiting

PRODUCTION
• cutting
• grinding
• assembling
• inspecting
• painting
• machining

STEP 4
Assign the Work and Delegate Authority

Bob — MARKETING   Loren — ACCOUNTING   Ian — PERSONNEL   Marie — PRODUCTION

STEP 5
Design a Hierarchy

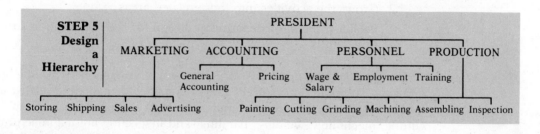

PRESIDENT

MARKETING   ACCOUNTING   PERSONNEL   PRODUCTION

General Accounting · Pricing · Wage & Salary · Employment · Training

Storing · Shipping · Sales · Advertising · Painting · Cutting · Grinding · Machining · Assembling · Inspection

FIGURE 7.1
The organizing process exemplified

fairly constant once a business is established. For example, the business will continue to seek a profit, and it will continue to employ people and other resources. But in time and with new plans, the ways in which basic activities are carried out will change. New departments may be created; old ones may be given additional responsibilities; some may cease to exist. New relationships between groups of decision makers may come into being as well. Organizing will create the new structure and relationships and modify the existing ones.

Step 2. Determine the Work Activities Necessary to Accomplish Objectives

What work activities are necessary to accomplish the identified organizational objectives? Creating a list of tasks to be accomplished begins with those that will be ongoing tasks and ends with the unique, or one-time-only, tasks. Hiring, training, and record keeping are part of the regular routine for running any business. But what, in addition, are the unique needs of this organization? Does it include assembling, machining, shipping, storing, inspecting, selling, advertising? Identify *all* activities necessary.

In an ongoing business, specific programs—which will be single-use plans—may require temporary reorganization within a business or department to handle them. A pilot project conducted for an ongoing business may identify which activities should be performed in a work unit or incorporated into the business.

Once managers know what tasks must be done, they are ready to classify and group these activities into manageable work units.

Step 3. Classify and Group Activities

This step asks managers to perform three processes:

1. Examine each activity identified to determine its general nature (marketing, production, finance, personnel, etc.).
2. Group the activities into these related areas.
3. Establish the basic department design for the organization structure.

In practice, the first two processes occur simultaneously. Selling, advertising, shipping, and storing can be considered marketing-related activities. Thus they are grouped under the Marketing heading. Assembly, cutting, machining, welding, painting, and inspecting are manufacturing processes; they can be grouped as Production. Personnel-related activities include hiring, training, developing, recruiting, and compensating.

In this situation, management has been classifying and grouping activities using the guidelines of homogeneity or similarity of activity. Work that is similar in nature (tasks, processes, or skills required) is placed together to achieve organizational objectives. This guideline is simple to apply, and it is logical. Grouping similar activities is based on the concept of division of labor and specialization. **Division of labor** is breaking down the work into its basic components—in our case, the basic activities—and assigning them to individuals who will then be specialists and perform the jobs more efficiently and effectively.

As the tasks are classified and grouped into related work units (production, marketing, accounting, and personnel), the third process, **departmentation**, is being finalized; that is, a decision is being made on the basic organizational format or departmental structure for the company. Groups, departments, and divisions are being formed on the basis of the objectives of the organization. Management will choose a departmental type from functional, geographic or territorial, customer, product line, or matrix options. We discuss these in detail later in this chapter.

Step 4. Assign Work and Delegate Appropriate Authority

Management has identified activities necessary to achieve objectives, has classified and grouped these activities into major operational areas, and has selected a departmental structure. The activities now must be assigned to individuals who are simultaneously given the appropriate authority to accomplish the task.

This step is critical in both the initial and ongoing organizing processes. The concept serving as the foundation for this step is the principle of *functional definition*—in establishing departments, the nature, purpose, tasks, and performance of the department must first be determined as a basis for authority. What does this principle mean in a business? It means that the activities determine the type and quantity of authority necessary. How much is needed to accomplish the tasks?

After the original organization is established, this step still retains its importance as adjustments in the nature of activity assignments are made. The nature, purpose, tasks, and expectations dictate the amount and type of authority the manager needs to be able to function. Authority does not come first; assignment of activities establishes the basis for authority.

Step 5. Design a Hierarchy of Relationships

This step requires the determination of both vertical and horizontal operating relationships of the organization as a whole. In effect, this step is putting together all the parts of the puzzle.

The vertical structuring of the organization results in a decision-making hierarchy showing who is in charge of each task, of each specialty area, and of the organization as a whole. Levels of management are established from bottom to top in the organization. These levels create the **chain of command**, or hierarchy of decision-making levels, in the company.

The horizontal structuring has two important effects: (1) It defines the working relationships between operating departments. (2) It makes the final decision on the span of control (the number of subordinates under the direction) of each manager.

The result of this step is a complete organization structure. This structure is shown visually by an **organization chart** (see Figure 7.2). The organization chart has its value to managers in depicting the basic framework of the organization. Figure 7.2 shows us that a chart can tell us:

1. Who reports to whom—the chain of command.
2. How many subordinates work for each manager—the span of control.
3. Channels of official communication through the solid lines that connect each job (box).
4. How the company is structured—by function, customer, or product, for example.
5. The work being done in each job—the labels on the boxes.
6. The hierarchy of decision making—where a decision maker for a problem is located.
7. How current the present organization structure is (if a date is on the chart).
8. Types of authority relationships—solid connections between boxes illustrate line authority, and dotted lines show staff and functional authority (which we examine later).

In addition, the chart is a trouble-shooting tool. It can help managers locate duplications and conflicts as a result of awkward arrangements. What the chart does not show are the degrees of authority, the informal communication channels, and the informal relationships.

The organizing process, like all managerial functions, is ongoing. The initial application of the process results in the organization's first organization structure and an organization chart. As the organization is activated and begins its systematic pursuit of goals, management monitors and controls its actions, successes, and failures. Changes and reassignments will take place. New plans will dictate organizational modifications after a new application of the organizing process. Organizing should not be viewed as a one-time process.

An example of new plans dictating organizational modifications is

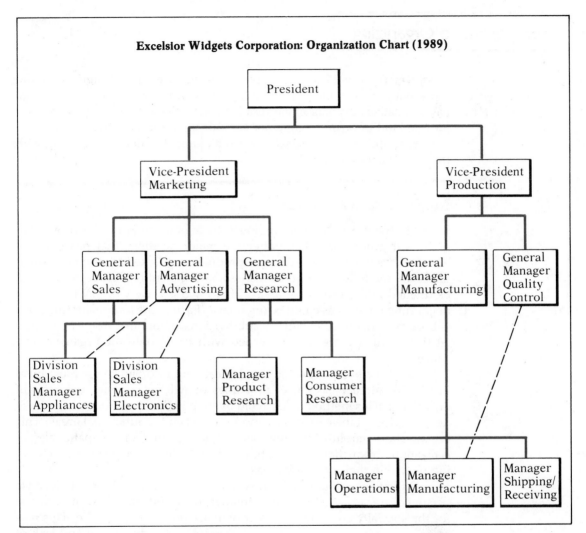

FIGURE 7.2
Organization chart showing the organization structure.
See the text for an explanation.

provided by Firestone Tire and Rubber Co. To pursue its new goals of (1) facilitating the management of Firestone's separate businesses as decentralized and autonomous units and (2) pursuing growth opportunities, the company reorganized its domestic operations. Rather than operating its domestic business as one unit, Firestone decided to have three separate groups—tire operations, automotive service, and specialty products.[2]

Now that we have been through the organizing process, let's examine the possible organizational design outcomes of the process.

Approaches to Organizing

Whatever the organization's approach to its structural design, it should represent the most effective and efficient use for all resources. Each design has its relative advantages and disadvantages. Remember, what works best for one kind of business may not be appropriate for another.

Five options are especially worth looking at in detail, beginning with the functional approach.

① The Functional Approach

Probably the most common approach to organizing is the functional approach. It groups activities under the major headings that nearly every business has in common—finance, production, marketing, and personnel. These are the functions of the business, and the entire organization would be divided into these major areas. Figure 7.3 is a view of just how these major functional areas could be organized. Each of the four major functions is broken down into its various subdivisions. (Note the absence of titles: At this point, we are not concerned with titles, only the organizational concept.)

The functional approach is a logical way to organize for most businesses. What each person or unit does or will do becomes the basis of organizing. This method helps avoid overlap in the execution of basic business activities. Lines are clearly drawn between the functional areas. This organization simplifies training because it provides for occupational specialization. Production or marketing, for example, can concentrate on training people in their specialty areas.

Difficulties can arise with this type of organizational format. Because personnel are separated from one another, their understanding and concern for the specialty areas outside their own are not easy to achieve. This narrowness of viewpoint can lead to communication difficulties and lack of cooperation between the functional areas, which can escalate to hostility; there could be a "production position" and a "marketing position" as a normal situation on organizational questions. If taken to the extreme, this narrow view can result in a specialty area placing its own welfare before the company's.

Another problem area for the functional structure pattern is that it does not develop generalists in the management area. The narrow viewpoint and specialized training develops staff members who are experts in their function, but as we have seen, the top level of management needs to be conceptual. There must be an understanding of the interrelationship and

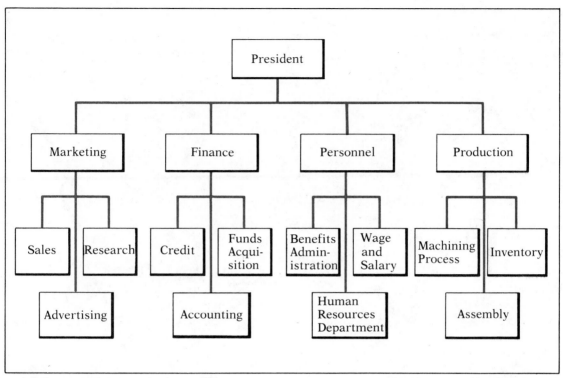

FIGURE 7.3
Organization chart for a company organized by function

dependency of all functions. The lack of generalism and potential internal rivalry that threatens a functional approach to organization makes economic growth as a system difficult.

② The Geographic Approach

Grouping activities for one department, or for an entire enterprise, under geographic heads or territories makes sense in various marketing, financial, and production companies. Marketing organizations—such as manufacturers' representatives—may wish to organize their sales efforts by regions of a state, the United States, or the areas of the world where they conduct their selling activities. Banks may decide to group their lending and other activities under similar headings. One look at the paper money (Federal Reserve Notes) in your wallet will tell you that the Federal Reserve System, which controls most of our nation's banks, has chosen a geographic approach; the system has divided the fifty states into twelve Federal Reserve Districts (see Figure 7.4).

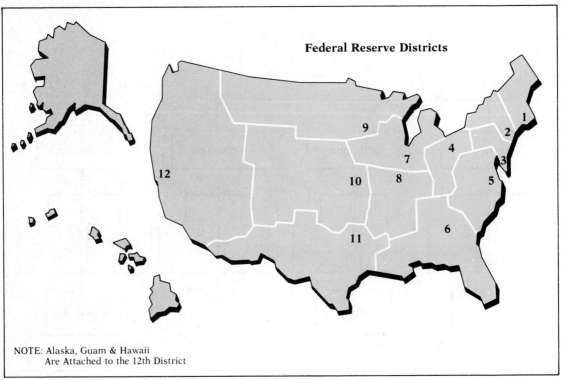

Federal Reserve Districts

NOTE: Alaska, Guam & Hawaii
Are Attached to the 12th District

FIGURE 7.4
The organization of the Federal Reserve System along geographic lines

Geographic patterns work best when different laws, currencies, languages, and traditions exist and have a direct impact on the ways in which business activities must be conducted. Regulations, taxes, and government permits are kinds of government rulings that dictate different approaches, plans, and strategies to marketing, production, and finance managers. What may be perfectly legal in one area may be illegal in another. What works well within one country or state may not be possible in another.

Manufacturers often have manufacturing facilities in several states in order to serve a mass market more efficiently and to take advantage of larger labor pools, transportation savings, and various tax advantages. Different climates can offer savings in several respects. The warmer sun-belt states mean lower heating costs and a closer proximity to sources of agricultural commodities.

In addition to aiding companies and managers in placing emphasis on or being responsive to local conditions, concerns, or needs, the geographic structure of organization furnishes a training ground to develop general management abilities. Managers are responsible for the activities in that geographic area. Decisions concerning that region will be made at

Source: Reprinted with special permission of King Features Syndicate, Inc.

that level and not forwarded up the chain of command. Better coordination for the activities in the geographic area is also a positive result of this approach.

A limitation for management to consider in adopting this format is cost—the cost of personnel and facilities. When a company makes the decision to expand geographically, it automatically incurs cost through duplication of personnel positions and additional building sites. The functional structure requires one sales manager. The territorial approach using seven separate geographic sales regions staffed by management personnel may require seven sales managers. Figure 7.5 illustrates this dilemma of organization.

3 The Product Line Approach

The establishment of an organization pattern based on product should be considered when attention, energy, and efforts need to be focused on an organization's particular products. This can be true if each product requires a unique strategy or production process or distribution system or capital sources. Or it could result if top management tries to focus the energy and talents of individuals on areas of expertise. Figure 7.6 illustrates this concept as it has been applied by General Motors Corporation.

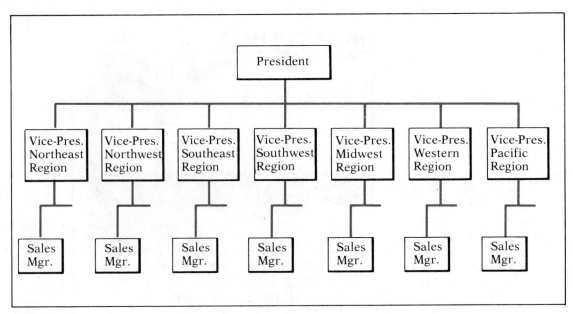

FIGURE 7.5
Geographic organization structure can lead to staffing duplication

Throughout its history, General Motors has been organized by product line. Originally (Figure 7.6, Part A), the company was organized under the separate product line divisions of Chevrolet, Buick, Oldsmobile, Cadillac, Pontiac, GMC Truck, and so on. Each product line division had functional divisions of manufacturing, finance, and distribution. In an effort to focus its energy on the small car field, General Motors reorganized its structure. While maintaining the product line organization, it now has two operating divisions: the Chevrolet-Pontiac division for small cars and the Buick-Oldsmobile-Cadillac division for larger models (Figure 7.6, Part B).

Such a divisional breakdown also works well in the manufacture of petroleum products, textbooks, or electronics, for example, because it allows a company to concentrate its research specialists on specific and related projects and problems. It allows a sales force to sell complementary products to a consistent group of buyers or purchasing agents. Competition occurs within the organization between product managers, sales managers, and others to outperform one another and to get a larger share of the organization's assets and resources. If carried to its extreme, this competition can be a disadvantage.

The major disadvantage is similar to that of the geographic structure—cost through duplication of business functions within each product line. Each needs marketing, finance, personnel, and production operations, which may be so specialized they are unable to serve more than one product line or division.

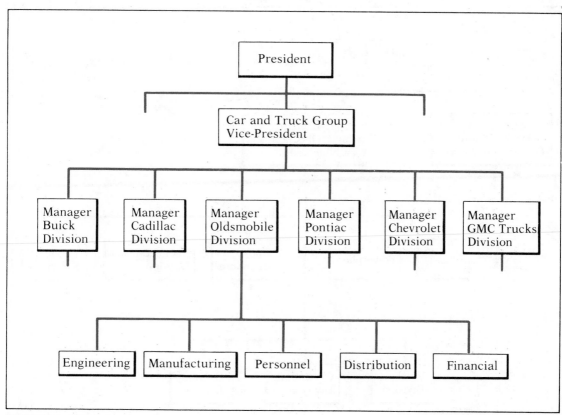

FIGURE 7.6, Part A
Organization chart illustrating General Motors Corporation's original product line organization

④ The Customer Approach

Organization around groups of customers makes economic sense when the customers are distinct enough in their demands, preferences, and needs to justify it. Governments almost always demand specialized treatment through their specifications, supervision of production requirements, competitive bidding practices, regulations on employment, and so on. A firm that seeks government contracts often has to have a separate department of specialists who do nothing more than try to interpret and apply various rules, regulations, and procedures that must be complied with in doing business with a government agency.

Catering to the needs of corporate (rather than government) customers, like Sears or Ward's, requires a different set of approaches, customs, and operations. And another set is needed by medical institutions, such as hospitals and clinics, whose customers are patients; these institutions design their patient care around medical service areas: emergency services,

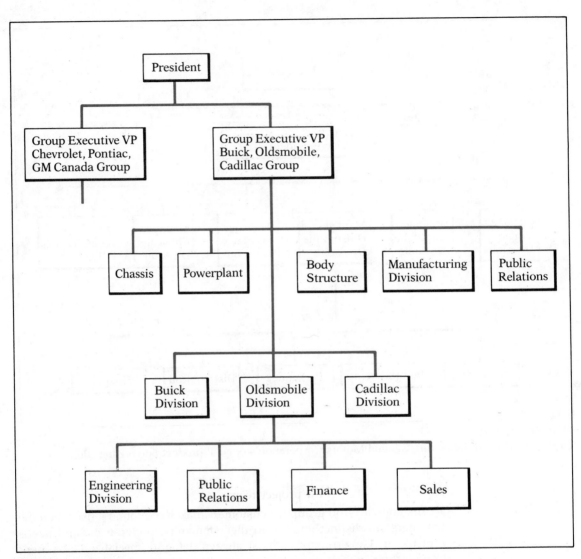

FIGURE 7.6, Part B
Organization chart illustrating General Motors Corporation's present product line organization

outpatient services, and x-ray are just a few examples. Dealing with corporate and institutional purchasing agents and buyers demands still different marketing approaches and skills from those needed to deal with individual consumers.

Figure 7.7 shows a customer structure. Just how far an organization should carry its customer approach depends on its internal decisions about how to best serve itself and its customers, patients, or clients. It may choose this approach for some but not all of its customers. Customers may be grouped simply as government and others, or as wholesale and retail.

FIGURE 7.7
Organization chart
for a company
organized by
customer

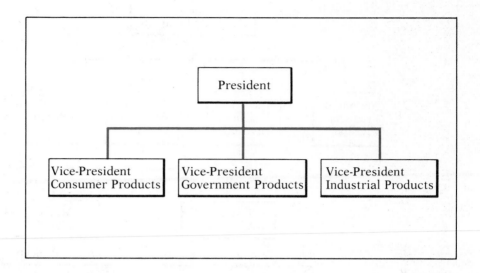

If the decision is made to use this approach with only some of a firm's customers, there will be difficulty in coordinating the customer-based department with departments organized on other patterns. The managers of the customer-structured departments may constantly be requesting special treatment for their particular needs. Another possibility is overspecialization: The facilities and personnel may become so specialized to solve the needs of their customers that they cannot be used for any other purpose—with the result of underutilization.

⑤ The Matrix Approach — *blends functions with project team*

A matrix organization pattern is a design blending the functional organization structure with a project team structure. Applications of this form are found in high-technology, project-based industries such as the aerospace, government contracting, consulting, and research and development businesses. Figure 7.8 presents a matrix organization structure for an aerospace project. The functional departments—production, materials, personnel, engineering, and accounts—are permanent parts of the organization. The various project teams—Venus, Mars, and Saturn—are created as the need arises and disbanded when the project is completed.

Members of the Venus project team are selected from the functional departments and are supervised for the duration of the project by the Venus project manager. During the course of the project, the technical team specialists have access to and can use the resources of their functional departments. This ongoing relationship of function and project, along with the lines of authority (downward from functional manager to technical representative and across from project supervisor to technical representative), composes a grid. This grid is also called a matrix.

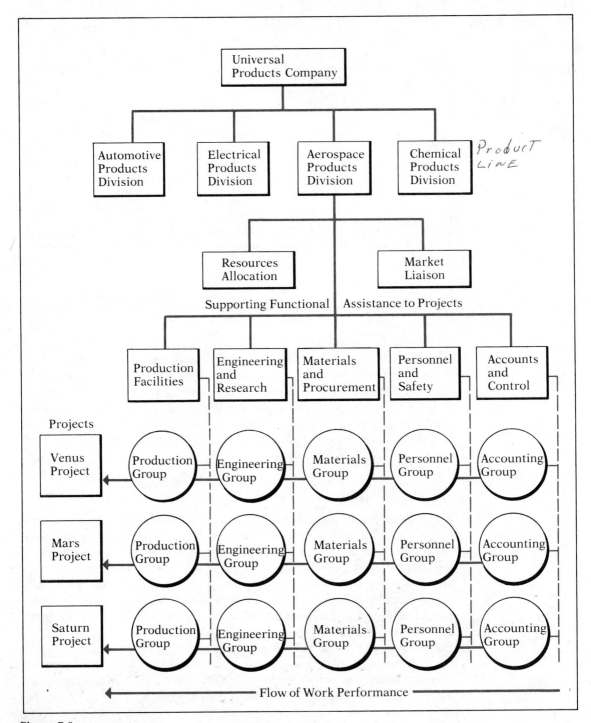

Universal
Products Company

Automotive
Products
Division

Electrical
Products
Division

Aerospace
Products
Division

Chemical
Products
Division

Product Line

Resources
Allocation

Market
Liaison

Supporting Functional | Assistance to Projects

Production
Facilities

Engineering
and
Research

Materials
and
Procurement

Personnel
and
Safety

Accounts
and
Control

Projects

Venus
Project

Production
Group

Engineering
Group

Materials
Group

Personnel
Group

Accounting
Group

Mars
Project

Production
Group

Engineering
Group

Materials
Group

Personnel
Group

Accounting
Group

Saturn
Project

Production
Group

Engineering
Group

Materials
Group

Personnel
Group

Accounting
Group

◄——————— Flow of Work Performance ———————

Figure 7.8
Matrix organization structure

Source: John F. Mee, "Matrix Organizations," *Business Horizons,* vol. 7, no. 2 (Summer 1964), p. 71. © 1964 by the Foundation for the
School of Business at Indiana University. Reprinted by permission.

The matrix approach utilizes the technical resources of an organization by efficiently allocating the expertise where and when it is needed. It should produce a coordinated effort because it focuses the functional expertise on a project, thus minimizing conflict between specialty areas. As flexible and efficient as a matrix structure is, it can have limitations. Project participation places a premium on interpersonal skills. These human skills are stressed in the constant interaction of the team members and because of the need to work with the functional departments. Additionally, there can be conflicts in terms of loyalty. Specialists do serve more than one master. They are asked to go in more than one direction. They work directly for both the functional manager and the project manager. This can create a strain on project members, the project manager, and the functional departments.

All these organizational patterns have appropriate applications. The challenge to the organization is to select the most suitable pattern to meet its objectives and to be responsive to the need to change the structure when the objectives change.

Major Organizational Concepts

Now that we have discussed the organizing process and potential organizational approaches, it is necessary to examine some major organizational concepts and principles that managers work with in developing a workable system. A working knowledge of authority, power, delegation, span of control, and the centralization vs. decentralization issue is essential to the ongoing process.

Authority: The Concept and Application

Step 4 of the organizing process—assignment of activities, with the appropriate authority—introduced the concept of authority. In this section, we develop the concept in detail: its nature, sources, importance, relationship to power, and types of authority. Our discussion also includes line and staff departments, and areas of possible concern about the types of authority.

Nature, sources, and importance of authority.   All managers in an organization have authority. They have different degrees of authority based on the level of management they occupy in the organization structure. **Authority** is a tool of a manager. It can be described as the *right to commit resources* (that is, to make decisions that commit an organization's resources), or the legal (legitimate) *right to give orders* (to tell someone to do or not to do something). Authority is the "glue" that holds the organization together. It provides the means of command. How does a manager acquire authority?

It has been said that "authority comes with the territory." This means that authority is vested in a manager because of the position he or she occupies in the organization. Thus authority is defined in each manager's job description or job charter. The person who occupies the position has its formal authority as long as he or she remains in the position. As the job changes in scope and complexity, so should the amount and kind of formal authority possessed.

Even though a manager has formal or legitimate authority, it is wise to remember that the willingness of employees to accept the legitimate authority is a key to effective management. The acceptance theory of authority focuses on the employee as the key to the manager's use of authority. In actuality, it is the interaction of formal authority and employee acceptance that provides for a positive experience.

It is possible for two managers to occupy identical positions of formal authority, with the same degree of acceptance of this authority by their employees, and still not be identically effective in the organization. Why? One manager may not possess the power to be as effective as another manager.

Relationship of authority to power. **Power** is the ability to exert influence in the organization. Having power can increase the effectiveness of a manager by enabling the manager to influence people to what is wanted beyond the scope of formal authority. Authority is positional—it will be there when the incumbent leaves. Power is personal—it exists because of the person. How does a person acquire power? The sources of power are these:

1. *Legitimate or position power.* Holding a managerial position with its accompanying authority provides a manager with a power base. The manager has the right to use power because of the might of the position. The higher a manager is in the organization hierarchy, the greater is the "perceived power," that power thought by the subordinates to exist (whether or not it really does). Vice-presidents wield, or can wield, a lot of power.

2. *Power to reward or punish.* The ability to grant favors or cause discomfort to others can serve as a basis of power. Preferential treatment, overtime, and expediting service (or, conversely, slowing service down) can provide the means to influence behavior and results. The "boss's" secretary normally possesses power well beyond the scope of the job. Controlling the boss's calendar and rationing out the time on the calendar is a prime example of reward or punishment.

3. *Referent or charismatic power.* This power is based on the kind of personality an individual has and how that personality is perceived by others. The adoration by others and desire to identify with and imitate a person are indications of this person's power.

4. *Expert power.* This power is possessed by persons who have demonstrated their superior skills and knowledge. They know what to do and how to do it. Others hope to stay on this expert's good side.

Types of authority. In an organization, different types of authority are created by the relationships between individuals and between departments. There are three types of authority:

Line authority defines the relationship between superior and subordinate. It is a direct supervisory relationship. Managers who supervise operating employees or other managers have line authority. Line authority flows downward in an organization directly from superior to subordinate, as Figure 7.9 illustrates.

Staff authority is advisory in nature. Managers whose role it is to provide advice or technical assistance are granted advisory authority. Advisory authority does not provide any basis for direct control over the subordinates or activities of other departments with whom they consult (see Figure 7.10). (Within the staff manager's own department, he or she exercises line authority over the department's subordinates.)

Line and staff departments. Line and staff authority are concepts that describe the authority granted to managers. Line and staff departments have different roles or positions within the organization structure.

Line departments, headed by a "line manager," are the departments established to meet the major objectives of the organization. Departments normally designated as line departments include production (of goods and services for sale to a market), marketing (to include sales, buying, advertising, and physical distribution), and finance (acquiring capital resources).

FIGURE 7.9
The flow of line authority is downward

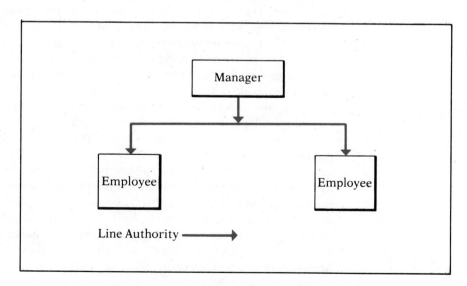

FIGURE 7.10
Staff authority is
advisory and
normally flows
upward

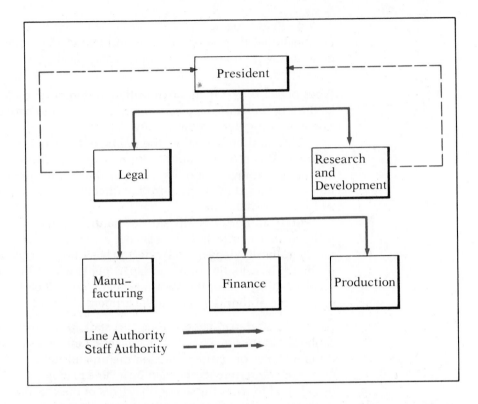

In functioning with the employees and departments under their control, line managers exercise line authority.

Staff departments provide assistance to the line departments and to each other. They can be viewed as making money indirectly for the company—through advice, service, and assistance. Traditional staff departments include legal, personnel, computer services, and public relations. These departments are created on the basis of the special needs of the organization. As an organization develops, its need for expert, timely, ongoing advice becomes critical. If the organization's resources can support a staff department, the department can be created to fill the gap. Staff departments can play a vital role in the success of a company.

There are some real dangers inherent in line–staff interaction that all management should be aware of. Because staff people must "sell" their ideas, there is a possibility that the line personnel will view the staff member as "pushy" or, in an extreme, as undermining the line managers. Staff managers need to develop tact and persuasive skills along with ideas. They also need to foster credibility for their ideas to be accepted: Bad advice can result in no audience the next time. Finally, line managers are inclined to feel that "the buck stops here" with them. In other words, because it is line managers who ultimately make the decisions, staff is not responsible for the results.

Functional authority is authority delegated to an individual or department over specific activities undertaken by personnel in other departments. Staff departments may be given functional authority to control their systems' procedures in other departments. A common specific example occurs in the personnel department, which must monitor and receive compliance in operating departments for recruitment, selection, and performance appraisal systems. See Figure 7.11.

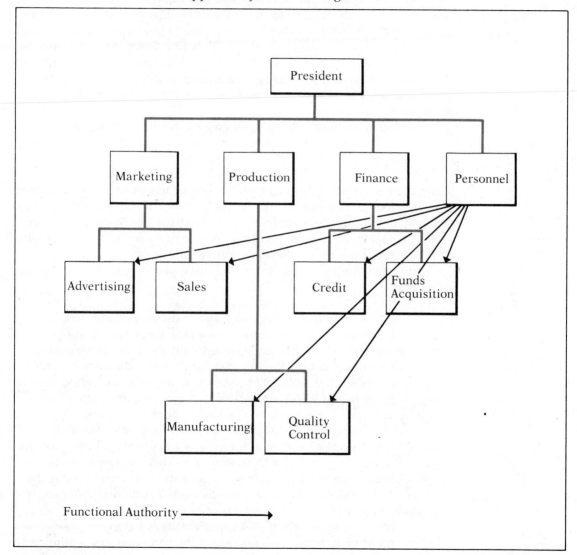

FIGURE 7.11
Functional authority crosses over departmental lines for specific activities. Personnel, for example, has authority for employment processes.

<u>Unity of command.</u>   A concern of all managers in the application of both staff and functional authority is violation of the principle of unity of command: This principle means that each person within that organization should take orders from and report to only one person.

Unity of command should be a guiding principle in any attempt to develop operating relationships. It would be ideal for each person to have only one boss. In reality, because of the operating relationships developed through staff departments, it is possible that organizational members will have more than one supervisor in given situations—or perceive that they do from the style with which advice is given. In business, a departmental manager or subordinate may receive guidance or directives on a given day from personnel on employment practices, from finance on budget time frames, and from data processing concerning user procedures. If possible, these situations should be minimized, or at least clarified, for the sake of all affected.

Now that authority has been discussed, how is it delegated?

Delegation

Delegation is a concept describing the passing of formal authority to another person. Superiors delegate, or pass authority down, to subordinates in order to facilitate work being accomplished. Delegation may become necessary when managers are absent from their jobs or just may be the philosophy of the manager in order to develop subordinates.

Whatever the reason for delegation, its application creates a sequence of events:

1. *Assignment of tasks.*   Specific tasks or duties that are to be undertaken are identified by the manager for assignment to the subordinate. The subordinate is then approached with the assignment (tasks).

2. *Delegation of authority.*   In order for the subordinate to complete the duties or tasks, the authority necessary to do them should be delegated by the manager to the subordinate. A guideline for authority is that it be adequate to complete the task—no more and no less.

3. *Acceptance of responsibility.*   **Responsibility** is the obligation to carry out one's assigned duties to the best of one's ability. Responsibility is not delegated by a manager to an employee, but the employee becomes obligated when the assignment is accepted. The employee is the receiver of the assigned duties and the delegated authority; these confer responsibility as well.

4. *Creation of accountability.*   **Accountability** is having to answer to someone for your actions. It means taking the consequences—either credit or blame. When the subordinate accepts the assignment and the authority, he or she will be held accountable or answerable for actions

taken. A manager is accountable for the use of her or his authority and performance. The manager is also accountable for the performance and actions of subordinates.

This four-step process should ensure that the process of delegation produces clear understanding on the part of the manager and of the subordinate. The manager should take the time to think through what is being assigned and to confer the authority necessary to achieve results. The subordinate, in accepting the assignment, becomes obligated (responsible) to perform, knowing that he or she is accountable (answerable) for the results.

Span of Control

The **span of control** or span of management is concerned with the number of subordinates each manager should have to direct. There is no correct number for the span of control. It is determined for each manager based on the interplay of the complexity and variety of the subordinates' work, the ability and training of the subordinates, the ability of the manager, and the company philosophy for centralization or decentralization of decision making.

As a general rule, the more complex a subordinate's job, the fewer should be that manager's number of subordinates. Another predictable guide is that the more routine the work of subordinates, the greater the number of subordinates that can be effectively directed and controlled. Because of these general rules, organizations always seem to have narrow spans at their tops and wider spans at lower levels. The higher one goes in the organization's hierarchy, the fewer will be his or her subordinates.

It is not uncommon to find a factory production supervisor with fifteen or more subordinates. (See Figure 7.12.) Why? Because persons who can be well trained to follow directions and routines will, once they master their tasks, require less of their supervisor's time and energies. They will know what they must do and exactly how to do it to meet their performance standards.

Conversely, it is uncommon to find a corporate vice-president with more than three or four subordinates. Why? Because middle and upper management employees perform little that is routine. Their tasks usually require ingenuity and creativity, and their tasks are nonrepetitive. Because the problems are more complex, they are more difficult to resolve. Managers at these levels require more time to plan and organize their efforts. When they turn to their bosses for direction and assistance, the boss needs to have the time available to render the assistance required. Because of this fact, generally the higher you go in an organization's hierarchy, the narrower will be the span of control. On the other hand, the lower you go in the hierarchy, the more subordinates a manager will have.

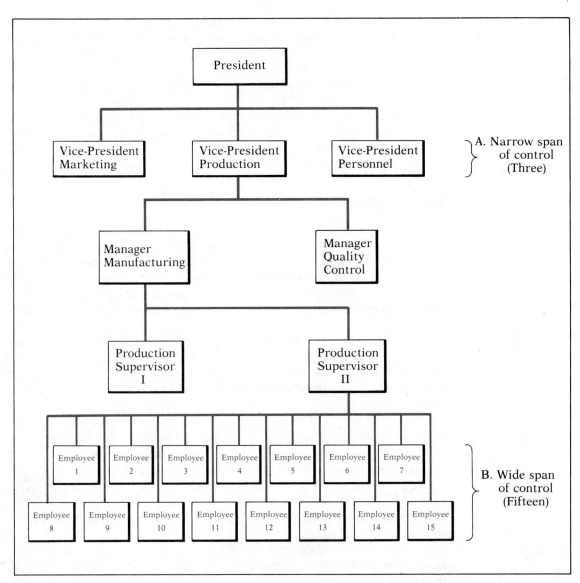

FIGURE 7.12
Narrow and wide spans of control

Just how many subordinates should any one manager have? The answer to this question depends on many factors and must be determined with a specific manager or job in mind. How much is the organization asking this manager to control? How are the tasks to be divided? What are the resources—people, money, and time—available? If a manager has too many people to supervise, his or her subordinates will be frustrated by their inability to get immediate assistance from or access to their boss. Time and other resources could be wasted; and plans, decisions, and actions might be delayed or made without proper controls or safeguards. On the other hand, if a manager has too few people to supervise, her or his subordinates might be either overworked or oversupervised and could become frustrated and dissatisfied.

Although one manager may be able to supervise six people effectively, another manager in the same job may not be able to do so. Why? Because no two managers are equal in their abilities and because their subordinates will have differing capabilities and levels of experience as well. The qualifications of the managers and their subordinates must be considered when creating spans of control. The more capable and experienced the subordinates, the more that can be effectively supervised by one competent manager. The less time needed to train and acclimate, the more there is to devote to producing output. In general, plans can be widened with the growth in experience and competence of personnel—thus the continuing need for training and development.

Another factor that can influence the span of control of a manager is the company's philosophy toward centralization or decentralization in decision making. What is this issue of centralization? Let's examine the concept and then relate it to the span of control.

Centralization vs. Decentralization

The terms *centralization* and *decentralization* refer to a philosophy of organization and management that focuses on either the selective concentration (centralization) or the dispersal (decentralization) of authority within an organization structure.[3] The question of where authority resides is resolved in an operating philosophy of management—either to concentrate authority for decision making in the hands of one or a few or to force it down the organization structure into the hands of many.

Centralization or decentralization is a relative concept when applied to organizations. The top-level management may decide to centralize all decision making: purchasing, staffing, operations. Or it may decide to set limits on what can be purchased at each level by dollar amounts, decentralize the hiring decisions to first-level management for clerical workers (retaining authority for managerial decisions), and let operational decisions be made where appropriate.

Some guidelines.   There are guidelines to follow in determining the degree of decentralization in a company:

1. The greater the number of decisions made at the lower levels of management, the more the company is decentralized.

2. The more important the decisions made at lower levels, the greater the decentralization. Purchasing decisions are a good measure. If the limit at the first level is $100,000, compared to another business in the same industry where the limit may be $1,000, the first company would be more decentralized.

3. The more flexible the interpretation of company policy at the lower levels, the greater the degree of decentralization.

4. The more widely dispersed the operations of the company geographically, the greater the degree of decentralization.

5. The less a subordinate has to refer to his or her manager prior to a decision, the greater the decentralization.

Relationship of centralization to span of control.   The company's philosophy of centralization or decentralization in decision making can influence the span of control of subordinate managers. A philosophy of decentralized decision making generally means that the span of control should be wider for each manager. This is so because decision making is forced down to subordinates, thus freeing up a manager's time commitments. This situation also generally means fewer levels of management in an organization.

Conversely, a philosophy of centralized decision making should result in a narrower span of control and more levels of management. If it is the philosophy of the company to have managers make the majority of decisions, the managers will closely supervise their subordinates and delegate little. Contacts with subordinates should increase in number and length, thus narrowing the span of control.

Despite the logic in this interrelationship of decision making and span of control, many times it is not true in practice. Managers with wide spans of control may choose not to delegate authority, and many times they are not as effective as they could be if they delegated. Additionally, the problem with this generalization is that other factors, as noted in the discussion on span of control, can be influential in determining how many subordinates a manager has.

Summary

- Planning must precede organizing, and the organizing process requires planning.
- Organizing determines the work to be done, classifies and groups the work, assigns the work, delegates the authority to do the work, and designs a hierarchy of decision-making relationships.
- Organizing creates an organization—a system of unified parts acting as a whole to achieve goals.

- The organizing process should be based on a knowledge and application of the organizing principles.
- The organizing process is a continuous one because new plans and goals may require changes in an organization's authority structure along with changes in the number and kinds of subdivisions needed to execute plans.
- Organizations may choose to divide their personnel and other resources along various departmental lines. The most popular approaches to organizing include the functional, geographic, product line, customer, and matrix approaches.
- Authority is a management tool. It is directly related to the position a manager holds. The type and amount of authority a manager needs depends on his or her function in the organization.
- The degree of centralization of decision making of an organization is the result of its management philosophy on the best way to serve its purposes.

Glossary of Essential Terms

accountability	Being answerable for the results of one's actions.
authority	The right to make decisions that commit the organization's resources or the legal right of a manager to tell someone to do or not to do something, also called formal or positional authority.
chain of command	The organizing principle concerned with the number of management positions in an organization and their unbroken connection to its top position.
delegation	The downward transfer of formal authority from one person to another.
departmentation	The creation of groups, subdivisions, or departments that will execute and oversee the various tasks that management considers essential.
division of labor	The study of tasks deemed essential, the breaking down of tasks into parts or steps, and the assigning of one or more of those parts to an individual or position.
functional authority	Authority over specific activities that are undertaken by personnel in other departments.
line authority	Direct supervisory authority from superior to subordinate.
line departments	Departments established to meet the major objectives of the organization.

organization	The result of the organizing process; it consists of a whole made up of unified parts (a system), acting in harmony to execute tasks to achieve goals, in an effective and efficient manner.
organization chart	A visual representation of the way in which an entire organization and each of its parts fit together.
organizing	The management activity that determines the work activities to be done, classifies and groups that work, assigns the activities and delegates authority to do the work, and designs a hierarchy of decision-making relationships.
power	A person's ability to influence results. It comes from expertise, charisma, or ability to reward or coerce, or from formal position.
responsibility	The obligation to carry out one's assigned duties to the best of one's ability.
span of control	The principle of organization that is concerned with the number of subordinates each manager should have to direct.
staff authority	Authority to serve in an advisory capacity; authority to advise.
staff departments	These assist all departments in meeting the objectives of the organization through advice or technical assistance.
unity of command	The organizing principle that states that each person in an organization should take orders from and report to only one person.
unity of direction	The organizing principle that states that each group of activities having the same objective should have one head.

Review Questions

1. Can you define this chapter's essential terms? If not, consult the preceding glossary.
2. How do the functions of planning and organizing relate to each other (1) in the initial development of a company and (2) during the modifications of the company's structure?
3. What are the three important benefits of the organizing process?
4. What are the five steps in the organizing process? Write a one-sentence description of what happens in each step.
5. What are the five kinds of approaches to organizing? Which of the approaches would you recommend for each of the following? Why?

Functional, Geographic, Product line, Customer, Matrix

a. a hardware store *PRODUCT LINE*
b. a company manufacturing and marketing one product *FUNCTIONAL*
c. a company with sales offices located in forty states *GEOGRAPHIC*
d. a company engaged in contract project work
e. a retail department store

formal auth

6. What are the three types of authority? What are the potential sources of authority? How do the two sources interact in reality? *LINE, STAFF FUNCTIONAL*

7. What is power? What are the sources of power? How does it differ from authority?

8. Explain why each of the organizing concepts or principles that follow is important to a manager.

pg.190 a. unity of direction *coordinating plans*
pg.210 b. unity of command *orders from 1 person*
AUTHORITY RELATIONSHIP pg.194 c. chain of command *decision making structure rel. between dep. number of people*
pg.210 d. delegation of authority *passing authority down to someone*
pg.211 e. span of control *NO. OF SUB. FEWER FOR MORE COMPLEX*
pg.213 f. centralization/decentralization *CONCENTRATION or DISPERSAL MAKE OWN CHOICES or*

References

1. Russell Robb, "Organization as Affected by Purpose and Conditions," in *Classics in Management*, ed. Harwood F. Merrill (New York: American Management Association, 1970), p. 147.

2. Matt O'Connor, "Firestone to Divide into Three Units, Change Its Name," *Chicago Tribune*, December 16, 1987, sect. 3, p. 3.

3. Harold Koontz and Cyril O'Donnel, *Management* (New York: McGraw-Hill, 1976), p. 375.

Readings

Baum, L. "Delegating Your Way to Job Survival." *Business Week* (1987), p. 206.

Block, Peter. *The Empowered Manager: Positive Political Skills at Work.* San Francisco: Jossey-Bass, 1987.

Buchholz, Steve and Thomas Roth. *Creating the High Performance Team.* New York: John Wiley & Sons, 1988.

Drucker, Peter. "The Coming of the New Organization." *Harvard Business Review* (January–February 1988), pp. 45–53.

Hickman, Craig and Michael Silver. *The Future 500: Creating Tomorrow's Organizations Today.* New York: New American Library, 1987.

Kiechel, Walter III. "Corporate Strategy for the 1990's." *Fortune* (February 29, 1988), pp. 34–42(6).

Larson, Erik and David Gobeli. "Matrix Management: Contradictions and Insights." *California Management Review*, 29, no. 4 (Summer 1987), pp. 126–138.

Nader, Ralph and William Taylor. *The Big Boys (Power and Position in American Business)*. New York: Pantheon, 1987.

Naisbitt, John and Patricia Aburdene. *Re-Inventing the Corporation.* New York: Warner Books, 1985.

Vicek, D. J., Jr. "Decentralization: What Works and What Doesn't." *Journal of Business Strategy*, 8 (Fall 1987), pp. 71–74.

C A S E S

7.1   Quality Controlled?

Juan Avilar was quite upset as he entered Jack Bailey's office on Friday morning. Juan had once again been overruled by Jack's quality control people and in front of his men on the first shift.

"Jack, I've had it with your pushy so-called quality control people. Each time they check my line they make changes with my people and I'm the last to know it."

"Easy, Juan," Jack said. "Sit down and tell me all the details."

"I've been over this with you before and you told me that your people would work with me. Twice this week they have stopped my line and told my people to make changes without seeing me first. Then this morning, while I'm helping Thompson with some routine maintenance, your Silly Sally starts to chew me out in front of my people."

"Just one minute, Juan. If Sally had words with you, I can't believe she would be abusive. I saw her this morning and got her point of view. According to her version, your people were ignoring a change that even you had agreed to about one week ago. She was only reminding you of that agreement, and she wanted to know why the change had not been made. Sally tells me that you were the one who was doing the chewing out, not her."

"Sure, go ahead, take her side. I don't know why I expected you'd listen to me. I just want to know who runs my shift—you and your people, or me."

"Juan, you know what the old man said about production and quality control. My people inspect your output at several stages along the line. They are the first to spot trouble, and they must have the power to stop defects."

"Look, Jack, let's get this settled now or I'm going to quit. I know that your people look for defects in my shift's output. I also know that my people are not stupid. They do not turn out defects on purpose. Nobody wants to make parts that are wrong. All I'm asking is that you stick to the agreement I thought we had. You promised that your people would work through me, not around me."

"That is precisely what Sally was trying to do this morning from what I can see. She went to you on the line because that is where you were. She asked you about the change that had not been made, and that is when, according to her, you blew your top."

"OK, forget about this morning. What about the other two instances this week when your people ordered changes made and I was not consulted? My people told me, after they made the changes, that they had been told to do so by QC. Can't you see what that does to my authority?"

"If my people did not see you first, it was because you were not around. What do you expect them to do? Should they let defects go on while they try to hunt you down? And how come you are the only shift manager who can't get along with quality control?"

For Discussion

1. Do Jack's people have functional authority?
2. What should quality control people do when the shift foreman is absent and defects appear?
3. Who should be responsible for quality control?

7.2 The Management Trainee

Trish was beginning to wonder if taking the job as a management trainee was a good idea. She was swamped with work and for the last three weekends had taken work home. Since going to work for Archer Finance, she has found her job slowly expanding to include bits and pieces from just about all parts of the company.

Josh Tillman was the general manager for all Archer's home office personnel and functions. The company was loosely organized by lending activities. Bowers was in charge of commercial loans and had three clerical assistants. Akins was in charge of consumer loans and had four clerks. Both women reported to Tillman. Tillman's partner, Mel Crenshaw, was assistant general manager in charge of collections and chaired the committee convened each week to review new loan applications. But as Trish soon found out, these lines were often crossed, and the managers felt free to use the clerical staff in a variety of assignments.

Trish was hired two months ago as an assistant to Josh Tillman. Tillman explained that her duties would be varied and designed to teach her the loan business. But what Tillman did not tell Trish was what she would be doing once her training had ended. Trish asked Tillman on two occasions what her assignment eventually would be, and each time he answered by saying it depended on her progress and the company's needs. So far, Trish has handled clerical tasks for Tillman, putting together data and processing it by computer to generate various kinds of management reports. She has also worked for Mel, creating computer-generated reports to help with the collections process. Last week, she began to work with Bowers, learning how loan applications were processed.

What happened to Trish today was beginning to be the norm, and Trish was not happy about it. She started the morning with loan applications and was quickly asked to drop her work and to join Mel in a committee meeting. Mel argued with Bowers for about fifteen minutes before getting her to agree to let Trish leave her department. Once in the meeting, Mel told Trish to take the notes for the session.

As the meeting was ending, Tillman showed up and demanded to know where his reports were. Trish replied that she had not had enough time to get them on the computer but would do so immediately. Mel overheard their conversation and reminded Trish that he needed the notes from the meeting typed and on his desk by 2 P.M. When Trish returned to her duties at commercial loans, Bowers told her to finish processing the loans on her desk and, if she needed help, to "borrow" a person or two from Marge Akins. Bowers then left the office for lunch.

Trish was almost at her limit of patience when Marge told her that she had no people to spare. After a few minutes of discussion about what Trish was doing in commercial loans, Marge asked Trish to bring in the applications she was working on to "see if they are being processed properly." Trish brought the applications to Marge who then looked them over carefully. "Who told you to batch them this way?" asked Marge. "Ms. Bowers did," replied Trish. "Well this method is not correct. It will mess up our filing system. Here, let me show you the proper way." Marge then proceeded to rearrange the work that Trish had spent two hours on this morning.

For Discussion

1. Which principles of organizing are being violated in this case?
2. In what ways are the violations occurring? Provide examples from the case to illustrate which principles of organizing are being violated.
3. What effects are the violations having on the people at Archer Finance?

C
H
A
P
T
E
R

8

Organizing: The Informal Organization

OUTLINE

The Organization Chart Doesn't Tell It All

The Informal Organization Defined

Types of Groups in the Informal Organization
- Horizontal Groups
- Vertical Groups
- Mixed Groups

Functions of the Informal Organization
- Why People Form Informal Groups
- Why Informal Groups Remain in Existence

Structure of the Informal Organization
- Leadership of the Group
- Nonleader Roles for Members
- Utilizing Group Roles

Significant Characteristics of Informal Organizations
- Development of Norms
- Development of Cohesion

Impact of the Informal Organization
- Negative Impact
- Positive Impact

Informal Communication—The Grapevine
- • Why Does the Grapevine Occur?
- • Characteristics of Grapevines
- • Patterns of Grapevines
- • Problems the Grapevine Can Cause

Strategies for Working with the Informal Organization

Summary

ESSENTIAL TERMS

cohesion	mixed group
grapevine	norm
horizontal group	sociogram
informal organization	vertical group
interaction chart	

LEARNING OBJECTIVES

After reading and discussing this chapter, you should be able to do the following:

1. Define this chapter's essential terms.
2. Explain the importance of a manager's recognizing and working with the informal organization.
3. Explain what is meant by the informal organization.
4. Discuss three types of informal groups characteristic of the informal organization.
5. Explain why people form informal groups and why the groups stay in existence.
6. Explain the basis of leadership within the informal organization.
7. Discuss two important characteristics of informal groups.
8. Describe the positive and negative impact of the informal organization on the formal organization.
9. Discuss strategies managers can use to work with the informal organization.

The Organization Chart Doesn't Tell It All

"You know, Frank, I've had quite a learning experience since I came here as a quality control supervisor. When I graduated from State with a degree in production systems, I thought I was ready to be a manager: I had all the latest theory on production, quality, and systems design, but the eight quality control technicians I was assigned have really taught me a thing or two.

"In some ways I supervise them . . . scheduling . . . techniques. In other ways, they work as a group to restrict my supervision. Let me give you some examples. Each one protects the other, so it's difficult to detect who's responsible for poor quality checks. Besides, they seem to have developed a quota on the number of checks they're going to make each day. Regardless of how much I have requested them to do, the results are basically the same. Oh, another thing; you know Henry? The one they call the 'guru' in G section? Well, despite my credentials, quite often my technicians take their problems to him.

"And another thing—they have information hot off the presses! Most of them eat together in the break area, but Carlos eats with his friends in the assembly area. It never fails; he brings back the latest information, both good and bad, and only sometimes accurate. Thank goodness I eat lunch with you and the other supervisors. It gives me the opportunity to get some things off my chest and find out what's happening in the company."

At this point Frank grins, nods knowingly, and replies: "Welcome to the club. It looks like you've had a good initiation into the workings of the informal organization around here. We all find it out: You have to work with both the formal and the informal organization to really be successful."

As the preceding conversation points out, functioning within the formal organization designed by management—of departmental structure, designated leaders (managers), decision-making guidelines, policies, procedures, rules—is a system of social relationships that, collectively, compose the informal organization. Managers need to understand this informal organization because it influences the productivity and job satisfaction of all organization members, managers as well as nonmanagers. Managers find out through experience that not everything in an organization takes place within the squares on the organization chart. People by nature refuse to stay in the boxes as drawn. They choose to operate within the confines of and with the support of the informal organization.

In this chapter, we examine the informal organization—its composition, functions, characteristics, impact on the formal organization, and strategies for working with the informal organization.

The Informal Organization Defined

The **informal organization** is a network of personal and social relationships that arise spontaneously as people associate with one another in a work environment.[1] It is composed of all the informal groupings of people within a formal organization. Memberships in most informal organizations change with time. Members are bonded together through the need for one another's company and the fact that they find their memberships beneficial to them in one or more ways. The informal organization presents a challenge for a manager because it consists of actual operating relationships not prescribed by the formal organization and, therefore, not shown on the company's organization chart.

The informal organization may be illustrated by only two workers whose habit it is to gossip and share their perceptions of company affairs and personnel; they may do so on the job, at break, or after work. Another example is one employee assisting someone in another department in solving a work problem. The informal organization should not be thought of as the domain of "workers" only. Managers form informal groups that cut across departmental lines. In addition, they actively participate in other

CAUTION PEOPLE NETWORKING

Source: Reprinted by permission: Tribune Media Services.

groups with nonmanagers. The informal organization exists everywhere. The lunch bunch, the coffee break group, and the company bowling team are other examples of informal groups.

Types of Groups in the Informal Organization

The informal organization is often looked at as groups of people. Informal groups may be described as horizontal, vertical, or mixed. These titles indicate whether the group members come from the same or different levels of the formal organization (see Figure 8.1).[2] Let's examine each one.

FIGURE 8.1
Types of groups in the informal organization

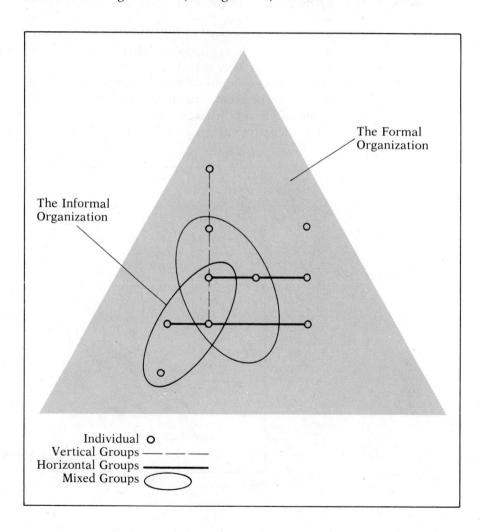

The Formal Organization

The Informal Organization

Individual ○
Vertical Groups — — —
Horizontal Groups ——————
Mixed Groups ⬭

Horizontal Groups

Horizontal groups include persons whose positions are on the same level of the organization. The groups can consist of all the members in the same work areas or membership developed across departmental lines. Members may be all management or all nonmanagement personnel. Regardless, horizontal groups are the common kind of informal groups by virtue of the ease of accessibility. Because all members operate at the same organizational level, they do not have a built-in vertical barrier to overcome.

Membership in a horizontal group is usually mutually beneficial to individuals. It promotes information sharing and provides mutual support: "We are all in this together," and "You help me and I'll help you." People in the same or related work areas often share the same problems, interests, and concerns.

An example of this mutual support exists in the group centered on the "old sage," one who gives other department members ongoing guidance for scheduling work, shares tricks of the trade, and helps with the pitfalls of the policy manual; in general, the old sage fulfills information needs while the group, in turn, provides the sage with current information, admiration, and a sense of competence and security.

Still another example can be found in an interaction between an operating department and another department, for which involvement is only supportive rather than primary. For example, members from five departments—production, sales, quality control, inventory, and shipping—regularly eat together, sharing problems and concerns while having lunch. The result is an alliance that helps resolve ongoing problems informally, expedite special orders, and create cooperation in general at the operating level. When a problem results, the response is not to turn to the boss. Rather, the "lunch buddy" in sales picks up the phone and requests a favor from his "lunch buddy" in shipping. "No problem," is the response.

At other times the informal group within a department can be bonded together because of the actions of a superior. Common concerns over security, communication, or equity can result in an informal group being formed. Within the same work area, individual similarities can be the reason for different informal groups to form. Age, experience, personalities, and race are other factors that can lead to the formation of informal groups.

Vertical Groups   SAME DEPARTMENT

Vertical groups include people on different levels of the formal organization's hierarchy. These people always come together within the same work areas. A vertical group in a production department might include a supervisor and one or more of his or her subordinates. Or a supervisor or group of supervisors might form a group with their boss. A vertical group can also be formed through skip-level relationships: A top-level manager may associate with a first-level manager, or an operating employee with a second-level manager. These relationships can be the result of outside interests or various employment relationships.

The organizational impact of these informal relationships can be both beneficial and detrimental to each party. The subordinate many times has access to inside information and a friendly ear to which to present his or her side of a story. In addition, the subordinate is usually perceived by others as someone who has political clout. A possible negative for the subordinate could be criticism from peers for playing politics.

From the boss's position, this informal group relationship provides quicker access to problems arising in the structure and improved communication. Another result is an improved public image because the fairness, openness, and accessibility of the boss are lauded by the subordinate. But risks for the superior include loss of objectivity with the subordinate and possible accusations of favoritism.

Mixed Groups

A **mixed group** is a combination of two or more persons whose positions are on different levels of the formal organization and in different work areas. A vice-president may develop a close relationship with the director of computer services in order to get preferential treatment. A production manager may cultivate an informal, social relationship with the director of maintenance for the same reason.

Mixed groups often form because of common bonds outside work. Members may come together because of common interests, club memberships, ethnic backgrounds, or other reasons.

The important point for a manager to realize is that informal groups do function quite naturally and often in the daily operations of the organization. They are an integral part of the interaction of managers and operating employees.

Once a manager knows what types of informal groups exist in the company, she or he will probably begin to wonder why the informal groups arise and why they remain in existence.

Functions of the Informal Organization

We have already discussed some reasons people form informal groups: common problems, interests, and concerns. There are others. Further, after groups are formed, they serve their members in additional ways in order to remain in existence.

Why People Form Informal Groups

Informal groups are formed for different reasons:

1. *Need for satisfaction.*   People have needs that in some cases are not met through the formal organization. The opportunity to fulfill security, affiliation, esteem, and sometimes self-actualization needs can encourage people to seek out and join others in an informal group. Eating with the same lunch group may meet affiliation needs. The department sports team may meet both friendship and ego needs.

2. *Proximity and interaction.*   A common reason people join groups is that they work near one another. This can be either through working in close proximity physically or because of frequent interaction. Horizontal informal groups are prime examples of this.

3. *Similarity.*   People may join informal groups because they are attracted to other people who are similar to themselves. Several persons with the same attitudes or beliefs may join one group. Other factors of similarity can be personality, race, sex, economic position, and perceived abilities. Generally, people associate with other people because they have the same beliefs and characteristics.[3]

Why Informal Groups Remain in Existence

Informal groups remain in existence because they serve four major functions.[4]

1. *They maintain the social and cultural values the group members hold in common.*   Individuals in the group are likely to share the same beliefs and values as a result of background, education, or cultural heritage. The many areas about which the group may have beliefs are reinforced and maintained by the group environment. Such belief areas are, for example, the work ethic, the job system, promotional patterns, and employment status (women, minorities, senior workers, trainees).

2. *They provide group members the opportunity for status and the opportunity for social interaction and fulfillment.*   Individuals can receive what the formal organization cannot or has not chosen to provide. In a large company, a worker may face an identity crisis—the feeling that "I'm just another number." The informal group provides this same worker with companionship, an audience for stories and experiences, and the chance to be important. Jose Alvarez is a case in point.

Jose is a technician on a car assembly line. As one of 750 technicians on the plant's organization chart, he often feels insignificant about his status and the role he plays in the company. "Just another cog in the wheel" is Jose's description of his job. But as a member of the company bowling team, he feels the situation is quite different. In addition to spending time with his friends bowling (and talking about bowling), Jose enjoys having been selected to captain the team. This special status provided by the group, to quote Jose, "has made coming to work enjoyable."

Another example is provided by Bill Locke. The nature of Bill's job as an environmental technician facilitates his interaction with all work groups day and night. During Bill's environmental analysis reviews in the work groups, he was able to acquire information to share with the president of the company on operating problems, personnel concerns, and overall climate factors. As the "unofficial organizational facilitator," Bill was given importance far beyond his formal organizational role.

3. *They provide information for their members.* The informal group develops its own system and channels of communication parallel to management's formal channels. The ability to acquire access to information for members is a major function of informal groups. Consider the following example:

Members of the general accounting department felt that they were being intentionally screened from organizational communication by their supervisor. Deadlines, major decisions affecting planning, and changes in operating philosophy were not being communicated. In response, the informal group developed its own communication system. Barbara, the group's "communication expert," previously worked with the secretary to the department head. She cultivated this relationship. In addition, Barbara had her own network of contacts in the personnel, auditing, and finance departments to provide and verify information. Using these four sources, Barbara was able to keep the group informed on the operations of the company.

4. *They influence the work environment.* Informal groups regulate or influence the behavior, dress, or work standards of their members through positive means—acceptance, support, affiliation—or through negative methods—threats of ostracizing noncomplying members. In the personnel office, Friday was "jeans day": Everyone wore blue jeans and casual clothes. This custom was observed by everyone but Henry Parker, who steadfastly continued to wear a shirt and tie. A constant barrage of comments by the informal group finally convinced Henry that this was not acceptable behavior. The shirt and tie disappeared, replaced by jeans.

The informal group can also regulate or influence the actions of management and other informal groups. An example is provided by the reaction of employees to the implementation of a new system for performance appraisal. The system—which provided category quotas, volumes of written documentation, and no appeal process—was boycotted by the informal group. Management's choice was clear: Fire all employees or modify the system. The system was modified.

As the groups function in the informal organization, group dynamics take place. The group members assume roles. How does a manager deal with a group? And what should a manager look for?

Structure of the Informal Organization

In informal groups, leaders emerge and member roles evolve. Let's examine each in detail.

Leadership of the Group

Just as in a formal organization, the informal group develops leader–follower relationships. Because of the number of informal groups in an organization, a person may be a leader in one group and a follower in another.

Leaders of informal groups arise for various reasons: age, seniority, charisma, work location, technical ability, or the opportunity to move around the work area freely—all can be reasons for assuming the leadership role. In horizontal groups, charismatic leadership is common. In vertical and mixed groups, the leader is usually the most senior person or the person holding the highest position in the formal organization.

There is a possibility that the group may have several leaders of varying importance to perform different functions. The group may look to one person as the expert on organizational matters and to another as its social leader. A third may be required on the matter of technical, job task questions. Usually one leader will exert more influence on the group than the others.

An illustration of the multiple leader concept is provided by Rex, Sherri, and Jack. Rex was referred to on matters of organizational politics, strategy, and systems. As a result of seniority and previous management experience, he was accorded the overall leadership role in the group. Jack was the acknowledged social leader. When parties, lunches, or get-togethers were desired by the group, Jack, because of his affiliative nature and social know-how, was placed in the leadership role. Sherri, the master craftsperson, assumed the leadership role in technical concerns. Whether it was using the correct procedures, assisting in developing proper techniques with new members of the group, or inventing shortcuts, Sherri was the person to whom the others turned.

Nonleader Roles for Members

In addition to the membership role in an informal group, there are other roles for members. Normally in an informal group, there is an inner core or primary group; a fringe group, which functions in and out of the group; and an out-status group, which though identified with the group, does not actively participate.[5] Figure 8.2 provides an illustration of this makeup.

    Is there a method available to identify the existence of informal groups and the composition of the groups? The answer is yes. Two tools can be used—a sociogram and an interaction (or informal organization) chart.

FIGURE 8.2
Composition of an informal group

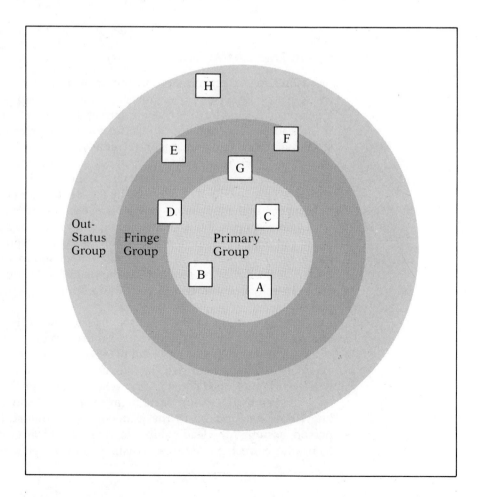

A **sociogram** is a diagram of group attraction. It was developed by J. L. Moreno over thirty years ago and is still applicable today. The sociogram is developed through a process of asking members whom they like or dislike and with whom they wish to work or not work.[6] It is based on the belief that group interactions are the result of people's feelings of like and dislike for one another.

The result of this process is the sociogram in Figure 8.3. The eight workers involved developed this pattern:

1. A, B, and C are a cohesive group and may form the inner core.
2. B is the star and assumes the leader characteristics as A, C, G, D, and E are all attracted to him.

FIGURE 8.3
A sociogram of the group shown in Figure 8.2

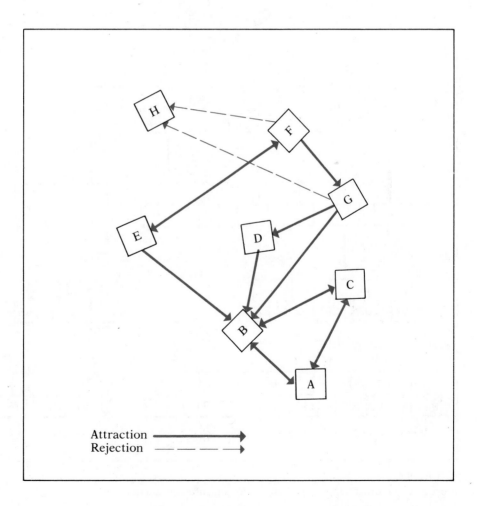

3. H is an isolate or out-status. No one is attracted to him, and he is rejected by G and F.

4. E and F are attracted to each other but appear to be on the fringe of the group.

An **interaction chart** is a diagram that shows the informal interactions people have with one another.[7] For any specific person, the chart can show with whom the person spends the most time and with whom the person communicates informally. Once this chart is developed, it can be compared with or even superimposed on the formal organization chart to illustrate differences. Figure 8.4 provides an illustration of the informal communication patterns that were developed from information known only to man-

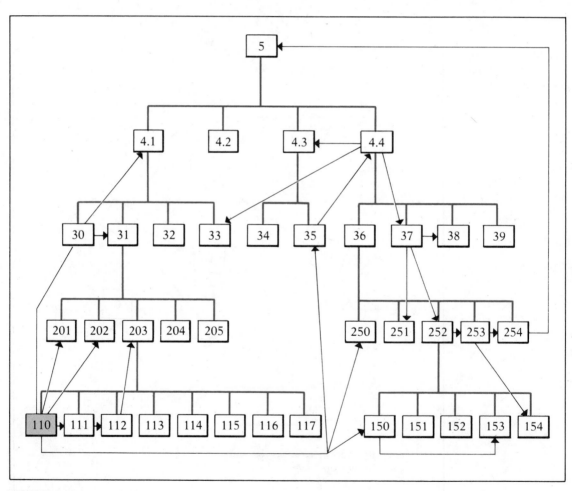

FIGURE 8.4
Informal communication patterns shown by an interaction chart

ager 110. The majority of the information communicated was transmitted outside the formal channels.

Rather than using a survey method, as in sociometrics, the chart is built as a result of observations of actual communications. The process is to record the quantity and duration of discussions taking place between individuals, noting who initiates the discussions with individuals, and who initiates discussions with the entire group.[8]

Utilizing Group Roles

Recognizing that informal groups exist is step one for a manager. The second step is identifying the roles members play within that group, and the third step is having the intelligence to use the information to work with the informal group. Why?

A manager works with employees on a daily basis. In doing this, the manager recognizes and adjusts to individual differences, values, and beliefs. At the same time the manager is working with a group or groups of employees who have a personality, values, and a culture. Managers need to be able to identify the leaders of these groups and work with them to influence the total group. It is not logical to try to influence a group by appealing to a fringe member. The leaders are at the core of decision making. By utilizing both the interaction chart and sociogram, a manager can identify the composition of groups.

An example of this approach was provided by Paula Fullmer, who had been selected to be president of a community college. The once well-functioning organization was now mired in its own problems, and its operating environment was characterized by factionalism. Paula's first action was to identify the various factions and their leaders. She then focused on influencing the behavior of these groups through their leaders and succeeded in aligning the groups and thus the individuals to the good of the organization.

Another set of information a manager needs besides the structure of leader–member roles is knowledge of the characteristics of a group. As a group interacts, it develops characteristics. Two characteristics a manager needs to recognize are group norms and cohesion.

Significant Characteristics of Informal Organizations

Development of Norms

Norms are standards of behavior that are accepted by all group members. A norm serves as a guideline. It tells group members what they can or cannot do under certain circumstances. Groups set their standards through consensus of ideas and activities or through the influence of the group's leader. Once these norms are established and agreed on by the group, they act as an internal control device on members.

At the executive level, vested suits, solid ties, gray suits, and "business" haircuts may be the standard for dress established by the leader. All rising young executives imitate this without question. The failure to adhere to this norm may result in a short career within the organization.

The story of Julie Gray provides an example of norms and of the results of violating the group's acceptable behavior codes. Going to work for the Brown Company was a double bonus for Julie. She got the challenging job she wanted, and she could carpool with her best friend who worked in the same building. Although Julie did not begin her work officially until 8:00 A.M., her ride-share needed to open the office by 7:30 A.M. This was perfectly agreeable to Julie. It gave her the chance to get started on the day's work. At first, Julie heard a lot of jokes from her fellow workers. "Eager beaver," "new kid on the block," or "trying to impress the boss." Julie took little notice. Soon, whenever Julie entered the room, all conversation stopped. No one was available to eat lunch when Julie wanted to go. Finally, Julie was taken aside by one of the group, who told her:

> Julie, you have to learn that we do things a certain way around here. We all know what our jobs are, how much we can do, and what is expected of us by management. You start working at 7:30. We get here at 8:00, have our coffee, talk a little, and start working at 8:30. What you're doing is putting us in a bad light with the boss. He'll start expecting us to be like you. We've been trying to tell you—either you change, or we'll make your life miserable.

Julie did change. She still arrived at 7:30, but she read the paper, wrote letters, and took care of other personal business until the group arrived. She then joined them for the morning routine.

Another example of the impact of norms on worker output is provided by a study done at the Western Electric Plant in Illinois in the late 1920s. In this study, researchers set out to prove the hypothesis that motivation to work, quantity of output, and quality of work were related to the social relationships among workers and those between workers and their boss.

Male workers were assigned to two groups, each of which wired and soldered electrical connections. An inspector was assigned to each group. The workers were isolated from their previous co-workers and subjected to the presence of an "observer"—a research assistant who kept records of output, rejects, and working conditions in both groups. The men were encouraged to work as they felt they should.[9]

The assistant recorded the following observations:

1. The groups split into two informal groups, each composed of wirers, solderers, and inspectors. Both informal groups developed their

unique patterns of behavior. Not all members of the two formal groups belonged to the two informal groups. (One informal group thought of itself as superior to the other.)

2. Each group developed norms as to what should be done and how. An upper limit on output was established by the groups. No individual should produce too much or too little. Those who did not conform felt ridicule and social pressures. Inspectors were pressured to become part of the group and to avoid acting officious.

3. The groups worked out their own violations of company policy on several issues. Contrary to policy, workers switched jobs. Output was reported by each person instead of through the supervisor. Each day they reported the standard figure the group had agreed on. Periodically, they reported less of what they had produced, thus saving finished work to be reported when they underproduced.

4. The workers in one of these informal groups thought of themselves as having higher status than the other group members because they were better producers. They were condescending in their attitudes and nagged the lower status group. Conflicts arose between the two groups. Since all were paid on the basis of output, the lower status group responded to the treatment by driving its production even lower. The two groups were caught in a self-defeating cycle.[10]

What is the message for management in both of these situations? Obviously, one message is that groups establish their norms, not management. The second, but not so obvious message, is that if management finds the norms unacceptable, management and the "group" will be on opposite sides. Management cannot change the group norms short of firing the group or disbanding it. Management's only choice is to work with the group and try to influence the group to change its norms.

Development of Cohesion

Cohesion is an important characteristic of informal groups; it is measured by the degree to which members share the group's goals and cooperate with one another. Cohesiveness is an indication of how much control the group has over its members: the more cohesive, the more the control. Factors such as stable membership, open communication, small group size, and physical isolation from other groups can lead to high cohesiveness.[11]

Informal groups develop differing degrees of cohesiveness as they function. Generally, the more cohesive the group, the greater its success in achieving goals and controlling its environment. A highly cohesive informal group has a singleness of purpose when dealing with outside influences, such as management and other groups. Because of this unity of purpose, the group can cause a lot of problems for management if it is in opposition to management, or it can achieve positive organizational results when operating in unison with management. On the other hand, informal groups displaying low cohesiveness may not be a major influence in either the informal environment or the formal organization.

An example of group cohesiveness is provided in the following scenario: For ten years, the fourteen secretaries of the Jimblot Corporation had been responsible for retrieving their functional divisions' mail from the centralized mailroom. During the workday, the secretaries made a minimum of three tours to the mailroom to deposit outgoing mail and collect incoming deliveries. This "ritual" gave the secretaries the opportunity to socialize, collect the latest information, and be freed from the work station. This norm was threatened when management proposed to provide a mail delivery and pick-up system in an effort to improve organizational productivity and eliminate a low-skilled portion of the secretarial job. The result—you guessed it! The secretaries banded together, presented an impregnable position, badgered their individual bosses, and totally resisted the change. The result of the group cohesiveness: Management abandoned the concept without even trying to implement it.

Impact of the Informal Organization

Now that we have examined the nature of the informal group, it is appropriate to consider the impact the informal organization can have on the formal organization. The groups that compose the informal organization can affect the formal organization negatively and positively. Let's discuss each category.

Negative Impact

There are four potential problem areas associated with the informal organization.[12]

1. *Resistance to change.*   The informal organization can resist change. In an effort to protect its values and beliefs, the informal group can place roadblocks in the path to any modifications in the work environment. A four-day compressed workweek or the hiring of minority workers could infringe on the values of the informal group, resulting in resistance to the change.

2. *Conflict.*   The informal group can create two "masters" for an employee. In an attempt to satisfy the informal group, the employee may come in conflict with the formal organization. The "lunch bunch" enjoys going together as a group, eating a leisurely meal, and analyzing

the business affairs of the company. The lunch bunch enjoys its 60-minute lunch each day even though management has authorized only a 30-minute lunch time. The employees' social satisfaction is in conflict with the employer's need for productivity.

3. *Rumor.* The informal communication system—the **grapevine**—can create and process false information or rumors. The creation of rumors can upset the balance of the work environment. In the next section of this chapter, we discuss rumor and the informal organization in greater depth.

4. *Pressure to conform.* The norms that the informal groups develop act as a strong inducement toward conformity. The more cohesive the group, the more accepted are the behavioral standards. Nonconforming in the person's reference group can result in gentle verbal reminders from the group but can escalate to harassment—ostracism, as illustrated in the account of Julie Gray, hiding tools, or rearranging the work area. It can even lead to physical abuse, as the following example illustrates.

One of the authors was involved in a sales training class where the group had gradually been escalating its punishment of Tom Olsen, the eager beaver. A week earlier, Tom had violated the group norm. During a practice sales presentation, Tom had humiliated the presenter, a fellow trainee. The group's accepted norm was to offer "minimal resistance" to their fellow trainees' sales pitches during presentations. Though reminded of the group's expected behavior, Tom humiliated a second trainee. Silence and ostracism were followed by constant phone calls during the night and the salting of Tom's food at group meals. Finally, Tom was held by his heels, upside down, outside a window on the tenth floor of the hotel! Physical punishment is a possibility in all informal groups.

Positive Impact

Despite the possibility of these problems, informal groups do have the potential to be helpful to managers. There can be five benefits for managers:[13]

1. *Makes the total system effective.* If the informal organization blends well with the formal system, the organization can function more effectively. The ability of the informal group to provide flexibility and instantaneous reactions will polish the plans and procedures developed through the formal organization.

2. *Provides support to management.* The informal organization can provide support to the individual manager. It can fill in gaps in the manager's knowledge through advice or through performing the work, for example, budgeting and scheduling. By performing effectively and

positively, it can build a cooperative environment. This, in turn, can mean more delegation to the employees and less time spent by the manager controlling employee behavior.

3. *Provides stability in the environment.*   The informal organization can provide acceptance and belonging. This feeling of being wanted by the group can encourage employees to remain in the environment, thus reducing turnover. Additionally, the informal organization provides a place for the person to vent frustrations. Being able to discuss them in a supportive environment may relieve emotional pressures.

4. *Provides a useful communication channel.*   The informal organization provides employees with the opportunity for social information, for discussing their work, and for understanding what is happening in the work environment.

5. *Encourages better management.*   Managers should be aware of the power of the informal organization in what is actually a check and balance system. Planned changes should be made with an awareness of the ability of the informal group to make the plan successful or unsuccessful.

One of the potential impacts (positive and negative) on the formal organization is the communication system developed by the informal organization. What is this system, and how does it function?

Informal Communication—The Grapevine

The informal communication system in an organization is known as the grapevine, and it is an important part of the organizational environment. To understand the effect of the grapevine, we need to examine its causes, patterns, characteristics, and problems.[14]

Why Does the Grapevine Occur?

The grapevine is the result of social interaction in an organization. Even in a formal organizational setting, informal communication will be present. People talk about their work, their frustrations, and their successes. Most often, they do so by way of the communication channel of the informal organization.

The activity on the grapevine is more a result of the situation in the work environment than of the natural inclination of the person. When the proper environmental factors arise, anyone can become a participant in the grapevine. What are these factors? Feelings of high anxiety and insecurity; familiarity with subject—be it friends or work; and the possession of new information. In addition, a person who holds a job with frequent access to information worth knowing or with the freedom to communicate may be an active participant in the process.

Characteristics of Grapevines

Among the significant characteristics of the grapevine are these two important facts: It is fast, and it can penetrate the tightest security. As a result, sometimes important information may be missing from the communications. Third, and also important, is the fact that the grapevine is easily accessible. The positive feature of this accessibility is that management can use it for feedback on the health of the organization. The process can translate organizational directives into employee language, or employees can be primed concerning the mood of a manager. The negative aspect of accessibility is that the grapevine can purposefully be used to carry totally erroneous information—information that can be both personally and organizationally damaging.

Patterns of Grapevines

There are four grapevine patterns, as shown in Figure 8.5. The most commonly used pattern is the cluster chain. This pattern involves the initiator (A) telling a "cluster"—in this case B, E, and L. Each employee in turn may tell another cluster. Not all people who receive information on the grapevine act as communicators.

Problems the Grapevine Can Cause

One problem with the grapevine is that it is not totally accurate. There is a tendency to omit some major pieces of information that have a bearing on accuracy. A second problem is rumor. Rumor is grapevine information that is communicated without evidence of truth. Rumor depends on interest and ambiguity.[15] If a subject is of no interest to a person, there is no cause for him or her to talk about it. And if all the facts are known, there is no room for rumor. Rumor, because it depends on interest and ambiguity, is subject to filtering of details. In addition, new details are added. Controlling rumor is discussed in the next section.

What can a manager do to function successfully with the informal organization?

FIGURE 8.5
Grapevine patterns

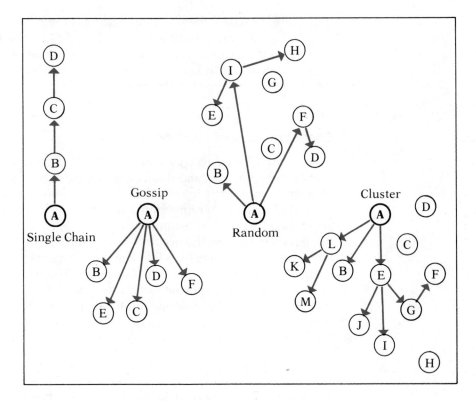

Strategies for Working with the Informal Organization

Every manager experiences the effects of the informal organization. Successful managers learn that the informal organization has benefits for the formal organization when managed correctly. What are key areas for managers?

A manager needs to start strategy development with a recognition and acceptance of the existence of the informal organization. The manager must try to develop an appreciation for the potential impacts (positive and negative) of the informal organization on the formal structure. This awareness will result in the realistic strategy of always considering the impact of any action on the informal organization before it is undertaken.

Another element of strategy development is to identify the informal groups and who heads them. Who are the leaders? What are the norms? How cohesive is the group? Two approaches, the sociogram and the informal organization chart, have been proposed as aids in this process. Another approach a manager can use to identify the informal leader is to watch for the arbitrator or mediator in disputes in the work unit. This role is an indication of informal power.

Once the research is done, the manager can be confident about what he or she is dealing with. Then the manager needs to develop strategies to align the informal organization's goals and activities with those of the formal organization. The manager must cultivate the informal organization. Four points for implementing this strategy can be:

1. Seek the support and cooperation of the informal leaders.
2. Provide open and complete communications by using both formal and informal channels.
3. Control rumor by:
   a. removing the causes of the rumor.
   b. applying efforts to counter erroneous rumors that can cause trouble, while letting the others die out.
   c. providing facts as quickly as possible.
   d. using a credible source to supply the facts.
   e. using face-to-face communication.
4. Keep the formal organization's activities from unnecessarily threatening the informal organization; in general, be sensitive to its existence.[16]

Summary

- The informal organization is the network of personal and social relationships that arises spontaneously in the organization. It is not shown on the formal organization chart.
- The informal organization influences the productivity and the degree of job satisfaction of organization members.
- Informal groups may be horizontal, vertical, or mixed—depending on who the members are and where they work. All have positive and negative features.
- Informal groups are formed to satisfy needs of the employees, or because of similarities of the members, or because of physical proximity.
- Informal groups remain in existence because they maintain the social or cultural environment, provide social satisfaction, provide information, and provide a means of control in the work environment.
- In informal groups, roles emerge, and the group develops characteristics. Multiple leadership roles are possible.

- Group norms that set standards for group behavior come about through the dictates of the group leader or consensus of its members' ideas and attitudes.
- Cohesion is measured by the degree to which members share the group's goals and cooperate. The more cohesive the group, the more success it will have in achieving its goals.
- The informal organization can affect the formal organization positively or negatively. Resistance, conflict, conformity, and rumor are negative outcomes. Supporting the formal system and manager, providing stability, communicating, and encouraging better management are positive impacts.
- The informal organization's communication system is known as the grapevine. It can provide both rumor and quality information.
- Informal groups are part of the formal organization. Managers need to develop strategies to work with the informal organization.

Glossary of Essential Terms

cohesion	The measure of a group's solidarity—the degree to which the members share resources and ideas, and the degree of their willingness to cooperate with one another.
grapevine	The communication system of the informal organization. It carries both rumors and messages.
horizontal group	An informal group composed of individuals within the same work areas or on the same level of the formal organization.
informal organization	The collection and interaction of informal groups within the formal organization.
interaction chart	A diagram that shows the informal interactions people have with one another at work.
mixed group	An informal group composed of persons in different work areas and at different levels of the formal organization.
norm	Any standard of conduct, or code, or pattern of behavior perceived by a group to be important for its members to honor or to conform to.
sociogram	A diagram of group attraction.
vertical group	An informal group composed of individuals who work in the same areas but on different levels of the formal organization.

Review Questions

1. Can you define this chapter's essential terms? If not, consult the preceding glossary.

2. Why does a manager need to recognize the existence of the informal organization and work with it?

3. "The informal organization consists of operating relationships not prescribed by the formal organization and therefore not shown on the company's organization chart." Explain this statement. *SPONTANEOUS*

4. What are the three types of informal groups in the informal organization? What is the composition of each group? *HORIZONTAL, VERTICAL, MIXED*

5. *pg.229* What are three reasons why people form informal groups? What are four reasons informal groups remain in existence? *BONDING NEED SATIS.*

6. *pg.231* How are leaders selected in the informal organization? How many leaders might an informal group have? Why?

7. *pg.235 237* Two characteristics describing informal organizations are norms and cohesion. What does each mean? Why are they important for a manager to recognize?

8. *pg.238-39* List and describe three positive and three negative impacts the informal organization has on the formal organization. *EFFECTIVE SYSTEM | RESIST CHANGE / SUPPORT TO MAN. | CONFLICT / STABILITY, COMMUN | RUMOR / SAT. CONFORM*

9. If you had to give advice to a manager on how to work with the informal organization, what should it include? *sup. + coop with leaders*

References

1. Keith Davis, *Human Behavior at Work: Organizational Behavior*, 7th ed. (New York: McGraw-Hill, 1985), pp. 329–331.

2. M. Dalton, *Men Who Manage* (New York: John Wiley & Sons, 1959).

3. Richard Hodgetts and Steven Altman, *Organizational Behavior* (Philadelphia: W. B. Saunders Co., 1979), pp. 142–144.

4. Davis, *Human Behavior at Work*, p. 336.

5. Theo Harmon and William G. Scott, *Management in the Modern Organization* (Boston: Houghton Mifflin, 1970), p. 432.

6. Stephen P. Robbins, *Organizational Behavior: Concepts and Controversies*, 3rd ed. (Englewood Cliffs, N.J.: Prentice-Hall, 1986), p. 205.

7. Davis, *Human Behavior at Work*, p. 337.

8. Robbins, *Organizational Behavior*, p. 203.

9. Ibid., p. 181.

10. F. J. Roethlisberger and W. J. Dickson, *Management and the Worker* (Cambridge, Mass.: Harvard University Press, 1939).

11. David R. Hampton, Charles E. Summer, and Ross A. Webber, *Organizational Behavior and the Practice of Management*, 5th ed. (Glenview, Ill.: Scott, Foresman, 1987), p. 200.

12. Davis, *Human Behavior at Work*, p. 333.

13. Ibid., p. 334.

14. Ibid., pp. 336–346. The majority of this information was adapted from the pages cited.

15. Gordon Allport and Leo Postman, *The Psychology of Rumor* (New York: Holt, Rinehart & Winston, 1947), p. 33.

16. Robert K. Mueller, "Corporate Networking: Building Channels for Information and Influence," *Free Press*, September 30, 1987, p. 4B.

Readings

Dyer, William G. *Team Building: Issues and Alternatives*. Reading, Mass.: Addison-Wesley, 1987.

Erkut, S. and J. P. Fields. "Focus Groups to the Rescue." *Training and Development Journal*, 41 (October 1987), pp. 74–76.

Half, Robert. "How Can I Stop the Gossip?" *Management Accounting*, 69 (September 1987), p. 27.

Hardaker, Maurice and Bryan Ward. "How to Make a Team Work." *Harvard Business Review* (November–December 1987), pp. 112–119(6).

Kennedy, Marilyn Moats. *Office Warfare: Strategies for Getting Ahead in the Aggressive '80s*. New York: Fawcett Crest, 1985.

Kotter, John. *Power and Influence: Beyond Formal Authority*. New York: Free Press, 1985.

Reich, Robert G. "Entrepreneurship Reconsidered: The Team as Hero." *Harvard Business Review* (May–June 1987), pp. 77–83.

Robbins, Anthony. *Unlimited Power: The Way to Peak Achievement*. New York: Fawcett Columbine, 1986.

Singh, Suman K. "The Bases and Issues of Ingroup Influences in a Work Organization." *Indian Journal of Industrial Relations*, 23, no. 4 (April 1987), pp. 423–432.

Zientara, Marguerite. *Women, Technology and Power*. New York: AMACOM, 1987.

8.1 Super Support

Six of the eight managers at Walston Products are having lunch together in the company lunchroom. Only Abe Stern, the company's president, and Mary Frisch, a supervisor, are absent. Let's listen in for a few minutes.

"How are profits this quarter?" asked Bill, the chief of sales.

"They should be the best ever—at least they are the best since I've been in charge of finance. We have never been higher in sales volume and lower in returns than we are right now. This year should break a lot of records."

Alice Armstrong, the personnel specialist joined in. "I think we can all take credit for the turnaround this company has seen over the past two years. I think I speak for all of us when I say that I've never worked with such a fine group as you all are. I've never seen more cooperation and group spirit before, and I've held several jobs in much larger companies."

"You know, Alice, you found a much-needed accountant for me last month, but she was sure inexperienced. The company she came from gave her a few bad habits and some really questionable accounting methods, but I nipped them in the bud. I think she is working out just fine now and is really eager to carry her load."

"You can take credit for that, Sarah. We needed someone in a hurry, and you took her under your wing. All your people think you are the greatest from what I hear."

Sarah blushed, and Max moved quickly to take her off the hook.

"As long as we are passing out praise, I'd like to thank Peter here for all the support he gave me when I first arrived. My team spirit comes from his care and feeding from my first day. I quickly sensed that Walston was my kind of company. I came from a place where you were lucky if your boss knew your name. Believe me, Walston is a great place to work. And by the way, thanks to you Charlie for helping me this weekend with the quarterly reports. I hated to see you miss your golf game, but I sure needed you on Saturday."

Charlie nodded and joined in. "Say, you know that we are all in this together. What are friends for? I only gave what I had to give, and I know that you would all do the same if the need arose. Lord knows I've seen you all give more than your share on many occasions."

"Say, where is Mary?" asked Alice.

"She's probably at her desk where she always is at lunch time. I feel sorry for her. Are any of you people close to her at all? I don't think I've heard anything but a 'hello' from her since she first arrived about a year ago."

"I don't think she likes to socialize," said Charlie. "She didn't attend the company outing last summer, and she missed our Christmas party. I think she just prefers to socialize elsewhere."

"Well, she is not a team player, and that bugs me," said Sarah. "I have tried to get her to join our luncheons on at least two occasions, and did I get a cold shoulder."

"Have any of us tried to bring her into the group besides Sarah?" asked Charlie.

The group members looked at one another and agreed that the time was right to talk with Mary again to try to bring her into the group. Charlie was volunteering to be the first to try tomorrow as the managers left the lunchroom.

For Discussion

1. What kind of informal group do these managers compose?
2. In what ways have they demonstrated the positive impact of the informal group?
3. What benefits of informal group membership has Mary not received by her lack of participation?

8.2 The Company Picnic

Barley Hastings was one happy man. This year's picnic marked the third anniversary of his company's founding, and his prospects had never looked better. Sales and profits were increasing, and to show his gratitude to all of his employees, Barley had decided to make this year's picnic better than the last two. The whole affair was catered and under a rented tent. Games and some valuable prizes were available for kids and adults alike. About sixty people were at the picnic. All but two of his twenty employees were present. Barley felt like a "patriarch" at a family reunion as he made his way from group to group.

"I wonder what's got the purchasing people so excited," Barley thought as he looked over the group and edged closer to it. Bill was angry about something, and the two others were looking shocked. Barley got close enough to overhear them but not close enough to join in.

"I'm not kidding you guys, that's what the supplier's man told me last week," said Bill.

"This is the first time I've heard about the supplier's change. How come you know and we don't?" asked Ruth.

"I got it straight from their top salesman when he bought me lunch. Maybe he shouldn't have told me, but he did, and I'm telling you now."

Barley thought about what he had overheard and knew exactly what Bill was talking about. "Damn," he thought, "I wish that salesman had kept his mouth shut. Those purchasing people are going to spread it all around, and I'm not ready to go public with it yet."

As he walked on, he wondered how the various groups had formed. The purchasing group seemed natural enough, but the group to his right was a mix of two managers from different departments and three workers from a third department. Barley decided to join in.

"Hi, Mr. Hastings. It's a great picnic and a great day for it."

"I agree. Hope everyone has had enough to eat. Don't hold back. There's plenty of food and drink."

After some friendly discussions, the conversation turned to business topics. Comments were made about the ways in which the company was growing and the fact that six new faces had been added over the last four months. Barley suddenly realized that one of the missing employees was from the department represented by the three workers. "Where's Albrite, today?" asked Barley. One of the workers was about to speak when Johnson gestered for him to hold off. Johnson then said that he was probably home with his "mommy," and the workers broke into laughter. (Barley thought about that comment later on. Albrite was the newest employee, and this was the first time Barley had a clue that he was not fitting in.) After a few more negative comments by Johnson about Albrite, Barley decided to move on.

The last group he visited before awarding the prizes consisted of the company's bowling team members, most of whom came from worker ranks and the accounting department. Barley complimented them on their 2nd place finish this year and talked about the prospects for next season. He was a little surprised to see them wearing their bowling shirts and noticed that all the team members wore mustaches. "Is a mustache part of your uniform?" asked Barley. "Nothing in writing about it," said Randle, "but you better not show up for practice without one." The group looked pleased with itself.

For Discussion

1. What kind of informal groups did Barley visit? Explain your answers.
2. What does the visit with the purchasing people tell you about informal groups?
3. What does Barley's visit with Johnson and his group tell you about informal groups?
4. What does the group that formed the bowling team tell you about informal groups? *NORMS + COHESIVENESS*

Staffing
and Directing

C H A P T E R 9

Staffing

OUTLINE

The Right Person in the Right Job

Staffing Defined

The Legal Environment of Staffing
- Equal Employment Opportunity
- Affirmative Action

Human Resource Planning
- Human Resource Forecasting
- Human Resource Inventory
- Comparison of Forecast and Inventory
- Role of the Individual Manager

Recruitment
- Sources of Applicants
- Role of the Individual Manager

Selection
- The Selection Process
- Role of the Individual Manager

Induction and Orientation
- Induction
- Orientation

Training and Development
- Training: Purposes and Techniques
- Development: Purposes and Techniques

Performance Appraisal
- What Are the Factors in Successful Appraisals?
- Types of Appraisal Systems
- Methods of Appraisal

Implementing Personnel Decisions
- Promotions
- Transfers
- Demotions
- Separations

Summary

ESSENTIAL TERMS

adverse impact	promotion
demotion	recruitment
development	selection
induction	separation
management by objectives	staffing
objective performance appraisal	subjective performance appraisal
orientation	training
performance appraisal	transfer

LEARNING OBJECTIVES

After reading and discussing this chapter, you should be able to do the following:

1. Define this chapter's essential terms.
2. Explain the importance of the staffing function and its relationship to planning and organizing.
3. List and describe the steps in the staffing process.
4. Explain the impact of equal employment opportunity and affirmative action on the staffing process.
5. Discuss the human resource planning process.
6. Outline the selection process, and describe each of the steps.
7. Distinguish between induction and orientation.
8. Define and distinguish between training and development.
9. Discuss the purposes and types of performance appraisal.

The Right Person in the Right Job

For an organization to survive and prosper, it must be able to identify, select, develop, and retain qualified personnel. People are the most important resource of an organization. They supply the talent, skills, knowledge, and experience to achieve the organization's objectives.

Through the planning function, management determined the objectives and formed the derivative plans for the organization. Management analyzed these objectives during the organizing function to determine what activities (developed then into a hierarchy of positions) were necessary to achieve the plans. The challenge at this point is for management to match personnel with the jobs identified.

This chapter has three purposes. One is to explain how an enterprise determines its personnel needs and how it then attracts and hires those persons. A second is to discuss the processes through which the organization develops its human resources throughout their tenure in the organization. The third purpose is to discuss how the legal environment affects the staffing process.

The activities we describe in the chapter are basic to all organizations. Each individual manager performs each of these basic human resource management activities with or without the assistance of human resource management staff specialists.

What is involved in the staffing process?

Staffing Defined

The **staffing** function can be viewed as consisting of a series of steps that managers perform to provide the organization with the right people in the right positions. Figure 9.1 illustrates the staffing process. The eight steps in the process are these:

1. *Human resource planning.* The purpose of human resource planning is to ensure that the personnel needs of the organization will be met. An analysis of the plans of the organization will determine what skills will be needed. Then management can review the present inventory of skills of the organization and develop a plan to provide the quantity and quality of personnel needed in the future.

2. *Recruitment.* After the human resource needs are determined, managers undertake recruitment to locate prospective employees. They

FIGURE 9.1
The staffing process

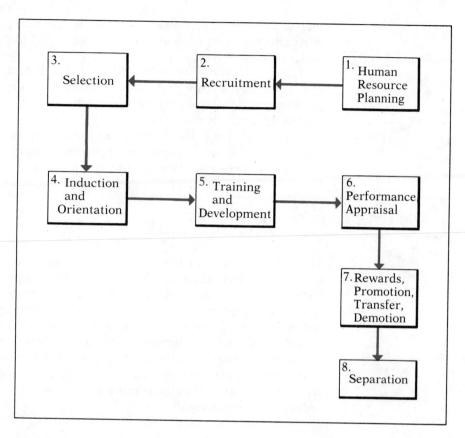

may accomplish it through newspaper and professional journal advertisements, employment agencies, contacts at trade schools or colleges, and internal sources of the organization.

3. *Selection.* The selection process involves evaluating the candidates and choosing the one whose credentials match job requirements. The steps in the selection process may include completing an application blank, interviews, reference checks, and physical examination.

4. *Induction and orientation.* This step integrates the selected employee into the organization. Processes include organizational socialization with the work group and becoming acquainted with the organization's policies and rules.

5. *Training and development.* Both training and development are concerned with improving the employee's ability to contribute to organizational effectiveness. Training involves the improvement of employee skills. Development concerns the preparation of the employee for additional responsibility or advancement.

6. *Performance appraisal.*   This step is one of appraising the employee's performance in relation to job standards and then providing feedback to the employee.

7. *Employment decisions: rewards, transfers, promotions, demotions.*   The appraisal of performance results in management's making employment decisions, areas of which are monetary rewards, transfers, promotions, and demotions.

8. *Separations.*   The dynamics of the staffing process involve both inflow and outflow of people. Managers are concerned with voluntary turnover, retirements, layoffs, and terminations.

The Legal Environment of Staffing

The staffing process of an organization is influenced by the legal environment. Major legislation has been enacted to provide for an employment environment in which both job applicants and present employees are free from discrimination in their pursuit of employment opportunities. In addition, legislation encourages employers to actively resolve the results of past discrimination by developing affirmative action plans.

Prior to examining the steps in the staffing process, we look at explanations of equal employment opportunity and affirmative action. When we later take up each of the staffing steps in detail, we will refer to these specific legal implications.

Equal Employment Opportunity

Employment choices made on the basis of race, color, religion, sex, age, or national origin are prohibited. It is unlawful for an employer to do either of the following:

1. To fail or refuse to hire or to discharge an individual because of race, color, religion, sex, age, or national origin.

2. To limit, segregate, or classify employees or applicants for employment in any way that would tend to deprive the individual of employment opportunities because of race, color, religion, sex, age, or national origin.[1]

These prohibitions are the result of federal laws. Their purpose is to prevent discrimination and to promote equal employment opportunities for all groups in our society. Discrimination that is either covert or overt is prohibited. Overt discrimination by an employer would mean purposefully not hiring or advancing a person because of sex, race, religion, color, age, or national origin. Covert discrimination is discrimination that may be the result of employment procedures, not of intentional practice. The effect is the same, though, and is unlawful.

An example of overt discrimination would be a manager's stating that he wants a "man for the job, not a woman" when either could do the job equally well. Covert discrimination may occur within the employment system. A test that results in minority groups' failing in a much greater percentage than whites is racially discriminatory if the test is not job related. This latter case is also an example of adverse impact. **Adverse impact** refers to any part of the employment process that results in a significantly higher percentage of a protected group being rejected for employment than the percentage of the nonprotected group. If the test is not job related, the failing testee can claim adverse impact.[2] Protected groups include women and those defined in federal law as minorities. Minorities are:

- Hispanics: Spanish-surnamed Americans.
- Oriental Americans: Asians or people from the Pacific Islands.
- Negroes: blacks not of Hispanic origin.
- American Indians: natives of North America.
- Eskimos: Alaskan natives.

The impact of most equal employment opportunity legislation is on the recruitment and selection of new employees, and on promotion, compensation, training, and discharge of present employees. Recruitment advertisements can no longer specify male or female. In the selection process, preemployment inquiries not related to job performance are prohibited. Questions on sex, age, marital status, race, religion, national origin, type of military discharge, color of hair and eyes, height, and weight are to be eliminated on the application blank and in interviews.[3] If tests are used, they should relate to job performance and be free of cultural bias. Employees should have equal opportunity for training, compensation, and advancement.

Exhibit 9.1 summarizes federal antidiscrimination laws. They specifically outlaw discrimination based on the criteria cited earlier and demand equal pay for those performing equal tasks. Handicapped people have special protection when they are employed by organizations doing business with the federal government.

Affirmative Action

Affirmative action goes beyond equal employment opportunity. It requires an employer to make an extra effort to hire and promote those in a protected minority. The purpose of *affirmative action* is to eliminate the present effects

EXHIBIT 9.1
Legislation Related to Staffing Function

Federal Legislation	Description of Provisions
1. Title VI 1964 Civil Rights Act	Prohibits discrimination based on race, color, or national origin. Applies to employers receiving federal financial assistance.
2. Title VII 1964 Civil Rights Act— Amended 1972	Prohibits discrimination based on race, color, religion, sex, or national origin. Applies to private employers of fifteen or more employees; federal, state and local governments; unions; and employment agencies.
3. Executive Orders 11246 and 11375 (1965)	Prohibits discrimination based on race, color, religion, sex, or national origin. Established requirements for affirmative action plans. Applies to federal contractors and subcontractors.
4. Title I 1968 Civil Rights Act	Prohibits interference with a person's exercise of rights with respect to race, color, religion, sex, or national origin.
5. Equal Pay Act of 1963	Prohibits sex difference in pay for equal work. Applies to private employers.
6. Age Discrimination in Employment Act of 1967— Amended 1978	Prohibits age discrimination against people between the ages of 40 and 70. Applies to all employers of 20 or more employees.
7. Rehabilitation Act of 1973	Prohibits discrimination on the basis of certain physical and mental handicaps by employers doing business with or for the federal government.
8. Vietnam Era Veterans Readjustment Act of 1974	Prohibits discrimination against disabled veterans and Vietnam era veterans.
9. Revised Guidelines on Employee Selection 1976, 1978, and 1979	Established a single set of guidelines for discrimination on the basis of race, color, religion, sex, and national origin. The guidelines provide a framework for making legal employment decisions about hiring, promoting, demoting, the proper use of tests, and other selection procedures.
10. Mandatory Retirement Act	Determined that an employee could not be forced to retire before age 70.

EXHIBIT 9.1
Continued

Federal Legislation	Description of Provisions
11. Privacy Act of 1974	Established the right of employees to examine letters of reference concerning them unless the right is waived.
12. Pregnancy Discrimination Act of 1978	Prohibits discrimination in employment based on pregnancy, childbirth, or related medical conditions.
13. Equal Employment Opportunity Guidelines of 1981—Sexual Harassment	Prohibits sexual harassment when such conduct is an explicit or implicit condition of employment, if the employee's response becomes a basis for employment or promotion decisions, or if it interferes with an employee's performance. The guidelines protect men and women.
14. Equal Employment Opportunity Guidelines of 1981—National Origin	Identifies potential national origin discrimination to include fluency-in-English job requirements and denying employment because of foreign training or education. Identifies national origin harassment in the work environment to include ethnic slurs and physical conduct with the purpose of creating an intimidating or hostile environment or unreasonably interferring with work.
15. Equal Employment Opportunity Guidelines of 1981—Religion	Determined that employers have an obligation to accommodate religious practices unless they can demonstrate this would result in undue hardship. Accommodation may be achieved through voluntary substitutes, flexible scheduling, lateral transfer, and change of job assignment.

of past discrimination, either overt or covert. When an organization takes an aggressive or affirmative role in recruiting, hiring, training, compensating, and upgrading jobs, the purposes of affirmative action should be achieved. The measurable result of affirmative action is for the organization's percentage of females, males, and minorities performing in job categories to be equal to the percentage of females, males, and minorities in the relevant job market.[4]

For most organizations, an affirmative action program is voluntary, but companies doing business for or with the federal government may be required to establish one. In doing so, the organization can implement either the good faith strategy or the quota strategy.[5] The *good faith strategy* focuses on identifying and eliminating obstacles to hiring and promotion of women and minorities. The idea is that by eliminating these obstacles to employment there will be increased utilization of women and minorities. The *quota strategy*, on the other hand, institutes a rigid code of hiring and promoting restrictions.

An affirmative action plan is just that—a plan. It plans for reaching out in recruiting to attract minorities and women. It plans to aggressively hire, train, and promote protected classes. The presence of an affirmative action commitment affects all staffing areas, especially human resources planning.

Human Resource Planning

The overall human resource planning process for an organization involves forecasting the demand for and supply of personnel. There are three elements to the planning: (1) forecasting the personnel requirements, (2) comparing the requirements to the inventory of potential candidates within the organization, and (3) developing specific plans for how many people to recruit (from outside) or whom to train (from inside). Figure 9.2 illustrates the human resource planning process. Let's examine the overall company process and the role of the individual manager.

Human Resource Forecasting

Human resource forecasting attempts to predict the organization's future demands for people and for jobs. The forecasting process can be simple or complex, depending on the kind of organization, its size, and the length of time considered in the forecast.

In forecasting the personnel requirements of the organization, management needs to consider the strategic plans of the organization and the normal employee turnover. Strategic plans determine the direction for the company and its need for people. The plans will dictate how many people will be needed (increase or decrease) to staff the organization and what skills and abilities they will need. The types of decisions made in planning can have different impacts on the manpower requirements of the organization: A decision to create a new product or new division may mean an

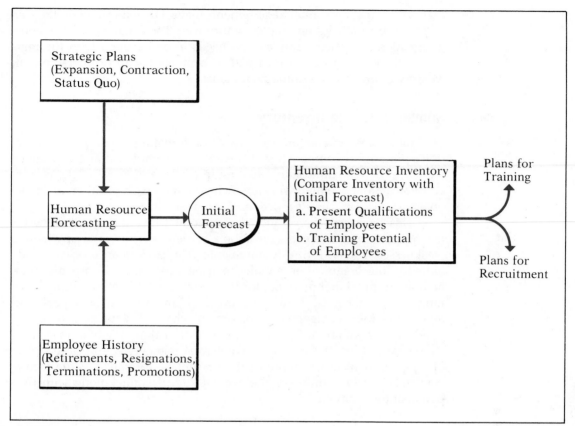

FIGURE 9.2
Human resource planning process

increase in the number of personnel and new positions, whereas plans to contract operations may lead to major workforce reductions. A strategy calling for maintaining the status quo may result in a decision to hire new employees only when present employees leave the company.

We can see how a company translates plans into actual personnel requirements with this illustration: A corporation that produces furniture decides to increase its production by 15 percent. Management analyzes the workload generated by the increase and determines:

- How much more work is required in terms of workhours.
- How much work is currently done by one person.
- How many people will be required to complete this additional work, based on what one person does.

After the personnel requirements have been developed, they are modified by statistics on employee turnover. The number of retirements, resignations, and terminations also needs to be included with the initial forecast. These figures in turn will be compared with the personnel inventory figures to determine final plans.

Human Resource Inventory

The human resource inventory provides information about the organization's present personnel. After the inventory is completed, an organization will have cataloged the skills, abilities, interests, and needs of the present workforce.[6] Management will know who occupies each position, his or her qualifications, length of service, and responsibilities.

This human resource audit (or personnel inventory) will allow the managers to match the organization's present personnel strengths and weaknesses against future requirements. The performance of each individual in the organization should be appraised. This will provide information on individual potential for increased responsibilities and for long-range training needs. Figure 9.3 provides an example of a personnel inventory—the management replacement chart. The process of developing this chart provides management with a departmental analysis of strengths and weaknesses, and a potential managerial succession plan. The replacement chart identifies the present performance of the incumbent manager in addition to the ages of key personnel along with their potential for promotion.

Comparison of Forecast and Inventory

Now that we have examined the personnel forecast and the personnel inventory, we want to know how the organization begins to prepare its human resource plan. We can look at our furniture manufacturer again for an example that can help clarify this process.

Management's strategic plans call for the addition of a data processing department within the next twelve months. The human resource planners go to work immediately defining the specific plans for personnel (do we recruit or train?) with the required skills in data processing; it is their task to fill the jobs designed by the organizational planners through job analysis. The inventory of present personnel is surveyed to determine if anyone is qualified to fill the new positions. It would answer these questions:

1. Do present employees possess the necessary prerequisites? If so, they should be considered.
2. If they do not possess the skills, can the skills be provided through training?

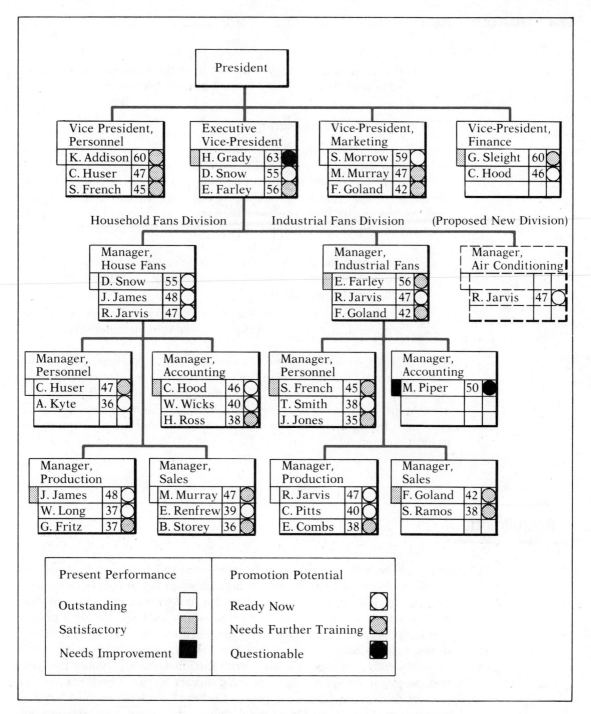

FIGURE 9.3
Management replacement chart
Source: Walter S. Wikstrom, *Developing Managerial Competence* (New York: National Industrial Conference Board, 1964), p. 99. Used by permission.

3. If the existing employees do not have the skills, where can persons with these skills be located outside the company?

Role of the Individual Manager

Regardless of whether the organization does or does not have the services of human resource planners, individual managers need to be actively involved with the human resource planning process. In any organization, the departmental managers should be the most knowledgeable management persons concerning their personnel needs. A manager can determine the need for additional or replacement personnel by two means:

1. Analyzing his or her workforce to determine who will be promoted, transferred, terminated, or leaving voluntarily through retirement or resignation.
2. Analyzing what new positions are justifiable through increased workload, new responsibilities, or changing technology.

If the analysis shows that there is a need for a new position, the manager should negotiate the approval of the position with her or his superior manager. If the rationale is sound, the position may be approved.

At this point, a job opening exists. Human resource planning (always influenced by affirmative action commitments) initiates the recruitment step to locate personnel.

Recruitment

In **recruitment** the organization is attempting to identify and attract candidates to meet the requirements of anticipated or actual position vacancies. Two devices used during this phase are the *job description* and *job specification*, both of which are developed as a result of job analysis. Before a pool of applicants is created, it is necessary to determine the job scope, function, duties, responsibilities, and relationships. The job description, as illustrated in Exhibit 9.2, provides a manager with the job demands. Notice the function, scope, and responsibilities of the customer service representative. The job specification (an example appears as Exhibit 9.3) identifies the education, experience, training, and behavioral abilities the person must have to perform in the job. Once armed with these tools, the manager can make contact with potential sources of applicants.

EXHIBIT 9.2
Job Description

I JOB IDENTIFICATION
POSITION TITLE: Customer Service Representative
DEPARTMENT: Policyholders Service
EFFECTIVE DATE: March 1, 1989

II FUNCTION
To resolve policyholders' questions and make corresponding adjustments to policies if necessary after the policy is issued.

III SCOPE
a) Internal
Interacts with other members of the department in researching answers to problems.
b) External (within company)
Interacts with Policy Issue for policy cancellations; with Premium Accounting on accounting procedures; with Accounting Department for processing checks.
c) External (outside company)
Interacts with policyholders to answer policy-related questions; with client company payroll departments to resolve billing questions; with the carrier to modify policies.

IV RESPONSIBILITIES
He/She will be responsible for:
a) Resolving policyholder inquiries on policies and coverage.
b) Initiating changes in policies with carriers at the request of the Insured.
c) Adjusting in-house records as a result of approved changes.
d) Corresponding with policyholders regarding changes as requested.
e) Reporting to the Department Manager any problems he or she is unable to resolve.

V AUTHORITY RELATIONSHIPS
a) Reporting relationships: reports to the manager of Policyholders Service.
b) Supervisory relationship: none.

VI EQUIPMENT, MATERIALS AND MACHINES
Typewriter, adding machine, and VDT.

VII PHYSICAL CONDITIONS OR HAZARDS
95% of the duties are performed either sitting at the desk or VDT.

VIII OTHER
Other duties as assigned.

EXHIBIT 9.3
Job Specification

I JOB IDENTIFICATION
POSITION: File/Mail Clerk
DEPARTMENT: Policyholders Service
EFFECTIVE DATE: March 1, 1989

II EDUCATION
Must have minimum of high school or equivalent.

III EXPERIENCE
Must have minimum of 6 months of filing experience involving developing, monitoring, and maintaining file system.

IV SKILLS
Typing skills: must be able to set up own work and operate typewriter. No minimum WPM.

V SPECIAL REQUIREMENTS
a) Must be flexible to the demands of the organization for overtime and change in workload.
b) Must be able to comply with previously established procedures.
c) Must be able to do detail work as illustrated by monitoring the location of the files and filing of files.
d) Must be able to apply systems knowledge as illustrated by anticipation of systems changes and creation of new procedures.

VI BEHAVIORAL CHARACTERISTICS
a) Must have high level of initiative demonstrated by recognizing a problem, resolving it, and reporting it to the Supervisor.
b) Must have interpersonal skills as demonstrated by being able to work as a team member and being cooperative with other departments.

Sources of Applicants

There are two sources of applicants—internal and external. Internal sources are the employees of the organization. A number of organizations have policies of promoting from within. This has a positive impact on the organizational members and the internal working environment. The opportunity for advancement has three distinct benefits: It can reduce turnover, provide incentive to learn jobs quickly, and assist in making the individual a functioning member of the organization faster because the person already knows the policies and expectations of the company.

There are also negatives from internal recruiting. Employees who do not get the jobs may become discontented. There is always the possibility that this policy, if taken to the extreme, can result in minimal "new blood" being brought into the organization; and that which is new is at a low position on the hierarchy. This may result in limited new ideas and stagnation.

One internal source is referrals of outside persons made by friends and relatives within the organization. Another method is to attract candidates by announcing job openings in company newsletters and posting position vacancies on bulletin boards. This provides all employees the equal opportunity to apply (if they see the notices). A third strategy is to conduct a search of the performance records of present employees with the intent of identifying qualified candidates and then encouraging them to apply for positions. This practice is not as popular as it once was because it may result in the organization's being accused of preselection for a job—that is, of not allowing all candidates for a position equal opportunity to be considered for the position. The practice is generally permissible if a manager does not seek candidates for openings in his or her own department, but encourages them to apply elsewhere.

A second potential source for candidates is outside the organization. Organizations can develop programs using on-site visits to colleges, trade schools, professional conferences, trade fairs, and high schools. This device allows the company to create impressions, answer questions, and screen applicants quickly.

Another tactic is to place advertisements in newspapers and trade journals or to place job requisitions with unions, school placement bureaus, and private or public employment agencies. The success in using these sources will depend on how well the organization has described its performance requirements and specifications. In 1987, a manufacturer of automobiles advertised 2,700 production jobs. Ninety thousand people applied![7]

There are limitations to the use of outside sources. One is the cost. It can be expensive to travel or have applicants travel, pay fees to agencies, or develop recruiting campaigns. A second limitation is the type of position being recruited for. The appropriate source is selected in terms of the position.

Role of the Individual Manager

The manager may have two roles in the recruitment process. For internal sources, the manager may be asked to identify potential candidates for openings in the organization on the basis of their performances while in the manager's department. These would be openings outside the manager's department, so it would be permissible to encourage employees to apply.

A second role is participation in recruiting trips. Often the line manager is asked to recruit at a college, trade fair, or professional association. When recruiting, a manager should be cautioned to present a realistic impression of the organization. Turnover is costly and is often based on unrealistic organizational expectations.

A final note on recruitment. Managers cannot rely on word of mouth or walk-in applicants to avoid charges of discrimination or to meet affirmative action commitments. Active recruitment is needed. In addition, the manager must keep in mind that recruitment by advertisements stating "wanted—male" or "wanted—female" is illegal.

When a pool of applicants has been created, the next phase is the selection process.

Selection

Selection is the process of deciding which candidate, out of the pool of applicants developed in recruitment, has the abilities, skills, and characteristics most closely matching job demands. The decision comes after the candidates go through a series of steps that compose the selection process. The normal selection philosophy is either to screen out the unqualified candidates at each step or to screen in the qualified ones; it's all a matter of perspective.

The Selection Process

Following is a discussion of the selection steps in the selection process shown in Figure 9.4.

Step 1: The application blank.   Prospective employees are requested to complete an application blank, which provides the manager with information on the education and experience of an applicant. In addition, it provides information about the applicant's previous growth and progress on the job as well as employment stability.[8] It can also show, simply by its requirements, a person's ability to follow instructions and his or her command of the language.

Step 2: Preliminary interview.   This step attempts to screen out the obviously unqualified from the pool of applicants. This interview may be conducted by the manager or a personnel specialist, using the information supplied on the application blank.

Step 3: Testing.   The purpose of employment testing is to determine the candidate's ability to perform the job. The kinds of tests used by employers vary and are subject to certain limitations. Aptitude tests attempt to measure

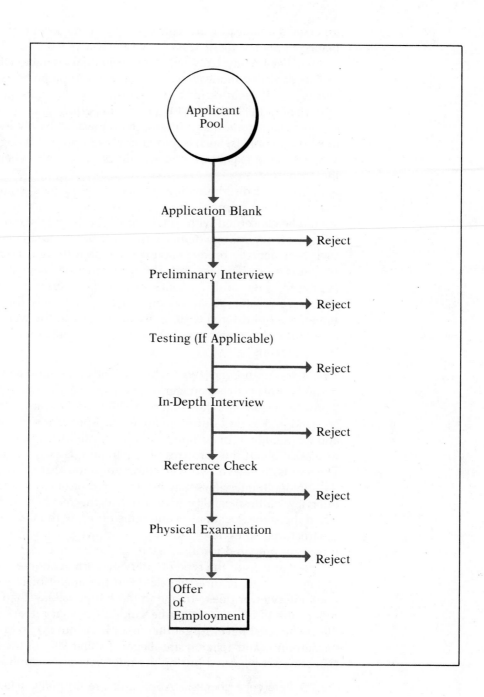

FIGURE 9.4
The selection
process

a person's ability to learn concepts and to master physical skills. Performance or achievement tests prove what a person can do at the time of testing. Personality tests measure individual characteristics and traits as well as particular motivations. They attempt to pinpoint particular strengths and weaknesses in order to match them to the prerequisites considered important in the jobholder for successful performance. Most tests need the expert administration and interpretation available only in testing agencies or by professionals, such as psychometrists and psychologists. For this reason, testing is expensive and should be used only when it is absolutely indispensable.

To avoid discrimination or charges of it, most companies use tests that have been approved or recognized as nondiscriminatory. Managers should be concerned with four points in testing: First, court decisions and federal agency rulings demand that test users must be able to show that their tests actually predict success on a job if those tests are used to make the decision to hire. Second, the tests must be valid—test what they are supposed to test and not some other area of performance. Third, the test should be reliable; it should provide approximately the same score each time it is administered to an individual. Fourth, the test must not exclude a significantly greater number of minority members than it does nonminority persons.

__Step 4: In-depth interviews.__   The in-depth interview will provide the applicant's prospective manager or managers (the candidate may have more than one person interview him or her) the opportunity to verify information on hand and to find out more about the applicant's interests, aspirations, and expectations. In addition, it will provide the opportunity to share information about the company, the job, and its environmental conditions. The aim is to have a two-way communication that is mutually beneficial.

In-depth interviews may be structured or unstructured. In a structured interview, little flexibility is allowed to the manager. All candidates are asked the same questions in the same order, with limited time to chat. An unstructured interview allows a free-flowing conversation; only overall topics are prepared for discussion by the interviewer.

Regardless of the type of interview format adopted, the effectiveness of the interview is directly related to the ability of the interviewer. The good interviewer does not spend more time talking than listening. In addition, the interviewer must be guided by what are acceptable inquiries. He or she must never forget that inquiries about age, marital status, ethnic background, and religion are illegal. Exhibit 9.4 shows us the questions that may not be asked during the interview or on application blanks.

__Step 5: Reference checks:__   Applicants are normally asked to supply personal or work references on the application blank. Personal references—ministers, doctors, friends—are of little value to an employer because ap-

EXHIBIT 9.4
What Employers Are and Are Not Allowed to Ask
on Employment Applications and in Interviews

	Acceptable Inquiry	**Discriminatory Inquiry**
Name	Additional information relative to change of name, use of an assumed name or nickname necessary to enable a check on applicant's work records.	The fact of a change of name or the original name of an applicant whose name has been legally changed.
Birthplace and Residence	Applicant's place of residence. Length of applicant's residence in state and/or city where the employee is located.	Birthplace of applicant. Birthplace of applicant's parents. Requirement that applicant submit birth certificate, naturalization, or baptismal record.
Creed and Religion	None.	Applicant's religious affiliation. Church, parish, or religious holidays observed by applicant.
Race or Color	General distinguishing physical characteristics such as scars, etc.	Applicant's race. Color of applicant's skin, eyes, hair, etc.
Photographs	None.	Photographs with application. Photographs after interview, but before hiring.
Age	If hired, can you furnish proof of age?	Date of birth or age of an applicant except when such information is needed for or to: 1. Maintain apprenticeship requirements based upon a reasonable minimum age. 2. Satisfy the provisions of either state or federal minimum age statutes. 3. Avoid interference with the operation of the terms and conditions and administration of any bona fide retirement, pension, employee benefit program.

continued

EXHIBIT 9.4
Continued

	Acceptable Inquiry	Discriminatory Inquiry
		4. Verify that applicant is above the minimum legal age (21), but without asking for a birth certificate.
		Age specifications or limitations in newspaper advertisements which may bar workers under or over a certain age.
Education	Academic, vocational, or professional education, and the public and private schools attended.	
Citizenship	Are you in the country on a visa which would not permit you to work here?	Any and all inquiries into whether applicant is now or intends to become a citizen of the U.S. or any other inquiry related to the aspect of citizenship.
National Origin and Ancestry	None.	Applicant's lineage, ancestry, national origin, or nationality. Nationality of applicant's parents or spouse.
Language	Language applicant speaks and/or writes fluently.	Applicant's mother tongue. Language commonly used by applicant at applicant's home. How the applicant acquired ability to read, write, or speak a foreign language.
Relatives	Names of relatives already employed by the company. Name and address of person to be notified in case of accident or emergency.	Name and/or address of any relative of applicant.
Military Experience	Military experience of applicant in the Armed Forces of the United States.	Applicant's military experience in other than U.S. Armed Forces.

EXHIBIT 9.4
Continued

	Acceptable Inquiry	Discriminatory Inquiry
	Whether applicant has received any notice to report for duty in the Armed Forces.	National Guard or Reserve Units of applicant.
		Draft classification or other eligibility for military service.
		Dates and conditions of discharge.
Organizations	Applicant's membership in any union or professional or trade organization.	All clubs, social fraternities, societies, lodges, or organizations to which the applicant belongs other than professional, trade, or service organizations.
	Names of any service organizations of which applicant is a member.	
References	Names of persons willing to provide professional and/or character references for applicant.	The name of applicant's pastor or religious leader.
	Names of persons who suggested applicant apply for a position with the employer.	
Sex and Marital Status	Maiden name of applicant.	Sex of applicant.
		Marital status of applicant.
		Dependents of applicant.
Arrest Record	Number and kinds of convictions for felonies.	The number and kinds of arrests of an applicant.
Height	None.	Any inquiry into height of applicant, except where it is a bona fide occupational requirement.

Source: Adapted from "Checklist to Avoid Bias Pitfalls," by James Strong. © Copyrighted, Chicago Tribune Company, all rights reserved, used with permission.

plicants do not normally list people who will provide negative information. Work references, on the other hand, have value, provided the reference will feel free to communicate. A telephone conversation between former manager and prospective manager is usually more useful for collecting information than a written inquiry because the applicant's former bosses can answer simply and directly with no tangible evidence that could be used

274 CHAPTER 9 Staffing

against them later. An employee who received a negative written reference could decide to use it as evidence in a defamation-of-character lawsuit against the author of that reference. Credit checks are considered discriminatory and are a questionable practice.

<u>Step 6: Physical examination.</u> Prior to tendering a job offer, some organizations require potential employees to take a physical examination. The purposes of the examination are to (1) prevent insurance claims for illnesses or injuries that occurred prior to employment by the company, (2) detect any communicable diseases, (3) certify that the person can physically perform the work. If there are physical requirements in the job description and job specifications, they must be valid. If they are not, the company may be accused of discrimination toward handicapped workers.

<u>Step 7: Offer of employment.</u> At this point, the top-ranking applicant is offered a job by management. This may involve a series of negotiations on initial salary, depending on the organization's compensation philosophy. A point to remember is that it is illegal to hire anyone who is not a U.S. citizen and unauthorized to work in the United States. Before an individual is hired, he or she must provide proof of citizenship or of authorization to work in the United States.

Role of the Individual Manager

The individual manager should be actively involved in the selection process. If the initial screening is not performed by the prospective applicant's manager, the in-depth interview will be. The manager should review the application blank and any test results in preparation for an in-depth interview.

After the interviews, the manager's further role in selection will be determined by the company's philosophy, size, degree of specialization, and the manager's ability. The manager may have the final decision on who is hired, may share the decision with his or her superior, or may have the decision made by the superior. In addition, the manager may be actively involved in the salary negotiations or have this taken care of by a superior or staff department. The manager needs to be comfortable with the hiring decision and, whenever possible, should be the person to make it.

If the candidate accepts the employment offer, the next phase—induction and orientation—commences.

④ | Induction and Orientation |

When an employee is hired, two processes are started: induction and orientation. The immediate goal of these processes is to bring the employee into the mainstream of the organization as quickly as possible. The purpose of the processes is to develop programs that turn "them" (new employees) and "us" (the company) into "we."

Induction

The purpose of **induction** is to provide the new employee with the necessary information about the company. It familiarizes the new person with the duties and benefits of employment. The employee receives pamphlets, fills in forms, gets a pass issued, and has fringe benefits explained. Management sees to it that the employee is provided with an explanation of the company history, its products or services, and the organization structure. The general purpose of this phase is to see that the employee learns where to go for answers and help, and what the important rules, policies, and procedures of the organization are.

The induction process is accomplished through an interaction of the employee, the immediate supervisor, and the personnel specialist if there is one. The time induction requires may be divided between one-to-one interactions and large-group education.

Orientation

Orientation continues what induction began. The new employee—having been exposed to the organization's formal systems, paperwork, and policies—is now introduced to the immediate working environment and co-workers. The purpose of this phase is to have the new employee become oriented to the working environment and operating reality.

The employee and manager will discuss specifics of the work: location, rules, equipment, procedures, and plans for training. In addition, the employee and manager have the opportunity to discuss and reinforce performance expectations that were initially discussed during the interview process. The new employee may be paired with an experienced employee for a period to help the socialization process. The pairing and one-to-one discussions are an attempt to reduce the employee's anxiety through meeting other people and allowing him or her the opportunity to discuss expectations and actual performance. The informal group further provides this type of feedback as the new employee interacts in the work environment.

The orientation phase is extremely important. Having the new employee become comfortable with the superior and the peer group is a "socialization" process as we discussed in Chapter 2. It needs to be planned and supported by management.

⑤ Training and Development

Training and development programs in an organization have different goals. Let's examine each in detail.

Training: Purposes and Techniques

Training supplies the skills, knowledge, and attitudes needed by individuals or groups to improve their abilities to perform their present jobs. Training for an employee is continuous throughout organizational life. First, training is used to give employees skills or to brush up existing skills to the level necessary to perform when new to the job. As the job changes or as an employee demonstrates the need for additional skills, the organization provides more training.[9]

Various training techniques can be employed by management. A person can be trained off the job in a classroom setting and then be sent to the workforce. Another approach is to use *OJT*, or on-the-job training. The person is trained while the job is being performed; training usually entails watching a fellow worker. A third approach is to use *vestibule training*: A simulated work environment is constructed; the trainee is placed in the environment to train without the pressure of meeting production figures.

One form of OJT that is successful is coaching of the employee by the supervisor. It has these basic steps:

1. Discussion of the process by the supervisor.
2. Demonstration of the task by the supervisor.
3. Individual performance by the trainee.
4. Feedback following the performance.

It is an informal, one-on-one teaching relationship between the manager and the employee. It has two main goals: to identify and encourage positive performance and to identify and remove barriers to negative performance.

Regardless of the type, training should be realistic. It should duplicate the actual means, materials, and environment the trainee should expect. Where possible, training programs and experiences should be designed with the trainee in mind. The ideal program would allow for constant feedback between trainee and trainer. It would allow people to progress at their own pace, accommodating individual differences. It also would allow one-on-one contacts between trainee and trainer. Finally, it should be conducted by people who know the material to be taught, know how to train, and want to conduct the training.

Development: Purposes and Techniques

Development, according to R. S. Schuler, "means preparing an employee for a future, but fairly well-defined job at a higher level."[10] Development programs get people ready for their and the organization's futures. Although training is often conducted "in-house" by organization employees, development usually takes place outside the immediate company environment and is often conducted by outside professionals. Development programs may send a person to a management seminar or workshop conducted by a university, a government agency, or an industry or a trade association. If the company offers a tuition refund for such a program, it encourages individuals to seek higher levels of formal education.

Development exposes people to skills, knowledge, and attitudes that will be helpful to them in higher positions. Efforts toward development often depend on an individual's personal drive and ambition and are not limited to company inventories of necessary skills or persons possessing them. Development activities such as management training programs may or may not be voluntary for individual workers, but in any case, they help participants prepare for the move into management or upgrade existing management skills. In most companies, there are more opportunities for development programs the higher one goes in management. Some companies offer their executives one year away, with pay, to earn their master's degree in business administration (MBA). Others, such as Xerox and Motorola, operate their own training and development centers, staffed in part with visiting professors and company managers.

In addition to seminars, workshops, college tuition refund programs, and leaves of absence for pursuit of advanced degrees, companies offer other development programs. Job rotation provides the opportunity for an employee to work on a variety of jobs in a work unit or in the organization. The rotation results in the person's developing an understanding of the interrelationship of activities and an overview of the work unit or organization. Internships, apprenticeships, or assistantships allow the individual to observe the work, ask questions, and imitate the practices of the incumbents.

Training and development programs attempt to meet the organization's demands for people. Both improve performances of individuals and of organizations. They reward ambition and act as incentives for a greater loyalty and commitment to the enterprise that offers them. They do so because they offer the means to gain greater security, to reach a higher level of job satisfaction, and to increase confidence and self-esteem. Companies that spend the time, money, and effort to develop and sponsor (or conduct) training and development programs are rewarded with a growing pool of talent capable of greater achievements and available for greater responsibilities.

Performance Appraisal

When an employee has received training and has performed in a job for a period of time, it is normal for an organization to conduct a performance appraisal.

Performance appraisal is a formal, structured system designed to measure the actual job performance of an employee compared to designated performance standards.[11] A manager should use appraisal to accomplish certain definite objectives:

1. Develop individual plans for improvement based on agreed-on goals, strengths and weaknesses.
2. Identify growth opportunities.
3. Document present job performance to provide superiors with information to make decisions on salary, promotion, demotion, transfer, and termination.
4. Provide the opportunity for formal feedback.

Organizations normally require managers to conduct formal performance appraisal sessions annually or semiannually. If the manager has supplied ongoing feedback to the employee between formal appraisal periods, then the appraisal session should merely provide the opportunity for formal documentation, open discussions, and the development of growth plans. Unfortunately, in many instances this is not the case. Performance appraisal can be used as the opportunity to "get" someone—hardly a constructive use. As we stated earlier, the purpose and expected result are documentation and planning.

What Are the Factors in Successful Appraisals?

The success of a performance appraisal is a function of the parties involved and the system used. Let's examine each factor.

The manager and the subordinate must be aware of the purposes behind a performance appraisal, and they must have faith in the process and the instruments or vehicles it uses. Each must take the time to prepare for the session. The manager needs to gather the results of his or her ongoing observations, specific performance records, ideas for improvement, and plans for growth and development; in addition, the manager must allow adequate time for reflection and summation. The employee has the same responsibilities.

Each party in the process must understand the appraisal system to be used and what criteria the employee is being measured against. If a manager holds all the cards or is making up the rules during the game, the employee will not receive a realistic performance appraisal; he or she will be confused, resentful, and disinclined to cooperate again.

The system must be appropriate for the job the employee is in. In some instances, a system is designed primarily for one category of personnel but is used for all employees; obviously, it will not be reflective of performance on the other jobs. In addition to being appropriate, the criteria to measure the employee should be specific. Finally, the criteria should provide for evaluating the employee against standards, not against another employee.

Types of Appraisal Systems

Performance appraisal systems have two components: One part is the criteria against which the employee is measured (for example, quality of work, knowledge, attitude); the other is the rating scale showing what the employee can achieve or perform on each criterion (good, 5 out of 10, 100 percent, etc.). As an example, consider that some of the criteria for measuring a student's performance are tests and classroom participation. The rating scale on a test might be 100 possible points; the rating scale on participation could be eight categories, ranging from "never volunteers" to "consistently creative participation."

There are two basic types of appraisal systems that can be used. Most systems are variations of these. Let's examine each system.

Subjective performance appraisal system. A subjective performance appraisal system is so titled because of the subjective (personal) viewpoint from which the appraiser makes his or her observations. Figure 9.5 (on page 282) provides an example of a subjective performance appraisal system. Notice the criteria—time management, attitude, knowledge of job, and communication. What does each category mean? What is attitude? What does "communication" refer to? Also notice the rating scale—excellent, good, fair, and poor. What does excellent mean to the rater? Or to you? How about good? Fair? Poor? What is the difference between good and fair?

A single problem faces both the manager and the employee. Rather than leading to dialogue about performance, the system can result in the two parties trying to defend interpretations of performance. Because of the lack of specific criteria (described factors of performance) and of a specific rating scale (increasing or decreasing descriptors of performance), the subjective appraisal system can result in the citing of critical incidents, comparisons to other employees, and judgments based on personality traits (positive and negative). Exhibit 9.5 illustrates a slightly less subjective system. Notice that the categories in the scale are described, as are the performance criteria. This is somewhat better, but still it is open to interpretation.

EXHIBIT 9.5
Subjective Performance Appraisal System

Work Philosophy/Habits

Factors/Performance Levels	1	2 3	4 5	6 7	8 9
1. Self-Improvement: Consider the desire to expand present capabilities in both depth and breadth. No opportunity to observe ( )	No interest in learning additional duties.	Limited interest in expanding job assignments, little interest in preparing for advancement.	Has demonstrated interest in additional assignments and shown some interest and preparation for advancement.	Has shown extra effort to learn additional job duties. Advancement preparation was or is being taken.	Very inquisitive concerning all phases of job-related assignments. Advancement preparation taken.
2. Attendance: Consider the regularity with which the employee reports to work.	Excessively absent.	Frequently absent.	Occasionally absent.	Rarely absent.	Almost never absent.
3. Punctuality: Consider number of occasions late. Punctuality is ( ) or is not ( ) essential for this job.	Excessively tardy.	Frequently tardy.	Occasionally tardy.	Rarely tardy.	Almost never tardy.

4. Work Planning: Consider how the workload is planned and organized for maximum efficiency.

No opportunity to observe ( )

Unsystematic, unable to organize workload.	Fair on routine but unable to organize variations effectively.	Efficient under normal conditions. Gives priority to important jobs.	Skillful in organizing and planning work. Meets emergencies promptly.	Exceptional efficiency; keeps priority items in proper perspective.

5. Conduct Under Stress: Consider the ability to perform under emotional stress or other pressure.

No opportunity to observe ( )

Easily rattled. Minimum pressure adversely affects job performance.	Pressure situations often limit job performance, easily rattled.	Has the ability to perform acceptably under stress, usually calm.	Tolerates pressure well. Responds coolly to crises.	Performs exceptionally well under pressure. Enjoys dealing with crises.

Principal strengths if any:

Principal needs or weaknesses if any:

What is the employee's potential for advancement?

    If so, to what job(s)?

What measures have been taken to improve this employee's worth to the Company?

Is the employee in the right job?

    If not, what would be more suitable?

Probationary Employee Only: Do you recommend retention of this employee?

Other comments:

Evaluated by _____ Relationship to Employee _____ How long have you been so associated? _____ Date _____

Reviewed by _____ Date _____

FIGURE 9.5
Subjective
performance
appraisal system

	Excellent	Good	Fair	Poor
Time Management		✔		
Attitude		✔		
Knowledge of Job	✔			
Communication			✔	

Objective performance appraisal system.   The second type of performance appraisal system is objective in design. Both the criteria for evaluation and the method of measurement in an objective performance appraisal are specific. Notice Exhibit 9.6. The criteria (production, turnover, quality control, absenteeism, and safety) are specific in nature. The rating scale has been replaced by specific goals or objectives to be reached in performance. The production goal, for example, is 15,000 units per month.

The employee knows what criteria the performance appraisal will be based on and what the measures will be (how performance measures up to goals). In this system, the employee and the manager establish goals

Source: Reprinted with special permission of King Features Syndicate, Inc.

EXHIBIT 9.6
Objective Performance Appraisal System

Goal-Setting Areas	Goals for 6 Months	Actual
Production: Actual units produced	15,000 per month	
Turnover: Percentage of personnel exiting a department per month	15%	
Quality Control: Percentage of units rejected per month	3%	
Absenteeism: Number of workhours lost from job due to absentee workers	10%	
Safety: Workhours lost	50 maximum	

together. They know what performance is based on and how it will be measured. Feedback is provided through reports. The employee knows where he or she stands at all times.

The objective system shown in Exhibit 9.6 is a derivation of **management by objectives** (MBO) and appraisal by results. Management by objectives is a one-on-one approach to improving performances of both individuals and the organization as a whole (see Chapter 5). It requires face-to-face meetings between managers and subordinates. Subordinates are asked to construct specific goals that will lead to improved performances. Supervisors suggest goals as well. Once specific goals are agreed on, they are assigned priorities, and times are set by which they should be achieved. Follow-up sessions are held periodically to review the progress being made, and adjustments to the goals are made as needed. Priorities may need to be changed as circumstances change, or new goals may have to be established. Additional resources may be needed to accomplish the goals. Individuals are evaluated on the number of goals they achieve, how they achieve them, and on the basis of how their performances have improved.

MBO, used as an appraisal system, depends on a commitment by top management. It begins in an organization at the top and filters down, on the basis of its success at the top and a preconditioning at lower levels to gain support for it. If it is to work, the people who are appraised with it must participate in goal setting. They need regular feedback and help in measuring their progress. Standards for performance must be agreed to by both manager and employee. When used properly, MBO develops strong commitments to progress toward goals, fosters an understanding of how one's position and efforts link to those of others, and gives a sense of equity to the entire appraisal process.[12]

Most applications of MBO to the appraisal process begin with clear and concise organizational objectives set by top management. These strategic goals dictate tactical goals required of departments, divisions, and individual employees. These short-term tactical goals are formulated by managers working together with their subordinates. Once goals have been agreed on, time limits are placed on each to facilitate the monitoring of the individual's progress. Throughout the appraisal period, comparisons are made between "what is" and "what should be." Revisions may be necessary either in the goals or in their time limits. New goals, time limits, or tactics to achieve goals may have to be mutually worked out.

Methods of Appraisal

The discussion to this point has centered on two methods of performance appraisal—manager appraisal of the subordinate and subordinate self-appraisal. In addition, peer appraisal can be used in a subjective appraisal system: The employee's peers are asked to evaluate him or her. This information is used as part of the manager's appraisal of the subordinate. Another method is upward appraisal, in which the subordinate evaluates the effectiveness of the superior, using a subjective system. Neither the peer nor upward system has had wide adoption.

Implementing Personnel Decisions

Through the process of performance appraisal, management acquires information to make employment decisions. For example, management can reward positive performance with an increase in pay by an amount based on the company's compensation program.

Other possible uses of the appraisal include decisions on promotions, transfers, demotions, and separations. These employment decisions not only affect employees but also influence the operation of the staffing process. These decisions result in individuals changing jobs or leaving the organization and in new jobs being created. Each possibility is examined next.

Promotions

One employment decision is a promotion. A **promotion** is a movement by a person into a position of higher pay and greater responsibilities. Promotions reward competence and ambition. They act as incentives to perform above the average in one's present job and to expand one's abilities, aptitudes, and knowledge through additional training and development.

Promotion decisions, even though they should be rewards for performance, are often influenced by other factors. Federal and state laws affect the ways in which promotions can be made. Affirmative action programs may dictate who or what kind of person gets the promotion. Perhaps promotion of the best qualified and most eligible will be blocked by seniority rules and the union agreement. Regardless, promotions should be based as much as possible on performance.

Transfers

A second employment decision is a transfer. A **transfer** represents a lateral move from one position to another that has similar pay and responsibility levels. Although there may be small differences between the jobs, they are relatively inconsequential. Management uses transfers most often to fill temporary vacancies. Sometimes, positions are created as a reward to allow a person to intern with or understudy another, higher job. These "assistant-to" positions help the transferee study the higher job up close and under the direct tutelage of the person who occupies it. Such moves are common when management is preparing to replace a person who is about to move up or out of the company.

Transfers are also used to staff a new operation, department, or division with a top-ranking, experienced nucleus of competent leaders. These persons will staff the operation over time, fleshing out the lower positions and, in some cases, providing for their own replacements.

Demotions

Another employment decision is demotion. A **demotion** is a movement from one position to another that has less pay or responsibility attached to it. Demotions can be used for punishment, but most organizations refuse it as an option, preferring instead to suspend the employee or assess a financial penalty through the forfeiture of pay. The reason for this reluctance is that a demotion staffs a position with an embarrassed and often angry worker who is not likely to be productive or any better behaved than she or he was in the former position. What this reluctance means is that a person who is promoted cannot usually return to his or her former position if he or she has trouble adjusting to the new one. This is especially true where the lesser position has already been filled.

Demotions have their place in staffing, however. When a demotion is made to keep an employee, presumably as a temporary measure, it can be an important staffing solution. If a person's job is being eliminated, he or she may be offered a position that represents a demotion. There is no shame or embarrassment attached to such a move, only concern for the individual. The hope is to give the person time to get retrained or qualified for a higher position. Some people survive the experience quite well, while others begin the search for other employment immediately, with or without their employer's knowledge or consent.

Separations

The last category of employment decision making by management is separation. **Separation** is the loss of an employee to an organization. If an employee has not performed well, management can terminate (involuntarily separate) the employee from the company. Separations also may happen naturally in the course of the business operations: People retire or resign. These separations are categorized as voluntary separations.

At times, it is necessary to temporarily separate employees from the company. A temporary separation is categorized as a *layoff* and is dictated by the level of business the company is experiencing. Companies have developed layoff procedures combining criteria of performance and seniority to determine the order of layoff.

Summary

- People are the most important of all an organization's resources.
- Staffing attempts to identify, attract, and retain qualified personnel. It begins with human resource planning and affects employees throughout their tenure in an organization.
- All aspects of staffing are affected by equal employment opportunity legislation. This legislation defines acceptable management actions during the staffing process. Affirmative action programs go beyond equal employment legislation. They attempt to develop plans for overcoming the results of past discrimination.
- Human resource forecasting attempts to predict the future demands for people and jobs for an organization. It is based on top management's strategic plans and on turnover.
- Human resource inventories list jobs and people in an organization. It must contain up-to-date information about individuals and the jobs that they perform.
- Recruitment involves finding people to meet the organization's demands for people with specialized skills, knowledge, and aptitudes.

- Selection evaluates the prospective candidates and chooses the one whose credentials most closely match job requirements.
- Induction and orientation involve providing a new employee with information about the company and with the opportunity to become familiar with the work, the supervisor, and the co-workers.
- Training tries to provide the employees with skills and attributes needed to perform in their jobs; development attempts to prepare employees for a future job.
- Performance appraisal involves measuring an employee's actual performance against designated performance standards. Success depends on the manager, the employee, and the system.
- Employment decisions that influence the staffing process in the organization are promotions, transfers, demotions, and separations.

Glossary of Essential Terms

adverse impact	The effect a selection device has when it excludes a significantly greater number of minority group members or women than other groups.
demotion	The movement from one position to another that has less pay or responsibility attached to it.
development	Preparing an employee for a future but fairly well-defined job at a higher level.
induction	Providing a person entering a company with the necessary information about the company.
management by objectives (MBO)	An approach to appraisals that requires subordinates to negotiate goals along with priorities and timetables for them in concert with their superiors.
objective performance appraisal	Appraisal system in which the criteria for performance and the rating scale are defined.
orientation	Bringing a person into the specific working environment with emphasis on socialization, the specific work, and the work environment.
performance appraisal	A formal, structured system designed to measure an employee's actual performance against designated performance standards.

promotion	Movement by a person into a position of higher pay and greater responsibilities.
recruitment	Finding people to meet the organization's demands for special skills, aptitudes, knowledge, and experience.
selection	Evaluating applicants and choosing the person who most closely meets job demands.
separation	A temporary or permanent way of losing employees.
staffing	The management activity that attempts to attract good people to an organization and to hold on to them.
subjective performance appraisal	Appraisal system in which the criteria for performance and the rating scale are not specifically defined.
training	Imparts skill, knowledge, and attitudes needed by individuals or groups to improve their abilities to perform in their present jobs.
transfer	A lateral move from one position to another having similar pay and a similar responsibility level.

Review Questions

1. Can you define this chapter's essential terms? If not, consult the preceding glossary.
2. Why is the staffing function important to an organization? What is the relationship of the staffing function to the functions of planning and organizing?
3. Identify the eight steps in the staffing process, and describe each step.
4. Distinguish between the purpose of equal employment opportunity and affirmative action in the staffing process.
5. What are the three elements involved in human resource planning?
6. Describe the basic steps in the selection process and the purposes of each.
7. Distinguish between the purposes of induction and orientation. What activities are included in an induction program? In an orientation program?
8. What is the purpose of development? What are three types of development experiences or activities? *seminars, tuition, school*
9. What are the four objectives of performance appraisal?

References

1. The Equal Employment Opportunity Act of 1972, Subcommittee on Labor of the Committee on Labor and Public Welfare, United States Senate (March 1972), p. 3.
2. John Klinfelter and James Thompkins, "Adverse Impact in Employment Selection," *Public Personnel Management* (May–June 1976), pp. 199–204.
3. James Ledvinka and Robert Gatewood, "EEO Issues with Pre-Employment Inquiries," *The Personnel Administrator*, 22, no. 2 (February 1977), pp. 22–26.
4. Howard Black and Robert Pennington, "Labor Market Analysis as a Test of Discrimination," *Personnel Journal*, 59 (August 1980), pp. 649–652.
5. Kenneth Marino, "Conducting an Internal Compliance Review of Affirmative Action," *Personnel*, 57 (March–April 1980), pp. 22–34.
6. R. S. Schuler, *Personnel and Human Resource Management* (St. Paul: West Publishing Co., 1981), pp. 75–76.
7. "Toyota Takes Pains, and Time, Filling Its Jobs at Its Kentucky Plant," *The Wall Street Journal* (December 1, 1987), p. 1.
8. Anthony Pell, *Recruiting and Selecting Personnel* (New York: Regents, 1969), pp. 96–98.
9. L. A. Klatt, R. G. Murdick, and F. E. Schuster, *Human Resources Management: A Behavioral Systems Approach* (Homewood, Ill.: Richard D. Irwin, 1978), p. 165.
10. Schuler, *Personnel and Human Resource Management*, p. 349.
11. Ibid., p. 221.
12. For additional insights to MBO as an appraisal process, see Anthony P. Raja, *Managing by Objectives* (Glenview, Ill.: Scott, Foresman, 1974); and H. Levison, "Management by Whose Objectives?" *Harvard Business Review* (July–August 1970), pp. 125–135.

Readings

Bernstein, Aaron. "Not So Fast, Baby." *Business Week* (February 29, 1988), pp. 48–52(2).

Hardesty, Sarah and Nehama Jacobs. *Success and Betrayal: The Crisis of Women in Corporate America*. New York: Simon & Schuster, 1987.

Jones, Constance. *Beat the MBAs to the Top*. Reading, Mass.: Addison-Wesley, 1987.

Paznik, Megan Jill. "Team Up with a Temp Service." *Administrative Management* (February 1988), pp. 25–29.

Schein, Edgar, ed. *The Art of Managing Human Resources*. New York: Oxford University Press, 1987.

Schneier, Craig, Richard Beatty, and Glenn McEvoy. *Personnel/Human Resources Management Today.* Reading, Mass.: Addison-Wesley, 1988.

Shipper, Frances and Frank Shipper. "Beyond EEO: Toward Pluralism." *Business Horizons,* 30, no. 3 (March–June 1987), pp. 53–61.

Smith, Michael. "Feedback as a Performance Technique." *Management Solutions,* 32, no. 4 (April 1987), pp. 20–29.

Stackel, Leslie. "The Flexible Work Place." *Employment Relations Today,* 14, no. 2 (Summer 1987), pp. 189–197.

Yate, Martin John. *Hiring the Best: A Manager's Guide to Effective Interviewing.* Boston: Bob Adams, 1987.

C A S E S

9.1 Making Do

"Thank you, Miss Perkins, for coming in. We will let you know as soon as we make our hiring decision." Muriel was getting desperate. She has interviewed four people in about as many weeks and has still not found a replacement for Edwards. "He'll be leaving next week, and if I don't find someone before he leaves, we won't be able to train Edwards' replacement properly," thought Muriel. She decided to go down to personnel and see for herself if anything new had developed.

"Hi, Allison. Have you been able to shake any more applicants lose from that workforce out there?"

"Muriel, I've been looking hard, but the labor market is tight for skilled technicians. We've spent about $5,000 on advertising, and we have found only the four people I've sent you. Won't any of them fit your needs?"

"None of them is really right. Their prime problem is a lack of up-to-date knowledge about the latest technology in superconductivity. Most of them have been out of school for years, and none of them has firsthand experience with the kind of research we need done."

"I wish you had given us more notice," said Allison. "We really should be advertising in scientific journals, but they need at least two months' lead time in order to print an ad."

"I gave you all the notice I had. Edwards just decided to move on, and when he told me he was leaving, I told you."

"I feel I should also tell you, Muriel, that we are not able to match benefits and pay for electronics people. Our industry is very competitive, and we won't be able to pay a new person what Edwards makes now."

As the week ended, Muriel had no new applicants to interview and decided to hire Lynn Perkins. "At least Edwards will have a week to work with her before leaving the company," thought Muriel. She called Lynn and offered her the research job. Lynn accepted and reported the following Monday for work. Muriel, as head of research, assigned Lynn to work with Edwards and crossed her fingers in the hope that the two would have enough time together to keep the project on target.

By Wednesday of Lynn's first week and Edwards' last, it was clear to all the parties that Lynn was a poor choice. As Edwards put it, "She just lacks the basics. She has never really worked in such a demanding laboratory environment and has to be told what to do in each step." Edwards was asked to stay on for another week but refused. "I've got other commitments," he said to Muriel, "and I can't stay past this Friday."

Muriel also found herself facing another problem. Paul Gambini, a junior lab assistant, was unhappy because he had not been asked to move up into the Edwards job. He resented Lynn and felt that his background was as good as, if not better than, hers.

"I didn't offer you the job because you are new at your present job," said Muriel. Paul countered by explaining that he has been working with Edwards for several months and knows more about the project than Lynn does. Although he is new to the company (he was hired when he graduated seven months ago), Paul feels that the job should have been offered to him. Muriel sensed that he was indeed hostile toward Lynn, and after talking with Lynn, she confirmed this feeling. Next week, Lynn would be Paul's boss in the lab, and Muriel was concerned about what that could lead to.

For Discussion

1. How can a company protect itself against the loss of an employee like Edwards?
2. What has Muriel failed to deal with so far in the staffing process? Provide examples from the case to support your answer.
3. What can be done about Lynn's situation now or in the near future?

9.2 Arthur's First Day

Michael Henderson was looking forward to Arthur Duffy's arrival. Mike had not had a chance to interview Arthur because of an illness in his family, but from all the reports Mike had received from personnel, Arthur was just the right person to fill the hole in Mike's shop. As Mike was reviewing his orientation program, Arthur appeared in the office. Mike greeted him and asked him to sit down. After some brief words about the weather and the trip to the plant, Mike got down to business.

After a few minutes of conversation, it became obvious to Mike that Arthur knew next to nothing about the company. Mike was also surprised to find out that Arthur had not been tested for his mechanical skills. After a phone call to personnel, Mike discovered that the results of Arthur's physical exam had not yet arrived. This meant that Mike could not put him to work. Irritated, Mike decided to show Arthur around the shop anyway and to introduce him to his co-workers.

Following the tour and the introductions, Mike took Arthur to lunch in the company cafeteria. During the meal, Mike cautioned Arthur about several things. First, Mike told Arthur to stay away from Jackson and his crowd because, Mike said, they were troublemakers and could cause problems for Arthur. Second, Arthur was cautioned not to join the union because, in Mike's words, "the top decision makers around here hate the union. If you join, your chances at a promotion will be shot." Finally, Mike warned Arthur to ignore any deviation from shop rules that he would witness once on the job. "I don't want you to pick up any bad habits," said Mike, "but I don't want you to squeal on anyone either."

When Arthur and Mike returned to Mike's office, a copy of the mechanical aptitude test was there. "Here is the test," said Mike as he handed it and a pen to Arthur. "Just sit here and do the best you can. It's no big deal, but company policy demands that you take it before you can work in the shop. When you're done, just give it to me and take off. I'll see you tomorrow at start-up time, and if we have the results of your physical, I'll put you to work in the shop."

While Arthur was taking the test, Mike returned to his pile of papers and proceeded to turn out the work as usual. During the next two hours, Mike entertained two visitors, took and made several phone calls, and disciplined a worker in front of Arthur. When Arthur finally finished, it was after 4 P.M., so Mike left the plant with him.

"Say, what are the hours here anyway?" asked Arthur.

"We start at 8 A.M. and quit at 5 P.M., with an hour for lunch. Any more questions?"

For Discussion

1. What specific errors in the staffing process are evident in this situation? What should be done to correct them?

2. What did Mike do with Arthur that you would not have done?

Human Motivation

OUTLINE

ESSENTIAL TERMS

equity theory
expectancy theory
hygiene factors
job enlargement
job enrichment

job rotation
motivation
motivation factors
needs
reinforcement theory

LEARNING OBJECTIVES

After reading and discussing this chapter, you should be able to do the following:

1. Define this chapter's essential terms.
2. Discuss the factors that stimulate and influence motivation.
3. List and give an example of the five need levels.
4. Discuss the impact of hygiene and motivation factors in the work environment.
5. Explain the characteristics of a person with high achievement needs.
6. Discuss the relationship of a person's expectations to motivated behavior.
7. Explain the relationship of reinforcement to motivation.
8. Explain how a person's level of motivation is influenced by equity.

How Do You Feel About Your Job?

The Hawthorne studies (Chapter 8) began a new phase in American management history. They started an investigation into the nature of people and their performances at work that will continue perhaps indefinitely. Most researchers believe that we have only scratched the surface in our search for understanding of the complexities of human nature.

Theories about human nature now recognize the need to consider many variables while attempting to analyze and interpret human behavior. People must be studied along with their jobs, their organizations, and other influences of the many different arenas in which they exist.

The need to continue investigations into the causes and consequences of human behavior at work has probably never been more necessary than it is now. The popular press and academic journals are filled with articles on the "blue-collar blues" and "white-collar woes." The book *Working*, by Studs Terkel, investigated the ways in which 133 people from many different occupational areas viewed their jobs. According to this book, many have experienced boredom and alienation. The price our nation and we consumers pay for worker alienation and dissatisfaction is huge. Our industries and economy are plagued with poor quality goods and services, high employee turnover and absenteeism, wasted time and materials that are lost to the production process, and ever-increasing costs for the things we need and buy. It is not difficult to understand why more than 35 percent of the new cars sold in America each year are foreign imports. It is difficult, however, to determine what individuals and organizations can do about it.

One area to examine in trying to determine the causes of boredom and dissatisfaction of workers on the job is motivation—the topic of this chapter, the first of two focusing on the management function of directing. Our major concerns in this chapter are to examine the concept of motivation and to present theories of motivation to assist managers in creating a supportive climate for performance. The next chapter focuses on leadership, the second major aspect of directing.

Motivation Defined

One of the continual challenges of management is the motivation of employees. As managers analyze their workforces, they can always see some people who outperform others of equal skill. A closer look might reveal instances in which a person with outstanding talents is consistently outperformed by someone having lesser talents. Why? These latter employees appear willing to exert more effort, to try harder, to accomplish their goals. Often these hard workers are described by their bosses as "motivated employees." The manager has made an accurate observation about motivation but has not given an explanation. What caused the workers to behave in that way? For the answer, we need to look at the person and a person's needs.

The Motivation Model

The needs of a person provide the basis for a motivation model. **Needs** are deficiencies a person is experiencing at a particular time. The needs may be physiological—body needs, such as food, water, air—or psychological—affiliation with others; self-esteem. The needs create a tension (stimulus) that results in wants. The person then develops a behavior or set of behaviors to satisfy the want. The behavior results in action toward goal achievement.[1]

Figure 10.1 illustrates the relationship of needs to performance. It contains an example of this model in action: A person is hungry (need); realizing this triggers a want (food); the person chooses to cook a hamburger (behavior), which he or she will eat (action to achieve the goal). Afterward, the person feels no hunger pangs (feedback).

As a manager, you are probably asking, "Is that all there is?" The answer is no. We have identified the foundation for motivation in this model, but there are influences on the motivated behavior of a person: Why did the person choose a hamburger instead of cereal? Why did the person cook the hamburger instead of buying it? Has the behavior been used before? If so, did it satisfy the need? Was the person still hungry?

Let's look at a more integrative approach, as shown in Figure 10.2.

The Integrated Motivation Model

Unsatisfied needs stimulate wants. As the person is choosing a behavior to satisfy the need, he or she must evaluate several factors:

1. *Past experiences.* All the person's past experiences with the situation at hand enter into the motivation model. These include experiences with a particular behavior, satisfactions derived, frustrations, effort required, and the relationship of performance to rewards.

2. *Environmental influences.* The person's behavior choices are affected by the environment, which is composed of the values of the organization as well as the expectations and actions of the manager.

3. *Perceptions.* The individual is influenced by his or her perceptions of the expected effort required to achieve performance, the absolute value of the reward, and the value in relation to what peers have received for the same effort.

FIGURE 10.1
Basic motivation
model

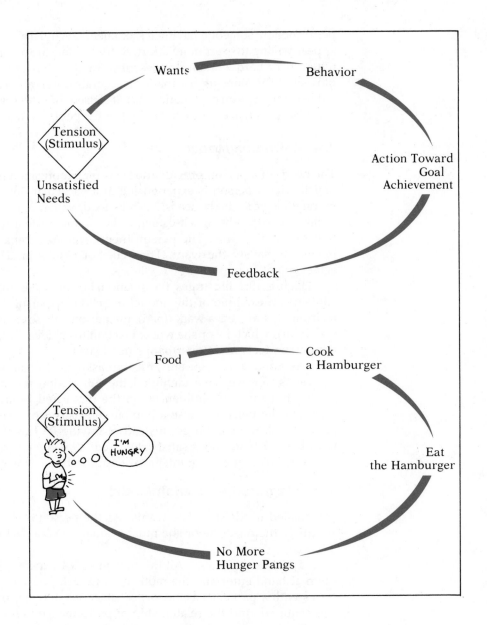

In addition to these three variables, skills and incentives (positive and negative results) have been added to the model. *Skills* are the person's capabilities (usually the result of training) for performing, and *incentives* are factors created by management to encourage workers to perform a task. Let's look at the process again: Unsatisfied needs stimulate wants. In con-

FIGURE 10.2
Integrated
motivation model

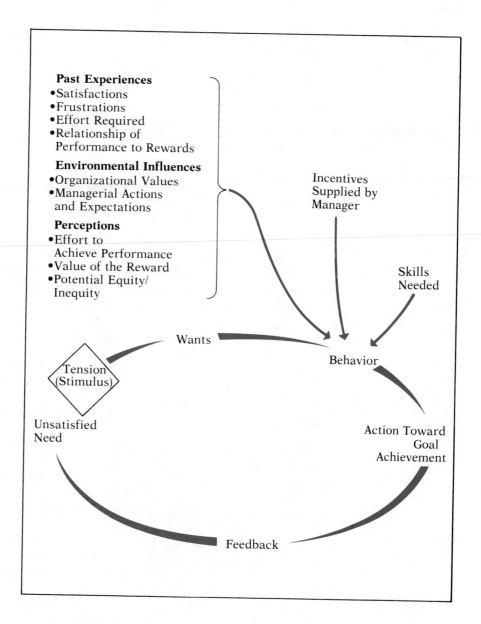

sidering behaviors to satisfy the wants, the person is evaluating the rewards or punishments associated with the performance (incentives); his or her abilities to take action (skills); and past experiences, environmental influences, and perceptions. This leads us to the definition of **motivation**: The interaction of a person's internalized needs and external influences that determines behavior designed to achieve a goal.

You are now able to explore some theories of motivation. The theories provide a manager with insight into motivated behavior. A starting point is to examine an employee's needs.

Motivation Theories That Focus on Needs

Maslow's Hierarchy of Needs

Psychologist Abraham H. Maslow has given us the theory of the hierarchy of needs. The hierarchy is based on four premises:[2]

1. Only an unsatisfied need can influence behavior; a satisfied need is not a motivator.

✗2. A person's needs are arranged in a priority order of importance. Thus the priorities (hierarchy) go from the most basic needs (water, food, shelter) to the most complex (ego and self-actualization).

3. As the person's needs are met on one level, the person advances to the next level of needs. He or she will focus on the first-level need until it is minimally satisfied before moving to the next level.

4. If satisfaction is not maintained for a once-satisfied need, it will become a priority need again. For example, if a person has satisfied safety needs and has advanced to the social needs level, safety will become a priority once again if the person is fired from her or his job.

The five levels.   Figure 10.3 shows the hierarchy of needs in their order of occurrence (priority). The first category is composed of physiological (physical) needs. These are the primary or basic-level needs consisting of water, air, food, shelter, and avoidance of pain. In the working environment, management tries to satisfy these needs primarily through salary and by eliminating threats to physical safety.

When the physiological needs are met to the satisfaction of the individual, safety needs become a priority as motivators. Expressions for our need for safety include employee unions, jobs with tenure, and desires for insurance and retirement programs. All of us desire a society in which we can be free from assault, tyranny, and other threats to our physical and emotional sense of security.[3] As with physiological needs, management attempts to satisfy safety needs primarily through salary.

The love needs (affiliation or social needs) become dominant when safety needs have been minimally gratified. People desire friendship, companionship, and a place in a group. Love needs include both giving and receiving.[4] These needs are met by frequent interaction with fellow workers and acceptance by others.

FIGURE 10.3
Abraham Maslow's
hierarchy of human
needs

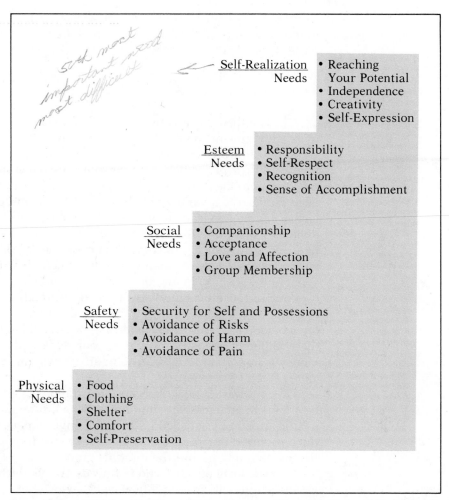

Source: Abraham H. Maslow, "A Theory of Human Motivation," *Psychological Review* 50 (1943): 370–396.

The next level in the hierarchy, <u>esteem needs,</u> includes the desire for self-respect and for the recognition of one's abilities by others. These conditions must be based on real and earned capacities and achievements in the individuals and on real respect from others. Satisfaction for these needs gives pride, self-confidence, and a true sense of importance. Lack of satisfaction of these needs can give a feeling of inferiority, weakness, and helplessness. Esteem needs can be met in an organization through recognition by peers and superiors of the person's work, by acquiring organizational titles, and by the accomplishment of work projects.

Maslow's highest need level, <u>self-actualization or self-realization</u>, refers to the desire for fulfillment. It represents the need to maximize the use of one's skills, abilities, and potential.

Implications for managers.   Maslow's theory has a number of implications for managers:

1. The theory is a general needs theory. Its categorization applies to all environments and not specifically to work.

2. A difficulty of working with needs theory is that people are unique in their perceptions and personalities. They can seek different satisfaction to the same need category in many ways. Each unsatisfied need can lead to a variety of behaviors, actions, and goals. Additionally, just as one motive leads to different behaviors, the same behavior in individuals can spring from different motives. The act of shopping for a new car, for instance, can come from many needs. Some people view an automobile as a way of gaining friends. Others view it as a statement about one's position in life, one's standard of living or status. Others see it primarily functionally; others, aesthetically; and so on. For this reason and others, it is dangerous to attempt to read motives by simply observing a person's actions or behavior. Figure 10.4 illustrates how money meets different needs for people. Recently 2,000 adults were asked why money is important to them. The figure shows how the majority of their answers can be categorized.

3. A thwarted need can cause frustration for an employee and will be a force in an employee until it is satisfied. It might be satisfied off the job, or it might be satisfied in the work environment in competition with the recognized organization. The esteem need, for example, can be satisfied by both unions and the informal group.

4. The level of satisfaction of needs always fluctuates. Once a need is satisfied, it will cease to influence behavior—but only for a time. Needs never remain fully satisfied.

Herzberg's Two-Factor Theory

A second needs theory was developed by psychologist Frederick Herzberg and his associates. The theory, called the two-factor or hygiene–motivation theory, uncovered one set of factors that produce job satisfaction and motivation and another set of factors that lead to job dissatisfaction. According to Herzberg, factors that can produce dissatisfaction are called hygiene factors. Those that can produce job satisfaction are called motivation factors.[5]

Hygiene factors.   Hygiene factors are the primary cause of unhappiness on the job. They are extrinsic to the job—that is, they do not relate directly

FIGURE 10.4
Money meets many
needs

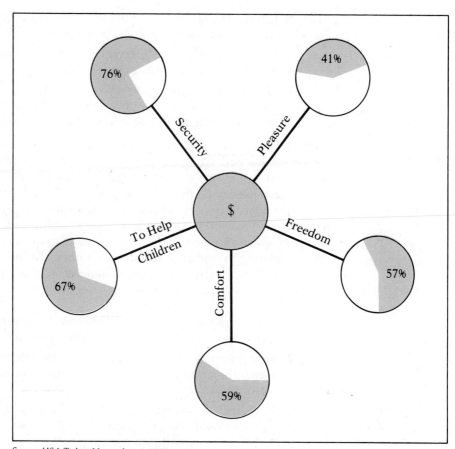

Source: USA Today, November 4, 1987, p. 1B

to a person's work, to its real nature. These are part of a job's environment—
its context, not its content. When an employer fails to provide these factors
in sufficient quality to its employees, job dissatisfaction will be the result.
When they are provided in sufficient quality, they will not necessarily act
as motivators—stimuli for growth or greater effort. They will only lead
employees to experience no job dissatisfaction.[6] These factors include:

1. Salary—adequate wages, salaries, and fringe benefits.
2. Job security—company grievance procedures and seniority privileges.
3. Working conditions—adequate heat, light, ventilation, and
   hours of work.
4. Status—privileges, job titles, and other symbols of rank and position.

5. Company policies—the policies of the organization and the fairness in administering those policies.

6. Quality of technical supervision—whether or not the employee is able to receive answers to job-related questions.

7. Quality of interpersonal relations among peers, supervisors, and subordinates—social opportunities as well as the development of comfortable operating relationships.

Motivation factors.   Motivation (or growth) factors are the primary cause of job satisfaction. They are intrinsic to a job because they relate directly to the real nature (job content) of the work people perform. When an employer fails to provide these factors in sufficient quality to employees, they will experience no job satisfaction. When they are provided in sufficient quality, they affect and provide job satisfaction and high performance. People require different kinds and degrees of motivation factors. What will be stimulating to one may not be to another. To individuals who desire them, motivation factors with the right amount of quality act as stimuli for psychological and personal growth.[7] These factors include:

1. Achievement—opportunity for accomplishment and for contributing something of value when presented with a challenge.

2. Recognition—acknowledgment that contributions have been worth the effort and that the effort has been noted and appreciated.

3. Responsibility—acquisition of new duties and responsibilities, either through the expansion of a job or by delegation.

4. Advancement—opportunity to improve one's organizational position as a result of job performance.

5. The work itself—opportunity for self-expression, personal satisfaction, and challenge.

6. Possibility of growth—opportunity to increase knowledge and develop through job experiences.

Figure 10.5 illustrates the hygiene–motivator factors. The hygiene factors operate in a range from no dissatisfaction, if they are present in the work environment, to high job dissatisfaction, if they are not present. The motivators, if present in the work environment, can provide high satisfaction. If not present, no satisfaction can result.

Figure 10.6 provides a comparison of Maslow's and Herzberg's view of needs. The hygiene factors are similar to Maslow's physiological, safety, and affiliation need levels. The motivation factors are similar to his esteem and self-realization needs.

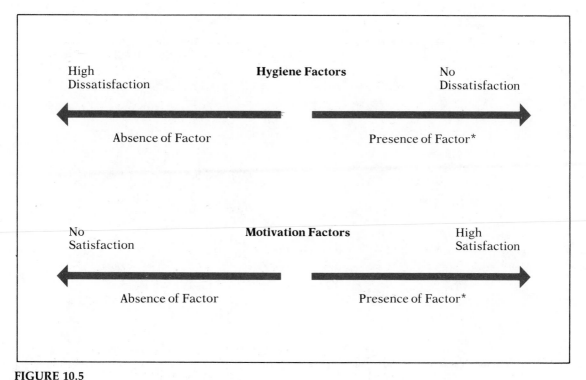

FIGURE 10.5
Herzberg's hygiene–motivator factors
*The quality of each factor present also influences each employee's level of satisfaction or dissatisfaction.

Implications for management. Herzberg's theory has the following implications for managers:

1. This theory relates specifically to the work environment, while Maslow's is a general theory applying to all environments.
2. Management can use the theory to focus its efforts on ensuring the presence of and quality in hygiene and motivation factors as a foundation on which to build motivation. In the absence of quality, employees may face an "unclean" environment, which can lead to dissatisfaction for the workforce.

McClelland's Need Achievement Theory

A third needs theory, developed through the work of David McClelland, relates to three needs: achievement, power, and affiliation.[8] Achievement

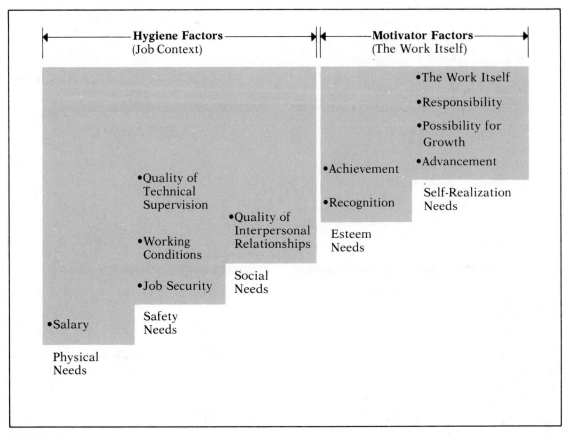

FIGURE 10.6
Comparison of Maslow's needs hierarchy and Herzberg's hygiene–motivator theories

relates to individual performance; power and affiliation are interpersonal in nature. The three are defined:

1. Achievement—desire to excel or achieve in relation to a set of standards.
2. Power—desire to control others or have influence over others.
3. Affiliation—desire for friendship, cooperation, and close interpersonal relationships.

Most of the study on the subject has focused on the achievement motivation. There are two points of note. It was observed that a strong achievement need was related to how well individuals were motivated to perform their work tasks. In addition, McClelland discovered that the achievement need could be strengthened by training.

The high achiever. The person who is described as a high achiever has the following characteristics:[9]

1. Achievers have a compelling need for personal achievement in doing the job or task, rather than for the rewards associated with it. The job and goal performance are what motivate the high achiever. This characteristic also means there is a strong need to excel in performing the task (for the means as well as the end). The high achiever wants to do it more efficiently than it has been done before, to do it better.

2. Achievers prefer to take personal responsibility for solving their problems rather than leaving the outcome to others. As a result, achievers can be viewed as loners, and at times appear to have difficulty delegating authority.

3. Achievers prefer to set moderate goals they think they can achieve. Their goal setting involves "stretching" to achieve the results because easy goals (high probability of success) would provide no challenge. Difficult goals (low probability of success) would mean the achiever is gambling on success; not only would the achiever not be in control of that situation, but also there could be no sense of achievement satisfaction from the event if it fails or is accomplished by happenstance.

4. Achievers prefer immediate and concrete feedback on performance. The rapid feedback is to assist achievers in goal measurement. The nature of the feedback needs to be in terms of goal performance (rather than personality variables) for the achiever to determine what needs to be done to improve performance.

Implications for management. McClelland's theory has the following implications for managers:

1. Managers should make a concerted effort to identify and to work with individuals with high achievement motivation. The ability to set goals and the desire for responsibility can be capitalized on in the work environment through delegation.

2. Achievers should be provided immediate, concrete feedback if their talents are to be utilized.

Figure 10.7 provides a comparison of the three needs theories. Each theory provides the manager with an understanding of the cause of behavior from a different viewpoint. Maslow's theory provides a hierarchy classification of needs. Herzberg provides a discussion of needs in relation to the job environment: hygiene factors, which are context related,

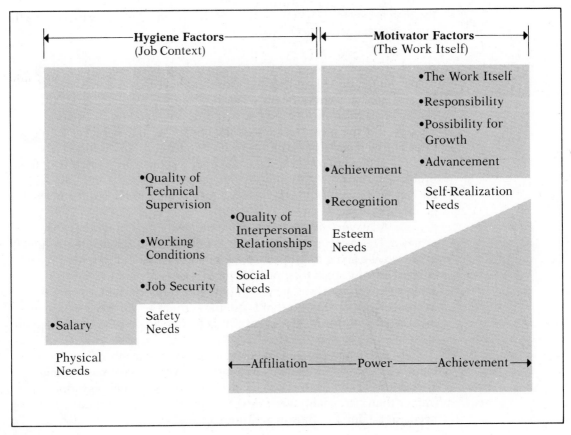

FIGURE 10.7
Comparison of Maslow's, Herzberg's, and McClelland's theories

and motivation factors, which are content related. McClelland's power and achievement relate to Maslow's higher order needs and to Herzberg's motivators.

Motivation Theories That Focus on Behaviors

Up to this point, we have discussed three motivation theories relating to the trigger for motivation, the needs of the individual. We are now ready to introduce three more theories indicating why people choose a particular behavior to satisfy these needs. These discuss the influences illustrated in Figure 10.2.

Expectancy Theory

Vroom's **expectancy theory** states that individuals will evaluate various behavior strategies on these bases: (1) the effort required for performance, (2) whether the performance will have a desired outcome, and (3) how valuable that outcome is to the employee. It includes three variables:[10]

1. Valence—How attractive is the reward? This is the strength or importance of the reward to the individual. It deals with the unsatisfied need of the individual.

2. Instrumentality—What is the possibility of a certain performance leading to the desired reward or outcome? This deals with the potential to achieve the desired outcome as the result of performance.

3. Expectation—Will the effort achieve performance? This entails an evaluation of how much effort the performance will take and the probability of achieving performance.

An example. John Friedman, an administrative assistant, has been requested at the last minute (Friday afternoon) to develop a presentation for his boss by Monday morning on the six-month budget results. A quick analysis shows John this will be a four-hour project. There are two behaviors immediately possible: stay and do the work, or take it home over the weekend.

Situation 1: Staying at work for the required four hours will result in a completed presentation by Monday (expectancy). John also knows from past experience that completing a project of this nature will be recognized by his boss and be lauded (instrumentality). John has a high regard for this recognition because it eventually will lead to a promotion. What bothers John is that working late on Friday will interfere with plans and may cause domestic problems (valence).

Source: Reprinted by permission of USF Inc.

Situation 2: Both the expectancy and instrumentality remain the same as with situation 1. The difference is that John's behavior is the result of the value of the reward. He has considered the value of the reward. By taking the work home, John will still receive his boss's recognition but will not receive negative recognition at home for interfering with social plans (valence).

In this process, John went through a series of questions: "Can I accomplish the task?" (Yes, it will take four hours, but I have the ability to do it.) "What's in it for me?" (When I do the task it can bring both positive and negative recognition [situation 1] or positive recognition [situation 2].) "Is it worth it?" (The positive is, but the negative isn't.)

Implications for managers.   The expectancy theory has these implications for managers:

1. The expectancy theory is heavily influenced by people's perceptions of outcomes to specific kinds of behavior. If an individual expects an outcome, possesses the competence to achieve it, and wants it badly enough, he or she will exhibit the behavior required by the boss and the organization. If a person expects that an undesirable outcome (from that person's point of view) will result from a specific behavior, she or he will be less inclined to exhibit that behavior. If a manager knows each individual subordinate, and knows their expectations and desires, the manager can tailor outcomes associated with specific behaviors.[11]

2. When managers are working with employees to develop motivated behavior, they need to be certain to do the following things:

   a. Find out what outcomes are perceived as desirable by employees and provide them. Outcomes the company provides may be intrinsic (reward, recognition, promotion) or extrinsic (pay, security). For an outcome to be satisfying to an individual employee, it must be perceived by the employee, be related to the needs and values that the individual wants to fulfill, and be consistent with the individual's expectations of what he or she should receive.[12]

   b. Effectively communicate desired behaviors and their outcomes. Employees need to know what is acceptable and what is not acceptable to the organization.

   c. Link rewards to performance. Once the acceptable performance level is attained, rewards should follow.

   d. Be aware that people and their goals, needs, desires, and levels of performance differ. The manager must set a level of performance that is attainable.

   e. Strengthen each individual's perceptions of his or her abilities to execute desired behaviors and achieve their outcomes. Provide guidance and direction.

Reinforcement Theory

A second theory that examines the "why" in behavior motivation has its foundations in the work of B. F. Skinner's operant conditioning.[13] The emphasis of **reinforcement theory** is that the behavior of a person in a situation is influenced by the rewards or penalties that person experienced in a similar situation. John, the administrative assistant in our previous example, received positive recognition from his boss for the extra effort on the project (weekend work). This was positive reinforcement of John's motivation and should influence John's behavior when the boss requests another last-minute project. Figure 10.8 provides an illustration of this situation.

The reinforcement theory introduces a major point for managers to understand about motivation—that much of motivated behavior is learned behavior.[14] The employee learns over time what type of performance is acceptable to the organization and what type of performance is not acceptable. This organizational learning that all employees go through becomes a factor in the motivation model by way of past experience (look again at Figure 10.2).

Types of reinforcement.   There are three main types of reinforcement behaviors available to managers: positive (reward), negative (punishment), and ignoring a subordinate's misbehavior. Of these three approaches, the first most often leads to long-range growth in individuals through lasting changes for the good in their behaviors.

FIGURE 10.8
The reinforcement process

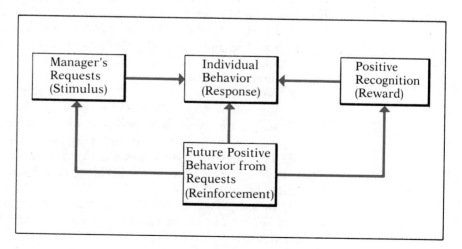

1. Positive reinforcement is provided after the desired behavior occurs, with the intention of increasing the probability that the desired behavior will be repeated. Positive reinforcers can be praise, pay, or promotions. These are normally regarded as favorable by employees and are likely to result in repeated behavior.

2. Punishment is an attempt to decrease the likelihood of a behavior recurring by applying negative consequences. Threats, punishments, docking pay, and suspensions are forms of punishment. The trouble with punishment as a response to behavior is that the person will learn what not to do, but will not necessarily learn what is the correct behavior.

3. Ignoring the misbehavior of subordinates will give the employee neither a positive nor a negative reinforcement. This technique can be used when the misbehavior is seen by the supervisor as temporary, nontypical, and not serious in its negative consequences. The supervisor's hope is that the misbehavior will be dropped in a short time; it will go away or disappear if ignored.

Reinforcement is affected by time. Whenever any type of reinforcement is applied to behavior, the closer the reinforcement is to the occurrence of the event, the greater the impact.

Implications for management. The reinforcement theory of motivation has the following implications for managers:[15]

1. Motivated behavior is influenced by learning what is acceptable and not acceptable to the organization.

2. If managers are working with employees to develop motivated behavior, they should:
   a. Be sure to tell individuals what they are doing wrong. If a person does not know why he or she is not getting rewards, the result may be confusion. Information allows a person to improve motivated behavior.
   b. Be careful not to reward all individuals the same. Rewards for individuals should be based on performance. If the same rewards are given for all performances, poor or average performance is reinforced, and high performance is ignored.

3. Tell individuals what they can do to get positive reinforcement. The establishment of a work standard lets all individuals know what is acceptable behavior.

4. Be sure to administer the reinforcement as close to the occurrence of behavior as possible. The appropriate reinforcement should immediately follow performance to get maximum impact.

5. Recognize that failure to reward can also modify behavior. If a manager does not praise a subordinate for meritorious behavior, the subordinate can be confused about the behavior a manager wants.

Equity Theory

A final view of motivation is provided by the **equity theory**: People are influenced in their behavior choices by the relative rewards they either receive or are going to receive. This theory is based on the assumption that people are motivated by a desire to be equitably treated at work.

People determine equity through the calculation of a simple ratio: what effort they are expected to invest on the job (their input) in relation to what they can expect to receive after investing that effort (their outcome or reward). This input–outcome ratio should provide us with a means of comparison with the ratios of other individuals or groups. Equity exists when the ratios are equivalent. Inequity exists (comes about) when, in the employee's mind, inputs exceed the relative or perceived values of outcomes.[16]

An example. Ellen McCann has been working as a salesperson for ten months. In this time, she has gone to sales school three times (achieving superior ratings in all categories), has consistently achieved 125 percent of sales quota, and has won two local sales contests. In recognition of this achievement, Ellen's boss had given her a $150 per month raise. Ellen's motivation has dropped noticeably in the past month. Why? She learned that a salesperson with no prior experience had been hired into the organization by her boss at $1,550 per month—$50 more than Ellen was making! As Ellen said, "It's not equitable! If they can do that, I'm going to start to look around."

This example illustrates two points about equity theory. First, there are different behaviors possible when persons believe they are the victims of inequity or are in a situation they perceive will lead to inequity. Their behaviors can lead to attempts to escape their situation ("I quit") or to attempts to put their input–outcome ratios in balance ("I'll do less" or "I want a raise").

A second point concerns the referent the person selects for comparison. There are two categories: other and system. The "other" category of referent can include those persons in the same job, same company, or same profession, or those with similar backgrounds or members of a circle of friends with whom the employee needs to compare himself or herself. The "system" as referent entails the individual's recognition of the presence of organizationwide policies and procedures: "If those people are allowed overtime, I should have overtime when I need it to complete my work." That is an example of comparison to the system.[17]

Implications for management. Equity theory has the following implications for managers:

1. Managers need to be concerned that an employee's motivation is affected by both the absolute rewards and the relative rewards available in the system.
2. Employees do make conscious comparisons of equity that influence their motivation levels.
3. There should be conscious efforts to establish and retain equity in the work environment.

Managing Motivation

We have explored six theories of motivation to provide information for managers who are striving to develop motivated employees. The theories of Maslow, Herzberg, and McClelland offer valuable insight into the needs that trigger motivated behavior. The theories on expectancy, reinforcement, and equity reveal the why of the motivation process—why employees display different types of motivated behavior. Each theory makes an important contribution to understanding the motivation of an employee, and each provides input for the model of motivation.

Now that the theory has been reviewed, we can consider the application: What can the individual manager do to develop motivated workers?

In this last section of the chapter, we present two concepts influencing the opportunity for motivation: redesign of the job and creation of a supportive climate.

Job Redesign

Since the Industrial Revolution, employers have been looking for more effective, efficient, and less expensive methods to manufacture standardized goods in quantity. Breaking jobs down into repetitive tasks led to the assembly line method of manufacture. The assembly line looks good on paper, but its application has led us to worker dissatisfaction, alienation, and boredom; it has also yielded declining productivity, rising costs, and a crisis of confidence in America's ability to provide quality goods and services.

Management trends in recent years have been attempts to deal with these problems in several ways. Jobs and organizations have been reexamined and redesigned in the light of modern motivational theories to put the challenge and other psychological rewards back into work. Management has taken many repetitive tasks away from jobs and given them to robots and other kinds of computer-assisted machinery. Training and development programs have been devised to get people ready and able to perform more demanding tasks and jobs.

Job redesign requires a knowledge of and concern for the human qualities people bring with them to the organization. Human qualities include such things as the needs and expectations of individuals, their perceptions and values, and their level of skills and abilities. Job redesign also requires knowledge of the job qualities—such things as the physical and mental demands made on individuals and the environment in which the job is performed. Job redesign usually tailors a job to fit the person who must perform it. The beginner gets pieces of the job in measured amounts until all the tasks have been learned and performed to standards. More experienced persons who are becoming bored with their jobs may be given more challenging tasks and more flexibility or autonomy in dealing with them.

The two directions approached in redesigning jobs are job scope and job depth. Job scope refers to the variety of tasks incorporated into the job, whereas job depth refers to the degree of discretion the person has to alter the job. The attempts at job redesign include job enlargement, job rotation, and job enrichment. Let's examine each approach.

Job enlargement. Job enlargement increases the variety or the number of tasks a job includes, not the quality or the challenge of those tasks. Often referred to as *job loading*, job enlargement may attempt to demand "more of the same" from an employee or to add other tasks containing an equal or lesser amount of meaning or challenge. Although some people need and want job enlargement, others do not. It can add to a person's individual job satisfaction and commitment to the job where people are suffering from an underload and the boredom that usually goes with it. Some people need to be kept constantly busy and occupied with routine that they understand and have mastered. Their "sense of competence" improves as their volume of output does. Some people simply seek more variety, not more challenge.

Job rotation. Job rotation assigns people to different jobs, or different tasks to people, on a temporary basis. The idea is to add variety and to expose people to the dependence of one job on others. Assembly line workers may be assigned one set of tasks one month and another set of tasks the month after that. Office workers may swap jobs for a time to learn additional dimensions of the office's responsibilities, to gain additional insights, and to enable them to substitute for one another in times of need. Job rotation can be used to cross-train and to facilitate permanent job transfers or promotions.

Job rotation can help stimulate people to higher levels of contributions and renew people's interests and enthusiasm. But once the novelty wears off and the new tasks are mastered, boredom and lack of interest can return.

Not everyone is suited for job rotation. Some fear the upset in routine that it represents. Others may feel that they are being used, especially if they are asked to do more demanding, less desirable, or more time-consuming work for the same amount of pay. The manager must keep in mind that individual perceptions of the nature, status, and desirability of tasks will vary with each person. Also, additional time and money may be required to keep rotation programs going. Production, along with morale, may suffer.

Job enrichment. Job enrichment applies Herzberg's motivation factors to a job, thus allowing those interested to satisfy some of their psychological needs. Herzberg refers to job enrichment as *vertical job loading*. In developing job enrichment, there are some specific areas to concentrate on:

1. *Variety of tasks.* Introduce new and more difficult tasks not previously handled.
2. *Task importance.* Give a person a complete natural unit of work. Also assign individuals specific or specialized tasks that enable them to become experts.
3. *Task responsibility.* Increase the accountability of individuals for their own work. Additionally, grant the employees additional authority in their activities.
4. *Feedback.* Make periodic or specialized reports directly available to the worker himself or herself rather than to a supervisor.

Experiments with job enrichment vary widely in their approaches, scope, and content. Most efforts at job enrichment allow people more control over their work. Some companies merely allow regular meetings between supervisors and workers to discuss mutual problems, and they solicit employee suggestions on methods improvement. Volvo pioneered the concept of having a team of workers work on the entire auto assembly operations to produce a single car. Many manufacturers have allowed skilled machine operators to set up their machines, maintain them, plan their flow as well as pace of work, and inspect their own output.

One of the most successful projects in our recent past involved the management and workers at General Motors' car assembly plant in Tarrytown, New York. In 1970, the plant had extremely poor production and labor relations. The plant manager, with the endorsement of top management and the labor unions involved, began a project to involve workers in decision making and to solicit their ideas for improvement. Initial successes led to the expansion of the project, utilizing volunteers and training programs in problem solving for management and workers. The cost exceeded $1.6 million but quality improved, absenteeism fell significantly, and unresolved grievances fell from about 2,000 in 1971 to 32 in 1978.[18]

Job enrichment is a useful tool to improve morale and performance. But not all jobs or job holders are good candidates for enrichment. Both Herzberg's research and the Tarrytown experiment tell us that job enrichment must take place in an atmosphere of mutual trust between labor and management. Participation must be voluntary, and management must be competent in its day-to-day operations as well as its efforts at job enrichment. Even so, members of both management and labor can be expected to resist some efforts at job enrichment. And once introduced, changes do not yield improvements overnight. Mistakes will be made, and setbacks will occur.

Job enrichment, once begun, should not be a short-term experiment. Whatever changes are made should match a job's level of challenge to the job holder's skills. Once a job is enriched, it may need to be enriched again. Once people experience the benefits of job enrichment, they will be reluctant to give them up. People may, for the first time at work, experience a sense of competence, autonomy, and recognition—and a sense of responsibility. These benefits will result in happier, motivated employees who would not welcome a return to their former circumstances.

Creating a Supportive Climate

Essential to the development of motivated employees is for a manager to provide a climate in which employees' needs can be met. What are the components of the environment? Some are adequate resources for goal accomplishment, support for reward systems, training, and a well-conceived organizational format. In addition, the manager's personal philosophy, actions, and expectations also shape the climate. Let's examine each of these parts of the manager's contribution.

The philosophy a manager has about work, people, his or her role in the organization, discipline, performance appraisal, coaching, training, or other interpersonal roles—all these form a basis for any action a manager implements. A managerial philosophy built on a positive premise—that people are ambitious, eager, do their work well, seek independence, respond to positives, and enjoy work—is a strong philosophy on which to establish definite and productive operating relationships.

The manager's actions are a product of her or his philosophy. What actions build a supportive climate? A starting point is assisting the employee in the attainment of his or her goals—by removing barriers, developing mutual goal-setting opportunities, encouraging positive risk taking, and providing stability. Two other actions can enhance the environment. Openly appreciating the contributions of the employee is the first. The other is to be sensitive to the employee's need for equity. The employee must feel that she or he is receiving a fair exchange for her or his input into the company and in comparison to other employees.

Management expectations for performance and behavior need to be developed and communicated to employees. For employees to function, they need to know what the manager really wants. There are two phases in this process. The first consists of developing and communicating the expectations of performance, group citizenship, individual initiative, and job creativity. The second involves consistency: The manager must be consistent in these expectations and in communicating them. The consistency will produce reinforcement, and the eventual result should be stability, anxiety reduction, and elimination of guessing games because the employees now know what the boss expects.

When these optimal organizational and personal ingredients are all meshed, the environment should be a supportive one that encourages motivated behavior.

Summary

- Motivation is stimulated by a person's needs and is influenced by a person's choices of actions.
- The various theories of motivation provide insight into the motivation of a person. All make a contribution to understanding motivation.
- Five main categories of need motivate us to behave in unique ways: physiological (physical) needs, safety or security, love or social, esteem, and self-realization or self-actualization.
- Herzberg's hygiene factors are the primary elements involved in job dissatisfaction. When they are present and possess sufficient quality (in each employee's mind), they can lead to no job dissatisfaction.
- Herzberg's motivation factors are the primary elements involved in job satisfaction. When they are provided and possess the desired degree of quality (in each employee's mind), they can stimulate personal and psychological growth.
- Achievement needs are related to task accomplishment and can be strengthened through training.
- Expectancy theory states that a person's behavior is influenced by the value of the rewards, the relationship of the rewards to the performance, and the efforts required for performance.
- According to reinforcement theory, motivation is learned by the employee. The consequences of behavior influence choices in subsequent similar situations.
- Equity theory states that employees compare their input–outcome ratios with other employees. This comparison influences their levels of motivation.

- Creating a supportive climate is a function of resources and the manager's philosophy, actions, and expectations.
- Job enlargement increases the variety or number of tasks, not their challenge or complexity.
- Job rotation exposes people to different tasks for varying lengths of time.
- Job enrichment provides motivation factors to a job on a continuing basis through more responsibility, control over the environment, and feedback.

Glossary of Essential Terms

equity theory	A motivation theory stating that people are influenced in their behavior choices (motivation) through the comparison of relative input–outcome ratios. People compare the ratios of their input (efforts) with outcome (rewards) to others' ratios to see if equity exists.
expectancy theory	A motivation theory stating that a person's behavior is influenced by the value of the rewards, the relationship of the rewards to the performance necessary, and the effort required for performance.
hygiene factors	Herzberg's list of causes most closely identified with unhappiness on the job. These extrinsic factors, if provided in the right qualities by management, can result in no job dissatisfaction.
job enlargement	Increases in the variety or the number of tasks a job includes, not the quality or the challenge of those tasks.
job enrichment	Designing a job to provide more responsibility, control, feedback, and authority for decision making.
job rotation	Sending people to different jobs on a rotating or temporary basis.
motivation	The interaction of a person's internalized needs and external influences (equity, expectancy, and previous conditioning) that determines behavior designed to achieve a goal.
motivation factors	Herzberg's list of conditions that can lead to an individual's job satisfaction. They are intrinsic to the job and offer satisfactions for psychological needs.
needs	Physical or psychological conditions in humans that act as stimuli for behavior until satisfactions for them have been provided or achieved.

| reinforcement theory | A motivation theory stating that the behavior choices of a person are influenced by the supervisor's reactions to them and the rewards or penalties experienced in a similar situation. |

Review Questions

1. Can you define this chapter's essential terms? If not, consult the preceding glossary.

2. What stimulates motivation? What are the three factors that influence an individual's choice of behavior to satisfy the stimulus?

3. List and explain the five categories of human needs identified by Abraham Maslow. Why are the needs arranged in a hierarchy?

4. What are Herzberg's hygiene and motivation factors? What is the importance of each set of factors to a manager?

5. When a person is described as a high achiever, what are her or his attitudes likely to be toward (a) goal setting, (b) feedback, (c) individual responsibility, (d) rewards?

6. Apply the expectancy theory to your classroom experience. Explain your motivation for grades in relationship to:
   a. the value of the reward (grade).
   b. the relationship of the reward to performance (tests, papers).
   c. the amount of effort to receive the grade (studying, number of hours).

7. Cite an experience you have had where your behavior (motivation) has been influenced by past consequences.

8. Describe the two factors used by a person in determining equity in a work situation.

TAPE
THURS.
NOV. 7

References

1. Keith Davis, *Human Behavior at Work: Organizational Behavior*, 7th ed. (New York: McGraw-Hill, 1985), p. 45.

2. Abraham H. Maslow, "A Theory of Human Motivation," *Psychological Review*, 50 (1943), pp. 370–396.

3. Ibid.

4. Ibid.

5. Frederick Herzberg, "One More Time: How Do You Motivate Employees?" *Business Classics: Fifteen Key Concepts for Managerial Success*, Harvard Business Review, 1975, pp. 16–17.

6. Ibid.

7. Ibid.

8. David C. McClelland, *The Achieving Society* (New York: Van Nostrand Reinhold, 1971).

9. David C. McClelland and David Burnham, "Power Is the Great Motivator," *Harvard Business Review* (March–April 1976), pp. 100–110.

10. Victor H. Vroom, *Work and Motivation* (New York: John Wiley & Sons, 1964).

11. For more detailed information and treatment, see Victor H. Vroom, *Work and Motivation* (New York: John Wiley & Sons, 1964); and L. W. Porter and E. E. Lawler, *Managerial Attitudes and Performance* (Homewood, Ill.: Richard D. Irwin, 1968).

12. Randall S. Schuler, *Personnel and Human Resource Management*, 3rd ed. (St. Paul: West Publishing Co., 1987), pp. 41–43.

13. B. F. Skinner, *Contingencies of Reinforcement* (New York: Appleton-Century-Crofts, 1969).

14. R. M. Tarpy, *Basic Principles of Learning* (Glenview, Ill.: Scott, Foresman, 1974).

15. W. C. Hamner, "Reinforcement Theory and Contingency Management in Organizational Settings," in *Organizational Behavior and Management: A Contingency Approach*, ed. H. L. Tosi and W. C. Hamner (New York: John Wiley & Sons, 1974), pp. 86–112.

16. J. Stacy Adams, "Toward an Understanding of Equity," *Journal of Abnormal and Social Psychology* (November 1963), pp. 422–436.

17. Paul S. Goodman and Abraham Fredman. "An Examination of Adam's Theory of Inequity," *Administrative Science Quarterly* (December 1971), pp. 271–288.

18. R. H. Guest, "Quality of Work Life: Learning from Tarrytown," *Harvard Business Review* (July–August 1979), pp. 77–85.

Readings

Beveridge, Don and Jeffrey Davidson. *The Achievement Challenge: How to Be a 10 in Business.* Homewood, Ill.: Dow Jones Irwin, 1988.

Burgher, Peter. *How to Earn More Using the Professional Excellence System for Managing Professionals.* Utica, Mich.: Agnes Press, 1985.

Garfield, Charles. *Peak Performers: The New Heroes of American Business.* New York: Avon Books, 1986.

Goodale, James. "Employee Involvement Sparks Diagnostic Conferences." *Personnel Journal*, 66, no. 2 (February 1987), pp. 79ff.

Harrison, R. "Harnessing Personal Energy: How Companies Can Inspire Employees." *Organizational Dynamics*, 16 (August 1987), pp. 4–20.

Herzberg, Frederick. "Workers' Needs: The Same Around the World." *Industry Week*, 234 (September 21, 1987), pp. 29ff.

Jasefowitz, Natasha. *You're The Boss: A Guide to Managing People with Understanding and Effectiveness.* New York: Warner Books, 1985.

Sherwood, Andrew. "A Baker's Dozen of Ways to Motivate People." *Management Solutions*, 32, no. 5 (May 1987), pp. 14–16.

Ullman, Joseph C. "Understanding Values: The Key to Managing?" *Business and Economic Review*, 33, no. 3 (April–June 1987), pp. 22–26.

Waterman, Robert H. Jr. *The Renewal Factor.* New York: Bantam Books, 1987.

C
A
S
E
S

10.1 What to Do About Joseph

Frank is worried about his subordinate and chief assistant, Joe. Until rather recently, Joseph Thomson has been an able and willing worker. But the signs of change are too clear to be ignored. About two weeks ago, Frank noticed that Joe was not his regular self. He was losing his sense of humor. When Frank kidded him about something in the past, Joe was quick to fight back with his own brand of kidding. For the past two weeks, Joe has just ignored Frank's efforts at humor or taken Frank's comments the wrong way.

Over the last ten days, Joe has been late to work two times. He has rarely been late more than once a year. He seems tired and drags through the day with little enthusiasm for his work. The work he turns in is up to standard, but the old spirit is gone. Frank asked Joe to take over a special project, and Joe made it very clear that he would if ordered to do so but would not volunteer to do it. Frank was beginning to have second thoughts about continuing to groom Joe to take over for him when he gets his promotion in 60 days.

Frank has tried to talk with Joe about these changes, but Joe is not willing to share his thoughts. Frank has asked around at work to see if he can gain any insights into Joe's behavior, but has been unable to discover anything of substance. Against his better judgment, Frank has decided to let his boss, Abel Farley, have a try at getting Joe to talk. After their visit, Abel called Frank into his office.

"Joe didn't say a whole lot, but I think part of his problem is his age. Joe is pushing fifty, and he thinks of himself as an aging man watching the world go by. He mentioned that his youngest child is graduating from college this summer and that he would soon be the only member of his family to not finish college."

"Well, boss, what can we do about midlife crisis?"

"If you aren't happy with his performance, tell him to shape up or ship out."

"I can't fire him for his attitude change. Maybe if I just let him have some time off to get a grip on himself . . ."

"Frank, why don't you just have a talk with his wife. See if she can suggest anything that might help. It's either that or just ignore his behavior if his work is to standards."

Frank let things go as they were and found that to be a mistake. Joe disappeared from the office for about an hour and didn't let Frank know where he was going. The last report Joe turned in had to be re-done. When Frank went looking for Joe, he found that he had taken his coat and left the office. It was 3 P.M. and Frank became concerned. He called Joe's home, and Joe's wife told him that Joe had come home because he wasn't feeling well. Joe's wife and Frank talked for several minutes, and she told Frank that her husband was worried about his inability to shake his depression. She also told Frank that she thought her husband was "scared to death" about taking over Frank's job. "I'm no psychologist," she said, "but I think he's afraid that he won't be able to live up to your expectations of him."

For Discussion

1. What needs seem to be at work in Joe? Provide examples from the case to support your answer.
2. What should Frank do now?
3. What does this case tell you about human motivation?

10.2 Differing Opinions

Two middle managers were discussing how they might better motivate their subordinate managers. Doris feels that the single most important "carrot" she can offer is a significant raise and increases in the cash value of fringe benefits. Frances holds that recognition in several forms is the best way to stimulate high performances. She believes that if people know what she expects from them and what the rewards for meeting those expectations will be, they will respond. The keys, Frances believes, are to set high standards, be available to help, and offer quick rewards for high quality performances. In Frances's words, "Nothing stimulates high performance so effectively as a pat on the back, a letter of commendation in a manager's file, and praise from higher ups in writing. Without these," Frances continued, "no person is going to get promoted."

"Frances, you are naive," said Doris. "Words are pretty cheap, and our people know it. Words, without the backing of money rewards, can't motivate anyone. I have tried praise, but in the case of Thomas Monroe, my newest subordinate, money did the trick. When Tom came on board last year, we had to hire him at the top end of his pay spread. I told him this in his interview. He knew that it would be at least twelve months before he could receive a decent raise. For the past ten months, he has been a mediocre performer. But since then, with his review approaching, he has become my star performer. If that doesn't prove my point, nothing will."

"Well," said Frances, "one case does not prove the rule for me. I have some experience in motivation, too, and it tells me that I am right, at least as far as my people are concerned. Most of my subordinates want to move up. We are fortunate to have a growing company with new branches opening up each year. Without my recommendation, my people know that they are going to stay where they are."

"Most of my people live for the here and now," said Doris. "Cash in hand or just out of reach is the ticket. Those who don't work for money are few and far between. The promise of a promotion won't pay today's bills, and it sure won't work to motivate new people. Most of my subordinates have only been here a few years. Most came up from various parts of the company. They know if they please me I will be generous. That's the secret to my reputation as well. When they look good, I look good."

At this point, Jeff Bradley came over. He had overheard their conversation and asked if he could join them. Frances said of course he could join them and asked if he had any opinions about motivating subordinates.

"I'm no expert on the subject," said Jeff, "but I have had six years experience as a manager and about five before that as a worker in two different companies. My basic philosophy is that people have different needs and expectations from work, and the better you can help them meet those needs and satisfy those expectations, the better they will perform for you." Jeff went on to tell them about one of his subordinates. "With Helen Aegis, punishment seems to work the best. I had talked with her on numerous occasions and until I took action to discourage her negatives, she didn't respond. But she is a widow and has two kids. The last thing she needs is to lose her job. She's a great performer now that she knows that my bark has a bite. Helen needs a job, and as long as she performs to the standards I set, she knows she'll have one."

For Discussion

1. Do you think that Doris is correct? Why or why not?
2. Is Jeff practicing the reinforcement theory? Why or why not?
3. Is Frances using the expectancy theory? Why or why not?
4. What does this case reveal about motivating employees?

Leadership

OUTLINE

ESSENTIAL TERMS

contingency model
continuum of leadership
   behavior
leadership

life cycle theory
Managerial Grid®
path-goal theory

LEARNING OBJECTIVES

After reading and discussing this chapter, you should be able to do the following:

1. Define this chapter's essential terms.
2. Discuss leadership as the result of the interaction of the leader, the led, and the work environment.
3. List and briefly explain the four essential leadership roles managers play.
4. Discuss the three factors that comprise a manager's leadership style.
5. Discuss the concept of situational leadership.
6. Discuss Fiedler's contingency theory.
7. Discuss the path-goal theory of leadership.

How to Get the Work Done

When you folks have some time, we need to discuss the India Project. I'd like your suggestions on how to reduce the delivery times to catch up on our initial commitment.

We need to *move* on this deadline. John, I want the cost estimates by 8:00 tomorrow morning. Gloria, likewise for the projections on personnel needs. I'll be expecting them.

What do you think we should do? We have examined and reexamined the situation. You're the experts. I'll trust your judgment. Can you bring me your decision by Friday?

These three situations provide illustrations of leadership in action. Note that the approach used by each manager is different, but the objective is the same—to achieve results through people. Managers who wish to be successful quickly realize that their most precious resource is people. The challenge for the manager is to provide the "right" amount and type of leadership to cultivate and develop the individuals.

This chapter is the second of two focusing on the management function of directing. In it, we examine leadership: the process of leadership, how leadership is determined, leadership roles, the elements of leadership styles, and specific leadership theories.

Leadership Defined

Whenever one person influences an individual or group toward accomplishing an objective, leadership occurs. **Leadership** is thus defined as the process of influencing a group or individual to set a goal or achieve a goal. It is a process involving the leader, the led (group or individual), and a particular goal or situation. It is behavioral in nature and involves personal interaction.

Management and leadership are not synonymous. Managers are required to plan, organize, staff, and control. They may or may not be effective in influencing their subordinates toward goal accomplishment. Ideally, all managers should be leaders, but many are not. A manager may be able to influence or direct organizational members, but because of an inability to perform the other management functions, the manager may fail to get individuals or a group to achieve organizational objectives.

On the other hand, constructive leadership is often found in non-managerial personnel. In the informal organization and on athletic teams, informal leaders influence the behavior of organization members. Many successful sports managers freely credit success to key players "who lead by actions as well as words."

Now that we have defined leadership, let's examine some examples of leadership roles.

Leadership Roles

In interacting with employees in the work environment, a manager must play four basic leadership roles: educator, counselor, judge, and spokesperson.[1] We consider the nature and importance of each.

Educator

All managers must perform the leadership role of educator. Managers fulfill this role by teaching employees job skills as well as acceptable behavior and organizational values. Managers accomplish much of behavioral education through the execution of their own daily work. Their work habits, attitudes, and behavior serve as a role model to all who observe them.

In addition to providing behavioral education, managers are ultimately responsible for the formal training of their employees. They may provide this skills training directly or arrange for it to be provided by others. Regardless of who ultimately performs the training, the manager should be knowledgeable about training principles, learning theory, and training techniques to perform this role.

Counselor

A second leadership role of a manager is counselor. This role involves listening, giving advice, and preventing and solving employees' problems. In performing this role, managers are fulfilling two expectations of employees: (1) awareness of and concern for the individual employee and (2) assistance in solving a problem.[2] The counselor role does not mean the manager is expected to solve all the employee's problems, but it does mean providing help in recognizing the basic problem and in searching for potential solutions.

Judge

Playing the leadership role of judge involves appraising subordinates' performances; enforcing policies, procedures, and regulations; settling disputes; and dispensing justice.[3] Appraising or evaluating performance requires a knowledge of the standards that are used to measure output. (We discussed this process in Chapter 9.) The enforcing of policies, procedures, and regulations is tied to communication and to training. People should be told, and shown, what limits and guidelines exist and how these apply to their specific situations. The function of settling disputes requires the exercise of tact and concern for resolution of conflicts. Dispensing justice entails giving credit and rewards as well as appropriate discipline.

Spokesperson

Managers act as spokespersons for subordinates when they relay their suggestions, concerns, and views to higher authorities. "Doing something" about subordinates' problems may mean going to bat for them on a higher management level. It may mean the manager will have to fight for changes to improve procedures, morale, and working conditions. In performing this leadership role, a manager must be willing to represent a subordinate's view even when she or he disagrees with it. (Disagreement could arise if the manager and the employee have different perceptions of a situation.)

Having looked at leadership in terms of role performance by a manager, let's now examine the nature of leadership—the interaction of the leader, the led (group or individual), and the organizational environment.

The Nature of Leadership

Initially it was thought that successful leadership was a result of the personality traits a person possessed. Thus leadership studies focused either on (1) identifying the traits of persons who were leaders versus those of nonleaders or (2) comparing the traits of successful leaders with the traits of unsuccessful leaders. Neither focus proved valuable because it was simply not possible to isolate a set of personality traits of effective leadership.[4]

A more viable theory is that leadership is a result of the interaction among the superior (leader), the subordinates (the led), and the organizational environment (work and the work situation). Leadership is in essence a special relationship between each manager and each individual or group, a relationship that in turn is influenced by the work environment. This unique blending dictates the appropriate leadership behavior to the manager, not vice versa.

For the manager, every situation is different. What works in one instance may not work in another. This situational approach requires that managers be flexible. The success or failure of a manager in providing leadership to an employee and the organization depends on how well the manager adjusts his or her leadership approach to the people involved and the circumstances or environment at that time.[5] There is no one correct approach for a manager; different styles need to be used with different subordinates and situations. Figure 11.1 illustrates the relationships within the leadership setting. A change in any one of the three components can affect the other two. Let's discuss each of the components of the leadership situation.

The Leader

The manager (leader) affects the leadership situation by his or her managerial philosophy, values, needs, and the strengths of or preferences for a leadership style. The styles a manager will use are influenced by each of these variables; therefore they merit a closer look.

A manager's philosophy about work and the people who perform the work will influence her or his approach to leadership. Douglas McGregor has hypothesized two sets of assumptions about people that serve as a philosophical base for leadership action.[6] Exhibit 11.1 illustrates the first set, known as *Theory X*. A manager basing an operating philosophy on Theory X would impose a directive leadership style on the individual or work group she or he is supervising. Coercion, negative motivation, and

FIGURE 11.1
The leadership situation

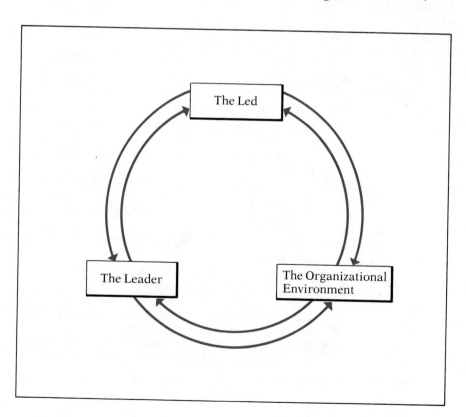

The Led

The Leader

The Organizational Environment

EXHIBIT 11.1
Theory X

1. The average human being has an inherent dislike of work and will avoid it if he can.
2. Because of this human characteristic about work, most people must be coerced, controlled, directed, and threatened with punishment to get them to put forth adequate effort toward the achievement of organizational objectives.
3. The average human being prefers to be directed, wishes to avoid responsibility, has relatively little ambition, and wants security above all.

EXHIBIT 11.2
Theory Y

1. The expenditure of physical and mental effort in work is as natural as play or rest. The average human being does not inherently dislike work. Depending on controllable conditions, work may be a source of satisfaction (and will be voluntarily performed) or a source of punishment (and will be avoided if possible).
2. External control and the threat of punishment are not the only means for bringing about effort toward organizational objectives. A person will exercise self-direction and self-control in the service of objectives to which he or she is committed.
3. Commitment to objectives is a function of the rewards associated with their achievement.
4. The average human being learns, under proper conditions, not only to accept, but to seek, responsibility.
5. The capacity to exercise a relatively high degree of imagination, ingenuity, and creativity in the solution of organizational problems is widely, not narrowly, distributed in the population.
6. Under the conditions of modern industrial life, the intellectual potentials of the average human being are only partially utilized.

refusal to allow employee decision making would probably be the actions of the manager.

Exhibit 11.2 depicts the second set of assumptions about work and human nature. A managerial philosophy founded on *Theory Y* will prepare a leader to work with people as individuals, to involve people in the process of decision making, to openly encourage people to seek responsibility, and to work with people to achieve their goals.

Source: Reprinted with special permission of King Features Syndicate, Inc.

The values a manager has will also influence the leadership environment. If the manager values independence, individual responsibility, initiative, and personal accountability, these values will be reflected in the managerial expectations, which in turn will shape the climate of the work environment. A manager whose value system includes the ideas that rewards, satisfaction, and recognition are a direct result of work will reflect that in his or her approach to employees.

The need for security, or perhaps some other need at a higher level, may influence a manager's leadership style. A high need for safety or security may result in the manager's being reluctant to let employees make decisions for fear of their mistakes. On the other hand, a manager functioning on a higher need level—say, working toward self-actualization—might encourage employee involvement.

The individual manager's leadership style strengths or preferences can influence the choices she or he makes. Each manager has individual strengths or possibly preferences for an approach in working with people. This preference or strength will serve as the predominant leadership style because the manager is more comfortable with it or has had success in its application.

The Led

The subordinates being led interact with the manager and environmental considerations in determining the leadership style. Individual employees have values, needs, abilities, and style preferences or expectations of a manager that ultimately influence the manager's approach.

The values of the work group influence leadership style. A work group valuing independence, unilateral decision making, quality of work life, and opportunity for initiative can influence a manager's style to be one of involvement, participation, and employee control of the resources for individual success. The opposite value system also requires an adjustment by the manager.

The needs of the individuals being supervised require a response in the manager's leadership style. An employee who exhibits a high concern for security in the work environment will require different leadership than an employee who is adventurous and seeks new areas of challenge.

The ability levels of employees are another influence on leadership approaches. An employee who has just been hired without previous experience on the job will function better with close, directive supervision: This will result in lack of confusion, increased learning rate, and a sense of security. The experienced worker, one who has demonstrated ability through performance, would chafe under the same close supervision. The manager in these situations should adopt appropriate leadership approaches. Figure 11.2 illustrates this necessity.

FIGURE 11.2
Adaptation of
Hersey and
Blanchard's life
cycle theory of
leadership

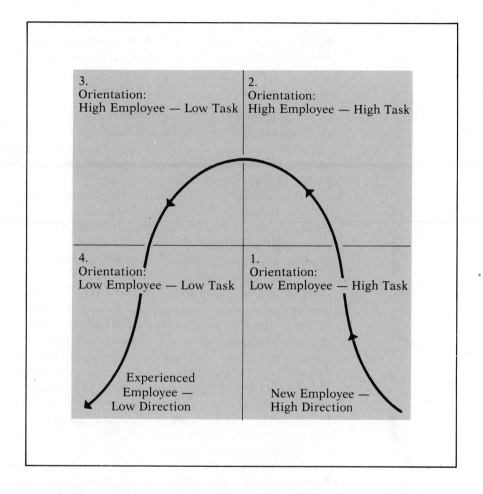

Hersey and Blanchard have provided an illustration of the variations in leadership requirements of a manager, variations based on the performance ability of the individual employee.[7] Known as the **life cycle theory**, it explains the changes in leadership necessary to respond to the organizational maturity of employees (see Figure 11.2). Notice the different approaches of a manager with an employee in block 1 (the new employee) and in block 4 (the experienced, secure employee.) The manager moves from high direction on the job to low·direction on an "as needed" basis.

Individuals and groups have leadership style expectations and preferences of their manager. If an individual or group has become accustomed to a directive leadership style, the introduction of a leader exhibiting little direction may cause confusion and indecision on the part of subordinates. At the other extreme, a group that is highly independent, responsive to individual goal setting, and good at group decision making is going to be dismayed by a leader who attempts to implement a directive style. Each group or individual has its own expectations for leadership styles.

The Environment

The third element of situational leadership is the environment—the work itself and the work situation. The variables in the work environment that influence the choice of leadership styles are the degree of structuring of the job, the amount of technology in the work environment, and the influence of upper level management.

Both a highly structured job (with severe limitations on individual decision making) and a highly automated work environment indicate that a directive leadership approach is called for. In other instances, where the job is creative (for example, in research biology), or where the work is the result of a team-centered environment, a participative style is indicated.

Upper level management may influence the style used by the individual manager in various environments. If the predominant style of a manager's boss is to be authoritarian in approach, there is a natural tendency for the manager to be influenced in this direction. Additionally, upper level management may require subordinate managers to use certain styles, not just influence them: Participative managers, for example, could prefer other managers to use that style for long-range team building.

The nature of leadership is that it is situational. The leadership approach of the manager will vary according to the interaction of the leader, the followers, and the work environment. In some instances, certain styles will be more effective than others. This is part of leading—adapting the style to the situation variables.

We have been looking at the ways different variables can determine the leadership styles of managers. Now it is reasonable to ask: What are these styles?

Leadership Styles

We have defined leadership as influencing others to achieve results. The approaches a manager uses to influence others are elements of the manager's leadership style. These elements, though described individually, in actuality are integrated in leadership. Managers' leadership styles are composed of three parts: how they choose to motivate, their decision-making styles, and their areas of emphasis (orientation) in the work environment.

Positive or Negative Motivation

Leaders influence others toward goal achievement through their approach to motivation. Depending on the style of the manager, the motivation can take the form of rewards or penalties.[8] Positive leadership style deals in praise and recognition, monetary rewards, increase of security, and additional responsibility. At the other end of the continuum (see Figure 11.3), negative leadership emphasizes penalties; loss of the job, suspension, and public reprimands are extremes of negative leadership.

FIGURE 11.3
Motivation
continuum

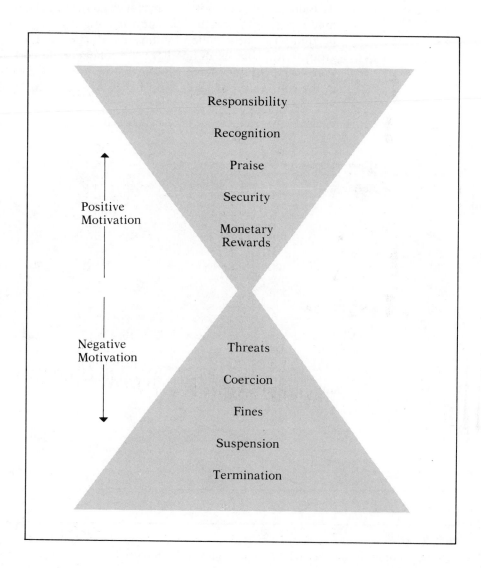

Positive
Motivation

Responsibility

Recognition

Praise

Security

Monetary
Rewards

Negative
Motivation

Threats

Coercion

Fines

Suspension

Termination

Positive leadership styles encourage development of employees through the creation of higher job satisfaction.[9] Negative leadership styles are based on threats and the ability to withhold items of value from an employee. The result of negative leadership may be an environment of fear, where the manager is viewed as a driver rather than a leader.

Decision-Making Style

A second element of a manager's leadership style concerns the degree of decision-making authority the manager grants to subordinates. These styles may range from absolute decision making by the manager, with no opportunity for participation by the subordinates, to decision making by the group within limits defined by the manager. Robert Tannenbaum and Warren H. Schmidt have presented this range of decision-making styles in the **continuum of leadership behavior** shown in Figure 11.4.[10] Any of

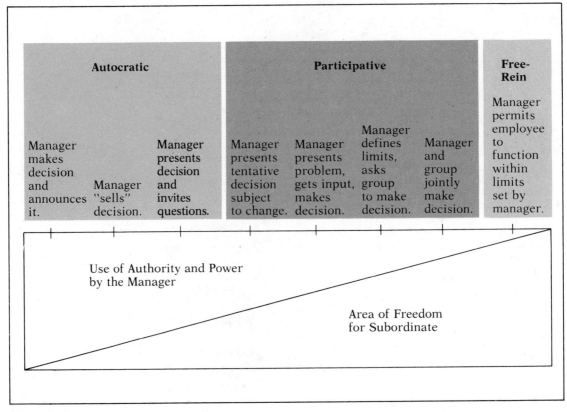

FIGURE 11.4
Continuum of leadership behavior (Tannenbaum and Schmidt)

these styles is an option a manager can choose to use based on the situation. Notice that the degree of involvement of the employee is greater as you move from left to right.

The range of styles shown on the continuum can be grouped under three headings: autocratic, participative, and free-rein. Let's discuss each in relationship to the continuum.

The autocratic leadership style. This style describes decision making solely by the manager. In its extreme case, the manager makes the decision and announces it to the work group. There is no opportunity for input into the decision-making process by the subordinates. Variations of this approach find the manager making the decision and then "selling" it to employees or making the decision and allowing the group the opportunity to ask questions. Once again, these style alternatives do not solicit employee input. When would these options be appropriate?

Depending on the situation, a manager may choose to use any of these variations of the autocratic style. One factor influencing this decision could be the individual employees. They may be new to the job and need direction or even be more comfortable with an autocratic approach. Other times, the situation may call for unilateral decision making: Perhaps there is not enough time for quality input from subordinates or the subordinates lack the information to be of assistance. Regardless, the autocratic style is applicable in some situations.

The participative leadership approach. This style is characterized by the manager's involving the subordinates in the decision. The involvement in decision making is a matter of degree and can range from the first to the last of the four arrays of participation that follow:

1. The manager presents a tentative solution subject to change based on employee input.
2. The manager presents a problem to the employees, solicits their input, and makes the decision.
3. The manager defines the limits of the problem, and the employees make the decision.
4. The manager and the employees jointly make the decision. (The manager and the employees have equality.)

As with the options of autocratic style, the manager's choices of involvement for employees will depend on the situation. It may be the manager's personal philosophy or preference to develop a democratic environment; it may not be. Employees might be more knowledgeable than the manager on a certain topic so that the manager is compelled merely to define the problem and then to solicit employee decision making.

The use of the participative leadership style requires the manager to genuinely use it—not just act as if it were being implemented. Managers often allow employee participation and decision making only on minor issues. The result: Participation comes to mean "subordinates give opinions, but the boss only listens sometimes and always decides."[11]

The free-rein style of leadership.   This style is characterized by the leader's encouraging the individual or group to function independently. The leader either sets limits and the followers work out their own problems, or the individuals set their own goals. In this style, the leader's role is to serve as a logistics specialist or representative of the group to outside groups.

The application of this style can be found with individuals or groups that the manager views as being knowledgeable, independent, or motivated. Additionally, if the work group is composed of high achievers, or is highly research oriented, this style has potential benefits.

The importance of this discussion on decision-making styles is that the manager is encouraged to vary the style in response to the employees and the situation. A new employee requires initially that decisions be made for him or her. The individual who later shows the ability and interest to become involved should be led through a form of participation. And the twenty-year veteran is a candidate for free-rein leadership. Managers need to vary their styles to achieve results. It requires practice and flexibility.

Task Orientation and Employee Orientation

The final element of leadership is the manager's perspective on the most effective way of getting work done. The two key areas are task orientation and employee orientation, which we look at now.

A manager who favors a task orientation places emphasis on getting the job done through better methods or equipment, control of the work environment, assigning and organizing work, one-person decision making, and monitoring through evaluation of performance. If this is the sole emphasis of a manager, the long-range implications for employees will be pronounced: It could lead to turnover, absenteeism, and decreased job satisfaction.[12]

An employee orientation, on the other hand, emphasizes concern for the human needs of subordinates. The managerial approach is to view employees as valuable assets to be cultivated and developed. Teamwork, positive relationships, trust, and solution of employee problems are the major focus of the employee-oriented manager. The behavioral implications of this emphasis are an increase in job satisfaction accompanied by a decrease in turnover and absenteeism.[13]

In actuality, these two perspectives are not mutually exclusive; a manager normally has some degree of both. A blend of both employee orientation and task orientation appears to be the working formula for most successful managers.[14]

Robert R. Blake and Jane S. Mouton have developed a leadership theory based on these two areas of emphasis.[15] Figure 11.5 provides an illustration of the application of this theory, the **Managerial Grid**.® Using concern for production (task orientation) and concern for people (employee orientation) as the axes, Blake and Mouton found they could plot five distinct management behaviors that result from the interplay of the two perspectives:

1. Managers exhibiting 9,1 (lower right) behavior emphasize a high concern for production and efficiency but a minimum concern for em-

FIGURE 11.5
The Managerial
Grid®

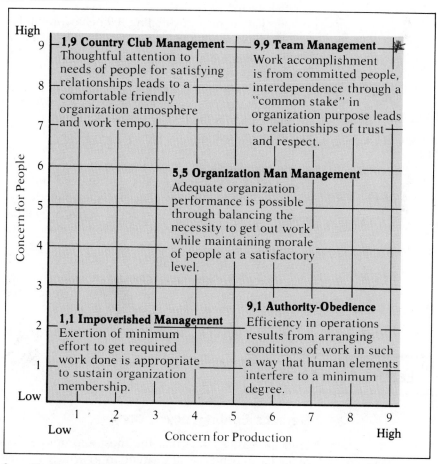

Source: The Managerial Grid figure from *The Managerial Grid III: The Key to Leadership Excellence*, by Robert R. Blake and Jane Srygley Mouton. Houston: Gulf Publishing Company, Copyright © 1985, page 12. Reproduced by permission.

ployees. This behavior is focused exclusively on tasks at the expense of relationships.

2. Managers exhibiting 1,9 behaviors emphasize a high concern for employees but a low concern for production. The focus is on developing personal relationships. This approach works well with competent people, with well-defined and proceduralized tasks, or in a situation in which the leader has strong confidence and control.

3. Managers exhibiting 1,1 behavior have little concern for people or for production. This combination is termed "impoverished management" because it represents a dissatisfied manager with little interest in the position.

4. The manager exhibiting 5,5 behavior emphasizes a moderate concern for people and production. A strong commitment is not made to either factor.

5. The manager exhibiting 9,9 behavior emphasizes a high concern for both production and employees. In this position, the manager views results as being achieved by "us" through goal setting along with emphasis on individual improvement and commitment.

The manager's leadership style (how the manager influences results) is composed of a number of elements. The manager adjusts the decision-making approach and motivational approach in terms of the situation. In addition, the perspective a manager has of the way to get results (emphasis on people or task or a combination of these) will affect the style chosen. The choices a manager makes will depend on the situation—individual employees, groups of employees, types of work, structure, personal preference of the manager, and upper level management's influence. Regardless of the combination the manager selects for each situation, the purpose is to influence. In providing the required leadership to a situation, the manager should avoid the six pitfalls of leadership (Figure 11.6).

There have been two theories of leadership developed incorporating these situational elements: Fiedler's contingency theory and House's path-goal theory. We examine each.

Leadership Theories

Fiedler's Contingency Theory

Fred E. Fiedler holds that the most appropriate style of leadership for a manager depends on the situation in which a manager works. The **contingency model**, which he developed, shows that the effectiveness of a leader is determined by the interaction of the manager's orientation (task or employee) with three situational variables: leader–member relationships,

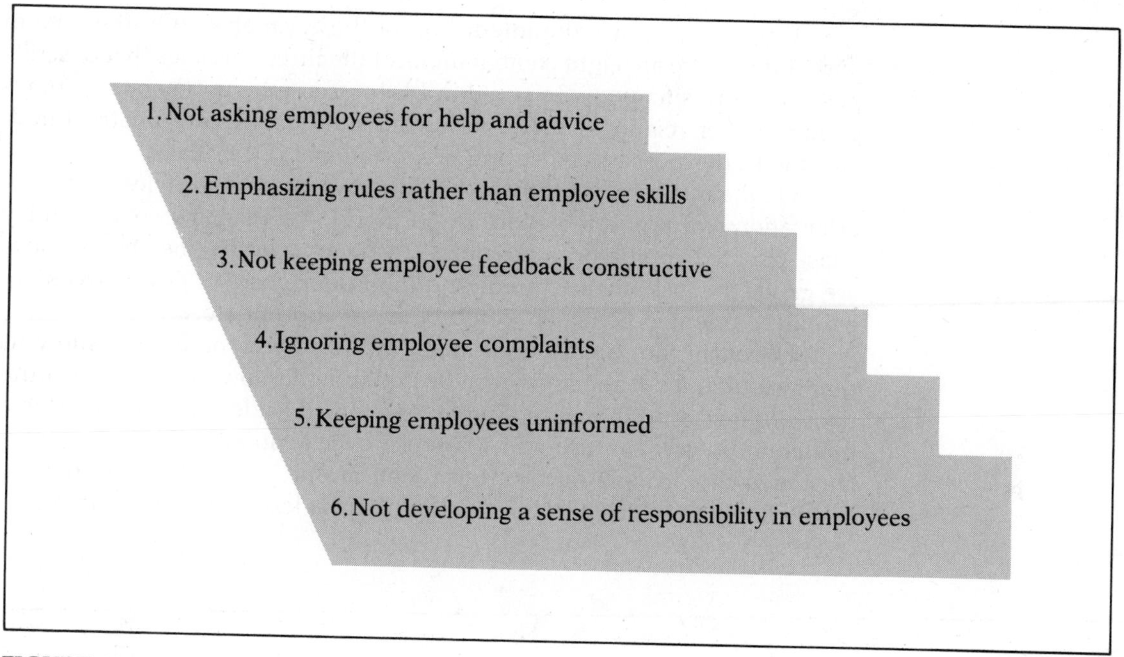

1. Not asking employees for help and advice

2. Emphasizing rules rather than employee skills

3. Not keeping employee feedback constructive

4. Ignoring employee complaints

5. Keeping employees uninformed

6. Not developing a sense of responsibility in employees

FIGURE 11.6

The six pitfalls of leadership

Source: Based on James K. Van Fleet, "The Deadly Sins of Supervision," *Success* (April 1987), p. 29.

task structure, and leader position power.[16] Having already discussed task and employee orientation in the previous section, we are now ready to examine the three variables so that we can understand the model of contingency theory.

Leader–member relations refers to the degree to which the leader is or feels accepted by the group. It is measured by the degree of respect, confidence, and trust the subordinates feel toward the superior. This factor is rated on a scale from good to poor. If the relationship is rated as good, the leader should be able to exercise influence over the subordinates easily. On the other hand, if there is friction or distrust (a poor rating), the manager may have to resort to favors to get performance.[17]

Task structure concerns the nature of the subordinate's job or task. It reflects the degree of structure in the job: A structured job would be routine in nature with prescribed processes. An example would be the position of file clerk. An unstructured job would have complexity and variety and room for creativity.

Leader position power describes the organizational power base from which the individual manager operates. To what degree can the leader punish or reward within the organization? The power can range from strong (vice-president of marketing) to weak (second staff assistant).

Figure 11.7 shows the interaction of these variables. On the bottom part of the figure are eight combinations of the three variables that describe possible work situations. In position III, for example, the manager enjoys good member relations, the tasks of the subordinates are unstructured, and the leader possesses a strong organizational power base.

On the upper half of the figure are the two orientation styles: employee orientation and task orientation. In position I, the manager could employ a task-oriented approach. In position IV, where the leader–member relations are good, the task unstructured, and the leader position power weak, an employee-oriented behavior would be more appropriate.

In conclusion, a close examination of Fiedler's model will show us that task-oriented leaders perform best with either low or high concentrations of power and influence. Employee-oriented leaders perform best with moderate power, control, and influence over a situation. A further conclusion is that leaders may perform well in one job and not in another. The position in which an organization places a leader makes a difference.

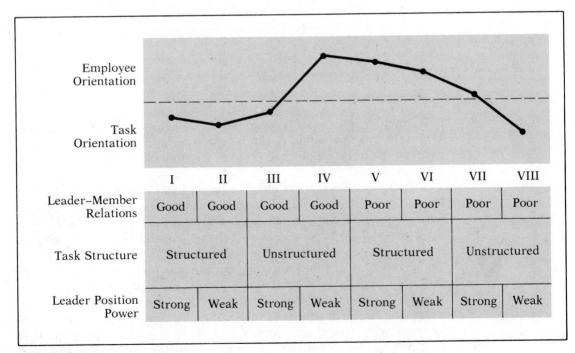

FIGURE 11.7

Interaction of leadership orientations with situational variables

Source: Reprinted by permission of the Harvard Business Review. An exhibit from "Engineer the Job to Fit the Manager" by Fred E. Fiedler (September–October 1965). Copyright © 1965 by the President and Fellows of Harvard College; all rights reserved.

Organizations can attempt to fit either the manager to the situation or the situation to the manager.

Path-Goal Theory

The **path-goal theory** of leadership is concerned with the ways in which a leader can influence a subordinate's motivation, goals, and attempts at achievement. It suggests that a leadership style is effective or ineffective on the basis of how the leader influences the perceptions of:

- Work goals or rewards of subordinates.
- Paths (behaviors) that lead to successful goal accomplishment.

The origin of this theory is in the expectancy theory of motivation (Chapter 10). We recall under that theory that an employee's motivations are influenced by the employee's perceptions of (1) his or her ability to accomplish a specific task, (2) the relationship of the rewards to the accomplishment of the task, and (3) the value of the rewards offered. The path-goal theory states that the leader can influence these perceptions of rewards and can clarify what employees have to do to achieve these rewards.

With this foundation in mind, let's examine the components of the path-goal theory: leader behavior and situational factors.

According to Robert J. House and Terrence R. Mitchell, subordinates are motivated by a leader's behavior.[18] This behavior influences both goal attractiveness and the paths available to reach the goals. Their theory contains two propositions concerning leader behavior:

1. Leader behavior is acceptable and satisfying to subordinates to the extent that they view such behavior as either an immediate source of satisfaction or an instrument to future satisfaction.
2. Leader behavior will increase subordinates' efforts if it links satisfaction of their needs to effective performance and supports their efforts to achieve goal performance.

These propositions tell managers to increase the number of outcomes available for effective performance, clear the paths to these outcomes of barriers, and help subordinates to see these outcomes as desirable.[19] To do this, the theory provides four types of leadership behaviors based on the work needed.[20] These are:

- *Instrumental behavior* (task oriented). It involves the planning, monitoring, and task assignment aspect of leadership. Instrumental behavior can be used to increase an employee's work effort or clarify outcomes.

- *Supportive behavior*. It involves the employee-oriented concern for the welfare and needs of subordinates. In addition, it includes creation of a warm, pleasant climate.
- *Participative behavior*. It involves using subordinates' ideas in decision making. A subordinate who operates independently and who has ability would respond favorably to this approach.
- *Achievement-oriented behavior*. This involves both developing a highly challenging climate for an employee and demanding good performance.

These leadership behaviors are based on the situational factors. There are two situational factors that influence leadership behavior:

1. The personal characteristics of the subordinates.
2. The environmental pressures and demands with which subordinates must cope to accomplish goals and satisfy personal needs.

Personal characteristics of a subordinate include the person's ability, self-confidence, and needs. These elements describe the performance level of the ability and the degree of confidence in performing the job. This factor of personal characteristics affects how subordinates view their leader and themselves. The stronger their abilities and beliefs in themselves, the less supervision they will tolerate from the boss.[21]

Environmental pressures include the influences on subordinates that they cannot control but which affect their abilities to perform the tasks effectively. Co-workers, the tasks assigned, and the leader's exercise of power are examples of these influences. Co-workers who are not cooperating can influence job performance and minimize an employee's perception of completing the job.

These situational variables do influence the manager's behavior. An employee who has high confidence and ability can be approached with an achievement-oriented style. Another who is unsure, but has ability, can be approached in a supportive manner. It is the situation that dictates the style. Managers need to be able to adjust.

Summary

- Leadership is the process of influencing a group or an individual toward the accomplishment of goal setting or goal achievement.
- Leadership and management are not synonymous.

- The four leadership roles a manager plays are educator, counselor, judge, and spokesperson.
- The nature of leadership of a manager is the result of the interaction of the leader, the led, and the organizational environment.
- The leader influences the leadership situation through her or his managerial philosophy, values, and needs as well as through the strengths or preferences of her or his leadership style.
- The subordinates affect the leadership situation through their values, needs, abilities, and style preferences or expectations.
- Environmental factors affecting leadership include job structure, the amount of technology, and upper level management influence.
- Leadership styles of a manager are dictated by the situation. Styles should vary according to the leader, the followers, and the environment.
- The elements of a manager's leadership style include motivational approach, decision-making style, and areas of emphasis (orientation) in the work environment.
- The leader can choose to motivate positively or negatively as part of leadership style.
- The decision-making options of leadership style refer to the degree of involvement of employees in the process. These options can be illustrated on a continuum of leadership behavior (see Figure 11.4).
- The three predominant leadership styles describing manager or employee decision making are autocratic, participative, and free-rein.
- In the work environment, a manager may emphasize task orientation or employee orientation as part of leadership style.
- Fiedler's contingency theory states that the effectiveness of a leader is determined by the interaction of the manager's orientation and three situational variables.
- Path-goal theory states that effectiveness of a leader is based on how the leader influences the employees' perception of work goals or rewards and their perception of the paths that lead to successful goal accomplishment.

Glossary of Essential Terms

contingency model	A theory of leadership (of Fiedler) that holds that the effectiveness of a leader is determined by the interaction of the leader behavior (orientation) and three variables: leader–member relations, task structure, and leader position power.

continuum of leadership behavior	Tannenbaum and Schmidt's visual representation of the various possible leadership approaches; the choice of one depends on the amount of decision making the leader is willing or able to share with subordinates. Positions along the continuum range from autocratic to free-rein approaches.
leadership	The process of influencing the group or individual toward the accomplishment of goal setting or goal achievement.
life cycle theory	A theory of leadership that states that the leadership approach varies with the maturity of the individual. An employee's maturity is viewed as his or her task-related ability and experience as well as willingness to accept responsibility.
Managerial Grid®	Blake and Mouton's visual representation of possible leadership behaviors, of which the one that occurs will result from the leader's orientation toward task or toward employee. A balance between the two extremes of orientation most often yields the most effective management behavior.
path-goal theory	A leadership theory concerned with the ways in which a leader can influence a subordinate's motivation, goals, and attempts at goal achievement.

Review Questions

1. Can you define this chapter's essential terms? If not, consult the preceding glossary.
2. What are the three variables that determine a manager's leadership style?
3. What are the four essential leadership roles managers play? What is involved in each?
4. What are the three factors that comprise a manager's leadership style? Discuss the elements of each factor.
5. "There is no one correct leadership style. A manager must be adjust the style based on the situation." Discuss this statement. able to adjust the style based on the situation." Discuss this statement.
6. What are the three variables that interact with a manager's orientation in Fiedler's contingency theory?
7. What are the four leadership behaviors in the path-goal theory of leadership? What are the two situational factors that influence the choice of leadership behavior?

References

1. W. R. Plunkett, *Supervision: The Direction of People at Work*, 4th ed. (Dubuque, Iowa: Wm. C. Brown Co., 1986), pp. 143–151.

2. A. A. Imberman, "Why Are Most Foreman Training Courses a Failure?" *Bedding*, 96, no. 6 (July 1969), pp. 40–41.

3. Plunkett, *Supervision*, p. 146.

4. Ralph M. Stodgill, "Personal Factors Associated with Leadership: A Survey of the Literature," *Journal of Psychology* (January 1948), pp. 35–71.

5. Oliver L. Niehouse, "The Myth of Consistency: There Are Certain Times When Managers Ought to Be Inconsistent and Unpredictable," *Success* (April 1987), p. 18.

6. Douglas McGregor, *The Human Side of Enterprise* (New York: McGraw-Hill, 1960), pp. 23–57.

7. Paul Hersey and Kenneth Blanchard, *Management of Organizational Behavior*, 2nd ed. (Englewood Cliffs, N.J.: Prentice-Hall, 1972), p. 135.

8. Keith Davis, *Human Behavior at Work: Organizational Behavior*, 6th ed. (New York: McGraw-Hill, 1986), p. 136.

9. Robert Keller and Andrew Szilagyi, "A Longitudinal Study of Leader Reward Behavior, Subordinate Expectancies, and Satisfaction," *Personnel Psychology* (Spring 1978), pp. 119–129.

10. Robert Tannenbaum and Warren H. Schmidt, "How to Choose a Leadership Pattern," *Harvard Business Review* (May–June 1973), pp. 162–180.

11. John Naisbitt, "Why Managers Must Be Facilitators: The Reasons Behind Participative Management Are Pragmatic and Profit Oriented," *Success* (April 1987), p. 12.

12. Rensis Likert, *The Human Organization* (New York: McGraw-Hill, 1976).

13. Ibid.

14. Peter Weissenberg and Michael J. Kavanagh, "The Independence of Initiating Structure and Consideration: A Review of the Evidence," *Personnel Psychology* (Spring 1972), pp. 119–130.

15. Robert R. Blake and Jane S. Mouton, *The Managerial Grid* (Houston: Gulf Publishing, 1964).

16. Fred E. Fiedler, "The Contingency Model—New Directions for Leadership Utilization," *Journal of Contemporary Business*, 3, no. 4 (Autumn 1974), pp. 65–80.

17. Ibid.

18. Robert J. House and Terrence R. Mitchell, "Path-Goal Theory of Leadership," *Journal of Contemporary Business*, 3, no. 4 (Autumn 1974), pp. 81–97.

19. Ibid.

20. Andrew Szilagyi, *Management and Performance* (Santa Monica, Calif.: Good-year Publishing, 1981), pp. 460–461.

21. House and Mitchell, "Path-Goal Theory."

Readings

Belker, Loren B. *The First-Time Manager: A Practical Guide to the Management of People*, 2nd ed. New York: AMACOM, 1986.

Bennis, Warren and Burt Namus. *Leaders, The Strategies for Taking Charge.* New York: Harper & Row, 1985.

Blanchard, Kenneth. *Leadership and the One-Minute Manager.* New York: Morrow & Co., 1985.

Byrd, Richard E. "Corporate Leadership Skills: A New Synthesis." *Organizational Dynamics*, 16, no. 1 (Summer 1987), pp. 34–43.

Carr-Ruffino, N. "How Do You Rate As a Manager?" *Executive Female*, 10 (July–August 1987), pp. 47–50.

Kirp, David and Douglas Rice. "Fast Forward: Styles of California Management." *Harvard Business Review* (January–February 1988), pp. 74–83.

Lieberman, Ernest. *Unfit to Manage: How Mis-Management Endangers America and What Working People Can Do About It.* New York: McGraw-Hill, 1988.

Maccoby, Michael. *Why Work: Leading the New Generation.* New York: Simon & Schuster, 1988.

Main, Jeremy. "Wanted: Leaders Who Can Make A Difference." *Fortune* (September 28, 1987), pp. 93–102(5).

Muczk, Jan and Bernard Reiman. "Has Participative Management Been Oversold?" *Personnel*, 64, no. 5 (May 1987), pp. 52–56.

11.1 Shock Therapy

Robert Manson is exhausted. He has just returned home from his first day as a trainee at Casa Del Sol, a neighborhood restaurant featuring Mexican cuisine. Bob has been hired to learn the business and eventually to take over its management once the owner, Jose Morales, leaves to open his second restaurant. After going through his mail and finishing a beer, Bob begins to reflect on the day's experiences.

The first thing that bothered Bob was the fact that Jose was an absolute dictator. He seemed to be the exact opposite of what his college course in supervision said a manager should be. Bob remembered how Jose shouted orders and instructions to almost everyone throughout the day. Even during the slack periods between meals, Jose was making constant demands on his people, Bob included. Not once could Bob remember Jose asking anyone's opinion or using the word "please." In spite of Jose's approach to management, the restaurant ran like a well-oiled machine. This fact puzzled Bob the most. Why, he thought, weren't the people resentful of Jose? They all did their jobs efficiently, and not once had Bob heard them complain.

Bob remembered one incident very clearly. A waiter had asked Jose if he could make a change in a procedure. After listening impatiently to the proposal, Jose responded as follows, "No good. Just do it like I trained you to, and we will all get along just fine. Everyone here does everything the same, and that's the way it is. You follow?" The waiter nodded his approval and went back to his duties.

Bob was worried that he could not operate the restaurant in Jose's style. He knew the values of participative management and felt that it was his natural style. He was afraid that he could not adjust to an autocratic style, especially since he believed it was a negative style, to be used when all other styles failed.

During his first day, Bob had studied the restaurant's procedures and questioned the wisdom behind a few of them. Now he felt he could not discuss them with Jose. He began to think his career in restaurant management would be a short one if he could not adjust to Jose's methods.

Bob liked Jose. All the people who worked for Jose seemed quite happy with their work. Jose had been civil and even friendly toward Bob throughout the day, but he demanded and got instant reactions from people. The restaurant was a successful business and offered Bob the promise of a very fine salary. Jose's methods certainly seemed to work, and the place was packed for three meals each day.

How can it be, Bob reflects, that such autocratic methods had produced such good results? Bob begins to search for his text on supervision.

For Discussion

1. Why do Jose's autocratic methods get good results?
2. What can you tell Bob about the usefulness of his preferred style of management at the Casa Del Sol?

11.2 Personal Selling

Parker Mendoza supervises fifteen sales professionals at the Chicago office of Trendy Products, Inc., an importer of the latest gift items from seven foreign countries. Besides his outside sales force, Parker supervises an office staff of two people. Three of his salespeople are in training, and the others have been in the field with an average of five years' experience in selling. When working with his new people, Parker spends one day each week with them in the field. He calls on retailers, mostly gift shops, and lets the new people watch as he makes the sales. After each call, he discusses what happened with the salesperson and uses each call as a demonstration of how to conduct personal selling.

With regard to supervising his experienced salespeople, Parker requires them to call the office twice each day to report their results, once in the morning before noon and once around 4 P.M. to summarize their days. He also requires that written summaries be filed each week that detail such things as the number of calls made, the sales written, the new prospects uncovered, and the complaints heard from customers.

The results of his supervision have been mixed. Two of the new people have yet to make a sale. Three of the experienced people have been complaining regularly about the burden of having to call in each day. One says it takes him away from calling on customers. One has told Parker that she feels it is unprofessional to have to make the calls. She is the top salesperson and has exceeded her sales goals in eleven of the past twelve months.

With his office staff, Parker is very willing to share decision making. In fact, two of his salespeople have mentioned that they run the office. As one of them put it, "Those two have Parker wrapped around their little fingers. He does not dare criticize them because he hates paperwork and would be lost without them." The office staff has received criticism from the salespeople who call in when Parker is not around and get no assistance or rude treatment. Complaints to Parker have not changed things.

At his monthly sales meeting with all of his salespeople in attendance, Parker announced that the new people would now be required to call in daily and that he intended to spend at least one day each month with each of his experienced salespeople in the field. As Parker put it, "Too many of you are not exceeding your sales goals. If you are doing anything wrong, I'll be with you to spot it. Customer complaints tell me that you don't get back to customers fast enough with answers."

Sheila Fergus interrupted Parker's next statement. "Parker, one of the reasons we take so long to respond to customers is that you won't let us make the decisions that have to be made. You are out of the office at least three days each week. Now you are telling us that you will be with each of us one day per month. How are we going to get to you in order to get your approval on things if you're in the field?"

For Discussion

1. What style of leadership is Parker using with each of his three groups: new salespeople, experienced salespeople, and the office staff?

2. What style of leadership would you recommend Parker adopt toward each of the three groups in Question 1?

3. Should Parker go ahead with his announced changes? Why or why not?

Controlling and Managing Change

Controlling: Prevention and Coping

OUTLINE

ESSENTIAL TERMS

controlling

diagnostic control

feedback control

feedforward control

prevention control

standard

therapeutic control

LEARNING OBJECTIVES

After reading and discussing this chapter, you should be able to do the following:

1. Define this chapter's essential terms.

2. Explain the interrelationship of planning and controlling.

3. Discuss the three steps in the control process.

4. Explain the concept of managerial standards.

5. Explain the concept of technical standards.

6. Discuss prevention, feedforward, and feedback controls.

7. List and discuss the six characteristics a manager must consider in designing a control system.

8. Explain two factors for making controls effective.

The Need for Controls

This chapter and the one that follows it examine controlling, the last of our five functions of management. Controlling is considered last because it affects and is affected by the other four functions, not because it is any less important. "A combination of well-planned objectives, strong organization, capable direction, and motivation have little probability of success unless there exists an adequate system of control."[1] Planning, organizing, staffing, and directing must be monitored to maintain their effectiveness and efficiency. Hence, there is a real need for competent people to plan, organize, and direct a control system that will work well.

In addition to the relationship of controlling to the other four functions of management, there is a very practical need for controlling. Organizational resources are limited. Their acquisition and use are critical to the survival of the organization. No person or organization should set resources in motion toward a goal and not monitor the progress of these resources. Coaches review game films to monitor progress toward game objectives; managers review performances of employees daily, weekly, and monthly to determine actual performance; and budget updates are sent to managers to compare actual spending with allocations. A sound organization operates under control—its progress is monitored to correct deviations or to revise critical plans.

This chapter is an overview of the controlling function. In it, we examine the process, types of controls, control characteristics, and methods for making control effective. In Chapter 13, we examine specific kinds of controls for nearly every type of business or organization.

Controlling Defined

Controlling establishes performance standards used to measure progress toward goals. The purpose of controlling is to determine whether people and the various parts of an organization are on target, achieving the progress toward their objectives that they planned to achieve. Planning chooses goals and maps out the necessary strategy and tactics. Controlling attempts to prevent failure (and to promote success) by providing the means to monitor the performances of individuals, departments, divisions, and the entire organization.

Robert J. Mockler has defined control this way:

Management control is a systematic effort to set performance standards with planning objectives, to design information feedback systems, to compare actual performance with these predetermined standards, to determine whether there are any deviations and to measure their significance, and to take any action required to assure that all corporate resources are being used in the most effective and efficient way possible in achieving corporate objectives.[2]

This definition provides us with the essential elements of control. Now we need to look at the control process and how it is developed.

The Control Process

The planning process determines objectives that eventually become the foundation for controls. The "first function," we have seen, is at the heart of all the others. Figure 12.1 shows the big picture, from the development of organizational objectives through individual objectives. The socioeconomic purpose is the fundamental reason the organization exists. The mission of the organization gives direction to planning and is the basic purpose for the organization's activities. Thus the strategic objectives and plans made at the top level of the organization are formulated in view of the organization's purpose and mission. From these plans flow the coordinated goals to be achieved by succeedingly lower levels of management in the organizational hierarchy. As the plans and goals are developed, there must be controls established to monitor the progress toward these goals. The feedback in the control process is intended to provide management with information on the progress of the various levels of plans, subplans, goals, objectives, strategy, tactics, or individual performances. Although the feedback may report progress as planned, it can also indicate that changes may be required in the plans and subplans themselves.[3]

An initial view of the control process reveals that it consists of three basic steps applicable to any persons, items, or processes being controlled. These steps are as follows:

1. Establish standards to be used in measuring progress, or lack of progress, toward goals.
2. Measure performance against standards, noting deviations from the standards.
3. Take actions necessary to correct deviations from standards.

These three steps happen continuously under the headings of Processes and Outputs in Figure 12.2.

FIGURE 12.1
The relationship of
planning and
controlling

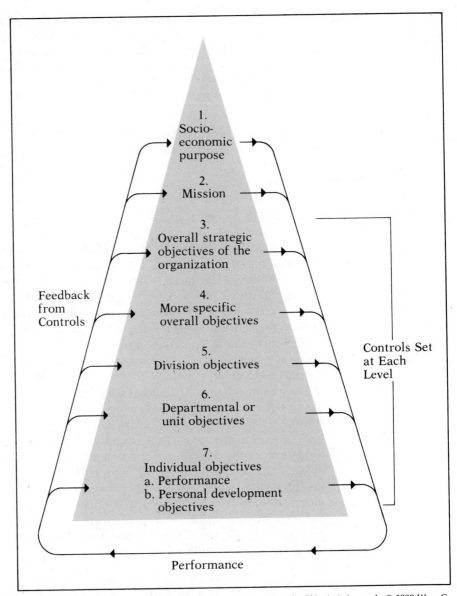

1.
Socio-
economic
purpose

2.
Mission

3.
Overall strategic
objectives of the
organization

4.
More specific
overall objectives

5.
Division objectives

6.
Departmental or
unit objectives

7.
Individual objectives
a. Performance
b. Personal development
objectives

Feedback
from
Controls

Controls Set
at Each
Level

Performance

Source: From George Odiorne et al., *Executive Skills: A Management by Objectives Approach.* © 1980 Wm. C.
Brown Company, Publishers, Dubuque, Iowa. Reprinted by permission of the author.

Establishing Standards

A **standard** is a measuring device, quantitative or qualitative, that is designed to help monitor the performance of people, capital goods, or processes. The exact nature of the standards to be used depends on what is

FIGURE 12.2
The control process
as a continuous
system

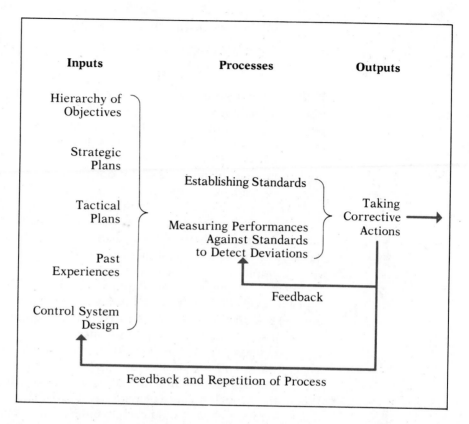

Inputs   **Processes**   **Outputs**

Hierarchy of
Objectives

Strategic
Plans

Establishing Standards

Tactical
Plans   Taking
                   Measuring Performances   Corrective
                      Against Standards   Actions
                    to Detect Deviations

Past
Experiences

Feedback

Control System
Design

Feedback and Repetition of Process

being monitored. Standards for comparison can apply to personnel, marketing, production, financial operations, and so on. Whatever the standards, however, they all can be assigned to one of two groups: managerial standards or technical standards.[4]

Managerial standards include such things as reports, regulations, and performance evaluations. All should focus on only the key areas and the kind of performance required to reach specific goals. They should be simple to understand, reviewed for appropriateness on a regular basis, and kept to a minimum. Managerial standards state the who, when, and why of the business.[5] Input from those who will use them is desirable when the managerial standards are being developed.

An example of a managerial standard is the sales manager's requirement of a monthly report from all salespersons; the report shows monthly progress on the key areas being monitored:

1. Total sales made in dollars and units.

2. Itemized sales by account name.

3. Potential sales to be made and status of sales in process.

4. An analysis of "lost sales" that states decisions made and why.

5. Report on sales calls made, including a review on established accounts and new accounts.

With this report, the manager is able to "control" the efforts of the sales force. An analysis of all the reports will show the sales manager who is performing as planned, when the performance is taking place (on schedule or not on schedule), and why the results are being achieved or not achieved.

Technical standards specify the what and how of the business. They apply to production methods and processes, to materials, machinery, safety equipment, parts, and supplies. Technical standards can come from internal and external sources. Safety standards, for example, may be dictated by government regulation or manufacturers' specifications for their equipment. Standards affecting parts of components manufacturing can be dictated by industry or customer specifications or by in-house capabilities.[6]

Examples of a technical standard are supplied by the production department in a business. Standards specifying machining tolerances, acceptable levels of quality, items produced per hour on an assembly line, and bid specifications developed by the engineering department—all are technical standards to guide performance and meet objectives.

Standards provide the who, what, when, why, and how to the control system. Who will take charge of this machine's maintenance? What will this person do to maintain it effectively and efficiently and control its use? When will the maintenance be performed? Why should it be done the way it is prescribed? How should each maintenance operation be performed?

As managers are developing and implementing standards in the control process, a point for them to remember is that the control process (like the processes that govern planning, organizing, staffing, and directing) is performed by operating employees. People need information to be successful in the control process. Managers need to take the time to provide information on the standards, what is being measured, and what the measuring information reveals. Is the standard an absolute? Is it strictly a warning signal? What is it supposed to indicate? Will it tell what the problem is and what to do about it? Or like a budget, will it just indicate that the standard is not being met? To be successful, managers must share this information if control standards and processes are to be effective.[7]

Measuring Performance

The first step in the control process has established the measuring device. The second step asks managers and others to measure the performance and determine if performance is in line with the set standards.

In possession of clear, simple standards that outline the acceptable and the unacceptable, managers can apply the standards to specific performances. This application often asks that comparisons be made between the "what is" and the "what should be." If the comparison yields results or measurements that are acceptable—within prescribed limits—no action need be taken. If the results show a trend away from the acceptable or show the unacceptable, action may be called for. Measurements must be taken regularly to discover any deviations as quickly as possible.

Consider this example: A machine operator is grinding metal parts to specific measurements (standards). Periodically throughout the grinding process, the machine operator measures the surface to be sure that it is within the tolerances set for the part—that is, within the ideal measurement plus or minus predetermined deviations. The operator may or may not measure each part throughout the grinding process depending on what the control procedures call for. After measuring the surface of a part, the operator notes an unacceptable surface—one ground beyond the limits. Next, the operator has to determine the cause of the deviation and take corrective action.

In the example, the measurement and comparison revealed that actual performance was below standard (an unacceptable surface, one ground beyond the limits). Another outcome of this step could be that the performance is well beyond, or above, the acceptable standard of performance. This discovery would also be a point of concern and should serve as a red flag for management. Why? It could mean the standard is not realistic and, therefore, not useful. It could also indicate that resources—personnel, equipment, and capital—are being used incorrectly. Such inappropriate use can result in lost opportunities for the organization.

As an example, consider a salesperson who repeatedly performs 200 percent above sales quota for a given territory. It could mean superior talent. It could also mean an inaccurate quota: The salesperson could be accomplishing the work in half the time allowed. Overachievement may mean underutilization of personnel, but before any action can be taken, further investigation is called for to determine what has happened.

Taking Corrective Action

Let us review a hypothetical control dilemma: Management has noted a deviation from a standard. A cause or causes for the deviation have been determined. Now, determining the precise action to take will depend on three things: the standard, the accuracy of the measurements that determined that a deviation exists, and the diagnosis of the person or device investigating the cause for the deviation. Standards can be too loose or too strict. Measurements may be inaccurate because of poor use of measuring devices or defects in the devices themselves. Finally, people can use poor judgment in determining the corrective actions to be taken.

Corrective actions can be prescribed by management in advance through polices, procedures, and practices. When such prescriptions exist, they help to shorten the reaction times to problems. But not every situation involving deviations from standards can be cured with a prescribed solution. When a customer fails to receive an order on time, a routine investigation is called for and conducted in a prescribed manner. But when employees violate work rules, the circumstances must be determined before any corrective action can be taken intelligently.

Sometimes corrective actions are automatic. When a thermostat senses temperatures below or above its setting, it triggers electrical current flow to increase or decrease temperature. Computer programs can prevent as well as detect deviations and then take corrective actions. Such is the case in many automated assembly lines using computer-guided equipment.

Some corrective actions may have to make exceptions to established policy, procedures, or practices. A customer demands a refund for a product having a defect not covered in the warranty. A refund may be made simply to keep a valued customer. Managers must be allowed some discretion to use their best judgments because most problems they face cannot be adequately proceduralized. No management procedure should be a substitute for judgment.

Finally, we must take great care in the most important step in the process of taking corrective action: detecting the causes for deviations. It is often easy to assume that we know what is wrong and why. But how often have we attempted to solve a problem that didn't exist at all? We have to remember that several diseases have the same symptoms; hence, failure to meet a goal may have more than one cause, each of which will, or may, require a unique solution.

Types of Controls

What types of controls are there, and what is their purpose? Work performed by organizations and their employees has a starting point (where inputs take place), a period of performance (where the inputs are meshed), and a final product (or output). Figure 12.2 showed this processing of work as a continuous system. Because of the nature of work and work flow, various types of controls have been developed. There are three basic types of controls: prevention, feedforward, and feedback. Each has its place in helping plans reach their potential. (As you read the explanation of each type of control, refer to Figure 12.3 for an illustration of when each control is applied.)

FIGURE 12.3
Types of controls

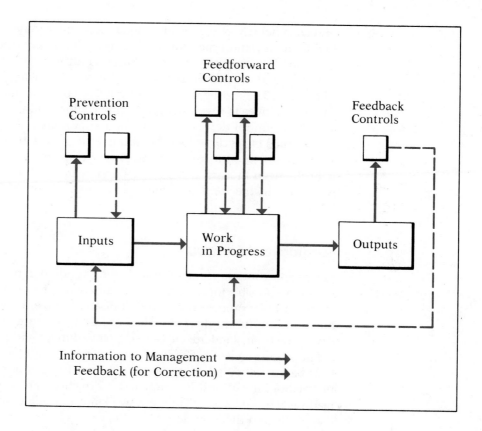

Prevention Controls

An ounce of prevention is worth a pound of cure. This old maxim is certainly true when a business's security, or your own, is involved. Better to prevent trouble than have to deal with its related problems. **Prevention controls** focus on establishing conditions that will make it difficult or impossible for deviations from norms to occur. Locks and bars on windows, safety equipment and safety procedures, and budgets—all are attempts to prevent problems.

One example of a prevention control is the development by companies of job descriptions and job specifications (see Chapter 9). The job description identifies the work that has to be done, thus clarifying working relationships, responsibility areas, and authority relationships. It assists in preventing the duplication of work and potential organizational conflict. The job specification identifies the abilities, training, education, and characteristics needed of a person to do the job. As a control device, it works to prevent a person who is totally unqualified from receiving the job, thereby saving money and time and precluding potential poor performance.

Another example of a prevention control is the implementation of induction and orientation programs by forward-thinking organizations (see Chapter 9). These programs are designed to ensure a smooth transition for a new employee to the systems and expectations of the organization. They are, as all control devices, focused at a critical area of the employee's organizational life cycle—from the hiring decision to actual job performance. They are intended to prevent the employee from being frustrated. They limit the need to learn through trial and error and minimize the need for resources, in the form of a manager's time, to correct deviations in the future.

Feedforward Controls

Prevention controls focus on establishing conditions that will make it difficult or impossible for deviations to occur and are therefore generally placed at the start of a process; they block or disarm trouble. **Feedforward controls**, however, are future directed: They are designed to detect and anticipate deviations from standards at various points throughout the processes. They are in-process controls. Feedforward controls are often called steering controls because they allow people to act on a process or activity while it is proceeding, not after it is completed. Corrections and adjustments can be made as the need arises. There are two kinds of feedforward control devices: diagnostic and therapeutic.

Diagnostic controls attempt to determine what deviation is taking or has taken place. They tell you what is wrong—not why. Diagnosis makes use of measurements that rely on the five senses. Perhaps the best kind of diagnosis occurs when the person most familiar with a situation uses his or her intuition and background experiences in discovering what has gone wrong. A physician's first line of attack on a patient's complaints involves that bank of previously acquired knowledge. Tests and other checks may be called on later to verify what the physician believes to be the proper diagnosis.

Diagnostic control devices include such things as gauges, meters, and warning lights. Some are designed to be interpreted (heard or seen) by people. Others can trigger electrical or mechanical actions to alert a person or computer that a deviation from a standard is taking place.

The sales manager who receives the monthly sales printout showing sales quota results is working with a diagnostic control device. It will indicate deviations from the acceptable standard but will not show why. The manager wonders: Is that normal at this time of the year, or is it based on performance? Analysis of the situation is necessary to confirm

Source: Reprinted with special permission of King Features Syndicate, Inc.

either possibility. Discovering the why can be the most difficult part of the process.

Therapeutic controls sense both the what and the why, and then they take corrective action. Control devices such as an engine speed governor and automatic transmission are designed to take necessary actions when conditions trigger them to do so. Engines have built-in controls, as do numerous kinds of equipment and machines. What they do and when is a result of their design and the interaction of their components. A computer at a bank will automatically print out a debit memorandum (showing a deduction from a depositor's account) when it receives a customer's check for a withdrawal. When such a check is received for more than the customer's balance, the computer puts the customer on an overdraft list, creates a debit memo for the bank's overdraft charge, and prepares the envelope for mailing the memo to the customer.

A manager conducting employee training using the coaching method (see Chapter 9) is utilizing a therapeutic control. When the trainee is performing the task, the manager is on the scene, observing if any deviations from the intended processes take place. If a deviation occurs, the manager observes it, diagnoses the reason for the incorrect technique, and corrects the deviation. The control and correction take place during the process—not two days after it has occurred.

Feedback Controls

Feedback controls are postaction controls and focus on the end results of the process. The information derived is not used for corrective action on a project because it has been completed. The feedback control provides information for a manager to examine and apply to future activities that are similar to the present one. The purpose is to help prevent mistakes in the future.

At the end of the year, for example, a manager should carefully review the analysis of the budget control report. What accounts were overdrawn? Why? Were there any accounts with a surplus? Why? Could funds that were not spent have been allocated to other accounts? Were all priorities met by the budget? At this time, the manager cannot modify budget expenditures or allocations for the previous year. But this information can provide a head start as the manager develops the budget plans for the upcoming year.

A practical illustration of a feedback control can be found in the expression "Boy, I'll never do that again that way!" Whether it applies to taking a vacation, driving across town on the expressway during peak traffic hours, or simply waiting to do birthday shopping until the last minute, all of us learn from experiences and apply those lessons to the next similar opportunity—a feedback control.

We have defined control, discussed the control process in depth, and examined the three types of controls. Now it is time to answer the following question: If an organization were to design a control system, what should be its characteristics?

Control Characteristics

"In the final analysis, for a control system to be effective, it requires the participation of the various company departments, the support of senior management, and the allocation of sufficient resources."[8] The best controls are those formed around the input from the various people and departments that will be affected by them.

Controls may have many different characteristics, but the most important are these:[9]

1. Acceptance by members of the organization.
2. Focus on critical control points.
3. Economic feasibility.
4. Accuracy.
5. Timeliness.
6. Ease of understanding.

Let's examine each of these characteristics.

1. Acceptance by the organization's members is crucial to a control's effectiveness and efficiency. Doing the right thing and doing things right both require people. Controls won't work unless people want them to. Too many controls, as well as too few, can lead to frustration and lack of motivation. Controls that appear to be arbitrary or unnecessary can have the same impact on a workforce. An example of controls that have negatively affected the work setting is provided by the increasing number of video display terminal operators who are monitored by their own computers. Employers in insurance, airline, telephone, and retail food store industries are using computers for recording when an operator is off a video display terminal or on an authorized or unauthorized break, counting keystrokes by the second, timing customer service transactions, and tracking errors. Although management views the control device as a positive approach to management because it measures work quantity and quality, employees do not share this perception. Comments like "meddlesome," "nuisance," "stressful," "invades privacy," and "abusive" typify employee reactions. Potential long-term outcomes of the employees' reactions are destroyed creativity, stifled initiative, and weakened desire to do a good job.[10]

2. Critical control points include all the areas of an organization's operations that directly affect the success of its key operations. The list of critical control points for the total enterprise would include such areas as sales, revenue, expenses, inventory levels, personnel turnover, safety for people and other assets, and more. In addition, each manager will have his or her own critical areas to control. The focus should be on those areas where failures cannot be tolerated and where the costs in time and money are the greatest. Having a salesperson document all activities during the day is a control method. But is it a control at the critical point? Wouldn't it be more effective to focus on key areas: on calls, sales, and new accounts?

3. The cost of the control or a control system must be weighed against the benefits it can return. The resources that will have to be expended may not return an equal or larger amount. An elaborate security system could include closed-circuit television, guards, and various alarms, but at what cost and to safeguard how much? A control system that requires the preparation of multiple pieces of paperwork, including requisition and justification forms, and several levels of authorization is overkill for the purchase of a gross of paper clips but is reasonable for the purchase of a four-color printing press.

4. Information must be accurate if it is to be useful. This character-

istic relates directly to the preceding discussion on feedforward controls used in diagnosing a deviation. Controls that offer inaccurate assessments feed decision makers the wrong input, which will cause them to produce incorrect responses (lack of action or inappropriate action and the waste of resources that go with both). A manager may report, for example, that production goals are not being met because "he does not have enough labor available." Investigation may reveal, however, that there is an adequate labor force, but the methods in use are inappropriate.

5. Timely information, like accurate information, must be given to those in charge if meaningful responses are to follow. Giving managers too much or unneeded information is as big a problem as not enough information. The purpose of a management information system (Chapter 13) is to gather, assemble, and interpret data, processing it into timely and accurate information that gets to those who need it. An illustration of this point is the reporting of budget expenditures. Budget printouts are helpful only when the appropriate manager receives them in a timely manner. In one organization, the printouts are received one month after the end of the month they describe. They do not reflect actual expenditures on the day received, nor realistic account balances. Because the automated control system is functioning a month behind, the manager has installed a manual bookkeeping control system. The result: accurate information at a cost of duplicated effort and personnel hours.

6. Complexity often means lack of understanding. The simpler the control, the easier it will be to understand and apply. If you have struggled with assembly instructions for a toy or hobby kit or garden equipment, you know firsthand how seldom one finds understandable instructions in writing. Controls often become complex because more than one person is responsible for creating, implementing, or interpreting them. Overlapping authority can cause confusion and duplication of effort. Complexity can also result when control users focus on mechanics and lose sight of the controls' purposes. This happens when one control leads to another: If one control is good, two are better. Refinements in reporting procedures often lead to additional controls and more control procedures and output. The result is a profusion of data, which tends to obscure the purposes behind the controls and to sidetrack control efforts.

Control characteristics aid in the design of the system. They serve as initial inputs for managers. After the system is implemented, what does a manager need to focus on to make the controls effective? Let's look at some key points for making controls effective.

Making Controls Effective

Controls are effective as long as they (1) do what they are intended for—prevent deviations, diagnose deviations, treat deviations, or provide information for future planning—and (2) do not create organizational problems that result in costs greater than the benefits of the control devices.

Update the Controls

Controls are effective only as long as they do what they are intended to do. When the control devices were designed, it was with a certain set of expectations and under specific circumstances. If these circumstances and expectations change within the organization, the control devices need to be reviewed and possibly updated or replaced. Why does this not happen regularly?

All of us, managers included, tend to get comfortable with the way things are. Everyone likes the security that accompanies routine. This desire for security and the resultant familiarity lead to an acceptance of systems or procedures that may have outlived their usefulness. "We've always done it that way" often becomes the excuse for avoiding the effort to reexamine, refine, and improve. After all, these efforts could bring discomfort and insecurity. But continually repeating the past means a lack of planning for the future. By relying on controls that are in place, organizations fail to make use of the preventive potential of the controlling process. The instant changes are planned or occur in operations, managers should begin to examine how adequate the present controls will be for the changes that are planned or already exist. Controls need to be current.

Monitor the Organizational Impact

A second critical area for managers to monitor in making controls effective is the degree of organizational impact, both on people and on systems, that controls have. It should be expected that control systems will affect employees and organizational operations, but extreme changes should be avoided.

When controls are developed, employees may resent them as unnecessary, strict, or demeaning. This point has already been stated in the preceding section on control characteristics. What can management do to make controls more acceptable and less threatening? Involvement of the employees in the design and implementation of the control is critical to reduce or eliminate anxiety and resentment. Involvement also results in commitment to the concept. In addition, controls should be realistic in terms of the standard of performance and the number of standards set. Standards should be attainable, not arbitrary. And managers must not overcontrol by setting more and more controls.

Controls also need to be monitored to limit the potential impact on organizational patterns and systems because controls can have side effects. For example, a control device can require an authorization for purchasing to be three levels of management higher than before the control was installed. What is the impact of this on morale, timeliness of decisions, and the decision-making environment? In addition, with the decision making located at higher levels, what has happened to the communication system in the organization?

One answer for management is to use program evaluation techniques to monitor the system. One technique, before-and-after comparison, looks at the environment before and after the system was installed to note any differences and why they occurred. Other available techniques operate with similar results. Regardless of the technique used, the impact of control is being evaluated.

The point of concern for managers is that controls need to be controlled. Managers need to review the controls periodically to guarantee applicability. They also must monitor the side effects of control on people and organizational systems by means of program evaluation.

Summary

- Controlling affects and is affected by planning, organizing, staffing, and directing.
- The acquisition and use of resources are critical to the survival of the organization. They should not be set in motion toward a goal without being monitored.
- Controlling requires managers to establish standards for performance, measure performances against those standards, and take the necessary actions to correct deviations from those standards.
- Standards need to be established in the areas of quantity and quality of output, costs, and time usage.
- Standards may be managerial or technical.
- Managerial standards include policies, rules, and reports; they state the who, what, and why of a business.
- Technical standards include safety, process and machine operations, and instructions and methods; they state the what and how of the organization.

- Prevention controls are based on anticipated deviations and attempt to make it impossible for them to occur.
- Feedforward controls are designed to detect and anticipate deviations from standards at various points throughout the process.
- Diagnostic control devices determine what deviation is taking or has taken place.
- Therapeutic controls determine what and why with regard to deviations. They trigger responses to problems.
- Feedback controls provide end-result information for future projects.
- Controls need to be acceptable to organization members, accurate, timely, focused on critical control points, economical, and easily understood.
- Keeping the control devices current with regard to objectives and expectations is critical in making control effective.
- It is necessary to monitor the degree of organizational impact of controls to assist in making control effective.

Glossary of Essential Terms

controlling   Establishing performance standards used to measure progress toward goals.

diagnostic control   A monitoring device or system that attempts to determine what deviation from a standard is taking or has taken place.

feedback control   A monitoring device or system designed to provide end-result information on a project for future planning.

feedforward control   A monitoring device or system designed to detect and to anticipate deviations from standards at various points throughout ongoing processes.

prevention control   Monitoring devices or systems designed to establish conditions that will make it difficult or impossible for deviations from standards to occur.

standard   A quantitative or qualitative measuring device designed to help monitor the performances of people, capital goods, or processes.

therapeutic control   A monitoring device or system designed to sense what deviations from standards are taking place and why and then to take a corrective action.

Review Questions

1. Can you define this chapter's essential terms? If not, consult the preceding glossary.

2. Why is the function of control critical to the success of the planning function?

3. Identify the three basic steps in the control process, and provide an example of each step.

4. What areas of a business do managerial standards apply to, and what three areas are stated in a managerial standard?

5. What areas of a business do technical standards apply to, and what do they specify?

6. What are the purposes of (a) prevention controls, (b) feedforward controls, and (c) feedback controls?

7. What are the six characteristics of controls discussed in this chapter, and why is each important? *ACCEPTANCE, TOLERATE, ECON FEASABILITY, ACCURATE, TIMELY, EASE OF UNDERSTANDING.*

8. Why do controls need to be updated as well as monitored for the degree of organizational impact they have?

References

1. Earl P. Strong and Robert D. Smith, *Management Control Models* (New York: Holt, Rinehart & Winston, 1968), p. 2.

2. Robert J. Mockler, *The Management Control Process* (Englewood Cliffs, N.J.: Prentice-Hall, 1972), p. 2.

3. George Odiorne, Heinz Weihrich, and Jack Mendleson, *Executive Skills: A Management by Objectives Approach* (Dubuque, Iowa: Wm. C. Brown Co., 1980), pp. x–xi.

4. Vincent G. Reuter, "A Trio of Management Tools Increases Productivity and Reduces Costs," *Arizona Business*, 22, no. 2 (February 1977), pp. 12–17.

5. Ibid.

6. Ibid.

7. Peter F. Drucker, *The Practice of Management* (New York: Harper & Row, 1954), p. 131.

8. Philip Gross, "How to Assess Your Internal Controls," *Inc.* (June 1981), p. 104.

9. Peter F. Drucker, *Management: Tasks, Responsibilities, Practices* (New York: Harper & Row, 1974), pp. 489–504.

10. Haya El Nasser, "Video Terminals Watch Workers." *USA Today* (February 15, 1987), p. 6B.

Readings

Ackoff, Russell L. *Management in Small Doses.* New York: John Wiley & Sons, 1987.

Allen, Brandt. "Make Information Services Pay Its Way." *Harvard Business Review* (January–February 1987), pp. 57–63.

Beniger, James. *The Control Revolution: Technological and Economic Origins of the Information Society.* Cambridge, Mass.: Harvard University Press, 1987.

Donnahoe, Alan. *Basic Business Statistics for Managers.* New York: John Wiley & Sons, 1988.

Johnson, H. Thomas and Robert Kaplan. *Relevance Lost.* Boston: Harvard Business School Press, 1987.

Mirabile, R. "Soft Skills, Hard Numbers (Quantify Managers' Competence)." *Training,* 24 (August 1987), pp. 53–56.

Odiorne, George. "Measuring the Unmeasurable." *Business Horizons,* 30, no. 4 (July–August 1987), pp. 69–75.

Sellers, Patricia. "Lessons from TV's New Bosses?" *Fortune* (March 14, 1988), pp. 115–130(6).

Silk, Leonard. *Economics in Plain English.* New York: Simon & Schuster, 1986.

Tucker, Frances, Seymour Zivan, and Robert Camp. "How to Measure Yourself Against the Best." *Harvard Business Review* (January–February 1987), pp. 8–10.

C
A
S
E
S

12.1   Getting Control

Wallace Struthers, the president of the GlenAire Bank and Trust, is discussing the statistics from his comptroller's report on the problems with the bank's automated teller machines with the members of his executive committee. "The figures are getting worse. According to a study by the American Bankers Association, about 18,000 crimes were committed at or with automated teller machines nationwide. Our bank's experience with losses from our ATMs parallels losses nationwide. About 90 percent of our losses come from people using stolen or lost ATM cards, about 5 percent from vandalism and break-ins to the ATMs, and the remaining 5 percent from robberies and muggings of customers at our remote ATM locations. Last year, the bank lost $12,954 because of these ATM-related crimes. This year, the comptroller estimates that our losses will exceed $15,000. Ladies and gentlemen, we have to tighten up on our controls over our three ATMs."

The bank's three automated teller machines are located as follows: One is at the bank, next to the drive-through lanes; the second is at the train station about fifty feet from the passenger depot in a telephone-booth-like structure; and the third is outside the local supermarket in a similar structure. All three machines are sheltered from the wind and rain and well lighted except for the occasional vandalism that breaks glass and destroys the lighting fixtures. All three have entrances that face a street and use folding doors. The booth at the train station has been the source of nearly 75 percent of the bank's losses to theft, vandalism, and fraud committed with stolen or lost cards.

The bank has only had automated teller machines for two years and has not installed any kind of surveillance equipment. It has relied on visual observation by bank personnel during banking hours for the machine at the bank and on public locations with high visibility from the street at the other locations. Obviously, this has not been adequate. Local police drive by all the machine locations at least once every hour of the day and night. The ATMs do not have any alarm devices to detect break-ins or tampering with them.

The problem with the stolen or lost cards is a tough one to deal with. Customers are issued a card when they sign up for the ATM service. Each cardholder has a six-number code that must be entered before the machines will accept the card. Once the numbers are entered, the card is inserted in a slot, and the transaction buttons are pressed to take cash from the cardholder's bank account. When the transaction is completed, the card is returned to a drop slot. Most cards that are lost have been left with the machine by the customers after each transaction. Obviously, the bank cannot do anything about stolen or lost cards until the customer notifies the bank. Then the bank programs its computer to reject any transaction using that card and its cardholder code. So far, more than 280 cards have been reported lost or stolen by customers.

For Discussion

1. As a member of the bank's executive committee, what security measures do you recommend to deal with the unauthorized use of ATM cards?
2. What kind of controls would you recommend to deal with vandalism problems?
3. What kind of controls would you recommend to deal with the problems of robbery and muggings at the ATM machines?

12.2 Keep 'em on Their Toes

Ethan Kress has built his business from scratch. Sixteen years and five stores to manage have given him the confidence to speak his mind about controlling operations. At the New York convention of independent hardware retailers, he did not hesitate to share his methods with colleagues who, like himself, run their own independent operations.

During the first day's lunch break, Ethan and several other entrepreneurs were discussing control of their multistore operations. Ethan explained that he favored a personal approach. He told the group about the visits he made every year to each of his three branch stores. Pretending to be a customer and dressed in his favorite gardening clothes, Ethan would wander the aisles looking for misplaced and mismarked merchandise. He would make mental notes on the orderliness of displays, the cleanliness of the store, the contacts that store personnel had with customers, and the accuracy of checkouts. When his visit was over, he would meet with the store manager and review his discoveries. He took special delight in one particular visit on finding dirty aisles, a discourteous clerk, and a particular item out of stock. He fired the manager on the spot and promoted the clerk with the most seniority. Ethan stayed with the store as its manager until things were in order again and the new man was able to take over. "I can tell you," said Ethan, "those unannounced visits of mine really keep my people on their toes."

For Discussion

1. Which kind(s) of control is Ethan using?
2. If you were one of Ethan's store managers, would his actions keep you "on your toes"? Why or why not?
3. What control characteristics do Ethan's visits have?

pg. 368   2, 4, 6

Some Forms
of Control

OUTLINE

ESSENTIAL TERMS

audit	information
balance sheet	Key Indicator Management
critical path	management information system
data	program evaluation review
human asset accounting	technique
income statement	ratio

LEARNING OBJECTIVES

After reading and discussing this chapter, you should be able to do the following:

1. Define this chapter's essential terms.
2. Describe the purposes for each of the general management controls.
3. Describe the purposes for each of the financial controls.
4. Describe the purposes for each of the production controls.

What Forms Do Controls Take?

Chapter 12 gave you an introduction to controlling as a function and process of management. This chapter introduces several of the most important controls and control processes in widespread use today. We look at general management controls, financial controls, production controls, and the functions of computers in the control process. Our primary objective in each area is to make you familiar with, not necessarily able to use, each kind of control or control process. Many of the controls examined here require in-depth knowledge beyond the content of this course and text.

General Management Controls

General controls considered here are these:

- The management information system.
- Key Indicator Management.
- Human asset accounting.
- Inventory control systems.

These are considered general management control tools because they help managers in more than one narrow area, such as production or finance. They may apply to all control efforts (as management information systems do) or to two or more areas (as inventory control systems do).

Management Information Systems

What is a management information system, and what are its purposes?

A **management information system** (MIS) is a formal method of providing management with accurate and timely information so that managers can make decisions and carry out the managerial functions and operations effectively. The information provided by the system relates to past, present, and future events both inside and outside the organization.[1] Notice the emphasis on information. An MIS provides information, not raw data, to managers for decision making. **Data** are unprocessed facts and figures that are of little use to managers.[2] On the other hand, **information** is data that have been deliberately selected, processed, and organized to be useful to an individual manager.[3] A sound MIS system identifies needs for information, identifies a source or sources of data, and designs the system to provide the information from the data. The point to remember is that the MIS is purposefully designed to meet the informational needs of the organization.

In developing an MIS, what factors need to be considered? According to William H. Sihler, four critical factors need to be considered in building, using, and evaluating any control system. These factors are:[4]

1. *Meet organizational objectives.* Is the system related to, and does it reinforce, the objectives of the organization? Is there congruence between the system and the goals, or is there disharmony and friction?

2. *Provide information flow.* Is the system well related to the organizational structure? Does information flow in an acceptable way to those who generate and use the data? Is coordination and consolidation of information effective and easy?

3. *Deliver the right quality and quantity of information.* Do the managers receive the information they require to do their jobs? Do they get too little information? Too much information? Does it tell them something useful about the activities that they have control over and that they can influence? Does it threaten them with punishment on account of activities for which they have neither responsibility nor authority?

4. *Provide timely information.* Is the information provided in time to be of use to the managers?

The last three points in Sihler's list relate specifically to a manager's *need* for information. Every organization, regardless of size, needs an MIS to collect, sort, interpret, summarize, and distribute information to those who need it in a timely, effective, and efficient manner. The foundation for management's decisions must be accurate, up-to-date information, so management must decide what information it needs and design the best means for obtaining it. The goal of an MIS is to provide what is needed (no more and no less) to those who need it (managers and other paid decision makers) at the right time and place and in the right form.

Let's consider the information needs of managers at various levels of management in an organization. Top-level managers need information on competitors, economic conditions, legal and political developments, and technology to plan with. For control purposes, they need reports on the overall financial picture of the organization. This information can be supplied on a monthly or quarterly basis for trend analysis.

Middle-level managers need information for their particular divisional operations. Whether the division is sales, production, personnel, or purchasing, the middle-level managers need information on trends or major types of fluctuations. The major difference between the information needs of top-level managers and middle-level managers is that much of the information is internal in nature for middle-level managers, and it is based on performance of subgroups.

Lower-level managers, because of the nature of their jobs, need daily information on performance. The needs vary by the position—a sales manager would want reports on daily sales, customer returns, new client contacts; production would need reports on wastage, quality rejects, units produced, manhour variations; personnel might need reports on daily openings, interviews performed, and employees hired.

As was previously stated, all organizations need to consciously develop an MIS system. Managers need an orderly flow of information on an ongoing basis with which to function. Initially this information can entail handwritten reports, summaries, statistics, or a series of reports from various functions flowing to a manager. (See Figure 13.1 for a view of an MIS system.)

FIGURE 13.1
A simplified MIS

As the needs of management become more sophisticated, the MIS will by design become more sophisticated. Figure 13.2 provides a view of a more detailed MIS. Notice that data from one operating department (Operating Division Data) when processed correctly provides information for three functional areas of management (engineering, geology, and accounting). Another observable phenomenon is that as both the quantities of information and the uses for the information increase, a decision may be made to integrate the MIS with a computer.

MIS and computers. If an organization decides to use a computer in its MIS, this choice is certain to aid the receivers of its output in the execution of all of their duties, not just their controlling efforts. Computers can speed the processing and increase the accuracy of data. Their small size and lower costs make them available to nearly every organization today: They can be purchased, leased, or time-shared (that is, time to use someone else's computer can be arranged for). A phenomenon that happens when computers are part of an MIS is that managers soon find many more applications for them than were originally envisioned. This in turn can mean an overload on facilities or personnel, eventually requiring an expansion of the system. Management should be aware at the outset of this possibility.

Establishing the MIS system. Whether or not the MIS is computerized, there are inherent problems for an organization when an MIS is to be established. Where there has been no formal system, there is likely to be the fear of the unknown, of change, of threat of reduced authority, and the use of "experts." Where there has been a formal system that now is to be computerized, the same inherent problems exist. What can be done to facilitate the improvement of the process? Here are some suggestions:

1. Involve the users in the systems design. The information specialists (such as systems design personnel and computer programmers) will not be using the information they help prepare and disseminate. What they need is the guidance of the people they are hired to serve.

2. Establish clear lines of direction, as well as control of the information-processing operations. Avoid confusion on authority, problem solving, and answers.

3. Construct clear procedures for gathering, sorting, interpreting, processing, and distributing data. Structure reduces fear of the unknown. How, when, and where need to be answered.

4. Use specialists where they are needed, and explain their roles to users. Establish the service role of the specialists rather than their alleged superiority or right to dictate orders to the users.

5. Build the staff in line with requirements for service. Don't overstaff for the sake of empire building, and don't understaff: Both will affect the quality of service.

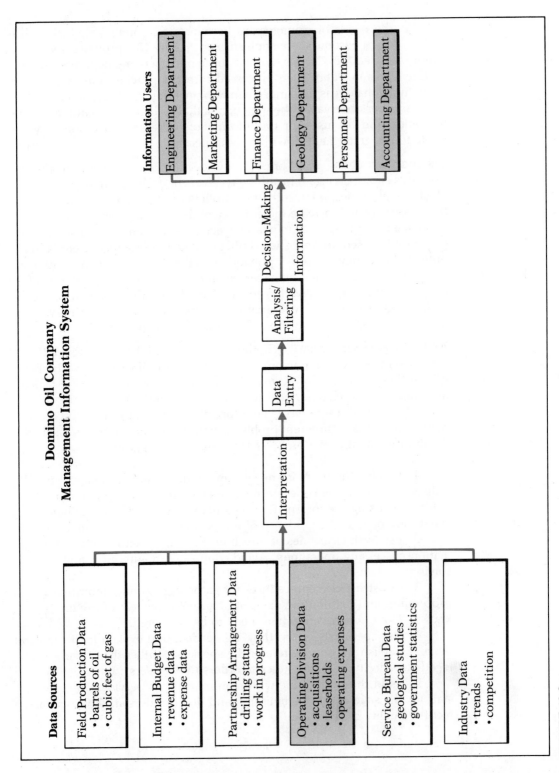

FIGURE 13.2
A sophisticated MIS

6. Centralize where possible. Decentralize when it is more effective and cost efficient to do so. Centralization brings concentrated resources and expertise.

Once an MIS is established, its operation must be flexible to meet the changing demands that will come. What existed yesterday may not remain today. Also, new kinds of information may be needed and in different presentation formats.

Problems with MIS.   No matter who develops the MIS, there are three problems that management must deal with. The first has to do with confidentiality and the need to safeguard data and information from unauthorized eyes. Some data should be restricted to locked files and reports for in-house use only. Data on current and future operations could damage a business's market position if it were to fall into the hands of the competition.

A second problem has to do with the quantity of information generated. MIS specialists often feel that unless they are creative in adding to their outputs, they may not be able to justify their positions or to add to their numbers. Care must be taken to consolidate information where possible and to monitor constantly the efficiency of the MIS output. The burdens for such vigilance fall on the MIS director and the recipients of the MIS output.

Third, when an MIS is introduced, the persons it is designed to serve will be asked to do something differently. Just as they receive from an MIS, they will be asked to give. Some data may be needed from their operations, so their roles may change so that they can supply the information. Preparation of the personnel will minimize this problem.

An MIS is something that all organizations need for their operations. The costs will be outweighed by the benefit in the long run—if the system is well thought out.

Key Indicator Management

Key Indicator Management (KIM) is a monitoring system that provides managers with information that, at a glance, provides the essentials they need.[5] Such an approach focuses on graphics—charts, tables, and graphs—to keep track of the key measures of company operations. "For each measure, a target is established and a monthly report created to show progress (or lack thereof) against a particular goal."[6] Rather than having to watch an entire operation, the manager can concentrate on the indicator. If the indicator is not on target, the manager must conduct further investigation into the operation.

Department heads, including the person in charge of the MIS department, select the targets and measuring devices through conferences with their supervisors. This extension and application of management by objectives and participative management helps companies as a feedforward control because it highlights trends along with interim or temporary successes and failures. KIM is an ongoing monitoring system that keeps track of operations as they progress.[7] It can watch over any key area or project on a temporary or permanent basis. Exhibit 13.1 shows an application of KIM. Note in the example that the key indicator has been identified as order entry (processing a customer order). The company is using as a measure the "customer order processing time (days)" with a target of three days. At a glance, the manager can see that the target this month has not been achieved (4.1 actual). It has not been achieved year-to-date or past year (4.4 and 4.7, respectively).

The following is a simplified approach to setting up a key indicator management system of monitoring:[8]

1. Identify the operating departments or functions to be measured.
2. Determine the items to be used in the measuring program.
3. Determine the measurement details.
4. Establish the targets (goals).
5. Prepare a periodic report.

Notice the process used by management. Just the areas of functions are identified. Then the critical items in each department to be monitored are

EXHIBIT 13.1

A Sample Application of Key Indicator Management

How a Key Indicator Report Can Promote Efficiency

Timing	Indicator	Measure	Target	This Month	Year to Date	Past Year	Range: Past 12 Months High	Low
The time it takes to process an order serves as an indicator of both efficiency and lead time needed to meet reliable promises to customers.	Order entry	Customer order processing time (days)	3.0	4.1	4.4	4.7	5.7	3.7

selected. The next phases involve exactly how to measure the success of these indicators and goal establishment by management. Reports are then generated in time frames directed by management. Steps 1 to 4 result in the isolation of factors that are critical to the success of the function.

Human Asset Accounting

Management has recognized for decades that its most valued resource is its people. But the money spent to recruit, hire, train, and develop people has traditionally been treated as an expense, not as an investment in valued resources. **Human asset** (or resource) **accounting** treats the money spent on and for employees as investment expenditures. Just as money that is spent to acquire a factory, computer, or other piece of capital equipment finds its way to the asset portion of the balance sheet, so too will the funds spent on human resources.

This accounting method takes two general approaches. The first records the money spent in recruiting, hiring, training, and developing employees and enters this amount as an asset on the company's periodic balance sheets, which are its representations of the owners' and the creditors' shares in the assets of the company. Periodically, this asset value is reduced by the value assigned to personnel lost through any permanent separation from the company. Such a method, though not common in corporate accounting offices, is one major attempt to highlight the dollars "invested" in employees and to control the amount of those dollars. Such an approach is not normally used, however, when calculating business tax returns, for it would lead to the payment of additional taxes. The exception is in the area of professional sports, where athletes are considered capital assets and can be depreciated.

The second approach, less common than the first, attempts to assign a dollar value to each employee's contribution to the company's profit. Such calculations are not easy to make, but general categories of employees can be created and dollar amounts assigned to each category on the basis of a percentage system. Arbitrary as such an approach may be, at least it is an effort to focus attention on people as resources, not just expenses.

A variation of human asset accounting is the use of staffing charts or staffing boards that value the human assets of the organization by assessing the long-term worth of the employees in terms of present and future contributions. This concept is shown in Figure 13.3. Note the coding of each of the managerial employees. They have been categorized in this way: promotable now, promotable in three years, promotable in five years, not promotable, and retirement status. In addition to this valuing of managerial talent, there is another coding that shows the quality of each incumbent manager's performance in her or his current job and the ages of key personnel (shown in parentheses).

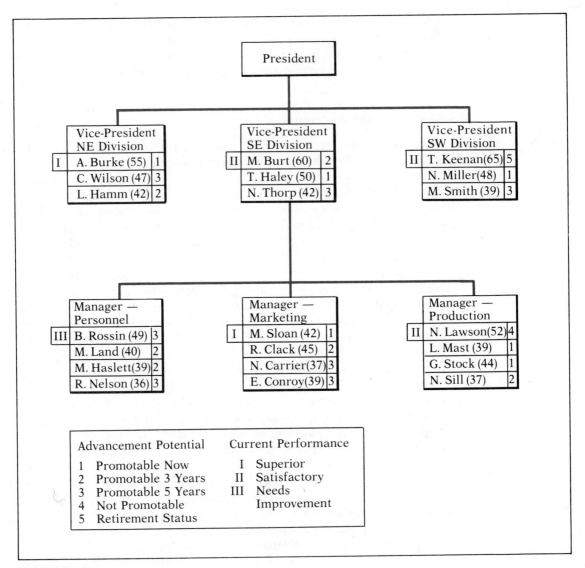

FIGURE 13.3
Staffing chart illustrating management replacement readiness

Inventory Control Systems

An *inventory control system* maintains an orderly flow of supplies, raw materials, or finished goods through an office, shop, or factory. Because items in any inventory represent costs, they need to be controlled. The purposes of inventory control systems for management are (1) to keep inventory levels and costs at desired minimums while (2) maintaining the proper safeguards over materials and (3) sustaining the proper flow of materials to places and people who need them.

All of us practice a kind of inventory control when we keep our checking accounts in order. We need to have enough money on hand to meet our current demands for cash and to think ahead to next month or perhaps beyond. Money must be there to cover the checks we write if we are to sustain our financial reputations and operations.

Costs connected with inventory control include the following:

1. Items in inventory.
2. Waste, spoilage, or damage.
3. Freight charges.
4. Security expenses—guards, insurance, alarm systems.
5. Obsolescence.
6. Storage costs—building space and maintenance.
7. Administrative costs—wages and salaries for moving items into and out of storage, keeping accurate counts, maintenance of storage equipment, procurement of and accounting for inventory items.

An organization might have to worry about several, less traditional costs as well: the costs connected with a shortage or unavailability of an item needed, the "opportunity cost," and interest expenses incurred when borrowing to carry inventories. The shortage cost is the cost when not having items on hand shuts down machines, stops work output and assembly lines, and more. The opportunity cost is the loss connected with the unavailability of the funds for other purposes because they are invested in inventory; this situation can necessitate borrowing to raise additional cash.

Exhibit 13.2 lists minimum requirements for a computerized inventory control system. Like most effective control systems, the inventory control system needs to be designed through consultation with those who must implement it and get information from it.

Financial Controls

Financial controls vary in their designs, applications, and frequency of use. What works well for one company may not work for another. We examine four control devices or methods that have an almost universal application to financial areas: budgets, control centers, financial statements, and their analysis through ratios and audits.

EXHIBIT 13.2

A Minimum Set of Requirements for a Computerized Inventory Control System

The list that follows sets down a minimum set of requirements for a computer inventory system.

1. It must uniquely identify every item in the inventory by an item number, and maintain an item file in the memory space.
2. It must maintain the count for the current number of each item on hand. This means that the system must recognize items received in and removed from inventory and must update the appropriate item file.
3. It must maintain the item cost in the item file.
4. It must compute the total dollar value of the inventory upon request. This is equivalent to multiplying the number on hand by the unit cost for each item and summarizing the value for the whole inventory.
5. It must compute and print out the dollar distribution of the inventory. This will also be expressed as a percentage of the total dollar value of the inventory.
6. It must produce a bill of materials for any item in the inventory. This means that each item in the inventory must have a pointer identifying the next higher and the next lower level of assembly. . . . The pointers can be the item numbers of the next higher or next lower level of assembly.
7. It must identify all shortages in the inventory. A shortage can be identified by finding an item file which indicates that a certain quantity has been withdrawn, but a lesser quantity has been received at the next higher level of assembly. This capability is extremely helpful in auditing and monitoring the inventory.
8. It must monitor and record time in the system.
9. It must compute a dynamic demand rate for each item in the inventory. This can be used for projecting, forecasting, and determining the reorder level and quantity for each inventory item.
10. It must compute the true cost of any item in the inventory by summing the costs of all its related subassemblies. Whenever a new cost figure is entered into the file, the system must automatically recompute item costs for all related items that are at a higher level than the item in question.
11. It must handle labor as an item in inventory in the same way that it handles a part. Each item of labor will have a unit cost equal to the hourly rate multiplied by the quantity of hours required to assemble that level of part.
12. It must project past information into the future, so that minimum on-hand requirements for each item in inventory can be changed to reflect current demand.
13. It must print a list of all critical items in the inventory—that is, all items whose current on-hand supply is below the required minimum. The system might also produce the purchase orders for those items.

EXHIBIT 13.2
Continued

14. It must produce scheduling information concerning the time when any item in the inventory should be assembled.
15. It must compute labor requirements for each item in the inventory.
16. It must search the entire inventory file and identify all items which have become inactive. An inactive item is one that has not been received in or removed from inventory, or one that has no higher or lower level of assembly.
17. It must be able to add and delete entire items from the inventory. This also includes the requirement of being able to change an existing item.

Budgets

The primary financial control for ourselves and every organization is a budget. As Chapters 5 and 12 pointed out, a budget is both a plan and a control. It is an estimate of income or expenses for a fixed period of time; and the particular estimates it contains become the standards against which future performances will be measured. If revenues (income) drop, expenditures probably should be curtailed. Or if expenditures are higher than expected, either more revenue must be produced or expenditures need to be slowed.

Budgets usually require input from those whose activities will be funded and controlled by them. Grass-roots budgeting asks each manager to project his or her unit's need for funds in specific categories—such as wages, salaries, and supplies. As these projections move up the management hierarchy, they are consolidated and become the budgets for ever larger units within the organization. This approach has several major advantages. First, those closest to an area know its funding needs better than any others. Those who have a hand and a voice in budget preparations are more likely to support them and live within them. Strategies formulated at higher levels will be affected by plans at lower levels. Bosses and their subordinates will both learn about each other's perspectives and functions in the process of the give and take in budgeting their operations.

Larger corporations have budget offices or centers within their financial management areas. The federal government has its Office of Management and Budget (OMB), which oversees the preparation of the federal budget and submits it to Congress for its approval. In like fashion, the corporate budget office will consolidate and prepare a corporate budget under the overall supervision of the chief financial officer; this office submits the budget to the finance or budget committee. It eventually receives the corporate seal of approval from the chief executive officer and the board of directors.

Exhibit 13.3 describes the three kinds of budgets prepared in most large corporations. These budgets are representative of an organization's comprehensive budgeting program. This program has two parts—operating and financial. Operating budgets include expense and revenue budgets for an entire organization or any of its parts for a fixed period. Financial budgets are represented by the cash and capital expenditure budgets, which spell out in detail where the organization intends to spend its money and where this money will come from.

Budgets will be effective control tools if they are based on adequate research, justifiable needs and expectations, and input from all levels they will control. In addition, budgets must be viewed as educated guesses etched in clay, not as facts carved in stone. They are feedforward controls in that they provide a means for continual monitoring of ongoing opera-

EXHIBIT 13.3
Kinds of Budgets Found in Most Large Businesses

Operating Budgets: (expenses vs. income)
Projections or estimates of the goods and services the organization expects to consume in the budget period. Includes expense budgets and revenue budgets for an entire organization or any of its parts for a fixed period.

Cash Budget
Projections or estimates of the amount of cash that will flow into and out of an organization or any of its parts for a fixed period. It includes income (cash from all sources, including borrowing) and outlay (cash payments for everything, including interest on borrowed funds).

Capital Expenditures Budget
Projections or estimates for the amount of money that will be needed to add fixed or long-term investment assets to the organization over a fixed number of months or years. Such assets include machinery and equipment that will be used by a business to create products or services and to conduct its regular operations.

"It's agreed then, we'll have our sales meeting on the sunny sands of St. Croix and, Wallace, I leave it to you to hide the cost somehow, somewhere, in some budget or other."

Source: Reprinted by permission: Tribune Media Services.

tions. As such, they must be adjusted periodically in the light of new and developing circumstances. Cuts may be necessary in some areas, while additional appropriations may be called for elsewhere.

Financial Control Centers

The cornerstone of every management control is the concept of *responsibility accounting*. The basic idea is simple: Each manager in a company has responsibility for a part of the total activity. The accounting system should be designed so that it yields a measurement of the financial effects of the activities that a manager is responsible for. This measurement can be stated in the form of a financial objective for each manager.[9]

To illustrate the preceding statement, Exhibit 13.4 explains the principal types of financial responsibility centers. Their existence in most large businesses bears witness to the fact that each manager has a contribution to make to cost control and to profits made by divisions and entire orga-

EXHIBIT 13.4
Principal Kinds of Financial Responsibility Centers in Large Businesses

Standard cost centers are exemplified by a production department in a factory. The standard quantities of direct labor and materials required for each unit of output are specified. The supervisor's objective is to minimize the variance between actual costs and standard costs. He or she also is usually responsible for a flexible overhead expense budget with the objective, again, to minimize the variance between budgeted and actual costs.

Revenue centers are best illustrated by a sales department where the manager does not have authority to lower prices to increase volume. The resources at the manager's disposal are reflected in the expense budget. The sales manager's objective is to spend no more than the budgeted amount and produce the maximum amount of sales revenue.

Discretionary expense centers include most administrative departments. There is no practical way to establish the relationship between inputs and outputs. Management can only use its best judgment to set the budget, and the department manager's objective is to spend the budgeted amount to produce the best (though still unmeasurable) quality of service possible.

Profit centers . . . are units such as a product division where the manager is responsible for the best combination of costs and revenues. The objective is to maximize the bottom line, the profit that results from the manager's decisions. A great many variations on this theme can be achieved by defining "profit" as including only those elements of cost and revenue for which the manager is responsible. Thus, a sales manager who is allowed to set prices may be responsible for gross profit (actual revenue less standard direct manufacturing costs). Profit for a product line marketing manager, on the other hand, might reflect deductions for budgeted factory overhead and actual sales promotion expenses.

Investment centers are units where the manager is responsible also for the magnitude of assets employed. Trade-offs are made between current profits and investments to increase future profits. Stating the manager's objective as maximizing return on investment or residual income (profit after a charge for the use of capital) helps the manager appraise the desirability of new investments.

Source: Reprinted by permission of the Harvard Business Review. Excerpt from "What Kind of Management Control Do You Need?" (March–April 1973). Copyright © 1973 by the President and Fellows of Harvard College; all rights reserved.

nizations. The president and the chief financial officer must decide on the type of financial objective to be specified for each organization unit and then determine how to calculate that measurement. A critical point in this decision is the selection of an objective for which a manager is responsible. Let's examine profit as a potential objective.

Profit should be used as a measure of financial responsibility only when it is possible to calculate it in such a way that a manager's "profit" increases as the result of actions for which he (or she) is responsible and which he (or she) has taken in the best interests of the company.[10]

Examine Exhibit 13.4 again. Note how the sales manager (revenue centers) is responsible for her or his profit contribution by generating revenue through sales, not by reducing costs. Similarly, the production department (standard cost centers) has control over only costs, not revenue. This control device focuses management's energy on controlling those factors actually within their scope of influence.

Financial Statements

There are two primary financial statements used by every organization that must live on a budget: the balance sheet and the income statement. The **balance sheet** focuses on the assets of an organization and who owns them—the organization or its creditors. The **income statement** focuses on the income and expenses of an enterprise and calculates the difference between them to arrive at a profit or a loss. Both provide a measure of feedback (after-the-fact) control over financial and other activities. Both are used as a base for budgeting, planning, and more. Both are prepared by bookkeepers and accountants.

The balance sheet.   Exhibit 13.5 illustrates the balance sheet for the Excel Corporation, a medical supply firm, and its subsidiaries for its 1989 fiscal year. It shows assets, liabilities, and stockholders' equity or net worth. *Assets* are what the company owns. The company's assets are normally broken down into current and fixed categories. *Current assets* are items that can normally be turned into cash within a short period of time (usually one year). These assets will include cash, securities, accounts receivable, inventories. *Fixed assets* are items that are used on a continuing basis to produce its goods and services—patents, property, equipment, trademarks, investments.

Liabilities are what the company owes. These consist of current and long-term debts. The first category—*current liabilities*—will have to be paid off during the current fiscal year. These include notes and accounts payable, taxes payable, and the current portion of long-term debt. *Long-term liabilities* include debt that is being reduced over a period longer than a year; mortgages and bonds are examples. The difference between assets and liabilities represents the owner's financial interests in the assets of the business.

The balance sheet is often expressed as an equation:

Assets = Liabilities + Owners' Equity

It is a "photograph" of the business, debt and equity positions with regard to its assets as of a specific date. As soon as the statement is prepared,

EXHIBIT 13.5

Balance Sheet for the Excel Corporation for Fiscal Year 1989

Assets

Cash	$ 12,912
Time deposits	312,335
Government-guaranteed and corporate debt securities, at cost which approximates market	35,029
Receivables	
Net	541,472
Inventories	645,818
Prepaid expenses and other current assets	143,234
Total current assets	1,690,800
U.S. government guaranteed securities held in Puerto Rico	49,600
Investments and other assets	70,546
Property, plant and equipment, net	827,131
Purchased patents, trademarks,and other intangibles, net	130,783
Goodwill, net	185,035
Total fixed assets	1,263,095
Total assets	$2,953,895

Liabilities and Stockholders' Equity

Notes payable—banks	$ 78,389
Notes payable—commercial paper	14,634
Current portion of long-term debt	58,822
Accounts payable and accrued liabilities	477,118
Federal, state and foreign income taxes	119,503
Total current liabilities	748,466
Long-term debt	558,256
Noncurrent payables and accrued liabilities	80,332
Deferred income taxes	67,932
Minority interest in foreign subsidiaries	11,614
Total liabilities	1,466,600
Stockholders' equity:	
Preferred Stock, par value $1 per share	
Authorized: 5,000,000 shares; Issued: none	
Common Stock, par value $1 per share	
Authorized: 150,000,000 shares	
Outstanding: 1989—79,660,849 shares	79,661
Capital in excess of par value of Common Stock	105,679
Retained earnings	1,301,955
Total stockholders' equity	1,487,295
Total liabilities and stockholders' equity	$2,953,895

changes start to take place in this debt and equity position. The value of the balance sheet rests in comparison from year to year and in the trends that appear. In addition, it yields financial data that can be used in various ratio calculations to take a measure of the company's financial health.

The income statement. Exhibit 13.6 is an income statement for the Right Corporation. It summarizes the accumulated income and expenses of the company for a one-year period. It, too, can be expressed as an equation:

Income − Expenses = Profit or Loss

The income statement provides the manager with a tool to review the expenses and revenue of the business on an ongoing basis. Income statements can be prepared for management control on any necessary time frame—daily, weekly, monthly. The categories provided by the income statement are the following:

1. Net sales—revenue from sales minus returns and allowances.
2. Costs of goods sold—cost to make or acquire the goods sold by the organization.
3. Gross profit—the cost of goods sold is subtracted from net sales to arrive at this figure.

EXHIBIT 13.6
Income Statement for the Right Corporation for Fiscal Year 1989

Revenue:	
Net Sales (Revenue)	$3,552,626
Less Cost of Goods Sold	1,665,786
Gross Profit	1,886,840
Operating Expenses:	
Marketing	1,066,271
Administrative and General	293,935
Research and Development	102,935
Interest	83,320
Total Operating Expenses	1,546,461
Income Before Taxes	340,379
Less Income Taxes	136,151
Net Profit	$ 204,228

4. Operating expenses—generally called overhead expenses. These include rent, advertising, utilities, insurance, and salaries not related to output.

5. Profit before taxes—subtract the operating expenses from the gross profit of the company to get a profit figure before taxes are deducted.

6. Taxes—the tax paid to the government on profit.

7. Net profit—the bottom line to the operations of the business.

Both balance sheets and income statements are prepared more often than annually. Most companies find it necessary to prepare them monthly and quarterly. The major purpose of the income statement is to measure the progression of costs and income, noting trends in the growth or decline of each item being monitored. Managers and their departments are evaluated in part on their contributions to the condition of the various categories (and specific accounts) on these statements.

Ratios

A **ratio** is an expression of the relationship between numbers. A ratio involves selecting two critical figures from a financial statement and expressing the relationship in terms of a percentage or ratio. Ratios help accountants and others measure progress toward goals and assess the financial health of their company's operations. On the surface a firm may appear to be sound—its balance sheet contains an impressive amount of current assets. But when its current assets are compared with its current liabilities using the liquidity ratio, as defined below, the company may find it has difficulty raising enough cash in a short period to meet its short-term debts. Ratios are compared in two ways: to past performances of the company and to performances of other companies in the same industry. One shows the progress of the company, while the second shows its operations relative to other firms.

Exhibit 13.7 describes the most frequently used ratios, how they are calculated, and for what purposes. We examine three of the most common types of ratios: liquidity, profitability, and debt.

1. *Liquidity Ratios.*   The ratio measures the ability of the enterprise to raise enough cash in a short period of time to meet its short-term debts. The most common liquidity ratio is the current ratio. It is determined by dividing current assets by current liabilities.

As an example: A company has $1,000,000 of current assets and $500,000 of current liabilities. Its current ratio is 2 to 1. (In other words, its current assets are two times its current liabilities.)

EXHIBIT 13.7
Important Ratios Used to Measure a Business's Financial Performance

Ratio	Obtained By	Purpose
Current assets to current liabilities	Dividing current assets by current liabilities.	To determine a firm's ability to pay its short-term liabilities.
Net profits to net sales	Dividing net profits after taxes by net sales.	To measure the short-run profitability of the business.
Net profits to tangible net worth	Dividing net profits after taxes by tangible net worth (the difference between tangible assets and total liabilities).	To measure profitability over a longer period.
Net profits to net working capital	Dividing net profits after taxes by net working capital (operating capital on hand).	To measure the ability of a business to carry inventory and accounts receivable and to finance day-to-day operations.
Net sales to tangible net worth	Dividing net sales by the firm's tangible net worth.	To measure the relative turnover of investment capital.
Net sales to net working capital	Dividing net sales by net working capital.	To measure how well a company uses its working capital to produce sales.
Collection period (receivables to credit sales)	First, dividing annual net sales by 365, to determine daily credit sales, and then, dividing notes and accounts receivable by average daily credit sales.	To analyze the collectibility of receivables.
Net sales to inventory	Dividing annual net sales by the value of the firm's merchandise inventory as carried on the balance sheet.	To provide a yardstick for comparing the firm's stock-to-sales position with that of other companies or with industry averages.
Fixed assets to tangible net worth	Dividing fixed assets (the depreciated book value of such items as buildings, machinery, furniture, physical equipment, and land) by the firm's tangible net worth.	To show what proportion of a firm's tangible net worth consists of fixed assets. Generally, this ratio should not exceed 100 percent for a manufacturer and 75 percent for a wholesaler or retailer.

continued

EXHIBIT 13.7
Continued

Current liabilities to tangible net worth	Dividing current liabilities by the firm's tangible net worth.	To measure the degree of indebtedness of the firm. Generally, a business is in financial trouble when this ratio exceeds 80 percent.
Total liabilities to tangible net worth	Dividing current plus long-term liabilities by tangible net worth.	To determine the financial soundness of the business. When this ratio exceeds 100 percent, the equity of the firm's creditors in the business exceeds that of the owners'.
Inventory to net working capital	Dividing merchandise inventory by net working capital.	To determine whether a business has too much or too little working capital tied up in inventory. Generally, this ratio should not exceed 80 percent.
Current liabilities to inventory	Dividing current liabilities by inventory.	To determine whether a business has too little or too much current debt in relationship to its inventory. If current debt is excessive, the firm may have to dispose of inventory quickly, at unfavorable prices, to meet its obligations.
Funded liabilities to working capital	Dividing funded liabilities (long-term obligations such as mortgages, bonds, serial notes, and other liabilities that will not mature for at least one year) by net working capital.	To determine whether the firm's long-term indebtedness is in proper proportion to its net working capital. Generally, this ratio should not exceed 100 percent.

Source: Adapted from *1970 Key Business Ratios* (New York: Dun & Bradstreet, 1971). By permission of Dun & Bradstreet Credit Services, a company of The Dun & Bradstreet Corporation.

2. *Profitability Ratios.*   This category of ratios is designed to put the profit picture into perspective from several points. Profits on total sales are obtained by dividing net profits after taxes by net sales; profitability of the owner's investment is obtained by dividing net profits after taxes by tangible net worth.

$$\text{Profits on Net Sales} = \frac{50,000 \text{ (profit)}}{1,000,000 \text{ (sales)}} = 5 \text{ percent}$$

To be meaningful, the ratio should be compared to past performances or to other firms in the same industry.

3. *Debt Ratios.*   These ratios are calculated to see if an organization can meet its long-term obligations.

An example is total debt divided by net worth. If the total debt of a business is $600,000 and the net worth is $1,200,000, the firm's assets are financed by 50 percent debt. If the industry average is 60 percent, there is no problem borrowing long-term capital. But if the industry average is 40 percent, the opportunities for borrowing are limited because of the debt the business has contracted.

Audits

Financial information is only as good as the data and interpretations on which it is based. Figures can lie, and liars can figure. Some kind of control is necessary to see to it that the data being used in information and control systems are accurate. **Audits** are formal investigations conducted to determine if records, reports, statements, and the data they are based on are correct and in line with the organization's rules and procedures. Audits may be conducted by insiders or outsiders to check on financial and management practices.

Internal audits.   Most companies establish regular routines to determine if people in all positions are doing what they should be doing accurately, effectively, and efficiently. In a sense, KIM and MBO are audit systems designed to let people determine and audit their own performances. Bosses routinely check or audit the work of their subordinates as well.

Most government agencies have internal investigative agencies to check on their various operations. Governments also have investigating agencies to check on compliance with governmental regulations. At the federal level, both the Office of Management and Budget (OMB) and the General Accounting Office (GAO) investigate the practices and procedures of various operations and report their findings of waste and irregularities to Congress. Internal audits have the advantage of keeping problems in-house and are conducted by persons who know the operations under scrutiny quite well. But internal investigations can yield cooperative coverups to protect friends and allies.

External audits.   When outsiders are employed to conduct investigations, objectivity is practically guaranteed. Public accounting firms provide trained accounting talent to examine financial records, statements, and procedures for corporations and others. The main purpose of choosing an outside auditor is to guarantee to insiders and interested outsiders (creditors, stockholders, etc.) that the financial data presented in financial documents give an accurate representation of events and that the examination is conducted in keeping with standard accounting practices and principles.

Production Controls

In this section, we examine three kinds of feedforward controls for production activities and projects: Gantt charts, critical path or network techniques, and quality control techniques. The first two are also aids to planning production. They provide ways to schedule and to keep track of progress on the basis of time. The latter keeps track of quality in production through regular or random inspections of the items of output through their various stages of production.

Gantt Charts

An early pioneer in scientific management was Henry L. Gantt, who is best known for his contributions to production planning and controlling. Gantt was the first to devise a reliable method for reserving machine time for jobs in production in order to promote the orderly flow of work from one machine to the next with a minimum loss of time or delays. His method, called a *Gantt chart*, has been adapted to other uses as well. Using a graph approach, it can track a project from its beginning to its end, comparing the time estimates for the steps involved with the actual time they require, and making adjustments in the start and ending times for the steps that follow.

Gantt charts work best for the scheduling and tracking of sequential events, the completion times of which will determine the total time for completing an entire project. They cannot handle highly complex operations that require many different kinds of sequential operations to begin or run simultaneously. Such projects (the building of a house, for example) require a network approach to scheduling and control.

Figure 13.4 depicts a Gantt chart. For Project A, there are three separate tasks: machining, assembling, and shipping. Brackets have been placed on the Gantt chart for the beginning and ending of each of the three tasks. A corresponding bar within each set of brackets is shaded in, representing actual completion of the tasks. The result is a graphic representation of the project. Notice that as of today, Project B is slightly ahead of schedule, and Project C is right on target.

FIGURE 13.4
Gantt chart for a manufacturing department

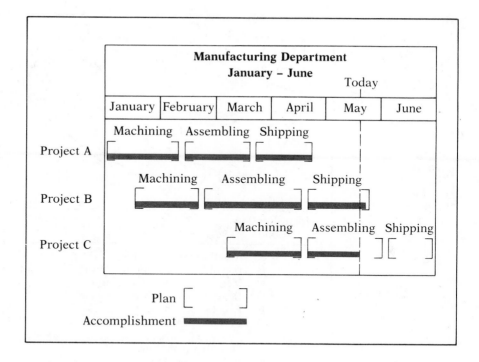

Network Techniques

Network techniques were designed to work with projects in which the activities or events are interrelated. This technique for scheduling and controlling uses events (circles) and activities (lines) that have time estimates assigned to them. Events are connected by activities and represent the beginning or starting point for some production operation. Activities lines or arrows show the time required to complete the event from which they emerge.

Figure 13.5 shows an example of network scheduling. It depicts the schedule for a project that involves 15 events and 18 activities. Event number 1 marks the start of activities A and B. Event number 2 marks the end of activity A, scheduled for 10 days, and the beginning of activity C, scheduled to take 2 days. To construct this network, each activity had to be listed, times had to be estimated and assigned for the completion of the activities, and the immediate predecessors for each activity had to be identified. Note that an activity cannot be started until its predecessor has been completed.

The completion time for the production effort equals the total times of the activities along the **critical path**—the longest possible path or route from the beginning to the end of the network (showing the longest time the job could take). The longest or critical path for Figure 13.5 is calculated below the figure.

FIGURE 13.5
A network (or critical path) diagram showing the activities for renewing a pipeline

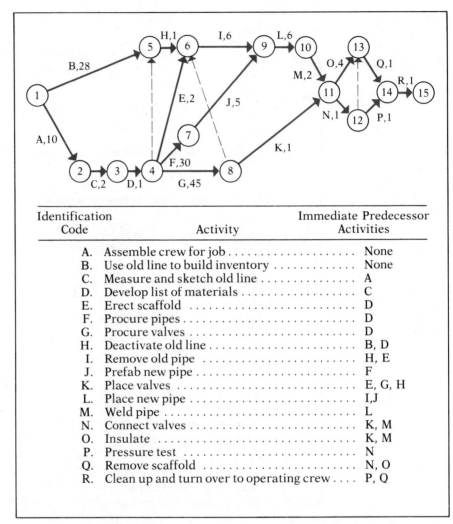

Identification Code	Activity	Immediate Predecessor Activities
A.	Assemble crew for job	None
B.	Use old line to build inventory	None
C.	Measure and sketch old line	A
D.	Develop list of materials	C
E.	Erect scaffold	D
F.	Procure pipes	D
G.	Procure valves	D
H.	Deactivate old line	B, D
I.	Remove old pipe	H, E
J.	Prefab new pipe	F
K.	Place valves	E, G, H
L.	Place new pipe	I, J
M.	Weld pipe	L
N.	Connect valves	K, M
O.	Insulate	K, M
P.	Pressure test	N
Q.	Remove scaffold	N, O
R.	Clean up and turn over to operating crew	P, Q

Source: From *Production-Inventory Systems: Planning and Control,* 3rd ed., by Elwood S. Buffa and Jeffrey G. Miller, pp. 611 and 622. © 1979 Richard D. Irwin, Inc., Homewood, Ill.

Activity		Time in Days
A	....	10
C	....	2
D	....	1
G	....	45
K	....	1
O	....	4
Q	....	1
R	....	1
Critical Path	=	65 days

This path represents the earliest possible completion time you can count on for the project, assuming that the worst combination of events is forced on you and that activities proceed according to their time estimates. If they do not, the changes will have to be recorded in the network and may cause a new critical path to emerge.

Program evaluation review technique (PERT) is a specific kind of network or critical path programming approach (see Chapter 5). It works best for new projects with which the production planners have little or no prior experience. PERT assigns four time estimates to activities: the optimistic, the most likely, the pessimistic, and the expected time. The expected time (the time the activity is actually expected to take) is based on a probability analysis of the other three time estimates. Critical path methods other than PERT do not make such estimates or assign probabilities to them.[11]

The PERT technique provides managers with a graphic view of the details of the project, from initiation to completion. It not only provides a good planning tool but also provides a control device by helping the manager spot trouble areas or see when the project is falling behind schedule. This in turn allows managers to take corrective action before the delay becomes critical.

Quality Control

There are degrees of quality. For some products intended for a one-time use (paper plates, foil cooking utensils, etc.), the product needs a very low level of quality and, therefore, little in the way of quality control. For items such as color television sets or major kitchen appliances, high standards must be set and substantial sums must be devoted to quality control personnel and methods. Quality control methods may take one form or a combination of forms. In most organizations, the methods used include inspection, testing, and sampling techniques.

Inspection. In this method of quality control, products are checked and examined against the standards designed for them. Inspections may be done by people, machines, or both. They may be feedback or feedforward controls depending on when in production they occur. Electronic eyes can inspect along moving lines of bottled products to sense proper fill levels and are capable of rejecting improperly filled bottles and shutting down the line for adjustments. Thus the electronic eyes are feedforward in nature. Final inspections of fully assembled products are usually feedback in nature. They will determine only that the assembly is not working properly; further analysis will have to be made to determine where any problems originated.

Most inspections are efforts at prevention and diagnosis. They attempt to keep close watch over the processes that are likely to fail or to cause the most trouble when they fail. When inspecting the output of processes, the inspector needs to know what is wrong and why; in addition, the inspector tries to determine trends away from acceptable standards.

How much inspection is enough? The answer rests in part in the nature of the item and in past history of the items in production. Units intended for life support in hospitals require 100 percent inspection of all of their components and processes. Manufacturers aware of past mistakes, along with operators with a history of producing rejected units, may want to inspect the output of certain machines or people quite closely until they are satisfied that all is well.

Testing. Testing may be a form of inspection. It applies to raw materials, work in the process of manufacture, and finished goods. Materials are tested in terms of their performance standards to determine strength, durability, and suitability for the users' purposes. Work in process is tested (electronic circuits, for example) to spot defects in human or machine efforts before they create too many rejects. Prototype testing (driving an experimental model of an automobile, for example) can lead to changes—modifications in design and manufacture—when the tester attempts to operate the equipment under the normal conditions in which it can be expected to operate.

Sampling techniques. Should all products be selected for inspection or only a few? Inspection and testing through sampling tries to spot problems and defects through the use of numbers. Sampling requires only a percentage of the items to be checked. This is based on the idea that a random sample is representative of the possible defects of the whole group of products.

The size of the sample to be tested or inspected can be determined statistically. Influences on the sample size are the value of the product, the potential for loss, and the extent of the loss if the product is sold with the defect. It is widely held that for large production runs of similar parts produced by standardized methods and machines, only 2 to 5 percent of items need to be inspected to determine trends. In determining who is watching which television show, rating services use a sample of households that represents less than 4 percent of American homes.

More important than a sample's size is the way in which the sample is taken. Samples need to be representative—possessing the characteristics to be monitored—and random—taken at nonuniform times and during the beginning, middle, and end of a run of manufacture. Most sampling techniques avoid regular samples, that is, samples taken at the same times throughout production runs.

Computers and Controls

Computers are aids to processing data into output with high degrees of speed and accuracy; they usually accomplish this feat at a lower cost than noncomputerized methods can. The four basic processing operations of computers include:

1. Sequencing (putting information in a predetermined order).
2. Merging (combining the new with the existing).
3. Calculating.
4. Summarizing (condensing information so that it can be utilized more effectively by management).[12]

Herein lies the key to effective and efficient use of computers: They are tools to aid management in decision making.

Computers can help managers in the execution of all of their functions by facilitating the various information systems that exist throughout their organizations. What benefit, after all, can be derived from information a manager receives after he or she makes a decision? Because of the speed, storage, and processing capabilities of the computer, it can provide timely and accurate information to the users. Reports that are being transmitted from various parts of the state, company, or world can be inputted, merged with one another or with existing information, analyzed for trends, and summarized immediately to aid managerial decision making. The computer provides management with the ability to receive information on which to make measurements and compare performance with standards (step 2 of the control process). This, in turn, allows management to make corrections in a timely fashion.

Despite what a computer can do to assist in the control process, there are some potential problems that management must face. Here is a partial list of problems that need to be addressed.[13]

1. *Benefits versus cost of the system.* The quality and quantity of the information received must be greater than the cost of developing, installing, and maintaining the computer system.

2. *Technological environment.* Management must be concerned with rapidly changing technology in the computer field. How can the company keep abreast of the latest developments? What will be the cost of doing so?

3. *Impact of the computer on personnel.* As we discussed in the section on MIS, computers mean change. What will be the impact on the people of the switch to computers? What jobs, if any, will be replaced?

What retraining is necessary? What will managers need to know to interact with the computer—for example, the capabilities, limitations, and costs; the keyboard skills necessary for access to the computer. What specialists are needed? How will they interact with regular personnel? Who will design the system? These questions will have to be addressed with a planned approach that involves those people affected by the decision.

4. *Centralized or decentralized computer system.*   Management may eventually have to make the decision for centralized or decentralized computer operations. This is not an easy decision to make and will include all the issues raised in the preceding problems as factors to be analyzed. A centralized system has the following strengths: All activities are carried out in one location; there is no duplication of staff and equipment, thereby minimizing costs; and contacts are simpler for decision making.

Those who favor decentralized computer operations point out these benefits: Every information-processing activity should be the responsibility of the unit most closely associated with it, and more managers today than ever before have an in-depth understanding of and need for computer services and capabilities.[14] Decentralized operations mean users have greater access to equipment, thereby resulting in timeliness of information and control of results.

Regardless of which decision an organization makes, if computers are to be effectively and efficiently used, they have to be available when they are needed to those who need them. They should be operated under a coordinated approach involving the user and the technical specialists.

Summary

- Management information systems collect, sort, interpret, summarize, and distribute up-to-date information in the right form at the right time to those who need it. An organization's MIS is at the heart of its planning and control efforts.
- Key Indicator Management relies on visual measurements taken at regular intervals and based on mutual (by boss and subordinate) selection of the indicators to be used.
- Human asset accounting places an emphasis on the dollar value of an organization's personnel. It treats the money spent on people as an investment, not just as an expense.

- Inventories of all kinds (supplies, raw materials, finished goods, etc.) must be controlled because they represent a sizable investment to most organizations.

- Budgets are both plans and controls. They should represent accurate estimates of income and expenses for a fixed period of time; and they need to be flexible.

- The concept of responsibility accounting indicates that each manager in a company has a responsibility for a part of the total activity. Each manager must have financial objectives by which his or her contributions and progress can be measured.

- Financial statements help summarize financial conditions and progress. The income statement and the balance sheet are the two most common financial controls.

- Ratios are used to judge the financial health of an enterprise. All require numeric information, most of which comes from the income statement or the balance sheet.

- Audits may be internal or external. They attempt to determine if what should be done is, in fact, being done.

- Production controls include inventory control systems, network scheduling, Gantt charts, and quality control measures.

- Computers aid businesses in all of their functions. They assist in providing timely and accurate information to users.

Glossary of Essential Terms

audit	An internal or external method of control, primarily financial, that determines if records, reports, statements, and data they are based on are correct and in line with established rules and procedures.
balance sheet	The financial statement and control that examines an organization's assets and the ownership interests in them.
critical path	The longest sequence of events and activities through a network production schedule.
data	Facts and figures that have not been processed.
human asset accounting	A control method that treats the money spent on and for employees as investments rather than expenses.
income statement	The financial statement and control that examines the organization's income and expenses.

information	Data that have been deliberately selected, processed, and organized to be useful to an individual manager.
Key Indicator Management	A monitoring and control system using mutually agreed-on key measures, represented visually and at regular intervals, to judge a manager's or department's progress or lack thereof.
management information system (MIS)	A formal method of providing management with accurate and timely information in order for decision making and managerial functions and operations to be carried out effectively.
program evaluation review technique (PERT)	A network method of production scheduling that assigns four possible completion times to activities: the optimistic, the most likely, the pessimistic, and the expected time. The expected time is based on a probability analysis of the other three time estimates.
ratio	The relationship between two or more numbers. Financial ratios can be used to judge the liquidity and profitability of an organization as well as the ability of an organization to pay its debts.

Review Questions

1. Can you define this chapter's essential terms? If not, consult the preceding glossary.
2. What purposes are served by the following general management controls: (a) a management information system, (b) Key Indicator Management, (c) human asset accounting, and (d) inventory control systems?
3. What purposes are served by the following financial controls: (a) budgets, (b) financial control centers, (c) a balance sheet, (d) an income statement, (e) ratios, and (f) audits?
4. What are the purposes of the following production controls: (a) a Gantt chart, (b) network techniques, and (c) quality control?

References

1. M. J. Riley, *Management Information Systems*, 2nd ed. (San Francisco: Holden Day, 1981), p. 5.
2. William M. Fouri, *Introduction to the Computer*, 3rd ed. (Englewood Cliffs, N.J.: Prentice-Hall, 1981), p. 495.

3. Steven L. Mandell, *Information Processing and Data Processing*, 3rd ed. (St. Paul: West Publishing Co., 1988), p. 9.

4. William H. Sihler, "Toward Better Management Control Systems," *California Management Review*, 14, no. 2 (1971), p. 33.

5. Robert L. Janson, "Graphic Indicators of Operations," *Harvard Business Review* (November–December 1980), pp. 164–170.

6. Ibid., p. 164.

7. Ibid.

8. Ibid., p. 170.

9. Richard F. Vancil, "What Kind of Management Control Do You Need?" *Harvard Business Review on Management 1975* (New York: Harper & Row, 1975), p. 446.

10. Ibid., p. 481.

11. James P. Fourre, *Quantitative Business Planning Techniques* (American Management Association, Inc., 1970), pp. 18–19.

12. Marjorie Lesson, *Basic Concepts in Data Processing* (Dubuque, Iowa: Wm. C. Brown Co., 1975), p. 6.

13. Robert H. Gregory and Richard L. Van Horn, "Value and Cost of Information," in *Systems Analysis Techniques*, eds. J. Daniel Auger and Robert W. Knapp (New York: John Wiley & Sons, 1974), pp. 473–489.

14. Frederick C. Sithington, "Coping with Computer Proliferation," *Harvard Business Review* (May–June 1980), p. 152.

Readings

Dale, B. and E. Barlow "Quality Circles: The View from Within." *Management Decision*, 25, no. 4 (1987), pp. 5–9.

Henry, David. *Handbook of Cost Reduction Techniques.* New York: Franklin Watts, 1986.

Hertz, David B. *The Expert Executive: Using Artificial Intelligence and Expert Systems for Financial Management, Marketing, Production, and Strategy.* New York: John Wiley & Sons, 1987.

Izzo, Joseph. *The Embattled Fortress: Strategies for Restoring Information Systems Productivity.* San Francisco: Jossey-Bass, 1987.

Janosko, Ann and Oscar Jensen. "Replacing Management's Crystal Ball with a Spreadsheet Program." *Planning Review*, 15, no. 4 (July–August 1987), pp. 21–29.

Kaplan, Robert S. "One Cost System Isn't Enough." *Harvard Business Review* (January–February 1988), pp. 61–66.

O'Learn, David and Efraim Turban. "The Organizational Impact of Expert Systems." *Human Systems Management*, 7, no. 1 (1987), pp. 11–19.

Rockart, John and Christina Bullen, ed. *The Rise of Managerial Computing.* Homewood, Ill.: Dow Jones Irwin, 1986.

Sepehri, Mehran. "Management Through Databases: Better Information, Not More Information." *Industrial Management*, 29, no. 1 (January–February 1987), pp. 7–11.

Sprague, Ralph Jr., ed. *Information Systems Management in Practice.* Englewood Cliffs, N.J.: Prentice-Hall, 1986.

C
A
S
E
S

13.1 Triton Wholesale

"We have got to do something about our inventory problem," said Fred. "We can't go on devoting space to tired and unsaleable merchandise. For the first time, we now know the extent of the problem. There are about two hundred boxes and crates of stuff that go as far back as 1957, the year of the founding of this business. There are another one hundred or so that are damaged or soiled items—useless to us and our customers."

Fred's partner was amazed at the size of the problem. Jack had no idea that so much merchandise was useless. "Think of the money we have tied up in that stuff," said Jack. "We should have been watching more closely. Taking a physical count has been our regular routine, but until this month, we never really put the numbers together with the saleability of the merchandise. What do you think we should do with the junk?"

"Jack, it's just the tip of an iceberg. This year alone we have lost $3,460 to shrinkage. That amount of inventory is just missing. It was probably stolen, but I can't be sure. And that leak we had last week caused another loss. When the sprinkler pipes froze and dropped water on the floor, we had another uninsured loss of $3,950, not to mention the cleanup and fixup costs. They were another $920. We've got to get a handle on these costs, or we'll be out of business."

"If we hadn't installed that computer, we still wouldn't know the extent of our inventory mess. It forced us to put every item in the computer's memory and focused our attention on the size of our problem. At least we know now what we have and what we don't and, most important, what it is all costing us."

"Jack, I estimate that our inventory is costing us about $532,000. Here's the breakdown." Fred handed Jack a sheet of paper with the following numbers:

Inventory on hand	$490,500
Shrinkage	3,460
Obsolete, damaged goods	35,240
Freight charges	3,150
Total	$532,350

"From now on, we have to enter every shipment in the computer the day it arrives. We have to compute the dollar value of our inventories to keep tabs on it. Right now our computer can tell us the following: the identity of each item and its location in storage, the physical count of each item in storage, the dollar value of the inventory, the length of time an item has been in the warehouse, and the minimum quantity to be kept on hand. It's up to us to keep this information current by entering each item we buy and sell into the computer the day each event takes place. This will give us all the information we need to keep a tight handle on the inventories."

For Discussion

1. What changes to Fred's list of inventories' costs would you recommend and why?
2. Are Fred and Jack using their computer to their best advantage? Why or why not?
3. What additional controls would you recommend to deal with their inventory problems?

13.2 Keeping Tabs

At the request of the board of directors of the Oxley school, Lester Fremont took over the weekend parking operations that used the school's parking lots. The school was located within a block of a major convention center and, at the request of the convention center's management, had agreed to let the center's patrons use the lots. Between 120 to 130 cars could be accommodated depending on how the cars were arranged. The lots were not striped, so different methods could be used.

Lester is a self-employed building contractor with family ties to several members of the school board. He had no experience with running parking operations until this time last year when he agreed to manage the parking lots. Lester rarely parked cars but did visit the lots several times each Saturday and Sunday to check on things. He hired three off-duty police officers to park cars. Each was paid $5 per hour, and two usually worked only two to three hours each day depending on how long it took them to fill the lots. When the last car was parked, one officer, Zackery Albers, would secure the lot and take the day's receipts to Lester's bank. The deposit receipt would then be mailed to Lester on the following Monday. The police officers were paid once each month using the hours recorded by Zackery on a time sheet. After deducting his management fee and the officers' wages, Lester sent a check for the balance to the school's treasurer on the first day of each month.

At last month's board meeting, the school treasurer gave his report to the board members, who noted a substantial decline in parking revenues. The board members were shocked to discover that the treasurer could not explain the decline and, further, that he could not even verify if the funds received were in the proper amount or not. Lester's accounting was all that the treasurer had to go on, and it consisted of merely a listing of the funds received for the month and the amounts subtracted for wages and Lester's 10 percent fee. The last three months have shown a steady decline and, when compared with the same three months of last year, represented a loss of $1,245 to the school. Several board members noted that convention business was up for the year and that this year was forecast to be a record for the center, at least as far as attendance at its functions was concerned. The board drafted a letter to Lester requesting his attendance at its next meeting.

Lester came prepared with his time sheets and the bank receipts. The meeting opened with a request to hear how Lester ran the parking operations. He explained that he depended on three police officers and that they took the $4 per car from each motorist as the cars entered the lots. The money was then given to Zackery, who deposited the total collected with the bank in person or through the night depository. Lester then produced the last three months' receipts and handed them to the treasurer. "As you can see," said Lester, "the amounts of the receipts total to the gross amount shown on my statements for each of the last three months." Lester told the board that he believed the totals were correct because he trusted his people. After all, he explained, they were police officers. Asked if he personally had ever totaled the funds collected on any of the parking days, Lester replied that he had not.

For Discussion

1. What factors could explain a legitimate decline in parking revenues?

2. As a school board member, what would you like to see Lester do?

3. If you were Lester, what controls would you implement to guarantee that all the money due from parkers is collected and deposited?

C
H
A
P
T
E
R

14

Managing Change and Conflict

OUTLINE

ESSENTIAL TERMS

change	organizational climate
change agent	organizational development
conflict	organizational learning

LEARNING OBJECTIVES

After reading and discussing this chapter, you should be able to do the following:

1. Define this chapter's essential terms.
2. Explain the concept of organizational climate, and describe its components.
3. Define change, and discuss the sources of change.
4. Identify the phases of change in an organization and the importance of this knowledge to a manager.
5. Explain the Greiner model for implementing organizational change.
6. Discuss the reasons why people resist change.
7. Discuss two models for changing people's behavior.
8. Explain the purpose of an organizational development program.
9. Identify the potential causes of conflict in an organization.
10. Explain three strategies for conflict management.

The Need to Understand Change and Conflict

Ideally, the organization should be a place where highly motivated people can work together to achieve both their individual goals and the goals of the organization. If management has done a good job of acquiring well-qualified individuals, the challenge becomes one of developing and maintaining a supportive organizational climate. This task is not easily accomplished. Two factors, change and conflict, influence the environment of an organization and can impede the efforts of individuals and groups toward goal accomplishment. Management needs to understand and manage these two factors.

The purpose of this chapter is to discuss the management of change and conflict. We first explore the phenomenon of change—what it is, why it happens, and how managers can best deal with change to minimize the disruption of the work environment. Additionally, we examine the concept of conflict—its causes and some strategies for managing it.

Before beginning our discussion of change and conflict, let's examine what is meant by the term *organizational climate*.

The Organizational Climate

"An organization reflects the history of its internal and external struggles, the types of people it attracts, its work processes and physical layout, the modes of communication, and the exercises of authority within the system."[1] These variables interact to create an organizational "personality." This personality, feel, or character is referred to as **organizational climate**; it is the internal environment in which the organization members function.[2]

The climate, or psychological environment, of an organization influences the people who work within it. Each organization has its own unique climate. John Kotter has developed a model that can assist us in describing the organizational climate.

Kotter Model of Organizational Climate

Kotter suggests that all organizations are made up of seven systems—one major control system and six supportive subsystems. Each of these systems acts with and is affected by every other system; no one system is independent. Together they compose the organization's personality or climate.[3] Let's look at each factor.

Key organization processes. The system of key organization processes is the central factor of an organization. It includes the way an organization goes about collecting and communicating information necessary to achieve its primary set of goals. It also includes how decisions are made as well as the production processes used in developing its products and services. The key organizational processes system is the most critical factor describing the climate because it is the most visible; thus it is the one by which people identify the company.

This central system or factor is affected by six other systems that create the total climate of the organization.

Employees and other tangible assets. All the resources of the organization make up one climate variable. The size and internal characteristics of an organization's employee population, plant and offices, equipment, tools, land, inventory, and money are unique to each firm. These are the resources with which the organization must work. The presence or absence and quality of these factors can create a prosperous or deprived climate.

Formal organization arrangement. The degree of structure in the organization is an element of climate. All the formal systems that have been designed to regulate the actions of an organization's machines and employees create a climate. Items included are the amount and type of job design, organizational structure, reporting hierarchy, rules, regulations, procedures, and standing plans.

Social system. The social system is composed of the norms and values shared by most employees. It is the set of relationships that exist among employees in terms of power, affiliation, and trust. What is the trust level between management and employees? Is the environment open? Is there communication? What roles do the informal organization and the grapevine play? The social system is one of the most crucial factors in establishing the organizational climate.

Technology. The factor of technology encompasses as elements the major techniques commonly used by employees while engaging in organizational processes. It also includes the underlying assumptions about the purpose of technology—for example, replacement of the human factor in the environment or providing the opportunity for better use of skills. The degree of technology in a situation can shape the organizational climate.

Dominant coalition. An organization's climate is very much affected by the objectives, strategies, personal characteristics, and internal relationships of the managers who oversee the organization and control its policy making. What is the leadership style of management? What is its impact? How do employees view management—as approachable or distant? Do the policies seem fair? Is the organization designed for performance rewards or social promotion?

External environment.   The external environment influences the other variables of the organizational climate. The factors composing the external environment include all possible suppliers (of labor, information, money, materials), markets, competitors, regulators, and associations that influence the organization's goods and services. Public attitudes, the state of technological development, the economy, the political system, demographics of people in a given area, and prices are some other factors shaping the organizational environment.

Importance of the Organizational Climate

The concept of organizational climate is not important by itself. What is important for a manager to realize is the sum total of its ingredients and its influence on the individual. The organizational climate is composed of many factors. These factors as a totality describe the personality of the organization. Further, the alteration of one factor can affect all the other factors and change the climate of the work environment. It is significant that the climate influences the people who work within it: The climate can be repressive or supportive depending on how it is managed. The key for management is to be aware of the factors that can alter a supportive climate, anticipate their occurrence, and manage for a positive result.

An example of the impact on the totality of the climate is the revolution in technology. The introduction of computers, with their speed and efficiency, affected business in major ways. No longer did time-consuming and tedious tasks, such as bookkeeping and payroll, have to be done manually. And automated inventory control systems replaced the end-of-the-month physical-count approach.

Additionally, that subsystem (technology) of the climate had an impact on other subsystems. Employees and other tangible assets were affected through the actual replacement of equipment and by the retraining or loss of personnel once considered essential to the organization. It also resulted in changes in rules and regulations. New procedures had to be developed to provide for the input and output systems of the computer—all within the realm of the formal organization. Finally, the director of data processing, because of the degree of specialized knowledge not understood by others, was placed in a significant decision-making position. This change affected the dominant coalition subsystem. The whole organizational climate had undergone a significant modification.

This example illustrates the alteration of the entire organizational climate by the adjustment of one variable. There are two related factors that can alter a climate—change and conflict. We examine both, beginning with the concept of change.

The Nature of Change

Change is a shift or alteration in the present environment. The shift or change may be in the way we perceive things or in how items are organized, processed, created, or maintained. Every individual and organization experiences change. Sometimes the change is planned for. Sometimes events beyond the individual's or organization's control initiate the change. In the former situation, there exists a greater possibility to predict what may happen and thereby to control events. In the latter instance, reaction to unforeseen events can be the response. Regardless, change does occur. Since it is certain to occur, change must be managed. A starting point to understanding change is to examine potential sources of change.

Sources of Change

Change may originate from inside or outside the organization. External sources of change may include technology, competition, government actions, economic variables, and social values. Government regulations on health, safety, and the conduct of business affect an organization. Equal Employment Opportunity Commission guidelines have been enacted that influence hiring, pay, training, and promotion decisions. Tax laws change. Economic conditions—such as recession, inflation, and interest rates—are sources of change. Finally, cultural changes in such areas as modes of dress, reasons for people working, composition of the workforce, and changes in traditional female and male roles can affect the organizational environment.

Internal sources of change might include managerial policies or styles, systems, and procedures; technology; and employee attitudes, with their resultant behavior. As an example, if a manager develops a new set of expectations for job performance, this change will influence the values and behaviors of the employees affected. The employees could adapt to these expectations or resist them. Or consider this: The development of a new pay system using weekly rather than monthly pay periods will require some major changes—in time frames, in amount of paper processed, and potentially in the technology (automated versus manual computation).

Knowing what change is and the potential sources of change is important for a manager. A second area of knowledge a manager needs is knowing when change is needed in an organization.

Identifying the Need for Change

Larry Greiner has developed a model that shows the evolution of change in an organization. Through research, Greiner found that there is a general pattern of growth for an organization and there are corresponding crises that demand change. The model expects change to be either evolutionary or revolutionary. Evolutionary change is gradual and constant, while revolutionary change is rapid and immediate.[4] Figure 14.1 shows the five phases of growth of an organization. Let's look at each phase.

Phase 1: Creativity.   This is the birth stage of an organization. It is marked by concerns for product and market, informal internal relationships, and an entrepreneurial style of management. But soon the need for capital, new products, new markets, and new employees forces the organization to change. A crisis of leadership occurs when management becomes in-

FIGURE 14.1
The Greiner model
of organizational
growth

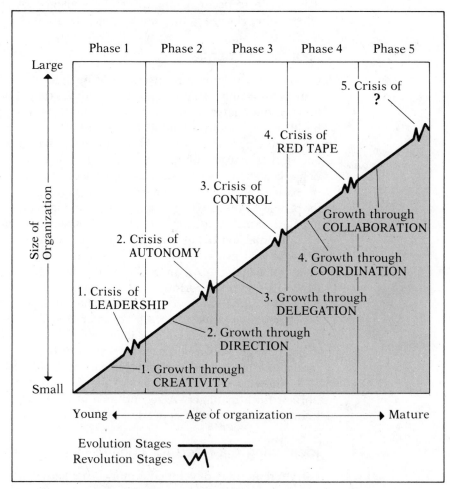

capable of reacting to the demands for structure as it grows. The organization enters a new phase.

Phase 2: Direction.   This phase is characterized by the implementation of rules, regulations, and procedures. Additionally, a functional organization structure is introduced; an accounting system for inventory and purchases is created; incentives, budgets, and work standards are established; and communications become more formal and impersonal. Eventually, there is a demand by lower level managers for greater delegation in decision making. This prompts another crisis and a revolutionary change in the organization.

Phase 3: Delegation.   Decentralization is the key to this phase. This is shown by greater responsibility being exacted from territorial managers, profit centers being created, top-level management beginning to practice *management by exception* (the conscious decision by a manager to enter into a situation on a "needs" basis—where that particular manager is needed to make a decision), and communications from top-level management becoming infrequent. The difficulty prompting a crisis occurs when top management senses that it is losing control over the organization. This leads to another revolution in the organization and another major change.

Phase 4: Coordination.   Management now attempts to seize control by emphasizing coordination. The organization is characterized by the merging of decentralized work units, the introduction of formal organizationwide planning, the increased exercise of control by staff personnel, and the restricting of capital expenditures. Although this phase generally exhibits growth, it is achieved at the price of red tape. Distance develops between line and staff personnel and between headquarters and field staffs. Paperwork bogs down the organization, and a new revolution takes place.

Phase 5: Collaboration.   This phase introduces a more behaviorally oriented and flexible system. Change produces more spontaneity in managing. Characteristics of the collaborative phase include team actions to solve problems, reduction of headquarters staff in number and modifications of the role to one of consulting rather than control, simplification of formal systems, and encouragement of an attitude toward risk taking and innovation.

This model graphically depicts the phases that organizations move through. It suggests there are predictable changes that organizations will encounter as they grow. Also at the heart of the model is the idea that solutions to one set of problems will ultimately breed new problems, causing the need for further change. Change as an organizational factor is a continuous process.

Managing Change

Once a manager has recognized and accepted the idea that change is inevitable and to a degree predictable, the next process is to develop strategies for managing it. An initial area for strategy development is for a manager to have a philosophy about the dynamics of change.

The Manager's Philosophy of Change

A manager's philosophy of change should encompass three elements—trust, organizational learning, and adaptiveness. Let's examine the importance of each.

Trust.   A critical ingredient in a manager's philosophy of change is how much emphasis is placed on trust in the work environment. Creating an environment where trust can be nurtured is vital to managers who wish to deal effectively with change. Numerous research studies have indicated that trust between employees and managers is the most important factor in having an effective, well-functioning organization.[5] Trust in this sense is defined as "an assured reliance on some person or thing, a confident dependence on the character, ability, strength, or truth of someone or something."[6] In a period of uncertainty or in adverse conditions, trust is a factor that allows individuals to continue to function while maintaining a hope that things will stabilize.

There are two essentials for trust to develop between managers and employees—a sense of adequacy and personal security. Adequacy refers to the feeling by each employee that he or she counts for something in the organization. Each person needs to have a knowledge that he or she means something to the organization and that her or his presence makes a difference in the overall performance of the firm. The second element of trust, personal security, is viewed as the degree to which each person feels that she or he can be openly honest and candid about personal observations without fearing any retaliation by management or others.

A high trust level between managers and employees can lessen the fear of change. Change threatens habits and security. If a manager has developed an environment of trust, employees will feel more comfortable as the organization moves through the crises of change. The reliance on or confidence in a manager can be the key to navigating troubled waters.

Organizational learning.   A second component of a manager's philosophy toward change is how the manager and the organization integrate new ideas into established systems to produce better ways of doing things. This concept, known as **organizational learning**, is a key element in developing a sound philosophy of change.

A manager can view organizational learning in either of two ways: single-looped or double-looped. A single-looped learning situation is one in which only one way or alternative exists in which to make adjustments; the organization has a prescribed way of doing things. When the actions of the organization do not follow the prescribed way, these actions are adjusted to meet the standards established. This attitude implies that the organization is not flexible and that there is a prescribed behavior for a situation. This in turn leads to more difficulty in adapting to change.

+ Double-looped learning, on the other hand, accepts the differences between the way things are supposed to be (espoused theory) and the way they actually work out (theory in use). A double-looped situation means more than one way or alternative exists. Change is made easier by approaching each situation not with a standardized behavior but with the idea of determining which behavior is best at meeting organizational goals. This theory of double-looped learning was developed by Frank Frielander, based on work by Chris Argyris and Don Schon; it opens the organizational environment for individual input.[7] If a manager believes there are numerous ways of reaching a goal, each employee is free to share ideas and the assumptions underlying the ideas. These ideas and assumptions can be examined in the light of change.

Adaptiveness. A third philosophical element is a managerial commitment to being prepared for change prior to the actual need for it. Managers who are adaptive rather than reactive will minimize wasted energy and maximize the use of time in a change situation. The development of a philosophy toward change enables the manager to approach change situations from an overall perspective. Establishing a climate of trust, focusing on adapting rather than reacting, and providing for flexibility through understanding organizational learning should enable the manager to be ready to manage organizational change.

Given these important ingredients, what is needed now is a rational approach for the manager to follow in change situations. Although there are several approaches, we focus on Larry Greiner's model for organizational change.

The Greiner Model for Organizational Change

The Greiner model outlines six phases of the dynamics of successful organizational change (Figure 14.2). This model has two parties involved—the change agent and the client. The **change agent** is the individual who is responsible for making change possible. The function of the agent is to make it possible for managers and employees to recognize the need for

FIGURE 14.2
The Greiner model
of the dynamics of
organizational
change

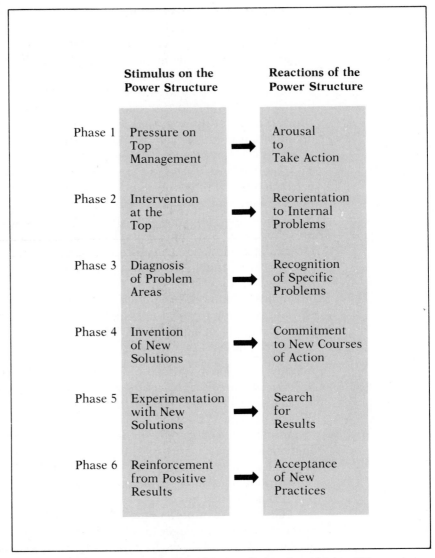

Source: Reprinted by permission of the Harvard Business Review. An exhibit from "Patterns of Organizational Change" by Larry E. Greiner (May–June 1967). Copyright © 1967 by the President and Fellows of Harvard College; all rights reserved.

change and to help initiate the required change. The change agent can exist within the organization or be brought in from outside. The *client* is the group or organization whose actions or attitudes are to be changed.[8] Let's examine each phase of the model.

Phase 1: Pressure and arousal.   In this phase, top management senses pressure from internal or external sources. Reactions to this pressure occur throughout the organization's power structure. Top management support at this point is critical: If a change program is to function, top management must sense the problems and support the necessary actions.

Phase 2: Intervention and reorientation.   This phase requires the selection of change agents who can begin the process of investigation and intervention. The change agents may be selected from competent insiders or outsiders.

Phase 3: Diagnosis and recognition.   This phase is highlighted by the gathering of data about the organization's problems by the change agent; these data come from those involved with or affected by the contemplated changes. Such a teaming approach involves the change agent, managers, and subordinates.

Phase 4: Invention and commitment.   There is a natural tendency to try to solve problems with old methods. To counteract this, the change agent takes an active role in encouraging new solutions and approaches to problems.

Phase 5: Experimentation and search.   This phase allows for temporary and controlled testing of both the problem's diagnosis and its treatment. The alternatives are reviewed for consistency and practicality.

Phase 6: Reinforcement and acceptance.   Where changes have improved organizational performances, the new solutions and methods may become permanent procedures and standards. This success leads to acceptance of change by the work group members.

The Greiner model provides the manager with a guide for managing change in the organization. But not all change is met with acceptance by organizational members. In many instances, it is resisted. Why? In this section, we provide some answers to that question.

Resistance to Change

People resist changes for many reasons. In some situations, change threatens security. In others, habits have provided a way to make decisions. In addition, people have selective perception of situations, which may inhibit change. Finally, some people resist change because of actual weaknesses in the proposed change.[9] We examine each reason briefly.

Desire for security.   Changes scare people. Individuals tend to find security in ways things have been done in the past. New technology, new systems, new procedures, and new managers can threaten a person's security and cause resistance. In addition, change often poses problems of power and control. "Will my influence still exist?" and "Where will I end up in the pecking order?" are reactions reflecting anxiety caused by change.[10]

Habits.   Habits provide a programmed method for decision making. "I can do this job blindfolded, with my hands tied behind my back": That may be a representative expression of the reason habit produces resistance to change. The present practices or behaviors require no extreme output of initiative or problem-solving energy. Learning new processes requires re-thinking or learning to think again.

Selective perception.   A person who has a biased interpretation of reality is guilty of selective perception. Reality is what the person thinks it is. This type of resistance can lead to stereotyping the arguments put forth for change—and to giving a stock reply to the stereotypes: "It's a management plot to do away with us." This resistance, a result of the person's attitudes and experiences, is difficult for a manager to deal with. In its extreme form, it perceives all actions of management as suspect.

Awareness of weaknesses in the proposed change.   A constructive type of resistance is evidenced by some organizational members who are aware of potential problems inherent in the proposed change. Knowing from ex-perience or from inside information that an idea will not work, these re-sisters can be valuable to management. They can help the organization save time, money, and energy.

Knowing why people resist change is critical to a manager. Once these causes are understood, the manager can develop approaches to work with those who are resisting a change.

Changing People's Behavior

Thus far we have concentrated on organizations as a whole and on man-aging changes in them. In this section, we deal with handling changes in individuals and their behaviors at work. The prime concerns are how to change skills, knowledge, and attitudes. We explore two approaches: Lew-in's model and force field analysis.

The Lewin Model

Many social scientists, psychologists, and educators have observed that people react differently to pressures for changes in their behaviors. Most will accept the need to learn new skills and to update their funds of knowl-edge. But most also resent pressures to change their attitudes. Accordingly, efforts in the workplace to change people's attitudes have been less suc-cessful than efforts to impart knowledge and skills. If attitudes that lie be-neath and support behaviors that are scheduled to be modified cannot be changed, changes in the behavior based on them will not take place or will be temporary at best. People will conform to management demands when managers are watching and regress to old habits and patterns of behavior when managers are absent.

Kurt Lewin has provided us with a very useful model that helps us understand how lasting changes can be brought about within organizations and to individuals. Lewin's model has three distinct phases: unfreezing, change, and refreezing.[11]

Phase 1: Unfreezing.   Managers as change agents spot deficiencies in subordinates' behaviors. The troublesome behaviors—those that lead to poor performance, conflicts, the need for discipline—and the causes of these behaviors are identified. Individuals are confronted with their current behaviors and the problems they cause. Attempts to convince the people to change are made by reducing their resistances to change and by offering methods and incentives for them to undergo changes. Pressures may be mounted against these individuals to make them uncomfortable and dissatisfied with their present behaviors. When people are upset enough to see the need for change, and want to change, phase 2 can begin.

Phase 2: Change.   When discomfort levels rise high enough, and individuals have the incentives to change, they will be looking for ways to reduce the tension in their lives: They will start questioning their present motives for and patterns of behavior. Now it is appropriate to present new role models and offer support to help people adopt new attitudes and patterns of behavior. New performance levels will begin to emerge. But if these are to be lasting effects, they must be supported and reinforced.

Phase 3: Refreezing.   New and approved attitudes and patterns of behavior are now recognized and rewarded. Any changes that create new problems for subordinates are identified and discouraged (back to phase 1). The old pressures that had created discomfort and problems for people disappear, and tensions are relieved. The new, more acceptable attitudes and the behaviors they support become part of the new work habits and routines.

Force Field Analysis

A second useful tool for visualizing the situations that are in need of change also comes from Kurt Lewin and is known as force field analysis. Figure 14.3, which illustrates this, depicts the change process as one that must overcome a person's or an organization's status quo or existing state of equilibrium—the balance between forces for change and forces that resist change. The change forces are known as *driving forces,* and the resisting forces are known as *restraining forces.*

Managers who contemplate making changes can diagnose the situation as it presently exists. They prepare a list of both driving and restraining forces and of the attitudes that support them. Change can then be attempted by weakening the restraining forces, strengthening the driving forces, or

FIGURE 14.3
A visual representation of a force field

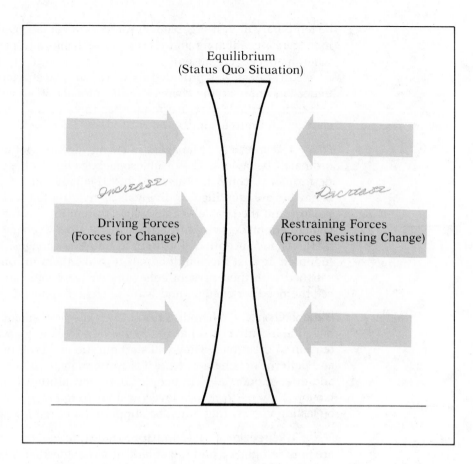

Equilibrium
(Status Quo Situation)

Increase

Decrease

Driving Forces
(Forces for Change)

Restraining Forces
(Forces Resisting Change)

both. Force field analysis is helpful in phases 1 and 2 of the Lewin model discussed previously.

Managing change, in organizations and individuals, is an ongoing process for managers. If this is done well, a good organizational climate can be maintained. Some organizations may make a thorough analysis of organizational problems and then implement a long-range program based on it. Such an approach is called organizational development (OD).

Organizational Development

The purpose of this chapter is to discuss how an individual manager manages change and conflict. **Organizational development**, by contrast, is a companywide long-term plan, rather than one undertaken by an individual manager. But in an effort to provide you with knowledge of change management, we include a brief explanation on the purposes of organizational development, its strategies, and evaluation processes.

Purposes of OD

The "primary purpose of OD is to bring about a system of organizational renewal that can effectively cope with environmental changes. In doing so, OD strives to maximize organizational effectiveness as well as individual work satisfaction."[12] It is the most comprehensive intervention strategy, involving all the activities and levels of management in ongoing programs that respond to internal and external sources. The OD process can be seen as a cyclical process in Figure 14.4.

OD Strategies

OD strategies consist of various tools, devices, and methods for introducing changes. Exhibit 14.1 describes the various strategies available to change agents for achieving their goals. OD practitioners may choose one or more of these depending on the circumstances they face. Limits on time, money, and their own personal skills with each strategy are just a few restrictions they may have to take into account. The choice of a strategy or strategies is usually the result of conferences and discussions involving those who will be most directly affected by them. Their experiences, personal feelings, and perceptions will help determine if their parts of the organization are ready for change and its techniques of introduction. Receptiveness of organizational members is crucial to the success of OD efforts. Consent of the governed is required before any implementation of strategies. It may take a good deal of time to pave the way for changes as well as to implement them.

Evaluating Effectiveness of OD

Since organizational development is an ongoing, long-term effort to introduce lasting change and to reshape an organization's technology, structure, and people, its successful implementation depends on significant investments of money and time. Both are needed to accurately diagnose problems, select strategies, and evaluate the effectiveness of the OD programs.

The primary evaluation uses the goals established when OD efforts and strategies began. Were they accomplished? If not, why not? The goals may have been unrealistic or too difficult to achieve over the time frame and with the resources allowed. Or inaccurate diagnosis of organizational problems may have caused the wrong goals to be set. Or changes may have been attempted before people were properly prepared to accept them. Or finally, changes may have occurred but have been only temporary.

Results of the OD evaluation will provide the feedback needed to redirect and improve programs, strategies, and change agents. In the final

FIGURE 14.4
A model for the
organizational
development
process

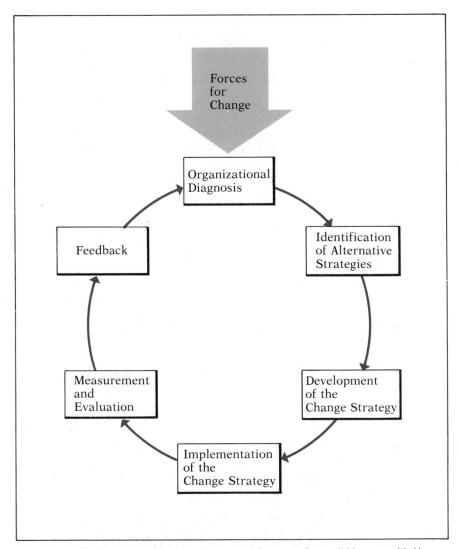

Source: Gene E. Burton, "Organizational Development—A Systematic Process," *Management World,*
March 1976. Reprinted from *Management World,* with permission from the Administrative Management
Society, Willow Grove, PA 19090. Copyright 1976 AMS.

analysis, OD, like any other management effort, is only as effective as the
quality of its inputs and the skills of the processors of those inputs will
allow it to be. Its success depends on participation and commitment by
those involved with achieving its expected outcomes. It must be based on
solid research, clear goals, appropriate methods, and effective change
agents. Most organizations recognize the value of using outsiders as change
agents: They bring unique and specialized skills and knowledge to their
tasks; they are objective in their approaches and may be better equipped
to sell their ideas, approaches, and management's goals.

EXHIBIT 14.1
Organizational Development Strategies

Diagnostic Strategies

Consultants:
: objective outsiders brought in to analyze and conduct audits of existing policies, procedures, and problems. Consultants can be individuals or groups and may act as change agents as well.

Surveys:
: interviews or questionnaires used to assess the attitudes, complaints, problems, and unmet needs of employees. Surveys are usually conducted by outsiders and guarantee anonymity to participants.

Group Discussions:
: periodic meetings conducted by managers to uncover problems and sources of discomfort and dissatisfaction that affect their subordinates.

Change Strategies

Training Programs:
: ongoing or special efforts to improve or increase skill levels, change or instill attitudes, or increase the knowledge needed to perform present jobs more effectively and efficiently.

Development Programs:
: ongoing or special efforts to get people ready for changes and promotions—to impart skills, knowledge, and attitudes needed for success in future positions.

Team Building Activities:
: projects and exercises designed to help people function as parts of an integrated whole rather than as individuals. Team building efforts instill a feeling of interdependence and an atmosphere conducive to information sharing and mutual cooperation.

Job Enrichment:
: efforts to increase one's influence and control over his or her job. Job enrichment seeks to provide missing motivational factors by expanding the duties and challenges available through work.

Management by Objectives:
: ongoing efforts to enable individuals to set goals and achieve them through individual effort and guidance from their managers.

continued

EXHIBIT 14.1
Continued

Meetings and Seminars:	meetings held to explore mutual problems and to seek mutually agreeable solutions. Such group sessions may be chaired by insiders or outsiders and may be used to prepare people for changes in advance of implementation.
Grid OD (Chapter 11):	a six-phase program for management and organizational development based on the managerial grid. The first two phases focus on management development. The last four phases are devoted to organizational development. The six phases are laboratory training seminar, team development, intergroup development, organizational goal setting, goal attainment, and stabilization.

OD is an expression of management's efforts to stay flexible. It recognizes that events inside and outside the organization can happen quite suddenly and create pressures for change. OD provides the personnel and mechanisms to deal with those changes and to control the evolution of change and its impact on the organizational structure, technology, and people.

Conflict—Its Nature and Sources

Conflict in a work environment is inevitable.[13] Whenever people must work together, there will be degrees of conflict. Why? Because people will not always be in perfect agreement on all issues, goals, or perceptions. This leads us to our definition of **conflict**—a "disagreement between two or more organizational members or groups arising from the fact that they must share scarce resources or work activities and/or from the fact that they have different status, goals, values or perceptions."[14] Additionally, conflict can be generated by the evolution of any of the stages of an organization's development.

Conflict is inherently neither positive nor negative. If conflict is managed correctly, it can be helpful (functional) in meeting the organization's goals. If it is not managed correctly, it can be destructive (dysfunctional).

To handle conflict, a manager needs to understand why conflict occurs. A starting point is to examine the sources.

Conflict can occur throughout the organization. Conflict can arise between the individual and the organization, between individuals, between groups and individuals, and between groups in the organization. The sources of the conflict include shared resources, differences in goals, differences in perceptions and values, disagreements in role requirements, nature of work activities, individual approaches, and the stage of organizational development.[15] We discuss each.

- *Shared resources.* Conflict can arise in an organization because limited resources must be shared by the organizational members. A manager of a work unit depends on the allocation of money, personnel, equipment, materials, and physical facilities to accomplish objectives. Some managers, despite the system used for allocation, will inevitably receive fewer resources than others. This can lead to lack of cooperation and eventually open conflict.

- *Differences in goals.* Individuals may have goals different from those of the organization. An individual's goal may require advancement within a three-year period. The organization may have a tradition of "seasoning" an employee over a longer period, say, seven years. There may be conflict in this situation.

  Also, formal groups within the organization may develop conflicting goals, a situation discussed in Chapter 4. For example, if production focuses its energies on manufacturing a product at the lowest possible cost, but the sales department is willing to accept unprofitable orders, conflict will arise.

- *Differences in perceptions and values.* Individuals have different value systems and different perceptions of a situation. These differences can lead to conflict in the work environment. For instance, an employee may place a high value on his time. He may really want to work but also prizes quality time with his family. A manager may request constant overtime or late work hours and not understand the employee's need to have family time. This is an obvious value system conflict.

  Different groups of employees can have conflicting perceptions too. Upper level management may perceive reports and procedures as valuable control devices designed to provide information. On the other hand, lower level employees may view the paperwork as busywork.

- *Disagreements in role requirements.* Role conflict can occur at all levels in the organization. An individual who is a member of a group can have conflicting demands placed on him or her by both the formal organization and the informal organization. Perhaps the informal group will seek out a worker as a leader, hoping for representation through her, and encouraging her assertiveness. But the formal organization may view the same person as just another employee, discouraging her input and attempting to control aggressiveness.

A second illustration can be noted in the area of line and staff interaction. The line manager may expect the staff person to give advice, be supportive to the organization, and be action oriented. The staff person may see her role as providing answers rather than advice, being analytical (sometimes critical) of the organization, and being reflective in order to review all potential alternatives. Conflict is inevitable.

- *Nature of work activities.* Conflict can result between individuals and groups concerning the quantity of work assigned as well as the relationship among the work units in performing the work. In the first situation, individuals and groups compare the workloads each has relative to the other. If there is inequity, there can be conflict.

  The second situation has two potential relationships. The group or individual may be dependent on another group or individual to complete work before starting its own. If the work is not on time or is of poor quality, open conflict can result. Another conflict situation can be created when two work groups or individuals are purposely placed in competition with each other. If management has set it up so that both groups have the opportunity to win, positive results can occur. But if it is a win–lose situation, conflict may be the outcome.

- *Individual approaches.* People have different styles and approaches in dealing with others and with situations. One person may be reflective, speak little, but deliver words of wisdom when ready to talk about a topic. Another person may be combative, as evidenced by an argumentative approach, immediate response with little thought, and pressure for agreement.

- *Stage of organizational development.* In the previous section of the chapter, we reviewed the various crises that can cause organizational change. These crisis conflicts are different depending on the stage of the development of the organization. The conflict may result from lack of or too much structure, inappropriate leadership, or overcontrol.

Knowing the potential sources of conflict is important to a manager, but developing strategies for dealing with it is critical to the organizational climate. We must remember that conflict is inherently neither positive nor negative: It can have either functional or dysfunctional consequences.

Managing Conflict

A manager needs to ensure that conflict does not become an end in itself. He or she must develop strategies to resolve potentially disruptive or dysfunctional conflict situations. Equally important, the manager needs to channel other conflict situations in constructive directions.[16] Prior to creating strategies, it is appropriate for the manager to develop a philosophical basis for dealing with conflict.

Philosophical Approaches to Conflict

A manager's philosophy about conflict will determine the approaches she or he takes in conflict situations. Stephen Robbins has identified three philosophical approaches to conflict.[17] Let's examine each.

Traditional view of conflict.   A manager may view conflict as unnecessary and harmful to an organization. If this is the philosophical foundation, the manager's reaction would be to fear its occurrence and to eliminate all evidence of conflict. If conflict does occur, the manager perceives it as his or her own failure to prevent it.

Behavioral view of conflict.   A second attitude toward conflict recognizes that conflict does frequently occur in organizations because of the nature of people, resource allocations, and organizational life. A manager holding this view would expect conflict. In addition, he or she might expect the conflict to turn out to be positive on occasions but more often to be harmful. With this philosophical foundation, the manager's reaction would be to attempt to resolve it or eliminate it once it occurs.

Interactionist view of conflict.   A more current philosophy about conflict is that it is inevitable in organizations and even necessary for organizational health. Further, no matter how well a company is developed and organized, conflict can and does occur. A manager operating with this philosophy would realize the challenge of conflict would be to manage it in order to maximize its positive potential for organizational growth or to minimize its negative effects.

What strategies are available to manage conflict?

Strategies for Managing Conflict

For conflict to be managed, the manager must first play the role of analyst to determine the following factors:

1. The type of conflict—between individuals, between individuals and groups, or between work groups.

2. The source of conflict—shared resources, differences in goals, role conflict, etc.

3. The level of conflict—how heated the situation is.

When these factors have been determined, the manager's challenge is to select the appropriate strategy. The manager may attempt to reduce the level of conflict or resolve the conflict. In special situations, he or she may attempt to increase the level of conflict. Let's discuss each approach.

Reducing the level of conflict.   In some situations, the manager may judge it appropriate to cool down the level of conflict as a final solution or an intermediate step to resolving the conflict. To implement the strategy, the manager may choose to provide the individuals or groups with a super-ordinate goal. With this strategy, the idea is to get everyone involved in the conflict situation to overlook or put aside individual differences and work toward another common goal.[18]

©1988 Tribune Media Services, Inc.
All Rights Reserved

"Well, Craigmeyer, I see we wasted our money sending you to that workshop on turning confrontations into constructive stepping stones for resolving conflict."

Source: Reprinted by permission: Tribune Media Services.

An example of this strategy can be seen in contract negotiations between management and unions. Each group has its own goals. The union wants high wages. Management—faced with fierce foreign competition and declining sales—would like to negotiate wages and benefits downward. These conflicting positions are replaced by another goal, a superordinate one, the continued existence of the organization; this goal supersedes the groups' individual goals.

Resolving conflict.   There are a number of approaches a manager can take to resolve conflict in a work environment.[19]

1. *Initiating compromise.*   With this approach, each party is required to give up something and find middle ground. In using this strategy, the manager and parties involved realize that there is not a win–lose outcome. The problem with this approach is that the conflict may recur because its root cause has not been removed.

2. *Initiating integrative problem solving.*   In this strategy, the manager is focusing on mutual problem solving by the parties involved. The conflicting groups or individuals are brought together with the idea of discussing the issues. At times, the group may work toward a consensus, seeking agreement by all on the best solution to a problem.

Another approach is for a confrontation session. In this process, the conflicting parties verbalize their positions and areas of disagreement. Unlike consensus seeking, this is a more heavily stress-related setting. The outcome hoped for is to find a reason for the conflict and resolve it. To be successful the manager acts as a mediator with one particular task—to force the parties into reaching a settlement. To get the desired outcome, a manager should use a method of operation that consists of the six distinct, consecutive segments listed in Exhibit 14.2.

3. *Initiating superordinate goals.*   Although this approach was also noted as a conflict reduction technique, it can be used to resolve conflict if the lower level goals of both parties are incorporated into the higher level goal.

Increasing the level of conflict.   There may be times when a manager would desire to increase the level of conflict and competition in a work environment. Situations in which a manager might initiate such action are these:[20]

- When organization members exhibit and accept minimal performance of peers.
- When people appear to be afraid to do anything other than the norm.
- When people passively accept events or behavior that should normally motivate action.

EXHIBIT 14.2
Six Steps for Mediating a Confrontation Session

1. Begin the discussions with the disputing parties.
2. Accumulate, from the disputing parties, all information that is relevant to the conflict. Provide each party the opportunity to present the problems, information, and factors from its own perception.
3. Develop a step-by-step agenda for all future discussions. The agendas should reflect phases in an overall strategy to resolve the conflict.
4. Initiate movement toward reaching a settlement. This step occurs only when the entire strategy has been designed.
5. Evolve from group meetings to separate sessions with each of the parties. In the individual sessions focus on solutions to the problem from an overall perspective.
6. Bring the parties back together to reach a mutual agreement that resolves the dispute.

Source: Adapted from Joseph B. Stulberg, "The Rewards of Conflict," *Success,* June 1987, p. 34.

The following five strategies are available to stimulate these situations:[21]

   1. *Bringing in outsiders.*   A manager may choose to bring in from outside the organization a person who does not have the same background, attitudes, or values as the present work group.
   2. *Changing the rules.*   In some instances, a manager may choose to either involve people not ordinarily included or exclude others normally included. This alteration of the "rules" can stimulate the environment. A manager attempting to open up the environment may ask an informal leader to attend "management only" meetings as a full participant. The result may be that both workers and manager gain new knowledge and change their actions.
   3. *Changing the organization.*   Another approach is to realign work groups and departments. A change in reporting relationships and the composition of work teams is designed to encourage the interaction of individuals with different experiences and perceptions.
   4. *Changing managers.*   In some instances, it is appropriate to insert a manager into a work group that can benefit from his or her dominant style of leadership. In other situations, the practice of rotating managers of work teams on a normal schedule can stimulate a group.
   5. *Encouraging competition.*   A final approach may be to encourage competition between groups or individuals. This can be done by offering bonuses, travel, time off, or certificates of merit. If a manager chooses

this method, he or she plans outcomes for the individuals or groups such as these:[22]

- Increase the cohesion within the group, and reduce internal differences.
- Focus on task accomplishment.
- Become more organized and efficient.

If the situation is not managed correctly, the competition can produce negative consequences between groups:[23]

- The other group is seen as an enemy.
- Communication between the groups can decrease or cease to exist.
- Open hostility can develop between the groups.
- One group can sabotage the efforts of another group.

Regardless of the strategy a manager selects in working with conflict, it will require skill and careful monitoring of the environment by her or him. As with the managing of change, conflict management requires ongoing sensitivity to the environment.

Summary

- Change and conflict are two factors that influence the organizational environment and can impede the efforts of individuals and groups toward goal accomplishment.
- An organization's climate is the personality of the organization. It is composed of a central system and six subsystems (according to the Kotter model).
- Change is a shift or alteration of the present environment.
- Change may arise from external or internal sources.
- A manager needs to be able to identify the need for change in an organization. The Greiner model provides management with a scheme for the evolution of change.
- A manager should develop a philosophy toward the phenomenon of change. The three elements of trust, organizational learning, and adaptiveness should compose this philosophy.
- The Greiner model for organizational change provides a manager with a rational approach to follow in change situations.

- A manager can expect resistance from those people affected by change.
- Management is faced with the challenge of changing people's attitudes, skills, and knowledge. Two models have application in this area. They are Lewin's model and force field analysis.
- Organizational development is a long-range program for change based on an analysis of organizational problems. It brings about a systematic renewal that can effectively cope with environmental changes.
- Conflict in a work environment is inevitable and is inherently neither positive nor negative. The effect of conflict depends on how it is managed.
- Conflict arises because people must share resources; or because they have different goals, values, perceptions, and styles; or because they disagree on roles. Conflict also arises as a result of a firm's stage of organizational development.
- A manager's philosophical approaches to conflict can reflect the traditional, behavioral, or interactionist view.
- A manager has a number of strategies for managing conflict. He or she can reduce the level of conflict or resolve it completely; in special situations, the manager may choose to increase the level of conflict in an organization.

Glossary of Essential Terms

change	A shift or alteration in the present organizational environment.
change agent	The individual responsible for introducing planned change in an organization. He or she may be an insider or outsider.
conflict	A disagreement between two or more organizational members or groups arising from the necessity for them to share scarce resources or work activities or from the fact that they have different status, goals, values, or perceptions.
organizational climate	The psychological environment or personality of an organization in which people must work.
organizational development	The long-range program for systematic renewal of an organization, based on an analysis of organizational problems.
organizational learning	The "how" behind the attempts by organizations and their managers to integrate new ideas into established systems to produce better ways of doing things.

Review Questions

1. Can you define this chapter's essential terms? If not, consult the preceding glossary.

2. What are the seven systems that compose the organizational climate? Describe each system. What knowledge of the organizational climate is important to a manager?

3. What is change? What are the two sources of change?

4. What are the phases of change in an organization? Why is it important for a manager to possess this information?

5. List the six phases for implementing organizational change proposed in the Greiner model. Explain each.

6. What are three reasons people resist change?

7. What are the "two forces" affecting change in the force field analysis model? How do these two forces affect the change process?

8. What is organizational development? What is its purpose?

9. List and explain four potential causes of conflict in an organization.

10. What strategies are available for conflict management? Give an example of each.

References

1. Daniel Katz and Robert L. Kahn, *The Social Psychology of Organization*, 2nd ed. (New York: John Wiley & Sons, 1978), p. 50.

2. Andrew J. Dubrin, *Fundamentals of Organizational Behavior* (New York: Pergamon Press, 1974), pp. 331–361.

3. Much of this section has been adapted from John P. Kotter, *Organizational Dynamics: Diagnosis and Intervention* (Reading, Mass.: Addison-Wesley, 1978), pp. 9–22.

4. Larry Greiner, "Evolution and Revolution as Organizations Grow," *Harvard Business Review* (July–August 1972), pp. 55–64.

5. Louis B. Barnes, "Managing the Paradox of Organizational Trust," *Harvard Business Review* (March–April 1981), pp. 107–118.

6. *Webster's Third International Dictionary* (Chicago: Encyclopedia Britannica, 1971), p. 2546.

7. Chris Argyris and Donald Schon, *Organizational Learning: A Theory of Action Perspective* (Reading, Mass.: Addison-Wesley, 1978).

8. Larry Greiner, "Pattern of Organizational Change," *Harvard Business Review* (May–June 1967), pp. 119–130.

9. Richard M. Hodgetts and Steven Altman, *Organizational Behavior* (Philadelphia: W. B. Saunders, 1979), pp. 353–355.

10. David A. Nadler, "The Fine Art of Managing Change," *The New York Times* (November 29, 1987), p. F3.

11. Kurt Lewin, "Frontiers in Group Dynamics: Concept, Method, and Reality in Social Science," *Human Relations*, 1, no. 1 (1947), pp. 5–41. See also Edgar H. Schein, "Management Development as a Process of Influence," *Industrial Management Review*, 2, no. 2 (May 1961).

12. Gene E. Burton, "Organizational Development—A Systematic Process," *Management World* (March 1976).

13. Joe Kelly, *Organizational Behavior*, rev. ed. (Homewood, Ill.: Richard D. Irwin, 1974), p. 570.

14. James A. F. Stoner, *Management*, 3rd ed. (Englewood Cliffs, N.J.: Prentice-Hall, 1986), p. 385.

15. See James G. March and Herbert Simon, *Organizations* (New York: John Wiley & Sons, 1958); and Dubrin, *Fundamentals of Organizational Behavior*.

16. Hodgetts and Altman, *Organizational Behavior*, p. 351.

17. Stephen Robbins, *Managing Organizational Conflict*, 3rd ed. (Englewood Cliffs, N.J.: Prentice-Hall, 1986), p. 321.

18. Hodgetts and Altman, *Organizational Behavior*, p. 351.

19. Stoner, *Management*, pp. 354–357.

20. Ibid., *Management*, p. 353.

21. Robbins, *Managing Organizational Conflict*.

22. Edgar H. Schein, *Organizational Psychology*, 2nd ed. (Englewood Cliffs, N.J.: Prentice-Hall, 1970), pp. 32–34.

23. Ibid.

Readings

Barczak, G. "Managing Large-Scale Organizational Change." *Organizational Dynamics*, 16 (Autumn 1987), pp. 22–35.

Benton, P. "The Greatest Challenge to Management (Technological Change)." *Management Today* (August 1987), pp. 71–72.

Cliff, Gordon. "Managing Organizational Conflict." *Management Review*, 75, no. 5 (May 1987), pp. 51–53.

Fink, Steven. *Crisis Management: Planning for the Inevitable*. New York: AMACOM, 1986.

Kakabadse, A. "Planning for Change." *Management Decision*, 25, no. 4 (1987), pp. 22–27.

Lynch, Robert. "The Shoot Out Among Nonteam Players." *Management Solutions*, 32, no. 5 (May 1987).

Martel, Leon. *Mastering Change*. New York: New American Library, 1986.

O'Toole, James. *Vanguard Management: Redesigning the Corporate Future*. New York: Berkley Books, 1985.

Peters, Tom. *Thriving on Chaos: Handbook for a Management Revolution*. New York: Alfred A. Knopf, 1988.

Walton, Richard E. *Innovating to Compete: Lessons for Diffusing and Managing Change in the Workplace*. San Francisco: Jossey-Bass, 1987.

C
A
S
E
S

14.1 A Minor Change

"They can't get away with this," said Allan, the shop steward. "There's no way I'm going to let this change go through without a fight. We will put all the union's muscle behind this effort to resist drug testing in the plant." Allan was reacting to the new memo circulated yesterday to all plant personnel. It detailed a "minor change" in the company—to conduct random tests of employees who had given management reason to suspect that they were using alcohol or other drugs. The memo was clear that testing would be done at the company's expense and that only workers would be tested. If a "positive" test result did occur, a second test would be conducted to verify the results of the first. Any employee who refused to be tested would be dismissed.

"Look, Allan," said the plant manager, "management is concerned as our whole society is today about drug-impaired workers and the costs they represent to this company and others. You know about the O'Brien case last month. He was high as a kite; everyone knew it, and he still was allowed to operate the overhead crane. You know what happened as a result. We don't want another case of lost time and medical bills."

"Mr. Munsun," said Allan, "you know that the union is opposed to this testing. It's an invasion of our employees' privacy. The testing has to be done with urine samples, and the figures I have read say that as many as 40 percent of the tests can yield false positives."

"Management is firm on this. Testing was not a program they decided on without much debate. Effective next month, your members will be tested if they give anyone in management cause to suspect that they are using drugs or under the influence of them. You had better get them used to the idea because that is how it is going to be."

The union quickly mobilized its members in opposition to the testing program. The press covered the local union's meeting, and the headlines in the two daily papers let the public know about the company's testing program. Management received many phone calls from community officials and members of the press inquiring about drug use in the plant. The local police chief talked to Munsun and told him that if illegal drugs were found, he wanted to be called in.

In the first week of the drug testing program, two workers refused to be tested and were fired. They filed a lawsuit claiming a violation of their rights to privacy and discrimination. One of the workers fired was the best designer in the company with an unblemished record for his fifteen years of employment. His loss threw two major programs into chaos. Within a month, development of a new product was so far behind schedule that it had to be scrapped. This loss led to the replacement of the head designer.

For the first time in the company's history, there was clear evidence that workers had deliberately destroyed company property. Sand was found in a milling machine's oil reservoir. Sand in the machine's oil had caused the failure of its $3,000 motor. This, like the firing of the two employees, did not go unnoticed by the local press.

Plant supervisors and team leaders have all reported an increase in worker-related problems. Many have noted increases in absenteeism and growing negative attitudes in plant employees, labor and management alike. The former plant environment was one of cooperation and mutual efforts aimed at problem solving. The environment now emerging is one of hostility and noncooperation. One supervisor had shifted from participative leadership to autocratic. In his words, "the fellas used to pitch in and respond nicely to requests. Now you have to threaten them with insubordination to get them to respond. It's almost like you're afraid to turn your back to them. Where is all this going to end?"

For Discussion

1. How has the "minor change" at this company affected each of the seven major organizational systems listed in your text? Provide examples from the case to support your answers.

2. What do you think about the way this testing program was introduced into the plant?

3. What assumptions lie beneath the company's drug testing program?

14.2 Conflicting Views

"You're from the old school," said Rita. "A little change never hurt anyone. You know the old saying that the only thing certain is change itself."

"Well," countered Gayla, "I believe that changes should be kept to a minimum and that conflict should be eliminated entirely. I don't want to go through another month like this last one. Don't you remember how so-called good friends were fighting with each other over such silly things as waste baskets and the color of desk blotters?"

Rita and Gayla were discussing the recent move from their rented quarters to the company's newly constructed regional office. Personnel and sections from three rented facilities were now in the process of taking over the new facility. Rita's group of sixteen people was the first to arrive and had its pick of spaces. Gayla's group was the last to arrive; its members found themselves on the third floor, overlooking the parking lot, and occupying the offices everyone else had rejected.

When Rita's people arrived, they were asked to visit the stockrooms in the basement to pick their desks, file cabinets, desk sets, and other accessories by marking the tags on each item with their names and sections. After Rita placed her people in their offices, she asked each of her subordinates to stake out a specific area or cubicle. Once each person had chosen a spot, Rita requested that the items chosen from stock be delivered and set up.

Things were a little different for Gayla and her group, however. When they arrived at the end of last month, there were just enough chairs, desks, desk sets, and so forth to equip each person's workstation. The stations were already set up on the third floor, in the rear quarter of the building. Exposures were north and east. The northern view was of the parking lot and the rear of a wholesale warehouse. The eastern view was of a busy interstate highway that ran parallel to the building about 100 feet away.

Needless to say, Gayla's people were complaining and moaning from the first day. The northeast corner of the top floor would mean cold winters, and the views were about as depressing as one could imagine. When Gayla's people found out that the others who had come ahead of them had been able to choose their own office furnishings, they really got upset. Gayla was having a very tough time trying to get her people to settle in and get productive. It did no good to explain to them that they were last because their lease had been the last to run out. Everyone suspected that higher-ups had it in for Gayla and that they were paying the price with lousy facilities. When reminded by other workers that their previous rented facilities had been considered better than anyone else's, Gayla's group members became somewhat defensive.

Over the last two weeks, Gayla was told by Rita and two other supervisors that her people were trying to swap wastebaskets and blotters with others in the building. In one instance, one of Gayla's people tore up a blotter and kicked a large dent in the wastebasket that belonged to a person who would not swap with her. What had been intended as good-natured kidding was being taken by the third-floor group as insulting remarks and conduct. Gayla sensed things were getting out of hand.

For Discussion

1. Which opening viewpoint do you support—Gayla's or Rita's? Why?
2. What philosophy toward conflict does each manager exhibit?
3. What are the causes of conflict in this situation?
4. What do you think of the way the company handled its moves and consolidation? How did this contribute to conflict?
5. What recommendations would you make to resolve or reduce the level of conflict?

Contemporary Management: Trends and Issues

Management
and Productivity

ESSENTIAL TERM

productivity

LEARNING OBJECTIVES

After reading and discussing this chapter, you should be able to do the following:

1. Define this chapter's essential term.
2. List three areas in which our federal government has contributed to our nation's decline in productivity and what actions it has taken to improve each area.
3. List two areas in which employees have contributed to our nation's productivity decline and what is being done or can be done about each area.
4. List two areas in which organized labor has contributed to our nation's decline in productivity and what is being or can be done about each area.
5. List two areas in which management in America has contributed to our nation's productivity decline and what is being or can be done about each area.

Productivity as the Key to Business Success

Most of what our textbook has presented thus far comes together in this chapter: All the past chapters have dealt with activities, factors, and functions of management as they affect the effectiveness and efficiency of a business enterprise. Effective businesses concentrate on producing the right product or service for their situation and capabilities. Efficient businesses concentrate on lowering costs or increasing output for each dollar invested in the business. Both approaches are essential in today's fast-changing markets and economies.

This chapter examines the concept of productivity. After defining this concept and looking at how it can be measured, we examine the major causes of low productivity and some of the remedies now being used by business around the world.

Productivity Defined

Productivity, in its most common form of measurement, is the measurement of how much input is needed to produce an amount of output. Productivity is usually expressed as a ratio between these two items. A *productivity index* (PI) is the result of dividing input into output. Output is measured in dollars or units, and input is measured in hours. To illustrate a measure of productivity, consider that you produced three school homework assignments in three hours of work. Dividing your output in units (3 assignments) by your input in hours (3), you arrive at a PI of 3 to 3, or 3 divided by 3, or 1.

Productivity Indexes

In general, two kinds of indexes can be used to measure productivity: the single-factor index and the combined-factors index. The single-factor index might use one of the following as a unit of input: hours of labor (direct or indirect), hours of machine time, tons of materials, or dollars of invested capital. A combined-factors index, or multifactor index, may combine such factors as labor, materials, and capital under some kind of formula and use it as an overall measure of an organization's total productivity gain or loss. Whichever index is used, it must be as simple as possible and thoroughly understandable to those who use it and react to its measurements.[1]

Productivity indexes help compare the performance of a company in its industry, plants in a company, departments within a manufacturing plant, and the contributions of those people or units of an enterprise that are not directly involved with producing what it sells. "Engineers, supervisors, and other white-collar employees make significant contributions to manufacturing productivity. . . ."[2] Their contributions need to be considered since all parts of an organization can be improved. The primary purpose behind all indexes is to focus management on critical aspects of all production processes and, therefore, to help lead to the improvement of performances. Productivity indexes help plot trends and spot those parts of an organization that are experiencing unusually strong or poor performances. All indexes have problems associated with them. None is a perfect measure. But an imperfect measure is often better than no measure at all.[3]

To keep track of our nation's productivity and to compare it to the productivity of other nations, the U.S. Department of Labor's Bureau of Labor Statistics has developed an extremely complicated aggregate productivity measure (our nation's PI). It is the ratio of our national output of goods and services—our gross domestic product—to the total hours of human labor needed to produce that output. Our gross domestic product is the measure in dollars, using the market value of our nation's businesses' output of goods and services. A PI is calculated for each year and then compared to a base year in order to note significant improvements or declines. Such comparisons are meaningful, however, only if the dollar figures for each year after the base year are adjusted for inflationary increases.

Using America's PI, the Bureau of Labor Statistics has calculated that productivity increased by an annual average of 1.2 percent from 1973 to 1981 and by 4 percent from 1981 to 1985. In 1986, U.S. productivity showed a downturn since it increased by only 3.7 percent, and in 1987, it increased by only 3.3 percent. See Figure 15.1 for the quarterly changes in America's productivity for the years 1986 and 1987. Exhibit 15.1 compares the growth in U.S. productivity (using output per hour invested in manufacturing) with eleven other heavily industrialized nations. According to the 1986 figures, Japan leads the pack, and the United States ranks ninth.

While aggregate measures may be useful for governments and nations, individual businesses need their own specialized productivity measures. Stanley B. Henrici, a retired general manager for Heinz USA and author of business articles and books, proposes that each company, whether a producer of goods or services, can create several productivity measures for the entire company or for its individual divisions. After adjusting for inflationary increases to its sales revenues, a retailer could track its productivity by dividing its net sales by the total of all the hours worked by its employees. Manufacturers could subtract purchases from revenues (both adjusted for inflationary increases) and divide the difference by the total hours worked by all employees. To measure changes from year to year, a

FIGURE 15.1
Quarterly changes
in America's
productivity, 1986–
1987

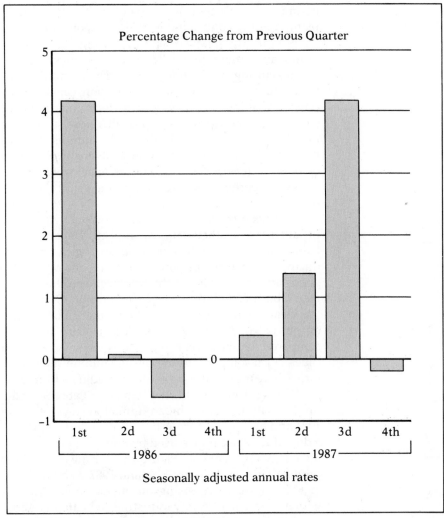

Source: U.S. Department of Commerce and U.S. Labor Department.

base year must be established for comparison purposes. Henrici's formula
for a manufacturer's current year is as follows:[4]

$$\frac{\text{Output}}{\text{per Hour}} = \frac{(\text{Product Revenues} - \text{Purchases}) \times \text{Inflation* Deflators}}{\text{Total Hours Worked}}$$

*Inflation deflators adjust the ratio's variables for inflationary increases in dollars received in revenue or
spent for purchases. If a company spent $400 in 1984 for 400 units of inventory, but had to spend $500
for the same 400 units in 1989, an inflation deflator would dictate the use of $400 in 1989's calculation of
purchases for calculating a meaningful PI. In other words, you can't increase or decrease your productivity
simply by spending or earning more money for the same unit volume of inventory or sales.

After this year's output is calculated, it can be compared to a base year as follows:

$$\text{Productivity Index (PI)} = \frac{\text{Output per Hour for Current Year}}{\text{Output per Hour for Base Year}}$$

By comparing its outputs and the inputs needed to achieve them, businesses can spot improvements or declines. Investigations can be conducted to determine why the company's PI is lower this year than last or why it has improved. Once the causes have been found, specific plans and goals can be developed to improve the company's efforts in many areas.

Many economists, managers, and research groups have looked at America's lagging productivity and come up with several related causes. We look next at these causes and what can be done to eliminate or reduce their impact on productivity growth.

Government Actions Affecting Productivity

The government is a key ingredient in the productivity picture. Through decisions regarding spending and taxation, regulation, and capital investment, the government has affected productivity.

EXHIBIT 15.1
Changes in Productivity for Twelve Industrialized Nations, 1960–1986*

Country	Output per Hour								
	1960	1965	1970	1975	1980	1983	1984	1985	1986
United States	62.2	76.6	80.8	92.9	101.4	112.0	116.6	121.7	126.0
Canada	50.7	65.0	75.6	88.6	98.2	106.9	110.2	112.7	112.1
Japan	23.2	35.0	64.8	87.7	122.7	142.3	152.2	163.7	168.2
Belgium	32.8	40.6	59.9	85.9	119.7	144.7	149.8	153.3	NA
Denmark	37.2	48.4	65.5	94.6	112.3	120.2	118.9	117.2	116.6
France	36.4	49.2	69.6	88.5	112.0	128.8	133.8	138.3	140.9
West Germany	40.3	54.0	71.2	90.1	108.6	119.1	123.5	128.9	131.4
Italy	36.5	52.9	72.7	91.1	116.9	126.6	134.7	136.8	138.4
Netherlands	32.4	42.1	64.3	86.2	113.9	127.5	141.2	145.6	NA
Norway	54.6	64.4	81.7	96.8	106.7	117.2	123.9	125.2	122.1
Sweden	42.3	58.5	80.7	100.2	112.7	125.5	131.0	134.5	136.4
United Kingdom	55.5	65.7	79.7	95.2	101.7	123.0	129.5	134.2	138.2

*1977 = 100.

Source: U.S. Labor Department, Bureau of Labor Statistics.

Government and Spending

America's federal government has the responsibility to look after its economy, to spend and tax, and to regulate commerce. Its actions affect nearly every person directly and create burdens or benefits for citizens and businesses. For its 1989 fiscal year, the federal government will spend more than $1 trillion. About $130 billion of those dollars will be borrowed funds. Since our nation began, the federal debt has grown to nearly $2 trillion. The interest on this debt amounts to about $150 billion each year.

Although heavy government borrowing has caused inflation in the past (inflation averaged 8.3 percent from 1978 to 1984), inflation has leveled off at about 3.5 percent for 1985 through 1987. But the cost for this leveling off has been higher interest rates for borrowed money needed by consumers and businesses. Interest rates for most types of loans have averaged above 10 percent for 1978 through 1988. Higher rates of interest create demands for higher wages, which cause the companies that grant them to have to raise prices: the wage–price spiral. As prices for American labor and products increase, foreign producers with lower labor costs and selling prices find America a ready marketplace. As we Americans pay more for energy, rent, borrowed funds, and our purchases, we have less to save and invest. Less money invested in businesses and less available to lenders means higher interest rates as all borrowers (large and small) compete for fewer available dollars. High interest rates cause businesses and consumers to put off spending. Less capital equipment is purchased, and less is spent for consumer goods; these decreases mean less expansion of business operations and fewer jobs.

Government and Regulations

Government actions, from the legislatures to the regulatory agencies, affect all aspects of our lives and the output and growth of our economy. According to the Small Business Administration, America's small businesses spend over $14 billion to complete millions of pages of government forms. Such burdens add to the cost of doing business and lessen productivity. Every dollar and every hour spent on government paperwork is one less for production of goods and services.

Federal regulations from federal agencies create the biggest burdens for American businesses. Fifty-seven federal regulatory agencies spend billions and employ almost 90,000 people to enforce thousands of economic and social regulations. Realizing the impact of government regulation on business productivity, the federal government has cut and delayed enforcement of many federal regulations. In many instances, before implementing new restrictions, agencies have been instructed to determine the costs of compliance and the benefits that the regulations are intended to yield. Various business representatives have asked that businesses be told

"*Your Majesty, according to our study the shoe was lost for want of a nail, the horse was lost for want of a shoe, and the rider was lost for want of a horse, but the kingdom was lost because of overregulation.*"

Source: Drawing by Dana Fradon; © 1980 The New Yorker Magazine, Inc.

what they must do and why, not how they must comply. They have pleaded for the right to determine their own methods. Such was the case with the requirements for improved gas mileage and emission controls with the auto industry; the desired results were achieved by manufacturers as promised. Exhibit 15.2 shows the results through 1987 of the federal government's efforts to deregulate industries.

Government and Capital Investment

High interest rates and runaway government spending discourage investment in capital equipment (tools, machinery, new plants and equipment) so necessary for businesses to stay competitive in world markets. With the costs of modernizing and updating facilities increasing, businesses may postpone attempts to improve their productivity through capital investments.

To help stimulate spending on capital improvements, the federal government has enacted major tax cuts and tax credits for investments in plants

EXHIBIT 15.2
Major Deregulation Legislation

Name of Act	Topic	Critical Points
Railroad Revitalization and Regulatory Reform Act (1976)	Railroad Rate Regulation	Provided an element of freedom for railroads to establish rates.
Airline Deregulation Act (1978)	Airline Competition	Directed the Civil Aeronautics Board to change its emphasis from regulating airline passenger service to encouraging competition between carriers; provided for the gradual lessening of the CAB's control over the airlines' rate setting; abolished the CAB as of January 1, 1985.
Motor Carrier Act (1980)	Truck Competition	Introduced elements of competition into the previously totally regulated motor carrier industry by (1) providing ease of entry and eliminating the requirement to document public need, (2) limiting restrictions on specific hauling practices, and (3) providing for price competition.
Depository Institutions Deregulation and Monetary Control (1980)	Bank Practices	Initial legislation directed at the deregulation of the banking industry; authorized interest to be paid on demand deposits; eliminated interest rate maximums; authorized mutual savings banks to make corporate, commercial, and business loans.

EXHIBIT 15.2
Continued

Staggers Rail Act (1980)	Railroad Rate Setting	Provided for price competition among railroads; declared rate control authority by the Interstate Commerce Commission was applicable only in markets dominated by railroads.
Thrift Institutions Restructuring Act	Savings and Loan Practices	Legislation directed at allowing thrift institutions to compete with commercial banks; allowed savings and loans to make commercial loans and to invest in nonresidential real estate.

Source: Business Economics.

and equipment over the past eight years. As a result, capital spending increased dramatically in 1984 and 1985, declined in 1986, and rose a modest 2.8 percent in 1987. Figure 15.2 shows the annual changes in capital spending by businesses from 1981 through 1987.

U.S. businesses planned to spend $385 billion on expansion and modernization of their facilities and equipment in 1987, up about 3 percent over 1986.[5] Nearly $15 billion of that amount was budgeted for office automation, a figure expected to increase to more than $20 billion by 1991.[6]

Employee Actions Affecting Productivity

Today's workers have been accused of not wanting to work, of being in love with leisure at the expense of employment commitments, of being sloppy and lacking pride in accomplishments, and of being lazy. One thing is certain: Today's worker is different from his or her counterpart of the 1960s and 1970s. Two major changes took place in those years: More women entered more job categories than ever before, and more workers entered

FIGURE 15.2
Capital spending by
U.S. businesses,
1981–1987

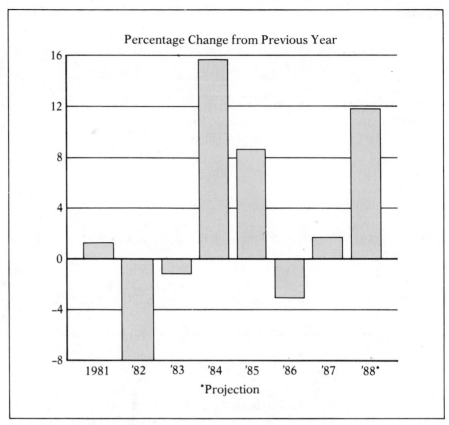

Percentage Change from Previous Year

*Projection

Source: U.S. Department of Commerce.

the job market with more skills than ever before. During the 1980s, the number of younger workers will drop—owing to a declining birth rate in the 1960s. The babies of the post–World War II baby boom are now in their late thirties and early forties. These workers are in, or entering, various career fields, and bring a variety of skills, attitudes, and values to the workplace.

The individual worker and manager must share some of the blame for low productivity. Those who loaf and fail to give their best to their jobs cost employers billions of dollars each year. Many major industries and companies are plagued with the problems of absenteeism, tardiness, restricted output by dissatisfied employees, and even sabotage.

Worker Attitudes Toward Work

According to a Louis Harris poll done in the fall of 1986, Americans are working harder and longer but are enjoying their jobs less. Seventy-one percent of the 1,250 people surveyed reported that they are certainly or probably working as hard as they can. But 40 percent of the 150 senior executives said that their subordinates could do more. Fifty-six percent of those polled said that the quality of their lives at work had improved over the previous ten years. The average office worker spent 6.5 hours a day at a desk or workstation. Asked what work characteristics were important to them, 82 percent responded in favor of a challenging job; 80 percent said good benefits; and 74 percent chose good pay, a free exchange of information, and making significant contributions.[7]

According to a poll by Robert Half International, a New York consulting and recruiting firm, 25 percent of Americans are not happy in their jobs. These people claim that they do not get enough recognition or money, that they want less stress or a better boss. Half's survey of vice-presidents and personnel directors also shows that as many as 27 million Americans are unhappy because they chose the wrong occupation or profession. Half recommends these cures: If you are unhappy with your boss, seek a transfer. If you are unhappy with your work, ask for new and different things to do; seek new skills to qualify yourself for a different job. Ask yourself what you *and* your company can do to remove the sources of your unhappiness.[8]

These survey results underscore the need for management to include Herzberg's motivation factors in many more jobs and the importance of career pathing and counseling. Unhappy workers are not motivated workers, and unmotivated people don't do much to improve their employer's productivity.

Employee Theft

According to the U.S. Bureau of Justice statistics, employee theft accounts for about 70 percent of retailers' losses to all types of crimes. Across U.S. industries, employee theft represents about 43 percent of all stock shrinkage. Federal convictions for embezzlement (stealing funds from one's employer) run about 1,700 per year. The impact on a victimized company can be serious enough to force it into bankruptcy. The impact of even small losses to employee thieves reduces the business's productivity and profits. Annually, retailers lose more than $1.5 billion, and only about 30 percent of those losses are to shoplifters and other outsiders.[9]

Theft of goods is not the only kind of theft experienced by businesses. Employees steal time and information. According to Reid Psychological Systems, a Chicago publisher of honesty tests, 75 percent of our nation's factory workers take a longer-than-permitted lunch or rest break without approval, nearly one-half come to work late or leave work early, and about one-third admit to taking sick days when they are not sick.[10] According to Robert Half International, theft of time by employees costs U.S. companies about $170 billion each year.[11]

Manufacturers, especially those involved with highly technical research, report theft by employees and others of trade secrets and the results of their expensive and time-consuming research. Such theft annually inflicts billions of dollars worth of damage in missed sales and wasted research and development costs. "Ideas slip out through executives, salesmen, and suppliers. Even cleaning workers have been caught selling trash to rivals. . . . Kellogg Company in April (1986) closed its Battle Creek (Mich.) plant to public tours when it learned that industrial spies from two foreign competitors had gathered valuable information during visits."[12]

Three primary factors influence employees to steal: need, opportunity, and rationalization. No matter how much a person earns, he or she could always use more. In general, the larger the thief's earnings, the larger the theft. Rationalizations include the theories that stealing from a business is not the same as stealing from an individual; the store or business earns so much that the amount stolen will not matter; I am underpaid, so I can even things out by stealing; and others are stealing, so why shouldn't I.[13] To deal with theft of information and trade secrets, industry spokespersons recommend the following:

- More vigorous prosecution by companies and states.
- Enactment of the Uniform Trade Secrets Act by more than the dozen states that now have it.
- Tighter security, especially computer security.
- Tightening up on the use of the Freedom of Information Act, which forces governmental agencies to release information to those who properly request it.
- Training employees on what to safeguard and how to do it.

Retailers have found that employee training can make a strong statement to the effect that theft by anyone will not be tolerated. Some vigorously prosecute those caught stealing. Others train employees on how to spot a shoplifter. Still others offer rewards for information leading to the prosecution or apprehension of employee thieves. More than ever, businesses are using innovative high-tech systems to include video monitoring, computerized monitoring of all cash transactions, sophisticated alarm and merchandise tagging systems, and intricate data entry procedures that must be followed in sequence to tap a computer's memory. Careful and professional screening of all applicants can help identify those who are or might be dishonest.

To deal with employees' theft of time, closer supervision is required. Managers are introducing telephone and video display terminal monitoring, and they are linking employee pay and benefits to the company's profits. Rewarding employees with perfect attendance records and keeping people busy through proper work assignments and monitoring of their progress have also helped reduce time theft.

Drugs at Work

More than 10 percent of adult Americans regularly use illegal drugs.[14] Drug use impairs one's ability to function properly. It has led to criminal acts, lost time from work, family breakups, and human suffering due to work-related accidents and personal illnesses. When you consider that about 10.5 million adult alcoholics and another 7.6 million adults in America have had serious drinking-related problems, the impact on our nation's productivity must be very great.[15] It has been estimated that drug use by employees costs their employers more than $33 billion each year in lost productivity.[16]

Attempts to Capture Greater Employee Commitment

Organizations have been experimenting with ways in which to capture their employees' enthusiasm and interest in both their work and their places of employment. Quality circles and quality of work life programs have led to efforts to enable workers in groups and as individuals to air their complaints, suggestions, and personal feelings and to get relief as well as rewards for their efforts. (Quality of work life, QWL, is a general label used to describe a variety of activities and programs intended to aid employees in their search for satisfaction of their needs. QWL uses training programs, development programs, group problem-solving sessions, labor–management groups, and attitude surveys. General Motors was the first major U.S. business to incorporate QWL activities into its collective bargaining agreement with the United Auto Workers in 1973. It made all QWL activities voluntary for all GM employees. QWL activities can improve the quality of work and the working environment for those employees who participate in them.)

The Bank of America's top management has developed several programs for helping employees who have problems or troubles because its members are convinced that troubled or dissatisfied workers cannot give their best to their jobs. An employee assistance department has been established and staffed in part with employee assistance officers. These people stand ready to discuss in confidence any work-related issue that is bothering a Bank of America employee. While employees are encouraged to talk with their supervisors first, they are not required to do so. Employee assistance officers will attempt to resolve any problems if the troubled employee gives them permission to do so.[17]

"Let's Talk it Over" is the Bank of America's formal grievance process for its nonunionized workforce. It provides six steps for resolving problems, from a worker–boss conference through a review by a committee made up of the heads of the personnel department, the legal department, and the executive officer of the complaining employee's division.[18] Similar programs exist in many other organizations—all aimed at letting individuals know that they matter, are appreciated, and can receive assistance when they need it.

According to E. Douglas White, senior vice-president of the American Productivity Center in Houston, today's worker has a far higher level of education and less concern for employment security than his or her parent or grandparent. Workers today realize the threat that foreign competition means to their employment and their employers.[19] Most realize, or soon will, that there is a greater need to cooperate with employers than to fight them.

Today's worker expects more from work than ever before. There are two questions that each employee is concerned about: What does my job require me to do? What is my reward for doing my job well?[20] Researchers from the nonprofit Public Agenda Foundation have interviewed hundreds of workers to find their problems and to communicate them to corporate and national leaders. They have found that today's workers consider a decent salary and workplace as rights, not as rewards. The things they said would motivate them to extra effort or enthusiasm appear in Exhibit 15.3. They are not new. Rather, they repeat what we have learned in earlier chapters about what motivates and stimulates people to excel. Most people

EXHIBIT 15.3
What Makes People Want to Work Harder and More Enthusiastically?

People are motivated to work hard when:
- Their tasks are interesting, varied, and involve some challenge, learning, and responsibility.
- They have enough information, support, and authority to get the job done.
- They help make decisions that affect their jobs because bosses recognize that they know their jobs best.
- They understand how their own work fits into the larger picture.
- They see rewards linked to performance, and understand how employees can advance.
- They are treated as individuals, personally important to the company.

Source: Public Agenda Foundation findings on individual motivation as reported in *Inc.*, April 1981, pp. 76–78.

simply want to feel wanted, to experience challenges, and to feel really useful in their jobs.[21]

As you know by now, workers are most often the source of useful information about how things can be made safer, better, more efficient, and less fatiguing. In Chapter 5, we talked to you about enlisting worker cooperation through worker participation programs and activities to include quality circles, training, and development programs. Many companies are currently using labor–management teams in which union and company officials pool their talents to improve working conditions and production operations. We examine changes in union–management relations next.

Union Actions Affecting Productivity

Rigid Job Structure

Historically, labor unions have had little appreciation for management plans and programs to make them partners. Most were suspicious that such plans for methods improvement were simply schemes to demand more work from members or to reduce employment. Unions feared that their members would accuse them of selling out to management. But things have been and still are changing.[22]

Since the 1930s, unions have become less craft oriented and more industrywide in their organizational efforts and memberships. The scientific management techniques that gave workers specialized tasks created narrow job descriptions and made it easy for workers to gain protection on the job through their unions. Unions allowed management to organize work as long as it was clearly defined. Unfortunately, elaborate divisions of work are not always efficient, and rigidly defined jobs make it difficult for management to adjust to changing demands from production. Today's industrial and clerical environments demand freedom to experiment and to redesign, enlarge, or enrich workers' jobs. When a market calls for short runs of specialized products, when demand is unpredictable, or when a product must change rapidly, old-style job definitions just don't apply.[23]

Strong unions do not need to demand rigid job definitions in order to adequately protect their workers. But the movement away from them has some unions uncertain about how to protect their members. As companies move into flexible job scheduling, assembly by teams, worker participation plans, and job rotations, the old work rules and grievance procedures don't seem to work. Unions in West Germany and Japan have become flexible and have formed partnerships with management to a greater extent than have American unions. Their flexibility has given their employers an edge when competing with American employers. Haruki Shimizu, general secretary of the Federation of Japanese Automobile Workers, points out that Japanese workers have a sense that their company is their base for living. What is good for the company will be good for them.[24] Hajime Nakai, president of Sanyo Electric Company's American subsidiary, SMC, points out that "in Japan, the union lives with the company and never pulls the trigger unless it finds itself in an extremely serious situation. It tries as much as possible to work with us on the same ground, because its members' future and prosperity are directly linked to ours. The important question for us (in America) right now is how to instill this concept in our American workers."[25]

Developing Progressive Labor Relations

The Japanese model for labor relations is based on a spirit of mutual sharing of concerns and on a common understanding that the company's welfare, survival, and growth should be the primary concerns for both labor and management. Employees are more flexible toward management's ideas because they do not fear layoffs. In fact, they are quite eager and willing to suggest labor-saving changes.

The concept of "lifetime employment" for which the Japanese have received so much credit is responsible for a number of benefits to both the company and the employees. But where this approach is taken (in the biggest Japanese companies that are successful in international markets), managements take more care in selecting, training, and advancing their personnel. An enormous effort is made to continually develop the skills and, therefore, the productivity of employees, individually and in groups. The Japanese are able to make these investments because they know their workers, with few exceptions, will be with the company for their entire careers.[26] Not so with most American workers, who are far more mobile and willing to move.

The concept of lifetime employment is not unique to Japan. Many U.S. employers have between 30 and 40 percent of their employees for all of their working lives. But American employers don't make this fact known to employees or managers although they could be using it to increase their workers' sense of self-worth and commitment to the company. American management tends to treat its people as less important assets than the Japanese firms do; American companies spend more money and time on technological improvements, thus fostering the adversary relationship between employer and employee.[27]

The United Auto Workers (UAW) was the first American union to commit itself to cooperation with management on quality of work life programs. Efforts to boost productivity at General Motors were proving of little use in the early 1970s because of workers who came in late, failed to report, and lacked involvement in their work. In 1973, the UAW and GM signed the first QWL agreement in U.S. history: Its underlying premise was that management would seek its rewards from improvements such as higher product quality and lower absenteeism. All QWL programs were to be voluntary, and none would be used to reduce manpower unilaterally or to increase production rates. The agreement has become a model for many other unions and has given QWL activities credibility in the eyes of union members and officials.[28]

Not all labor leaders and rank and file members are convinced yet because old suspicions die hard. But industries under pressure from foreign competition have led the way into QWL efforts to improve their productivity. Most have met with significant success. Labor leaders have found that their members will respond when given the correct information they need to decide for or against QWL proposals and contracts. Several unions have sent regular representatives to the Productivity Forum, along with some corporate executives and government representatives. Together, they explore ways to improve productivity and working relationships.[29]

The 1987 United Auto Workers agreement with Ford Motor Company illustrates organized labor's stand in helping their members by also helping their members' companies stay competitive. It included significant job-security provisions, wage increases, work rule changes, and reductions on having work done by outside suppliers (outsourcing). The three-year contract ensures the jobs of 104,000 blue-collar workers and requires Ford to recall one laid-off worker for every two workers who retire, resign, or die. To discourage the use of overtime, the agreement requires that $1.25 be paid into a special union training fund for each hour of overtime used. Wages will rise by 3 percent for each year of the contract, the first increases to base pay of $13.42 per hour since 1984. In exchange, the union agreed to new, widespread work rule changes to help Ford become more flexible in its human resource uses.[30] In 1987, Ford employees received an average profit-sharing bonus of more than $3,000 per employee. The recent and huge Ford profits are a result in part of labor's concessions over previous years and the emphasis on quality products to meet today's car-buyer's needs.

Management Actions Affecting Productivity

Poor Management Practices

In an interview published in *U.S. News & World Report*, Professor Robert Hayes of the Harvard Business School identified several management causes behind our declines in productivity. He points out an American management tendency to be myopic—to sacrifice long-term planning and objectives for short-term gains. Large bonuses linked to last year's profit performance tend to encourage such myopia. Managers face pressures from stockholders, boards of directors, and their own compensation systems to show profit growth in the present. A result, for example, was the delay in the auto industry in introducing fuel-efficient cars and the tire industry's delay in providing American-made radials—both of which gave foreign competition an edge, along with a strong product recognition in the minds of American consumers. According to Hayes, "The best way we can compete against foreign firms is to keep offering better products. But in many industries, management avoids introducing new products because it essentially makes old assets and old skills obsolete, temporarily lowering return on investment."[31]

Professor Hayes points out two additional problems: (1) frequent executive turnover leading to major changes in strategy and (2) corporate diversification. The old tradition of working one's way to the top of an organization's management hierarchy has given way to "importing" talent at various levels when problems occur. Typically, these managerial imports lack firsthand experience with the business and bring in friends to get results fast. Corporate strategies change, with the result that initiative from below can be stifled. When the corporation becomes too diversified, it gets involved with too many things that are unfamiliar to to those in charge. Valuable time is spent getting familiar with operations. Few managers are able to cope with the problems that different companies in different industries represent.[32]

Part of the blame for time wasted by workers belongs to managers who fail to manage their subordinates adequately. The principal areas of weakness, according to Theodore Barry & Associates of Los Angeles, include poor scheduling of work, unclear communication of assignments, improper staffing and coordination of work, and poor discipline. According to Barry's management studies (more than fifty since 1974), management spends too much time on technology and too little on human resource management. "Production supervisors don't manage their work groups effectively, middle management doesn't provide needed control systems, and upper management doesn't appreciate the complexities of workforce management."[33] See Figure 15.3 and Appendix A.

These are the identified problems from a management viewpoint. But what are the solutions? They include a commitment at the top, more research and development, training, retraining, better management of time and paperwork, and flexible manufacturing.

Commitment at the Top

As with so many other management programs and activities, efforts at improving productivity must start and be supervised from the top. Tenneco's chief executive officer, James L. Ketelsen, knows this and began his

FIGURE 15.3
The management causes behind time wasted by employees, given in percentages

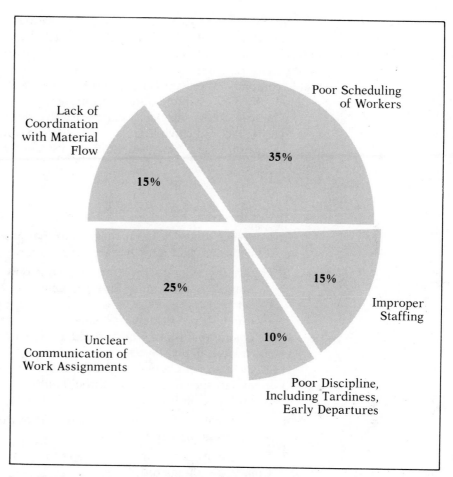

Source: Theodore Barry & Associates, Los Angeles.

company's efforts at improving productivity by making it the most important long-term goal for the future. In a memo to the company's various division heads, he stated: "Productivity gains are a consequence of the interplay of many factors working simultaneously—capital, labor, union–management relations, incentives, and finally, management itself. With productivity gains difficult to obtain, and equally difficult to maintain, management needs to give this matter constant attention if progress is to be made." Ketelsen appointed Tenneco's director of its management development program as the director of productivity programs at the corporate level. The director's initial tasks were to assess the techniques already in use and to examine alternatives before developing a plan.[34]

The president of Boise Cascade, Jon H. Miller, is personally involved in developing the company's approach. He formed a corporate-level task force and then established task forces for the company's five operating divisions. Miller asked a senior production executive to spend a year at the American Productivity Center to learn measurements and techniques and to work on various projects. When the manager returned, he took over the productivity direction. "We are not trying to impose one method on the whole company. We want each group to develop the methods most appropriate for their own operations and industry."[35]

What can an organization's chief executive do to tackle the problem of increasing its productivity? C. Jackson Grayson, founder and president of the Houston-based American Productivity Center, has these suggestions:[36]

1. Get involved.

2. Convince others in top management that productivity gains are a major goal that must be given high priority.

3. Ensure that a long-term strategic plan is developed to:
   a. identify opportunities for improvement.
   b. set goals.
   c. establish productivity measures.
   d. ensure that those who succeed are rewarded.
   e. involve all employees.
   f. keep a continuous flow of information going.
   g. assign specific functions throughout the organization. Include both line and staff.

4. Ensure that productivity efforts are part of the company's regular business plan and budget.

5. Realize that gains come from doing things harder and better and from doing things differently.

This last point means changes in organization, management styles, the roles of workers and of first-line supervisors, and labor relations. All these changes involve taking risks.

Fred K. Foulkes, professor of management at Boston University's Graduate School of Management, conducted a study of twenty-six of America's largest nonunion industrialized companies to determine what they had in common with regard to attributes, attitudes, and policies. His studies suggest that such companies benefit most from the flexibility they have to improve productivity in both the short and the long run. The experiences of the companies studied suggest that companies willing to take creative approaches to employee relations can improve their productivity. The executives of the companies studied believed that they achieved higher productivity than they could have if they had been unionized.[37]

Professor Foulkes's nine major findings are shown in Exhibit 15.4. Together, they illustrate a pervasive management concern for employees that has allowed managers at every level to do the following:

- Deal directly with employees.
- Experience a lack of an adversary relationship with workers.
- Experiment more freely with employee relation plans.
- Foster a climate of cooperation between themselves and other employees.

After all, that is what is really needed to improve productivity.

EXHIBIT 15.4
Nine Common Attributes, Attitudes, and Policies of Twenty-Six Large Nonunion Industrialized Companies

1. **A Sense of Caring**
   Top management's commitment to employees is demonstrated through symbols, policies, and practices. A few examples include common fringe benefits, few visible status symbols, promotion.

2. **Carefully Considered Surroundings**
   Care is taken in choosing a plant location, determining plant size, and deciding what work will be done "in house." Plant workforces are kept small to encourage personal contact. Work that is traditionally union work is farmed out. Militant or aggressive union environments are avoided.

3. **High Profits, Fast Growth, and Family Ties**
   Many of the companies are high-technology growth firms, dominant in their markets and leaders in their industries. Thus they offer employment and advancement opportunities, job security, and profits worth sharing. A significant number are owned by one or a few families.

4. **Employment Security**
   The companies go for steady work, not seasonal or government contract work that can cause production fluctuations. They cut pay for all in hard times to keep everyone on. They reduce the workforce by attrition. Vacation time can be banked.

5. **Promotion from Within**
   This policy—along with training, education, career counseling, and job posting—attracts, keeps, and develops good people. Training for larger jobs on company time or at company expense breeds loyalty and enthusiasm, and promotes high levels of productivity.

continued

EXHIBIT 15.4
Continued

6. **Influential Personnel Departments**
   These companies consider personnel specialists to be extremely important and spend the money needed to keep them professional and up-to-date. They carry weight with and are often part of top management.

7. **Competitive Pay and Benefits**
   Compensation is at or above union scales. Pay and benefits are well publicized and explained. Heavy emphasis is placed on merit raises instead of routine, across-the-board increases. Profit-sharing and stock-purchase plans help employees identify with the company.

8. **Managements That Listen**
   Attitude surveys, regular meetings, random interviews, and access to higher levels of management by all employees characterize the nonunion company. An open-door policy is encouraged at all management levels, and appeals and grievance procedures exist. Some companies even hire professional arbitrators for difficult issues.

9. **Careful Grooming of Managers**
   Careful selection includes panel interviews and assessment centers. Supervisors are carefully trained and their rewards are linked to their abilities to apply their training. Competence means promotion.

Source: Reprinted by permission of the Harvard Business Review. From "How Top Nonunion Companies Manage Employees" by Fred K. Foulkes (September–October 1981). Copyright © 1981 by the President and Fellows of Harvard College; all rights reserved.

Research and Development

In 1987, a total of $127 billion was spent in the United States on research and development, up 7.4 percent over 1986. About 50 percent of the funds were spent by businesses, about 48 percent by government, and about 3 percent by nonprofit institutions such as foundations, colleges, and universities.[38]

Research and development is crucial to the future of a nation's economic growth, as it is to the future of an industry and an individual business. New properties of materials are uncovered, new facts are discovered, new uses for old materials and new products are invented. *Pure research* leads to knowledge for its own sake. *Applied research* tries to convert the results of pure research into new products and new technologies. Research and development has led the computer industry from vacuum tubes to microchips. It has resulted in such new products as video tapes, laser disks, computer graphics, and desktop printing.

At the 3M Company, research into adhesives discovered a substance that would stick to a surface just enough to allow things to stay together and to be separated without harming their surfaces. The product that came out of this pure research was the now famous Post-It Notes. Unless companies continue to invest in research and development, they will have no new products to bring to market and will find they are unable to compete with those who do invest in research and development.

According to a survey of 500 scientists and technology decision makers conducted by *Research & Development* magazine in 1988, the United States leads the world in R&D by a slim margin; 48 percent of those polled believed the United States is in the lead, while 46 percent gave the lead to Japan. The current race in R&D between these two countries is for products and applications for superconductors. Research has discovered unusual ceramics that carry electricity with no loss of energy when cooled to −283° Fahrenheit. The eventual payoffs could be railroad trains that operate on a cushion of air at 300 miles per hour and computers that operate at speeds one hundred times faster than today's models.[39]

Although U.S. R&D efforts tend to be efforts by individual companies and nonprofit institutions, Japanese efforts have been cooperative ventures. Today, 120 U.S. firms and 60 universities are working with superconductivity pretty much on their own. In Japan, the Ministry of International Trade and Industry (MITI) has, once again, organized research groups to work on superconductivity. Eighty-eight companies including Sony and Nissan have combined their talents and funds to conduct laboratory research, and the Japanese government has committed $61 million to aid in the use of the new technology in transportation, materials development, and transmission of electricity over power lines. In 1988, the U.S. government contributed $98 million to such R&D, about half was devoted to defense-related work.[40]

MITI-organized research groups have created breakthroughs in steel production, computers, and semiconductors. Japanese companies have shown a great skill at taking American inventions and discoveries and converting them into marketable products. Sony took the discovery of the transistor by AT&T Bell Laboratories and made the world's first transistor radio. Japanese companies have taken the U.S. discovery of semi-conductors and used it to drive most American companies out of the consumer electronics market. Americans win Nobel prizes for their research discoveries, but the Japanese take the technology and develop products with it.[41]

The Japanese are not the only foreigners challenging America with their R&D. Students from many nations now occupy about 20 percent of the desks at our colleges and universities that grant Ph.Ds. More than 40 percent of patents granted by the U.S. Patent Office are now awarded to foreigners.[42]

Training

With the rapidly changing world of business making increased demands on all kinds of businesses to respond to challenges from foreign competitors, managements have looked to ways to cut costs and improve methods and facilities. One answer has been to train new hires and existing personnel to take on the demands of new technologies and changing work environments. U.S. companies spend about $30 billion each year to train their people.[43] Training increases an employee's usefulness to himself or herself and to employers. The skills, knowledge, and attitudes gained through training increase people's and businesses' abilities to compete more effectively and efficiently. William Wiggenhorn, director of training at Motorola, Inc. in Illinois, reports that training efforts in the areas of process control and problem-solving methods have returned about thirty times the dollars invested through increased efficiencies.[44]

To effectively use modern technology and computer integrated manufacturing, workers and managers need to understand them. Training prepares them to work together in integrated teams that help design, utilize, and control new processes. Today's plants call for a high degree of participation in decision making at all levels by nearly all employees. Committees, brainstorming sessions, quality circles, and other kinds of interactive group approaches need trained leaders and participants if they are to be effective.

Retraining

In 1987, labor costs in the average manufacturing company represented about 15 percent of production costs. Experts seem to agree that cutting costs by cutting people has gone about as far as it can.[45] When a company terminates or lays people off for long periods, it often loses them forever. When production needs to pick up again, a new round of hiring must take place to acquire the people needed. Most companies have found that it is less expensive to keep people on and to retrain them for the jobs that it will need in the future. Hallmark, the greetings card company, maintains a continuous retraining program, giving their workers new and a broader range of skills. To keep people busy during slack periods, Hallmark cross-trains people, gives them additional training, switches production among its plants, and puts people to work on different tasks.[46]

Digital Equipment Corporation (DEC) recently found itself with too many managers, production workers, and underused technology. To replace its out-of-date plant, DEC designed a new assembly system that would use product groups, less direct labor, and flexible manufacturing techniques. It then identified the skills the new system would need and the skills its people had. A mismatch occurred—too many assemblers, supervisors, and technicians and not enough computer operators, programmers, process controllers, and other specialists. In 1984, DEC began extensive retraining, then reassignments, of personnel. Since the program began, 4,500 people have left the company, 3,800 have assumed new duties, and 2,200 to 2,500 people have been retrained each year.[47]

Better Management of Time and Paperwork

According to Robert Half International surveys, executives waste a good deal of their time on meetings and reading memos. The first study of one hundred large corporations found that top managers spend an average of 16.5 hours each week in meetings. Those executives surveyed said that 30 percent of their time in meetings was a complete waste of time.[48] The second survey of one hundred vice-presidents and personnel directors found that 39 percent of all office memos are unnecessary and wasteful. According to this study, the average executive spends eleven weeks a year reading memos. Seventy-six percent of those surveyed felt memos are too long, and 58 percent felt the copies go to too many people.[49]

Paperwork costs American businesses more than $100 billion each year according to Margaret Magnus, editor of *Personnel Journal*. In its recent study, the journal found that for every $1 spent to print forms, $20 to $80 are spent to process, copy, distribute, and destroy forms. According to the *Personnel Journal* study, some possible cures are reducing the number of memos and forms, using electronic bulletin boards and mail, and video conferencing.[50]

Flexible Manufacturing

With names like computer integrated manufacturing (CIM), computer aided design (CAD), computer assisted manufacturing (CAM), and flexible manufacturing, U.S. producers are moving toward the latest in efficient and cost-effective manufacturing facilities. A truly modern factory can produce several products on the same assembly line at high speeds and for short runs. Its many parts are linked by computers and can respond to changing needs more quickly than their aging counterparts. "The ultimate flexible factory could be programmed to roll out many different types of products, made on the same day to customer order, eliminating expensive inventories."[51] Flexible CIM equipment, when tailored to meet individual producers' needs, allows them to respond rapidly to changes in the marketplace and to adjust their outputs to meet customer requirements.

Three American factories are close to the ultimate in flexible manufacturing:

- GE's plant in Louisville, Kentucky, produces different styles of refrigerators on the same line.[52]

- Cypress Semiconductor Corporation in San Jose, California, produces seventy-one kinds of superfast computer chips, each meeting a specific customer need.[53]
- Ford Motor Company's Norfolk, Virginia, truck plant uses laser-assisted robots to align and drive rivets and to deburr automatic transmission housings.[54]

When a manufacturer makes the decision to move into CIM, it must commit to "coordinate design and manufacturing functions to minimize the number of parts and labor needed to make a product." When IBM made its decision to make its own computer printers, it decided to reduce its parts from 150 to 60. It succeeded in reducing the parts for its typewriters from 3,000 to 1,000 and increased the reliability of both products in doing so. IBM's manufacturing facilities demonstrate another hallmark of flexible manufacturing: just-in-time delivery of parts needed, minimizing storage and handling and investment in parts inventories.[55]

Ramchandran Jaikumar, associate professor at the Harvard Business School, observes that, "With a few exceptions, the flexible manufacturing systems installed in the United States show an astonishing lack of flexibility. In many cases they perform worse than the conventional technology they replace. The technology is not to blame; it is management that makes the difference."[56] Glen Allemendinger from Harbor Research notes that American companies are moving cautiously, for the most part, into CIM in an evolutionary way—creating islands of automation.[57]

Summary

- Productivity as it is most commonly measured compares outputs in units or dollars with inputs in human or machine-time hours.
- Productivity can be increased by (1) increasing outputs or (2) reducing inputs. Outputs are increased through aggressive marketing. Inputs can be reduced through the more efficient use of capital goods and labor, by working harder and smarter, and by using production time more effectively.
- Our federal government has hurt our nation's productivity through its huge deficits, by the tight-money policy that fights inflation but supports high interest rates, and by excessive regulations.
- Individuals have hurt their employer's productivity and our nation's by stealing time and by withholding efforts.
- Organized labor has hurt our nation's productivity by resisting management's efforts to improve work and output through restrictive work rules.

- Managements have hurt their companies' productivity by concentrating on near-term at the expense of long-term goals and plans (plans to modernize, update, and replace aging capital equipment) and by ignoring the inherent value of the individual.

- All groups in our economy have shown awareness of the problem our nation and their companies face with regard to productivity and are taking concrete, positive steps to improve the areas over which they have some control.

Glossary of Essential Terms

productivity   The measurement of the amount of input needed to generate any given amount of output. It is the basic measurement of the efficiency of businesses.

Review Questions

1. Can you define productivity? If not, consult the preceding glossary.
2. In what ways has our federal government adversely affected our nation's productivity? What is it doing about each? What more can it do?
3. In what ways are individual employees adversely affecting their employers' productivity? What can each of us do to improve our own productivity?
4. In what ways has organized labor hurt our nation's and companies' productivity? What is being done to change the situation?
5. In what ways has American management hurt their companies' productivity? What is management doing to correct the situations?

References

1. W. Bruce Chew, "No-Nonsense Guide to Measuring Productivity," *Harvard Business Review* (January–February 1988), p. 114.
2. Ibid., p. 115.
3. Ibid., p. 118.

4. Stanley B. Henrici, "How Deadly Is the Productivity Disease?" *Harvard Business Review* (November–December 1981), pp. 127–129.

5. "Businesses Plan to Boost Capital Spending by 2.8%," *Chicago Tribune*, June 10, 1987, sect. 3, p. 1.

6. Karen Loeb, "USA Snapshots: Office-Automation Sales," *USA Today*, June 8, 1987, p. 1E.

7. Carol Kleiman, "Hate Your Job? Welcome to the Club," *Chicago Tribune*, October 18, 1987, sect. 8, p. 1.

8. Mark Memmott, "We Work More and Like It Less," *USA Today*, May 19, 1987, p. 1B.

9. Scott Matulis, "Employee Theft: The Inside Job," *Entrepreneur* (March 1988), p. 82; Sam Meddis, "White-Collar Crime Doesn't Pay; Federal Convictions Up," *USA Today*, September 28, 1987, p. 12A.

10. "Fibbing on the Job," *Chicago Tribune*, November 16, 1987, sect. 4, p. 1.

11. "At Work: Clocking Time Stolen from Our Jobs," *USA Today*, November 26, 1986, p. 4B.

12. "Information Thieves Are Now Corporate Enemy No. 1," *Business Week*, May 5, 1986, p. 120–121.

13. Matulis, *Entrepreneur* (March 1988), p. 85.

14. "We All Pay Heavy Cost of Drug Use," *USA Today*, March 1, 1988, p. 11A.

15. Dan Sperling, "Say 'No' to Alcohol This Weekend," *USA Today*, April 5, 1988, p. 1D.

16. *USA Today*, March 1, 1988, p. 11A.

17. "Listening and Responding to Employees' Concerns" (an interview with A. W. Clausen), *Harvard Business Review* (January–February 1980), p. 104.

18. Ibid., p. 104.

19. "Big Talent Search Among Rank and File," *U.S. News & World Report*, November 30, 1981, p. 55.

20. "Special Report: The Turned-Off Worker," *Inc.* (April 1981), p. 76.

21. Ibid., p. 78.

22. Charles G. Burck, "What's in It for the Unions," *Fortune*, August 24, 1981, p. 88.

23. Michael J. Fiore, "Why Unions Don't Work Anymore," *Inc.* (March 1982), p. 17.

24. *Newsweek*, September 8, 1980, p. 62.

25. "How the Japanese Manage in the U.S.," *Fortune*, June 15, 1981, pp. 97–98, 102–103.

26. Robert H. Hayes, "Why Japanese Factories Work," *Harvard Business Review* (July–August 1981), pp. 64–65.

27. Ibid., p. 64.

28. *Fortune*, August 24, 1981, p. 89.

29. Ibid., p. 92.

30. James Warren, "Ford, Auto Union Reach an Accord," *Chicago Tribune*, September 18, 1987, sect. 1, p. 5.

31. "Major Cause of Business Problems: Poor Managers" (an interview with Professor Robert H. Hayes, Harvard Business School), *U.S. News & World Report*, December 8, 1980, pp. 69–70.

32. Ibid., p. 70.

33. "Lower Productivity? Blame Bosses: Report," *Chicago Tribune*, October 19, 1979, Sect. 4, p. 9.

34. C. Jackson Grayson, "What Every CEO Should Know About Productivity," *Chief Executive*, no. 15 (Spring 1981), p. 36.

35. Ibid., p. 37.

36. Ibid., p. 38.

37. Fred K. Foulkes, "How Top Nonunion Companies Manage Employees," *Harvard Business Review* (September–October 1981), p. 90.

38. Rod Little, "USA Snapshots: Who Funds R&D Programs," *USA Today*, June 23, 1987, p. 1B.

39. John Hillkirk, "Japanese Capitalize on USA Research," *USA Today*, March 2, 1988, pp. 1B–2B.

40. Ibid.

41. Ibid.

42. "America's R&D Performance: A Mixed Review," *Business Week*, April 20, 1987, p. 59.

43. Tom Peters, "Hardware Before Humans: Firms Spend on Plant, Scrimp on Training," *Chicago Tribune*, October 12, 1987, sect. 4, p. 9.

44. Ibid.

45. Bill Saporito, "Cutting Costs Without Cutting People," *Fortune*, May 25, 1987, p. 27.

46. Ibid.

47. Ibid., p. 30.

48. Jim Spencer, "Let's Do Lunch," *Chicago Tribune*, December 11, 1986, sect. 5, p. 2.

49. "Execs Waste Time Reading Memos," *USA Today*, April 8, 1987, p. 7B.

50. Lawrence M. Fisher, "Clipping Paper Costs," *The New York Times*, December 13, 1987, sect. 3, p. 1.

51. William R. Neikirk, "U.S. Manufacturers Wary on Automation," *Chicago Tribune*, July 5, 1987, sect. 1, pp. 1, 14.

52. Ibid. p. 14.

53. "Revving Up the American Factory," *The New York Times*, January 11, 1987, sect. 3, p. 1.

54. Richard A. Wright, "Ford Steering Robots to New Frontiers of Automation," *Chicago Tribune*, November 15, 1987, sect. 18, p. 22.

55. *The New York Times*, January 11, 1987, sect. 3, p. 8.

56. Neikirk, *Chicago Tribune*, July 5, 1987, sect. 1, p. 14.
57. Ibid.

Readings

Chew, W. Bruce. "No-Nonsense Guide to Measuring Productivity." *Harvard Business Review*, no. 1 (January–February 1988), pp. 110–118.

Grayson, C. Jackson, Jr. and Carla O'Dell. *American Business: A Two Minute Warning.* New York: Free Press, 1988.

Hartman, Curtis and Steven Pearlstein. "The Joy of Working." *Inc.* (November 1987), pp. 61–63, 66–67, 70–71.

Juran, J. M. *Juran on Planning for Quality.* New York: Free Press, 1988.

Kotkin, Joel. "The Great American Revival." *Inc.* (February 1988), pp. 52–54, 56, 60, 62–63.

Matulis, Scott. "Employee Theft: The Inside Job." *Entrepreneur* (March 1988), pp. 82–88.

Miller, William C. *The Creative Edge: Fostering Innovation Where You Work.* Reading, Mass.: Addison–Wesley, 1987.

Nasar, Sylvia. "Competitiveness: Getting It Back." *Fortune* (April 27, 1987) pp. 217–218, 220–221, 223–225.

Peters, Tom. *Thriving on Chaos: Handbook for a Management Revolution.* New York: Alfred A. Knopf, 1987.

Waterman, Robert H., Jr. *The Renewal Factor.* New York: Bantam Books, 1987.

C
A
S
E
S

15.1   Boosting Production

Dell Webster surveyed the ocean from his suite while his wife mixed the drinks. The last five days had been filled with great experiences. Both he and his wife were finishing up their all-expenses-paid vacation—his reward for being the top salesperson in his region. With two more days to go and new islands to visit, Dell was wondering if he would be able to get back into the swing of things at his office. The company had really done things right, Dell thought, as he pushed the buttons for room service. "What will it be tonight, honey?" he asked his wife.

Dell's company had sent the top salespeople from its ten regions to the Virgin Islands for one week of fun and sun. Last year, it sent them to Hawaii. Next year, Samuelson, the sales vice-president, was planning to send them to London. "Nothing is too good for my people," said Samuelson. "After all, without you we would have no production. Money spent on rewarding my sales staff is money spent to boost production." With these words, he closed the last company-wide sales meeting at the company's headquarters in Denver.

The top salesperson in the entire company, Maria Davis, got the trip to the islands and the keys to a new car. This year alone, the company estimated that it would spend $26,000 to pay for the trips, another $12,000 to pay for the car, and about $45,000 to pay all the salespeople their bonuses. The vice-president of finance was protesting to Samuelson that things were getting too expensive. Samuelson replied that every dollar spent to reward salespeople would generate two extra dollars in sales over the next year. He had the figures to prove it. Two years ago, the company spent $58,000 to reward salespeople, and sales the next year increased by $131,000. Last year, sales rewards totaled $67,500, and sales this year hit a record high, increasing by $151,000.

For Discussion

1. In what ways do the dollars spent to reward salespeople boost production and productivity?

2. What do you think of Samuelson's claim that dollars spent to reward salespeople will return to the company as sales dollars?

3. If Samuelson is correct, should the company spend even more money to reward its salespeople? Why or why not?

15.2 Charlie's Puzzle

Charlie Dietrick was puzzled. As he sipped his usual cup of morning coffee, he thought back over the events of the plantwide meeting he attended yesterday. All the office and factory managers had been assembled for a briefing on what his company had planned to launch as an all-out war to boost productivity. The CEO, Al Henderson, had made it clear that within thirty days he expected plans to increase productivity on his desk. All Charlie had to do was to put a few good ideas down on paper and give them to his boss for consolidation with the suggestions from others in his group. But without additional funds, Charlie thought that his ideas could not be implemented. Henderson had made it clear that no new funding would be available. Any ideas would have to be implemented within existing, budgeted funds.

"Here we go again," thought Charlie. "Another all-out war. Seems that we just had one a few months back to improve safety in the plant. Well I guess my salvation rests in waiting them out. This will pass in time like all the others. But I need some ideas to submit, or the boss will get nuts."

Charlie picked up his phone and called his fellow manager in purchasing. "Sally, it's Charlie. Have you got a few minutes? You do? Great. I'll see you in your office in five minutes."

On his way to Sally's office, Charlies passed two of his subordinates at the pay phone near the plant entrance. "How come you guys aren't on the loading dock?" asked Charlie.

"We had kind of an emergency out there. Sam didn't show up today, so we're calling Jackson to get him to come in."

"Why didn't you guys call me? Jackson is out sick. Leave him be. And why does it take two of you to call him, anyway? Now there are three of you absent from the dock."

"Sorry boss. Phil here didn't have Jackson's number and asked me to call. He has a few things he wants to discuss with Jackson, so we thought we'd kill two birds with one call."

Charlie got his people on their way and walked a few doors farther on. "That's the last time I cover for Jackson," Charlie thought. "He's probably been drinking again. He's getting worse every month." Just then Charlie noticed his forklift truck operator walking toward him. After a few minutes discussion, the problem became clear. The night shift apparently had failed to perform the required maintenance last night, and now the truck had a burned motor bearing. "Call this number, Edith, and see if they can get a repair going today. That truck is so old it will probably be down tomorrow with some other darn problem."

When Charlie finally reached Sally's office he had a throbbing headache. "Hi, Sally. Before we get started talking about increasing our department's productivity, can I have an aspirin?"

For Discussion

1. What happened during Charlie's day to give him a few ideas about improving productivity? Provide examples from the case problem.

2. What would lead you to believe that the CEO's "war" to increase productivity might not succeed?

Management and Society

OUTLINE

ESSENTIAL TERMS

ethics   social audit

morals   social responsibility

LEARNING OBJECTIVES

After reading and discussing this chapter, you should be able to do the following:

1. Define this chapter's essential terms.

2. Discuss the meaning of responsibility as it applies to managers in this chapter.

3. List and describe the three phases in the evolution of managers' social responsibilities.

4. State two tests to determine if an intended action will be ethical or unethical.

5. List four ways in which a business and its managers can build into their organization a true sense of social responsibility.

The Three Cs of Business Ethics

According to authors Robert C. Solomon and Kristine R. Hanson, "business ethics is nothing less than the full awareness of what one is doing, its consequences and complications." Their three Cs of business ethics are *compliance, contributions,* and *consequences.*[1]

Compliance involves living and behaving according to the law, corporate codes of ethics, company rules, principles of morality, community expectations, and such general concepts as equity. Managers must go further than the simple obedience to what the law demands. Shortcuts in quality that lead to customer dissatisfaction with a product may be "legal," but they are hardly encouragement for repeat business. Treating employees with respect and fairness is not required by law, but it is essential for building trust and a productive workforce.

Contributions include giving customers value for their patronage, giving employment, helping individuals and society to meet their needs, and making improvements to the quality of life for employees and community members alike. In 1986, American corporations gave $4.5 billion to charities such as the United Way, the arts, and education.[2] But their people gave far more in service to community organizations such as neighborhood schools, scouting programs, community cleanup programs, and volunteer services.

Consequences of business actions can be either positive or negative for the company, society, and other individuals and groups. Consequences may be intended or unintended, anticipated or unanticipated. In 1988, Texaco agreed to pay $1.25 billion in fines to the U.S. Energy Department to settle claims, going back to 1973, that the company had illegally overcharged customers for a variety of oil products.[3] The consequences: lost revenues, bad public relations, and consumers left without money they were entitled to keep.

To Whom Are Managers Responsible?

Never before have so many conflicting demands been made on those who hold the reins of power. Managers in the public and the private sector face pressures from within their working environments and outside them. Individuals and groups demand more for themselves and their constituencies even while refusing to give more in the way of taxes and commitment. The rapid pace of change in our society and the explosion in technology and information make it imperative that we all continue to grow, to read, to listen, to study—just to stay abreast of what is new in our environments.

The pressure on business managers is increasing because of the need many organizations feel to accommodate the new breed of worker. Efforts at increasing productivity must be successful, not just because of the pressure from competitors but also because of the pressures from the economic environment (such as inflation, the costs of credit, and the push from government and special-interest groups to modify traditional methods of operations). It is with this latter area (increasing pressures rather than competition) that this chapter is most concerned.

At its essence, a business is a complex system of interacting groups. The primary members of this system are the capital owners, employees, and the consumers of the business's output. The owners risk capital and expect fair profits. Employees invest their energy, efforts, and imaginations and expect appropriate monetary and psychological income. Consumers supply the income from which all the system's bills are paid and expect fair value for the dollars they spend.[4] "Together, and *only* together, can they produce the output they subsequently share. What each member receives is constrained by what other members require, and no member can in the long run enjoy a disproportionate share."[5]

The basic problem or dilemma faced by managers is the same today as it has been for several decades: to balance the conflicting demands as they attempt to allocate and manage their organization's use of scarce resources. But the past decade has made this balancing act far more difficult and necessary than it ever has been. Forces outside the individual enterprise have never before been so well organized and forceful in presenting their demands and expectations. And external variables (those beyond the direct control of managers) have never changed so rapidly or had so much of a direct impact on day-to-day management decisions. (See Figure 16.1.)

Finally, we must remember that individual citizens, through their elected representatives, create the public policy (the laws and rules) that "govern the relationships among the members of the system and between the business system and the rest of society."[6] Since businesses operate in a society, society has the right to regulate them and to expect that they will provide essential consumer goods and services in a safe and efficient manner.

How Management Is Linked to Responsibility

Individuals and responsibility are linked in three ways.[7]

1. When we speak of someone being responsible, we often mean that he or she should be made to answer for actions or failure to act (accountability). That person should take the blame or the credit.

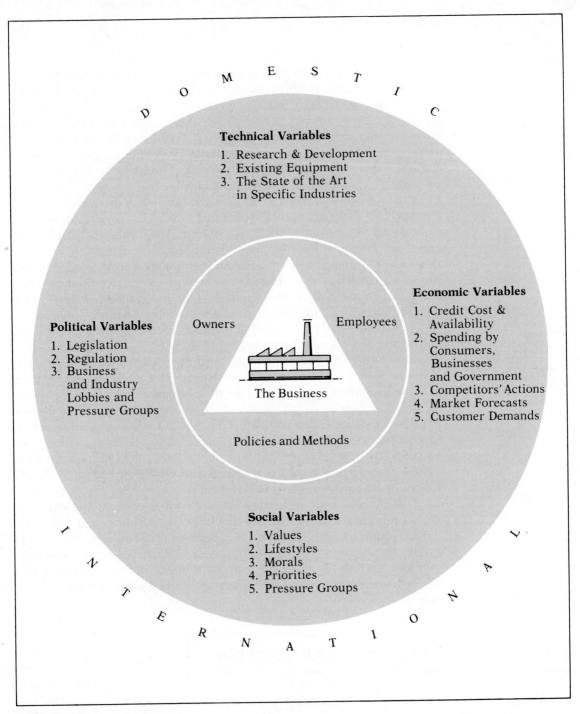

FIGURE 16.1
Business as a subsystem in society and the variables that affect its abilities to make decisions

2. People are responsible for playing roles and following rules. Lawyers are responsible for defending their clients; doctors are responsible for treating their patients; managers are responsible for executing their jobs in line with their organization's rules and policies.

3. People are responsible if they are trustworthy and reliable. Others respect and trust their abilities to make judgments and informed decisions.

Other chapters have addressed points 1 and 2 above as they relate to managers. This chapter is concerned with point 3. After all is said and done, managers are in fact stewards who have in their custody the faith and trust of many other individuals and groups. They are entrusted with the tasks of looking out for others' interests while looking out for their own. Responsible people act with the interests of other persons in mind.

The Evolution of Managers' Responsibilities

Management has passed through three phases since the founding of American businesses. It has moved from the classical or enlightened self-interest phase, through the social awareness phase, into the social responsibility phase of the 1980s. Each of these phases exists to some extent in American businesses, but the movement is strongly in the direction of the third phase in most large organizations.

The Classical Phase

Since Adam Smith's monumental book, *An Inquiry into the Nature and Causes of the Wealth of Nations* (1776), entrepreneurs (owner-managers) have recognized the basic responsibilities they have to maximize profits by producing a product or service with maximum efficiency. By serving themselves, they provide others with needed goods or services. Those who are successful are rewarded in the marketplace with patronage and profits. As long as they operate within the law, they are free to operate as their judgment dictates. Professional managers are responsible to the owners and have to consider their interests as primary. People in a market are free to express their moral values through free choice (or rejection). Their choices create a moral climate in enterprises that serve the market. The only social responsibilities a manager has are to make profits and obey the law.[8]

The classical view was restated recently by Nobel prize-winning professor of economics, Milton Friedman, as follows:[9]

1. In an economic system based on private property, the managers are employed by owners to make as much money as possible while conforming to the law and to ethical custom.

2. Managers are exclusive agents for their employers and owe primary responsibility to them.

3. The corporate executive is an agent for stockholders and should not make decisions about social responsibilities and social investments because those represent tax decisions. Such matters are government functions.

Such arguments tend to ignore several facts:

1. The ownership and management of large corporations are quite separate.

2. Managers have a great deal of flexibility to act in a wide variety of situations without the owners' direct orders or involvement.

3. Managers are people with morals and ethical codes of behavior who exercise individual judgments regularly.

Not exercising some measure of social responsibility will invite additional government efforts to force social responsibilities onto a business. Such governmental intervention has been the state of affairs in America since the 1930s.

The Social Awareness Phase

This phase is often called the "hand of government" phase or the "activist" phase. It is characterized by the conviction that managers hold the reins of enormous economic and political power that can be used to promote social goals and cure social ills: It is the responsibility of those in government to regulate the use of these powers to prevent abuses and to promote good.[10]

Businesses are permitted to exist by government because they provide employment, they yield tax revenues, they produce needed goods and services, and they serve to allocate resources to essential tasks. The government sets desired goals and the means to achieve them, which often call for the regulation of commerce and of managerial decision making. Managers must pursue rational economic goals and obey the regulations and laws of governments. They sense and apply these to their day-to-day operations.

The *social awareness* phase has been marked by following the letter of the law and not its true intent or spirit. Businesses did only what was mandated and with no enthusiasm. Quotas for minorities were set, and once reached, minorities were ignored. Court battles were waged to define the law and the limits of the government's authority. Tokenism was an early hallmark of this phase.

This phase began in the New Deal era of the 1930s and has continued to the present with a proliferation of government agencies and commissions to oversee the exercise of commerce and to set and determine how to reach a variety of goals designed to improve society and deal with economic problems. The social awareness phase places managers in a passive mode—accepting and reacting to changes imposed by governments at several levels. (See Figure 16.2.)

The Social Responsibility Phase

Although there is no common, widespread agreement on the definition of the term **social responsibility**, we use it to mean "the moral and ethical content of managerial and corporate decisions, that is, the values used in

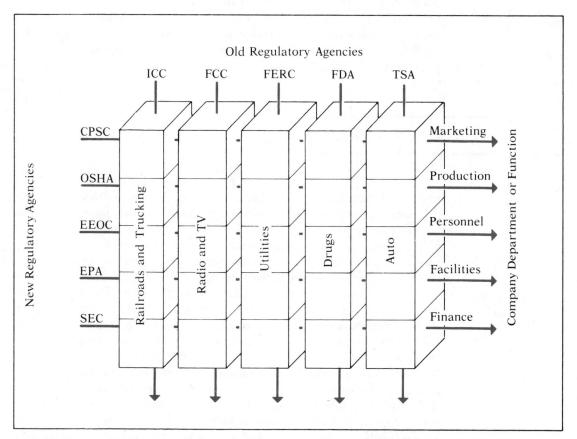

FIGURE 16.2
Focus of the old and the new federal regulatory agencies on American business. The older agencies (pre-1960) regulated specific industries, whereas the new ones regulate nearly every industry.
Source: Adapted from Grover Starling, *The Changing Environment of Business*, Third Edition (Boston: MA: PWS-KENT, 1988), p. 45.
©1988 by PWS-KENT Publishing Co. Reprinted by permission of PWS-KENT Publishing Company, a division of Wadsworth, Inc.

business decisions over and above the pragmatic requirements imposed by legal principle and market economy."[11] An organization has social responsibility if it recognizes, through its managers, that it has an obligation to respond to society's moral and ethical values and acts to ensure that its actions help meet the needs of society.

The social responsibility phase is very strong in our economy at present. It represents a socioeconomic managerial philosophy and asserts that managers have responsibilities to react positively to the community's demands for social programs for improved quality of life. They must attempt to evaluate the changes in the expressions of public and national goals and to modify their goals and programs to meet the demands of the society they serve.[12]

This phase requires managers to anticipate possible changes and to adopt an active mode in forecasting and planning to meet the new demands that society may require. After a look at the moral and ethical demands on managers, we return to the concept of social responsibility and how the modern manager and organization have incorporated it into their regular operations.

Managers, Morals, and Ethics

You will recall that our definition of corporate or business social responsibility included the "moral and ethical content of managerial and corporate decisions." **Morals** are concepts of right and wrong that form a system of principles on which decisions can be based. The Ten Commandments are a set of moral principles that govern the conduct of many people in their relationships with others. A person has a "moral point of view" if he or she (1) is careful (not impulsive) in mapping out alternatives and their consequences and clear about goals and purposes and (2) considers the effects of actions, actual or intended, on others.[13] This moral viewpoint is characterized by respect for the lives of others and involves taking their needs and interests into account while making decisions and before taking actions.

Ethics is concerned with standards of honesty and honorable human conduct. It focuses on how people's plans and intentions will affect others and on the circumstances surrounding those plans and intentions. A person's or group's ethics are influenced by the morality of individuals. "Religious beliefs and training, educational background, political and economic philosophy, socialization through family and peer group influences, and work experience all come together to produce a personal moral code of ethical values with associated attitudes."[14]

Thinking Ethically

Authors Robert C. Solomon and Kristine Hanson offer the following rules to individuals who want to think about the ethical implications to their intended actions:[15]

1. Consider other people's well-being, including the well-being of nonparticipants.
2. Think as a member of the business community and not as an isolated individual.
3. Obey, but do not depend solely on, the law.
4. Think of yourself—and your company—as part of society.
5. Obey moral rules.
6. Think objectively.
7. Ask the question "What sort of person would do such a thing?"
8. Respect the customs of others, but not at the expense of your own ethics.

Thinking about intended actions while using these eight rules will help you think about the contribution and the consequences that will flow from the acts. The eight rules remind us that we are all part of something larger than ourselves. Our actions have impacts on others, and therefore, they and those impacts must be considered before we act.

Many of the decisions managers face each day do not have moral or ethical consequences; in general, these are the decisions that will not affect others. But every time a decision will have an effect on others, ethics comes into the decision-making process. Consider the following situations:

1. The company allows twenty-minute coffee breaks. All the members of Department A take thirty or more minutes. As the supervisor of Department A, what should you do?
2. Mary knows that the head buyer for the company is receiving gifts from vendors, a practice specifically prohibited by company policy. What should she do?
3. A major appliance manufacturer is considering closing a small plant in your state. It is profitable, but the company could make more profits if it transferred assembly operations to Mexico. Unfortunately, 3,000 jobs are at stake, along with the economy of a small town. What should its managers decide?

These kinds of decisions are not easy to make; without a moral base to managers' thinking, they would be purely economic decisions with a focus on profits. All of us need self-respect, which comes by following our consciences and acting in moral and ethical ways. An organization that lacks a moral point of view in making its major decisions can compromise the ethics and morals of its employees or force them to compromise their consciences' dictates. There may come a time during your employment, if it hasn't come already, that you will be asked or ordered to compromise your morals and act in an unethical manner. How will you react? What will you do?

The value of ethics is that they help individuals and groups determine which actions are acceptable—the most beneficial or the least harmful—before undertaking them. Each of us has an ethical code of conduct that influences us and acts as a frame of reference when considering alternatives. Our morals give us a conscience and shape our perceptions of what is permissible and what is not. Our consciences give us a sense of guilt when we act contrary to our moral and ethical senses.

Ethics Programs and Codes

In 1987, the Business Roundtable, an advisory and research group comprising the chief executives of 200 major corporations, sponsored a study of the ethics programs at ten companies. According to the director of the study, Andrew D. Sigler of Champion International Corporation, "you need a culture and peer pressure that spells out what is acceptable and isn't and why. [A program] involves training, education, and followup."[16] To make a program effective, the report by the Roundtable recommends the following:[17]

- Greater commitment of top management to ethics programs.
- Written codes of ethics that clearly communicate management's expectations.
- Programs to implement the company's guidelines.
- Strict enforcement of the codes.
- Surveys to monitor compliance.

The record of the past few years tells us that even those companies that have long emphasized the need for ethical behavior among their managers can make mistakes in judgment. Boeing has had a widespread emphasis on ethics since 1964, but in 1984, the company illegally used inside information to gain a government contract. Chevron U.S.A. Inc. agreed to pay $1.5 million as a civil penalty to settle a 1986 violation of the Clean Water Act in 1988.[18] That same year, two Beech-Nut Nutrition Corporation executives were found guilty of intentionally distributing phony apple juice intended for babies. The product was labeled as pure apple juice but was largely sugar, corn syrup, and other ingredients.[19]

About 75 percent of our nation's 1,200 largest corporations had established ethics codes in 1986. Ethicists and corporate managers agree that a code is the first step to guaranteeing ethical conduct. But a study by Washington State University reports that ethics codes do not deter corporate crime. This study of 485 U.S. manufacturers was scheduled for release in 1987. Without top-level management commitment and enforcement of a code, it is just not enough. "Ethical behavior means doing the right thing for a wide range of constituencies. No business can succeed over time unless it does the right things for the constituencies it serves," according to Ed Hood, vice-chairman and executive officer of General Electric. The constituencies he is referring to are the owners, customers, employees, suppliers, and the company's community.[20]

Various groups, such as lawyers and doctors, have established and published codes of ethical behavior that govern their conduct with clients, patients, or customers. Many businesses have established ethical codes for managers, purchasing agents, salespeople, and others who deal with the public. These codes attempt to regulate human conduct of business affairs. They can, if enforced, prevent legal and public relations problems.

Motivations for Managers' Unethical Conduct

Saul W. Gellerman, author and dean of the University of Dallas Graduate School of Management, believes that four basic rationalizations lie beneath unethical behavior by managers. Exhibit 16.1 lists the four rationalizations.

EXHIBIT 16.1
Four Commonly Held Rationalizations That Can Lead
to Misconduct by Managers

- A belief that the activity is within reasonable ethical and legal limits—that is, that it is not "really" illegal or immoral.
- A belief that the activity is in the individual's or the corporation's best interests—that the individual would somehow be expected to undertake the activity.
- A belief that the activity is "safe" because it will never be found out or publicized; the classic crime-and-punishment issue of discovery.
- A belief that because the activity helps the company the company will condone it and even protect the person who engages in it.

Source: Reprinted by permission of the Harvard Business Review. Excerpt from "Why 'Good' Managers Make Bad Ethical Choices" by Saul W. Gellerman (July–August 1986). Copyright © 1986 by the President and Fellows of Harvard College; all rights reserved.

Regarding the first rationalization, how can a manager know how far is too far? When dealing with gray areas, how is a manager to know if intended actions are on the side of right or not? Professor Gellerman offers the following suggestions:[21]

- When in doubt, don't.
- Don't try to find out "how far is too far."
- Superiors who push you to do things better, faster, cheaper will turn on you when you cross the line between right and wrong.
- Remember that managers "are paid to know which risks are worth taking."

In dealing with the second rationalization, Professor Gellerman calls for an outside, independent auditing agency that would report to outside directors on how management's successes have been achieved. Insiders tend to interpret intended or actual actions taken by management in a more favorable light than outsiders, as government investigators might.[22] In 1987, Chrysler Corporation admitted to disconnecting odometers on cars driven by Chrysler executives for up to 400 miles and then reconnecting them and selling those cars as new. Chairman Lee Iacocca acknowledged that he had known about the practice for nine months but had been assured by company lawyers that it was not a "problem."[23]

Regarding the third rationalization, Professor Gellerman suggests increasing the frequency of audits and spot checks as a deterrent, "especially when combined with three other simple techniques: scheduling audits irregularly, making at least half of them unannounced, and setting up some checkups soon after others."[24] A problem at Hertz Corporation was uncovered by an internal audit that was triggered by a postal inspector. It seems that Hertz's Boston office was "creating damage estimate reports from nonexistent body shops." Customers were charged $13 million more than they should have been for repairs to cars they damaged from 1978 to 1985. Customers were billed a retail rate, but Hertz actually paid much less to fix the cars.[25]

The fourth rationalization can be countered by a top management that exerts a strong moral influence and does not condone loyalty against the law or against common morality or against society itself. "To put it bluntly, superiors must make it clear that employees who harm other people allegedly for the company's benefit will be fired."[26] In the Hertz case cited above, nineteen managers lost their jobs because of the overcharging. When Motorola Inc. discovered that fifty-nine employees were falsifying costs on defense contract work, twenty managers were fired or had their salaries frozen or promotions denied. The remaining thirty-nine were warned that failing to follow company rules would lead to their dismissal.[27]

Business Ethics Today: A Report Card

The three surveys below represent the views of business executives and others, in the United States and worldwide, on the condition of business ethics. The first survey cites the ethical issues considered most important by managers around the world. The second points up the need for ethical training and where managers think it should take place. The third is an overview of ethics in the United States.

According to the 1987 International Survey of Corporate Ethics conducted by the Conference Board, these are the top five ethical issues facing business:[28]

Employee conflicts of interest	91%
Inappropriate gifts received by employees from outsiders	91%
Sexual harassment of employees	91%
Unauthorized payments received	85%
Affirmative action	85%

The survey consulted the CEOs and senior managers in 300 companies worldwide.

A 1987 survey of 722 executives in America's 1,000 largest corporations gives us the following opinions:

Most people are at least occasionally unethical in their business dealings	84%
Companies should provide all employees with some ethics training	84%
Ethics should be taught in every business course	87%

Fifty-six percent of executives surveyed believed people have become less ethical in the past twenty years, while 8 percent felt there has been an improvement. The survey was conducted by the executive search firm of McFeely Wackerle Jett.[29]

A 1987 survey of 8,180 American professionals, including business executives, business school deans, accountants, attorneys, bankers, clergy, teachers, and lawmakers, tells us that America has the highest standard of business ethics. The survey by Touche Ross, one of America's largest accounting firms, asked individuals to rank nations by their standards of ethics. The United States was first, England second, Canada third, Switzerland fourth, and West Germany fifth. Other results were as follows:[30]

U.S. business is highly ethical	15%
Ethics in the U.S. have improved over the last 100 years	62%
Ethics have improved over the last 20 years	37%
Ethics have declined over the last 20 years	33%
U.S. business is reasonably ethical	81%
High ethical standards strengthen a company's competitive position	63%

Ethics Tests

Different people and groups have different criteria that they apply to determine if an intended action, or inaction, is the right course to follow. The Golden Rule states that we should treat others as we ourselves wish to be treated. It works well if the people who apply it have all of their faculties and are aware of the social conventions. The concept of "the greatest good for the greatest number" is another test applied to situations in order to determine what the right behavior should be. It works well if the consequences and circumstances are fully understood and foreseen. Regardless of what test is applied, human judgment is involved. Few of us are able to know with certainty all the circumstances and consequences surrounding us and our actions at any given time.

Doing what is legal or allowed by law will not necessarily be the ethical route to take. Refraining from illegal conduct may not ensure ethical conduct either. Laws permit and forbid many human patterns of behavior that you and I would not appreciate or condone. The purpose of the law is not to dictate morals or ethics. It is simply to dictate the will of a society's majority. And as we all know, majority opinions have a way of becoming minority viewpoints with different circumstances and the passage of time. Our nation's experiment with Prohibition (1920–1933) is but one example. It helped create organized crime, made most adults lawbreakers, and engendered an abiding disrespect for the law and law enforcement that lasted until Prohibition was repealed.

Managers and the Law

Criminal activities in business include many kinds of illegal activities, from individuals who steal time and money from their employers to managers who defraud other businesses and the public through decisions to commit

their companies to illegal paths or practices. Cases involving large sums of money and large corporations hit the headlines fairly regularly. But crimes committed by smaller businesses rarely do. Once convictions are obtained, penalties paid, and violators fired, the public soon forgets the specifics of the violations but remembers that businesses are quite capable of illegal practices.

Problems Facing Business

According to research done by the National Business Crime Information Network, theft of merchandise was the most common business problem in 1987, as it was in 1986. The top five problems in the order of their importance for 1987 were:[31]

- Theft of goods.
- Employee mistreatment.
- Procedure or policy violations.

- Vehicle safety violations.
- Theft of cash.

The accounting firm of Ernst & Whinney surveyed 240 companies in 1987 and found that 51 percent had experienced some form of computer fraud. The survey estimates indicate that this problem costs U.S. businesses between $3 billion and $5 billion each year. The FBI estimates that the average loss on a company hit by computer crime is $600,000, or about twenty-five times higher than the loss experienced from other, more common crimes.[32]

Most crimes committed against a business are motivated by a desire for personal gain. Most crimes committed by business executives against outsiders are motivated by a desire to keep their jobs. As Stanley Sporkin, the Security and Exchange Commission's enforcement chief puts it, "In many instances where people are not lining their own pockets, you can only explain corporate crime in terms of 'produce or perish.' "[33]

Illegal activities along with unethical ones often begin because a chief executive officer is unable or unwilling to police the entire organization. Executives who do not look too closely at the activities of subordinates convey the message that they do not want to know. "As long as I don't know what you are doing, do it but don't tell me about it." If a chief executive really wants to police the organization, she or he can establish policies, committees, and enforcement procedures—as well as publicize the fact that the company is serious about legal behavior. Most important are the examples and tone at the top. They must indicate a serious commitment to legal and ethical behavior.

Individuals and Ethics

A 1987 *USA Weekend* poll asked 614 randomly selected adults from across the United States how they felt about lying. Here are some of the poll's findings:[34]

- 61 percent think it is OK to lie, at least sometimes.
- 40 percent have lied to employers to skip work.
- 15 percent have lied on their job applications.
- 57 percent say that they have been in a position where the only choice they had was to lie.

Internal Revenue Service commissioner, Lawrence Gibbs, reports that American taxpayers and businesses voluntarily paid only 83 percent of the income taxes they owed in 1987. The IRS reports that more than half the $85 billion in taxes that was owed but not paid was owed by individuals who file tax returns but fail to report income from extra jobs, small businesses, or other nonwage but legal sources.[35]

Finally, consider the three C's of ethics and the following event. The rear door on an armored truck flew open on a busy freeway near downtown Columbus, Ohio. Money bags and cash were scattered along the highway for about a mile before the driver realized what was happening. The cash drew crowds of people, and about $1 million disappeared from the pavement, along with the people who scooped it up. Two months afterward, only a small fraction of the money had been turned in by citizens of Columbus.[36]

Corporate Responsibility for Criminal Acts

In 1909, the U.S. Supreme Court held that corporations "could be held liable, as individuals can be, for crimes involving intent." In recent years, this corporate liability has meant large fines and criminal convictions for corporate managers, board members, and owners. In 1985, three managers from Film Recovery Systems Inc., an Illinois company, were convicted of murder and given twenty-five-year sentences for knowingly creating work conditions resulting in a strong possibility of death to their workers. According to figures from the U.S. Bureau of Labor Statistics, job-related injuries and fatalities have risen about 12 and 14 percent, respectively, from 1983 to 1987. Almost half the fifty states now have some form of corporate criminal-liability law, and most are using them more vigorously—prosecuting business owners for criminal negligence.[37]

Managing for Social Responsibility

Professors Goodpaster (ethics) and Matthews (corporate policy) at the Harvard Business School believe individuals and organizations can act from a moral point of view. Groups are made up of individuals, and groups act as a unit or a person in many instances. Groups have guidelines and rules that determine their authority and how they are to use it. Groups generate decisions (output) that is the result of the interactions of their members. Groups can be moral, just as they can be efficient, productive, or competent.[38]

Many organizations have built in a variety of safeguards to promote a sense of moral and social responsibility. They have codes of conduct for various groups, policies to govern managerial behavior and uniformity of approaches to problems, internal audits to determine progress and adherence to rules and procedures, and research programs to build better products and a safer, more productive working environment. In 1970, for example, General Electric created a public policy committee, staffed by members of its board of directors, to create social programs and keep track of their progress and achievements.[39] The larger the enterprise, the more likely it is to have a separate department to plan for and oversee organizational efforts to be socially responsible and to see to it that environmental and safety regulations are followed.[40]

About three-quarters of our nation's largest corporations have adopted written codes of ethics. But if these are to be truly meaningful and actually affect the conduct of business employees, training and enforcement efforts are needed. Allied Corporation of New Jersey holds three-day ethics seminars five times a year at which managers, clergy, and philosophers use case studies to apply ethical standards. Polaroid Corporation holds regular conferences that deal with moral questions raised by new technologies and the trend toward self-regulation in industries.[41] Michael Rion, a former corporate responsibility director and director of Hartford Seminary in Connecticut, believes a company wishing to act in good conscience needs a written code of ethics, widespread staff support, a continuing management development program with an emphasis on ethical behavior, and a policy of consistent management backing so that honest employees know their leaders do not appreciate coverups.[42]

The organization that accepts the view that it has obligations to persons other than its insiders, and makes managerial decisions on every level from a moral point of view, is an organization that is socially responsible. Its leadership at the top demonstrates this moral position in either an active or a passive mode of operations: That is, it will either react and adapt to changes forced on it, or it will adapt and take the lead in meeting social challenges. In either event, three things will occur:

1. It will fix the area of the social responsibility.
2. It will develop policies and procedures (see Exhibit 16.2) for following dictates and implementing socially mandated changes.
3. It will audit the results of its efforts.

When an organization is truly committed to meeting its social responsibilities, it reflects that commitment in its routine approaches to management decision making and its ongoing planning operations.

One of the first organizations to make an attempt to incorporate social and political forecasting into its planning efforts was General Electric. In 1967, it established a Business Environmental Studies unit in its corporate-level personnel and industrial relations component. The BES was a broad survey of the prospective business environment that was thought likely to exist in the 1970s. The planning and forecasting unit considered the interaction of several variables—such as the rising level of education, changing

EXHIBIT 16.2
A Recommended Policy to Govern Business Social Actions

In developing policies governing social actions, companies are reexamining their profit concepts. The following profit objective statement is suggested for companies reevaluating their responsibilities:

> It is the policy of the company to take action in the name of social responsibilities but not at the expense of the rising profit level required to maintain the economic strength and dynamism desired by top management. Actions taken in the name of social responsibility should enhance the economic strength of the company and/or the business community. The overall mission of the company is two pronged: to set forth and achieve corporate objectives both internally and externally, that meet specified social challenges in areas ranging from product quality to quality of life; and to increase the company's earnings per share at a rate that meets shareowner/ profit expectations *and* these new social requirements.

A number of companies have adopted similar profit policy statements.

Source: George A. Steiner, "Institutionalizing Corporate Social Decisions," *Business Horizons*, December 1975.

attitudes toward work, and increasing pluralism and individualism. Its women's rights study of 1970 enabled GE to publish its own affirmative action guidelines on equal opportunity for women a year before the federal guidelines were issued.[43]

The Social Audit

Social responsibility, to be truly effective and pervasive in an organization, needs the backing of all managers. It needs to be part of daily operations, not subordinate to them. The manager needs to know what is being done in terms of social responsibility, what can be expected in the future, and what the results have been for past actions and plans.

The **social audit** is a report (feedback) on the social performance of a business. No uniform or widely accepted standards for making the audit or for reporting its findings exist at present, but many businesses do report on their performances.[44] General Motors uses a narrative summary in its corporate annual report. A major Chicago bank uses its social audit for internal purposes and to prepare public relations press releases. A complete social audit would attempt to report in dollar amounts the balance sheet items and the income and expenses connected with social responsibility actions and programs. An example of this would be a company that invested in pollution control measures and equipment and subsequently experienced reduced expenses or actual income from that investment. Dow Corning recovers hydrogen and chlorine previously lost (toxically) to the atmosphere and experiences a 33 percent return each year on its pollution control investment.[45]

Whatever methods are used, a social audit is becoming standard procedure for many of our nation's largest businesses. It usually includes a summary of corporate activities under these headings: charitable contributions, support of local community groups and activities, minority employment, employment of the handicapped, employment of women, pollution control, health and safety measures, support for minority enterprises, and efforts to improve the quality of work life for employees. Progress may be stated in terms of goals set and met as well as in monetary terms. Those who benefit are clearly labeled, and the extent to which they benefit is quantified when possible. The results of the social audit should be shared with all employees so that awareness of the commitment to and success of programs can be reinforced. People responsible for successes should be identified and rewarded.

Ethical Issues for the 1990s

Employers, employees, and society are often in conflict when it comes to dealing with five key issues facing them today in the workplace. Exhibit 16.3 highlights these five basic issues. What is being done and what should be done to balance employees' rights to privacy and the employers' rights to manage their companies?

1. *Drug-testing.* "Drug use costs American industry nearly $50 billion a year in absenteeism and turnover."[46] Employee theft, much of it drug-related, costs employers about $10 billion each year. "Failing to ensure a safe and drug-free workplace can subject an employer to millions in liability claims when people are injured by an errant employee or faulty product."[47] About 50 percent of our nation's largest companies test job applicants for drugs, and another 20 percent are considering doing so.[48]

2. *AIDS.* Acquired immune deficiency syndrome (AIDS) has infected thousands of people worldwide. In the United States, over 70,000 people have AIDS. These victims are protected by both federal and state laws that protect the handicapped. Though employers may treat AIDS victims properly, they are facing the problem of co-workers who do not want to share facilities and work with these people. Large employers

EXHIBIT 16.3
Five Basic Ethical Issues Facing Business in the 1990s

Drug-Testing	Seven states have passed laws restricting drug tests. Random testing in private industry is under legal attack, and the Supreme Court has agreed to decide whether testing government employees violates the Fourth Amendment.
AIDS	Employees with AIDS are covered by laws protecting the handicapped. But few companies have educated their work forces to prevent discrimination by co-workers.
Lie Detector Tests	The first federal law restricting the use of polygraphs is now being drafted from bills passed recently by the House and Senate. Similar laws already exist in 31 states.
Computer Surveillance	Federal and state restraints on employer monitoring of computer work and telephone conversations are under discussion. Meanwhile, companies have increasing access to electronic data bases that contain vast amounts of personal information on employees.
Genetic Screening	Lab tests can determine whether employees have genetic traits that make them susceptible to certain diseases. Some authorities say legislation is needed to prevent employers from using such tests to screen job applicants.

Source: "Privacy," John Hoerr et al. Reprinted from the March 28, 1988, issue of *Business Week* by special permission, copyright, © 1988 by McGraw-Hill, Inc.

and industries are moving toward policies that call for programs of education to remove the fear of AIDS from the workplace.[49]

3. *Lie detector tests.*   Recent surveys show that about 30 percent of our nation's largest employers and about 50 percent of retail businesses use lie detectors in preemployment screening and to investigate thefts in the workplace. Effective December 1988, federal law now prohibits private employers from requiring or requesting polygraph or lie detector tests from current or prospective employees.

4. *Computer surveillance.*   Thousands of U.S. workers have their output monitored by computers everyday at work. Many companies record employee phone calls. Sometimes this monitoring is done without the employees' knowledge. The Communications Workers of America union is asking Congress for a law that would prohibit secret monitoring in all industries and require beeps on the phone to indicate that a supervisor is listening. Massachusetts is considering a similar law.[50]

5. *Genetic screening.*   Tests exist that can identify a person's predisposition to diseases like heart disease and cancer. Such tests can be used to deny people employment, insurance, and promotions.[51]

All these issues pose difficult questions and relate to a person's right to privacy. They affect a person's feeling of self-worth and the employer's right to run a business.

Your Individual Role

You are entering the world of business decision making when you become a member of management's team. You will take all of your talents and values to work with you. You will enter an environment structured by others with constraints and aids to help you succeed. Above all, you take your integrity. It is a precious gift, but it can be compromised and lost. Organizations have discovered this, as have governmental agencies.

As a manager, you are a steward—a custodian of the trust of others. You must represent and defend the interests of those who put you in office and those whose work keeps you there. But you will need to take a longer view, to have a wider perspective that reaches outside the organization and into the community, state, and nation of which you are an active part. The mandates of government are givens, and you will learn to live with them. Few people argue today against such existing laws and institutions as social security, worker's compensation, and the Fair Labor Standards Act. But managers and businesses as a community opposed them when they were first proposed.[52]

As a manager, you must try to sense the mood of the times and the demands that will be made on you and your employer in the future. If your company has no built-in approach to social responsibility, you may be able to get those in power interested in doing something about it. Both you and your employer have a right to take a stand, "sell" it, and defend it when social, moral, or legal issues are raised. Like individual organizations, industries, and businesses in general, you have a right to be heard and to make your standards known. Just as you have obligations to many people and groups, your employer does also. Your duty is to meet your responsibilities and to help your employer meet its.

Summary

- Greater pressures from more groups than ever before are being felt by managers in the execution of their basic functions.
- External groups—such as governments, environmentalists, conservationists, and civil rights groups—are demanding that private enterprise do more in the way of helping to reduce society's ills.
- Managers are trustees of the public's trust, the owners' trusts, and the employees' welfare.
- Businesses are trustees of the public's trust and exist because the public—society—allows them to. They must be willing to respond to society's needs and demands on them.
- Organizations, like individuals, can and do act morally and ethically as well as immorally and unethically. They can be and are held accountable for their actions under both the law of society and the law of the marketplace.
- Today's larger businesses have adopted an active approach in their exercise of corporate social responsibility by making social responsibility a goal, part of their forecasting and planning, and part of the institution's approach to decision making and problem solving.
- Just as society has a right to make its needs and demands known to managers and businesses, so too, do those individuals and groups have a right to let society know their needs and points of view.

Glossary of Essential Terms

ethics A branch of philosophy concerned with what is honest and honorable in human conduct, its motives, and its ends. It is based on a system of moral principles and values.

morals Concepts of right and wrong that form a system of principles on which decisions can be based.

social audit A report (feedback) on the social performance of a business. It may be formal, informal, quantitative or qualitative, public or private.

| **social responsibility** | The moral and ethical content of managerial and corporate decisions; it is concerned with the values used in business decisions, over and above the pragmatic requirements imposed by legal principle and the market economy. |

Review Questions

1. Can you define this chapter's essential terms? If not, consult the preceding glossary.
2. In what way does the term *responsibility* apply to managers and organizations in this chapter?
3. What are the three phases that managers have passed through with regard to their concern for social responsibilities?
4. How can one determine if intended actions are ethical or moral?
5. How can managers build social responsibility into their organizations?

References

1. Robert C. Solomon and Kristine Hanson, *It's Good Business* (New York: Atheneum, 1985), pp. 20–21.
2. Julie Stacey, "USA Snapshots: Individuals Lead in Giving," *USA Today*, May 27, 1987, p. 1B.
3. "Texaco Is Facing Another Big Payout," *The New York Times*, February 28, 1988, p. 16.
4. Douglas S. Sherwin, "The Ethical Roots of the Business System," *Harvard Business Review* (November–December 1983), p. 184.
5. Ibid.
6. Ibid.
7. Kenneth E. Goodpaster and John B. Mathews, Jr., "Can a Corporation Have a Conscience?" *Harvard Business Review* (January–February 1982), pp. 133, 138.
8. Ibid., p. 136.
9. Milton Friedman, "The Social Responsibility of Business Is to Increase Its Profits," *New York Times Magazine*, September 13, 1970, p. 142.
10. Robert H. Bock, "Modern Values and Corporate Responsibility," *MSU Business Topics* (Spring 1980), pp. 10–12.
11. Ibid., p. 8.

12. George A. Steiner, "Institutionalizing Corporate Social Decisions," *Business Horizons* (December 1975), pp. 15–16.

13. William K. Frankena, *Thinking About Morality* (Ann Arbor: University of Michigan Press, 1980), p. 26.

14. Thomas W. Dunfee, "Employee Ethical Attitudes and Business Firm Productivity," *The Wharton Annual (1984)*, University of Pennsylvania, Pergamon Press, p. 76.

15. Robert C. Solomon and Kristine Hanson, *It's Good Business* (New York: Atheneum, 1985), pp. 46–49.

16. John A. Byrne, "Businesses Are Signing Up for Ethics 101," *Business Week*, February 15, 1988, pp. 56–57.

17. Ibid., p. 57.

18. "Chevron to Pay Big Pollution Fine," *Chicago Tribune*, January 24, 1988, sect. 7, p. 4.

19. "2 Execs Guilty in Fake-Juice Case," *Chicago Tribune*, February 18, 1988, sect. 1, p. 10.

20. Joel Dresang, "Companies Get Serious About Ethics," *USA Today*, December 9, 1986, p. 2B.

21. Saul W. Gellerman, "Why 'Good' Managers Make Bad Ethical Choices," *Harvard Business Review* (July–August 1986), pp. 88–89.

22. Ibid.

23. Tom Peters, "The News Is That Iacocca's Response Made News," *Chicago Tribune*, July 27, 1987, sect. 4, p. 6.

24. Ibid., p. 90.

25. "Hertz Is Doing Some Body Work—On Itself," *Business Week*, February 15, 1988, p. 57.

26. Gellerman, *Harvard Business Review* (July–August 1986), p. 90.

27. "Motorola Disciplines 59 in Defense Cost Case," *Chicago Tribune*, April 1, 1988, sect. 3, p. 3.

28. Marty Baumann, "USA Snapshots: Ethics in Business," *USA Today*, November 27, 1987, p. 1B.

29. "At Work: How Do Your Office Ethics Compare?" *USA Today*, September 30, 1987, p. 4B.

30. "U.S. Places 1st in Ethics Survey," *Chicago Tribune*, December 18, 1987, sect. 2, p. 3.

31. Richard Latture, "USA Snapshots: Bad for Business," *USA Today*, February 26–28, 1988, p. 1A.

32. Mark Lewyn, "Computerline: Average Take of Computer Fraud: $600,000," *USA Today*, May 7, 1987, p. 6B.

33. Irwin Ross, "How Lawless Are Big Companies?" *Fortune*, December 1, 1980, p. 62.

34. Gregory Katz, "It's the Truth: A Lot of Us Lie, at Least a Little," *USA Weekend*, March 6–7, 1987, p. 4.

35. "Tax Cheats Keep $84.9 Billion," *Chicago Tribune*, March 18, 1988, sect. 1, p. 14.

36. "Highway Cash Case Nearing Quiet Close," *Chicago Tribune*, December 21, 1987, sect. 1, p. 9.

37. Joseph P. Kahn, "When Bad Management Becomes Criminal," *Inc.* (March 1987), pp. 46–48, 50.

38. Goodpaster and Matthews, "Can a Corporation Have a Conscience?" pp. 134–135.

39. Steiner, "Institutionalizing Corporate Social Decisions," p. 18.

40. Vernon M. Buehler and Y. K. Shetty, "Managerial Response to Social Responsibility Challenge," *Academy of Management Journal* (March 1976), p. 69.

41. Robert Cross, "Corporate Conscience: Putting Big Business on Its Best Behavior," *Chicago Tribune*, January 3, 1985, sect. 5, p. 1.

42. Ibid., p. 6.

43. Ian H. Wilson, "Socio-Political Forecasting: A New Dimension to Strategic Planning," *Michigan Business Review* (July 1974).

44. Steiner, "Institutionalizing Corporate Social Decisions," p. 18.

45. Michael G. Royston, "Making Pollution Prevention Pay," *Harvard Business Review* (November–December 1980), pp. 7–8.

46. "Privacy," John Hoerr et al., *Business Week*, March 28, 1988, p. 61.

47. Ibid.

48. "Testing for Drugs Becoming Routine," *Chicago Tribune*, April 10, 1988, sect. 8, p. 1.

49. Hoerr, *Business Week*, March 28, 1988, p. 63.

50. Ibid., p. 65.

51. Ibid.

52. John T. Dunlop et al., "Business and Public Policy," *Harvard Business Review* (November–December 1979), p. 86.

Readings

Barry, Vincent. *Moral Issues in Business*, 3rd ed. Belmont, Calif.: Wadsworth, 1986.

Cadbury, Adrian. "Ethical Managers Make Their Own Rules." *Harvard Business Review* (September–October 1987), pp. 69–75.

Grothe, Mardy and Peter Wylie. *Problem Bosses: Who They Are and How to Deal with Them*. New York: Facts on File, 1987.

Hoerr, John et al. "Privacy." *Business Week*, March 28, 1988, pp. 61–65, 68.

Leap, Terry L. "When Can You Fire for Off-Duty Conduct?" *Harvard Business Review* (January–February 1988), pp. 28–30, 34, 36.

Patton, Arch and John C. Baker. "Why Won't Directors Rock the Boat?" *Harvard Business Review* (November–December 1987), pp. 10–12, 16, 18.

Peters, Tom. *Thriving on Chaos: A Handbook for a Management Revolution.* New York: Alfred A. Knopf, 1987.

Rappaport, Alfred. *Creating Shareholder Value: The New Standard for Business Performance.* New York: Macmillan, 1986.

Seymour, Sally. "The Case of the Willful Whistle-Blower." *Harvard Business Review* (January–February 1988), pp. 103–109.

Weaver, Paul H. *The Suicidal Corporation: How Big Business Fails America.* New York: Simon & Schuster, 1988.

C
A
S
E
S

16.1   A Question of Ethics

Betty has a problem. She has just discovered that her best friend is dating Calvin Pritz, a former manager in her company, Felton Information Services. The romance is serious and a violation of Sam Felton's unwritten guideline: No employee may become romantically involved with managers or employees of competitive businesses and keep his or her job. Betty's friend and fellow manager at Felton, Clara, is dating a vice-president of a rival computer software company and is in violation of Sam's policy.

Clara has been dating Calvin for almost six months. So far, she has confided only in Betty. As far as Betty knows, no one else at Felton is aware of Clara's situation. Clara told Betty only after being teased for several weeks about a "secret." Clara is a rising star at Felton, close to becoming a vice-president, and eager to keep her career intact.

In the past, one manager had quit over this issue. Sam discovered the relationship between a top-ranking supervisor in the new products division and a woman who sold competitors' products. That supervisor was given an ultimatum: Quit or cut off the relationship.

He told Sam that the relationship was over, but after three months, Sam discovered that it was not. The supervisor was fired by Sam himself. As Sam put it, "We work in a highly competitive environment. If word leaks out about our business plans and products, we could be last in the marketplace. A romantic relationship, more than any other, can compromise our market position."

After the supervisor's dismissal, rumors began to circulate that the romantic relationship had been discovered through telephone monitoring. Sam's executive secretary, Eva Brown, let it slip one day that numbers called by Felton employees on company phones were cataloged and traced to individuals. Most of the managers think that this is how the supervisor's connection with his girlfriend was discovered.

Betty is worried that she will not be able to keep Clara's secret. She has a close personal relationship with Sam Felton and is debating whether or not she should just tell Sam before he finds out through some other source. "What will happen to me," Betty thought, "if Sam finds out and then finds out that I knew about the relationship?"

For Discussion

1. What are the ethical issues in this case?
2. What is Clara's ethical responsibility?
3. What should Betty do and why?

16.2   Three Times This Week

Gloria was annoyed as she busied herself with the shop closing routines. Three times this week she had been approached by people wanting something from her. As a new business on the block, Gloria had little capital to spare. She did wonder if she had been a little too quick to say no to all of their requests.

The first person appeared on Monday of her fourth full week of operations. A man from the local chapter of the Knights of Columbus had asked Gloria if she would put a sign for their upcoming fundraiser in her window. Gloria had refused, stating that if she did it for him she would have to do it for all the organizations in town. Besides, it would make her window display appear unbalanced.

The second visitor was from the local chamber of commerce. It was putting a book together that would offer senior citizens discounts from various merchants around town. Gloria refused to be a part of the program because besides offering discounts, she would have to pay a $45 fee to be included in the coupon booklet.

Just this morning a third person appeared representing a local bank that she was just starting up. It was minority-owned and operated and specialized in loans to improve the property in its neighborhood and the surrounding areas. Its funds were federally insured, and it was looking for new depositors, especially the commercial and retail businesses in the community. Gloria said that her money was with a more established bank and would stay there. She was not one for taking risks and making unnecessary changes in her routines.

For Discussion

1. What view toward social responsibility does Gloria exhibit? Explain your choice.
2. How could you help Gloria reevaluate her three missed opportunities?

International Management

OUTLINE

Controlling and the International Manager
  • Characteristics of Controls
  • Control Problems
Summary

ESSENTIAL TERMS

culture   multinational corporation
international management

LEARNING OBJECTIVES

After reading and discussing this chapter, you should be able to
do the following:

1. Define this chapter's essential terms.

2. Explain why business corporations establish foreign
   operations.

3. Discuss the influences of the environment and culture on the
   actions of an international manager.

4. Identify and discuss the variables an international manager
   must consider in performing the planning function.

5. Identify and discuss the three organizing phases through
   which a multinational organization evolves.

6. Describe the staffing and compensation problems encountered
   in international management.

7. Describe the influence of employee attitude and
   communication on the directing function of an international
   manager.

8. Describe the characteristics of control systems and the specific
   problems of control in international management.

International Management

As probably never before in our nation's history, managers in all kinds of businesses are paying attention to what is going on across our borders and overseas. American businesses are part of a global economy regardless of how large or small they are and regardless of where they are located. The value of our dollar in relation to foreign currencies directly affects business and consumer decisions around the world. A strong dollar during the middle 1980s has meant cheaper imports, an exporting of American jobs, and a growing trade imbalance (trade deficit) for America. For foreign businesses, a strong dollar has meant a growing American market for foreign goods and services and an increase in the inflow of U.S. dollars with which to shop around the world.

FIGURE 17.1
The annual U.S. trade deficit, 1981–1987

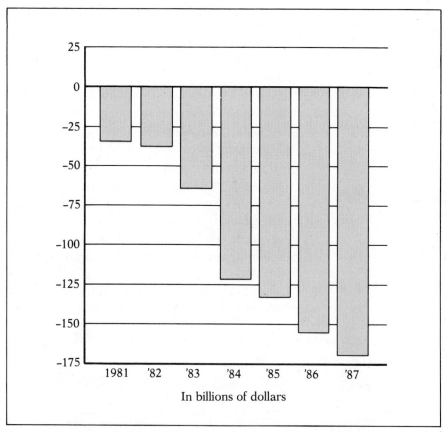

In billions of dollars

Source: U.S. Department of Commerce.

The U.S. Balance of Trade

In 1987, the United States ran a record trade deficit with its trading partners of $171.2 billion. Figure 17.1 shows that trade deficits have been with the United States in every year since 1981. For the first three months of 1988, trade deficits were averaging about $13 billion monthly. While exports have been rising, so too have imports. America's largest categories of imports are automobiles, oil, clothing, electrical machinery, and agricultural commodities. Its leading exports are aircraft, agricultural commodities, data processing and office equipment, industrial machinery, electrical machinery, and chemicals. With Japan alone, America had a trade deficit of $52 billion in 1987, up from $51.4 billion in 1986.[1]

Foreign Investments in America

In 1986, foreigners invested about $30.5 billion in America, bringing total foreign investments in the United States to about $210 billion.[2] Figure 17.2

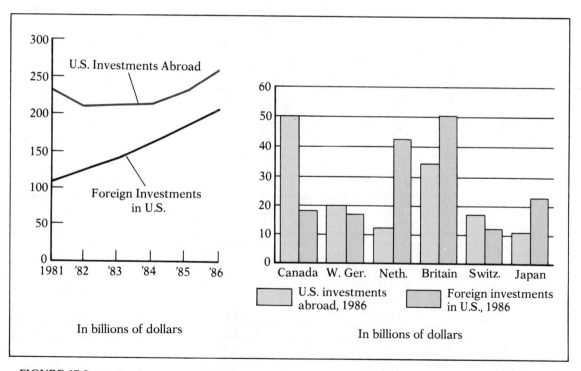

FIGURE 17.2
Total U.S. investments abroad and foreign investment in the U.S., 1981–1986. Investment positions for the U.S. and six of its largest trading partners, 1986
Source: U.S. Department of Commerce.

"Ladies and gentlemen, the meeting is now open. The first order of business is to wave our little American flag and our little company flag."

Source: Reprinted by permission: Tribune Media Services.

shows total investment positions for the six largest foreign investors. Most of the dollars invested in America in 1986 were invested in manufacturing ($13.7 billion) followed by retail trade ($5 billion) and real estate ($4 billion).[3] In addition, foreigners invested about $13 billion in 1987 in our federal government's debt. Foreigners then held about $269 billion in U.S. Treasury securities and own about 13 percent of our nation's $2.1 trillion in debt.[4]

U.S. Investments Abroad

By 1987, U.S. companies had invested a total of about $260 billion in foreign countries. Much of it was invested in overseas business operations and real estate. U.S. companies have about $50 billion invested in Canada, about $35 billion invested in Great Britain, and about $20 billion invested in West Germany. See Figure 17.2 for a summary of U.S. investments overseas.[5]

The Multinational Corporation

Foreign trade means dollars, jobs, and tax revenue to the economies of states as well as of countries. Ohio has made this discovery with its import of Honda manufacturing and assembly operations, as has Tennessee with its Nissan operations. Nearly all of our country's top 1,000 corporations do business with and have their own operations in foreign countries. Many of these companies are classified as **multinational corporations**—companies with operating facilities, not just sales offices, in several foreign countries.[6] Thousands of our small businesses provide products and services to these large corporate customers. In addition, these small businesses have their own lists of customers abroad and have established their own sales outlets abroad. As the world grows and develops, so too will hundreds of local and national economies. The managers of those businesses that are part of international trade have become engaged in **international management**—managing resources (people, capital goods, money, inventories, and technology) across national boundaries and adapting management principles and functions to the demands of foreign competition and environments. The demands on such managers have never been greater than they are today. Throughout the remainder of this chapter, we examine the ways in which the manager's job is affected by involvement in commerce with foreign governments, businesses, and individuals.

The International Manager

All businesses involved in international trade, whether they are multinational corporations or small international suppliers, require the services of men and women who love a challenge—the challenge of working in the ever-changing environment of international trade. Such people need to thrive on the unexpected, the new, the different, and the unique. If they are to work abroad, outside their native lands, they need a love of or sincere interest in the host country's people, traditions, history, and culture. They must have expertise in the host country's language, business customs, economy, and commercial laws. And above all, they need to be patient and flexible.

The international manager working in a host country can be a native of that country, a native of the parent company's country, or a native of a third country. Most multinational corporations employ a mixture of the three in their foreign operations. (By law, some countries require a certain number of their citizens to be employed in the management ranks of the operations they host.) Before sending a manager to a foreign country, the parent company will usually see to it that a certain amount of training is absorbed. Courses and seminars in the host country's history, customs, laws, language, and other areas help prepare the manager and his or her family members for what awaits abroad. In large multinational corporations, newly arrived managers and their families participate in various orientation activities in a host country. Most new managers have a chance to understudy experienced managers before they take on too much responsibility.

The Twenty-first Century Executive

In 1988, *U.S. News & World Report* conducted interviews with scores of executives, management consultants, and business school professors to identify the paramount traits that tomorrow's executives should possess. Here are the findings in brief:[7]

- Global strategist: Working as deftly in Tokyo as in Toledo, he sees—then seizes—markets worldwide. The future CEO must have an understanding of how to manage in an international economy.
- Master of technology: A fast-moving manager must use high tech to stay ahead. The future CEO must stay in touch with innovations and harness the new technology to make new and better products.
- Politician par excellence: Knowing which buttons to press can cut red tape. Local and national regulations, international treaties, trade barriers, and changing currency values will occupy more of the CEO's time in the future.
- Leader/motivator: Old-time charisma is nice, but CEOs must coach teams as well as command them. Increasingly, CEOs must be able to assemble and work with teams of knowledge workers, pooling expertise and striving for a consensus.

International managers perform the same functions—planning, organizing, staffing, directing, and controlling—that all other managers perform, and they attempt to apply all the principles this text has examined. The difference for the international manager is one of application. The environment of international business has a variety of unique circumstances and demands on the manager that must be understood before principles and functions can be effective. In the remainder of this chapter, we examine that environment and the major differences that exist when a manager attempts to plan, organize, staff, direct, and control a business activity in a host country.

The Environment of the International Manager

The manager of an international company must perform managerial functions in an environment far more complex than that of a manager in a company not engaged in international operations. Why? The environment the international manager faces is the *total world environment*. That is, it is the sum total of the environments of every country in which a company has its foreign affiliates. This environment consists of four basic elements: legal, cultural, economic, and political.[8] Exhibit 17.1 identifies the variables found in each element in the environment.

But what does this mean to the international manager? The manager needs to be constantly monitoring all these variables of the specific countries involved to see which ones will have a positive or negative impact on the company's operations. Remember, this environment is dynamic and often volatile. A manager whose company is engaged in international financial activities, for example, needs to monitor currency convertibility, inflation rates, and currency stability. Or, a manager whose company is trying to decide whether to establish a manufacturing plant or to expand its production capacity needs to analyze the political stability of the area, the government's attitude toward foreign businesses, social unrest, and foreign policy.

EXHIBIT 17.1

A Look at the Environmental Factors Involved in the Legal, Cultural, Economic, and Political Environments

Legal Environment

- Legal tradition
- Effectiveness of legal system
- Treaties with foreign nations
- Patent/trademark laws
- Laws affecting business firms

Cultural Environment

- Customs, norms, values, beliefs
- Language
- Attitudes
- Motivations
- Social institutions
- Status symbols
- Religious beliefs

continued

EXHIBIT 17.1
Continued

Economic Environment

- Level of economic development
- Population
- Gross national product
- Per capita income
- Literacy level
- Social infrastructure
- Natural resources
- Climate
- Membership in regional economic blocks (European Economic Community)
- Monetary and fiscal policies
- Nature of competition
- Currency convertibility
- Inflation
- Taxation system
- Interest rates
- Wage and salary levels

Political Environment

- Form of government
- Political ideology
- Stability of government
- Strength of opposition parties and groups
- Social unrest
- Political strife and insurgency
- Governmental attitude toward foreign firms
- Foreign policy

Source: From Arvand V. Phatak, *International Dimensions of Management,* Second Edition (Boston: PWS-KENT Publishing Company, 1989), p. 6. © 1989 by PWS-KENT Publishing Company; 1983 by Wadsworth, Inc. Reprinted by permission of PWS-KENT Publishing Company, a division of Wadsworth, Inc.

Another environmental concern of the international manager is the uniqueness of each international environment. A technique or style that works in one environment may not be entirely applicable in another. As an example, a manager who plans to utilize a particular leadership style—participative—must consider the cultural environment of the specific country where this is to be introduced—its customs, norms, values, beliefs. If the country has its values or norms focused on a respect for authority, this participative style will not be as effective as it would in a country that values a democratic approach to leadership.

A final consideration about the environment of the international manager: The manager must monitor the total environment, not just environments of countries where the firm has operations. In the international environment, both opportunities and threats can arise anywhere in the world. It is necessary, therefore, that the international manager be alert to global developments no matter where they occur.[9]

Another major difference for the international manager is the cultural dilemma. Though touched on briefly as an environmental factor in this section, it is worth further investigation because it influences the application of all the management functions and principles in international management.

The Cultural Dilemma
of the International Manager

To accomplish the company's objectives, the international manager works daily with the cultures of different nations and regions within those nations that differ from his or her own cultural background. **Culture** is the distinctive way of life of a group of people—their complete design for living, which involves knowledge, beliefs, arts, morals, and customs.[10] It is imperative that an international manager from the United States understand the cultures of countries in which he or she operates. The manager not only must understand the culture but also how that culture differs from or is similar to American culture. Analysts who have studied the performance and problems of corporations and individuals abroad have discovered that it is the problems related to working with a different culture that are likely to influence the success or failure of the undertaking.[11]

To avoid this prescription for failure, an international manager has two missions. First, the manager must fully understand his or her own culture. The next task is to study the culture of the country where the company plans to expand its operations. Only in this way can the manager be certain not to force his or her own cultural values or expectations on foreign nationals and expect them to behave as he or she would. International managers must recognize the influence of culture and modify their own personal behavior and managerial approaches.

If this is the key to success for the international manager, let's take a moment to examine the culture and value orientations that are typical of American and most western societies. The values representative of the U.S. culture include the following:[12]

1. *Individualism.* Individualism describes the attitude of independence of the person who feels a large degree of freedom in the conduct of his or her personal life. The result of individualism is a device for self-expression and individual accomplishment. This value may not be shared in other cultures.

2. *Informality.* Informality has two components. First, the American culture does not place a great deal of importance on tradition, ceremony, or social rules. Second, the "style" in American culture is to be direct and not waste time in the conduct of meetings and conversation. Neither of these values may be significant when conducting business in Latin America or the Middle East.

3. *Materialism.* Materialism in America has two elements. First, there is a tendency to attach status to physical objects—a certain brand of car or clothing made by a name designer. Second, because of vast natural resources, Americans are inclined to buy objects and then discard them while they still have a functional value. Both of these behaviors, if exhibited in other societies, may create problems for the international manager.

4. *Change.* Change is viewed as part of the U.S. culture, but it is also perceived as something an individual can influence. We can bring about change. In other societies, this same cultural value may not exist. Change is seen as inevitable but as a phenomenon that occurs naturally—a part of the overall evolution of people and their world. Change is accepted; it is predetermined. There is no deliberate attempt to influence or bring it about.

5. *Time orientation.* Time in the American culture is seen as a scarce and precious resource. As a result, there is an emphasis on the efficient use of time. This belief dictates the practices of setting deadlines and of making and keeping appointments. But in other societies, time is often viewed as an unlimited and never-ending resource. This attitude is why people in some cultures tend to be quite casual about keeping appointments or meeting deadlines.

As we discussed, knowing his or her own culture is the first step for an international manager. The second phase of the education process involves analyzing the culture of the country where the company is expanding operations. What should be analyzed? One suggested approach is to evaluate five dimensions:[13]

1. *Material culture.* The international manager needs to evaluate the technology and the technological know-how for producing goods in a country, the manner in which the country makes use of these abilities, and the resulting economic benefits to the society.

2. *Social institutions.*   The influence on individuals of social institutions—business, family, social class, politics—needs to be recognized.

3. *Man and universe.*   The values and beliefs of people in other cultures may be influenced greatly by religion and superstition. The international manager needs to understand that these elements are an integral part of the cultural dilemma.

4. *Aesthetics.*   This dimension is composed of the art, folklore, music, and drama of the culture. These factors can be important in interpreting the symbolic meanings of artistic expressions. Failure to interpret these correctly can create problems for an international manager.

5. *Language.*   The most difficult dimension for the international manager is language. Not only does a manager need to speak the language of the host country, an international manager must also understand the interpretations of the language as they differ from the definitions in a dictionary.

Having described the international manager and evaluated the environmental and cultural differences to be encountered, it is now appropriate to discuss the management functions—planning, organizing, staffing, directing, and controlling—and their practice in international management.

Planning and the International Manager

As we have already seen in Chapter 4, planning is the manager's attempt to prepare for tomorrow today. Regardless of whether a manager is developing plans for a domestic company or an international one, this looking to the future depends on the assumptions, premises, or conditions that planners accept as true and real, based on their experiences or those of others, and the resulting forecasts or expectations that these same planners formulate with regard to the likely or probable state of events or conditions at some time in the future. In other words, planning on an international level involves the same planning elements: assessing the environment, developing assumptions, and then forecasting based on the assumptions. But planning for an international company is usually far more complex than planning for domestic operations. Why?

A company engaged only in domestic operations is required to monitor and assess primarily the environmental variables of one country in developing its assumptions and forecasts. In an international company, a manager must monitor the changes in the environment of the countries the company has operations in, must determine if these independent environments will influence each other, and then must determine how these overall changes will influence the particular area the manager is responsible for.

In developing plans, the international manager is monitoring and assessing a set of unique variables, including the following:[14]

1. *Political instability and risk.*   Planning involves determining potential changes in governments as well as changes in policy by those governments toward foreign firms and their practices.

2. *Currency instability.*   The future of exchange rates needs to be factored into the planning process, for major fluctuations can bring disaster or significant gains, depending on the accuracy of company assessment.

3. *Competition from state-owned enterprises.*   Planning must consider the presence of and competitive activity from state-owned enterprises. Because they are heavily subsidized by their government, they do not have to earn profits or returns on investments comparable to private competitors. As a result, pricing practices or bidding practices will not be the same.

4. *Nationalism.*   A major variable to be considered by the international manager is the desire for independence by nations. This can result in a company's operations being nationalized (taken over), local controls being imposed on hiring of foreign nationals, import controls being implemented, and limitations being placed on the export profits of the company's host country.

As can be seen from these variables, planning for the international manager is far more complicated than for the manager's domestic counterpart. The consequences of the lack of proper assessment and planning can be devastating. Inadequate preparation can result in a failure to enter a foreign market at the right time or by the right means (licensing someone to produce a product rather than establishing a company-owned production facility or allocating financial resources to ventures that are then immediately nationalized).

Knowing that planning is both critical and difficult on an international level, companies have approached the assessment and planning function in a number of ways. Some allow one person to work at it part time in addition to other duties. Others use a separate unit within corporate headquarters staffed by a group of specialists who report to a vice-president or the chief executive officer. Both approaches may use outside talent, such as consultants, government reports and employees, host country citizens, and managers from the parent company's foreign operations.[15] The effectiveness of the assessment efforts depends on whether a company can decide how to (1) apportion responsibility for gathering and analyzing information between line and staff managers and between in-house personnel and outside consultants; (2) build credibility and effectiveness into the analysis so that the organization takes it seriously; and (3) bring an understanding of the importance of analysis into corporate operations, particularly capital budgeting and long-term planning.[16] These assessments lead to forecasts that various levels of managers then use to differing degrees when constructing their plans. The aim of all the efforts at assessing, interpreting, forecasting, and creating strategies and tactics is to create a unity within management of the multinational corporation and to be a good corporate citizen in the host countries.

Standardization vs. Customization

For too long, American companies have produced standardized products developed for American consumers and then tried to sell these same designs to foreigners. But in today's global markets, customers around the world demand products with features different than those that Americans find appealing. Boeing introduced its 737 model about twenty years ago, and when its sales began to decline, it turned to foreign markets to save the plane. By studying how pilots flew in developing countries and their flying conditions and needs, Boeing redesigned its 737 to land more softly on asphalt runways that were softer than concrete and shorter than runways in other nations. With engines with added thrust, wings redesigned to allow for shorter landings, and low-pressure tires to keep the plane on the ground after touchdown, Boeing found that the 737 became the best selling plane in the history of jet aircraft.[17]

Nixdorf Computer of Germany builds minicomputers and office automation equipment around a single but flexible design. It then tailors the machines to meet specific customer needs. "Nixdorf spends 10 percent of its R&D budget sending research teams of salesmen, product developers, and production people to talk to customers. The tactic cements the relationship between company and customer." Custom-designed equipment keeps customers tied to a producer, and that means future business.[18]

Organizing and the International Manager

Companies develop organization structures to achieve objectives. As the objectives of the organizations change, the organization structures need to change (Chapter 7). An organization on an international level operates under the same set of guidelines.

As organizations extend their operations to host countries, their internal organization structures must change. The structures chosen at any given time in a firm's evolution depend on the extent of the operations abroad, their locations and contributions to the parent company, and the degree of experience and competence possessed by both parent and host country managers. The structure chosen must be able to cope with the social, political, and economic differences that exist between the parent and its host country operations. The structure developed to launch overseas operations will not be adequate when the company moves from simple sales outlets to full-fledged manufacturing, sales, and distribution in two or more host countries. Whatever structure is chosen must be able to balance foreign and domestic operations and their tendencies to seek dominance and control, one over the other. A decision about the degree of centralization of authority and decision making must be made and reexamined as the organization's operations expand and meet new challenges.

Although the organization structure utilized by a company depends on its objectives, the typical evolution for multinational organizations takes them through three phases: preinternational division phase, international division phase, and global structure phase.[19] A major point to note as we trace the evolution of these phases is that in a domestic company, a two-dimensional structure (functional and product or functional and territorial) is often used to meet the objectives. In the international arena, a three-dimensional structure is eventually required, which combines functional, product, and territorial patterns to provide functional expertise, product know-how, and knowledge of the area for the company.

The Preinternational Division Phase

The first stage usually accommodates the company just starting out in foreign markets. Normally when a company initiates the international venture, it is on the basis that it has a technologically advanced product that is needed in the marketplace and can stand on its own. The result is the selection by the company of an export department or the addition of an export manager to the marketing department that already exists to carry out the firm's international objectives. (See Figure 17.3.)

The International Division Phase

When a parent company realizes it needs additional specialists and that it must plan for (rather than react to) international opportunities and threats, it takes the second step in integrating foreign operations into the management operations of the domestic firm. The international division is usually directed by a vice-president who reports directly to the president or chief executive officer (CEO) of the parent company. (See Figure 17.4.)

The head of the division is given line authority over all activities abroad. The formation of this division in effect segregates the company

FIGURE 17.3
The initial organization structure utilized in international business usually involves the addition of an export department to an already existing marketing department.

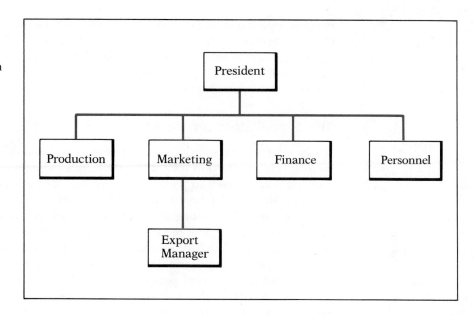

FIGURE 17.4
A simplified corporate structure containing an international division

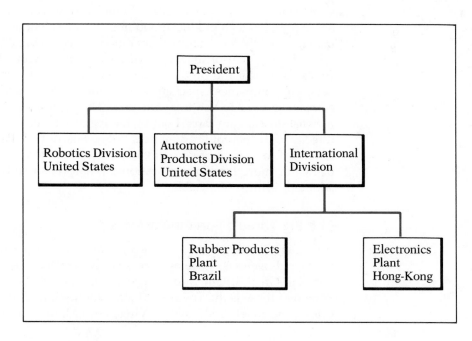

into two differentiated parts—domestic and international. The division may contain various staff or functional services to serve all the international branches (such as legal, economic research, finance, and marketing support personnel), but the responsibilities for production and marketing usually reside in the international host country branches.[20]

The Global Structure Phase

As the international operations continue to evolve and the business becomes increasingly involved in international business activities, top management makes a commitment to perceive the organization in a global perspective. At this point, the company has entered the global structure phase. Decisions that previously were made separately by domestic and international parts of the company are now made at the corporate headquarters for the total enterprise. Corporate decisions are made with a total company perspective for the purpose of achieving the company's overall mission and objectives.

The shift to a global perspective needs to be accompanied by an organization structure that will achieve these objectives. The structure will evolve into one with functional, product, or geographic features. The final structure will be based on worldwide product groups, worldwide area groups, or a mixture of the two.[21]

The product group approach works best for diverse and widely dispersed product lines and for those with relatively high technology or research and development activities. Command and control lines pass through a vice-president of a product group from the president or CEO to the general managers of the host country operations. (See Figure 17.5, Part A.)

The regional or area approach works best with a narrow group of similar products and products that are closely tied to local consumer markets. Oil companies, specialty food manufacturers, and rubber products companies tend to use this structure. The typical functions of the international division are carried out by the regional managers, who must report directly to the parent headquarters.[22] (See Figure 17.5, Part B.) An example of a need to change organizational structure is exemplified by the joining of two or more foreign corporations. Whatever organization structure is adopted, it must be flexible.

The Big Three's Foreign Partners

All America's largest auto producers have foreign partners in the United States and overseas. General Motors has no less than six, four are Japanese, one is in Great Britain, and the other is in South Korea. Probably the best known of these is the Toyota-GM joint venture in California that produces Chevrolet models and Toyota FX-16s. Ford Motor Company has three for-

**FIGURE 17.5,
PART A**
A simplified
corporate structure
integrating
worldwide product
groups

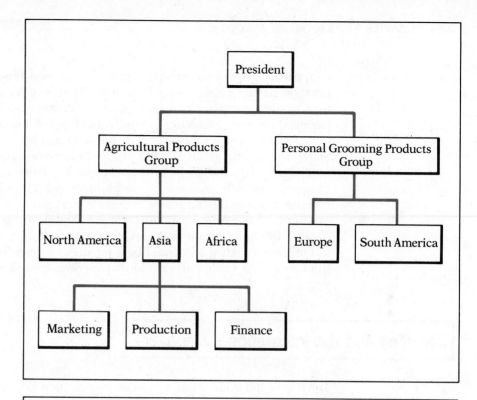

**FIGURE 17.5,
PART B**
A simplified
corporate structure
integrating regional
divisions

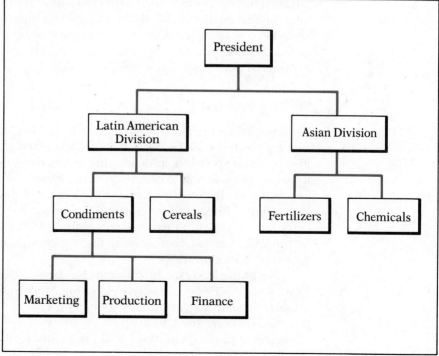

eign partners, one each in Japan, South Korea, and Taiwan. Chrysler Corporation has an alliance with Mitsubishi Motors of Japan that builds cars for Chrysler in Japan and in Illinois. Its overseas operations also include partnerships with Lamborghini and with Alfiere Maserati in Italy.[23]

Since 1964, the Japanese alone have opened 640 plants in the United States, employing about 160,000 people in forty-two states.[24] In the automobile industry, the alliances between the Big Three and the foreign car companies (mostly Japanese) have brought with them an inflow of parts manufacturers that build plants near the American company that uses their products. These American and Japanese–American car companies spent nearly $4 billion of their earnings to buy parts from seventy parts plants in the United States, all owned by a Japanese parent. The result is a shift from American-made parts made by American-owned producers.[25]

Staffing and the International Manager

The role of the staffing function in an organization is to identify and acquire qualified human resources to ensure the success of the organization. In the international environment, staffing fulfills this mission. But two major concerns need to be noted. One is the general staffing problem of identifying qualified employees, and the other is the problem involved in compensating managerial personnel. Let's examine each.

Staffing Problems

Finding qualified persons to fill jobs with multinational corporations' host country positions can be difficult, especially when attempting to find qualified technical specialists in developing or less developed countries. Initially, it may be possible only if citizens from the parent country or a third country are recruited. Eventually, through training and development programs, host country citizens can be groomed for various jobs. Surveys done among executives of U.S. multinational corporations indicate that the major problem in their foreign operations is finding enough qualified personnel in particular host countries.[26]

For example, Texas Instruments has been making semiconductors in Japan since the 1960s. It started by sending Americans to Japan. They hired a Japanese staff that eventually took control of the Japanese operations. But the company tried to keep its American ways of hiring, rewarding managers, and compensating. It did not work well. The company finally adopted the Japanese methods of recruiting and rewarding, "including bonuses and a promotion system based strongly on seniority. Today TI is the only American semiconductor company with duplicate memory chip factories in the U.S. and Japan." In 1985, the company won the prestigious Deming Prize for quality control for its Japanese operations.[27]

Compensation Problems

Compensating host country managers in line with parent country practices seldom works. Customs and host country competition demand specific changes. Levels of taxes, inflation, and the relative value of currencies must be considered. The American custom of rewarding managers for their department's or division's success must be tempered with the contribution it makes to the whole enterprise and the kinds of barriers it has had to overcome. Although the Japanese, Germans, and English create benefits for individual recipients, other peoples and their multinational corporations do not.[28] Factors such as the value of seniority, the cost of living in a host country, and the level of status a manager is viewed to possess by peers must be considered and compensation adjusted accordingly.

Directing and the International Manager

People are not the same around the world. They have different languages, cultures, customs, traditions, and attitudes about work and working. These differences make the directing function—specifically, supervision and communicating—more challenging than it would be if just one country's populace were involved. Next we focus on some of the major differences and the challenges they represent to a parent company's management.

Employee Attitudes

A few of the differences employees have around the world revolve around their attitudes about company loyalty, the roles of each gender and caste, the value of work in their lives, and the value of time. In France and Germany, for example, a great deal of value is placed on where one attended school and on what one's parents do for a living. An "old boy" network and caste system exists that limits promotability in these cultures. Peter Drucker, author and management consultant, has found that the number one reason why foreign nationals join American multinationals is to overcome such traditional prejudices. Similar caste distinctions exist in Japan and other countries. One's status among managers in a Japanese environment is never in doubt, and each member of a discussion or group is clearly aware of his or her status before serious discussions take place.[29]

On the other hand, in Japan, company loyalty is strong among Japanese nationals. Their unions are more cooperative than U.S. unions are with management, and Japanese workers are more committed to making things better in their companies than are U.S. workers. Japanese executives in the United States (10,500 work for 1,200 Japanese firms in the United States) are consistently amazed at how Americans compartmentalize their lives, keeping family, job, and friendships quite separate. "The Japanese, who have a strong spirit of company loyalty, find most of the friendships in the work environment."[30] The normal mode of operation for Japanese managers is to be subtle, to suggest. Though they dislike and generally do not give direct orders, they have found that in America they must.[31]

Communication Problems

An international manager may be presented with a number of communication dilemmas. Not only words, but body language as well differs from one ethnic or cultural group to another. For example, it is considered an insult by Arabs to cross your feet or legs or to show the bottoms of your shoes to them. The parent company may wish to transact business in English and dollars, but it will have to adjust to Japanese, Korean, German, and other languages and currencies. The manager in a host country may be Swiss, the parent company may be American, and the host country may be France. Some method to reconcile the communications difficulties needs to be effective if the multinational corporation is to be successful. Relying on translators can be tricky. Host country nationals may pretend lack of understanding when it is in their interest to do so. Certain words do not have direct translations or will come out with an imprecise meaning. Host country managers need a working knowledge of the language of their workforces and an understanding of their customs as well.

Consider just one problem of giving a gift to a foreign national. The choice of a gift can cause embarrassment or trouble for the giver if the country's customs and traditions are not understood. Exhibit 17.2 outlines a few rules that apply to gift giving abroad. Note item 14, and avoid giving a clock to a Chinese national.

Another area of communications difficulties for host country managers has to do with negotiating with host country nationals. Negotiations take place with suppliers, unions, government officials, and various trading partners. Exhibit 17.3 presents eleven tips for negotiating. Together they say, "When in Rome, do as the Romans do." A Japanese negotiator will consider you rude if you reposition a chair even a few inches. In Spain, the American "OK" sign formed with the thumb and forefinger is a vulgar gesture. In Finland, you may be asked to negotiate in a sauna.[32]

EXHIBIT 17.2
Some Tips on How to Avoid the Pitfalls in Gift-Giving Abroad

1. Don't rely on your own taste.
2. Don't bring a gift to an Arab man's wife; in fact, don't ask about her at all. Bringing gifts for the children is, however, acceptable.
3. In Arab countries, don't admire an object openly. The owner may feel obligated to give it to you.
4. Do not bring liquor to an Arab home. For many Arabs, alcohol is forbidden by religious law.
5. Don't try to outgive the Japanese. It causes great embarrassment and obligates them to reciprocate even if they cannot afford it.
6. Do not insist that your Japanese counterpart open the gift in your presence. This is not their custom and can easily cause embarrassment on the part of the recipient.
7. As a courtesy, hold your gift with two hands when presenting it to a Japanese business person, but do not make a big thing of the presentation.
8. Be careful when selecting colors or deciding on the number of items. The color purple is inappropriate in Latin America because it is associated with Lent.
9. Avoid giving knives and handkerchiefs in Latin America. Knives suggest the cutting off of the relationship, and handkerchiefs imply that you wish the recipient hardship. To offset the bad luck, the recipient must offer you money.
10. Logos should be unobtrusive.
11. In West Germany, red roses imply that you are in love with the recipient. Moreover, perfume is too personal a gift for business relationships.
12. In the People's Republic of China, expensive presents are not acceptable and cause great embarrassment. Give a collective gift from your company to theirs.
13. In China, a banquet is acceptable, but you will insult your hosts if you give a more lavish banquet than the one given you.
14. A clock is a symbol of bad luck in China.

The most important rule is to investigate first. After all, no one laughs at gift gaffes. True, it is the thought that counts: the thought you give to understanding the culture and the taste of the people with whom you plan to negotiate.

Source: Reprinted by permission of the *Harvard Business Review.* Excerpt from "It's the Thought That Counts" by Kathleen K. Reardon (September–October 1984). Copyright © 1984 by the President and Fellows of Harvard College; all rights reserved.

EXHIBIT 17.3
How Americans Should Adjust Their Negotiating Behaviors to Fit the Styles of the Host Country Executives

1. *I can go it alone.* Use team assistance wisely. Don't hesitate to include extra members on your team such as financial or technical experts. The extra expense may be an excellent investment. Also, observation of negotiations can be a valuable training experience for younger members of the organization. Even if they add little to the discussion, their presence may make a difference.

2. *Just call me John.* The way to make foreign clients more comfortable is to follow *their* traditions and customs. American informality and egalitarian views are simply out of place in most countries in the world. Status relations and business procedures must be carefully considered with the aid and advice of your local representatives.

3. *Pardon my French.* Ideally, U.S. negotiators should speak the local language, although in practice this is seldom possible. Americans usually travel overseas for short trips, and the investment in executive time for extensive language training appears unwarranted. However, American representatives should recognize the conversational disadvantages when foreign executives use an interpreter even though they understand English. Even a rudimentary knowledge of key foreign terms or numbers may aid the American.

4. *Check with the home office.* An important part of the preparations for any negotiation is the determination of authority limits—both theirs and yours. Americans should weigh the disadvantages of having full authority against the expenses of communication with the home office. Not having the final say may be a useful strategy for maintaining the proper interpersonal relationship and harmony, particularly in international negotiations.

5. *Get to the point.* We Americans depend on tightly written contracts and corporate lawyers for protection against the unscrupulous. Since in many places in the world legal systems are not as dependable, foreign executives invest much time in establishing personal relationships. Americans bargaining in foreign countries must be patient and plan to spend more time in non-task sounding. Let the other side bring up business and put your wristwatch in your coat pocket. Moreover, remarks such as "We will need to get our legal staff to review this proposal" can quickly sour international deals. Other countries see us as a nation of lawyers in a world where law is used to handle business agreements that are in trouble, not at the beginning of the discussions. Be careful of open references to "legal review." For the foreigner, it may be a signal that the business relationship will be short-lived.

EXHIBIT 17.3
Continued

6. *Lay your cards on the table.* Foreign executives seldom lay their cards on the table. They are more likely to hold an ace or two in reserve. Often, initial demands will be irritatingly high from the American point of view. Most foreign executives expect to spend more time negotiating and expect to make concessions. You should adjust your initial offer accordingly and anticipate having to ask the same questions in several ways to get what we would call straight answers.
7. *Don't just sit there, speak up.* Recognize that silence can be a much more powerful negotiating tool than good arguments. Consider its uses, but in particular be aware of its use against you. Look at your notes, fiddle with your pen, anything, but let *them* break the silence.
8. *Don't take no for an answer.* Take the situation in Japan as a good example. The correct strategy for Americans negotiating with Japanese or other foreign clients is a Japanese strategy: ask questions. When you think you understand, ask more questions. Carefully feel for pressure points. If an impasse is reached, don't pressure. Suggest a recess or another meeting. Large concessions by the Japanese side at the negotiation table are unlikely. They see negotiations as a ritual where harmony is foremost. In Japan, minds are changed behind the scenes.
9. *One thing at a time.* Avoid making concessions on any issue until the group has fully discussed all issues. This is good advice for bargaining with American clients too. Also, do not measure progress by the number of issues that have been settled. In other countries different signals may be much more important.
10. *A deal is a deal.* Recognize differences in what an agreement means across cultures. A signed contract does not mean the same thing in Tokyo, Rio, or Riyadh as it means in New York.
11. *I am what I am.* Flexibility is critical in cross-cultural negotiations. Americans must adapt to the circumstances of world economic interdependence. Our power at the international negotiation table will continue to erode as our trading partners develop industrially. We must change our negotiating style accordingly.

Source: Reprinted by permission of the Harvard Business Review. Excerpt from "Negotiators Abroad—Don't Shoot from the Hip" by John L. Graham and Roy A. Herberger, Jr. (July–August 1983). Copyright © 1983 by the President and Fellows of Harvard College; all rights reserved.

Controlling and the International Manager

The management function of control involves the three-step process developed in Chapter 12. It includes (1) establishing standards to be used in measuring progress, or lack of progress, toward goals; (2) measuring performance against standards, noting deviations from standards; and (3) taking actions necessary to correct deviations from standards. In international management, this control process is identical. What we need to focus on are the characteristics of control systems in an international company and the unique problems of control.

Characteristics of Controls

Multinationals use a variety of controls to monitor and adjust the performance of their foreign affiliates. These fall into two groups: direct controls and indirect controls.[33] Let's examine each.

Direct controls include the use of such devices as periodic meetings, visits by the home country's top-management team to the foreign subsidiaries, and the staffing of the foreign affiliates by home country nationals. In addition, regularly scheduled management meetings can be held to discuss the performance of the foreign affiliates.

The indirect control devices used by companies to control foreign subsidiaries are the various sets of reports that each foreign subsidiary must submit to top management, which detail its performance during a specific period. The main criteria used to measure performance include return on investment and profits. In the same family as the reports are a whole array of budgetary and financial controls that are imposed through budgets and various types of financial statements, such as the balance sheet, profit-and-loss statement, cash budget, and financial ratios depicting the financial health of each subsidiary.

Control Problems

As with planning, control and the problems associated with it are far more complex in a multinational company than in one that is purely domestic in operation. This is because the multinational operates in more than one cultural, economic, political, and legal environment.

Control is made difficult by everything from language difficulties to legal restrictions. Most companies rely on (1) regular reporting procedures; (2) evaluation measures such as the degree of the host operation's productivity growth, its ability to meet corporate objectives, its penetration into the market, and its profitability; and (3) regular on-site inspections. But these reporting procedures can be complicated by language and currency differences, screening of information by host country managers, and different delivery methods. Also, control methods can be affected by local unions, legal restrictions, customs, and general lack of comparability to parent company standards. On-site inspections must be carried out by experienced observers who have an understanding of the above problems. Finally, the geographic distance from parent to host country can make time delays in reporting and reception of orders routine.

Some of the best run plants in America are managed by the Japanese. An example of implanting control is exhibited by the Japanese in America. The Honda facility in Ohio, Nissan's plant in Tennessee, and the Toyota/GM NUMMI plant in California are just three examples. At NUMMI, productivity is about twice as good as that of any other GM plant.[34] The Nissan plant uses 351 robots (some of Norwegian design), 3,300 people, the latest in equipment and methods from Japan, and a 782-acre site to manufacture 256,000 vehicles a year. Opened in 1983, it is considered one of the most efficient plants in the world. Its vehicles are now produced at less cost than the comparable Nissan vehicles can be produced for in Japan. Key personnel are trained in Japan to use Japanese-style worker teams, quality control, just-in-time delivery methods, and fiber-optic monitoring in the robot painting department.[35]

Summary

- The American economy is part of a world economy.
- Since the 1950s, American companies have been investing in foreign business operations, and foreigners have been investing in American business operations.
- Multinational corporations own or jointly operate business activities in several foreign countries.
- The international manager needs an in-depth understanding of a foreign country—its people, customs, laws, history, and language.
- The international manager performs the same functions of management (planning, organizing, staffing, directing, and controlling) as the manager of a domestic company, but the international environment requires the additional understanding of unique circumstances and demands on their application.

- The environment the international manager faces is the total world environment.
- The international manager must deal daily with the cultures of different nations and regions within these nations that differ from his or her own cultural background.
- Planning in an international environment is far more complex than planning for domestic operations only.
- Planning on an international level requires the manager to assess political instability and risk, currency instability, competition from state-owned enterprises, and nationalism.
- Although the organization structure utilized by an international company depends on its objective, the typical evolution for a multinational corporation takes the company through three phases: the preinternational division phase, the international division phase, and the global structure phase.
- Staffing problems in international management center on finding a number of qualified persons to fill jobs and in compensating managers.
- The differences in employee attitudes about work and working and the difficulty of communication make the directing function challenging for the international manager.
- In the control function, an international manager relies on both direct and indirect controls.
- Problems in control are caused by language difficulties, legal restrictions, currency differences, customs, lack of comparability to parent company standards, and geographic distance.

Glossary of Essential Terms

culture	The distinctive way of life of a group of people; their design for living, which includes knowledge, beliefs, arts, morals, and customs.
international management	Managing resources across national borders and adapting management principles and functions to the demands of foreign competition and environments.
multinational corporation	Companies with operating facilities—not just sales offices—in several foreign countries.

Review Questions

1. Can you define this chapter's essential terms? If not, consult the preceding glossary.
2. Why do business corporations establish foreign operations?
3. What are the five variables an international manager should evaluate when analyzing a society's culture?
4. Describe each of the four variables an international manager should assess in developing plans.
5. What is the level of commitment of an international organization's top management in the global structure phase of organizational development? What three options are available in this phase?
6. What particular compensation problem is encountered in international management?
7. What communication problems can be encountered in international management?
8. What two groups of control devices are relied on in international management?

References

1. Elaine S. Povich, "Surge in Exports Cuts Trade Deficit," *Chicago Tribune*, February 13, 1988, sect. 1, p. 1.
2. "Foreign Investment in U.S. Up," *Chicago Tribune*, June 25, 1987, sect. 3, p. 3.
3. "Business Facts: Foreign Investments in U.S. Businesses," *Chicago Tribune*, July 15, 1987, sect. 3, p. 1.
4. "Business Facts: U.S. Government Debt Held by Foreigners," *Chicago Tribune*, February 4, 1988, sect. 3, p. 1.
5. *Chicago Tribune*, June 25, 1987, sect. 3, p. 3.
6. Carl Heyel, ed., *The Encyclopedia of Management*, 3rd ed. (New York: Van Nostrand Reinhold, 1982),
7. Clemens P. Work et al., "The 21st Century Executive," *U.S. News & World Report*, March 7, 1988, pp. 48–51.
8. Arvind V. Phatak, *International Dimensions of Management* (Boston: Kent, 1983), p. 5.
9. Ibid., p. 7.

10. Harlan Cleveland, Gerald J. Mangone, and John C. Adams, *The Overseas Americans* (New York: McGraw-Hill, 1960).

11. Phatak, *International Dimensions of Management*, p. 19.

12. Ibid., p. 22.

13. Melville J. Herskovits, *Man and His Works* (New York: Alfred A. Knopf, 1952), p. 17.

14. Phatak, *International Dimensions of Management*, pp. 41–42.

15. Stephen J. Kobrin, "Assessing Political Risk Overseas," *The Wharton Magazine*, 6, no. 2 (Winter 1981–82), pp. 25–27.

16. Thomas W. Shreeve, "Be Prepared for Political Changes Abroad," *Harvard Business Review* (July–August 1984), p. 112.

17. Andrew Kupfer, "How to Be a Global Manager," *Fortune*, March 14, 1988, p. 52.

18. Louis S. Richman, "Lessons from German Managers," *Fortune*, April 27, 1987, p. 270.

19. Phatak, *International Dimensions of Management*, p. 67.

20. Heyel, *The Encyclopedia of Management*, p. 498.

21. Ibid., pp. 498–499.

22. Ibid., p. 499.

23. Doug Carroll, "Consolidations Make Carmakers' World Smaller," *USA Today*, May 4, 1987, p. 6B.

24. John Hillkirk, "Japanese to Open More USA Plants," *USA Today*, December 23, 1987, p. 1B.

25. R. C. Longworth, "Japan's Script Has Made-in-USA Cast," *Chicago Tribune*, May 13, 1987, sect. 3, p. 3.

26. U. E. Weichmann and L. G. Pringle, "Problems That Plague Multinational Marketers," *Harvard Business Review* (July–August 1979), p. 120.

27. Andrew Kupfer, "How to Be a Global Manager," *Fortune*, March 14, 1988, p. 58.

28. Heyel, *The Encyclopedia of Management*, p. 636.

29. John L. Graham and Roy A. Herberger, Jr., "Negotiators Abroad—Don't Shoot from the Hip," *Harvard Business Review* (July–August 1983), p. 162.

30. William A. Stoever, "Japanese Boss, American Employees," *The Wharton Magazine* (Fall 1982), p. 46.

31. Ibid., p. 48.

32. Arnold Schechter, "Speaking the Language Eases Distance," *USA Today*, March 7, 1985, p. 3D.

33. Phatak, *International Dimensions of Management*, p. 135.

34. John Hillkirk, "Factories Get More Competitive," *USA Today*, August 3, 1987, p. 2B.

35. John Hillkirk, "Nissan Gears Up in USA," *USA Today*, October 28, 1987, p. 4B.

Readings

Alden, Vernon R. "Who Says You Can't Crack Japanese Markets." *Harvard Business Review* (January–February 1987), pp. 52–56.

Bartlett, Christopher A. "Managing Across Borders." *Sloan Management Review* (Summer 1987), pp. 7–17.

"Competitiveness: 23 Leaders Speak Out." *Harvard Business Review* (July–August 1987), pp. 106–123.

Connoly, Seamus G. *Finding, Entering and Succeeding in a Foreign Market.* New York: Prentice-Hall, 1987.

Kirkland, Richard Jr. "How to Be a Global Manager." *Fortune*, March 14, 1988, pp. 52–58.

Mitroff, Ian I. *Business Not as Usual.* San Francisco: Jossey-Bass, 1987.

Porter, Michael E., ed. *Competitiveness in Global Industries.* Boston: Harvard Business School Press, 1986.

Rennie, John C. *Exportise.* Boston: Small Business Foundation of America, 1987.

Tolchin, Martin and Susan Tolchin. *Buying into America: How Foreign Money Is Changing the Face of Our Nation.* New York: Times Books, 1988.

VanMesdag, Martin. "Winging It in Foreign Markets," *Harvard Business Review* (January–February 1987), pp. 71–74.

CASES

17.1 Down Mexico Way

Nick Carson has just returned from a trip to Mexico. He has been conducting negotiations with a South Korean manufacturer to supply the plastic parts his new plant will need when it is completed in about three months. His plant will supply several foreign-owned plants in Mexico with a variety of components, and his production will require several plastic moldings that the South Korean company is willing to supply.

Nick's expansion into Mexico represents his first foreign operation. His company, located in Kentucky, has grown rapidly by feeding parts to a variety of foreign-owned companies that have recently opened in the Midwest. His newest customer is located in southern

California and will be supplied by the Mexican plant once it is in full operation. Nick will have three plants in operation when the Mexican plant opens. The two in Kentucky are managed from a central headquarters with two plant managers reporting to Nick. Nick is thinking of letting his son run the Mexican plant and report directly to Nick in Kentucky.

Nick chose Mexico because of its average hourly wage of $1.05, its nearness to his California customers, and the growing market of foreign-owned companies in Mexico. He does not think any special requirements will be imposed on his company because of the new plant. The Mexican government has made Nick's expansion possible by providing him with important tax concessions and with a low-cost loan to build the plant, things that Kentucky will do for foreigners but not for natives like Nick. If all goes according to plan, Nick plans to move the production from one of his Kentucky plants to his Mexican plant.

Over the past five years, Nick's customers have steadily grown in number and changed in nationality. Today, more than half Nick's business is done with foreign-owned multinationals doing production in the Midwest. Another third of his business will be in California, and that is also with foreign-owned manufacturers. With the potential for many new customers in Mexico, Nick feels he has positioned himself properly for expansion into the next decade.

For Discussion

1. How do you think Nick's formal organization will change with the addition of the Mexican plant?
2. What staffing problems can Nick expect to deal with?
3. Do you see any potential problems for Nick given his customer base? If so, what are they?

17.2   Getting Ready to Negotiate

Ellison Endicott, III, was busy with the details of the upcoming negotiations with the "camel drivers" as he liked to call them. As the third

Endicott to head the company, Ellison believed it was his duty to carry on the tradition of handling important company negotiations in person. He liked to meet the people his company would deal with in a one-on-one fashion. It was the style his father liked and one that Ellison felt most at home with. The negotiations with the Arabs would go better, he felt, if each person got to know the other. Not one for formalities, Ellison preferred a handshake to a contract. Ellison knew his business and wanted to know, firsthand, every individual who had big bucks to spend for his company's products.

"We have two weeks to prepare our pitch," said Ellison. He and his sales professionals were meeting to determine their approach to the negotiations. "Have we got a translator on board?" asked Ellison.

"We do," replied Patterson, the vice-president of marketing.

"Pat, I want these negotiations to run smoothly. It will be our first big step into the Middle East. Those camel drivers have big bucks to spend, and most of them are ours. We want to get some of them back here in the good old U.S.A."

"Mr. Endicott," said Pat, "I've done a little research on the country and its customs. The whole place is dry, and the women wear veils in public. It's about as chauvinistic an environment as you can find. Their government is run by a royal family, and most of the key jobs are held by a small, inner circle of brothers and first cousins of the king."

"What have you got on the main man we will be seeing, Ali Ben Yassur?"

"He's got three wives and about ten kids. Near as I can tell, he is a distant relation to the king or has close ties to him at the very least. He's in his fifties and has the power to make deals."

"Who's in charge of getting the gifts for Ali, his wives, and kids?"

"I am, Mr. Endicott," replied Walters, Patterson's second in command. "I have perfume, sports equipment, and an engraved watch. I spent most of the $1,000 you allowed me to spend."

"Fine, fine," said Ellison. "I don't want to appear to be chintzy. Nothing gets the other guy indebted to you quicker than nice gifts.

Just be sure they are wrapped right and get on the plane when we do."

"We have the reservations, Mr. Endicott. I've allowed two full days for business conferences if we need them. We arrive at 8 P.M. their time and meet with Ali at 10 A.M. the following day. Carter from legal, Walters, you, and me all have separate rooms on one floor at the hotel."

"I want all of you to be with me when we meet Ali. I want the meeting to be informal. I will do all the talking through the translator. You did get that kid from our embassy, didn't you?"

"Yes, Mr. Endicott. His name is Bently Smith-Overson. He's from England and has worked for our embassy for about a year. He will be with us for the two days if we need him."

"Sounds like a good man. Carter, I will be checking with you throughout the talks, so stay close. I'll be pushing for our usual terms, but I will be demanding cash up front, the day of delivery. They have the money, and I'm not compromising on that. It's not our usual way, but I don't want any hassles like trying to collect our money in a foreign country. If we compromise early with these people, we may find later negotiations a lot tougher. We don't want to appear weak. My strategy is always the same. I lay my cards on the table and stand firm on all the terms."

For Discussion

1. What parts of Endicott's strategy are likely to cause him problems?
2. What additional preparations would you urge Endicott and his people to make before they meet with Ali?
3. What bias or perceptions does Endicott have that are the foundation for his "international strategy"?

APPENDIX A   Managing Your Time

Time is a precious resource. We all have exactly the same number of hours in each day, so the essential difference among us is how we use those hours. Many of us waste hours because we see them as "free"—they represent no direct cost to us. We learn that time is one resource that, once spent, is nonrenewable. Time and money must be budgeted if we are to get the best use from them.

Time Is Money

Most people do not really know what their time is worth. If you are paid an hourly wage, you may think that the pay you receive for one hour is the value of your time. That is only part of the value each of your hours has. What about the cost of your fringe benefits? Studies tell us that the average employee receives benefits that equal about 35 percent of his or her paycheck. That's an additional value of 35 cents for each dollar received in a paycheck. Exhibit A shows you the way you can place an accurate price on your time. It assumes a forty-hour workweek and details figures for both salaried and hourly paid individuals.

After you use the exhibit to calculate your time's value, ask yourself if the money you receive for each hour you spend is worth it, given how you spent each hour. Is reading the daily paper for twenty minutes each morning at work really giving you the return that the dollars those minutes represent are worth? If not, you will see how certain blocks of time may be used to greater advantage. You will be able to decide which tasks really belong at work and which should be left for when you are not on the payroll.

Budgeting Your Time

If you are going to use your time in more productive ways, you have to attempt to control it and to eliminate, as much as possible, others' control over it. Budgeting will help you improve on the ways you use time because

EXHIBIT A
What My Time at Work Is Worth

Weekly Salary	Benefits 35% of Salary	Total Salary	Value per Hour	Value per Minute
$250	$ 87.50	$337.50	$ 8.44	$ .14
350	122.50	472.50	11.81	.20
500	175.00	675.00	16.88	.28

Pay per Hour	Benefits	Total Hourly Pay	Value per Minute
$ 5	$1.75	$ 6.75	$ .11
10	3.50	13.50	.23
15	5.25	20.25	.34

it is a plan for using time designed by you. Creating a budget begins with knowing how you use time now and how much time you will have available for use. Next, you must know what influences exist on your use of time, and plan with those limits in mind.

Time Logs

Exhibit B is an example of a daily time log. It allows you to keep track of how you are spending your time each day. It lists sets of tasks connected with both regular and unexpected activities. Regular activities are those connected with the routines of each day at work. The unexpected represent unplanned-for interruptions that are usually connected with someone else's desire to include you in his or her day. Try to get rid of as many of these as you can. Request that uninvited guests reserve their conversations to breaks and mealtimes. Uninvited callers can be requested to put their requests in the form of short memos that can be dealt with at your leisure. At the end of each day, review your time log results by asking yourself the following questions:

- What did you spend time on that you should not have?
- Did you plan to use your time in any ways? Did those plans work out? Why or why not?

EXHIBIT B
Daily Time Log

Use this log to keep track of how you spend your time at work, away from work, or both. Use multiples of 5-minute intervals, and keep track in minutes.

Regular Activities	Mon	Tue	Wed	Thur	Fri	Sat	Sun	Totals
Time spent with others								
1. Evaluating/praising/disciplining								
2. Attending scheduled meetings								
3. Training/coaching								
4. Making telephone calls								
5. Meals and breaks								
6. Other (specify) _____								
Time spent alone								
1. Reading memos, letters, reports								
2. Preparing reports and correspondence								
3. Planning and scheduling work								
4. Efforts at self-development								
5. Travel time: to and from scheduled events								
6. Other (specify) _____								
Unexpected Activities								
1. Receiving telephone calls								
2. Communicating with "drop-ins"								
3. Attending "last minute" meetings								
4. Dealing with unexpected problems								
5. Other (specify) _____								
Totals								

- What uses of your time can be eliminated?
- What patterns or trends are emerging in how you use your time? How have others influenced your use of time?
- What have you learned about yourself today? How will tomorrow be different?

Budgeting time works in the same ways that budgeting money does. Both require thought and some degree of trial-and-error experimentation. Both begin with givens—the blocks of time or money already committed to achieve goals. Money budgets include rent, other major categories of fixed expenses (expenses that do not change from week to week or month to month), and savings. Time budgets are concerned with the time you have available to use productively—the time left to you after sleeping, eating, commuting, etc.

When you know your available time to program for productive uses, you are ready to budget. Divide your work into projects or units. Examine each with an eye toward its importance and the amount of time you think each will take to complete. Assign your work priorities such as "urgent," "routine," and "due within one week." Block out the time you will need for each task, and spread that time over specific hours of specific days you have available.

If you have never really worked at budgeting your time, you will experience some frustrations. You will plan, but your plans will be interrupted by events that you failed to foresee. Start your budgeting with the next full week in mind.

Daily Planners

Exhibit C is an example of a daily planner. It asks you to plan your days by considering the specific goals that you wish to accomplish first. By listing these in the order you wish to accomplish them, you will give yourself specific targets to be hit throughout the day. After listing your goals, use the activities section to list the specific actions, people, and events that you need to reach your goals. Remember that daily planners are just one tool to help you make more efficient and effective use of your time. They are not set in concrete. They can be changed to flex with the day as it unfolds. But regular use of them can help you take charge of your day and learn from the experiences of each day.

When reviewing your daily planners, ask yourself the following questions:

- Did I accomplish what I expected to accomplish? If not, why not?
- Were my estimates of time realistic? If not, why not?
- What have I learned that will improve my planning?

EXHIBIT C
Daily Planner

Start by listing your major objectives for the day in the order in which you wish to accomplish them. Under the Activities section, list the specific tasks you need to perform to reach your objectives and the estimated starting and ending times for each. Complete the Results section at end of day.

My Objectives for Today:

_____ 19 _____

1. _____
2. _____
3. _____
4. _____
5. _____

Activities (who, what, when, where, how)	Starting Time	Ending Time
1. _____		
2. _____		
3. _____		
4. _____		
5. _____		
6. _____		
7. _____		
8. _____		
9. _____		
10. _____		

Results:

_____

What to Carry Over to Tomorrow:

_____
_____
_____

Time management is helped by keeping track of how you spend time, but the essence of good time management is more concerned with how you should spend your time. Using a daily time log and a daily planner will tell you what you are or plan on doing with your time, not what you *should* be doing with it. If all that you are listing are your meetings, appointments, tasks, and deadlines, you are not really managing your time. To move away from simple listings to more effective planning, consider answers to the following questions when scheduling your time:

- What do I need to do to accomplish my goals?
- What needs to be done to benefit my people?
- What must be done to improve my department?
- What can be done to help me advance in my career?

These questions need to be asked each day, and they must consider both the near-term and long-range views connected with each.

Barriers to Effective Time Use

Your primary barrier is yourself—your health, mental states, routines, habits, rituals, and attitudes about time and tasks. All of us procrastinate: We put off tasks or delay starting them because we dread doing them. They represent discomfort, inconvenience, or worse. Procrastination can also occur because we lack confidence in our abilities to perform certain tasks or because we don't know how to get started.

If the tasks require doing, you can avoid procrastination by using a "sandwich" approach: Schedule tasks you fear or find uncomfortable between tasks that are enjoyable. And give yourself a reward of some kind after successfully dealing with a task you don't particularly care to perform. Celebrate with a few moments of congratulations and a cup of coffee.

Many people make the mistake of equating the hours worked with the concept of productivity. The more hours worked, the more productive they feel they are. But studies and our own experiences tell us that, at some point, the hours invested begin to pay back less and less. Fatigue sets in, and our minds get foggy. Our judgments and results become flawed.

According to a 1988 study by Accountemps, employees have periods of time each day in which they are mos. and least productive. Twenty-three percent of those polled in a nationwide survey believed they were most productive in the early morning, 66 percent said the middle of the morning was their best time, and only 1 percent felt their most productive time was the early afternoon.[1] What is your most productive time each day? To what tasks do you routinely devote that time?

Others influence your use of time in positive and negative ways. Your boss may dictate your tasks and some of the priorities for them. Such decisions may or may not represent effective or efficient uses of your time. People who interrupt your day may do so in many ways. They drop in without an appointment to visit or discuss their problems. The phone is probably the largest reason for interruptions. It has a way of ringing and drawing your attention away from your work at irregular intervals.

All kinds of interruptions can be discouraged and reduced. Respectfully request that people make appointments so that you can prepare for their visits and schedule your time to include those visits. Ask you boss for regular times for passing requests, feedback, or instructions. Have someone screen your calls. Request that those who call you regularly put their thoughts in writing instead of talking on the phone. Dealing with memos can be more effective than dealing with phone calls. Restrict your socializing to normal break times or to after-hours conversations. Exhibit D offers a few additional suggestions on how to save time.

EXHIBIT D
Some Tips on Saving Time

1. Develop routines, procedures, work habits, and patterns that use your time more effectively. Update and refine them as your circumstances change.
2. Schedule time for relaxation and change-of-pace activities.
3. Keep a notepad handy for jotting down those insights and ideas that occur periodically.
4. Put waiting times to good use.
5. Put time saved on tasks to good use.
6. Label and attempt to remove unnecessary interruptions.
7. Use these magic words when approaching tasks:

   combine, simplify, eliminate, rearrange, delegate.

8. Program difficult tasks for your peak hours of efficiency.
9. Establish a respect for time as a valuable resource that is not to be wasted. Break down your hours on the job into the dollars that they represent.
10. Remember that leisure is enjoyed only when you are free of guilt, worry, and anxiety over work yet undone.

Improving Routines

In this section are some suggestions for improving the basic routines that many people face each day at work. Specifically, we look at handling the in-basket of work on your desk, processing paperwork, and maintaining your files.

A person's in-basket is the pile of papers waiting for processing. Reports, memos, records of all kinds, mail, and various publications help fill our in-baskets each day. The first step is to glance at each with an attempt to categorize or group them into several piles. Then determine the degree of importance or urgency that they represent. As you pick up each piece of paper, decide if it is a "keeper," discard," or "pass-along." A keeper is something you will want to save to work on yourself or to file for future reference. A discard is something we read or skim and determine has no lasting value. Junk mail is an example of a discard. Pass-alongs are things we should read but pass to others or assign to subordinates for their attention and consideration.

After your three piles are created, file your discards in the "circular file" (the wastebasket), pass along the pass-alongs, and devote your attention to assigning priorities to each of the remaining pieces of paper. Try to avoid handling each piece more than these two times. Items that carry deadlines for action should be logged on your weekly calendar twice— once on the day they are due and once on a date prior to the deadline that will give you a start-up time and allow sufficient time for their completion. Items for file should carry a suspense date—a date when their value will be lost and they are no longer worth saving. In this way, your files can be purged periodically of obsolete and outdated material.

For keepers that require your time and attention, decide just what action is necessary—a letter, a phone call, a conference. Log these on your calendar according to the priorities you establish. Integrate the new work due today with the work you planned to accomplish for today. Make any adjustments in scheduling that you believe to be necessary. Collect the trivial, less time-consuming tasks for a one- or two-hour block one day each week. Delegate them, if possible, and work out regular procedures for dealing with routine, recurring tasks.

As you deal with each item on your agenda for the day, keep at it until you finish. Keep a notepad handy for ideas that occur to you and that will help with or influence other tasks. Keep in mind that phone calls interrupt your schedule and concentration as well as those of others. Think twice before you pick up the phone to get someone else involved in your problems. Maybe a memo or some research on your part is a better solution.

Reference

1. Marcia Staimer, "USA Snapshots: Workers at Best Before Noon," *USA Today*, March 25, 1988, p. 1B.

APPENDIX B   Managers and Stress

Stress can be defined as the perceived discomfort arising from a lack of fit between the individual and the demands he or she feels compelled to meet.[1] It is the body's reaction to conditions that make demands on it. Although the source of stress can be one's family, one's psychological makeup, or one's job and working environment, we focus here on only the last-named source.

All people in the work environment, both managers and subordinates, are subject to job-related stress. Not all stress is negative; in fact, some people respond in a positive way to being "stressed." But excessive job-related stress for an extended period "can cause physical illness and psychological disturbance with psychosomatic as well as physical changes. While stress is an inevitable part of living and working, excessive pressure costs dearly in ill health, lost productivity, and increased personal problems."[2]

The Nature of Stress

Sources of Stress

From a clinical perspective, there are three general ways that stress actions arise:

1. *Stimulus-based stress.* The feeling of stress in an individual is caused by the stimulant or stressor. The stressor can vary from individual to individual. An example would be a feeling of stress stimulated by an employee having to meet with a manager for a performance appraisal session.

2. *Response-based stress.* The source of stress in this situation is not from a stimulant but from the response a person must make. The stressor is the psychological or physiological response of the individual. For example, when an employee is asked to change

behavior from an established pattern, this psychological or behavior change can cause stress.

3. *Stimulus-response-based stress.* In this situation, stress arises from
   a joint reaction to a stimulus and the accompanying response.
   For example, when a manager changes a report deadline, the
   change in deadline is a stress stimulant. In turn, the response
   the person must make—acceptance of an earlier deadline with
   no opportunity to modify it—can cause stress.

Knowing the general sources of stress can be important to a manager.
In working with employees and in evaluating personal stress, it is important
to realize that stress is unique to the individual and the situation. What
then are the specific conditions at work that can cause stress?

1. *Physical work environment.* This includes noise, temperature, pollution, vibration, and motion.
2. *Group conflicts.* This includes a lack of cohesiveness and inter-
   group conflict.
3. *Management style.* For a manager, this includes having to use a
   management style that is in conflict with a style preference; for a
   subordinate, it includes not being managed with an acceptable
   style. In both instances, stress can be produced.

In addition, conditions that cause stress include the reality of the perception that you

- Have too much work to do and not enough time to do it in.
- Are in doubt about how to proceed in solving a problem or mak-
  ing a decision.
- Feel that you lack control over the things that are affecting you.
- Are uncertain about your responsibilities (are experiencing role
  ambiguity).
- Are in conflict with others or dealing with others who are in con-
  flict with one another.
- Are required to do work that you don't want to do.
- Have responsibility for others.

According to a 1987 poll taken by *USA Today*, 80 percent of workers
say their jobs are a source of stress and 30 percent felt their jobs were very
stressful. What follows are the causes of stress at work and the percentages
of those polled who chose the causes:[3]

Type of work done	64%
Lack of communication	50
Understaffing	46
Employer's demands	44
Preoccupation with work	38
Incompetent supervisors	32
Not allowed to do a good job	32
Co-workers	32
Too many work hours	31
Incompetent subordinates	29

Signs of Stress

All of us respond differently to stress situations. Intense stress can affect people both physically and emotionally. Physical and emotional signs of stress in a person include high blood pressure; gastrointestinal disorders; high pulse rate; excessive use of medication and other kinds of drug abuse; and feelings of fear, tension, and depression. Behavioral changes can also be symptomatic of stress. These include a drop in normal work performance, missing meetings and deadlines, tardiness, absenteeism, and withdrawal from others at work.

Reactions to Stress

Reactions to stress vary from individual to individual. Two common responses are "flight or fight." Flight is a reaction to stress in which an individual attempts to avoid confronting the stressor. The person, either physically or psychologically, attempts to get away from the threatening situation. The fight syndrome, on the other hand, enables people to solve problems or to adjust to a new environment. People exhibiting the fight syndrome love a challenge and will fight through their problems using the physical and psychological stimulation that stress causes to help them overcome difficulties. Such people are strong competitors and have a low tolerance for accepting defeat or frustrations.

Depending on how people react to stress, it can cause them to achieve more than they otherwise would—to reach their potential. Some people thrive on the stress that changes bring and work best with the pressures of deadlines and a shortage of resources. Between 1975 and 1983, researchers at the University of Chicago studied several hundred executives at the Illinois Bell Company. The researchers concluded that the persons who handled stress the best had a personality trait they called "hardiness." Hardiness was defined as a style of thinking, a kind of world view that involves commitment, control, and challenge coupled with a strongly positive attitude toward life. As an answer to stress, hardiness was judged to be twice as effective as any other factor. According to the researchers, commitment is the ability to get involved with work. Control is the belief that you can influence events around you and have a willingness to act on that belief.[4]

Hardiness can be developed in adults but is usually formed in childhood. Learning that attitude involves the ability to put events into a personal perspective, deciding how they will affect you, imagining ways to change events, and putting those ideas into action.[5] People with hardiness tend to view change as a natural part of life and its developmental nature. Change and stress are viewed as stimuli to growth. People without hardiness tend to feel and act like passive victims of circumstances and tend to get sick in the face of stressful situations.

Clay Sherman, president of Management House, Inc., a Chicago management consulting firm, offers the following advice on how to cope with stress:[6]

- *Physical escape.* Sports after work, a walk during lunch or just walking away from your desk. "Go somewhere else and work for an hour."
- *Mental escape.* Daydream, look at snapshots of family.
- *Recreation.* Joke with a friend, go to a game room.
- *Socialize.* Talk about the problem with friends.
- *Vent.* Cry, yell, throw something. "Get it out of your system."
- *Problem solving.* Attack your work, confront the problem co-worker.

Managing Stress

Organizations and managers within the organizations have recognized the need for and are placing a priority on managing stress in the work environment. The motivation comes not only from humanitarian concerns and the observed loss in productivity but also from the fact that managers and companies are facing legal risks today. Employees and courts in many states are recognizing that job stress can cause physical and psychological harm. "Now courts divide claims of psychological injury into those arising from a discrete, identifiable accident and those arising from the effects of repetitive events, no one of which can be identified as causing the injury."[7] Courts are now allowing workers to be compensated for psychological injuries, and state workers' compensation boards allow compensation for psychological injuries that result from an accident involving physical injuries. This requires organizations and managers to examine scientific research about job stress, to understand how the various courts are treating employees' stress-related workers' compensation claims, and to take preventive measures to lessen their legal liability for such claims.

Individual Manager Actions

When managers spot a worker or fellow manager with stress symptoms, they can no longer afford to overlook them. Such people can be identified through frequent and direct contact and through a survey of their attitudes about their work and working environment. Once spotted, managers have an obligation to intervene in some way. Lessening stress-producing factors in a person's job or job environment is one kind of intervention; referring employees to a physician is another kind. Further, a subordinate may need additional training, help with a project, or a reduction in the noise level of the work area. Removing or reducing the conditions that can cause stress will help subordinates become more productive and healthier performers. Managers who can recognize job stress and its symptoms and who can help reduce the causes of stress or help their employees deal with their stress stand a better chance of keeping their employees healthy and productive than managers who fail to make such efforts.

Organizational Programs

Employee assistance programs are designed to help employees with a variety of problems. Most are designed to help people become healthier and more productive. In a 1986 survey of 293 companies nationwide, Hewitt Associates, a benefits consulting firm, found that 43 percent of the businesses surveyed have some kind of assistance program. An additional 10 percent were considering the addition of one or more assistance programs. Ninety-nine percent of the companies with employee assistance programs had one to deal with alcohol and drug abuse, 92 percent had a program to deal with psychological problems, 91 percent had a program to deal with marital or family problems, and 83 percent had a program designed to deal with stress.[8] Other employee assistance programs dealt with financial and legal matters. In various ways, all the programs uncovered by the survey dealt either with stress directly or with the problems that lead to stress in one's life and job.

Many companies have created special programs to lower stress or enable employees to cope with stress better. Examples of these programs include providing:

- Facilities for physical exercise ranging from jogging tracks to full gyms with instructors and organized classes.

- Quiet rooms for meditating and reading (many have their own libraries).
- Courses to teach employees stress reduction and coping techniques that deal with the "whole" person and include topics such as diet and nutrition, exercise, and time management.
- On-site or off-site confidential counseling concerning personal or career problems.

References

1. Laurie Larwood, *Organizational Behavior and Management* (Boston: Kent Publishing, 1984), pp. 182–183.
2. J. M. Ivancevich, M. T. Matteson, and E. P. Richards, III, "Who's Liable for Stress on the Job?" *Harvard Business Review* (March–April 1985), p. 61.
3. "Work Poll: Stress on the Job," *USA Today*, June 16, 1987, p. 7B.
4. Laura Kavesh, "Stress Meets Its Master—It's Called Hardiness," *Chicago Tribune*, August 16, 1984, sect. 5, p. 1.
5. Ibid., pp. 1, 6.
6. Kevin Maney, "Don't Let Stress Get the Best of You: Learn to Cope and Find Outlets," *USA Today*, June 16, 1987, p. 7B.
7. Ivancevich, et al., *Harvard Business Review* (March–April 1985), p. 62.
8. Carol Kleiman, "Firms Extending Hand to Troubled Employees," *Chicago Tribune*, April 26, 1987, sect. 8, p. 1.

Glossary

accountability Being answerable for the results of one's actions.

adverse impact The effect a selection device has when it excludes a significantly greater number of minority group members or women than other groups.

alternative A potential course of action that is likely to eliminate, correct, or neutralize the cause of a problem.

aptitude A fundamental capacity or talent—such as reasoning, verbalizing, and calculating—that may be innate or acquired.

assumptions The premises or conditions that planners accept as or know to be true and real because of their past experiences or those of others.

audit An internal or external method of control, primarily financial, that determines if records, reports, statements, and data they are based on are correct and in line with established rules and procedures.

authority The right to make decisions that commit the organization's resources or the legal right of a manager to tell someone to do or not to do something, also called formal or positional authority.

balance sheet The financial statement and control that examines an organization's assets and the ownership interests in them.

brainstorming A group effort at generating ideas and alternatives, using inside experts who focus on one issue or problem.

breakeven analysis A quantitative planning technique relating costs, revenue, and profit. It determines at what point income and expenses are equal—where an organization breaks even.

budget A single-use plan for predicting sources and amounts of income and how it is to be used.

budgeting A planning technique that attempts to formalize in writing the financial resources to be allocated for specific purposes.

chain of command The organizing principle concerned with the number of management positions in an organization and their unbroken connection to its top position.

change A shift or alteration in the present organizational environment.

change agent The individual responsible for introducing planned change in an organization. He or she may be an insider or outsider.

cohesion The measure of a group's solidarity—the degree to which the members share resources and ideas, and the degree of their willingness to cooperate with one another.

committee A group of people who volunteer or are appointed to serve as investigators, problem solvers, or decision makers.

communication The transmission of information and understanding from one person or group to another.

communication barrier Objects or behaviors that can interfere with communication effectiveness.

conceptual skill The ability to view the organization as a whole and see how the parts of the organization relate and depend on one another. Deals with ideas and abstractions.

conflict A disagreement between two or more organizational members or groups arising from the necessity for them to share resources or work activities or from the fact they have different status, goals, values, or perceptions.

contingency model A theory of leadership (of Fiedler) that holds that the effectiveness of a leader is determined by the interaction of the leader behavior (orientation) and three variables: leader–member relations, task structure, and leader position power.

continuum of leadership behavior Tannenbaum and Schmidt's visual representation of the various possible leadership approaches; the choice of one depends on the amount of decision making the leader is willing or able to share with subordinates. Positions along the continuum range from autocratic to free-rein approaches.

controlling Establishing performance standards used to measure progress toward goals.

crisis team Key people located throughout the organization who come together in an emergency to take charge and make the necessary decisions to deal with its impact on the organization.

critical path The longest path through a production flowchart or diagram from start to finish.

culture The distinctive way of life of a group of people; their design for living, which includes knowledge, beliefs, art, morals, and customs.

data Facts and figures that have not been processed.

decision The result of making a judgment or reaching a conclusion.

decision making A rational choice among alternatives—making a judgment or reaching a conclusion.

decision tree A graphic representation of the actions a manager can take and how these actions relate to future events.

delegation The downward transfer of formal authority from one person to another.

Delphi technique A forecasting technique using the opinions of outside experts.

demotion The movement from one position to another that has less pay or responsibility attached to it.

departmentation The creation of groups, subdivisions, or departments that will execute and oversee the various tasks that management considers essential.

development Preparing an employee for a future but fairly well-defined job at a higher level.

diagnostic control A monitoring device or system that attempts to determine what deviation from a standard is taking or has taken place.

division of labor The study of tasks deemed essential, the breaking down of tasks into parts or steps, and the assigning of one or more of those parts to an individual or position.

equity theory A motivation theory stating that people are influenced in their behavior choices (motivation) through the comparison of relative input–outcome ratios. People compare the ratios of their input (efforts) with outcome (rewards) to others' ratios to see if equity exists.

ethics A branch of philosophy concerned with what is honest and honorable in human conduct, its motives, and its ends. It is based on a system of moral principles and values.

expectancy theory A motivation theory stating that a person's behavior is influenced by the value of the rewards, the relationship of the rewards to the performance necessary, and the effort required for performance.

feedback A receiver's reaction to a message, through which a receiver becomes a sender.

feedback control A monitoring device or system designed to provide end-result information on a project for future planning.

feedforward control A monitoring device or system designed to detect and to anticipate deviations from standards at various points throughout ongoing processes.

fixed costs Costs unconnected to and separate from the costs of manufacturing a product or selling it.

forecast Planners' expectations about the likely or probable state of events or conditions at some time in the future.

functional authority Authority over specific activities that are undertaken by personnel in other departments.

game theory An operations research technique that attempts to predict how people or organizations will behave in competitive situations.

grapevine The communication system of the informal organization. It carries both rumors and messages.

horizontal group An informal group composed of individuals within the same work areas or on the same level of the formal organization.

human asset accounting A control method that treats the money spent on and for employees as investments rather than expenses.

human skill The ability to interact with other people successfully. To understand, work with, and relate to individuals and to groups of people.

hygiene factors Herzberg's list of causes most closely identified with unhappiness on the job. These extrinsic factors, if provided in the right qualities by management, can result in no job dissatisfaction.

impersonal communication Communication in which the participants do not interact directly.

income statement The financial statement and control that examines the organization's income and expenses.

induction Providing a person entering a company with the necessary information about the company.

informal organization The collection and interaction of informal groups within the formal organization.

information Data that have been deliberately selected, processed, and organized to be useful to an individual manager.

interaction chart A diagram that shows the informal interactions people have with one another at work.

interest Areas of activity that capture your imagination and curiosity and have a special appeal.

international management Managing resources across national borders, and adapting management principles and functions to the demands of foreign competition and environments.

interpersonal communication Communication delivered in either a face-to-face or voice-to-voice method.

job enlargement Increases in the variety or the number of tasks a job includes, not the quality or the challenge of those tasks.

job enrichment Designing a job to provide more responsibility, control, feedback, and authority for decision making.

job rotation Sending people to different jobs on a rotating or temporary basis.

Key Indicator Management A monitoring and control system using mutually agreed-on key measures, represented visually and at regular intervals, to judge a manager's or department's progress or lack thereof.

leadership The process of influencing the group or individual toward the accomplishment of goal setting or goal achievement.

life-cycle theory A theory of leadership that states that the leadership approach varies with the maturity of the individual. An employee's maturity is viewed as his or her task-related ability and experience as well as willingness to accept responsibility.

limiting factors Constraints managers work with that rule out potential alternatives.

line authority Direct supervisory authority from superior to subordinate.

linear programming A quantitative planning technique that attempts to determine the best way to allocate resources, when given the possible alternate uses for and limitations on the resources.

line departments Departments established to meet the major objectives of the organization.

management The process of setting and achieving goals through the execution of five basic management functions that utilize human, financial, and material resources.

management information system (MIS) A formal method of providing management with accurate and timely information in order for decision making and managerial functions and operations to be carried out effectively.

management by objectives (MBO) An approach to appraisals that requires subordinates to negotiate goals along with priorities and timetables for them in concert with their supervisors.

managerial grid Blake and Mouton's visual representation of possible leadership behaviors, of which the one that occurs will result from the leader's orientation (toward task or toward employee). A balance between the two extremes of orientation most often yields the most effective management behavior.

managers Those in positions of authority who make decisions to commit resources toward the achievement of goals.

maximize Make the best possible decision. Requires ideal resources—information, time, personnel, equipment, and supplies.

medium The method chosen to deliver a message.

message The information being transmitted in the communication process.

mission The formal statement about the central purpose behind the organization's existence—its reason to be.

mixed group An informal group composed of persons in different work areas and at different levels of the formal organization.

morals Concepts of right and wrong that form a system of principles upon which decisions can be based.

motivation The interaction of a person's internalized needs and external influences (equity, expectancy, and previous conditioning) that determines behavior designed to achieve a goal.

motivation factors Herzberg's list of conditions that can lead to an individual's job satisfaction. They are in-

trinsic to the job and offer satisfactions for psychological needs.

multinational corporation Companies with operating facilities—not just sales offices—in several foreign countries.

needs Physical or psychological conditions in humans that act as stimuli for behavior until satisfactions for them have been provided or achieved.

network A quantitative planning technique using activities and events to chart the flow of a project from start to finish and to calculate the shortest possible completion time for the project.

norm Any standard of conduct, or code, or pattern of behavior perceived by a group to be important for its members to honor or to conform to.

objective A goal or target that an individual or an organization intends to achieve through planning and plans.

objective performance appraisal Appraisal system in which the criteria for performance and the rating scale are defined.

obsolescence The condition in which a person or machine is no longer able to perform management's expectations.

operating plan A plan that focuses on the implementation or ongoing part of a manager's planning responsibilities.

organization (1) A group of two or more people that exists and operates to achieve clearly stated, common objectives. (2) The result of the organizing process; it consists of a whole made up of unified parts (a system), acting in harmony to execute tasks to achieve goals, in an effective and efficient manner.

organizational climate The psychological environment or personality of an organization in which people must work.

organizational development The long-range program for systematic renewal of an organization, based on an analysis of organizational problems.

organizational learning The "how" behind the attempts by organizations and their managers to integrate new ideas into established systems to produce better ways of doing things.

organization chart A visual representation of the ways in which an entire organization and each of its parts fit together.

organizing The management activity that determines the work activities to be done, classifies and groups that work, assigns the activities and delegates authority to do the work, and designs a hierarchy of decision-making relationships.

orientation Bringing a person into the specific working environment with emphasis on socialization, the specific work, and the work environment.

path-goal theory A leadership theory concerned with the ways in which a leader can influence a subordinate's motivation, goals, and attempts at goal achievement.

payback analysis Evaluation of investment alternatives by comparing the lengths of time necessary to pay back their initial costs.

performance appraisal A formal, structured system designed to measure an employee's actual performance against designated performance standards.

planning Setting objectives and determining the means (courses of action) to reach those objectives.

policy Broad guidelines to aid managers at every level in making decisions about recurring situations or functions.

power A person's ability to influence results. It comes from expertise, charisma, or ability to reward or coerce, or from formal position.

prevention control Monitoring devices or systems designed to establish conditions that will make it difficult or impossible for deviations from standards to occur.

problem The difference between a desirable situation and what actually happens—the "what is" compared with the "what should be."

procedure Plans that answer how to do something.

productivity The measurement of the amount of in-

put needed to generate any given amount of output. It is the basic measurement of the efficiency of businesses.

program A single-use plan for solving a problem or accomplishing a group of related activities needed to reach a goal.

program evaluation review technique (PERT) A network method of production scheduling that assigns four possible completion times to activities: the optimistic, the most likely, the pessimistic, and the expected time. The expected time is based on a probability analysis of the other three time estimates.

programmed decision Resolution by routine decision-making steps or procedures of a recurring challenge or problem.

project management The overseeing of a project by a project manager who must plan, organize, staff, and control those tasks needed to reach the desired outcome.

promotion Movement by a person into a position of higher pay and greater responsibilities.

quality circle A general planning technique involving workers and their supervisors in determining ways to improve methods, reduce waste and costs, and improve quality.

queueing (waiting line) models An operations research technique used to assist managers in deciding what length of waiting line or queue would be preferable.

ratio The relationship between two or more numbers. Financial ratios can be used to judge the liquidity and profitability of an organization as well as the ability of an organization to pay its debts.

receiver The person or persons intended as the audience for a message.

recruitment Finding people to meet the organization's demands for special skills, aptitudes, knowledge, and experience.

reinforcement theory A motivation theory stating that the behavior choices of a person are influenced by the supervisor's reactions to them and the rewards or penalties experienced in a similar situation.

responsibility The obligation to carry out one's assigned duties to the best of one's ability.

role Behaviors a manager is required to enact as he or she functions in the organizational environment. The role is influenced by the job description and the expectations of superiors, subordinates, and peers.

rule Plans that dictate human behavior or conduct at work.

satisfice Make the best possible decision you can with the time and information you have available.

selection Evaluating applicants and choosing the person who closely meets jobs demands.

sender The person or persons initiating a message.

separation A temporary or permanent way of losing employees.

simulation A model of a real or an actual activity or process that behaves like the real activity or process.

skill Mental or muscular-motor ability to do something well; a specific proficiency.

social audit A report (feedback) on the social performance of a business. It may be formal, informal, quantitative or qualitative, public or private.

socialization The process through which new members of an organization gain exposure to its values and norms, its policies and procedures, and the behaviors expected from new people.

social responsibility The moral and ethical content of managerial and corporate decisions; it is concerned with the values used in business decisions, over and above the pragmatic requirements imposed by legal principle and the market economy.

sociogram A diagram of group attraction.

span of control The principle of organization that is concerned with the number of subordinates each manager should have to direct.

staff authority Authority to serve in an advisory capacity; authority to advise.

staff departments These assist all departments in meeting the objectives of the organization through advice or technical assistance.

staffing The management activity that attempts to attract good people to an organization and to hold on to them.

standard A quantitative or qualitative measuring device designed to help monitor the performances of people, capital goods, or processes.

strategic plan A decision about long-range goals and the course of action to achieve those goals. Strategic plans influence the construction of tactical plans.

strategic planning Planning that focuses on organizational direction, involving all levels of management.

subjective performance appraisal Appraisal system in which the criteria for performance and the rating scale are not specifically defined.

system A group of interrelated parts, operating as a whole, to achieve stated goals or to function according to a plan or design.

tactical plan A decision about short-term goals and the courses of action that will enable an organization to achieve those goals. Tactical plans help achieve strategic goals.

technical skill The ability to use the processes, practices, techniques, and tools of the specialty area a manager supervises.

therapeutic control A monitoring device or system designed to sense what deviations from standards are taking place and why and then to take a corrective action.

training Imparts skills, knowledge, and attitudes needed by individuals or groups to improve their abilities to perform in their present jobs.

transfer A lateral move from one position to another having similar pay and a similar responsibility level.

unity of command The organizing principle that states that each person in an organization should take orders from and report to only one person.

unity of direction The organizing principle that states that each group of activities having the same objective should have one head.

variable costs Costs connected to the manufacture or sale of a product.

vertical group An informal group composed of individuals who work in the same areas but on different levels of the formal organization.

Bibliography

Adams, J. Stacy. "Toward an Understanding of Equity." *Journal of Abnormal and Social Psychology*, November 1963, pp. 422–36.

Albert, J.L. "Census Survey Shows Higher Education Pays." *USA Today*, October 2, 1987, p. 11A.

Allport, Gordon and Leo Postman. *The Psychology of Rumor*. New York: Holt, Rinehart & Winston, 1947.

"America's R&D Performance: A Mixed Review." *Business Week*, April 20, 1987, p. 59.

Argyris, Chris and Donald Schon. *Organizational Learning: A Theory of Action Perspective*. Reading, Mass.: Addison-Wesley, 1978.

"At Work: Clocking Time Stolen from Our Jobs." *USA Today*, November 26, 1986, p. 4B.

"At Work: Hard Work Remains Key Rung on Corporate Ladder." *USA Today*, November 4, 1987, p. 4B.

"At Work: How Do Your Office Ethics Compare?" *USA Today*, September 30, 1987, p. 4B.

"At Work: Resume Report: Keep It Simple." *USA Today*, December 2, 1987, p. 4B.

Auger, J. Daniel and Robert W. Knapp, eds. *Systems Analysis Techniques*. New York: John Wiley & Sons, 1974.

Barnes, Louis B. "Managing the Paradox of Organizational Trust." *Harvard Business Review*, March–April 1981, pp. 107–18.

Baumann, Marty. "USA Snapshots: Ethics in Business." *USA Today*, November 27, 1987, p. 1B.

"Big Talent Search Among Rank and File." *U.S. News & World Report*, November 30, 1981, p. 55.

Black, Howard and Robert Pennington. "Labor Market Analysis as a Test of Discrimination." *Personnel Journal*, no. 59, (August 1980), pp. 649–52.

Blake, Robert R. and Jane S. Mouton. *The Managerial Grid*. Houston: Gulf Publishing Company, 1964.

Blake, Robert R. and Jane S. Mouton, et al. "Breakthrough in Organizational Development." *Harvard Business Review*, November–December 1964, pp. 135–138.

Bock, Robert H. "Modern Values and Corporate Responsibility." *MSU Business Topics*, Spring 1980, pp. 8–12.

Buehler, Vernon M. and Y. K. Shetty. "Managerial Response to Social Responsibility Challenge." *Academy of Management Journal*, March 1976, pp. 66–78.

Burck, Charles G. "What Happens When Workers Manage Themselves?" *Fortune*, July 27, 1981, p. 62.

Burck, Charles G. "What's in It for the Unions?" *Fortune*, August 24, 1981, pp. 88–92.

Burton, Gene E. "Organizational Development: A Systematic Process." *Management World*, March 1976.

Business Classics: Fifteen Key Concepts for Managerial Success. Harvard Business Review, 1975.

"Businesses Plan to Boost Capital Spending by 2.8%." *Chicago Tribune*, June 10, 1987, sect. 3, p. 1.

"Business Facts: Foreign Investments in U.S. Businesses." *Chicago Tribune*, July 15, 1987, sect. 3, p. 1.

"Business Facts: U.S. Government Debt Held by Foreigners." *Chicago Tribune*, February 4, 1988, sect. 3, p. 1.

Byham, W. C. "Starting an Assessment Center the Correct Way." *The Personal Administrator*, February 1980, pp. 27–32.

Byrne, John A. "Businesses Are Signing Up for Ethics 101." *Business Week*, February 15, 1988, pp. 56–57.

Carroll, Doug. "Consolidations Make Carmakers' World Smaller." *USA Today*, May 4, 1987, p. 6B.

"Chevron to Pay Big Pollution Fine." *Chicago Tribune*, January 24, 1988, sect. 7, p. 4.

Chew, W. Bruce. "No-Nonsense Guide to Measuring Productivity." *Harvard Business Review*, January–February, 1988, p. 114

"Chrysler Prepared to Return to Europe." *Chicago Tribune*, January 24, 1988, sect. 7, p. 7.

Churchill, Niel C. "Budget Choice: Planning vs. Control." *Harvard Business Review*, July–August 1984, p. 151–152.

Classics in Management, revised ed. Harwood F. Merrill, ed. American Management Association, 1970.

Cleveland, Harlan, Gerald J. Mangone, and John C.

Adams, *Overseas Americans*. New York: McGraw-Hill, 1960.

Coakley, Michael. "Even Mighty Exxon Mired in Ooze of Oil Uncertainty." *Chicago Tribune*, February 28, 1982, sect. 5, p. 5.

Cohen, Nadia. "What Employers Dislike the Most." *Chicago Tribune*, January 20, 1985, sect. 8, p. 1.

Cross, Robert. "Corporate Conscience: Putting Big Business on Its Best Behavior." *Chicago Tribune*, January 3, 1985, sect. 5, p. 1.

Dalton, M. *Men Who Manage*. New York: John Wiley & Sons, 1959.

Davis, Keith. *Human Behavior at Work: Organizational Behavior*. 7th ed. New York: McGraw-Hill, 1985.

Detz, Joan. "The Adaptive Leader." *Success*, June 1987, p. 46.

Dresang, Joel. "Companies Get Serious About Ethics." *USA Today*, December 9, 1986, p. 2B.

Drucker, Peter F. *Management: Tasks, Responsibilities, Practices*. New York: Harper & Row, 1974.

Drucker, Peter F. *Managing for Results*. New York: Harper & Row, 1964.

Drucker, Peter F. *The Practice of Management*. New York: Harper & Row, 1954.

Dubrin, Andrew J. *Fundamentals of Organizational Behavior*. New York: Pergamon Press, 1974.

Dunfee, Thomas W. "Employee Ethical Attitudes and Business Firm Productivity." *The Wharton Annual (1984)*, University of Pennsylvania, Pergamon Press, p. 76.

Dunlop, John T. et al. "Business and Public Policy." *Harvard Business Review*, November–December 1979, pp. 85–97.

The Equal Employment Opportunity Act of 1972. Subcommittee on Labor of the Committee on Labor and Public Welfare, United States Senate, March 1972, p. 3.

"Execs Waste Time Reading Memos." *USA Today*, April 8, 1987, p. 7B.

Fayol, Henri. *General and Industrial Management*. London: Sir Isaac Pitman & Sons, 1949.

"Fibbing on the Job." *Chicago Tribune*, November 16, 1987, sect. 4, p. 1.

Fiedler, Fred E. "The Contingency Model—New Directions for Leadership Utilization." *Journal of Contemporary Business*, no. 4, 1974, pp. 65–80.

Fiedler, Fred E. and Martin M. Chemers. *Leadership and Effective Management*. Glenview, Ill.: Scott, Foresman, 1974.

Fiore, Michael J. "Why Unions Don't Work Anymore." *Inc.* (March 1982), p. 17.

Fisher, Lawrence M. "Clipping Paper Costs." *The New York Times*, December 13, 1987, sect. 3, p. 1.

"Foreign Investment in U.S. Up." *Chicago Tribune*, June 25, 1987, sect. 3, p. 3.

Foulkes, Frederick K. "How Top Nonunion Companies Manage Employees." *Harvard Business Review*, September–October 1981, pp. 90–96.

Fouri, William M. *Introduction to the Computer*. 3rd ed. Englewood Cliffs, N.J.: Prentice Hall 1981.

Fourre, James P. *Quantitative Business Planning Techniques*. New York: American Management Association, 1970.

Frankena, William K. *Thinking About Morality*. Ann Arbor: University of Michigan Press, 1980.

Friedman, Milton. "The Social Responsibility of Business Is to Increase Its Profits." *New York Times Magazine*, September 13, 1970, p. 142.

Gellerman, Saul W. "Why 'Good' Managers Make Bad Ethical Choices." *Harvard Business Review*, July–August 1986, pp. 88–89.

Goodman, Paul S. and Abraham Fredman." An Examination of Adam's Theory of Inequity." *Administrative Science Quarterly*, 1971, pp. 271–88.

Goodpastor, Kenneth E. and John B. Matthews, Jr. "Can a Corporation Have a Conscience?" *Harvard Business Review*, January–February 1982, pp. 132–41.

Graham, John L. and Roy A. Herberger, Jr. "Negotiators Abroad—Don't Shoot from the Hip." *Harvard Business Review*, July–August 1983, p. 162.

Grayson, C. Jackson. "What Every CEO Should Know About Productivity." *Chief Executive*, no. 15, 1981, pp. 36–40.

Gregory, Robert H. and Richard L. Van Horn. "Value and Cost of Information." *Systems Analysis Techniques*, edited by J. Daniel Auger and Robert W. Knapp. New York: John Wiley & Sons, 1974, pp. 473–489.

Greiner, Larry E. "Evolution and Revolution as Organizations Grow." *Harvard Business Review*, July–August 1972, pp. 37–46.

Greiner, Larry E. "Patterns of Organization Change." *Harvard Business Review*, May–June, 1967, p. 119.

Gross, Philip. "How to Assess Your Internal Controls." *Inc.*, June 1981.

Guest, R.H. "Quality of Work Life: Learning from Tarrytown." *Harvard Business Review*, July–August 1979, pp. 77–85.

Hackman, J.R. and G.R. Oldham. *Task Design*. Reading, Mass.: Addison-Wesley, 1980.

Hall, D.T. and M.A. Morgan. "Career Development and Planning." *Contemporary Problems in Personnel*, rev. ed., edited by W.C. Hamner and Frank L. Schmidt. Chicago: St. Clair Press, 1977.

Hammer, W. C. "Reinforcement Theory and Contingency Management in Organizational Settings." *Or-*

ganizational Behavior and Management: A Contingency Approach, edited by H.L. Tosi and W. C. Hammer. New York: John Wiley & Sons, 1974.

Hampton, David R., Charles E. Summer, and Ross A. Webber. *Organizational Behavior and the Practice of Management,* 5th ed. Glenview, Ill.: Scott, Foresman, 1987.

Harmon, Theo and William G. Scott. *Management in the Modern Organization.* Boston: Houghton Mifflin, 1970.

Harvard Business Review on Human Relations. New York: Harper & Row, 1979.

Harvard Business Review on Management. New York: Harper & Row, 1975.

Hawken, Paul. "Problems, Problems." *Inc.,* September 1987, pp. 24–25.

Hayes, Robert H. "Why Japanese Factories Work." *Harvard Business Review,* July–August 1981, pp. 56–66.

Henrici, Stanley B. "How Deadly Is the Productivity Disease?" *Harvard Business Review,* November–December 1981, pp. 127–29.

Hersey, Paul and Kenneth Blanchard. *Management of Organizational Behavior,* 2nd ed. Englewood Cliffs, N.J.: Prentice-Hall, 1972.

Herskovits, Melville J. *Man and His Works.* New York: Alfred A. Knopf, 1952, p. 17.

"Hertz Is Doing Some Body Work—On Itself." *Business Week,* February 15, 1988, p. 57.

Herzberg, Frederick. "One More Time: How Do You Motivate Employees?" *Business Classics: Fifteen Key Concepts for Managerial Success. Harvard Business Review* 1975, pp. 13–22.

Heyel, Carl, ed. *The Encyclopedia of Management,* 3rd ed. New York: Van Nostrand Reinhold, 1982, p. 495.

"Highway Cash Case Nearing Quiet Close." *Chicago Tribune,* December 21, 1987, sect. 1, p. 9.

Hillkirk, John. "Factories Get More Competitive." *USA Today,* August 3, 1987, p. 2B.

Hillkirk, John. "Japanese Capitalize on USA Research." *USA Today,* March 2, 1988, pp. 1B–2B.

Hillkirk, John. "Japanese to Open More USA Plants." *USA Today,* December 23, 1987, p. 1B

Hillkirk, John. "Nissan Gears Up in USA." *USA Today,* October 28, 1987, p. 4B.

Hodgetts, Richard and Steven Altman. *Organizational Behavior.* Philadelphia: W. B. Saunders Company, 1979.

Hoerr, John et al. "Privacy." *Business Week,* March 28, 1988, p. 61.

House, Robert J. and Terence R. Mitchell. "Path-Goal Theory of Leadership." *Journal of Contemporary Business,* no. 4, 1974, pp. 81–97.

"How the Japanese Manage in the U.S.," *Fortune,* June 15, 1981, pp. 97–98, 102–03.

Imberman, A. A. "Why Are Most Foreman Training Courses A Failure?" *Bedding,* no. 6, 1969, pp. 40–41.

"Information Thieves Are Now Corporate Enemy No. 1." *Business Week,* May 5, 1986, p. 120–21.

Janson, Robert L. "Graphic Indicators of Operations." *Harvard Business Review,* November–December 1980, pp. 164–70.

Kahn, Joseph P. "When Bad Management Becomes Criminal." *Inc.,* March 1987, pp. 46–48, 50.

Katz, Gregory. "It's the Truth: A Lot of Us Lie, at Least a Little." *USA Weekend,* March 6–7, 1987, p. 4.

Katz, Robert L. "Skills of an Effective Administrator." *Harvard Business Review,* September–October 1974, pp. 90–102.

Katz, Robert L., Daniel and Robert L. Kahn. *The Social Psychology of Organization,* 2nd ed. New York: John Wiley & Sons, 1978.

Keller, Robert and Andrew Szilagyi. "A Longitudinal Study of Leader Reward Behavior, Subordinate Expectancies, and Satisfaction." *Personnel Psychology,* Spring 1978, pp. 119–29.

Kelley, Joseph. *Organizational Behavior,* rev. ed. Homewood, Ill.: Richard D. Irwin, 1974.

Klatt, L. A., R. G. Murdick, and F. E. Schuster. *Human Resource Management: A Behavioral Systems Approach.* Homewood, Ill.: Richard D. Irwin, 1978.

Kleiman, Carol. "Hate Your Job? Welcome to the Club." *Chicago Tribune,* October 18, 1987, sect. 8, p. 1

Kleiman, Carol. "Sunny Forecast for Class of '88." *Chicago Tribune,* December 18, 1987, sect. 2, p. 1.

Klinfelter, John and James Thompkins. "Adverse Impact in Employment Selection." *Public Personnel Management,* May–June 1979, pp. 199–204.

Kobrin, Stephen J. "Assessing Political Risk Overseas." *The Wharton Magazine,* 6, no. 2, Winter 1981–82, pp. 25–27.

Koontz, Harold and Cyril O'Donnel. *Management.* New York: McGraw-Hill, 1976.

Kotter, John P. *Organizational Dynamo: Diagnosis and Intervention.* Reading, Mass.: Addison-Wesley, 1978.

Kupfer, Andrew. "How to Be a Global Manager." *Fortune,* March 14, 1988, p. 52.

Latture, Richard. "USA Snapshots: Bad for Business." *USA Today,* February 26–28, 1988, p. 1A.

Ledvinka, James and Robert Gatewood. "EEO Issues with Pre-Employment Inquiries." *The Personnel Administrator,* no. 2, 1977, pp. 22–26.

Lesson, Marjorie. *Basic Concepts in Data Processing.* Dubuque, Iowa: Wm. C. Brown Co., 1975.

Levison, H. "Management by Whose Objectives?" *Harvard Business Review,* July–August 1970, pp. 125–35.

Lewin, Kurt. "Frontiers in Group Dynamics: Concept,

Method, and Reality in Social Science." *Human Relations*, no. 1, 1947, pp. 5–41.

Lewyn, Mark. "Computerline: Average Take of Computer Fraud: $600,000." *USA Today*, May 7, 1987, p. 6B.

Likert, Rensis. *The Human Organization*. New York: McGraw-Hill, 1976.

"Listening and Responding to Employees' Concerns." (An interview with A. W. Clausen), *Harvard Business Review*, January–February 1980, p. 104.

Little, Rod. "USA Snapshots: Experience Counts." *USA Today*, February 19, 1988, p. 13.

Little, Rod. "USA Snapshots: Who Funds R&D Programs." *USA Today*, June 23, 1987, p. 1B.

Loeb, Karen. "USA Snapshots: Office-Automation Sales." *USA Today*, June 8, 1987, p. 1E.

Loeb, Karen. "USA Snapshots: The Trouble with Resumes." *USA Today*, October 2, 1987, p. 1B.

Longworth, R. C. "Japan's Script Has Made-in-USA Cast." *Chicago Tribune*, May 13, 1987, sect. 3, p. 3.

"Lower Productivity? Blame Bosses: Report." *Chicago Tribune*, October 19, 1979, sect. 4, p. 9.

McClelland, David C. *The Achieving Society*. New York: Van Nostrand Reinhold, 1971.

McClelland, David C. "Power Is the Great Motivator." *Harvard Business Review*, March–April 1976, pp. 100–10.

McGregor, Douglas. *The Human Side of Enterprise*. New York: McGraw-Hill, 1960.

"Major Cause of Business Problems: Poor Managers." (An interview with Professor Robert H. Hayes, Harvard Business School), *U.S. News & World Report*, December 8, 1980, pp. 69–70.

Mandell, Steven L. *Information Processing and Data Processing*, 3rd ed. St. Paul: West Publishing Co., 1988, p. 9.

March, James G. and Herbert Simon. *Organizations*. New York: John Wiley & Sons, 1958.

Marino, Kenneth. "Conducting an Internal Compliance Review of Affirmative Action." *Personnel*, March–April 1980, pp. 22–23.

Marshall, Verena and Ron Cacioppe. "A Survey of Differences Between Managers and Subordinates." *Leadership and Organizational Development Journal*, no. 4, 1986, p. 17–25.

Maslow, Abraham H. "A Theory of Human Motivation." *Psychological Review*, 50, 1943, pp. 370–96.

Matulis, Scott. "Employee Theft: The Inside Job." *Entrepreneur*, March 1988, p. 82.

Mayfield, Marlys. *Thinking for Yourself: Developing Critical Thinking Skills Through Writing*. Belmont, Calif.: Wadsworth, 1987.

Mayo, Elton. *The Human Problems of an Industrial Civilization*. New York: Macmillan, 1933.

Meddis, Sam. "White-collar Crime Doesn't Pay; Federal Convictions Up." *USA Today*, September 28, 1987, p. 12A.

Mee, John F. "Matrix Organizations." *Business Horizons*, no. 2, 1964, pp. 70–72.

Memmott, Mark. "At Work: 6 Keys to Exec Success." *USA Today*, March 18, 1987, p. 9B.

Memmott, Mark. "Forward Thinkers Plan Careers Backward." *USA Today*, October 7, 1987, p. 5B.

Memmott, Mark. "We Work More and Like It Less." *USA Today*, May 19, 1987, p. 1B.

"Metro Report: Hot Spots: Inc.'s Annual Ranking of America's Cities." *Inc.*, March 1988, p. 74.

Mintzberg, Henry. "The Manager's Job: Folklore and Fact." *Harvard Business Review*, July–August 1975, pp 49–61.

Mockler, Robert J. *The Management Control Process*. Englewood Cliffs, N.J.: Prentice-Hall, 1972.

"Motorola Disciplines 59 in Defense Cost Case." *Chicago Tribune*, April 1, 1988, sect. 3, p. 3.

Mullins, Marcy Eckroth. "Why Employees Quit." *USA Today*, February 29, 1988, p. 5B.

Nadler, David A. "The Fine Art of Managing Change." *The New York Times*, November 29, 1987, p. F3.

Naisbitt, John. "Why Managers Must Be Facilitators: The Reasons Behind Participative Management Are Pragmatic and Profit Oriented." *Success*, April 1987, p. 12.

El Nasser, Haya. "Video Terminals Watch Workers." *USA Today*, February 15, 1987, p. 6B.

Neikirk, William R. "U.S. Manufacturers Wary on Automation." *Chiacgo Tribune*, July 5, 1987, sect. 1, pp. 1, 14.

Niehouse, Oliver L. "The Myth of Consistency: There Are Certain Times When Managers Ought to Be Inconsistent and Unpredictable." *Success*, April 1987, p. 18.

Odato, James M. "Tips to Keep Career on the Fast Track." *USA Today*, March 9, 1988, p. 4B.

Odiorne, George, Heinz Weihrich and Jack Mendleson. *Executive Skills: A Management by Objectives Approach*. Dubuque, Iowa: Wm. C. Brown Co., 1980.

Osborn, Alex F. *Applied Imagination*. New York: Charles Scribner's Sons, 1953.

Pell, Anthony. *Recruiting and Selecting Personnel*. New York: Regents, 1969.

Peters, Tom. "Hardware Before Humans: Firms Spend on Plant, Scrimp on Training." *Chicago Tribune*, October 12, 1987, sect. 4, p. 9.

Peters, Tom. "The News Is That Iacocca's Response

Made News." *Chicago Tribune*, July 27, 1987, sect. 4, p. 6.

Phatak, Arvind V. *International Dimensions of Management*, 2nd ed. Boston: PWS-KENT, 1989.

Plunkett, W. R. *Business*. Dubuque, Iowa: Wm. C. Brown Co., 1982.

Plunkett, W. R. *Introduction to Business: A Functional Approach*. Dubuque, Iowa: Wm. C. Brown Co., 1977.

Plunkett, W. R. *Supervision: The Direction of People at Work*, 4th ed. Dubuque, Iowa: Wm. C. Brown Co., 1986.

Porter, L. W. and E. E. Lawler. *Managerial Attitudes and Performance*. Homewood, Ill.: Richard D. Irwin, 1968.

Povich, Elaine S. "Surge in Exports Cuts Trade Deficit." *Chicago Tribune*, February 13, 1988, sect. 1, p. 1.

Raja, Anthony P. *Managing by Objectives*. Glenview, Ill.: Scott, Foresman, 1974.

Reich, Robert B. "Regulations by Confrontation or Negotiation?" *Harvard Business Review*, May–June 1981, pp. 82–83.

Reuter, Vincent G. "A Trio of Management Tools Increases Productivity and Reduces Costs." *Arizona Business*, February 1977, pp. 12–17.

Revving Up the American Factory." *The New York Times*, January 11, 1987, sect. 3, p. 1.

Richman, Louis S. "Lessons from German Managers." *Fortune*, April 27, 1987, p. 270.

Riley, M. J. *Management Information Systems*, 2nd ed. San Francisco: Holden Day, 1981, p. 5.

Robb, Russell. "Organization as Affected by Purpose and Conditions." *Classics in Management*, edited by Harwood F. Merrill. New York: American Management Association, 1970, p. 147.

Robbins, Stephen P. *Managing Organizational Conflict*. Englewood Cliffs, N.J.: Prentice-Hall, 1974.

Robbins, Stephen P. *Organizational Behavior: Concepts and Controversies*, 3rd ed. Englewood Cliffs, N.J.: Prentice-Hall, 1979.

Roethlisberger, F. J. and W. J. Dickson. *Management and the Worker*. Cambridge, Mass.: Harvard University Press, 1939.

Rosenberg, Arthur M. and Jim Murray. "Can We Talk?" *Modern Office Technology*, 4, February 1988, pp. 40–46.

Ross, Irwin. "How Lawless Are Big Companies?" *Fortune*, December 1, 1980, pp. 57–64.

Rossman, M. L. "Bridging the Communications Gap Between Marketing and Operations." *Marketing News*, 21, July 3, 1987, p. 31.

Royston, Michael G. "Making Pollution Prevention Pay." *Harvard Business Review*, November–December 1980, pp. 6–22.

Runcie, John F. "By Days I Make the Cars." *Harvard Business Review*, May–June 1980, pp. 106–15.

Saporito, Bill. "Cutting Costs Without Cutting People." *Fortune*, May 25, 1987, p. 27.

Sayles, Leonard R. and George Strauss. *Human Behavior in Organizations*. Englewood Cliff, N.J.: Prentice-Hall, 1980.

Schechter, Arnold. "Speaking the Language Eases Distance." *USA Today*, March 7, 1985, p. 3D.

Schein, Edgar H. *Career Dynamics: Matching Individual and Organizational Needs*. Reading, Mass.: Addison-Wesley, 1978.

Schein, Edgar H. "Management Development as a Process of Influence." *Industrial Management Review*, no. 2, May 1961.

Schein, Edgar H. *Organizational Psychology*, 2nd ed. Englewood Cliffs, N.J.: Prentice-Hall, 1970.

Schein, Edgar H. "Organizational Socialization and the Profession of Management." *Industrial Management Review*, Winter 1968, pp. 1–16.

Schuler, Randall S. *Personnel and Human Resource Management*. St. Paul: West Publishing Co., 1981.

Sherwin, Douglas S. "The Ethical Roots of the Business System." *Harvard Business Review*, November–December 1983, p., 184.

Shreeve, Thomas W. "Be Prepared for Political Changes Abroad." *Harvard Business Review*, July–August 1984, p. 112.

Sihler, William H. "Toward Better Management Control Systems." *California Management Review*, no. 2, 1971.

Sithington, Frederick C. "Coping with Computer Proliferation." *Harvard Business Review*, May–June 1980, pp. 152–64.

Skinner, B. F. *Contingencies of Reinforcement*. New York: Appleton-Century-Crofts, 1969.

Snyder, Leonard. "An Anniversary Review and Critique: The Tylenol Crisis." *Public Relations Review*, Fall 1983, p. 24–34.

Solomon, Robert C. and Kristine Hanson. *It's Good Business*. New York: Atheneum, 1985, pp. 20–21.

"Special Report: The Turned-Off Worker." *Inc.*, April 1981, p. 76.

Spencer, Jim. "Let's Do Lunch." *Chicago Tribune*, December 11, 1986, sect. 5, p. 2.

Sperling, Dan. "Say 'No' to Alcohol This Weekend." *USA Today*, April 5, 1988, p. 1D.

Stacey, Julie. "USA Snapshots: Individuals Lead in Giving." *USA Today*, May 27, 1987, p. 1B.

Steiner, George A. "Institutionalizing Corporate Social Decisions." *Business Horizons*, December 1975, pp. 12–18.

Stodgill, Ralph M. "Personal Factors Associated with Leadership: A Survey of Literature." *Journal of Psy-*

chology, January 1948, pp. 35–71.

Stoever, William A. "Japanese Boss, American Employees." *The Wharton Magazine*, Fall 1982, p. 46.

Stoner, James A. F. *Management*. Englewood Cliffs, N.J.: Prentice-Hall, 1982.

Strong, Earl P. and Robert D. Smith. *Management Control Models*. New York: Holt, Reinhart & Winston, 1968.

Stulberg, Joseph P. "The Rewards of Conflict." *Success*, June 1987, p. 34.

Szilagyi, Andrew. *Management and Performance*. Santa Monica, Calif.: Goodyear Publishing, 1981.

Tannenbaum, Robert and Warren H. Schmidt. "How to Choose a Leadership Pattern." *Harvard Business Review*, May–June 1973, pp. 162–80.

Tarpy, R. M. *Basic Principles of Learning*. Glenview, Ill.: Scott, Foresman, 1974.

"Tax Cheats Keep $84.9 Billion." *Chicago Tribune*, March 18, 1988, sect. 1, p. 14.

"Testing for Drugs Becoming Routine." *Chicago Tribune*, April 10, 1988, sect. 8, p. 1.

"Texaco Is Facing Another Big Payout." *The New York Times*, February 28, 1988, p. 16

"Tired of Tires." *USA Today*, December 23, 1987, p. 1B.

Tosi, H. L. and W. C. Hamner, ed. *Organizational Behavior and Management: A Contingency Approach*. New York: John Wiley & Sons, 1974.

"Toyota Takes Pains, and Time, Filling Its Jobs at Its Kentucky Plant." *The Wall Street Journal*, December 1, 1987, p. 1.

"2 Execs Guilty in Fake-Juice Case." *Chicago Tribune*, February 18, 1988, sect. 1, p. 10.

"U.S. Places 1st in Ethics Survey." *Chicago Tribune*, December 18, 1987, sect. 2, p. 3.

Vancil, Richard F. "What Kind of Management Control Do You Need?" *Harvard Business Review on Management 1975*, New York: Harper & Row, 1975, p. 446.

Vroom, Victor H. "A New Look at Managerial Decision Making." *Organizational Dynamics*, no. 4, 1973, pp. 66–80.

Vroom, Victor H. *Work and Motivation*. New York: John Wiley & Sons, 1964.

Warren, James. "Ford, Auto Union Reach an Accord." *Chicago Tribune*, September 18, 1987, sect. 1, p. 5.

"We All Pay Heavy Cost of Drug Use." *USA Today*, March 1, 1988, p. 11A.

Webster's Third International Dictionary. Chicago: Encyclopedia Britannica, 1971, p. 2546.

Weichmann, U. E. and L. G. Pringle. "Problems That Plague Multinational Marketers." *Harvard Business Review*, July–August 1979, p. 120.

Weissenberg, Peter and Michael J. Kavanaugh. "The Independence of Initiating Structure and Consideration: A Review of the Evidence." *Personnel Psychology*, Spring 1972, pp. 119–30.

Whiting, Charles S. "Operation Techniques of Creative Thinking." *Advanced Management*, October 1955, pp. 24–30.

Wikstrom, Walter S. *Developing Managerial Competence*. New York: National Industrial Conference Board, 1964.

Wilson, Ian H. "Socio-Political Forecasting: A New Dimension to Strategic Planning." *Michigan Business Review*, July 1974, pp. 15–24.

Work, Clemens P. et al. "The 21st Century Executive." *U.S. News & World Report*, March 7, 1988, pp. 48–51.

Wright, Richard A. "Ford Steering Robots to New Frontiers of Automation." *Chicago Tribune*, November 15, 1987, sect. 18, p. 22.

Index